THE NEW OXFORD SCHOOL ATLAS

Editorial Adviser
Patrick Wiegand

© Oxford University Press 1990
© Maps copyright Oxford University Press

Oxford University Press Walton Street, Oxford OX2 6DP
Oxford New York Toronto
Delhi Bombay Calcutta Madras Karachi
Petaling Jaya Singapore Hong Kong Tokyo
Nairobi Dar es Salaam Cape Town Melbourne Auckland

and associated companies in
Berlin Ibadan

Oxford is a trade mark of Oxford University Press

ISBN 0 19 831650 X (non net) ISBN 0 19 831678 X (hardback)

First published 1990
Reprinted 1990

Printed in Hong Kong

Oxford University Press

Contents

4 Latitude and Longitude

The earth is a small, blue planet.
Seen from space it has no right way up.

An imaginary grid is used to pinpoint the position of any place on earth. This grid consists of lines called parallels of latitude and meridians of longitude. Both are measured in degrees.

Latitude
Parallels of latitude measure distance north or south of the equator. The equator is at latitude 0°. The poles are at latitudes 90°N and 90°S.

Longitude
Meridians of longitude measure distance east or west of the Prime Meridian. The Prime (or Greenwich) Meridian is at longitude 0°. The 180° line of longitude, on the opposite side of the earth, is the International Date Line.

The equator divides the earth into halves: the Northern Hemisphere and the Southern Hemisphere. The Prime Meridian and the 180° meridian together also divide the earth into halves: the Western Hemisphere and the Eastern Hemisphere.

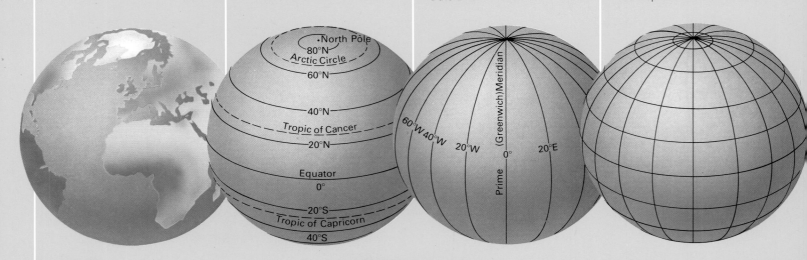

When used together, lines of latitude and longitude form a grid. The position of places on the surface of the earth can be located accurately using this grid.

To locate places really accurately, each degree of latitude and longitude can be divided into 60 minutes. Minutes can be divided into even smaller units called seconds.

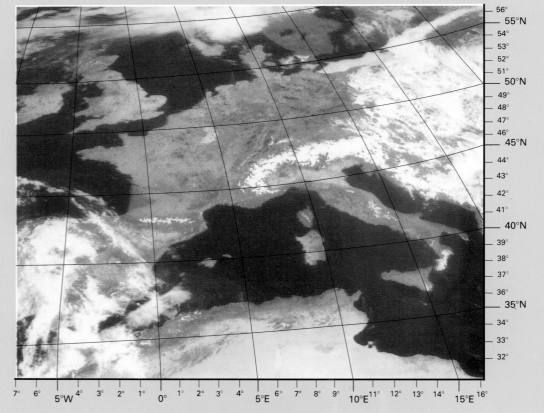

Extract from a Meteosat view of Europe, 35,790 km above the equator. (This is an enlargement of the photograph of the earth shown at the top of the page.)

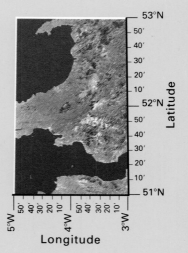

Extract from the Landsat image of the British Isles shown on page 28. This extract shows part of Wales at a scale of 1 : 4 500 000.

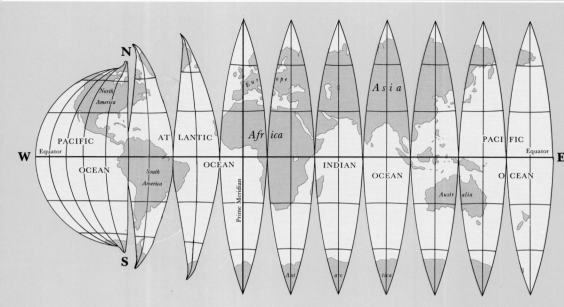

The most accurate way of looking at the earth's land and sea areas is to use a globe. Maps, however, are more convenient to use than globes. This map has been made by unpeeling strips, or gores, from the globe's surface. The map is difficult to use because gaps are left in the land and sea.
Grids of parallels and meridians that are used to turn a globe into a flat map are called map projections. It is impossible to flatten the curved surface of the earth without stretching or cutting part of it. It is important that the projection used for a world map is suitable for the purpose.

The **Oblique Aitoff projection** is also equal area. The arrangement of the land masses allows a good view of routes in the northern hemisphere. The position of North America and Asia on either side of the Arctic is shown clearly.

Mercator's projection was designed for navigators. Any straight line on the map is a line of constant compass bearing. Straight lines are not the shortest routes, however. Shape is accurate on a Mercator projection but the size of the land masses is distorted. Land is shown larger the further away is it from the equator.

——— Line of constant compass bearing

- - - - Shortest route

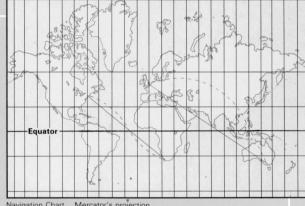

Navigation Chart. Mercator's projection.

Peters' projection is an equal area projection. The land masses are the correct size in relation to each other, but there is some distortion in shape. This projection has been used to emphasize the size of the poor countries of the South compared with the rich countries of the North.

——— Brandt Line

▨ Rich North

▨ Poor South.

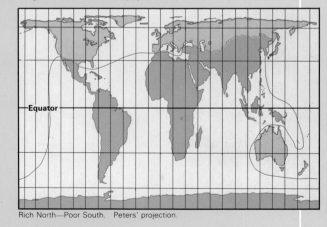

Rich North—Poor South. Peters' projection.

Gall's projection gives a reasonable compromise between accuracy of shape and area. A modified version is used in this atlas as a general purpose world map. This map shows states which have gained their independence since 1945.

▨ States independent since 1945.

States independent since 1945. Gall's projection.

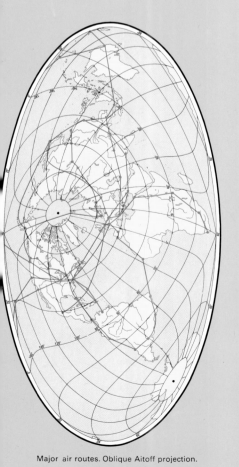

Major air routes. Oblique Aitoff projection.

Understanding Topographic Maps

Topographic maps show the main features of the physical and human landscape. There are small differences in the symbols and colours used for the maps of the British Isles and those for the rest of the world.

British Isles Maps

Boundaries

international

national

county

region (Scotland)

district (N. Ireland)

Communications

motorway

primary road

A road

● motorway junction

● motorway service area

railway

canal

⊕ international airport

✈ other airport

Cities and towns

◁ built-up areas

■ over 1 million inhabitants

● more than 100 000 inhabitants

• smaller towns

Scale 1:1 000 000

0   25km

Scale is shown by a representative fraction and a scale line.

Non British Isles Maps

Boundaries

international

disputed

internal

national park

Communications

motorway

other major road

track

railway

canal

✈ major airport

Cities and towns

◁ built-up areas

■ over 1 million inhabitants

● more than 100 000 inhabitants

• smaller towns

+ historic sites

Physical features

 seasonal river/lake

marsh

salt pan

ice cap

sand dunes

coral reef

Place names
Local spellings are used. Anglicised and other common spellings are shown in brackets. This atlas has been designed for English speaking readers and so all places have been named using the Roman alphabet. Compare this extract of the map of Southern Asia with the same map printed in Bengali.

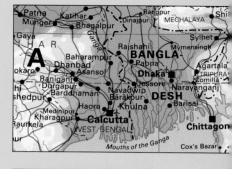

Type style
Contrasting type styles are used to show the difference between physical features, settlements and administrative areas. Physical features (except for peaks) are shown in italics.

e.g. *Hautes Fagnes*   *Maas*

Peaks are shown in condensed type.

e.g. Hohe Acht 746

Settlement names are shown in upper and lower case.

e.g. Valkenswaard

Administrative areas are shown in capital letters.

e.g. LIÈGE

The importance of places is shown by the size of the type and whether the type face is bold, medium or light.

e.g. Malmédy   Bergheim   **Duisburg**

Land height
Colours on topographic maps refer only to the height of the land. They do not give information about use or other aspects of the environment.

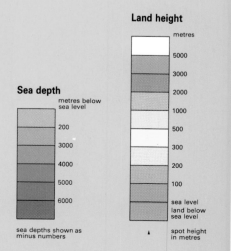

Sea depth

metres below sea level

200

3000

4000

5000

6000

sea depths shown as minus numbers

Land height

metres

5000

3000

2000

1000

500

300

200

100

sea level

land below sea level

▲ spot height in metres

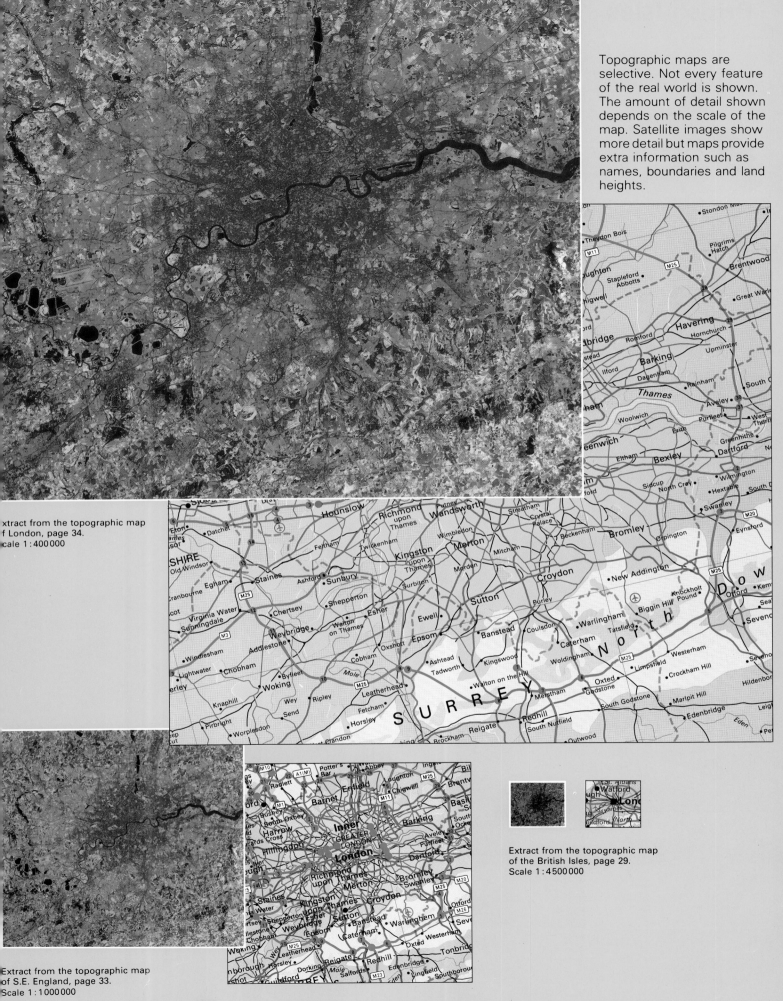

Topographic maps are selective. Not every feature of the real world is shown. The amount of detail shown depends on the scale of the map. Satellite images show more detail but maps provide extra information such as names, boundaries and land heights.

Extract from the topographic map of London, page 34.
Scale 1:400 000

Extract from the topographic map of S.E. England, page 33.
Scale 1:1 000 000

Extract from the topographic map of the British Isles, page 29.
Scale 1:4 500 000

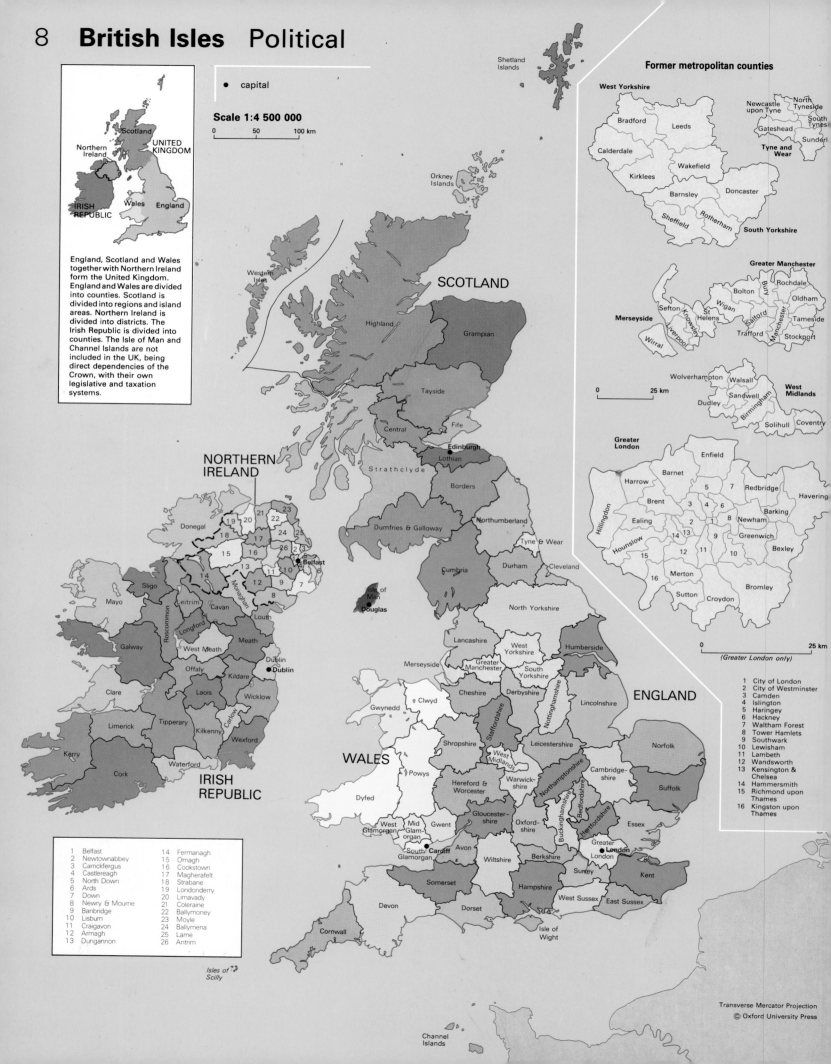

● capital

Scale 1:4 500 000

0   50   100 km

UNITED KINGDOM
Scotland
Northern Ireland
Wales   England
IRISH REPUBLIC

England, Scotland and Wales together with Northern Ireland form the United Kingdom. England and Wales are divided into counties. Scotland is divided into regions and island areas. Northern Ireland is divided into districts. The Irish Republic is divided into counties. The Isle of Man and Channel Islands are not included in the UK, being direct dependencies of the Crown, with their own legislative and taxation systems.

Shetland Islands

Former metropolitan counties

West Yorkshire
Bradford   Leeds
Calderdale
Kirklees   Wakefield
Barnsley   Doncaster
Sheffield   Rotherham
South Yorkshire

Newcastle upon Tyne   North Tyneside
Gateshead   South Tynes
Sunderl
Tyne and Wear

Greater Manchester
Bolton   Bury   Rochdale
Wigan   Oldham
Sefton   St Helens   Salford   Manchester   Tameside
Merseyside   Knowsley   Trafford   Stockport
Liverpool
Wirral

Wolverhampton   Walsall   **West Midlands**
Dudley   Sandwell   Birmingham   Solihull   Coventry

Greater London
Enfield
Harrow   Barnet
Brent   5   7   Redbridge
Hillingdon   3   4   6   Havering
Ealing   8   Newham   Barking
Hounslow   14   13   1   2   9   Greenwich
15   12   11   10   Bexley
16   Merton   Bromley
Sutton   Croydon

0   25 km

SCOTLAND

Western Isles
Orkney Islands

Highland
Grampian
Tayside
Central   Fife
Edinburgh
Lothian
Strathclyde
Borders
Dumfries & Galloway
Northumberland
Tyne & Wear
Cumbria   Durham   Cleveland

NORTHERN IRELAND

Donegal
19 20 21 23
18 17 22 24 25
15 16 26 2 3
13 4 5 6
14 11 10 Belfast
Monaghan 12 9 7
8

Sligo
Mayo
Leitrim   Cavan
Roscommon   Longford   Meath
Galway   West Meath
Offaly   Kildare
Clare   Laois   Wicklow
Limerick   Tipperary   Kilkenny   Carlow
Kerry   Waterford   Wexford
Cork

IRISH REPUBLIC

Dublin

Isle of Man
Douglas

North Yorkshire
Lancashire   West Yorkshire   Humberside
Merseyside   Greater Manchester   South Yorkshire
Cheshire   Derbyshire   Nottinghamshire   Lincolnshire

0   25 km
(Greater London only)

ENGLAND

Clwyd
Gwynedd
Staffordshire   Leicestershire   Norfolk
Shropshire   West Midlands   Warwickshire   Northamptonshire   Cambridgeshire   Suffolk

WALES
Powys
Hereford & Worcester   Bedfordshire
Dyfed   Gwent   Gloucestershire   Oxfordshire   Buckinghamshire   Hertfordshire   Essex
West Glamorgan   Mid Glamorgan
South Glamorgan   Cardiff
Avon   Wiltshire   Berkshire   Surrey   Greater London   London   Kent
Somerset   Hampshire   West Sussex   East Sussex
Devon   Dorset
Cornwall   Isle of Wight

Channel Islands
Isles of Scilly

1	Belfast	14	Fermanagh
2	Newtownabbey	15	Omagh
3	Carrickfergus	16	Cookstown
4	Castlereagh	17	Magherafelt
5	North Down	18	Strabane
6	Ards	19	Londonderry
7	Down	20	Limavady
8	Newry & Mourne	21	Coleraine
9	Banbridge	22	Ballymoney
10	Lisburn	23	Moyle
11	Craigavon	24	Ballymena
12	Armagh	25	Larne
13	Dungannon	26	Antrim

1	City of London
2	City of Westminster
3	Camden
4	Islington
5	Haringey
6	Hackney
7	Waltham Forest
8	Tower Hamlets
9	Southwark
10	Lewisham
11	Lambeth
12	Wandsworth
13	Kensington & Chelsea
14	Hammersmith
15	Richmond upon Thames
16	Kingston upon Thames

Transverse Mercator Projection
© Oxford University Press

British Isles Physical

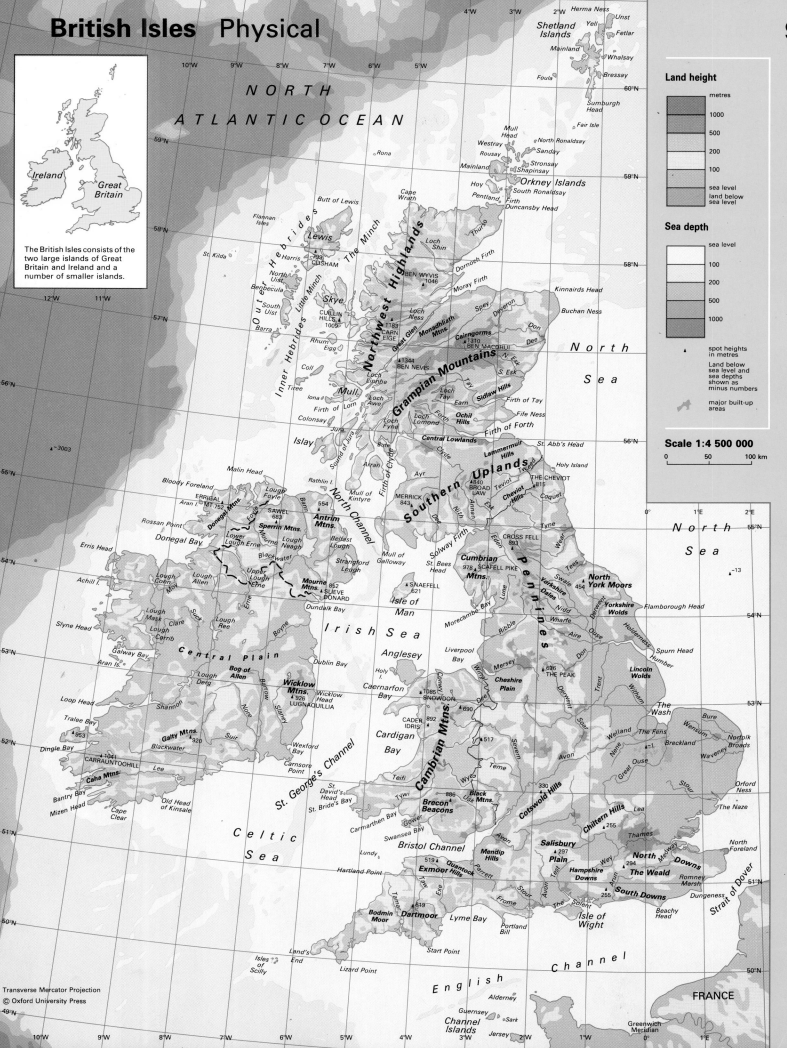

The British Isles consists of the two large islands of Great Britain and Ireland and a number of smaller islands.

Land height

metres
1000
500
200
100
sea level
land below sea level

Sea depth

sea level	
100	
200	
500	
1000	

▲ spot heights in metres

Land below sea level and sea depths shown as minus numbers

major built-up areas

Scale 1:4 500 000

0   50   100 km

Transverse Mercator Projection

© Oxford University Press

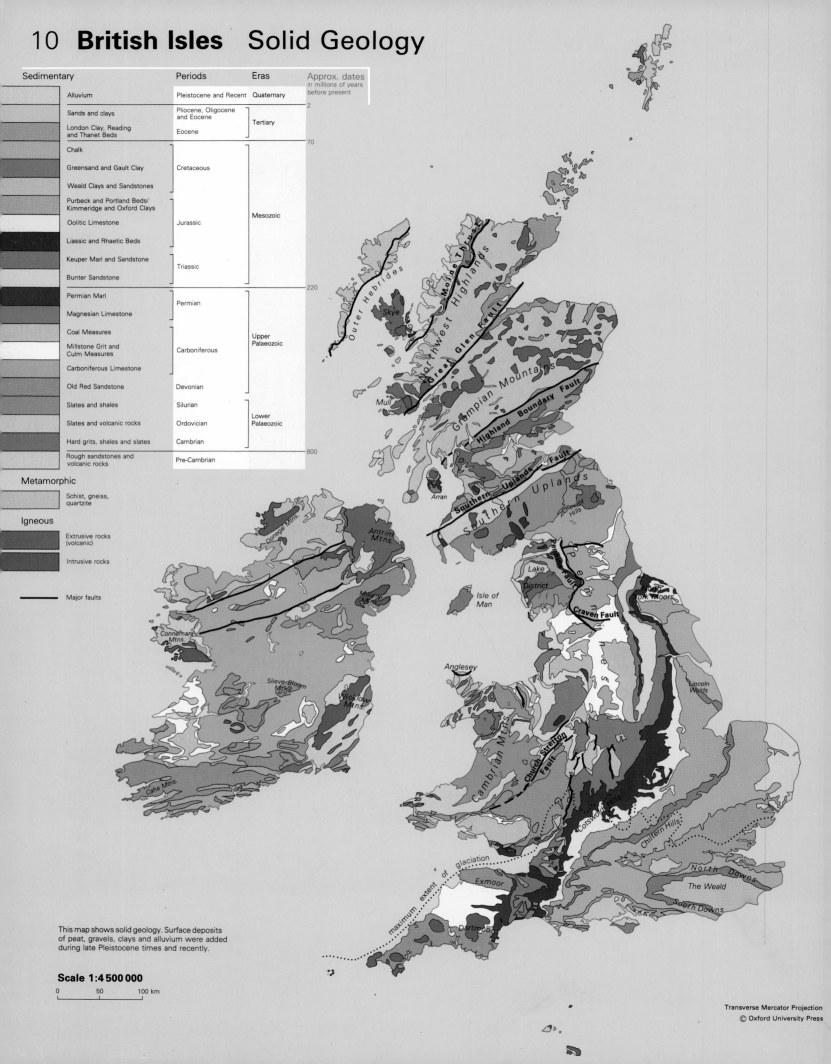

Sedimentary	Periods	Eras	Approx. dates in millions of years before present
Alluvium	Pleistocene and Recent	Quaternary	
Sands and clays	Pliocene, Oligocene and Eocene	Tertiary	2
London Clay, Reading and Thanet Beds	Eocene		
Chalk			70
Greensand and Gault Clay	Cretaceous		
Weald Clays and Sandstones		Mesozoic	
Purbeck and Portland Beds/ Kimmeridge and Oxford Clays			
Oolitic Limestone	Jurassic		
Liassic and Rhaetic Beds			
Keuper Marl and Sandstone	Triassic		
Bunter Sandstone			220
Permian Marl	Permian		
Magnesian Limestone			
Coal Measures		Upper Palaeozoic	
Millstone Grit and Culm Measures	Carboniferous		
Carboniferous Limestone			
Old Red Sandstone	Devonian		
Slates and shales	Silurian		
Slates and volcanic rocks	Ordovician	Lower Palaeozoic	
Hard grits, shales and slates	Cambrian		600
Rough sandstones and volcanic rocks	Pre-Cambrian		

Metamorphic

Schist, gneiss, quartzite

Igneous

Extrusive rocks (volcanic)

Intrusive rocks

——— Major faults

This map shows solid geology. Surface deposits of peat, gravels, clays and alluvium were added during late Pleistocene times and recently.

Scale 1:4 500 000

0   50   100 km

British Isles Soils

Upland peat | Lowland fen peat | Alluvial gley | Gley

Poorly drained soils

- Upland peat and peat bog. Well-leached acid peat formed by high rainfall.
- Lowland fen peat. Alkaline peat formed by water-logging in low areas.
- Alluvial gleys. Gleying from low lying location such as flooding by sea or river.
- Gleys. Gleying from underlying impermeable parent material, usually clay.

Well drained soils

- Brown earths. Subsoil formed from weathering of parent material.
- Argillic brown earths. Subsoil formed by the accumulation of clay leached from above.
- Podzols. Subsoil has an accumulation of iron and/or aluminium.
- Rendzinas and brown calcareous soils. Shallow and moderately deep soils over limestones and chalk.
- major urban areas.

Brown earth | Argillic brown earth | Podzol | Rendzina

Scale 1:4 500 000

0   50   100 km

Transverse Mercator Projection
© Oxford University Press

Actual surface temperature

°C
17
16
15
14
13
12
11
10
9
8
7
6
5
4
3
2
1
0
-1
-2

⌒ isotherms reduced to sea level

→ warm currents

→ cold currents

January

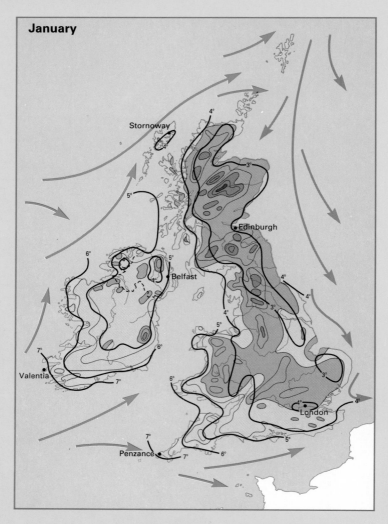

Stornoway
Edinburgh
Belfast
Valentia
London
Penzance

Climate graphs for selected British Isles stations
(1951–80 averages)

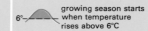
6° growing season starts when temperature rises above 6°C

Stornoway

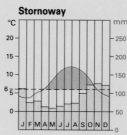

Height above sea level: 15 metres
Mean annual rainfall: 1096 mm
Mean January temperature: 4.0°C
Mean July temperature: 12.6°C

Edinburgh

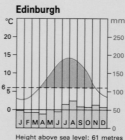

Height above sea level: 61 metres
Mean annual rainfall: 642 mm
Mean January temperature: 3.0°C
Mean July temperature: 14.3°C

July

Stornoway
Edinburgh
Belfast
Valentia
London
Penzance

Belfast

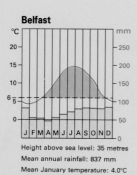

Height above sea level: 35 metres
Mean annual rainfall: 837 mm
Mean January temperature: 4.0°C
Mean July temperature: 14.6°C

London (Kew)

Height above sea level: 6 metres
Mean annual rainfall: 599 mm
Mean January temperature: 4.4°C
Mean July temperature: 17.4°C

Valentia

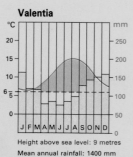

Height above sea level: 9 metres
Mean annual rainfall: 1400 mm
Mean January temperature: 6.6°C
Mean July temperature: 14.8°C

Penzance

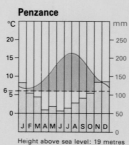

Height above sea level: 19 metres
Mean annual rainfall: 1131 mm
Mean January temperature: 6.9°C
Mean July temperature: 16.1°C

Scale 1 : 10 000 000

0   100   200 km

Transverse Mercator Projection

© Oxford University Press

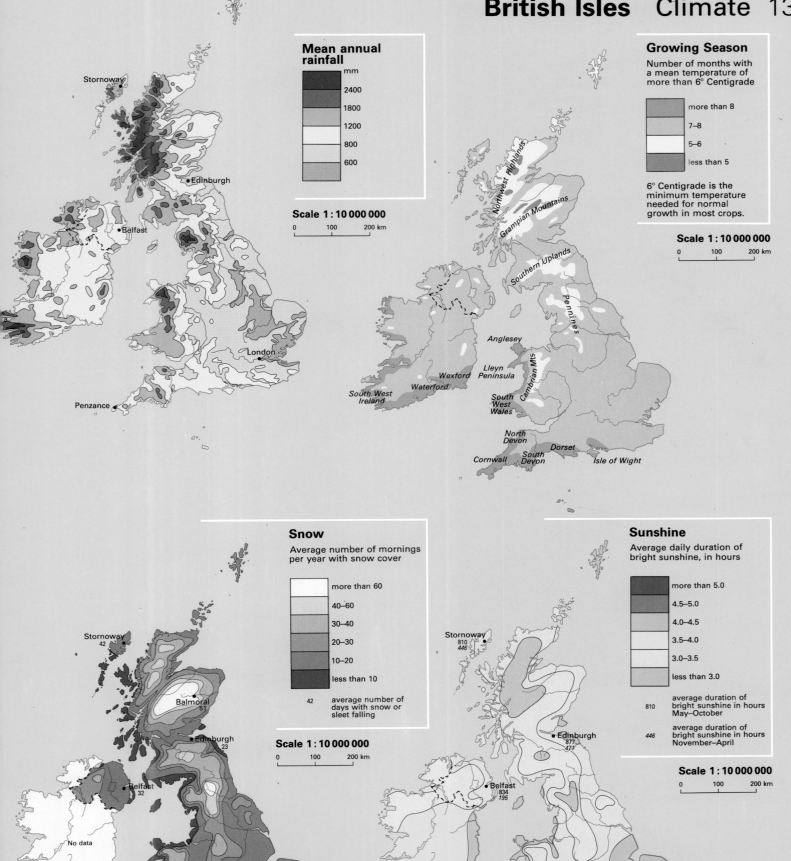

Mean annual rainfall

mm
2400
1800
1200
800
600

Scale 1 : 10 000 000

0   100   200 km

Stornoway
Edinburgh
Belfast
London
Penzance

Growing Season

Number of months with a mean temperature of more than 6° Centigrade

more than 8
7–8
5–6
less than 5

6° Centigrade is the minimum temperature needed for normal growth in most crops.

Scale 1 : 10 000 000

0   100   200 km

Northwest Highlands
Grampian Mountains
Southern Uplands
Pennines
Anglesey
Lleyn Peninsula
Cambrian Mts
Wexford
Waterford
South West Ireland
South West Wales
North Devon
Cornwall
South Devon
Dorset
Isle of Wight

Snow

Average number of mornings per year with snow cover

more than 60
40–60
30–40
20–30
10–20
less than 10

42   average number of days with snow or sleet falling

Scale 1 : 10 000 000

0   100   200 km

Stornoway
42
Balmoral
51
Edinburgh
23
Belfast
32
No data
Valentia
927
379
London
22
Penzance
4

Sunshine

Average daily duration of bright sunshine, in hours

more than 5.0
4.5–5.0
4.0–4.5
3.5–4.0
3.0–3.5
less than 3.0

810   average duration of bright sunshine in hours May–October

446   average duration of bright sunshine in hours November–April

Scale 1 : 10 000 000

0   100   200 km

Stornoway
810
446
Edinburgh
877
471
Belfast
834
195
London
1060
497
Penzance
1142
596

Transverse Mercator Projection

© Oxford University Press

Population density

Persons per square kilometre

	more than 1500
	1000–1500
	500–1000
	250–500
	100–250
	50–100
	10–50
	0–10

Cities and towns

- ⬤ over 1 million inhabitants
- ● 500 000 to 1 million inhabitants
- • 100 000 to 500 000 inhabitants
- · 25 000 to 100 000 inhabitants

On this map the population of the Inner London Boroughs is shown using one symbol. The Outer London Boroughs each have their own symbol.

- – – – international boundary
- ——— county boundary

Scale 1 : 4 500 000

0   50   100 km

Population growth 1801–1981

Population in millions

British Isles

England & Wales

Scotland

Irish Rep.

N. Ireland

1801 '31 '61 '91 1921 '51 '81

Note:
No census was taken in 1941.
Irish data available separately as Irish Republic or Northern Ireland from 1931.

UK: birth and death rates per 1000 population, 1971–85

births

deaths

'71 '73 '75 '77 '79 '81 '83 '85

Total population, 1986	
United Kingdom	56.76 million
Irish Republic	3.54 million
Isle of Man	0.06 million
Channel Islands	0.14 million

Population structure of the UK, 1984

Year of birth

Age at mid 1984

males   females

1894
1904
1914
1924
1934
1944
1954
1964
1974
1984

90
80
70
60
50
40
30
20
10
0

500 400 300 200 100 0 thousands

0 100 200 300 400 500 thousands

········· projection to the year 2001

Transverse Mercator Projection

© Oxford University Press

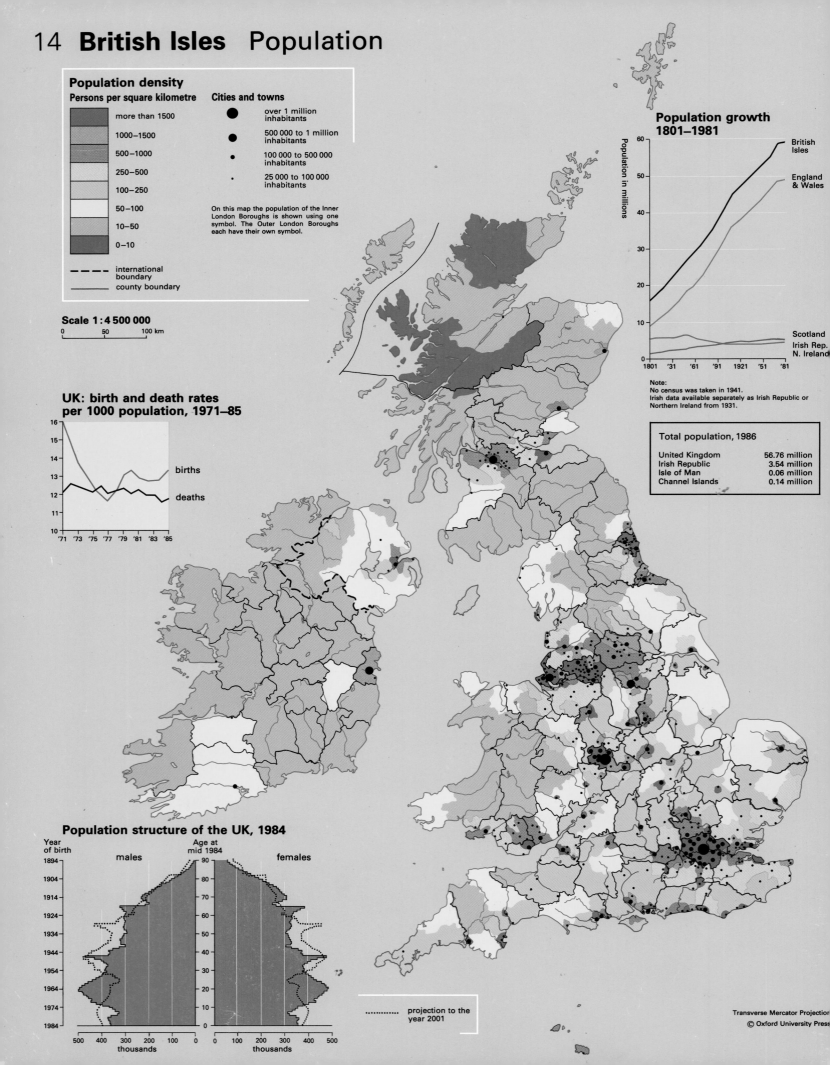

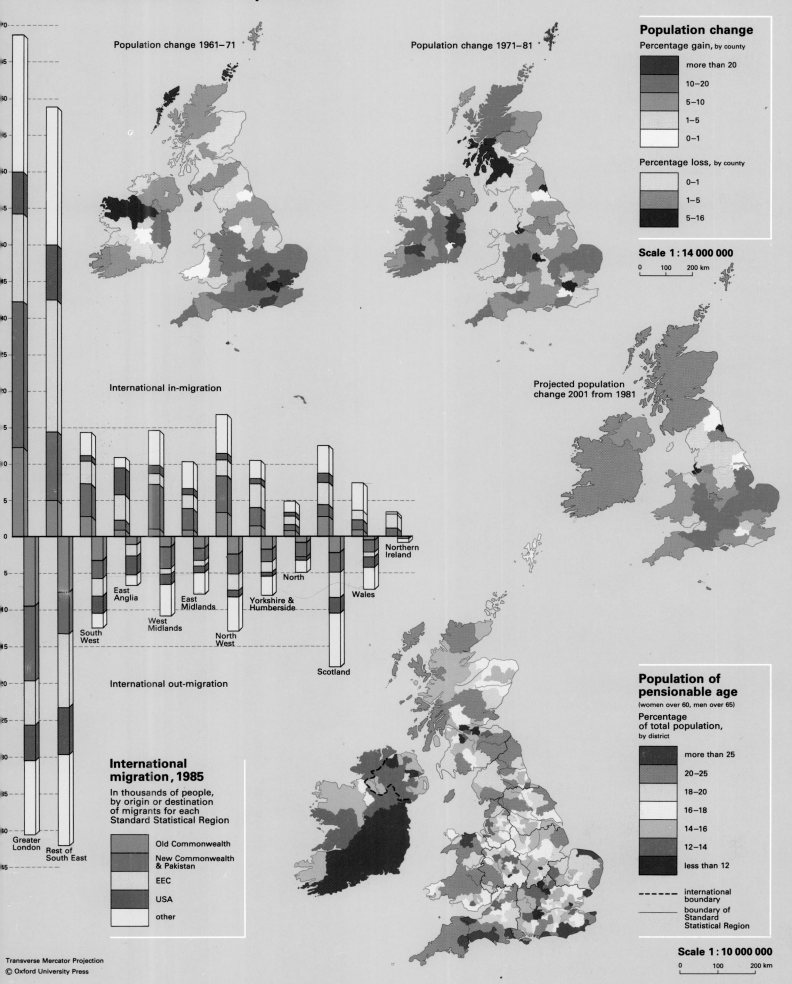

Population change 1961–71

Population change 1971–81

Population change

Percentage gain, by county

- more than 20
- 10–20
- 5–10
- 1–5
- 0–1

Percentage loss, by county

- 0–1
- 1–5
- 5–16

Scale 1 : 14 000 000

0   100   200 km

Projected population change 2001 from 1981

International in-migration

East Anglia

South West

West Midlands

East Midlands

Yorkshire & Humberside

North West

North

Wales

Scotland

Northern Ireland

Greater London

Rest of South East

International out-migration

International migration, 1985

In thousands of people, by origin or destination of migrants for each Standard Statistical Region

- Old Commonwealth
- New Commonwealth & Pakistan
- EEC
- USA
- other

Population of pensionable age

(women over 60, men over 65)

Percentage of total population, by district

- more than 25
- 20–25
- 18–20
- 16–18
- 14–16
- 12–14
- less than 12

- - - - international boundary

——— boundary of Standard Statistical Region

Scale 1 : 10 000 000

0   100   200 km

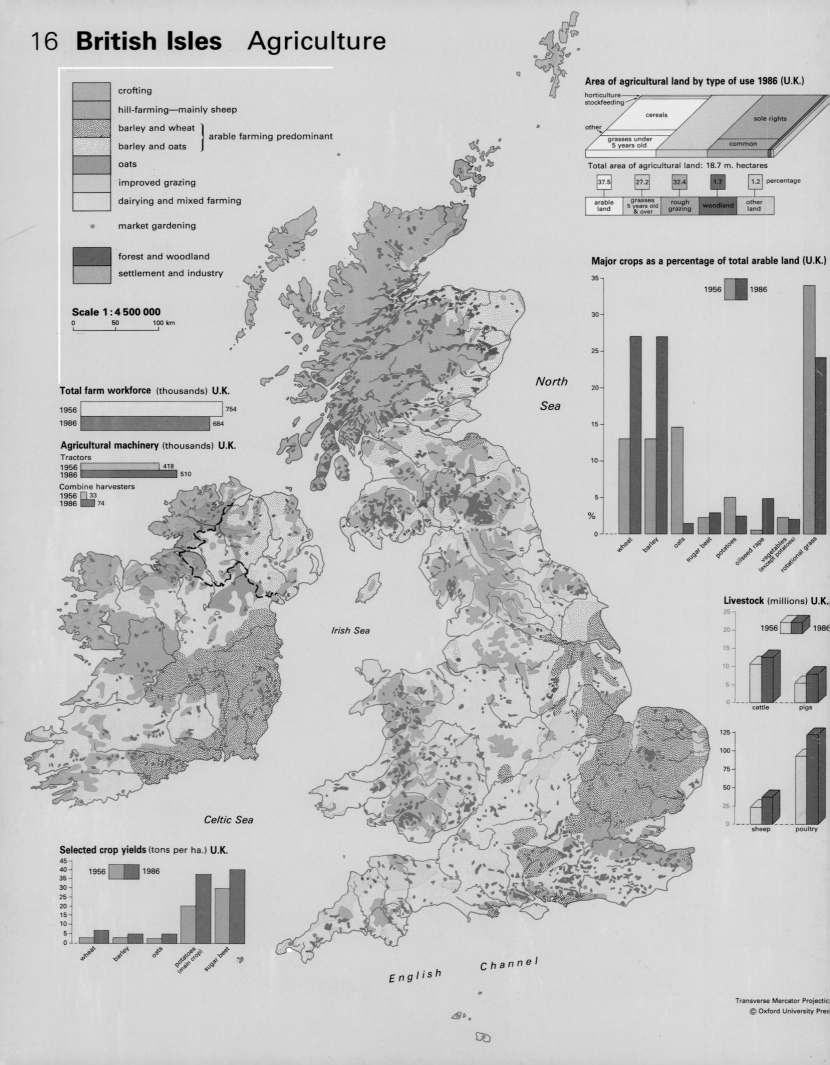

Legend:
- crofting
- hill-farming—mainly sheep
- barley and wheat } arable farming predominant
- barley and oats }
- oats
- improved grazing
- dairying and mixed farming
- • market gardening
- forest and woodland
- settlement and industry

Scale 1 : 4 500 000

0   50   100 km

Area of agricultural land by type of use 1986 (U.K.)

horticulture
stockfeeding
cereals
other
grasses under 5 years old
sole rights
common

Total area of agricultural land: 18.7 m. hectares

37.5	27.2	32.4	1.7	1.2	percentage
arable land	grasses 5 years old & over	rough grazing	woodland	other land	

Total farm workforce (thousands) U.K.

1956	754
1986	684

Agricultural machinery (thousands) U.K.

Tractors
1956	418
1986	510

Combine harvesters
1956	33
1986	74

Major crops as a percentage of total arable land (U.K.)

1956   1986

wheat, barley, oats, sugar beet, potatoes, oilseed rape, vegetables (except potatoes), rotational grass

Livestock (millions) U.K.

1956   1986

cattle, pigs, sheep, poultry

Selected crop yields (tons per ha.) U.K.

1956   1986

wheat, barley, oats, potatoes (main crop), sugar beet

North Sea

Irish Sea

Celtic Sea

English Channel

Transverse Mercator Projection
© Oxford University Press

Sea depth

metres
100
200
500
1000

sand banks

sea areas
(used in weather forecasts)

major built-up areas

Fishing ports
(tonnes of fish landed UK 1987, Ireland 1986)

○ more than 95 000
◦ 10 000–95 000
· 1000–10 000

Fish processing centres
(number of employees)

▲ more than 1000
▴ 50–1000

Major fishing grounds

plaice
sole
cod
haddock
herring
mackerel
shrimps
nephrops
(Dublin Bay prawn, langoustine, scampi)

Scale 1 : 9 000 000

0   100   200 km

SOUTH EAST ICELAND

FAEROES

BAILEY

FAIR ISLE

VIKING

NORTH UTSIRE

HEBRIDES

Whalsey
Lerwick
Scalloway

Kirkwall
Kinlochbervie
Scrabster
Stornoway
Wick
Lochinver
Ullapool

CROMARTY

Lossiemouth
Buckie
Macduff
Fraserburgh
Portsoy
Banff
Peterhead
Conon Bridge

SOUTH UTSIRE

ROCKALL

Mallaig

Aberdeen

FORTIES

FISHER

Oban

Arbroath

MALIN

FORTH

Glasgow
Pittenweem
Tarbert
Edinburgh
Eyemouth
Campbeltown
Duns
Moville
Ayr
Greencastle
Rathmullen
Kincasslagh
Burtonport
Killybegs

Kirkcudbright
Annan

North
Sea

GERMAN

TYNE

North Shields
Hartlepool
Whitehaven

Dogger
Bank

Portavogie
Ardglass
Annalong
Kilkeel

Clougherhead

DOGGER

BIGHT

Clay Deep

Rossaveel
Galway
Skerries
Howth
Holyhead

IRISH
SEA

Whitby
Scarborough
Bridlington

Fleetwood

Kingston upon Hull
Grimsby

Silver
Pit

HUMBER

Dingle
Valentia
Cromane
Castletownbere
Kinsale

Cobh
Dunmore East
Kilmore Quay

Boston

CHANNEL

Milford Haven

Lowestoft

FASTNET

LUNDY

THAMES

Warminster

Southend on-Sea

Bovey Tracey
Plymouth
Newlyn
Truro
Brixham

DOVER

WIGHT

SOLE

PORTLAND

FINISTERRE

PLYMOUTH

BISCAY

sandbanks
▲ **light-vessel**
vehicle ferry route
hovercraft route
jetfoil route
channel tunnel
(under construction)
principal railway
motorway
main road

to London
Chatham
M26 M2
Ramsgate
Maidstone
Canterbury
to London
A20(T)
Ashford
M20
Dover
Folkestone
A259(T)
A21(T)
Hastings
A289(T)

to Zeebrugge
to Oostende

Strait of Dover

Calais
(projected)
Fréthun
Dunkerque
N1
N42
St.-Omer
Boulogne-sur-Mer
to Lille, Bruxelles
Hazebrouck
A26
A25

English Channel

to Paris
to Paris

Scale 1 : 2 000 000

0   25   50 km

Modified Conical Orthomorphic Projection
© Oxford University Press

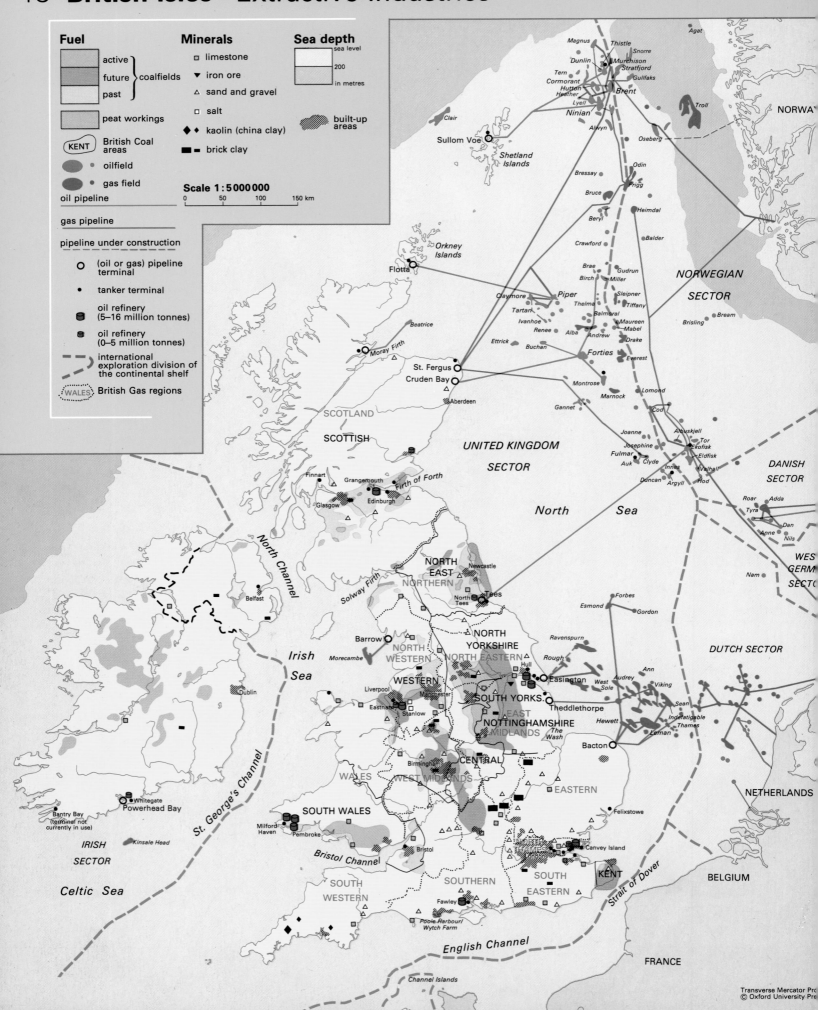

Fuel

coalfields
- active
- future
- past

peat workings

KENT British Coal areas

oilfield

gas field

oil pipeline

gas pipeline

pipeline under construction

○ (oil or gas) pipeline terminal

• tanker terminal

oil refinery (5–16 million tonnes)

oil refinery (0–5 million tonnes)

– – – international exploration division of the continental shelf

WALES British Gas regions

Minerals
- □ limestone
- ▼ iron ore
- △ sand and gravel
- ▢ salt
- ◆ kaolin (china clay)
- ▬ brick clay

Sea depth

sea level
200
in metres

built-up areas

Scale 1:5 000 000

0   50   100   150 km

NORWAY

Magnus   Thistle
Snorre
Dunlin   Murchison   Stratfjord
Tern   Gullfaks
Cormorant   Hutton
Heather   Brent
Lyell
Ninian   Alwyn   Troll
Oseberg
Clair   Odin
Sullom Voe   Frigg
Shetland   Bressay   NORWEGIAN
Islands   Bruce   SECTOR
Heimdal
Beryl   Balder
Crawford
Brae   Gudrun
Birch   Miller   Brisling
Orkney   Sleipner   Bream
Islands   Claymore   Piper   Thelma
Flotta   Tartan   Tiffany
Ivanhoe   Balmoral
Beatrice   Renee   Alba   Maureen
Ettrick   Andrew   Mabel
Moray Firth   Buchan   Drake
Forties
St. Fergus   Everest
Cruden Bay   Montrose   Lomond
Aberdeen   Marnock
Gannet
SCOTLAND   Cod
Joanne   Albuskjell
SCOTTISH   Josephine   Tor   DANISH
Fulmar   Ekofisk   SECTOR
UNITED KINGDOM   Auk   Clyde   Eldfisk
SECTOR   Innes   Valhall
Duncan   Argyll   Hod
Roar   Adda
North   Sea   Tyra
Dan
Finnart   Anne   Nils
Grangemouth   Firth of Forth
Glasgow   Edinburgh   WEST
GERMAN
SECTOR
NORTH   Nam
EAST   Newcastle
NORTHERN
North   Tees   Forbes   DUTCH SECTOR
Belfast   Tees   Esmond   Gordon
Solway Firth   Ravenspurn
Barrow   NORTH
NORTH   YORKSHIRE   Rough
WESTERN   NORTH   Hull   West Sole
Morecambe   EASTERN   Easington   Audrey   Viking
Dublin   WESTERN   Ann
Liverpool   SOUTH YORKS.   Theddlethorpe   Sean
Irish   Eastham   Thames
Sea   Stanlow   EAST   Rough   Indefatigable
NOTTINGHAMSHIRE   Hewett   Leman
MIDLANDS   The Wash
Bacton
Birmingham   CENTRAL
WALES   WEST MIDLANDS
EASTERN
Whitegate   NETHERLANDS
Powerhead Bay   SOUTH WALES   Felixstowe
Bantry Bay   Milford   Bristol
(terminal not   Haven   Pembroke
currently in use)   Canvey Island
Kinsale Head   London
IRISH   Bristol
SECTOR   Bristol Channel   KENT
SOUTH   SOUTHERN   SOUTH   Strait of Dover
WESTERN   EASTERN   BELGIUM
Celtic Sea   Fawley
Poole Harbour/   English Channel
Wytch Farm   FRANCE

St. George's Channel

North Channel

Channel Islands

Transverse Mercator Pro
© Oxford University Pre

Legend

major built-up areas

Forestry

forest and woodland

forest parks

Paper mills
Annual production (tonnes)

- more than 100 000
- 25 000–100 000

Water

—— Water Authority boundary (England and Wales)

Regional Council boundary (Scotland)

Water Service Divisions (Northern Ireland)

Surface water

rivers

21 ● major reservoirs (with capacity in millions of cubic metres of water)

Groundwater

highly productive aquifers (porous rock)

highly productive aquifers (jointed rock)

NB Although chalk is slightly porous, the main groundwater flow is through fissures

▼ major public supply groundwater pumping station (more than 20 000 cubic metres/day)

Scale 1 : 4 500 000

0   50   100 km

High forest tree species in Great Britain

percentage of all species

100 — 75 — 50 — 25 — 0

- Sitka spruce
- Scots pine
- Lodgepole pine
- Norway spruce
- Japanese/Hybrid larch
- other conifers
- Oak
- Beech
- Ash
- Birch
- other broadleaved species

Domestic water use in England and Wales, 1986

average litres per person per day

130 — 100 — 75 — 50 — 25 — 0

- flushing WC
- baths and showers
- washing machines
- hand washing, drinking, cooking, cleaning, outside use, etc.

Water use in England and Wales

thousand megalitres per day

40 — 30 — 20 — 10

water supply

Central Electricity Generating Board

industry ← agriculture

1976   1980   1986

Map labels

SHETLAND ISLANDS

ORKNEY ISLANDS

WESTERN ISLES

12 ● Loch Calder

HIGHLAND

Loch Glass 26

26 ● Loch Ness

GRAMPIAN   Inverurie   Aberdeen

Glen More

Fort William

25 ● Blackwater Res.
10 ● Loch of Lintrathen

18 Loch Turret   TAYSIDE

64 19 Glen Finglas Res.

Loch Arklet 12   Loch Katrine

Loch Lomond 70   CENTRAL   FIFE   Glenrothes

Loch Thom   Carron Valley Res.

Queen Elizabeth

Ardyll

11 ● LOTHIAN

Portmore Loch

STRATHCLYDE   BORDERS

Fruid Res. 11   12 Talla Res.
23 ● Daer Res.   64 Megget Res. 20

19   The Border

Loch Bradan   200 Kielder Res.

DUMFRIES & GALLOWAY   NORTHUMBRIAN

Galloway   Peudhoe

22 ● Derwent Res.

41 Cow Green Res.
41 ● Thirlmere   15   Selset Res. 20

Workington   85 Haweswater   Balderhead Res.

Grizedale   North Riding

Barrow-in-Furness

ISLE OF MAN   NORTH WEST   22 Grimwith Res.

12   YORKSHIRE   Tadcaster

Stocks Res.   Burnley

Blackburn   Halifax

Darwen   11 ● Covenham Res.

Rivington linked reservoirs   17 Radcliffe   28 Ladybower Res.

Longdendale linked reservoirs 19

Ellesmere Port   Delamere

Shotton 11   60

Alwen Res.   Llyn Brenig

Snowdonia   Llyn Celyn 74

Lake Vyrnwy 59   Blithfield Res. 18   Foremark Res. 13

WELSH   SEVERN-TRENT   Rutland Water 124

50 ● Llyn Clywedog   Birmingham   ANGLIAN

Claerwen Res. 35   Caban-Coch Res. 20   Pitsford Res. 18

43   Draycote Water 23   59 ● Gratham Water

Llyn Brianne Res. 61

Usk Res. 12   25 ● Abberton Res.

15   Talybont Res. 12   Dean & Wye Valley   27 ● Hanningfield Res.

Taf Fechan 22 Llandegfedd Res.   High Wycombe   Purfleet Northfleet

Newport   THAMES   Dartford   Sittingbourne

Llangynwyd   Thatcham   Snodland Aylesford Maidstone

Chew Valley Lake 20   New   21 ● Bewl Water

Watchet   WESSEX   SOUTHERN

Wimbleball Lake 21

SOUTH WEST

34 Roadford Res.

28 Colliford Lake Res.

Ireland labels

Ards

Glenariff

Gortin Glen   NORTHERN

Drum Manor

Ballyshannon Res. 170   WESTERN   Parkanaur

Florence Court   SOUTHERN   Gosford   EASTERN

Rossmore   Castlewellan Tollymore

Lough Key   Killykeen   13 Silent Valley Res.

Dún Á Rí   Slieve Gullion

Portumna   Donadea   Dublin

Parteen Weir Res.   168 ● Pollaphuca Res.

465 ●   Avondale

Currachase

J. F. Kennedy

Carrigadrohid Res.   57 Inishcarra Res.

Gougan Barra   33   Farran

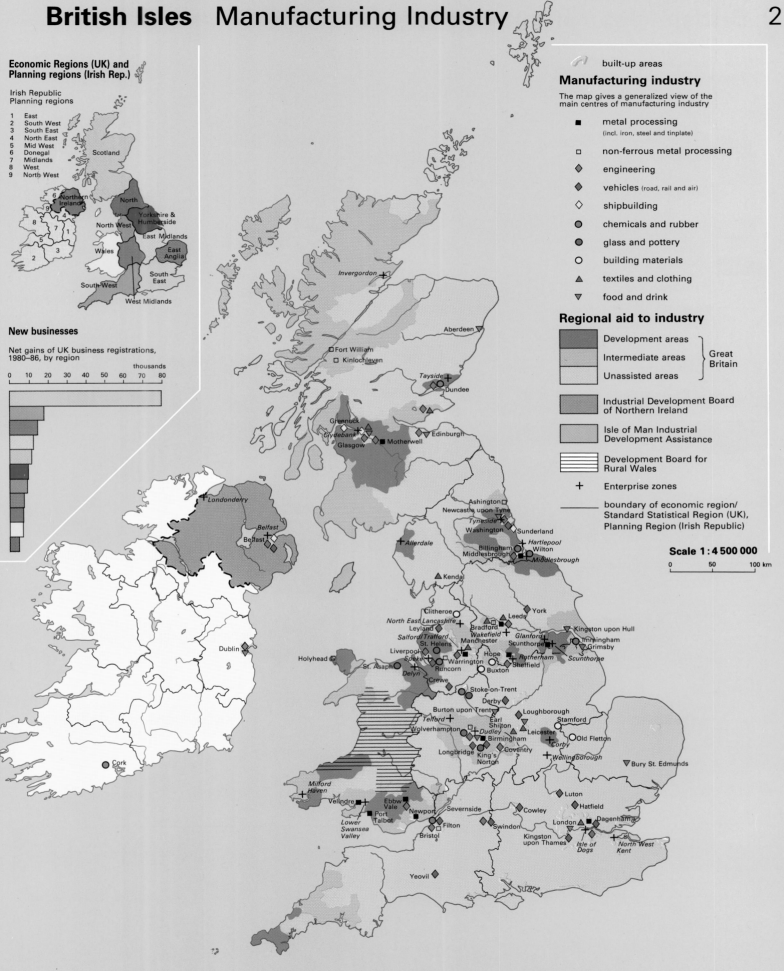

Economic Regions (UK) and Planning regions (Irish Rep.)

Irish Republic
Planning regions

1 East
2 South West
3 South East
4 North East
5 Mid West
6 Donegal
7 Midlands
8 West
9 North West

New businesses

Net gains of UK business registrations, 1980–86, by region

thousands
0 10 20 30 40 50 60 70 80

built-up areas

Manufacturing industry

The map gives a generalized view of the main centres of manufacturing industry

■ metal processing (incl. iron, steel and tinplate)
□ non-ferrous metal processing
◆ engineering
◆ vehicles (road, rail and air)
◇ shipbuilding
● chemicals and rubber
● glass and pottery
○ building materials
▲ textiles and clothing
▽ food and drink

Regional aid to industry

Development areas ⎫
Intermediate areas ⎬ Great Britain
Unassisted areas ⎭

Industrial Development Board of Northern Ireland

Isle of Man Industrial Development Assistance

Development Board for Rural Wales

+ Enterprise zones

— boundary of economic region/Standard Statistical Region (UK), Planning Region (Irish Republic)

Scale 1 : 4 500 000

0 50 100 km

Transverse Mercator Projection
© Oxford University Press

British Isles Employment

Employment by region, 1987
Percentage of total employed

- Distribution, hotels, catering, repairs
- Banking, finance, insurance, business services and leasing
- Public administration and other services
- Transport and communication
- Metal goods, engineering and vehicles industries
- Other manufacturing industries
- Construction
- Energy and water supply
- Metals, minerals and chemicals
- Agriculture, forestry, fishing

- - - - international boundary

——— boundary of Standard Statistical Region

Scale 1:7 000 000

0   100   200 km

50%
40
30
20
10
0

UK data based on Standard Industrial Classification, 1980.
Irish Republic data based on Industrial Classification, 1981 Census of Ireland.

Job gains in Great Britain, 1966–84

Total 3.3 million
- private services
- finance
- health
- teaching
- distribution
- public administration

Job losses in Great Britain, 1966–84

Total 5.4 million
- building
- public utilities
- general industry
- textiles and clothing
- heavy industry
- primary industry (mining and agriculture)
- 'growth' industries (electronics and chemicals)

Map regions labelled: Scotland, Northern Ireland, Irish Republic, North, Yorkshire & Humberside, North West, East Midlands, Wales, East Anglia, South West, South East, West Midlands

Employment structure analysis, Great Britain 1986

Total employed population   21 105 000
Production and construction industries   6 635 000
  of which manufacturing industries   5 137 000
Service industries   14 161 000

0%   10%   20%   30%   40%   50%   60%   70%   80%   90%   100%

- Distribution, hotels, catering, repairs
- Banking, finance, insurance, business services and leasing
- Public administration and other services
- Transport and communication
- Metal goods, engineering and vehicles industries
- Other manufacturing industries
- Construction
- Energy and water supply
- Metals, minerals and chemicals
- Agriculture, forestry, fishing

Lower labels:
Wholesale distribution, Retail distribution, Hotels and catering, Others, Banking and finance, Business services, Others, Public administration and defence, Education, Medical and other health services, Others including social, recreational and personal services, Railways, Other inland transport, Postal services and telecommunications, Others, Mechanical engineering, Electrical and electronic engineering, Motor vehicles and parts, Others, Food, drink and tobacco, Textiles, Footwear and clothing, Timber and wooden furniture, Paper, printing and publishing, Others, Coal extraction and solid fuels, Others, Chemical industry, Others

Employees by industry based on the Standard Industrial Classification 1980

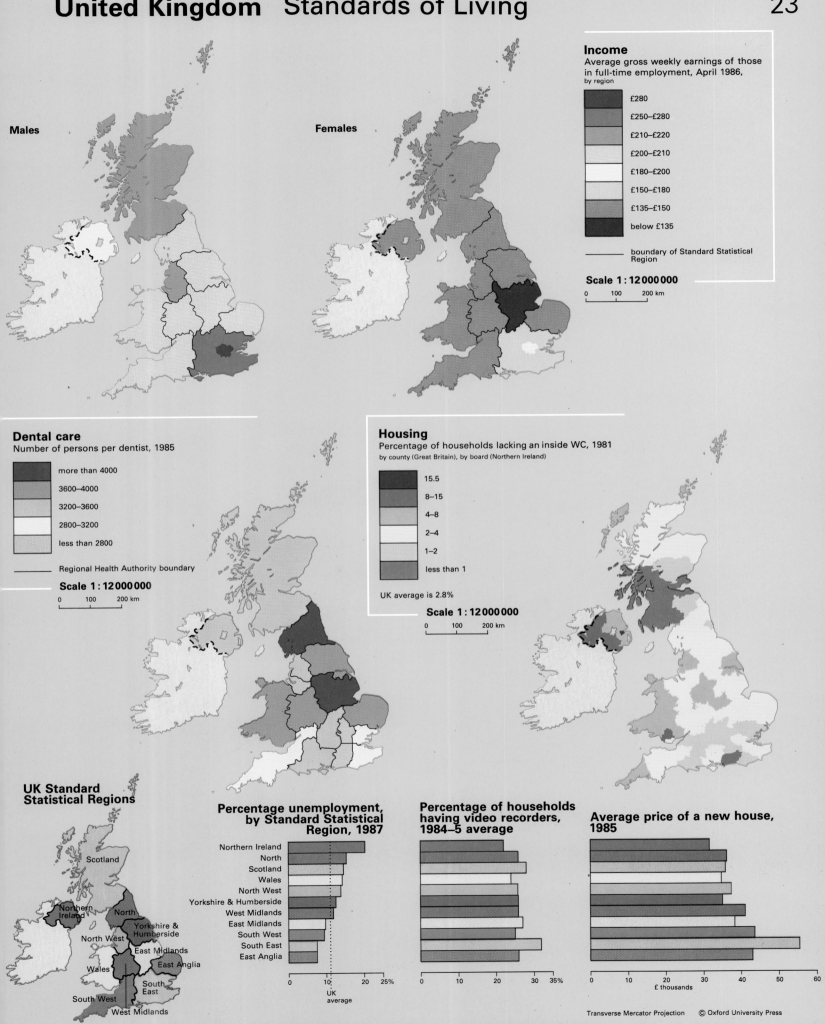

Males

Females

Income
Average gross weekly earnings of those in full-time employment, April 1986, by region

- £280
- £250–£280
- £210–£220
- £200–£210
- £180–£200
- £150–£180
- £135–£150
- below £135

— boundary of Standard Statistical Region

Scale 1 : 12 000 000
0   100   200 km

Dental care
Number of persons per dentist, 1985

- more than 4000
- 3600–4000
- 3200–3600
- 2800–3200
- less than 2800

— Regional Health Authority boundary

Scale 1 : 12 000 000
0   100   200 km

Housing
Percentage of households lacking an inside WC, 1981
by county (Great Britain), by board (Northern Ireland)

- 15.5
- 8–15
- 4–8
- 2–4
- 1–2
- less than 1

UK average is 2.8%

Scale 1 : 12 000 000
0   100   200 km

UK Standard Statistical Regions

Scotland

Northern Ireland

North

North West

Yorkshire & Humberside

East Midlands

Wales

East Anglia

South East

West Midlands

South West

Percentage unemployment, by Standard Statistical Region, 1987

Northern Ireland
North
Scotland
Wales
North West
Yorkshire & Humberside
West Midlands
East Midlands
South West
South East
East Anglia

0   10   20   25%

UK average

Percentage of households having video recorders, 1984–5 average

0   10   20   30   35%

Average price of a new house, 1985

0   10   20   30   40   50   60
£ thousands

Transverse Mercator Projection   © Oxford University Press

Legend:
- motorways
- main roads
- principal railways
- Channel tunnel (under construction)
- vehicle ferry routes
- ● major container terminals

Scale 1 : 4 500 000

0   50   100 km

Transverse Mercator Projection

© Oxford University Press

Legend

Airports
Passengers in 1987

- more than 15 million
- 1–15 million
- less than 1 million

Airways

UK controlled airspace

other airways (beyond UK controlled airspace)

limit of Flight Information Region (FIR)

Ports
Cargo handled in 1987 (tonnes)

- more than 20 million
- 5–20 million
- 95 000–5 million

Waterways

navigable rivers

canals

major freight waterways

Scale 1 : 4 500 000

0   50   100 km

Map Labels

Unst
Sullom Voe
Shetland Islands
Scatsta
Lerwick
Sumburgh

Orkney Islands
Orkney
Kirkwall

Wick

Stornoway

Benbecula

Cromarty Firth
Inverness
Peterhead

Caledonian Canal
Aberdeen

Tiree
Montrose
Dundee
Perth
Crinan
Forth
Forth
Clyde
Clyde
Glasgow
Edinburgh
Islay
Berwick-upon-Tweed
Prestwick
Ayr

Londonderry
Foyle
Coleraine
Bann
Larne
Carrickfergus
Belfast
Belfast Harbour
Cairnryan
Stranraer
SCOTTISH FIR
LONDON FIR
Newcastle
Blyth
Tyne
Carlisle
Sunderland
Seaham
L. Neagh
Upper L. Erne
Lower L. Erne
L. Allen
Warrenpoint
Erne
Silloth
Whitehaven
Workington
Tees/Hartlepool
Tees-side
Whitby
Horan (Knock)
Greenore
Douglas
Barrow-in-Furness
Scarborough
L. Ree
Drogheda
Isle of Man
Heysham
Lancaster
Lancaster
Leeds/Bradford
Ouse
Galway
Shannon
Grand Canal
Dublin
Fleetwood
Blackpool
Leeds & Liverpool
R. Ouse
R. Hull/
R. Humber
Goole
Kingston upon Hull
Hull
L. Derg
Dun Laoghaire
Anglesey Marine Terminal
Liverpool
Liverpool
Garston
Aire & Calder
R. Trent
Immingham/Grimsby
Barrow
Holyhead
Mostyn
Hawarden
Manchester Ship Canal
Manchester
Witham
Shannon
Nore
Caernarfon
Shropshire Union
Trent
Boston
Shannon Estuary
New Ross
Arklow
Llangollen
Trent & Mersey
Soar
East Midlands
King's Lynn
Suir
Blackwater
Waterford
Rosslare
Grand Union
Wisbech
Norwich
Yare
Great Yarmouth
Lowestoft
Lee
Cork
Cork Harbour
Birmingham
Coventry
Nene
Cambridge
Gt Ouse
Fishguard
Severn
Avon
Oxford
Ipswich
Mistley
Colchester
Harwich
Felixstowe
Milford Haven
Gloucester/Cheltenham
Luton
Stansted
Brightlingsea
Swansea
Neath
Sharpness
Blackwater
Port Talbot
Cardiff
Newport
Thames
Lea
London City
London
Southend-on-Sea
Barry
Bristol
Heathrow
Battersea Heliport
Medway
Whitstable
Ramsgate
Watchet
Bridgwater
Kennet & Avon
Gatwick
Manston
Dover
Folkestone
Southampton
Shoreham
Newhaven
Lydd
Bournemouth
Portsmouth
Littlehampton
Exeter
Poole
Cowes
Exmouth
Teignmouth
Par
Fowey
Plymouth
Penzance Heliport
Falmouth
Tresco
Isles of Scilly
St. Mary's

SHANNON FIR

Alderney
Guernsey
St. Peter Port
Channel Islands
Jersey
St. Helier

National Parks

Areas of Outstanding Natural Beauty (England, Wales and Northern Ireland);
National Scenic Areas (Scotland)

Green Belt and proposed Green Belt (United Kingdom)

Heritage Coast (defined and proposed in England and Wales);
Coastal Conservation Zones (Scotland)

• major reserves

● internationally recognized sites
(including Special Protection Areas,
'Ramsar' Sites and Biosphere Reserves)

★ World Heritage Sites
(natural and cultural)

major built-up areas

Scale 1 : 4 500 000

0   50   100 km

The term Green Belt is now being
adopted in new development
plans in Northern Ireland.
It is gradually replacing the
Areas of Special Control, drawn
around the towns and larger
villages to control urban sprawl.

The National Parks were
joined in 1988 by the
similarly constituted
Broads Authority.

Pseudo natural colour satellite image

This composite image of the British Isles has been created from 52 smaller, separate images obtained by Landsat satellite. Scanners from the satellite sense the reflection of the earth in small picture elements or pixels. For each pixel reflected radiation is recorded from several parts of the electromagnetic spectrum. This information has been reprocessed by computer to simulate a natural colour to the land areas. Adjustments have been made for the curvature of the earth when the pixels were pieced together.

British Isles

Boundaries
international
internal

Communications
motorway
other major road
railway
✈ major airport

Cities and towns
⬡ major built-up areas
■ over 1 million inhabitants
● more than 100,000 inhabitants
• smaller towns

Land height

metres
1000
500
200
100
sea level
land below sea level

▲ spot height in metres

Scale 1 : 4 500 000

0   50   100 km

Transverse Mercator Projection
© Oxford University Press

South West England

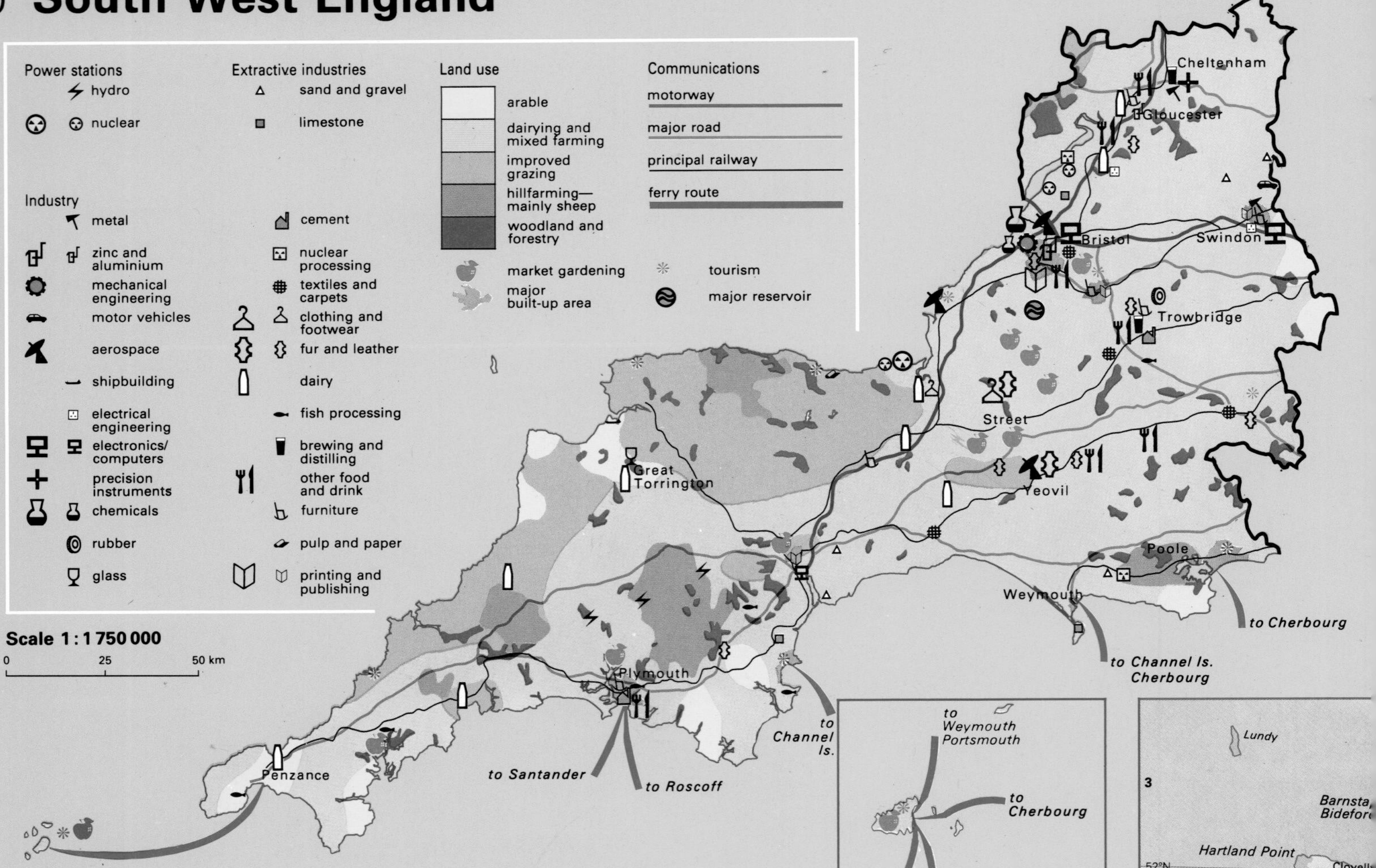
Power stations
hydro
nuclear
Extractive industries
sand and gravel
limestone
Land use
arable
dairying and mixed farming
improved grazing
hillfarming—mainly sheep
woodland and forestry
market gardening
major built-up area
tourism
major reservoir
Communications
motorway
major road
principal railway
ferry route
Industry
metal
zinc and aluminium
mechanical engineering
motor vehicles
aerospace
shipbuilding
electrical engineering
electronics/computers
precision instruments
chemicals
rubber
glass
cement
nuclear processing
textiles and carpets
clothing and footwear
fur and leather
dairy
fish processing
brewing and distilling
other food and drink
furniture
pulp and paper
printing and publishing
Cheltenham
Gloucester
Bristol
Swindon
Trowbridge
Street
Yeovil
Great Torrington
Poole
Weymouth
Plymouth
Penzance
to Cherbourg
to Channel Is. Cherbourg
to Channel Is.
to Santander
to Roscoff
to Weymouth Portsmouth
to Cherbourg
to St-Malo
to St-Malo
Scale 1 : 1 750 000
0
25
50 km

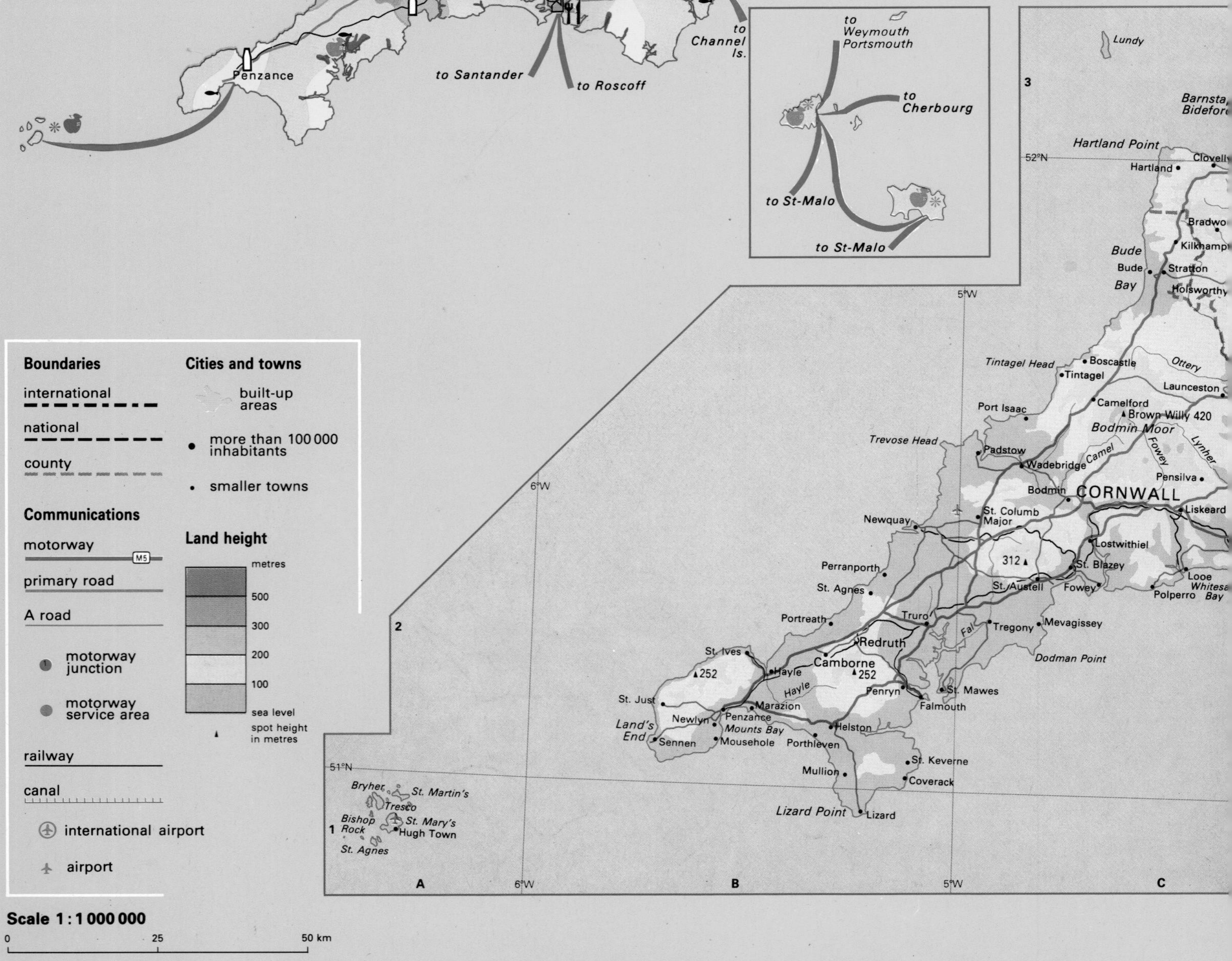
Boundaries
international
national
county
Cities and towns
built-up areas
more than 100 000 inhabitants
smaller towns
Communications
motorway
M5
primary road
A road
motorway junction
motorway service area
railway
canal
international airport
airport
Land height
metres
500
300
200
100
sea level
spot height in metres
Lundy
Barnstaple
Bideford
Hartland Point
Clovelly
Hartland
52°N
Bradworthy
Kilkhampton
Bude
Bude Bay
Stratton
Holsworthy
Tintagel Head
Boscastle
Tintagel
Ottery
Launceston
Port Isaac
Camelford
Brown Willy 420
Bodmin Moor
Trevose Head
Padstow
Camel
Fowey
Lynher
Wadebridge
Pensilva
Bodmin
CORNWALL
Liskeard
Newquay
St. Columb Major
Lostwithiel
Perranporth
312
St. Blazey
St. Agnes
St. Austell
Fowey
Looe
Polperro
Whitesand Bay
Portreath
Truro
Fal
Tregony
Mevagissey
St. Ives
Redruth
Dodman Point
252
Hayle
Camborne
252
St. Just
Hayle
Penryn
St. Mawes
Marazion
Falmouth
Land's End
Newlyn
Penzance
Mounts Bay
Helston
Sennen
Mousehole
Porthleven
St. Keverne
51°N
Mullion
Coverack
Bryher
St. Martin's
Tresco
Lizard Point
Lizard
Bishop Rock
St. Mary's
Hugh Town
St. Agnes
1
2
3
A
B
C
6°W
5°W
Scale 1 : 1 000 000
0
25
50 km

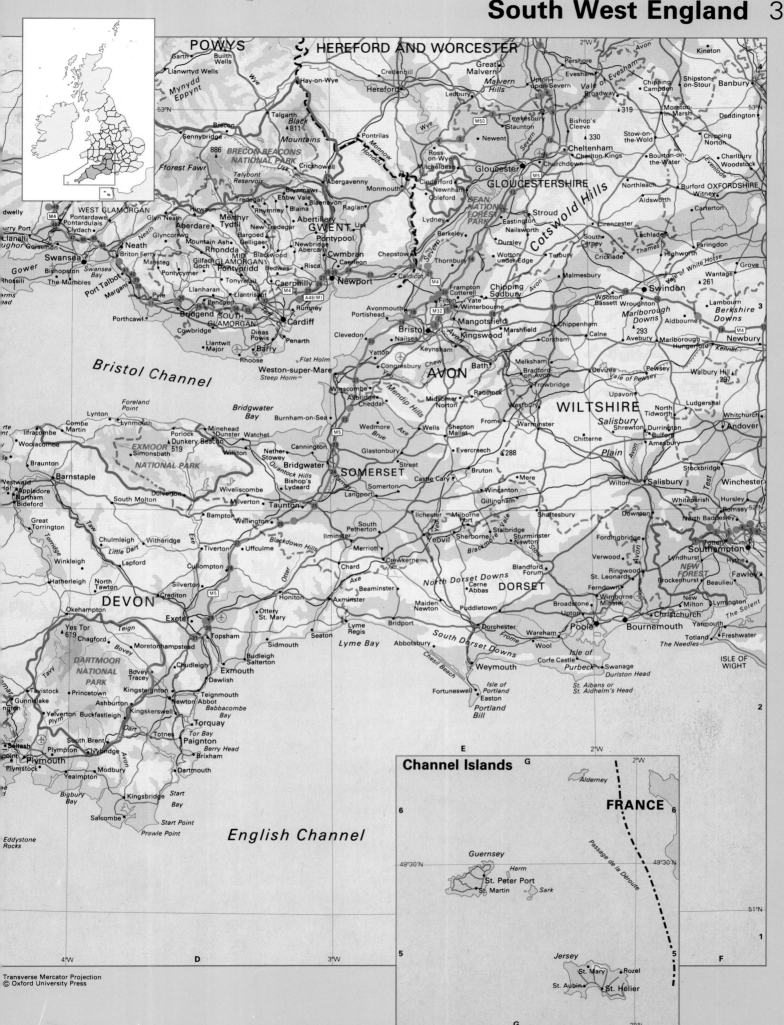

Land use

- arable
- dairying and mixed farming
- improved grazing
- hillfarming— mainly sheep
- woodland and forestry

market gardening

major built-up area

tourism

major reservoir

Communications

- motorway
- major road
- principal railway
- ferry route

Scale 1 : 1 750 000

0   25   50 km

Power stations

- coal
- coal/oil
- oil
- gas
- nuclear

Industry

- iron and steel
- metal
- aluminium
- mechanical engineering
- motor vehicles
- rail vehicles
- aerospace
- electrical engineering
- electronics/ computers
- precision instruments, optics
- jewellery
- oil refining
- glass
- cement

Extractive industries

- coal
- sand and gravel
- limestone

- bricks and tiles
- nuclear processing
- textiles and carpets
- clothing and footwear
- fur and leather
- dairy
- fish processing
- sugar refining
- brewing and distilling
- other food and drink
- furniture
- pulp and paper
- printing and publishing

Boundaries

county

Communications

motorway   M1

primary road

A road

- motorway junction
- motorway service area

railway

canal

- international airport
- other airport

Cities and towns

built-up areas

- over 1 million inhabitants
- more than 100 000 inhabitants
- smaller towns

Land height

metres
300
200
100
sea level
land below sea level

spot height in metres

Scale 1 : 1 000 000

0   25   50 km

King's Lynn
Norwich
Peterborough
Cambridge
Bedford
Banbury
Ipswich
Felixstowe
Harwich
Oxford
Reading
London
Fawley
Portsmouth
Newhaven
Dover
Folkestone

to Oslo
Kristiansand
Esbjerg
Hamburg
Hoek van Holland
Göteborg

to Zeebrugge

to Vlissingen

to Dunkerque

to Zeebrugge
Oostende
Calais
Boulogne

to Channel Is.
Cherbourg
St-Malo
le Havre
Caen

to Dieppe

WARWICKSHIRE
Rugby
Daventry
Southam
Stratford-upon-Avon
Gaydon
Byfield
Wood Halse
Kineton
Weed
Chipping Campden
Shipston-on-Stour
Banbury
Broadway
Brackley
Bishop's Cleeve
330
Stow-on-the-Wold
Moreton-in-Marsh
Deddington
Cheltenham
Charlton Kings
Bourton-on-the-Water
Chipping Norton
Bicester
GLOUCESTERSHIRE
Northleach
Burford
Charlbury
Woodstock
OXFORDSHIRE
Kidlington
Cotswold Hills
Aldsworth
Witney
Oxford
Wheatley
Cirencester
Carterton
South Cerney
Lechlade
Abingdon
Cricklade
Thames
Highworth
Paringdon
Dorc
Vale of White Horse
Didcot
Harwell
Wallir
Swindon
Grove
Wantage
East Ilsley
Goring
Wootton Bassett
Wroughton
261
Lambourn
Pangbourn
Marlborough Downs
Aldbourne
Berkshire Downs
Calne
293
Avebury
Newbury
BERKSHIRE
Devizes
Marlborough
Hungerford
Kennet
Thatcham
Pewsey
Vale of Pewsey
Walbury Hill
297
Kingsclere
Tadley
Upavon
Ludgershall
Basings
WILTSHIRE
North Tidworth
Overton
Oakley
Salisbury
Shrewton
Durrington
Bulford
Andover
Whitchurch
Chitterne
Amesbury
HAMPSHIRE
Plain
Avon
Stockbridge
New Alresford
Wilton
Salisbury
Winchester
51°N
Whiteparish
Hursley
Twyford
Downton
Romsey
North Baddesley
Eastleigh
Bishop's Waltham
Fordingbridge
Wickham
Waterlooville
Verwood
Lyndhurst
Southampton
Totton
Hythe
Hedge End
Fareham
St. Leonards
Ringwood
NEW FOREST
Fawley
Stubbington
Ferndown
Brockenhurst
Beaulieu
Gosport
Wimborne Minster
New Milton
Lymington
Cowes
Christchurch
Poole
Bournemouth
Yarmouth
Fishbourne
Ryde
Bembridge
Totland
Freshwater
ISLE OF WIGHT
Newport
Sandow
The Needles
The Solent
Shanklin
Swanage
Durlston Head
St. Catherine's Point
Ventnor

Transverse Mercator Projection
© Oxford University Press

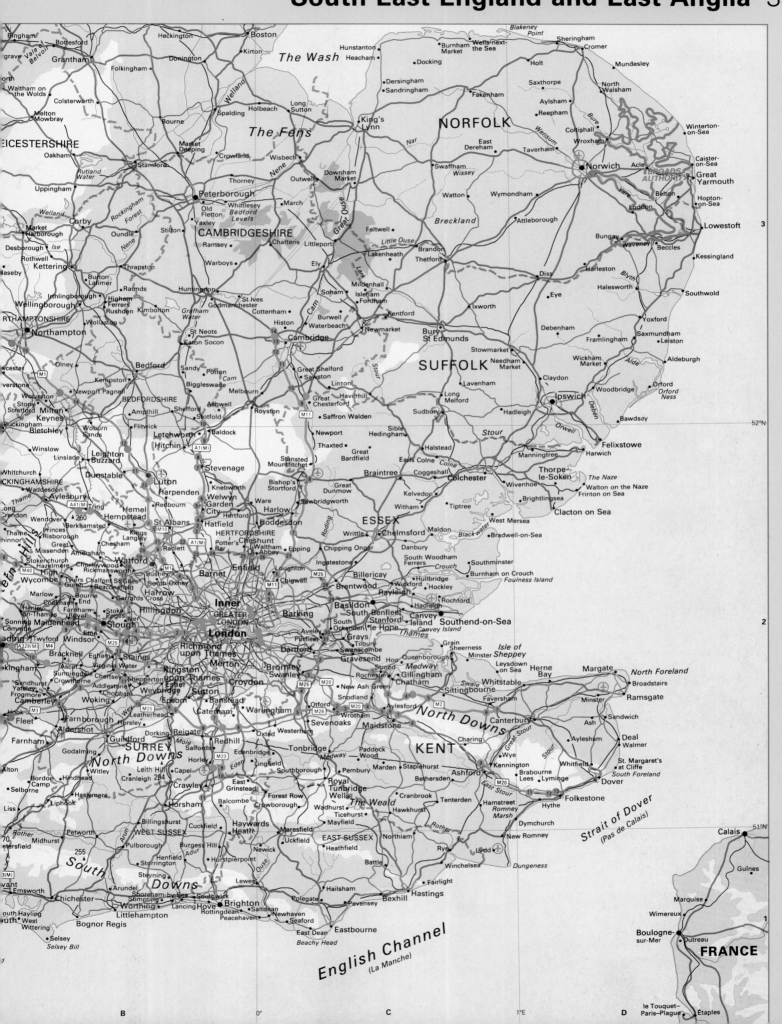

For legend see page 32.

Scale 1 : 400 000

0 10 km

Transverse Mercator Projection
© Oxford University Press

BEDFORDSHIRE

HERTFORDSHIRE

ESSEX

BUCKINGHAMSHIRE

GREATER LONDON

BERKSHIRE

SURREY

KENT

Chilterns

North Downs

Epping Forest

Place names (north to south, approximate):

Broughton, Cranfield, Marston Moretaine, Langford, Shefford, Henlow, Stotfold, Milton Keynes, Woburn Sands, Lidlington, Ampthill, Maulden, Clophill, Chicksands, Shillington, Letchworth, Baldock, Bletchley, Aspley Guise, Flitwick, Hitchin, Newton Longville, Great Brickhill, Toddington, Streatley, Barton-le-Clay, Stewkley, Hockliffe, Leighton Buzzard, Stanbridge, Billington, Dunstable, Eaton Bray, Caddington, Luton, Kings Walden, Stevenage, Whitwell, Walkern, Braughing, Clavering, Newport, Thaxted, Brent Pelham, Quendon, Henham, Elsenham, Great Bardfield, Stansted Mountfitchet, Stebbing, Wing, Linslade, Mentmore, Edlesborough, Whipsnade, Markyate, Welwyn, Knebworth, Watton at Stone, Puckerage, Standon, Hadham Ford, Bishop's Stortford, Takeley, Great Dunmow, Felsted, Cheddington, Ivinghoe, Daghall, Harpenden, Wheathampstead, Tewin, Hertford, Much Hadham, Spellbrook, Hatfield Heath, High Roding, Great Waltham, Little Waltham, Marsworth, Aston Clinton, Tring, Potten End, Berkhamsted, Great Gaddesden, Redbourn, Welwyn Garden City, Ware, Widford, Sawbridgeworth, Hunsdon, Sheering, Harlow, Matching Green, Chelmsford, Writtle, Wendover, Hemel Hempstead, St. Albans, Hatfield, Essendon, Hoddesdon, Roydon, Stanstead Abbotts, Great Baddow, Galleywood, Botley, Bovingdon, Chesham, Kings Langley, Chiswell Green, London Colney, Colney Heath, Welham Green, Brookmans Park, Cuffley, Cheshunt, Lower Nazeing, Epping, Thornwood Common, North Weald Bassett, Chipping Ongar, Great Missenden, Prestwood, Chalfont St. Giles, Abbots Langley, Radlett, Shenley, Potter's Bar, Waltham Abbey, Theydon Bois, Stondon Massey, Ingatestone, Stock, Amersham, Holmer Green, Little Chalfont, Chorleywood, Watford, Borehamwood, Bushey, Enfield, Loughton, Chigwell, Stapleford Abbotts, Brentwood, Billericay, Hazelmere, Tylers Green, Rickmansworth, South Oxhey, Barnet, Edgware, Southgate, Chingford, Woodford, Redbridge, Grays Hill, High Wycombe, Loudwater, Beaconsfield, Chalfont St. Peter, Harefield, Stanmore, Finchley, Hendon, Wood Green, Edmonton, Waltham Forest, Romford, Havering, Hornchurch, Basildon, Flackwell Heath, Gerrards Cross, Ruislip, Kenton, Golders Green, Haringey, Tottenham, Hornsey, Leyton, Wanstead, Ilford, Barking, Dagenham, Upminster, Stanford le Hope, Bourne End, Cookham, Burnham Beeches, Harrow, Brent, Wembley, Camden, Islington, Hackney, West Ham, Newham, Rainham, Linford, Chadwell St. Mary, Maidenhead, Bray, Taplow, Stoke Poges, Farnham Royal, Hillingdon, Uxbridge, Greenford, Ealing, Willesden, Paddington, Westminster, City of London, Tower Hamlets, Woolwich, South Ockenden, Aveley, Purfleet, West Thurrock, Grays, Fifield, Slough, Iver, West Drayton, Southall, Brentford, Hammersmith, Kensington & Chelsea, Fulham, Battersea, Southwark, Greenwich, Erith, Greenhithe, Swanscombe, Northfleet, Tilbury, Eton, Windsor, Datchet, Hounslow, Richmond upon Thames, Putney, Wandsworth, Lambeth, Brixton, Lewisham, Eltham, Bexley, Dartford, Gravesend, Old Windsor, Berkshire, Feltham, Twickenham, Wimbledon, Streatham, Catford, Sidcup, North Cray, Wilmington, Hextable, Higham, Bracknell, Ascot, Egham, Staines, Ashford, Sunbury, Kingston upon Thames, Merton, Mitcham, Beckenham, Bromley, Swanley, South Darenth, Instead Rise, Virginia Water, Sunningdale, Chertsey, Shepperton, Surbiton, Morden, Orpington, Eynsford, Hartley, Strood, Bagshot, Camberley, Lightwater, Windlesham, Chobham, Weybridge, Addlestone, Walton on Thames, Esher, Croydon, Ewell, Sutton, New Addington, Knockholt Pound, West Kingdown, Culverstone Green, Snodland, New Ash Green, Frimley, Knaphill, Byfleet, Cobham, Oxshott, Epsom, Banstead, Purley, Warlingham, Biggin Hill, Tatsfield, Caterham, Otford, Kemsing, Seal, Ightham, Borough Green, West Malling, Deep Cut, Pirbright, Woking, Ripley, Send, Leatherhead, Ashtead, Tadworth, Kingswood, Coulsdon, Woldingham, Westerham, Sevenoaks, Wrotham, Ditton, Farnborough, Worplesdon, Fetcham, Horsley, West Clandon, Merstham, Woldingham, Oxted, Limpsfield, Crockham Hill, Sevenoaks Weald, Shipbourne, Wateringbury, Mereworth, Ash, Onslow Village, Guildford, Dorking, Westcott, Brockham, Reigate, Redhill, South Nutfield, Godstone, South Godstone, Marlpit Hill, Edenbridge, Hildenborough, Yalding, Puttenham, Shalford, Shere, Gomshall, North Holmwood, Salfords, Outwood, Leigh, Tonbridge, Paddock Wood, Godalming, Bramley, Wonersh, North Downs, Leith Hill, Beare Green, Capel, Charlwood, Horley, Smallfield, Lingfield, Dormansland, Penshurst, Fordcombe, Hindhead, Elstead, Milford, Witley, Chiddingfold, Rowly, Ockley, Ewhurst, Cranleigh, Ifield, Crawley, Copthorne, East Grinstead

Roads/motorways: M1, A1(M), M11, M25, M10, M40, M4, M3, M20, M23, M26, A41(M), A1(M)

Grand Union Canal

Thames, Lea, Roding, Mole, Wey, Eden, Medway

West and East Midlands

LINCOLNSHIRE
NOTTINGHAMSHIRE
DERBYSHIRE
SOUTH YORKSHIRE
LEICESTERSHIRE
NORTHAMPTONSHIRE
CAMBRIDGESHIRE
BEDFORDSHIRE
BUCKINGHAMSHIRE
WARWICKSHIRE
WEST MIDLANDS
SHROPSHIRE
CHESHIRE
GREATER MANCHESTER
HEREFORD AND WORCESTER
CLWYD
POWYS
WALES
PEAK DISTRICT NATIONAL PARK
BRECON BEACONS NATIONAL PARK
The Wash
The Fens
Lincoln Wolds
Sherwood Forest
Vale of Belvoir
Cannock Chase
Wenlock Edge
Malvern Hills
Vale of Evesham
Black Mountains
Liverpool Bay
Spurn Head
Humber
Birmingham
Sheffield
Liverpool
Manchester
Nottingham
Leicester
Derby
Coventry
Lincoln
Stoke-on-Trent
Wolverhampton
Peterborough
Northampton
Chester
Shrewsbury
Worcester
Hereford
Gloucester
Luton
Bedford
Grimsby
Boston
King's Lynn
53°N
52°N

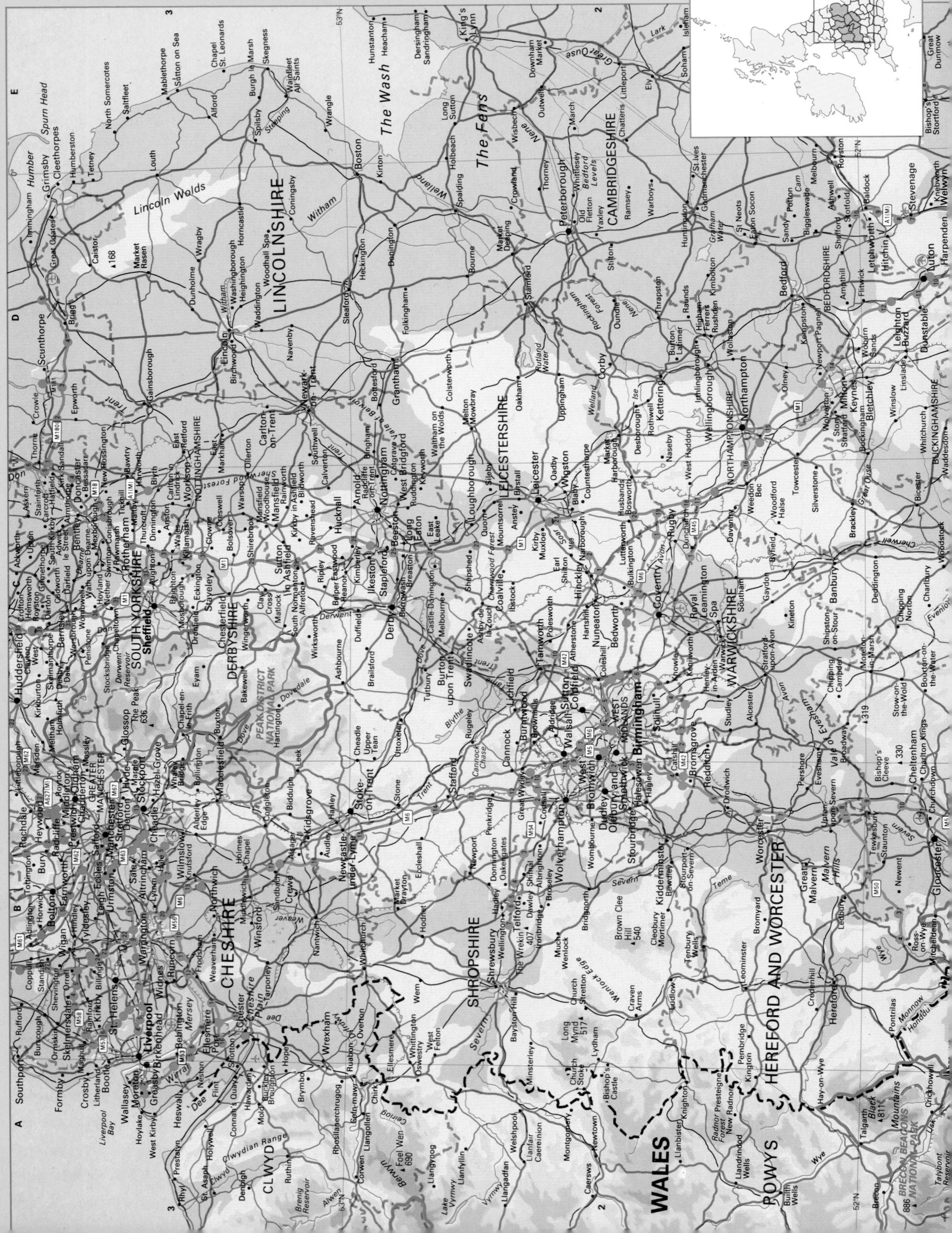

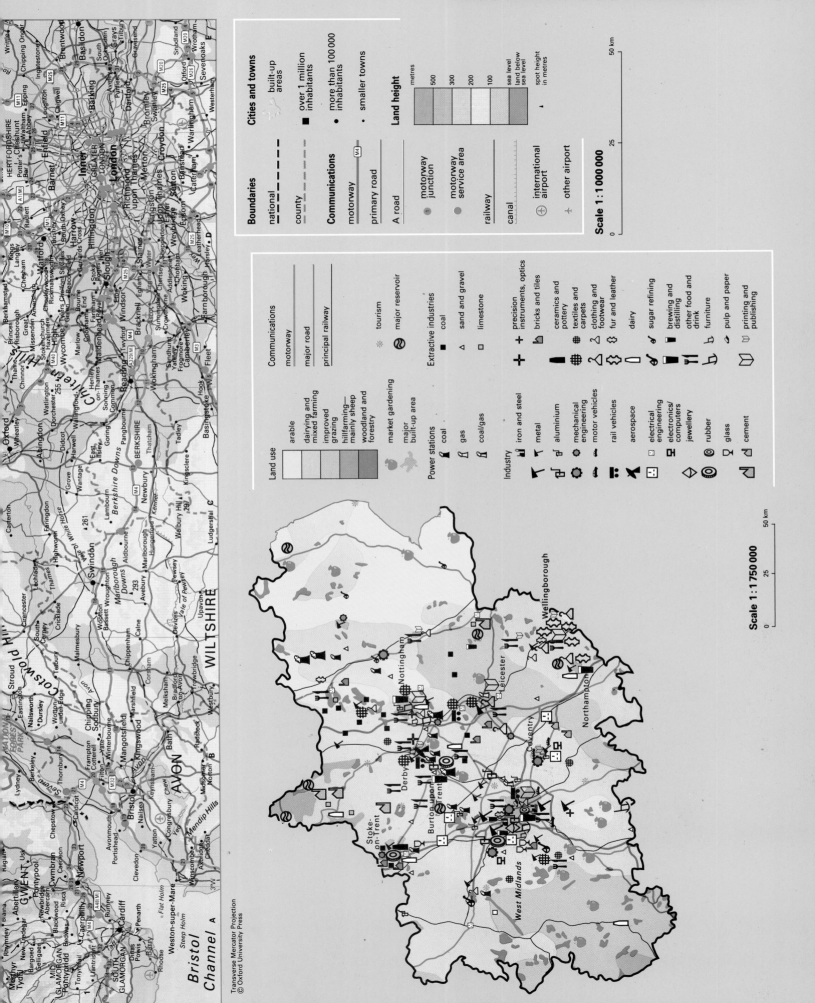

Boundaries

national

county

Communications

motorway M4

primary road

A road

motorway junction

motorway service area

railway

canal

international airport

other airport

Cities and towns

built-up areas

over 1 million inhabitants

more than 100 000 inhabitants

smaller towns

Land height

metres

500
300
200
100
sea level
land below sea level

spot height in metres

Scale 1:1 000 000

0   25   50 km

Land use

arable

dairying and mixed farming

improved grazing

hillfarming— mainly sheep

woodland and forestry

market gardening

major built-up area

Communications

motorway

major road

principal railway

tourism

major reservoir

Extractive industries

coal

sand and gravel

limestone

Power stations

coal

gas

coal/gas

Industry

iron and steel

metal

aluminium

mechanical engineering

motor vehicles

rail vehicles

aerospace

electrical engineering

electronics/ computers

jewellery

rubber

glass

cement

precision instruments, optics

bricks and tiles

ceramics and pottery

textiles and carpets

clothing and footwear

fur and leather

dairy

sugar refining

brewing and distilling

other food and drink

furniture

pulp and paper

printing and publishing

Scale 1:1 750 000

0   25   50 km

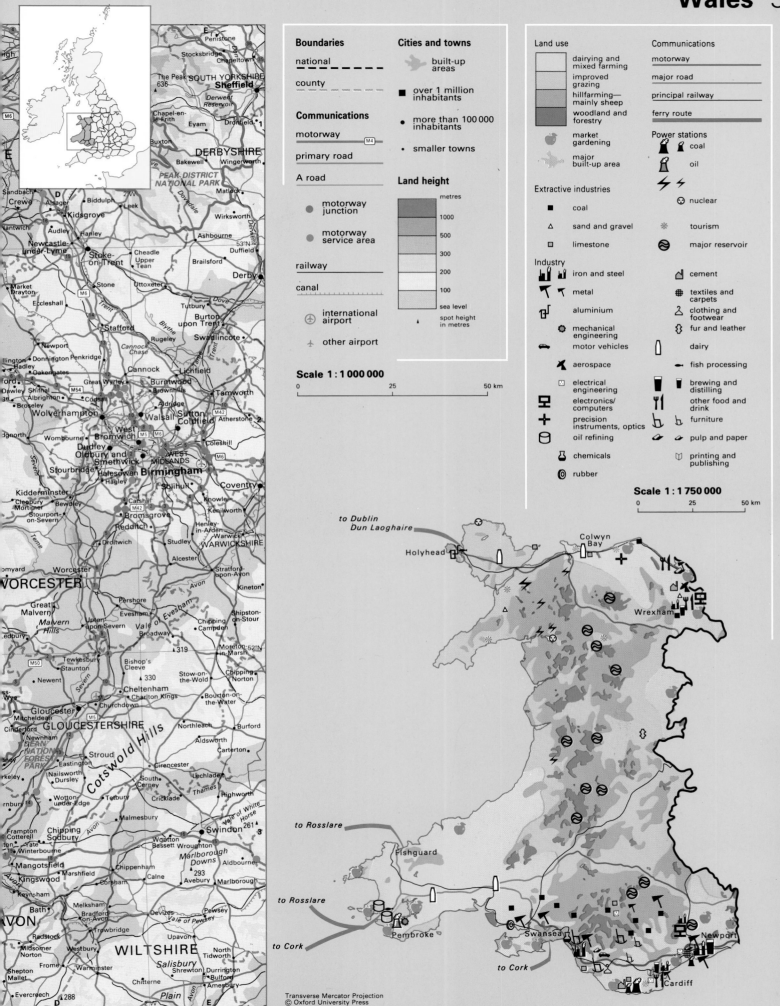

Boundaries
national
county

Communications
motorway
primary road
A road
motorway junction
motorway service area
railway
canal
international airport
other airport

Cities and towns
built-up areas
over 1 million inhabitants
more than 100 000 inhabitants
smaller towns

Land height
metres
1000
500
300
200
100
sea level
spot height in metres

Scale 1:1 000 000
0   25   50 km

Land use
dairying and mixed farming
improved grazing
hillfarming—mainly sheep
woodland and forestry
market gardening
major built-up area

Extractive industries
coal
sand and gravel
limestone

Industry
iron and steel
metal
aluminium
mechanical engineering
motor vehicles
aerospace
electrical engineering
electronics/computers
precision instruments, optics
oil refining
chemicals
rubber

Communications
motorway
major road
principal railway
ferry route

Power stations
coal
oil
nuclear
tourism
major reservoir

cement
textiles and carpets
clothing and footwear
fur and leather
dairy
fish processing
brewing and distilling
other food and drink
furniture
pulp and paper
printing and publishing

Scale 1:1 750 000
0   25   50 km

Transverse Mercator Projection
© Oxford University Press

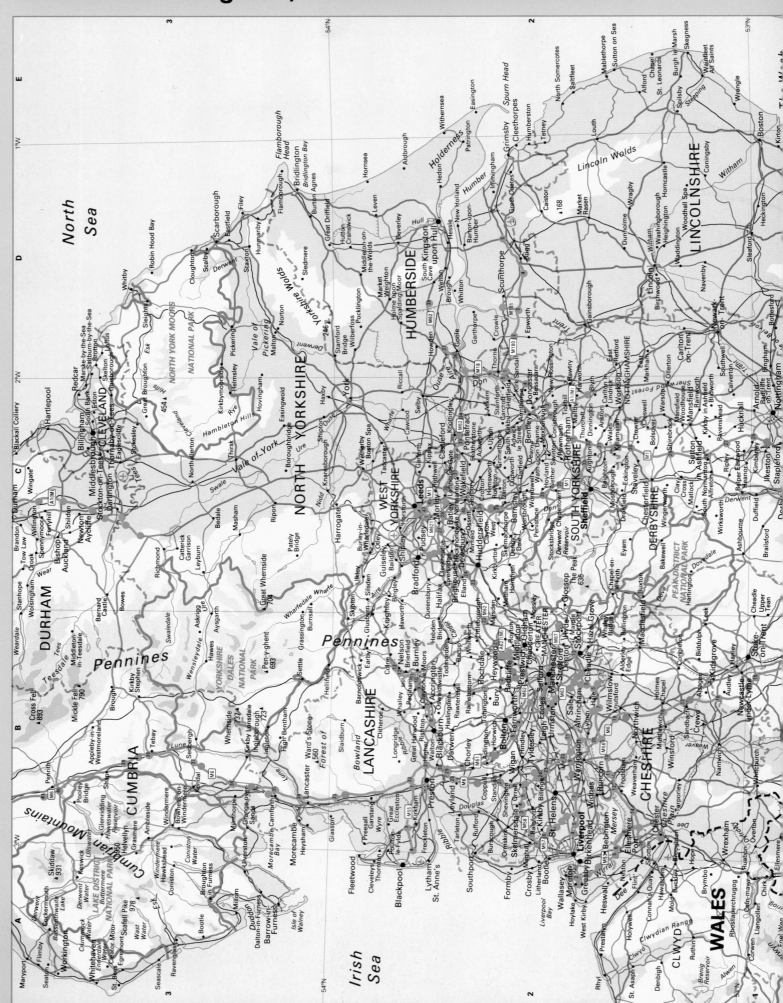

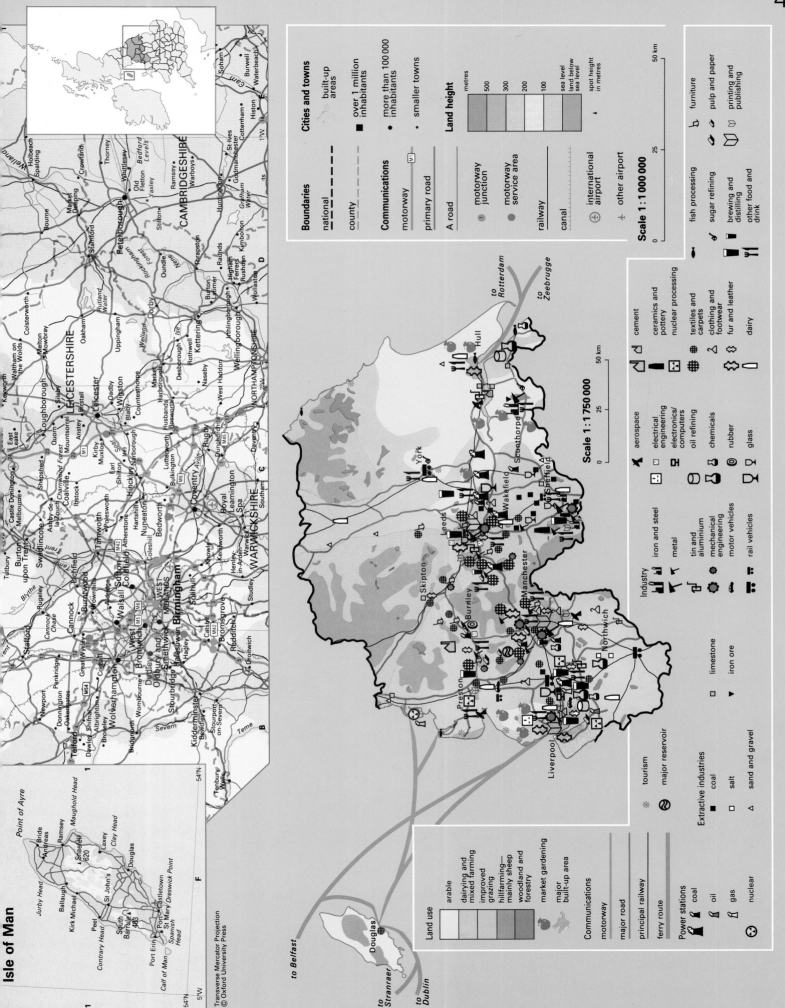

A · B · C · D

3°00'W · 2°40'W · 2°20'W · 2°00'W

Morecambe Bay

Morecambe · Torrisholme · Halton · Brookhouse
Heysham · Lancaster · Settle
Overton · Scotforth · Ward's Stone 560 ▲ · Airton

54°00'N

Lune · Glasson · Galgate · Long Preston
Cockerham · Wyre · Hellifield
Forest of Bowland
Stocks Res.
Ribblesdale

Fleetwood · Knott End-on-Sea · Stake Pool · Slaidburn
Rossall Pt. · Preesall · Oakenclough · Hodder · Gisburn
Stalmine · **LANCASHIRE** · Barnoldswick · Earby · Silsden
Cleveleys · Garstang · Waddington · West Bradford · Glusburn
Thornton · Calder · Chipping · Clitheroe · Colne · Keighley
Wyre · Brock · Longridge · Hurst Green · Nelson · Trawden · Haworth
Poulton-le-Fylde · Great Eccleston · Ribble · Billington · Whalley · Brierfield · Oxenhope
Blackpool · Barton · Samlesbury · Great Harwood · Calder · Padiham · Burnley
Great Marton · Broughton · Fulwood · Clayton-le-Moors · Rishton · *Hebden Water*
M55 · Preston · Walton-le-Dale · Blackburn · Accrington · Hebden Bridge
Kirkham · Higher Walton · Oswaldtwistle · *Forest of Rossendale* · Todmorden
Freckleton · Warton · Bamber Bridge · Darwen · Haslingden · Rawtenstall · Bacup
Lytham St. Anne's · Lytham · *Ribble* · Longton · Hutton · Leyland · Ripponden
Hesketh Bank · Much Hoole · Euxton · Edgworth · Ramsbottom · Whitworth · Littleborough
Beconshall · Tarleton · Bretherton · Chorley · Toppings · Tottington · Rochdale · Milnrow
Banks · Croston · Charnock Richard · Bradshaw · Bury · Heywood · Shaw · Marsden
Southport · Rufford · Adlington · Horwich · Little Lever · Middleton · Royton · Delph
Ainsdale · Scarisbrick · Coppull · Standish · Bolton · Radcliffe · *Saddleworth*
Burscough Bridge · Newburgh · Shevington · Aspull · Westhoughton · Farnworth · Whitefield · Failsworth · Uppermill · *Moor*
Formby · Ormskirk · Dalton · Wigan · Hindley · Walkden · Kearsley · Prestwich · Chadderton · Oldham · Mossley
Great Altcar · Aughton · Skelmersdale · Orrell · Ince in Makerfield · Abram · Leigh · Swinton · Pendlebury · Failsworth
Hightown · Lydiate · Rainford · Billinge · Ashton in Makerfield · Tyldesley · Atherton · Salford · Ashton-under-Lyne · Stalybridge
Crosby · Maghull · Kirkby · Haydock · Golborne · Eccles · Manchester · Droylsden · Dukinfield · Audenshaw
Litherland · Aintree · Knowsley · Newton-le-Willows · Culcheth · Urmston · Stretford · Denton · Hyde · Hadfield
Bootle · **MERSEYSIDE** · West Derby · St. Helens · Prescot · Risley · Irlam · Partington · Sale · Bredbury · Glossop
New Brighton · Huyton-with-Roby · Whiston · Rainhill · Great Sankey · Warrington · Altrincham · Hale · Cheadle · Romiley · Marple
Wallasey · **Liverpool** · Childwall · Thelwall · Stockton Heath · Lymm · Stockport · Hazel Grove
Moreton · Seacombe · Birkenhead · Allerton · Halewood · Widnes · Runcorn · Bramhall · High Lane · New Mills
Hoylake · Greasby · Bebington · Speke · Manchester Ship Canal · Handforth · Poynton
West Kirby · Irby · Pensby · *Wirral* · Eastham · Ellesmere Port · Ince · Elton · Frodsham · Weaver · Mobberley · Wilmslow · *Bollin* · Whaley Bridge
Heswall · Neston · Willaston · Ness · Burton · Ledsham · Helsby · *Delamere Forest* · Barnton · Knutsford · Alderley Edge · Bollington
Baguilt · *Dee* · Upton · *Mersey* · Dunham-on-the-Hill · Weaverham · **CHESHIRE** · Prestbury · Macclesfield
Halkyn · Connah's Quay · Shotton · Blacon · Chester · Frodsham · Cuddington · Northwich · Hartford · Chelford
Northop · Queensferry · Mancot · Lache · Duddon · Davenham · Moulton · Goostrey
WALES · Ewloe · Hawarden · Broughton · Tarvin · Kelsall · Delamere · Wharton · Cranage · Marton
Mold · Buckley · *Dee* · Tarporley · Winsford · Middlewich · Holmes Chapel · Macclesfield

53°40'N · 53°20'N

Liverpool Bay

Shropshire Union Canal · *Trent & Mersey Canal* · *Macclesfield Canal* · *Rochdale Canal* · *Leeds & Liverpool Canal*

Transverse Mercator Projection
© Oxford University Press

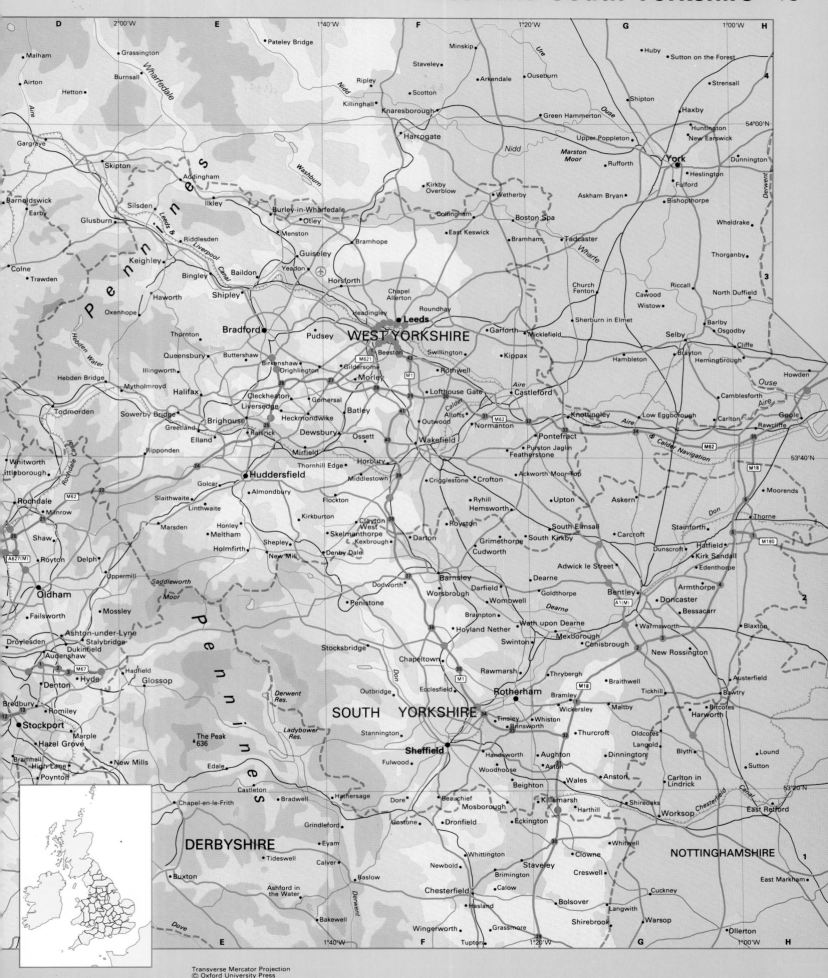

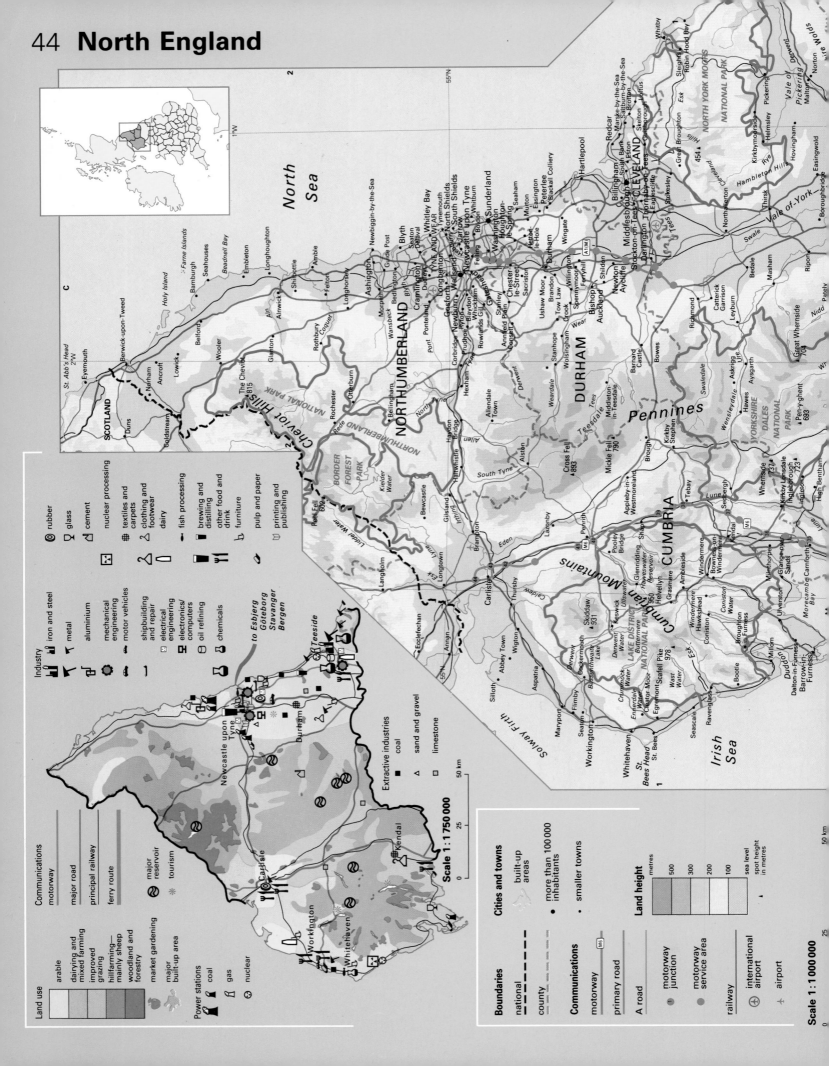

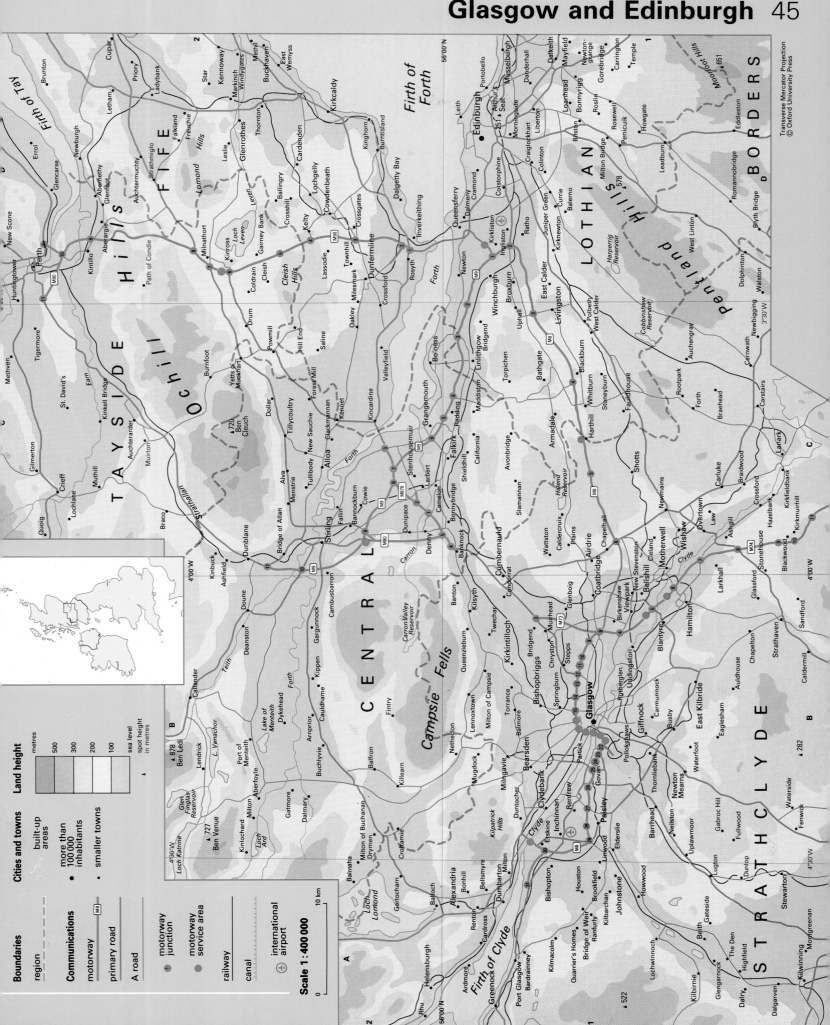

Transverse Mercator Projection
© Oxford University Press

Boundaries
region

Communications
motorway ▬M8▬
primary road
A road

● ● motorway junction
● motorway service area
━━━ railway
╌╌╌ canal
✈ international airport

Cities and towns
built-up areas
● more than 100 000 inhabitants
• smaller towns

Land height

metres	
500	
300	
200	
100	
sea level	

▲ spot height in metres

Scale 1 : 400 000
0   10 km

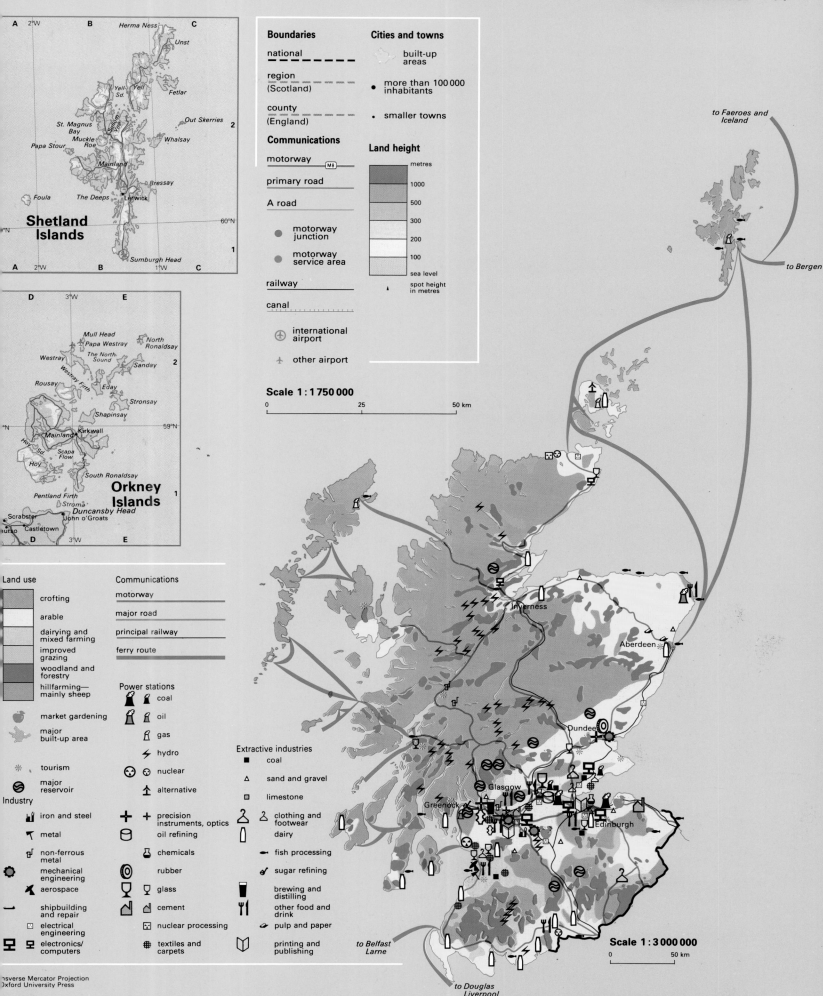

Shetland Islands

Herma Ness
Unst
Yell
Yell Sd.
Fetlar
Out Skerries
St. Magnus Bay
Muckle Roe
Papa Stour
Sullom Voe
Mainland
Whalsay
Bressay
Foula
The Deeps
Lerwick
Sumburgh Head
60°N
2°W
1°W

Orkney Islands

Mull Head
Papa Westray
North Ronaldsay
Westray
The North Sound
Sanday
Rousay
Westray Firth
Eday
Stronsay
Shapinsay
Mainland
Kirkwall
Hoy Sd.
Scapa Flow
Hoy
South Ronaldsay
Pentland Firth
Stroma
Duncansby Head
Scrabster
John o'Groats
Castletown
59°N
3°W

Boundaries
national
region (Scotland)
county (England)

Communications
motorway — M8
primary road
A road
● motorway junction
● motorway service area
railway
canal
⊕ international airport
✈ other airport

Cities and towns
built-up areas
● more than 100 000 inhabitants
• smaller towns

Land height
metres
1000
500
300
200
100
sea level
▲ spot height in metres

Scale 1 : 1 750 000
0   25   50 km

Land use
crofting
arable
dairying and mixed farming
improved grazing
woodland and forestry
hillfarming— mainly sheep
market gardening
major built-up area
* tourism
major reservoir

Communications
motorway
major road
principal railway
ferry route

Power stations
coal
oil
gas
hydro
nuclear
alternative

Industry
iron and steel
metal
non-ferrous metal
mechanical engineering
aerospace
shipbuilding and repair
electrical engineering
electronics/ computers
precision instruments, optics
oil refining
chemicals
rubber
glass
cement
nuclear processing

Extractive industries
■ coal
△ sand and gravel
□ limestone
clothing and footwear
dairy
fish processing
sugar refining
brewing and distilling
other food and drink
pulp and paper
printing and publishing
textiles and carpets

to Faeroes and Iceland
to Bergen

Inverness
Aberdeen
Dundee
Glasgow
Greenock
Edinburgh

to Belfast Larne
to Douglas Liverpool

Scale 1 : 3 000 000
0   50 km

Transverse Mercator Projection
Oxford University Press

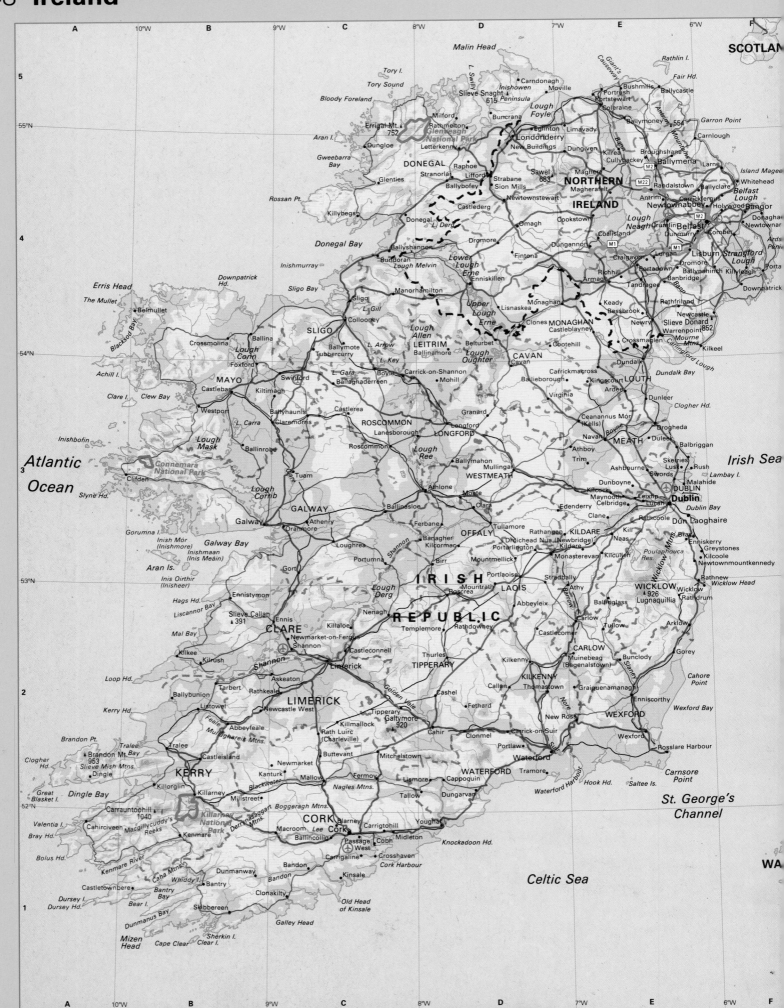

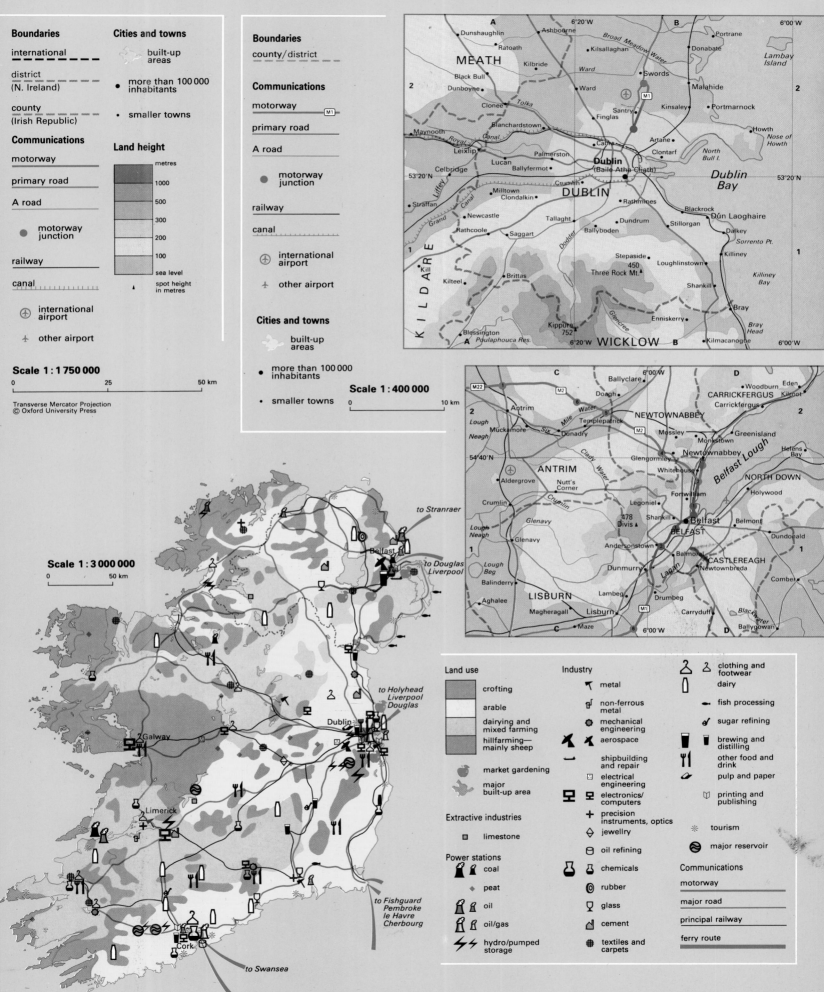

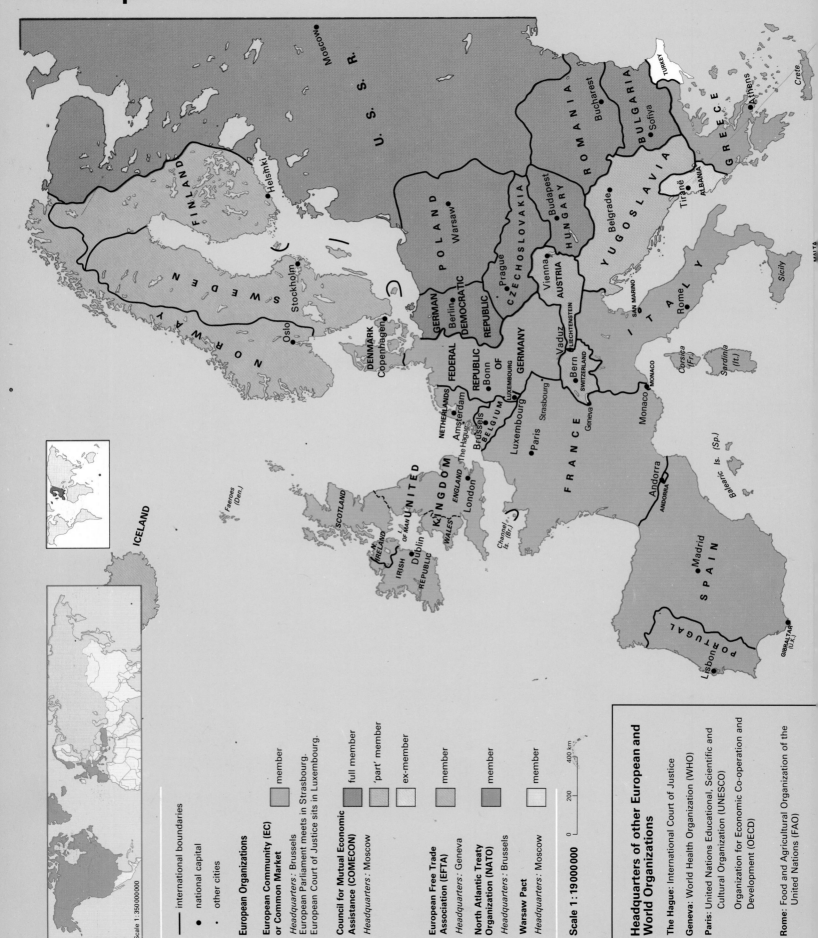

Scale 1:350 000 000

ICELAND

Faeroes
(Den.)

European Organizations

European Community (EC) or Common Market
member

Headquarters: Brussels
European Parliament meets in Strasbourg.
European Court of Justice sits in Luxembourg.

Council for Mutual Economic Assistance (COMECON)
full member
'part' member
ex-member

Headquarters: Moscow

European Free Trade Association (EFTA)
member

Headquarters: Geneva

North Atlantic Treaty Organization (NATO)
member

Headquarters: Brussels

Warsaw Pact
member

Headquarters: Moscow

international boundaries
national capital
other cities

Scale 1:19 000 000

0   200   400 km

Headquarters of other European and World Organizations

The Hague: International Court of Justice

Geneva: World Health Organization (WHO)

Paris: United Nations Educational, Scientific and Cultural Organization (UNESCO)
Organization for Economic Co-operation and Development (OECD)

Rome: Food and Agricultural Organization of the United Nations (FAO)

Conical Orthomorphic Projectio

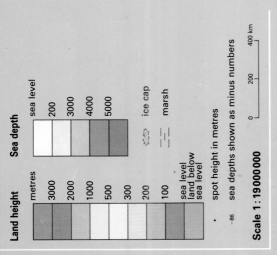

Land height

metres	
3000	
2000	
1000	
500	
300	
200	
100	
sea level land below sea level	

Sea depth

sea level	
200	
3000	
4000	
5000	

ice cap
marsh

• spot height in metres
−86 sea depths shown as minus numbers

Scale 1:19 000 000

0 200 400 km

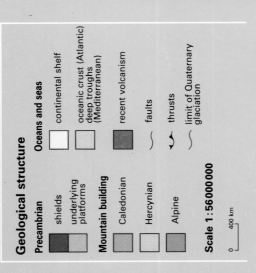

Geological structure

Precambrian
shields
underlying platforms

Mountain building
Caledonian
Hercynian
Alpine

Oceans and seas
continental shelf
oceanic crust (Atlantic)
deep troughs (Mediterranean)

recent volcanism
faults
thrusts
limit of Quaternary glaciation

Scale 1:56 000 000

0 400 km

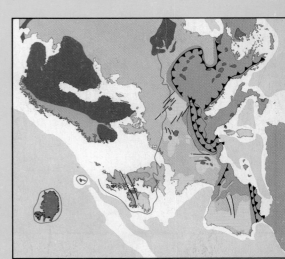

© Oxford University Press

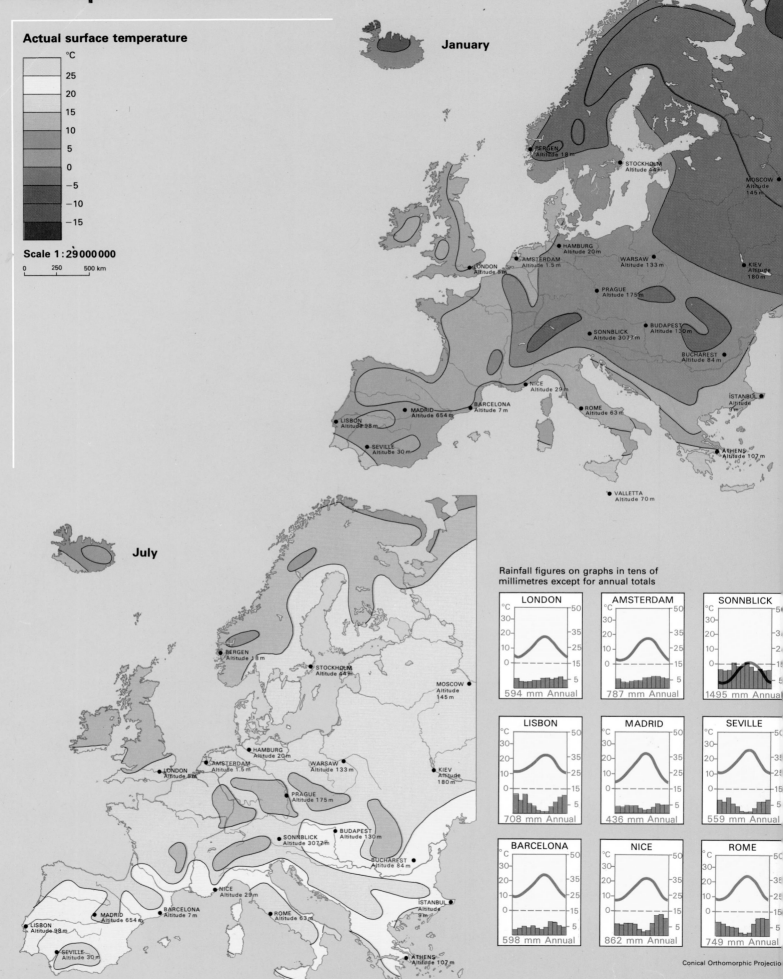

Actual surface temperature

°C
25
20
15
10
5
0
-5
-10
-15

Scale 1:29 000 000

0   250   500 km

January

BERGEN
Altitude 18 m

STOCKHOLM
Altitude 44 m

MOSCOW
Altitude
145 m

HAMBURG
Altitude 20 m

AMSTERDAM
Altitude 1.5 m

WARSAW
Altitude 133 m

KIEV
Altitude
180 m

LONDON
Altitude 5 m

PRAGUE
Altitude 175 m

SONNBLICK
Altitude 3077 m

BUDAPEST
Altitude 130 m

BUCHAREST
Altitude 84 m

NICE
Altitude 29 m

BARCELONA
Altitude 7 m

ROME
Altitude 63 m

İSTANBUL
Altitude
9 m

MADRID
Altitude 654 m

LISBON
Altitude 98 m

SEVILLE
Altitude 30 m

ATHENS
Altitude 107 m

VALLETTA
Altitude 70 m

July

BERGEN
Altitude 18 m

STOCKHOLM
Altitude 44 m

MOSCOW
Altitude
145 m

HAMBURG
Altitude 20 m

AMSTERDAM
Altitude 1.5 m

WARSAW
Altitude 133 m

KIEV
Altitude
180 m

LONDON
Altitude 5 m

PRAGUE
Altitude 175 m

SONNBLICK
Altitude 3077 m

BUDAPEST
Altitude 130 m

BUCHAREST
Altitude 84 m

NICE
Altitude 29 m

BARCELONA
Altitude 7 m

ROME
Altitude 63 m

İSTANBUL
Altitude
9 m

MADRID
Altitude 654 m

LISBON
Altitude 98 m

SEVILLE
Altitude 30 m

ATHENS
Altitude 107 m

VALLETTA
Altitude 70 m

Rainfall figures on graphs in tens of
millimetres except for annual totals

LONDON
594 mm Annual

AMSTERDAM
787 mm Annual

SONNBLICK
1495 mm Annual

LISBON
708 mm Annual

MADRID
436 mm Annual

SEVILLE
559 mm Annual

BARCELONA
598 mm Annual

NICE
862 mm Annual

ROME
749 mm Annual

Conical Orthomorphic Projectio

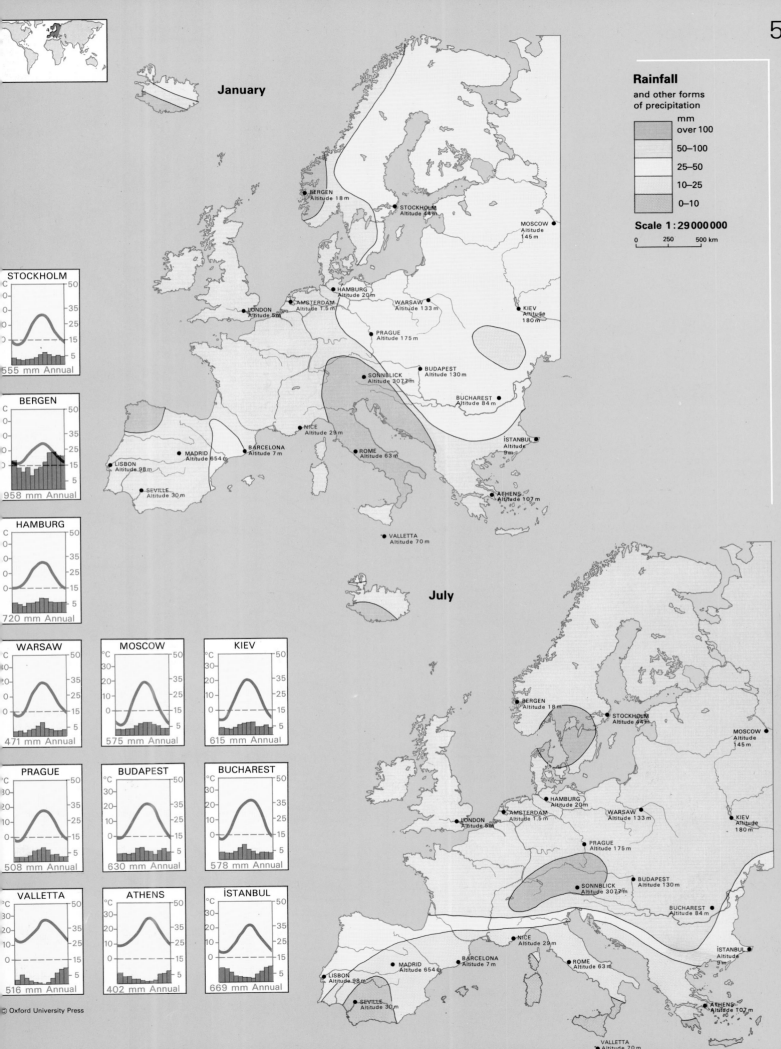

January

Rainfall
and other forms
of precipitation

mm
over 100
50–100
25–50
10–25
0–10

Scale 1:29 000 000

0   250   500 km

July

STOCKHOLM
555 mm Annual

BERGEN
958 mm Annual

HAMBURG
720 mm Annual

WARSAW
471 mm Annual

MOSCOW
575 mm Annual

KIEV
615 mm Annual

PRAGUE
508 mm Annual

BUDAPEST
630 mm Annual

BUCHAREST
578 mm Annual

VALLETTA
516 mm Annual

ATHENS
402 mm Annual

İSTANBUL
669 mm Annual

© Oxford University Press

BERGEN
Altitude 18 m

STOCKHOLM
Altitude 44 m

MOSCOW
Altitude 145 m

HAMBURG
Altitude 20 m

AMSTERDAM
Altitude 1.5 m

LONDON
Altitude 5 m

WARSAW
Altitude 133 m

KIEV
Altitude 180 m

PRAGUE
Altitude 175 m

SONNBLICK
Altitude 3077 m

BUDAPEST
Altitude 130 m

BUCHAREST
Altitude 84 m

NICE
Altitude 29 m

İSTANBUL
Altitude 9 m

MADRID
Altitude 654 m

BARCELONA
Altitude 7 m

ROME
Altitude 63 m

LISBON
Altitude 98 m

SEVILLE
Altitude 30 m

ATHENS
Altitude 107 m

VALLETTA
Altitude 70 m

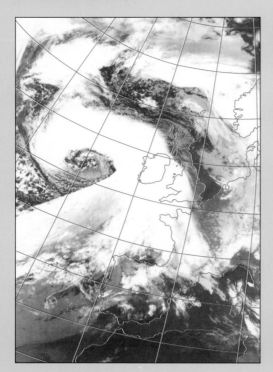

31 January 1988, 1526 hours GMT

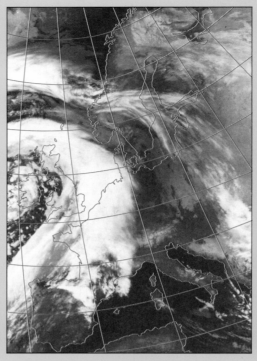

1 February 1988, 0340 hours GMT

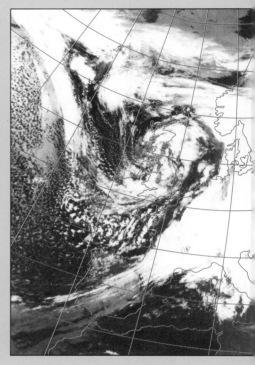

1 February 1988, 1515 hours GMT

Weather summary for the United Kingdom 1 February 1988

Scotland had a period of continuous rain or sleet, with snow in places overnight, the snow principally across higher ground but for a time, snowfall was reported from lower levels. By the end of the night, the weather had turned dry in most places, though heavy rain continued in the far north and extreme east. During the day, as the depression crossed from the southwest, periods of heavy rain developed, with further snow over the mountains.

Across Northern Ireland, England and Wales, heavy overnight rain, with a short period of sleet and snow in the north, had all but cleared by dawn, then the daytime weather was dominated by clusters of heavy, squally showers, these accompanied by hail and thunder. The showers during the morning were most prominent in Wales and the west, but by afternoon, all areas were at risk, with large clusters of heavy showers and squally, stormy winds.

Winds were very strong across England and Wales, with gales or severe gales widespread, with gusts reported widely 45 to 60 knots, and around exposed western and southwestern coasts, gusts above 80 knots, with report of 90 knots from Lands End Coastguard. (Plymouth/Mountbatten reported a gust of 70 knots, the highest February value on record.)

Temperatures were generally above normal, notably so in the southern half of the country, though the mildness was tempered by the strength of the wind.

Cloud amount

○	0	◑	5
◐	1 or less	◕	6
◔	2	◕	7 or more
◑	3	●	8 (oktas)
◒	4		

Weather

= mist

≡ fog

؛ drizzle

, rain and drizzle

· rain

✸ rain and snow

✳ snow

Air pressure
isobars at 4 mb intervals
—— 1024 ——

Temperature

05 in degrees Celsius

Wind speed (knots)

◎ calm

○— 1–2

○⌐ 3–7

○⌐ 8–12   for each additional
half-feather
○\ 13–17   add 5 knots

Fronts

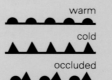

warm

cold

occluded

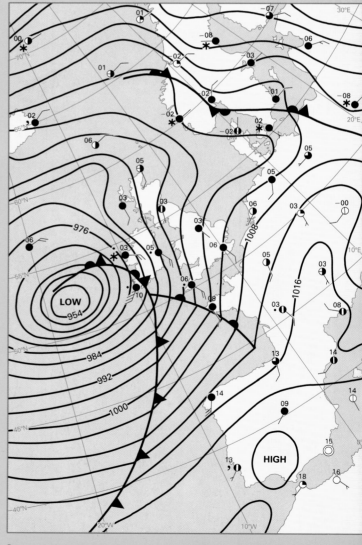

Synoptic chart for 31 January 1988 at 1800 hours GMT

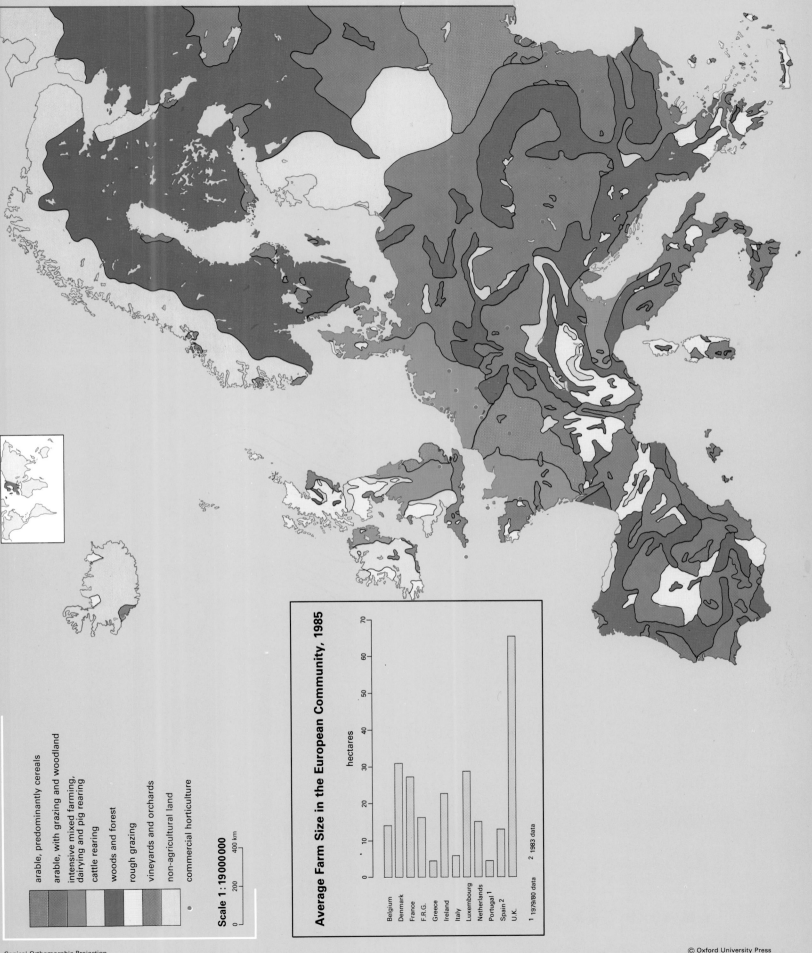

arable, predominantly cereals

arable, with grazing and woodland

intensive mixed farming,
dairying and pig rearing

cattle rearing

woods and forest

rough grazing

vineyards and orchards

non-agricultural land

commercial horticulture

Scale 1 : 19 000 000

0   200   400 km

Average Farm Size in the European Community, 1985

hectares

Belgium
Denmark
France
F.R.G.
Greece
Ireland
Italy
Luxembourg
Netherlands
Portugal [1]
Spain [2]
U.K.

1 1979/80 data   2 1983 data

Conical Orthomorphic Projection

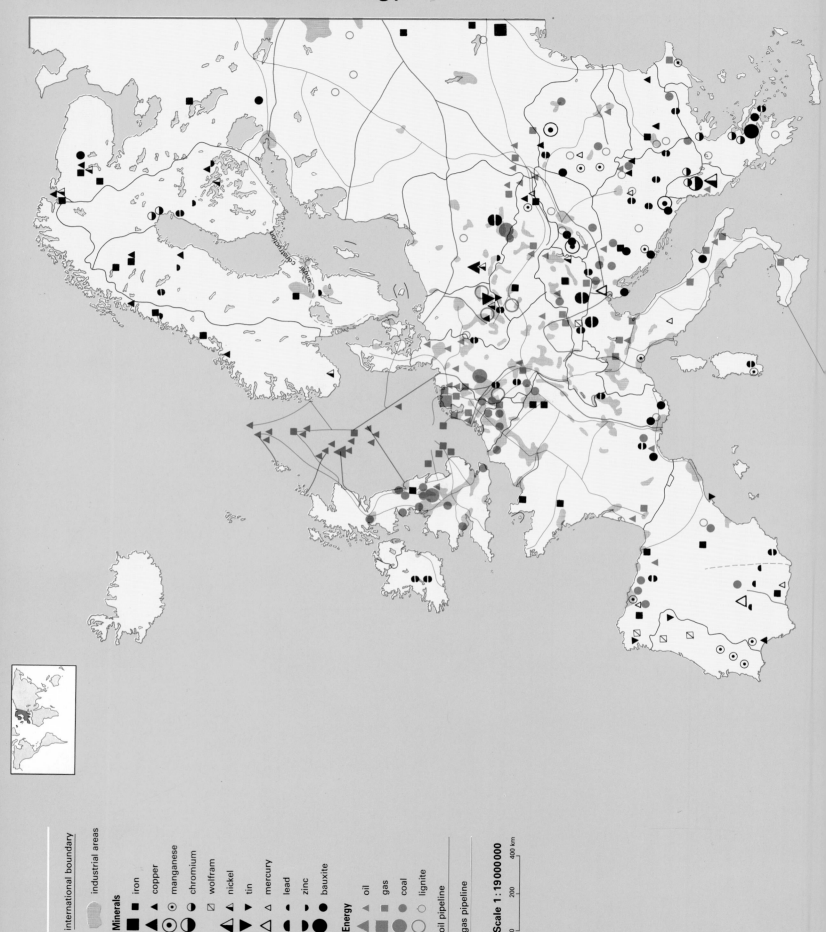

international boundary

industrial areas

Minerals

		iron
		copper
		manganese
		chromium
		wolfram
		nickel
		tin
		mercury
		lead
		zinc
		bauxite

Energy

	oil
	gas
	coal
	lignite

oil pipeline

gas pipeline

Scale 1:19000000

0   200   400 km

Conical Orthomorphic Projection

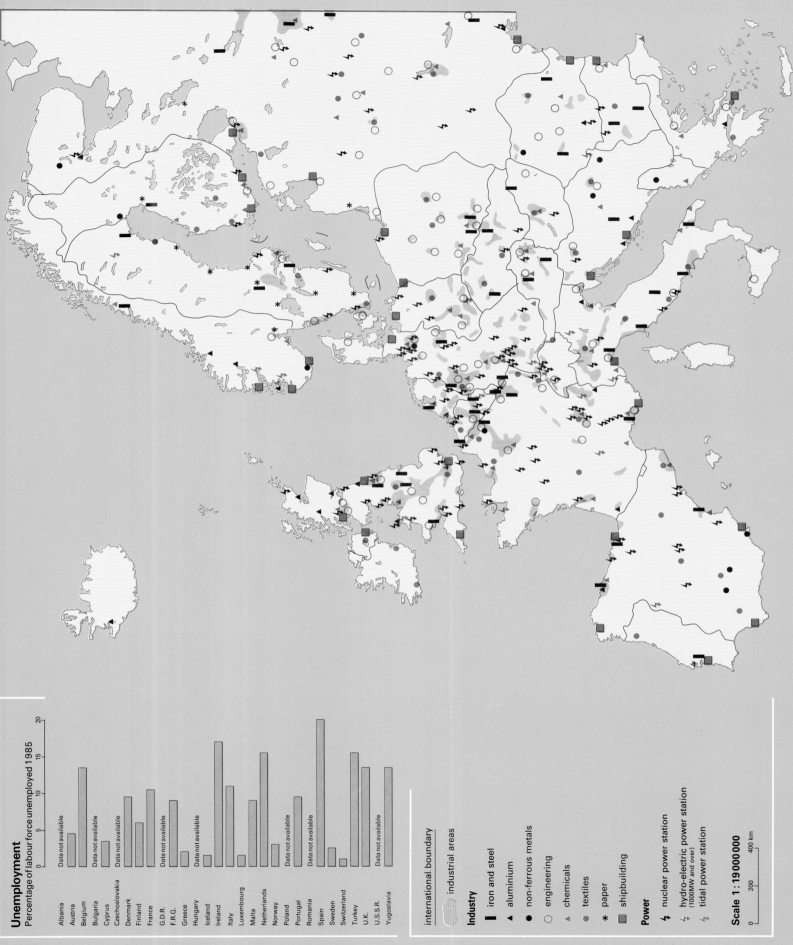

Unemployment
Percentage of labour force unemployed 1985

Albania	Data not available
Austria	
Belgium	
Bulgaria	Data not available
Cyprus	
Czechoslovakia	Data not available
Denmark	
Finland	
France	
G.D.R.	Data not available
F.R.G.	
Greece	
Hungary	Data not available
Iceland	
Ireland	
Italy	
Luxembourg	
Malta	
Netherlands	
Norway	
Poland	Data not available
Portugal	
Romania	Data not available
Spain	
Sweden	
Switzerland	
Turkey	
U.K.	
U.S.S.R.	Data not available
Yugoslavia	

international boundary

industrial areas

Industry

▬ iron and steel

▲ aluminium

● non-ferrous metals

○ engineering

◤ chemicals

● textiles

✳ paper

◼ shipbuilding

Power

ϟ nuclear power station

ϟ hydro-electric power station
(1000MW and over)

ϟ tidal power station

Scale 1:19 000 000

0   200   400 km

© Oxford University Press

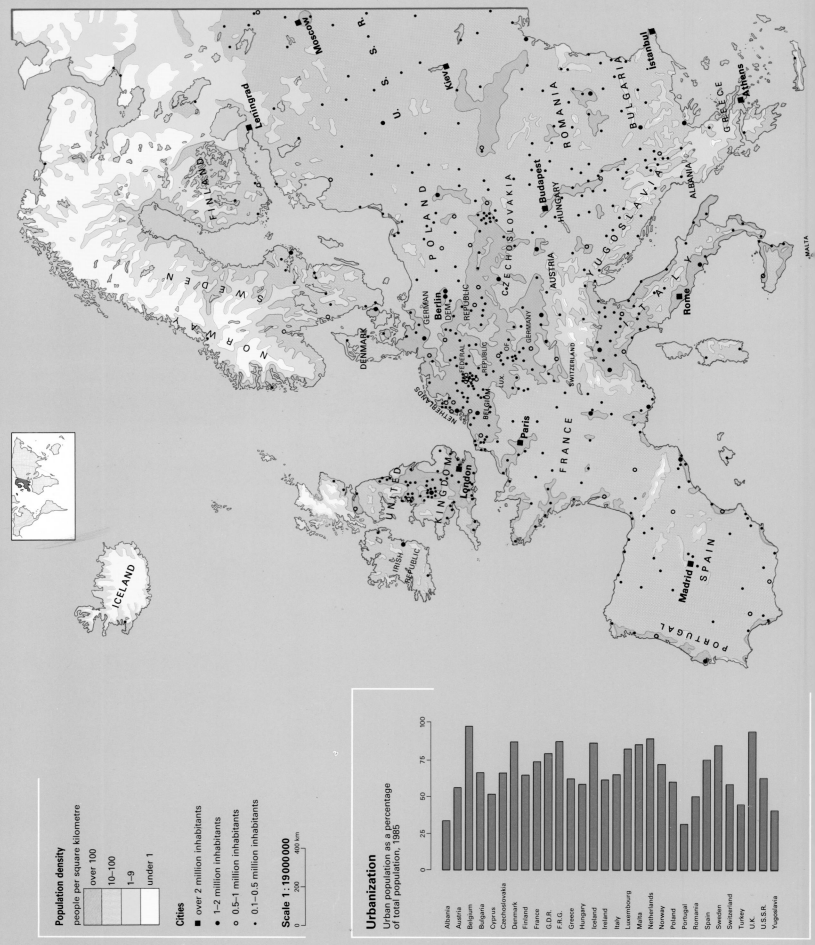

Population density

people per square kilometre

over 100
10–100
1–9
under 1

Cities

■ over 2 million inhabitants
● 1–2 million inhabitants
○ 0.5–1 million inhabitants
· 0.1–0.5 million inhabitants

Scale 1:19000000

0   200   400 km

Urbanization

Urban population as a percentage
of total population, 1985

Albania, Austria, Belgium, Bulgaria, Cyprus, Czechoslovakia, Denmark, Finland, France, G.D.R., F.R.G., Greece, Hungary, Iceland, Ireland, Italy, Luxembourg, Malta, Netherlands, Norway, Poland, Portugal, Romania, Spain, Sweden, Switzerland, Turkey, U.K., U.S.S.R., Yugoslavia

© Oxford University Press

Conical Orthomorphic Projection

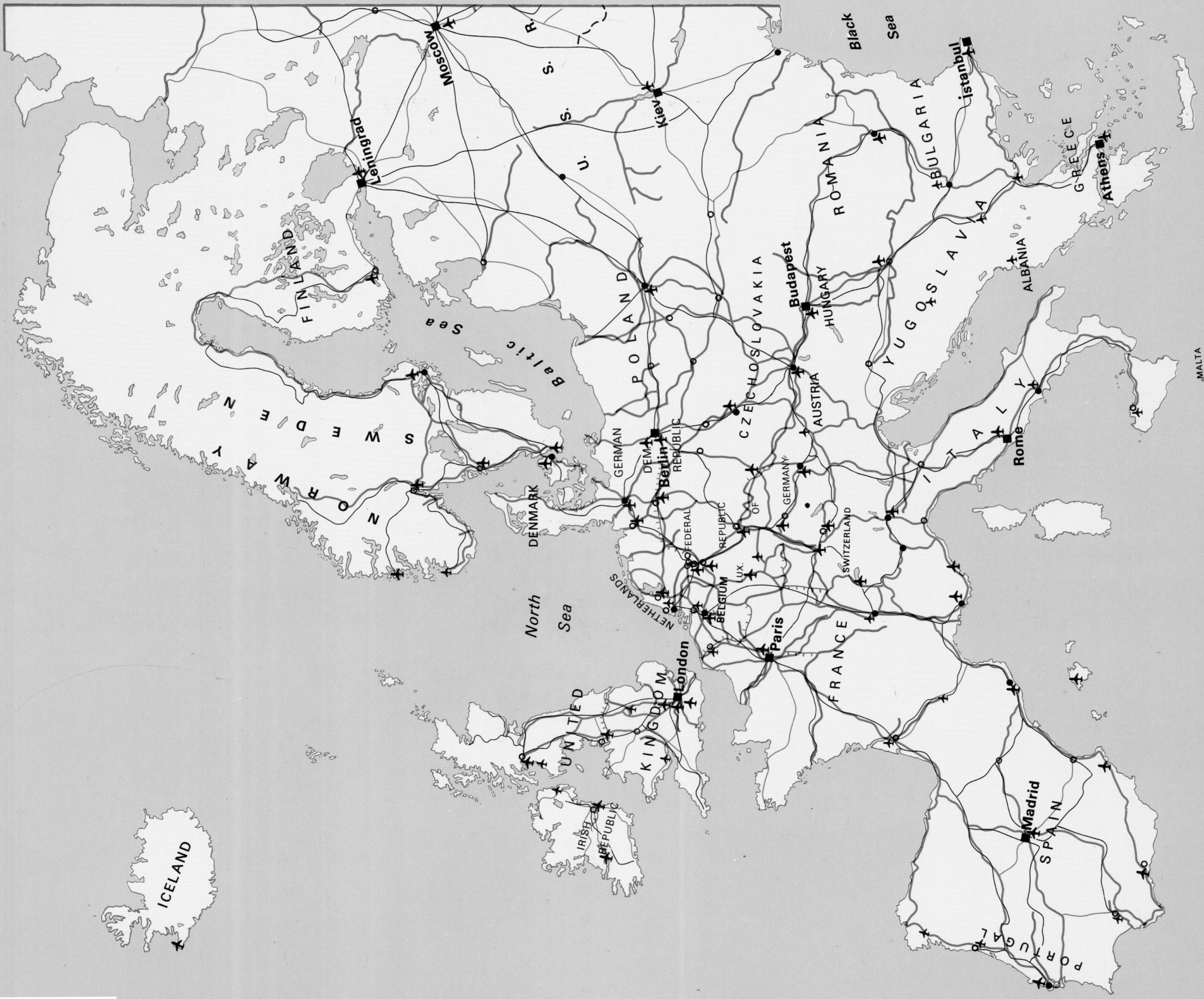
Black Sea
Moscow
Leningrad
Kiev
U. S. S. R.
Istanbul
BULGARIA
ROMANIA
GREECE
Athens
ALBANIA
YUGOSLAVIA
MALTA
FINLAND
Baltic Sea
POLAND
CZECHOSLOVAKIA
Budapest
HUNGARY
AUSTRIA
ITALY
Rome
SWEDEN
NORWAY
GERMAN DEM. REPUBLIC
Berlin
FEDERAL REPUBLIC OF GERMANY
SWITZERLAND
LUX.
BELGIUM
NETHERLANDS
DENMARK
North Sea
Paris
FRANCE
London
UNITED KINGDOM
IRISH REPUBLIC
ICELAND
Madrid
SPAIN
PORTUGAL

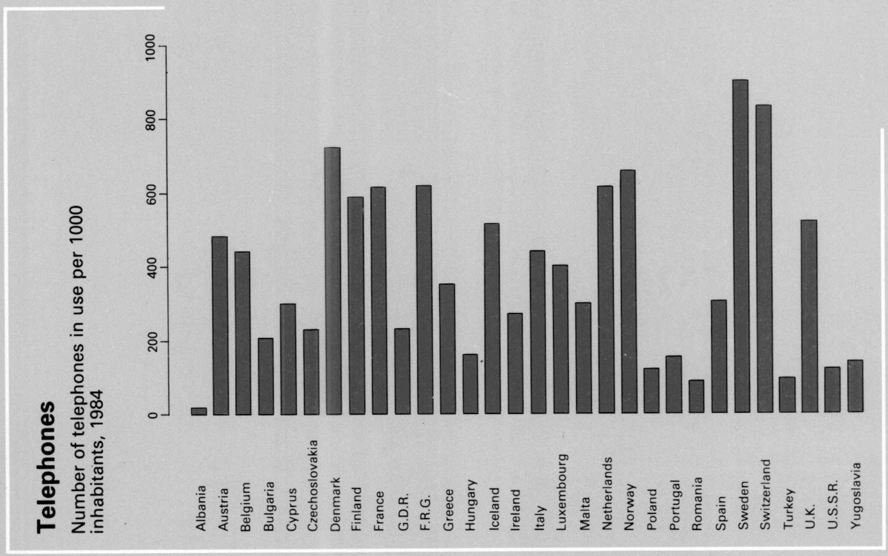
Telephones
Number of telephones in use per 1000 inhabitants, 1984
0
200
400
600
800
1000
Albania
Austria
Belgium
Bulgaria
Cyprus
Czechoslovakia
Denmark
Finland
France
G.D.R.
F.R.G.
Greece
Hungary
Iceland
Ireland
Italy
Luxembourg
Malta
Netherlands
Norway
Poland
Portugal
Romania
Spain
Sweden
Switzerland
Turkey
U.K.
U.S.S.R.
Yugoslavia

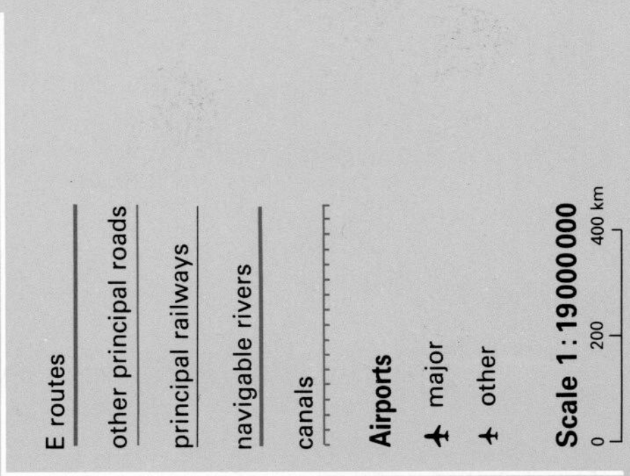
E routes
other principal roads
principal railways
navigable rivers
canals
Airports
major
other
Scale 1:19 000 000
0
200
400 km

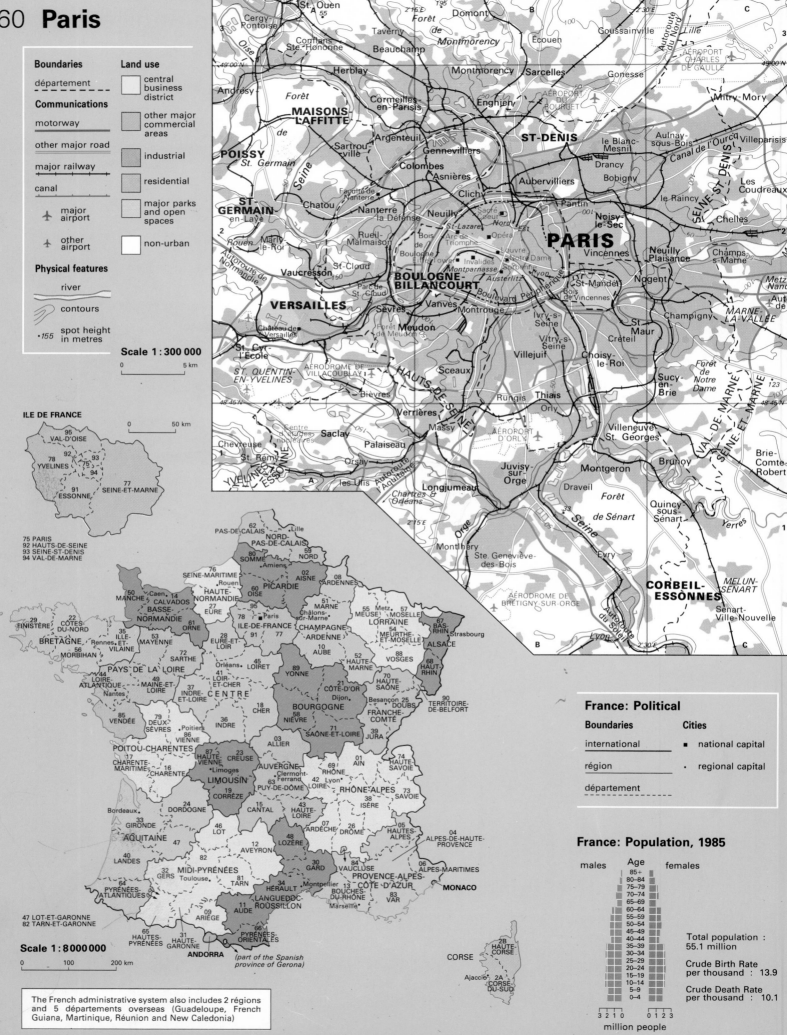

Boundaries

international — · — · —

Communications

motorway

other major road

railway

canal

✈ major airport

Cities and towns

⬭ built-up areas

■ over 1 million inhabitants

● more than 100 000 inhabitants

· smaller towns

Physical features

marsh

ice cap

Land height

metres
3000
2000
1000
500
300
200
100
sea level
land below sea level

▲ spot height in metres

Scale 1 : 5 000 000

0   50   100 km

Conical Orthomorphic Projection

© Oxford University Press

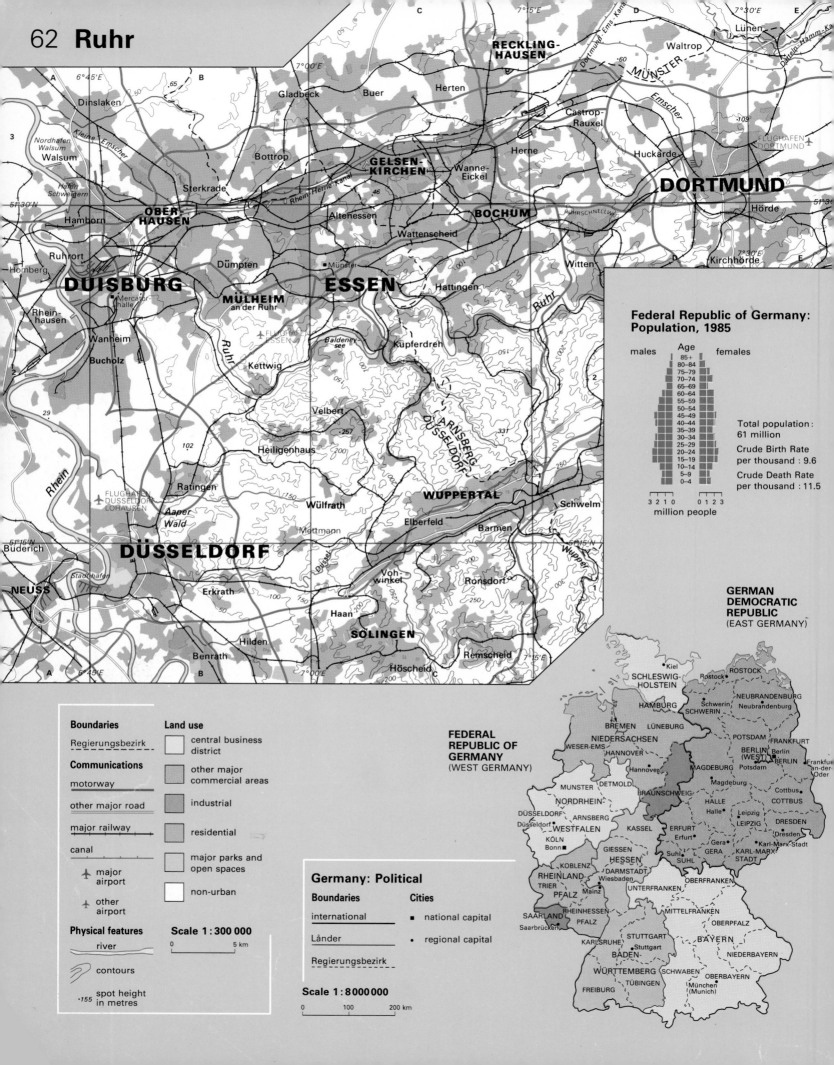

62 Ruhr

Federal Republic of Germany: Population, 1985

males | Age | females

85+
80–84
75–79
70–74
65–69
60–64
55–59
50–54
45–49
40–44
35–39
30–34
25–29
20–24
15–19
10–14
5–9
0–4

3 2 1 0   0 1 2 3
million people

Total population: 61 million

Crude Birth Rate per thousand : 9.6

Crude Death Rate per thousand : 11.5

Boundaries
Regierungsbezirk

Communications
motorway
other major road
major railway
canal
✈ major airport
✈ other airport

Physical features
river
contours
·155 spot height in metres

Land use
central business district
other major commercial areas
industrial
residential
major parks and open spaces
non-urban

Scale 1 : 300 000
0   5 km

Germany: Political

Boundaries
international
Länder
Regierungsbezirk

Cities
■ national capital
● regional capital

Scale 1 : 8 000 000
0   100   200 km

FEDERAL REPUBLIC OF GERMANY (WEST GERMANY)

GERMAN DEMOCRATIC REPUBLIC (EAST GERMANY)

Boundaries

international

internal

Communications

motorway

other major road

railway

canal

✈ major airport

Cities and towns

◁ built-up areas

■ over 1 million inhabitants

● more than 100 000 inhabitants

• smaller towns

Physical features

marsh

ice cap

Land height

metres

3000

2000

1000

500

300

200

100

sea level

land below sea level

▲ spot height in metres

Scale 1:3 500 000

25   50 km

Benelux: Political

Boundaries
international
région
province

Cities
■ national capital
• provincial capital

Scale 1:4 000 000

0   50   100 km

Boundaries
international
internal

Communications
motorway
other major road
railway
canal
✈ major airport

Physical features
marsh

Cities and towns
built-up areas
■ over 1 million inhabitants
● more than 100 000 inhabitants
• smaller towns
▲ spot height in metres

Scale 1:2 000 000

0   25   50 km

Land height

metres
500
300
200
100
sea level
land below sea level

Conical Orthomorphic Projection   © Oxford University Press

NETHERLANDS

GRONINGEN
FRIESLAND
DRENTHE
OVERIJSSEL
NOORD-HOLLAND
ZUID-HOLLAND
UTRECHT
GELDERLAND
ZEELAND
NOORD-BRABANT
LIMBURG

Leeuwarden
Groningen
Assen
Zwolle
Haarlem
Amsterdam
Arnhem
's-Gravenhage (Den Haag, The Hague)
Utrecht
Middelburg
's-Hertogenbosch

BELGIUM
VLANDEREN
WEST-VLANDEREN
OOST-VLANDEREN
BRABANT
ANTWERPEN
LIMBURG
HAINAUT
WALLONIE
NAMUR
LIÈGE
LUXEMBOURG

Brugge (Bruges)
Gent (Gand)
Antwerpen (Anvers)
Bruxelles (Brussel, Brussels)
Hasselt
Maastricht
Liège
Mons
Namur
Arlon

LUXEMBOURG
Luxembourg

North Sea

Waddeneilanden (West Frisian Islands)
Ostfriesische Inseln (East Frisian Is.)

NETHERLANDS

BELGIUM

FRANCE

GERMAN REPUBLIC

LUXEMBOURG

U.K.
Strait of Dover (Pas de Calais)

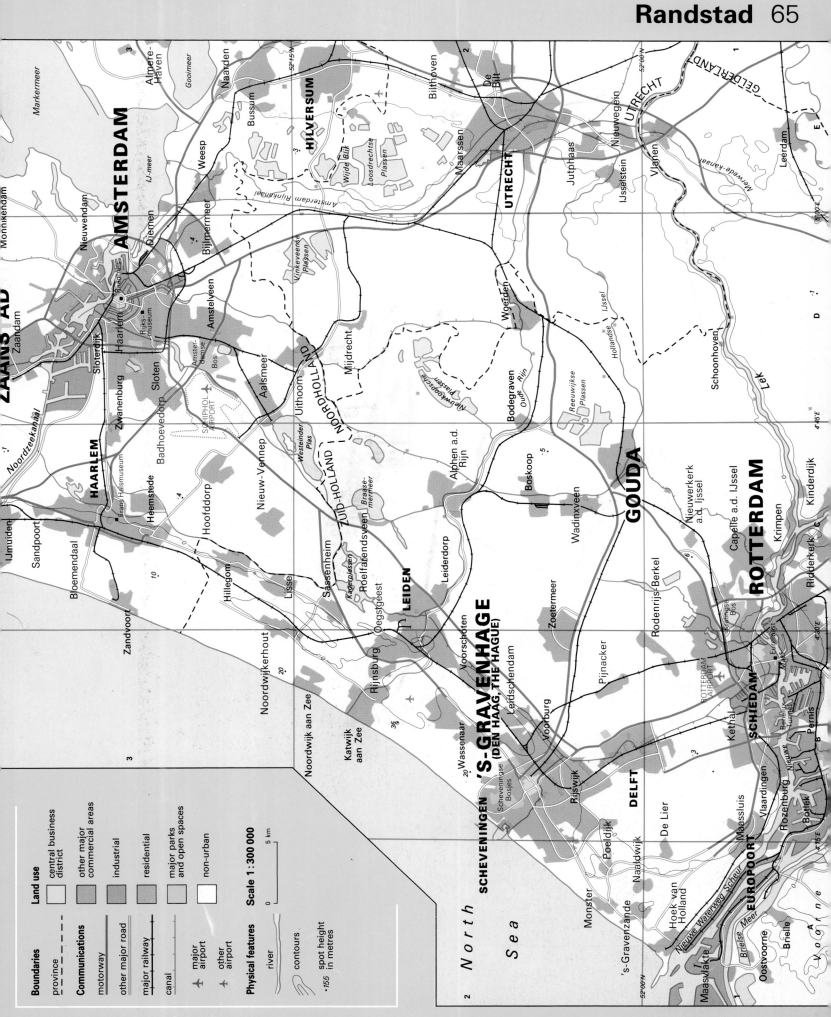

Boundaries

Communications

province

motorway

other major road

major railway

canal

Physical features

river

contours

·155 spot height in metres

✈ major airport

✈ other airport

Land use

central business district

other major commercial areas

industrial

residential

major parks and open spaces

non-urban

Scale 1:300 000

0   5 km

ZAANSTAD

Markermeer

Monnikendam

Almere-Haven

Gooimeer

Naarden

Bussum

Weesp

HILVERSUM

Bilthoven

De Bilt

GELDERLAND

Nieuwendam

AMSTERDAM

Zaandam

Diemen

IJ-meer

Wijde Blik

Loosdrechtse Plassen

Maarssen

UTRECHT

Nieuwegein

Leerdam

Merwede-kanaal

Noordzeekanaal

Haarlem

Sloterdijk

Rijksmuseum

Amstelveen

Bijlmermeer

Amsterdam Rijnkanaal

Vinkeveense Plassen

Mijdrecht

Woerden

Jutphaas

IJsselstein

Vianen

IJssel

HAARLEM

Zwanenburg

Badhoevedorp

Sloten

Amsterdamse Bos

Aalsmeer

Uithoorn

NOORD-HOLLAND

Nieuwkoopse Plassen

Bodegraven

Oude Rijn

Reeuwijkse Plassen

Schoonhoven

Hollandse IJssel

Lek

Frans Halsmuseum

SCHIPHOL AIRPORT

Westeinder Plas

ZUID-HOLLAND

Alphen a.d. Rijn

Boskoop

GOUDA

Nieuwerkerk a.d. IJssel

Capelle a.d. IJssel

Krimpen

ROTTERDAM

Ridderkerk

Kinderdijk

Heemstede

Hoofddorp

Nieuw-Vennep

Braassemermeer

Wadinxveen

Rodenrijs-Berkel

IJmuiden

Sandpoort

Bloemendaal

Hillegom

Lisse

Sassenheim

Roelofarendsveen

Kagerplassen

Leiderdorp

LEIDEN

Zoetermeer

Pijnacker

Kralingse Bos

SCHIEDAM

Maas

Zandvoort

Noordwijkerhout

Oegstgeest

Rijnsburg

Voorschoten

'S-GRAVENHAGE (DEN HAAG, THE HAGUE)

Leidschendam

Voorburg

ROTTERDAM AIRPORT

Kethel

Benelux Tunnel

Vlaardingen

Nieuwe Maas

Pernis

Noordwijk aan Zee

Katwijk aan Zee

Wassenaar

Scheveningse Bosjes

Rijswijk

DELFT

De Lier

Maassluis

Rozenburg

Botlek

SCHEVENINGEN

North Sea

's-Gravenzande

Monster

Poeldijk

Naaldwijk

Hoek van Holland

Nieuwe Waterweg

Scheur

Maasvlakte

EUROPOORT

Brielse Meer

Oostvoorne

Brielle

Voorne

Bay of Biscay

ATLANTIC OCEAN

MEDITERRANEAN Sea

FRANCE

SPAIN

PORTUGAL

ANDORRA

MOROCCO

ALGERIA

Pyrenees / Pirineos / Pirineos

Cordillera Cantabrica (Cantabrian Mts.)

Balearic Islands (Spain)

Mallorca

Menorca

Ibiza

Formentera

Cabrera

Strait of Gibraltar

Gulf of Valencia

Costa Blanca

Costa del Sol

Costa Brava

Sierra Morena

Sierra Nevada

La Mancha

Cities (selected labels): La Coruña (Coruña), El Ferrol del Caudillo, Ortigueira, Luarca, Avilés, Gijón, Oviedo, Mieres, Santander, Torrelavega, Reinosa, Baracaldo, Bilbao, San Sebastián, Biarritz, Bayonne, Vigo, Pontevedra, Santiago de Compostela, Lugo, Villalba, Ponferrada, León, Orense, Verín, Bragança, Vila Real, Braga, Guimarães, Porto (Oporto), Vila Nova de Gaia, Matosinhos, Aveiro, Viseu, Coimbra, Figueira da Foz, Leiria, Caldas da Rainha, Tomar, Santarém, Sintra, Cascais, Lisboa (Lisbon), Almada, Barreiro, Setúbal, Sines, Beja, Aljustrel, Évora, Portalegre, Elvas, Badajoz, Mérida, Cáceres, Trujillo, Plasencia, Castelo Branco, Guarda, Covilhã, Ciudad Rodrigo, Salamanca, Zamora, Valladolid, Palencia, Burgos, Logroño, Miranda de Ebro, Vitoria, Pamplona, Jaca, Huesca, Tudela, Zaragoza, Calatayud, Soria, Tarazona, Barbastro, Lérida (Lleida), Tarrasa, Sabadell, Manresa, Gerona, Figueras, San Feliú de Guixols, Badalona, Hospitalet, Barcelona, Tarragona, Reus, Tortosa, Vinaroz, Benicarló, Castellón de la Plana, Sagunto, Valencia, Alcira, Teruel, Cuenca, Guadalajara, Alcalá de Henares, Madrid, Leganés, Móstoles, Getafe, Aranjuez, Toledo, Talavera de la Reina, Ávila, Segovia, Sigüenza, Daroca, Alcañiz, Almansa, Albacete, Villarrobledo, Manzanares, Ciudad Real, Valdepeñas, Puertollano, Almadén, Don Benito, Almodóvar, Peñarroya-Pueblonuevo, Córdoba, Jaén, Andújar, Linares, Úbeda, Baza, Guadix, Granada, Motril, Almería, Adra, Málaga, Marbella, Ronda, Antequera, Lucena, Écija, Utrera, Sevilla (Seville), Carmona, Jerez de la Frontera, El Puerto de Sta. María, Cádiz, San Fernando, Sanlúcar de Barrameda, Algeciras, La Línea de la Concepción, Gibraltar (U.K.), Ceuta (Sp.), Huelva, Ayamonte, Tavira, Faro, Olhão, Lagos, Portimão, Silves, Elche, Alicante, Orihuela, Murcia, Cartagena, Lorca, Águilas, Hellín, Elda, Alcoy

Tanger (Tangiers), Tétouan, Asilah, Larache, Ksar-el-Kebir, Kénitra, Oujda, Melilla (Sp.), Nador, Al Hoceima

Alger (Algiers), Boufarik, Blida, Médéa, Tizi Ouzou, Dellys, Cherchell, Ech Cheliff, Miliana, El Bayadh, Oran, Arzew, Mostaganem, Relizane, Mascara, Tiaret, Sidi Bel Abbès, Tlemcen, Aïn Témouchent, Beni Saf, Saïda, Djelfa, Bou Saâda, Mohammadia, Bougzoul, Ksar El Boukhari

Rivers: Ebro, Duero / Douro, Tejo / Tajo (Tagus), Guadiana, Guadalquivir, Miño / Minho, Júcar, Segura, Turia

Spot heights (metres): 2321, 2142, 2468, 2592, 2020, 2019, 1991, 3482 Mulhacén, 3404, 3141, 2921, 2381, 2455, 1832, 2308, 2142

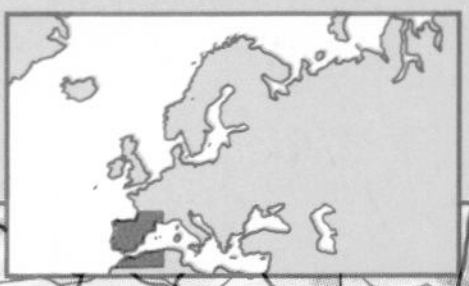

Scale 1 : 6 250 000

0 — 50 — 100 km

Legend

Boundaries
- international

Communications
- motorway
- other major road
- railway
- canal
- ✈ major airport

Cities and towns
- built-up areas
- ■ over 1 million inhabitants
- ● more than 100 000 inhabitants
- • smaller towns

Physical features
- seasonal river/lake
- marsh
- ▲ spot height in metres

Land height

metres
3000
2000
1000
500
300
200
100
sea level

Balearic Islands (Spain)

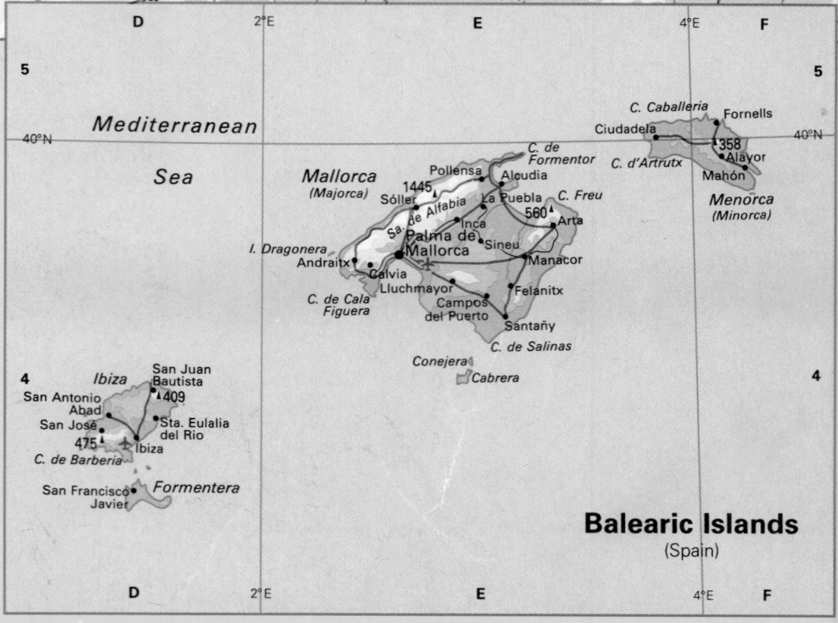

Mediterranean Sea

Mallorca (Majorca), Menorca (Minorca), Ibiza, Formentera, Cabrera

Ciudadela, Fornells, Alayor, Mahón, C. Caballería, C. de Formentor, Pollensa, Alcudia, La Puebla, Artá, Manacor, Felanitx, Santañy, Sineu, Inca, Sóller, Palma de Mallorca, Andraitx, Calvía, Lluchmayor, Campos del Puerto, San Antonio Abad, San José, San Francisco Javier, San Juan Bautista, Ibiza, Sta. Eulalia del Rio

I. Dragonera, Conejera, C. de Cala Figuera, C. de Barberia, C. de Salinas, C. Freu, C. d'Artrutx

Spot heights: 1445, 1409, 560, 475, 358

Scale 1 : 3 000 000

0 — 25 — 50 km

Conical Orthomorphic Projection

© Oxford University Press

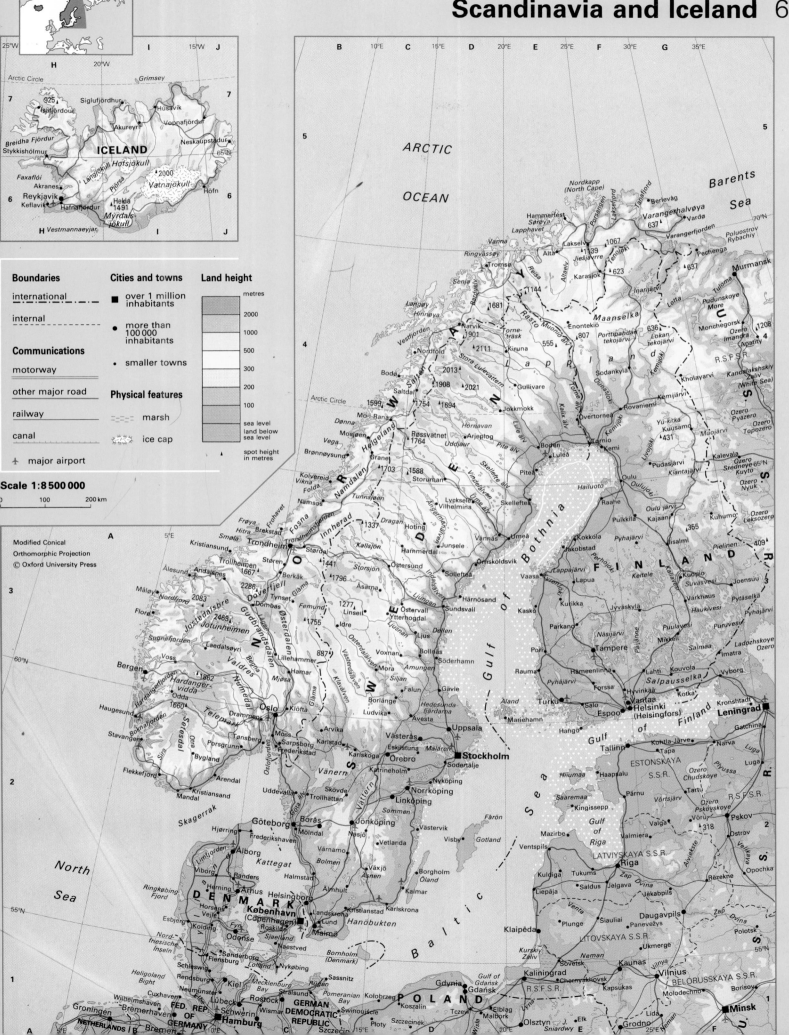

ICELAND

Boundaries
international
internal

Communications
motorway
other major road
railway
canal

✈ major airport

Cities and towns
■ over 1 million inhabitants
● more than 100 000 inhabitants
• smaller towns

Land height

metres
2000
1000
500
300
200
100
sea level
land below sea level
▲ spot height in metres

Physical features
marsh
ice cap

Scale 1:8 500 000

0   100   200 km

Modified Conical
Orthomorphic Projection
© Oxford University Press

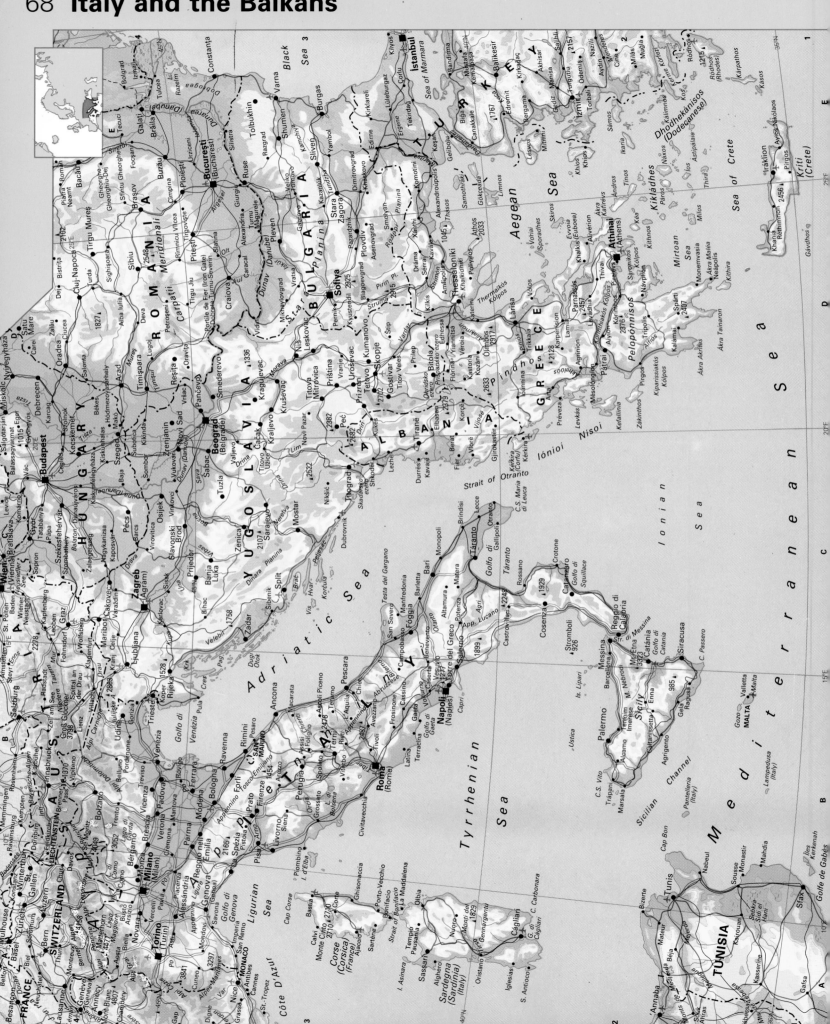

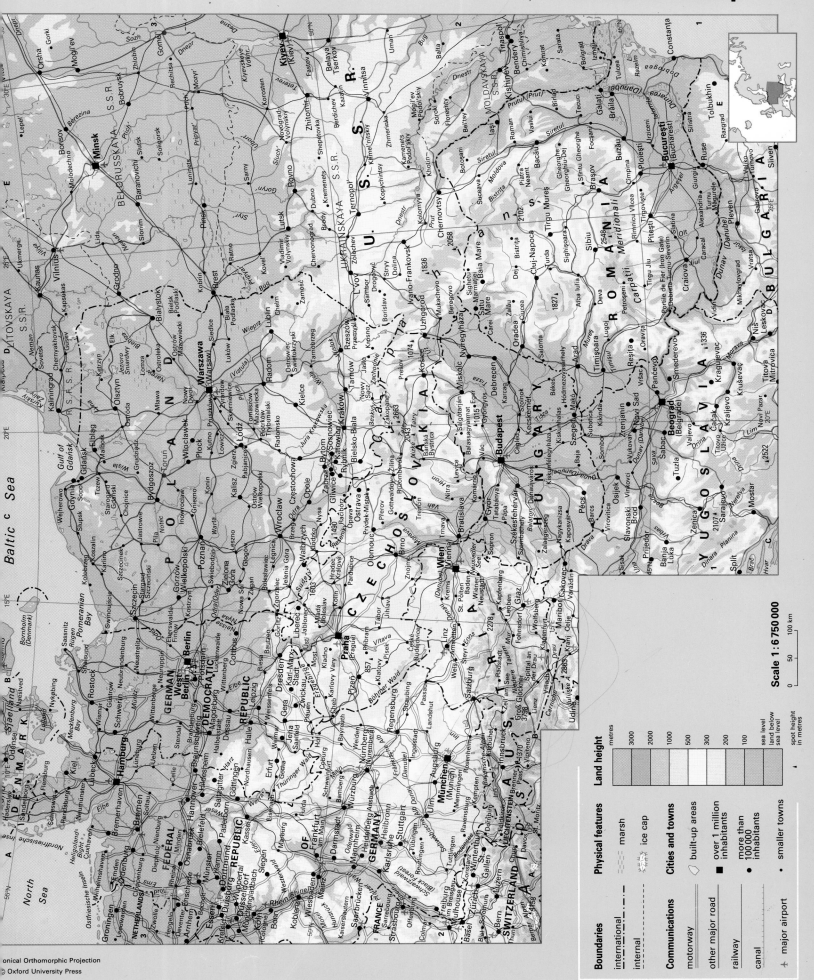

Scale 1 : 6 750 000

0   50   100 km

Boundaries
international
internal

Communications
motorway
other major road
railway
canal
✈ major airport

Physical features
marsh
ice cap

Cities and towns
built-up areas
■ over 1 million inhabitants
■ more than 100000 inhabitants
● smaller towns

Land height
metres
3000
2000
1000
500
300
200
100
sea level
land below sea level
▲ spot height in metres

Conical Orthomorphic Projection
© Oxford University Press

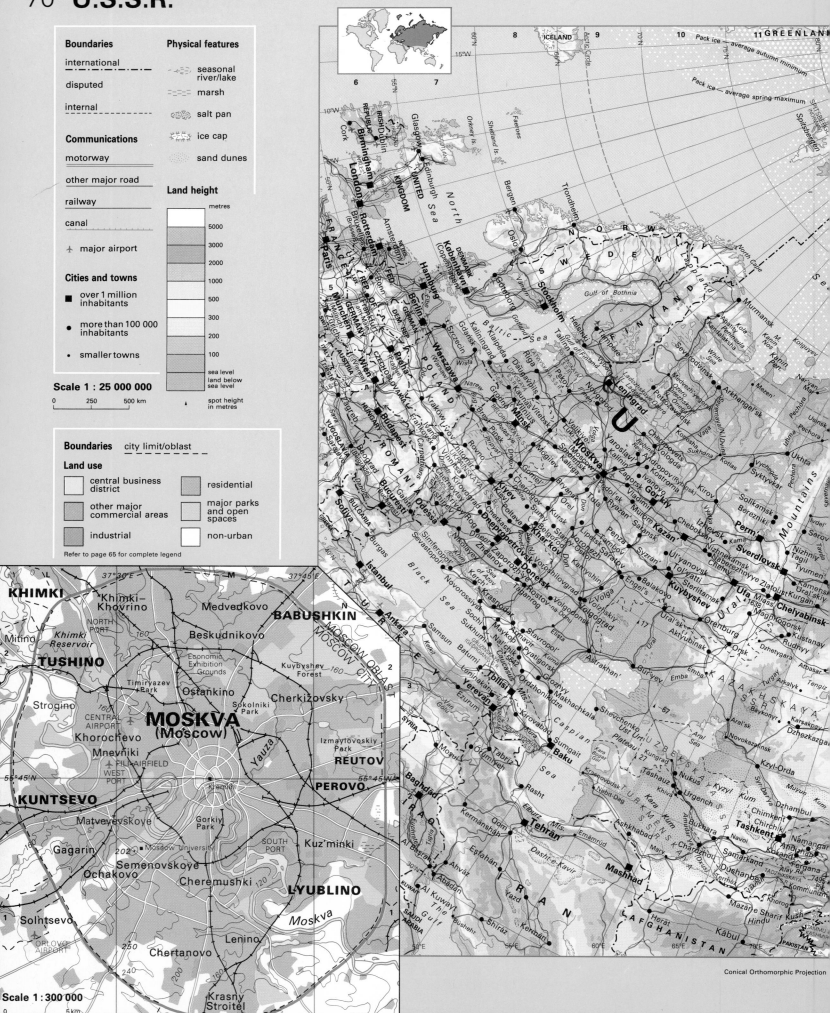

Boundaries
international
disputed
internal

Communications
motorway
other major road
railway
canal
✈ major airport

Cities and towns
■ over 1 million inhabitants
● more than 100 000 inhabitants
• smaller towns

Scale 1 : 25 000 000

0   250   500 km

Physical features
seasonal river/lake
marsh
salt pan
ice cap
sand dunes

Land height
metres
5000
3000
2000
1000
500
300
200
100
sea level
land below sea level
▲ spot height in metres

Boundaries   city limit/oblast

Land use
□ central business district
▨ other major commercial areas
▓ industrial
▨ residential
▨ major parks and open spaces
□ non-urban

Refer to page 65 for complete legend

Scale 1 : 300 000

0   5km

Conical Orthomorphic Projection

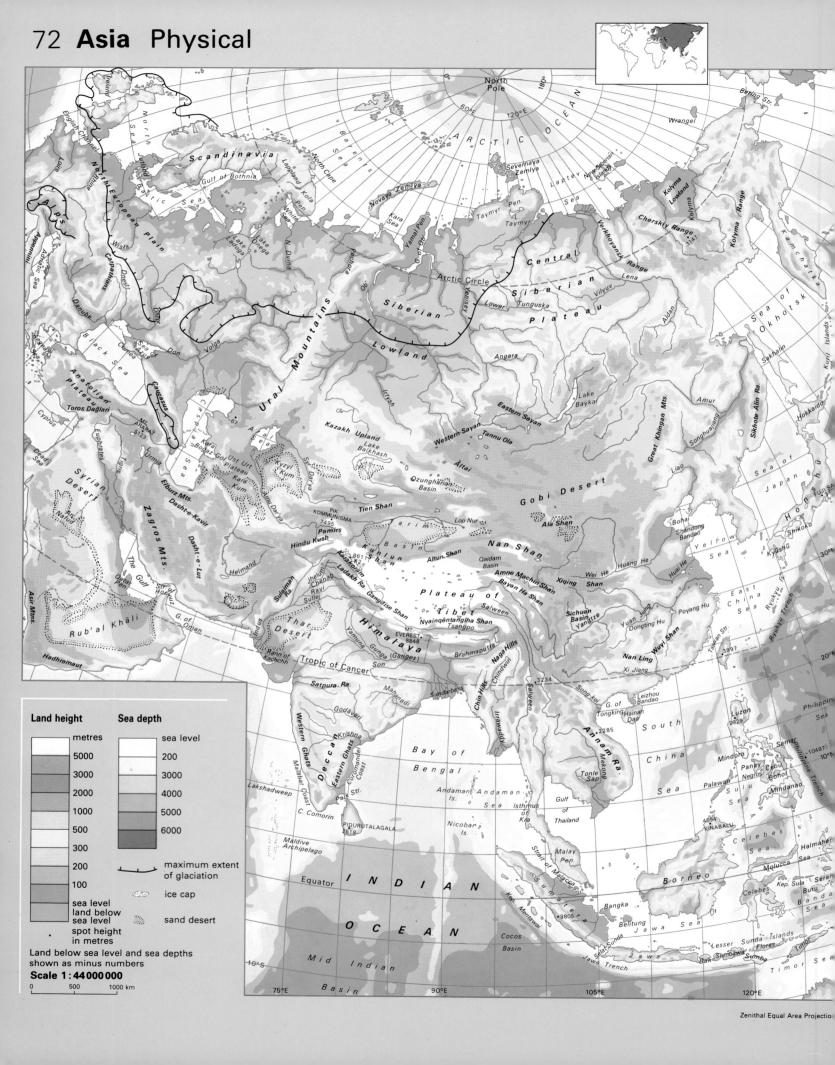

Land height

metres

	5000
	3000
	2000
	1000
	500
	300
	200
	100
	sea level

land below sea level

· spot height in metres

Land below sea level and sea depths shown as minus numbers

Scale 1:44 000 000

0   500   1000 km

Sea depth

sea level

	200
	3000
	4000
	5000
	6000

maximum extent of glaciation

ice cap

sand desert

Zenithal Equal Area Projection

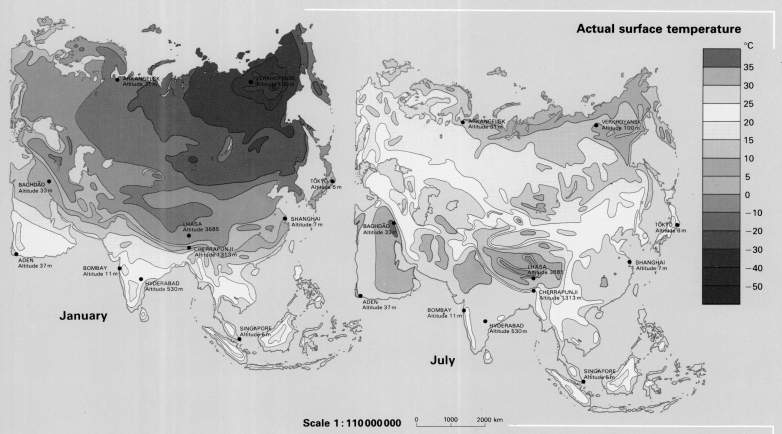

Actual surface temperature

°C
- 35
- 30
- 25
- 20
- 15
- 10
- 5
- 0
- −10
- −20
- −30
- −40
- −50

January

July

Scale 1 : 110 000 000

0   1000   2000 km

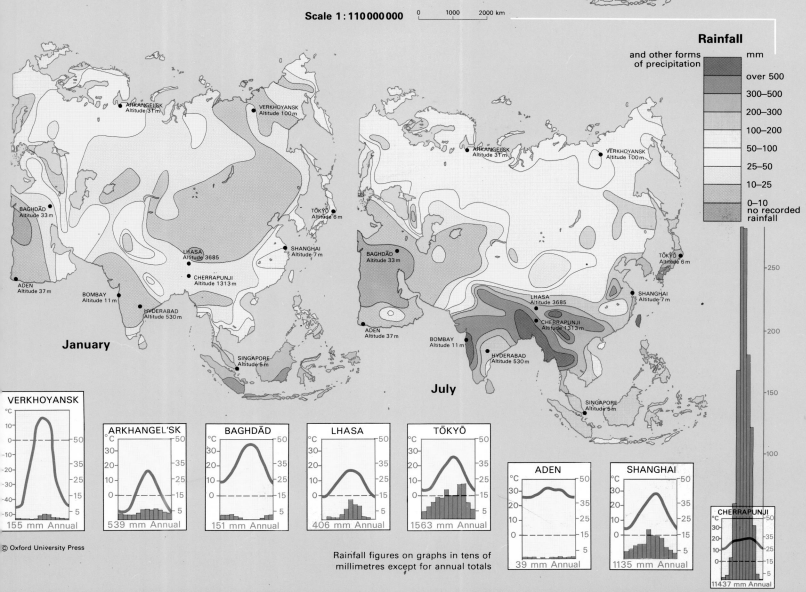

Rainfall

and other forms
of precipitation   mm

- over 500
- 300–500
- 200–300
- 100–200
- 50–100
- 25–50
- 10–25
- 0–10
- no recorded rainfall

January

July

VERKHOYANSK
155 mm Annual

ARKHANGEL'SK
539 mm Annual

BAGHDĀD
151 mm Annual

LHASA
406 mm Annual

TŌKYŌ
1563 mm Annual

ADEN
39 mm Annual

SHANGHAI
1135 mm Annual

CHERRAPUNJI
11437 mm Annual

Rainfall figures on graphs in tens of
millimetres except for annual totals

arable, predominantly cereals

arable, predominantly paddy

general arable

arable with cash crops

irrigated crops

grazing and dry farming

deciduous forest, farming and grazing

mixed forest, farming and grazing

tropical rain forest, lumbering, crops

coniferous forest, lumbering

desert, nomadic herding

marsh or swamp

tundra and high altitude desert

ice cap

Scale 1 : 44 000 000

0   500   1000 km

BOMBAY
°C
30
20
10
0
70
50
35
25
15
5
2078 mm Annual

HYDERABAD
°C
30
20
10
0
50
35
25
15
5
157 mm Annual

SINGAPORE
°C
30
20
10
0
50
35
25
15
5
2282 mm Annual

Rainfall figures on graphs in tens of millimetres except for annual totals

Zenithal Equal Area Projectio

© Oxford University Pres

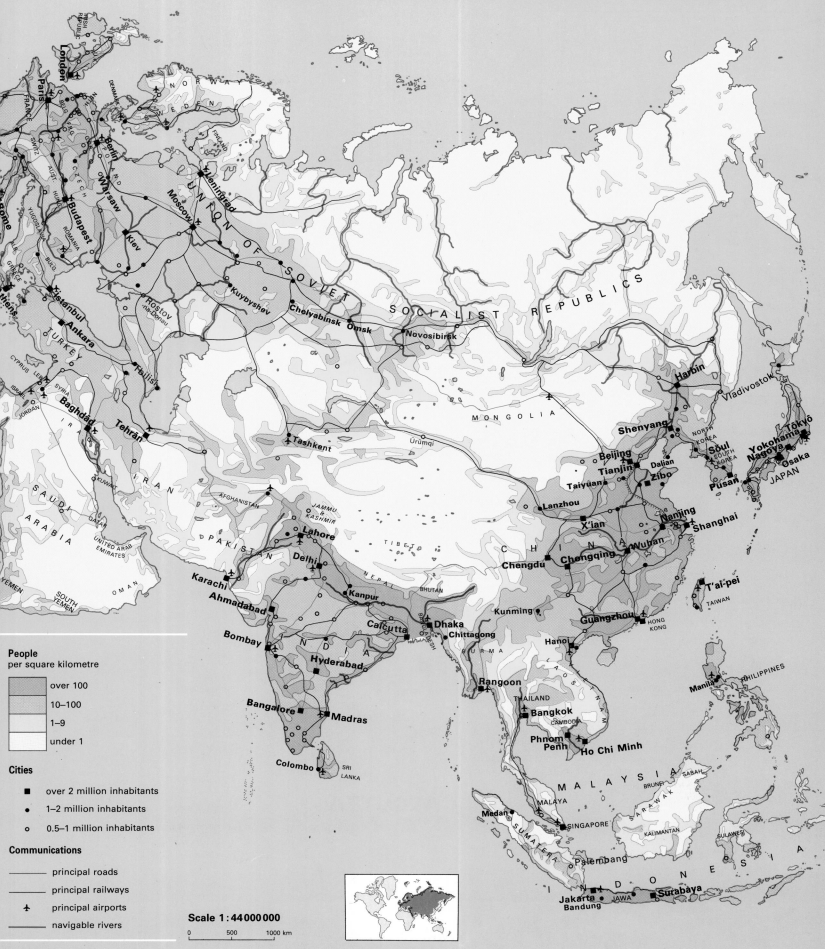

People
per square kilometre

- over 100
- 10–100
- 1–9
- under 1

Cities

- ■ over 2 million inhabitants
- ● 1–2 million inhabitants
- ○ 0.5–1 million inhabitants

Communications

- principal roads
- principal railways
- ✈ principal airports
- navigable rivers

Scale 1 : 44 000 000

0   500   1000 km

Zenithal Equal Area Projection

© Oxford University Press

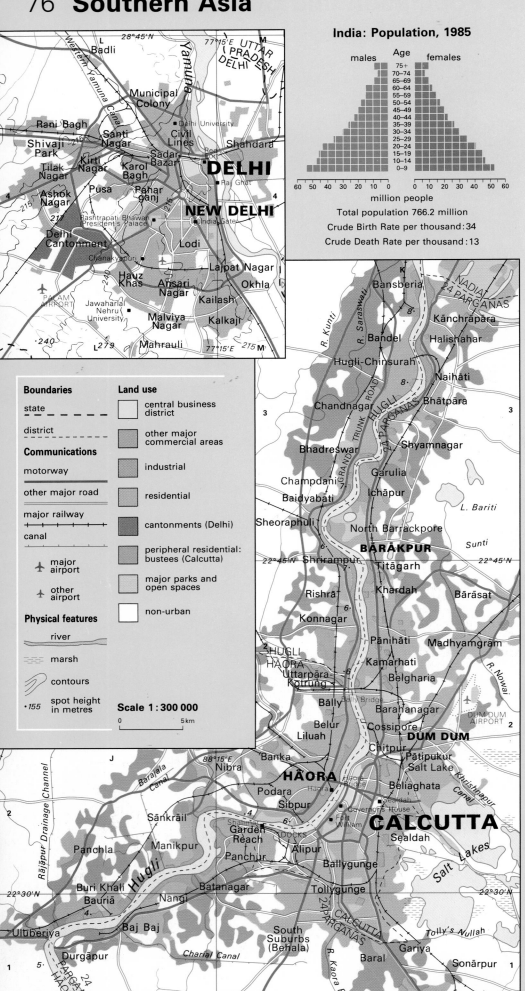

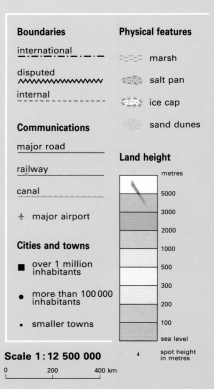

India: Population, 1985

males — Age — females

75+
70–74
65–69
60–64
55–59
50–54
45–49
40–44
35–39
30–34
25–29
20–24
15–19
10–14
0–9

60 50 40 30 20 10 0 | 0 10 20 30 40 50 60

million people

Total population 766.2 million

Crude Birth Rate per thousand: 34

Crude Death Rate per thousand: 13

Boundaries
state
district

Communications
motorway
other major road
major railway
canal
✈ major airport
✈ other airport

Physical features
river
marsh
contours
·155 spot height in metres

Land use
central business district
other major commercial areas
industrial
residential
cantonments (Delhi)
peripheral residential: bustees (Calcutta)
major parks and open spaces
non-urban

Scale 1 : 300 000

0 — 5km

Boundaries
international
disputed
internal

Communications
major road
railway
canal
✈ major airport

Cities and towns
■ over 1 million inhabitants
● more than 100 000 inhabitants
• smaller towns

Physical features
marsh
salt pan
ice cap
sand dunes

Land height
metres
5000
3000
2000
1000
500
300
200
100
sea level
▲ spot height in metres

Scale 1 : 12 500 000

0 — 200 — 400 km

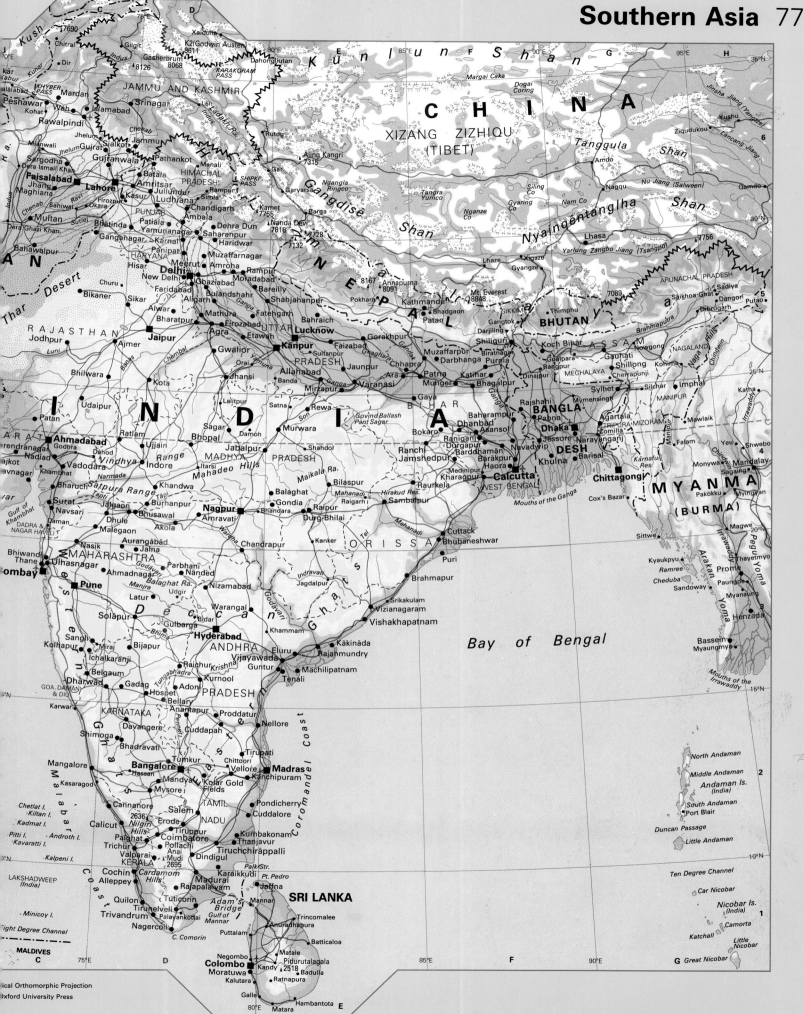

Israel & Lebanon
Scale 1:4 000 000

0   50   100 km

Conical Orthomorphic Projection

Boundaries

international

disputed

internal

Communications

motorway

other major road

railway

canal

✈ major airport

Cities and towns

■ over 1 million inhabitants

● more than 100 000 inhabitants

● smaller towns

+ historic sites

Physical features

seasonal river/lake

marsh

salt pan

ice cap

sand dunes

Land height

	metres
	5000
	3000
	2000
	1000
	500
	300
	200
	100
	sea level
	land below sea level

▲ spot height in metres

Scale 1:12 500 000

0   125   250 km

© Oxford University Press

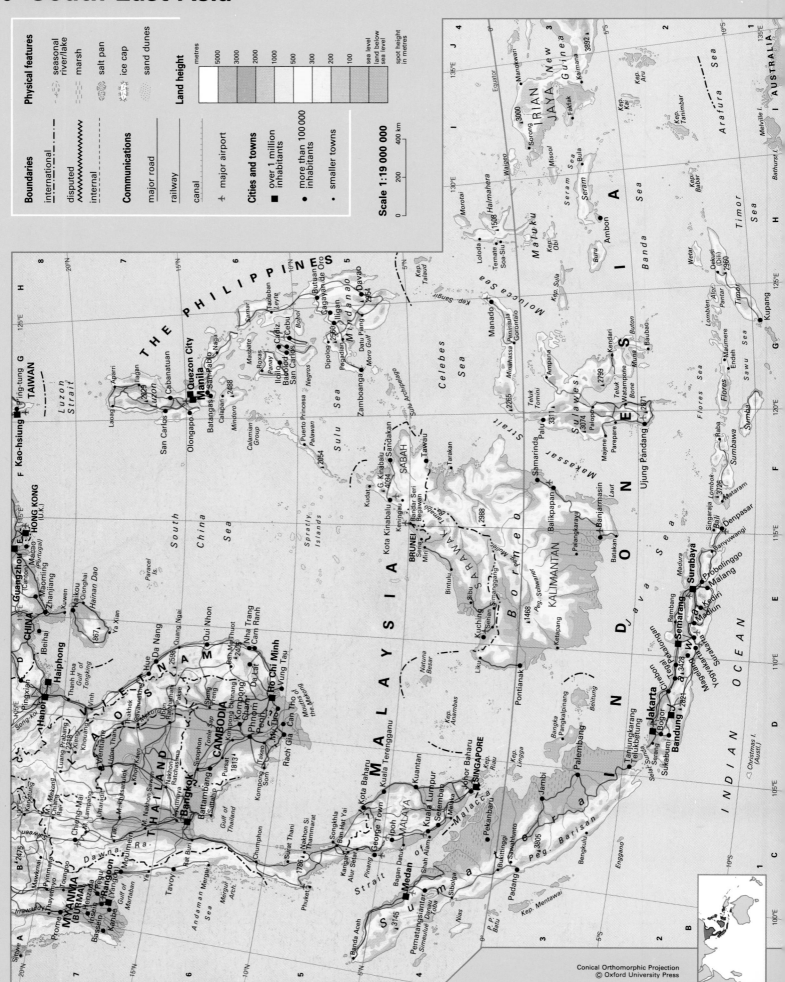

Boundaries
international
disputed
internal

Communications
major road
railway
canal

Cities and towns
■ over 1 million inhabitants
● more than 100 000 inhabitants
• smaller towns
✈ major airport

Physical features
seasonal river/lake
marsh
salt pan
ice cap
sand dunes

Land height
metres
5000
3000
2000
1000
500
300
200
100
sea level
land below sea level
spot height in metres

Scale 1:19 000 000

0   200   400 km

Conical Orthomorphic Projection
© Oxford University Press

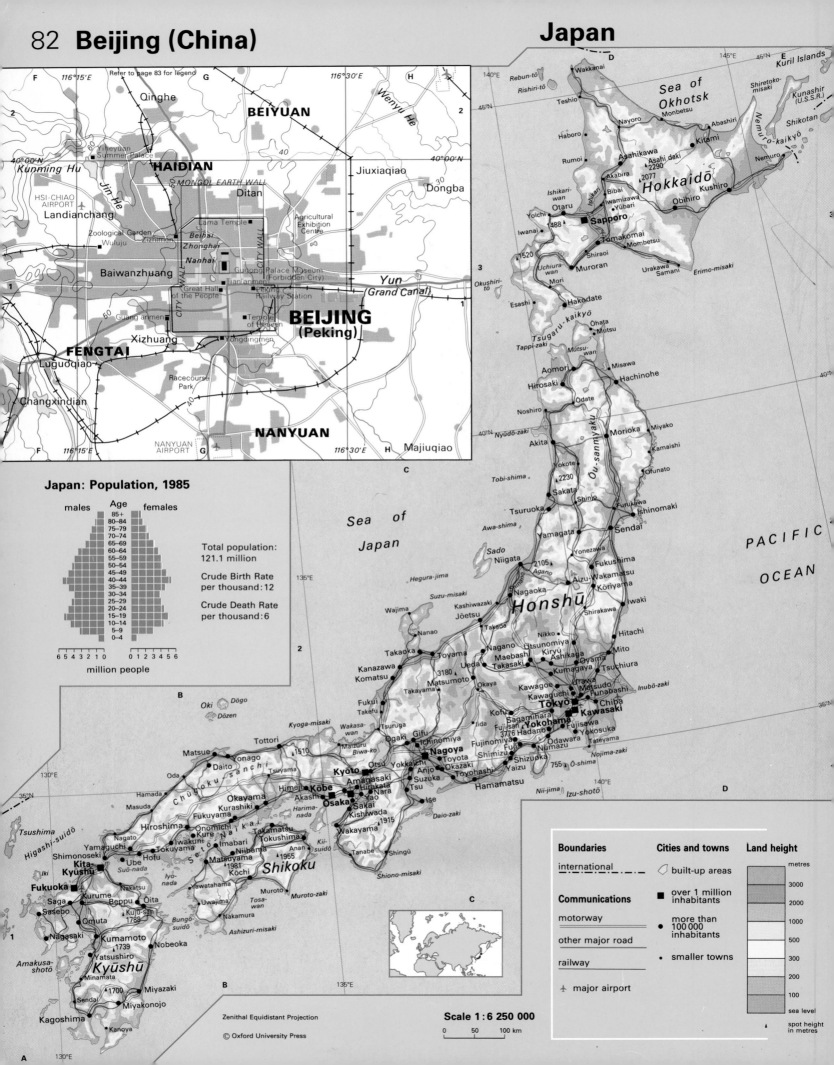

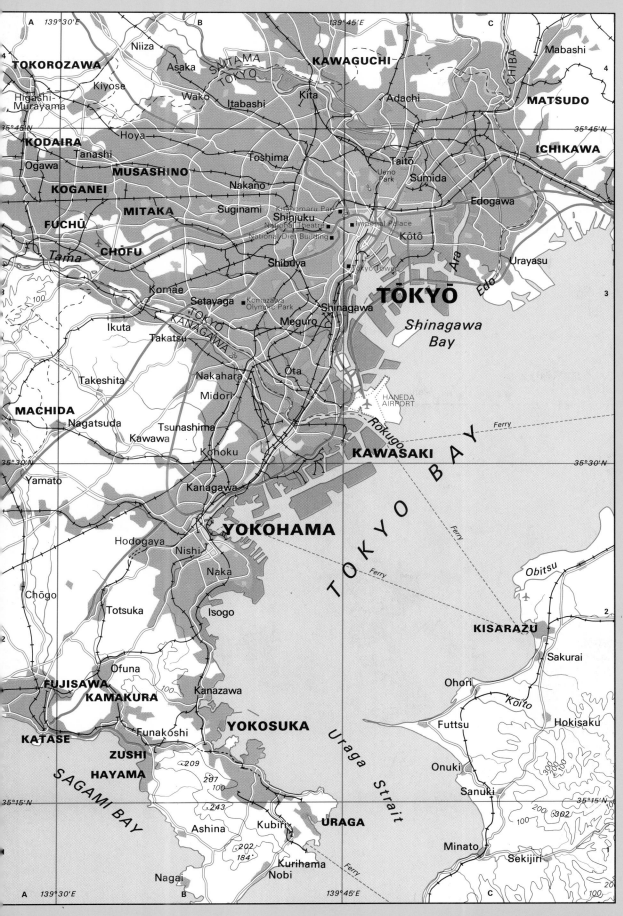

Boundaries

prefecture (Tokyo)

Communications

motorway

other major road

major railway

canal

✈ major airport

✈ other airport

Physical features

∼ river

contours

·155 spot height in metres

Land use

central business district

other major commercial areas

industrial

residential

major parks and open spaces

non-urban

Scale 1 : 300 000

0   5km

TOKOROZAWA
Niiza
Asaka
Kiyose
Higashi-Murayama
Wako
Itabashi
Kita
KAWAGUCHI
SAITAMA TOKYO
Mabashi
CHIBA
Adachi
MATSUDO
KODAIRA
Hoya
Tanashi
Ogawa
Toshima
Taitō
ICHIKAWA
MUSASHINO
Nakano
Ueno Park
Sumida
KOGANEI
Suginami
Edogawa
MITAKA
Kitanomaru Park
Shinjuku
National Theatre
Imperial Palace
Kōtō
FUCHŪ
National Diet Building
Urayasu
CHŌFU
Tama
Shibuya
Tokyo Tower
TŌKYŌ
Ara
Edo
Komae
Setayaga
Komazawa Olympic Park
Shinagawa
Shinagawa Bay
Ikuta
Meguro
Takatsu
Ōta
Takeshita
Nakahara
Midori
HANEDA AIRPORT
Rokugo
Ferry
MACHIDA
Nagatsuda
Tsunashima
Kawawa
Kohoku
KAWASAKI
TOKYO BAY
Yamato
Kanagawa
Obitsu
YOKOHAMA
Hodogaya
Nishi
Ferry
Naka
Ferry
Chōgo
Totsuka
Isogo
KISARAZU
Sakurai
Ofuna
Kanazawa
Ohori
FUJISAWA
KAMAKURA
Kōito
Funakoshi
YOKOSUKA
Futtsu
Hokisaku
KATASE
ZUSHI
HAYAMA
·209
Onuki
·207
Uraga Strait
SAGAMI BAY
·243
URAGA
Sanuki
Ashina
Kubiri
Minato
·202
·184
Sekijiri
Nagai
Kurihama Nobi
Ferry

139°30'E 139°45'E

35°45'N 35°30'N 35°15'N

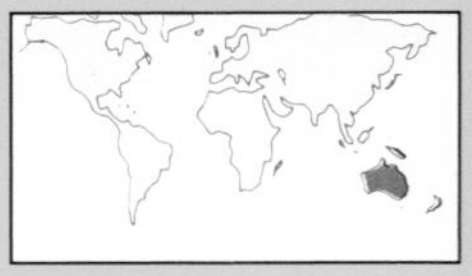

Actual surface temperature

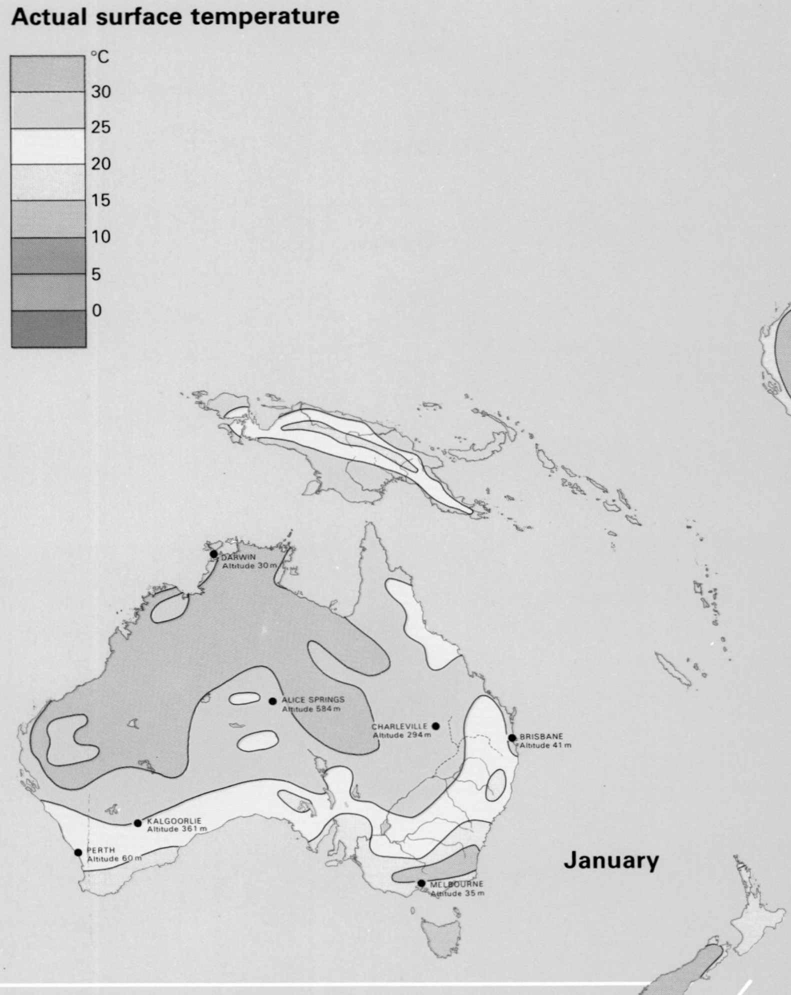

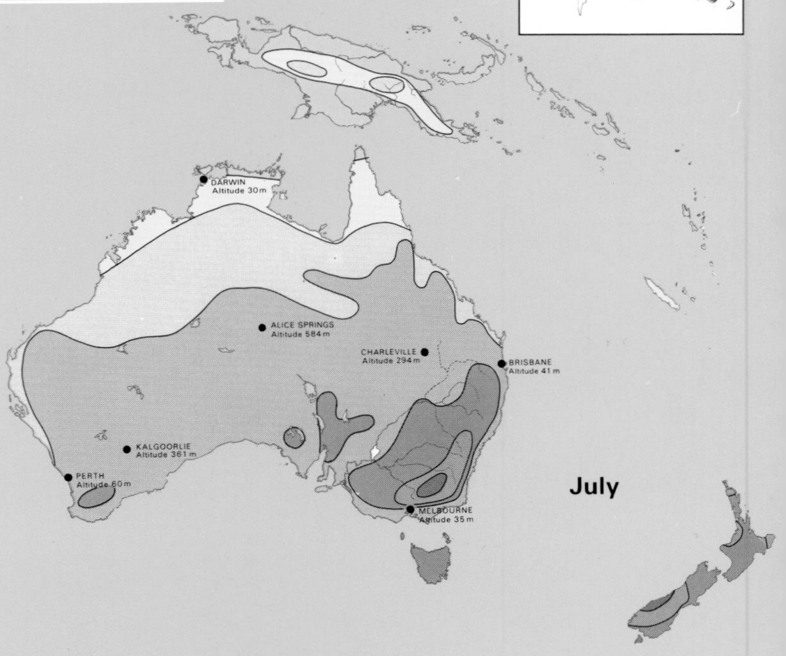

°C
30
25
20
15
10
5
0
DARWIN Altitude 30 m
ALICE SPRINGS Altitude 584 m
CHARLEVILLE Altitude 294 m
BRISBANE Altitude 41 m
KALGOORLIE Altitude 361 m
PERTH Altitude 60 m
MELBOURNE Altitude 35 m
January

DARWIN Altitude 30 m
ALICE SPRINGS Altitude 584 m
CHARLEVILLE Altitude 294 m
BRISBANE Altitude 41 m
KALGOORLIE Altitude 361 m
PERTH Altitude 60 m
MELBOURNE Altitude 35 m
July

Scale 1 : 60 000 000 0 500 1000 km

DARWIN Altitude 30 m
ALICE SPRINGS Altitude 584 m
CHARLEVILLE Altitude 294 m
BRISBANE Altitude 41 m
KALGOORLIE Altitude 361 m
PERTH Altitude 60 m
MELBOURNE Altitude 35 m
July

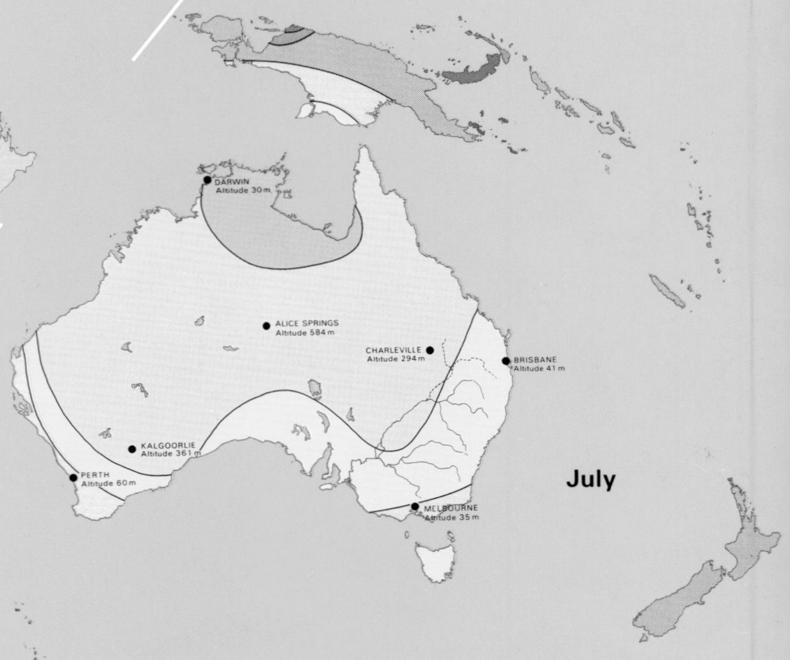

Rainfall

and other forms of precipitation

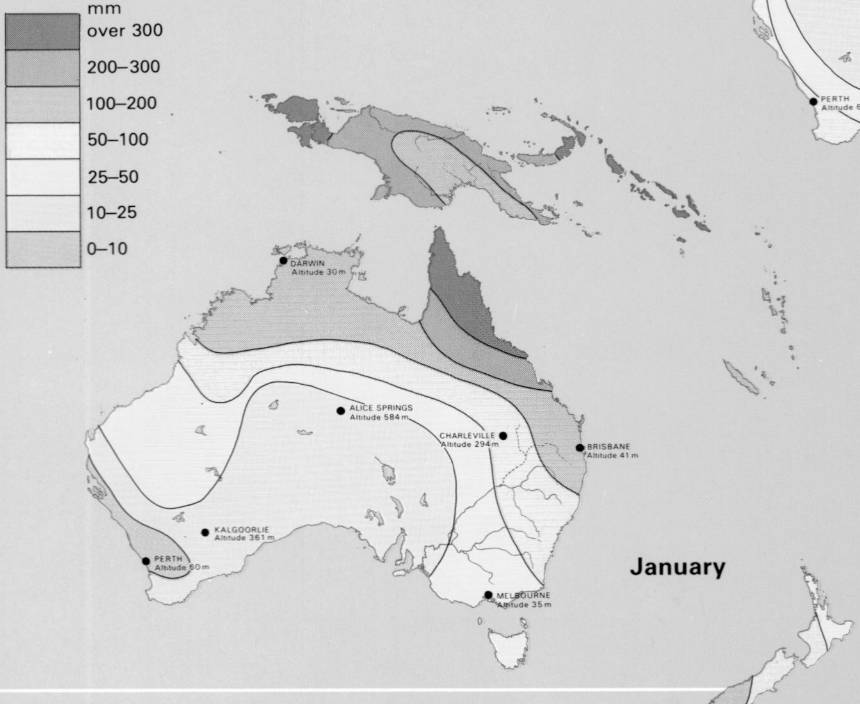

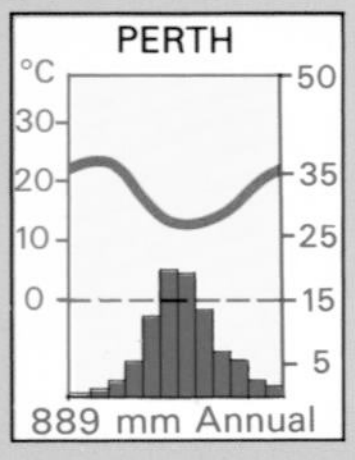

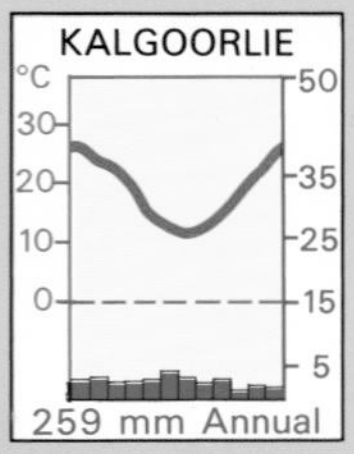

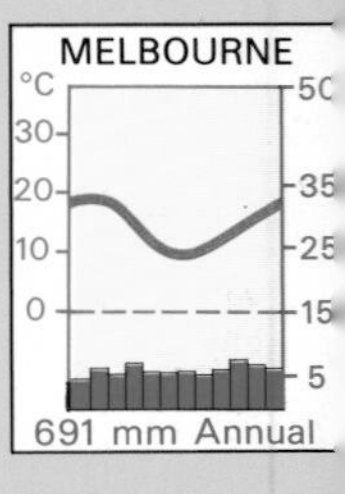

mm
over 300
200–300
100–200
50–100
25–50
10–25
0–10
DARWIN Altitude 30 m
ALICE SPRINGS Altitude 584 m
CHARLEVILLE Altitude 294 m
BRISBANE Altitude 41 m
KALGOORLIE Altitude 361 m
PERTH Altitude 60 m
MELBOURNE Altitude 35 m
January

PERTH
°C
30
20
10
0
50
35
25
15
5
889 mm Annual

KALGOORLIE
°C
30
20
10
0
50
35
25
15
5
259 mm Annual

MELBOURNE
°C
30
20
10
0
35
25
15
5
691 mm Annual

Scale 1 : 60 000 000 0 500 1000 km

Modified Zenithal Equidistant Projection

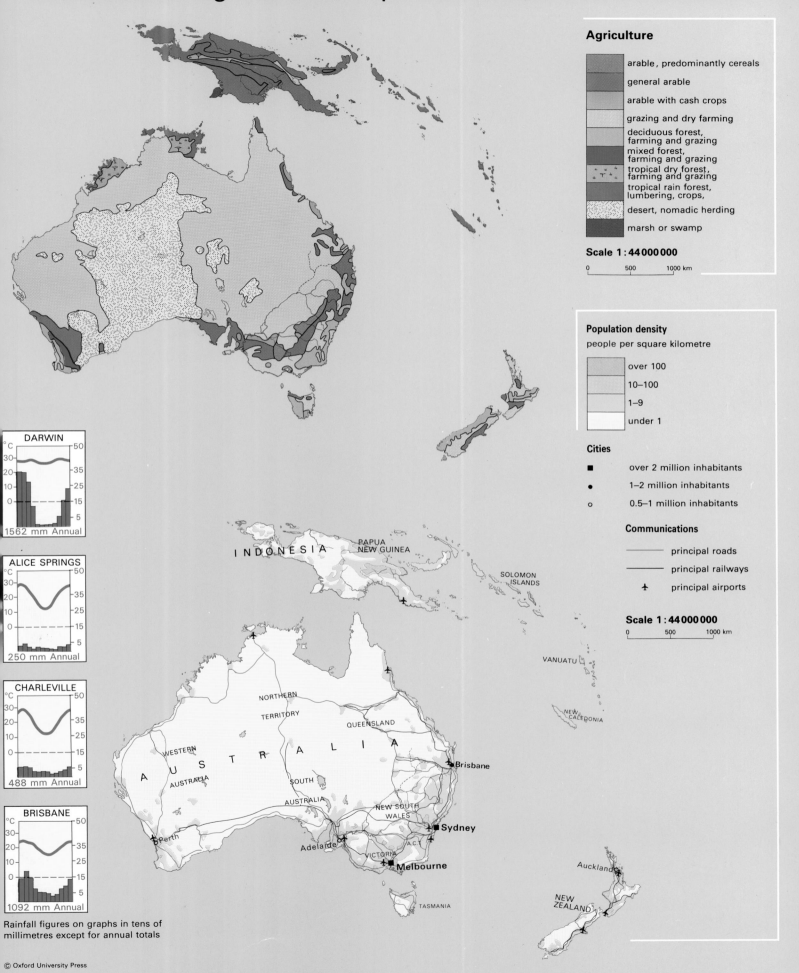

Agriculture

- arable, predominantly cereals
- general arable
- arable with cash crops
- grazing and dry farming
- deciduous forest, farming and grazing
- mixed forest, farming and grazing
- tropical dry forest, farming and grazing
- tropical rain forest, lumbering, crops,
- desert, nomadic herding
- marsh or swamp

Scale 1 : 44 000 000

0   500   1000 km

Population density

people per square kilometre

- over 100
- 10–100
- 1–9
- under 1

Cities

- ■ over 2 million inhabitants
- ● 1–2 million inhabitants
- ○ 0.5–1 million inhabitants

Communications

- —— principal roads
- —— principal railways
- ✈ principal airports

Scale 1 : 44 000 000

0   500   1000 km

DARWIN
°C   50
30   35
20
10   25
0   15
5
1562 mm Annual

ALICE SPRINGS
°C   50
30   35
25
10
0   15
5
250 mm Annual

CHARLEVILLE
°C   50
30   35
25
10
15
5
488 mm Annual

BRISBANE
°C   50
30   35
20
10   25
0   15
5
1092 mm Annual

Rainfall figures on graphs in tens of
millimetres except for annual totals

INDONESIA

PAPUA
NEW GUINEA

SOLOMON
ISLANDS

VANUATU

NEW
CALEDONIA

AUSTRALIA

WESTERN
AUSTRALIA

NORTHERN
TERRITORY

QUEENSLAND

SOUTH
AUSTRALIA

NEW SOUTH
WALES

Brisbane

A.C.T.

VICTORIA

Perth

Adelaide

■ Sydney

■ Melbourne

Auckland

TASMANIA

NEW
ZEALAND

© Oxford University Press

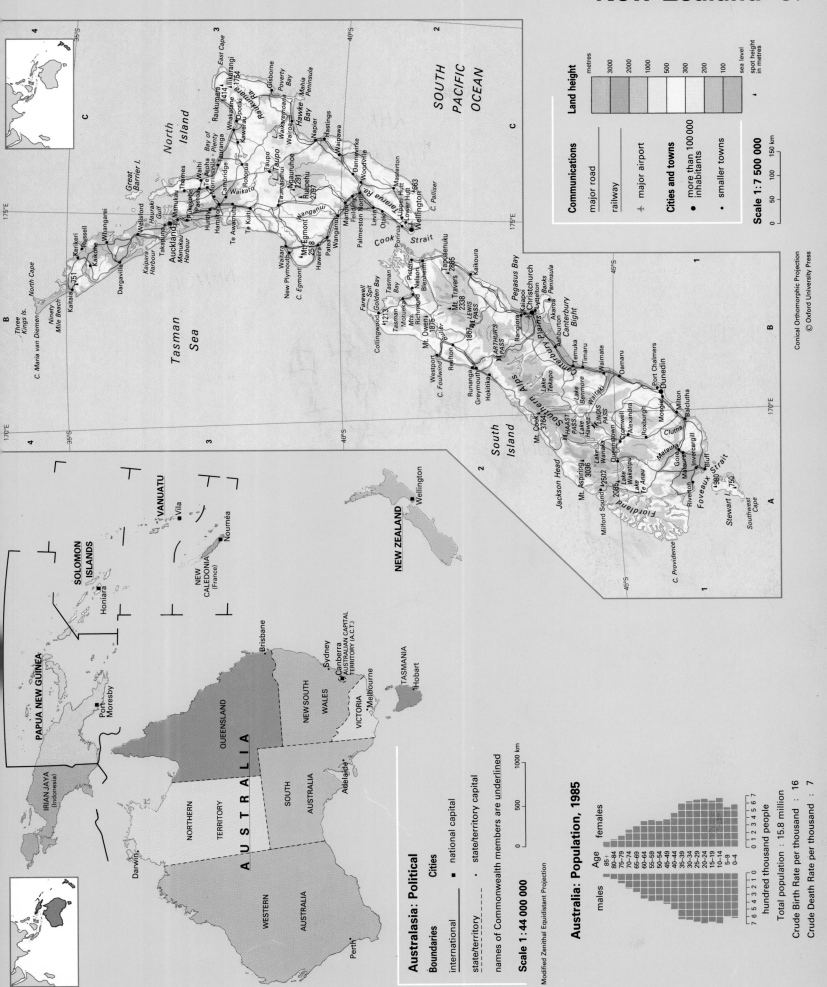

Land height

metres	
3000	
2000	
1000	
500	
300	
200	
100	
sea level	

▲ spot height in metres

Communications

major road
railway
✈ major airport

Cities and towns

● more than 100 000 inhabitants
• smaller towns

Scale 1:7 500 000

0 50 100 150 km

Conical Orthomorphic Projection

© Oxford University Press

SOUTH PACIFIC OCEAN

North Island

Tasman Sea

South Island

South Pacific Ocean

Cook Strait

Australasia: Political

Boundaries — **Cities**

international ▬ national capital
state/territory ▬ state/territory capital

names of Commonwealth members are underlined

Scale 1:44 000 000

0 500 1000 km

Modified Zenithal Equidistant Projection

PAPUA NEW GUINEA
IRIAN JAYA (Indonesia)
SOLOMON ISLANDS — Honiara
VANUATU — Vila
NEW CALEDONIA (France) — Nouméa

AUSTRALIA
WESTERN AUSTRALIA
NORTHERN TERRITORY
QUEENSLAND
SOUTH AUSTRALIA
NEW SOUTH WALES
VICTORIA
TASMANIA

Darwin
Perth
Adelaide
Brisbane
Sydney
Canberra (AUSTRALIAN CAPITAL TERRITORY (A.C.T.))
Melbourne
Hobart
Port Moresby

NEW ZEALAND — Wellington

Australia: Population, 1985

Age — males / females

85+
80-84
75-79
70-74
65-69
60-64
55-59
50-54
45-49
40-44
35-39
30-34
25-29
20-24
15-19
10-14
5-9
0-4

7 6 5 4 3 2 1 0 — 0 1 2 3 4 5 6 7
hundred thousand people

Total population : 15.8 million
Crude Birth Rate per thousand : 16
Crude Death Rate per thousand : 7

Land height

metres
5000
3000
2000
1000
500
300
200
100
sea level
land below sea level
. spot height in metres

Sea depth

sea level
200
3000
4000
5000
6000

Land below sea level and sea depths shown as minus numbers

sand desert

Scale 1 : 44 000 000

0 500 1000 km

NORTH ATLANTIC OCEAN

Mediterranean Sea

Black Sea

Caspian Sea

20°W 15°W
35°N
30°N
25°N
20°N

Str. of Gibraltar
Madeira Is.
Canary Is.
C. Blanc
C. Vert
Senegal
Fouta Djallon

Haut Atlas
Atlas Saharien
Grand Erg Occidental
4165
Grand Erg Oriental
El Erg Iguidi
Erg Chech
Tanezrouft
Hoggar
Adrar

G. of Gabès
Gulf of Sirte

Sahara Desert
Tibesti
3415

Bodélé
Niger

L. Chad
Chari

Jebel Marra

C. Bon

133
Qattara Depression
Libyan Desert
Western Desert
Kufrah Oasis
Nubian Desert

Nile Delta
Sinai
G. of Suez
Red Sea Hills
L. Nasser
4820

White Nile
Blue Nile
Atbara
Danakil
Bab el Mandab
3268
C. Guardafui

An Nafud
Tropic of Cancer
Asir Mts

Sudd
Bahr el Ghazal
Bomu
Uele
Zaïre (Congo)
Lomami
Sangha
Oubangui
2829

Ethiopian Highlands
Ogaden
Shebele
Juba

East Rift Valley
L. Turkana
L. Kyoga
L. Victoria
MT. RUWENZORI 5120
Serengeti
KILIMANJARO 5895
Mitumba Mts
L. Tanganyika
Pemba I.
Zanzibar

Jos Plateau
Kainji Res.
Volta
Volta
Benue
Adamawa Mtns
4095 Sanaga

Bight of Benin
Niger Delta
Bight of Bonny
Gulf of Guinea
C. Palmas
C. Lopez
Guinea Depression

Mai Ndombe
Kasai
Cuango
Lulua
Lualaba

West Rift
5340

INDIAN OCEAN
Equator
Aldabra Is.
Comoro Archipelago

SOUTH ATLANTIC OCEAN
Ascension I.
St. Helena
Angola Depression

Angola Plateau
2610
Cunene
Cuito
Cubango

L. Bangweulu
Muchinga Mts
Rovuma
L. Nyasa (L. Malawi)
Zambezi
Kariba L.
Okavango Basin
Makgadikgadi Salt Pan

Mozambique Channel
Madagascar
Ankarata Mts
2658

Namib Desert
Kalahari Desert
Limpopo
Orange
Vaal
High Veld
Drakensberg
3482
Gt. Karoo
C. of Good Hope
C. Agulhas
C. St. Francis
Mozambique Depression

Tropic of Capricorn

0° 5°E 10°E 15°E 25°E 30°E 35°E 45°E 50°E
5°N 5°S 10°S 15°S 20°S 25°S 30°S 35°S

Africa: Political

— international boundary
• national capital
Names of commonwealth members are underlined

Scale 1 : 80 000 000
0 500 1000 km

MOROCCO
ALGERIA
TUNISIA
Alger Tunis
Rabat Sale
CEUTA (Sp.)
MELILLA (Sp.)
Tarabulus (Tripoli)
LIBYA
EGYPT
Cairo

WESTERN SAHARA
MAURITANIA
Nouakchott
MALI
NIGER
CHAD
SUDAN
Khartoum
Ndjamena
Niamey
Bamako
Ouagadougou
BURKINA

CAPE VERDE IS.
Praia Dakar
SENEGAL
THE GAMBIA
Banjul
Bissau
GUINEA BISSAU
GUINEA
Conakry
SIERRA LEONE
Freetown
Monrovia LIBERIA
CÔTE D'IVOIRE
Yamoussoukro
GHANA
Accra
Abuja
NIGERIA
BENIN
TOGO
Porto Novo
Lomé

DJIBOUTI
Djibouti
Addis Abeba
ETHIOPIA
SOMALIA
Mogadishu

CENTRAL AFRICAN REPUBLIC
Bangui
CAMEROON
Yaounde
Malabo
EQU. GUINEA
São Tomé
SÃO TOMÉ AND PRÍNCIPE
GABON
Libreville
CONGO
Brazzaville
ZAÏRE
Kinshasa
CABINDA (Angola)

UGANDA
Kampala
KENYA
Nairobi
RWANDA
Kigali
BURUNDI
Bujumbura
Dodoma
TANZANIA

Luanda
ANGOLA
ZAMBIA
Lusaka
MALAWI
Lilongwe
Harare
ZIMBABWE
MOZAMBIQUE
COMOROS
Moroni
Aldabra Is. (Seychelles)
Antananarivo
MADAGASCAR

Windhoek
NAMIBIA
Walvis Bay (S. Africa)
BOTSWANA
Gaborone
Pretoria
Mbabane
SWAZILAND
Maputo
REPUBLIC OF SOUTH AFRICA
Maseru
LESOTHO

Zenithal Equal Area Projection

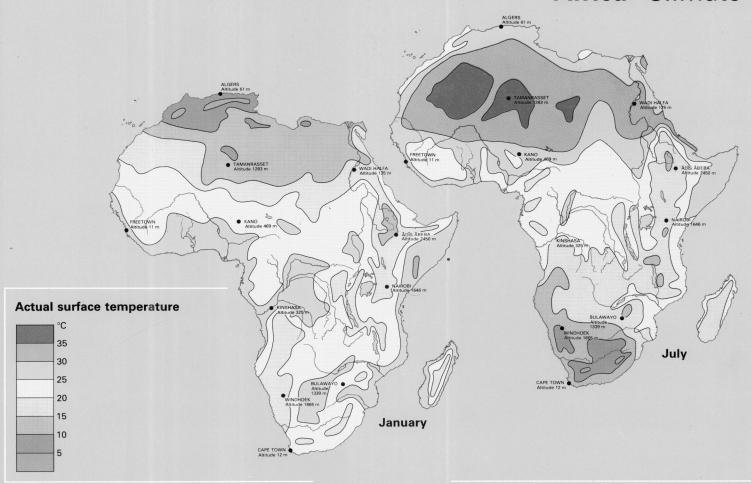

Actual surface temperature

°C
35
30
25
20
15
10
5

January

July

Scale 1 : 80 000 000

0   500   1000 km

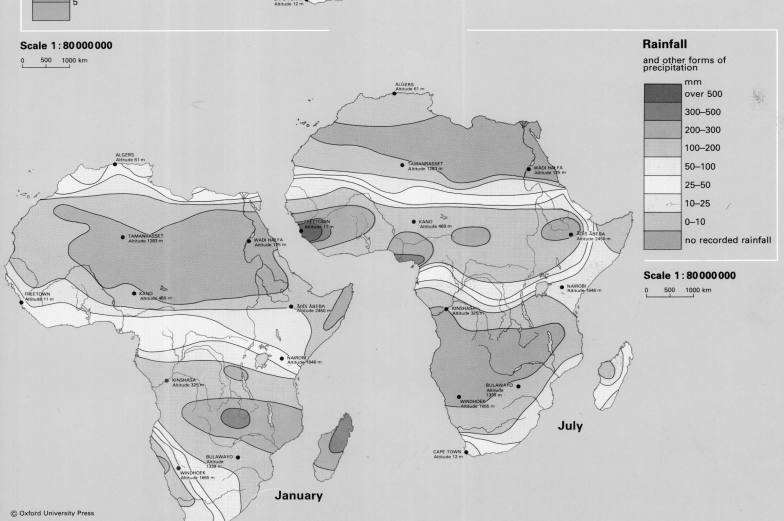

Rainfall

and other forms of precipitation

mm
over 500
300–500
200–300
100–200
50–100
25–50
10–25
0–10
no recorded rainfall

Scale 1 : 80 000 000

0   500   1000 km

January

July

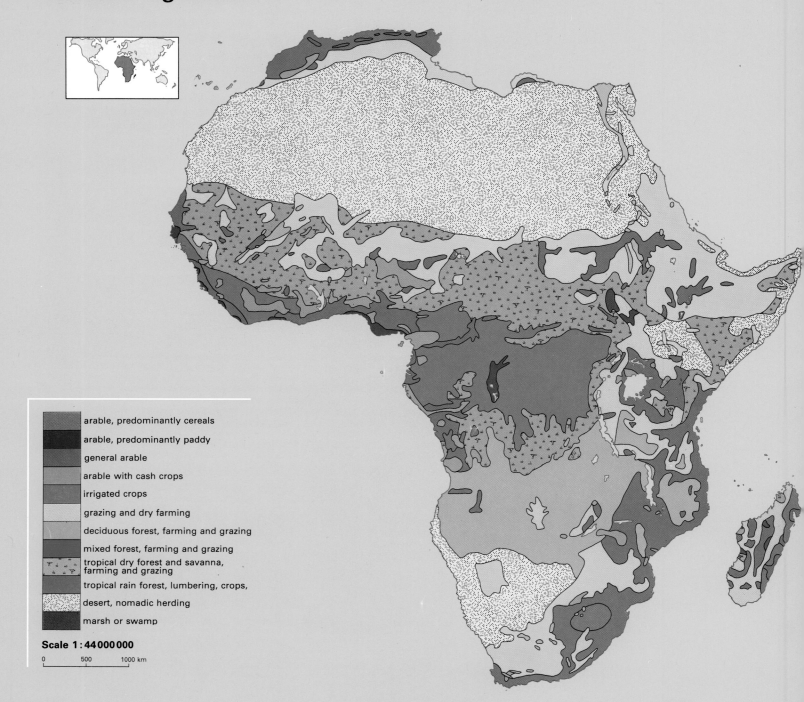

arable, predominantly cereals

arable, predominantly paddy

general arable

arable with cash crops

irrigated crops

grazing and dry farming

deciduous forest, farming and grazing

mixed forest, farming and grazing

tropical dry forest and savanna, farming and grazing

tropical rain forest, lumbering, crops,

desert, nomadic herding

marsh or swamp

Scale 1 : 44 000 000

0   500   1000 km

Tsetse fly

infected areas

Rainfall figures on graphs in tens of millimetres except for annual totals

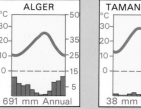

ALGER

691 mm Annual

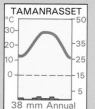

TAMANRASSET

38 mm Annual

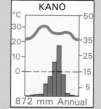

KANO

872 mm Annual

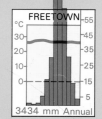

FREETOWN

3434 mm Annual

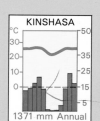

KINSHASA

1371 mm Annual

Zenithal Equal Area Projection

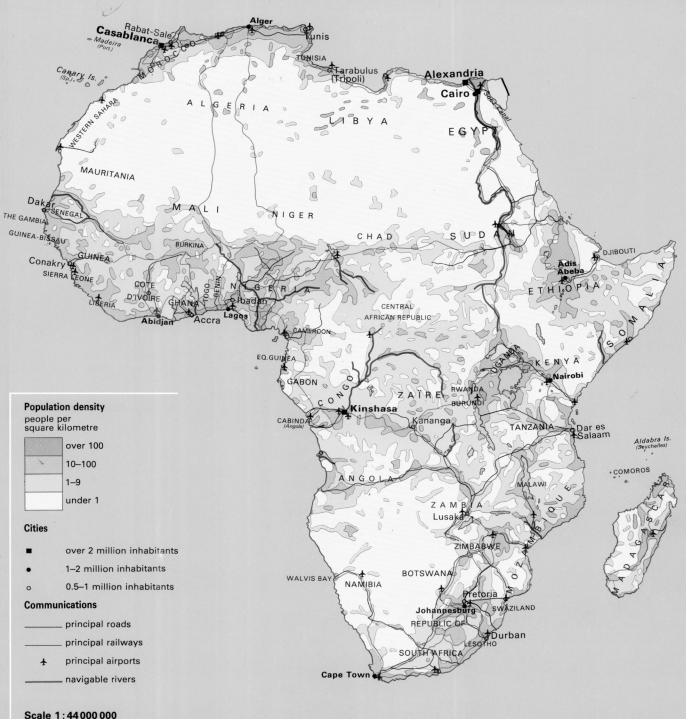

Population density
people per
square kilometre

- over 100
- 10–100
- 1–9
- under 1

Cities

- ■ over 2 million inhabitants
- ● 1–2 million inhabitants
- ○ 0.5–1 million inhabitants

Communications

- —— principal roads
- —— principal railways
- ✈ principal airports
- —— navigable rivers

Scale 1 : 44 000 000

0   500   1000 km

Rabat-Sale
Casablanca
Madeira (Port.)
Alger
Tunis
TUNISIA
Tarabulus (Tripoli)
Alexandria
Cairo
Suez Canal
MOROCCO
Canary Is. (Sp.)
WESTERN SAHARA
ALGERIA
LIBYA
EGYPT
MAURITANIA
Dakar
SENEGAL
THE GAMBIA
GUINEA-BISSAU
Conakry
GUINEA
SIERRA LEONE
LIBERIA
CÔTE D'IVOIRE
MALI
NIGER
BURKINA
CHAD
SUDAN
DJIBOUTI
Ādīs Ābeba
ETHIOPIA
SOMALIA
GHANA
TOGO
BENIN
Ibadan
NIGERIA
Lagos
Abidjan
Accra
CAMEROON
EQ. GUINEA
CENTRAL AFRICAN REPUBLIC
GABON
CONGO
ZAIRE
RWANDA
BURUNDI
UGANDA
KENYA
Nairobi
CABINDA (Angola)
Kinshasa
Kananga
TANZANIA
Dar es Salaam
Aldabra Is. (Seychelles)
COMOROS
ANGOLA
MALAWI
MADAGASCAR
ZAMBIA
Lusaka
MOZAMBIQUE
ZIMBABWE
WALVIS BAY
NAMIBIA
BOTSWANA
Pretoria
Johannesburg
SWAZILAND
REPUBLIC OF
Durban
LESOTHO
SOUTH AFRICA
Cape Town

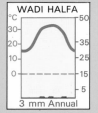

WADI HALFA
°C / 50
30 / 35
20 / 25
10 / 15
0 / 5
3 mm Annual

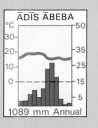

ĀDĪS ĀBEBA
°C / 50
30 / 35
20 / 25
10 / 15
0 / 5
1089 mm Annual

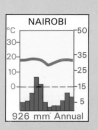

NAIROBI
°C / 50
30 / 35
20 / 25
10 / 15
0 / 5
926 mm Annual

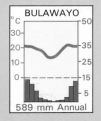

BULAWAYO
°C / 50
30 / 35
20 / 25
10 / 15
0 / 5
589 mm Annual

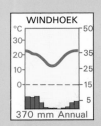

WINDHOEK
°C / 50
30 / 35
20 / 25
10 / 15
0 / 5
370 mm Annual

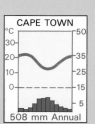

CAPE TOWN
°C / 50
30 / 35
20 / 25
10 / 15
0 / 5
508 mm Annual

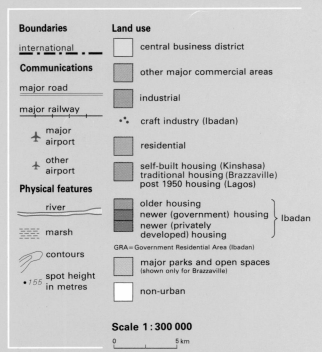

Boundaries

international ·—·—·

Communications

major road

major railway ——+——+——

✈ major airport

✈ other airport

Physical features

~~~ river

marsh

contours

•155 spot height in metres

Land use

central business district

other major commercial areas

industrial

craft industry (Ibadan)

residential

self-built housing (Kinshasa) traditional housing (Brazzaville) post 1950 housing (Lagos)

older housing
newer (government) housing } Ibadan
newer (privately developed) housing

GRA = Government Residential Area (Ibadan)

major parks and open spaces (shown only for Brazzaville)

non-urban

Scale 1 : 300 000

0   5 km

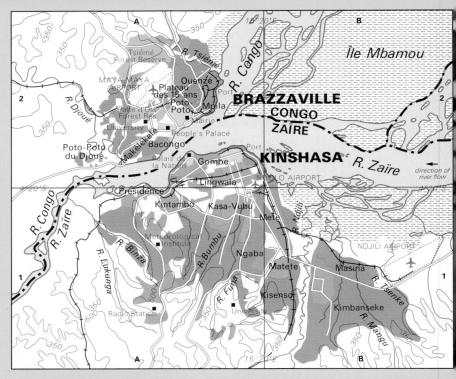

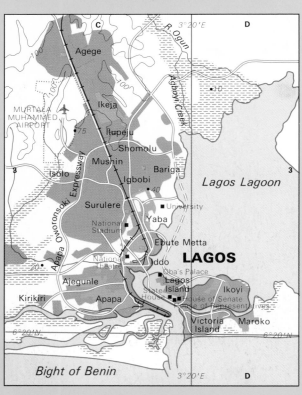

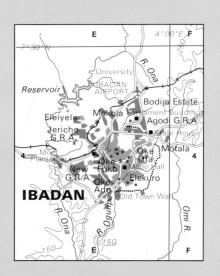

Population growth in selected tropical African cities, 1950–80

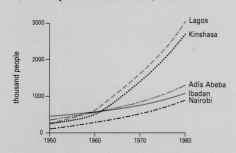

Zaire: Population, 1980

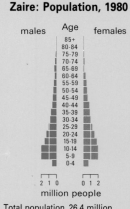

males   Age   females

Total population 26.4 million

Crude Birth Rate per thousand : 45

Crude Death Rate per thousand : 16

Nigeria: Population, 1983

males   Age   females

Total population 92.2 million

Crude Birth Rate per thousand : 50

Crude Death Rate per thousand : 17

Egypt: Population, 1983

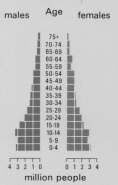

males   Age   females

Total population 45.9 million

Crude Birth Rate per thousand : 37

Crude Death Rate per thousand : 10

© Oxford University Press

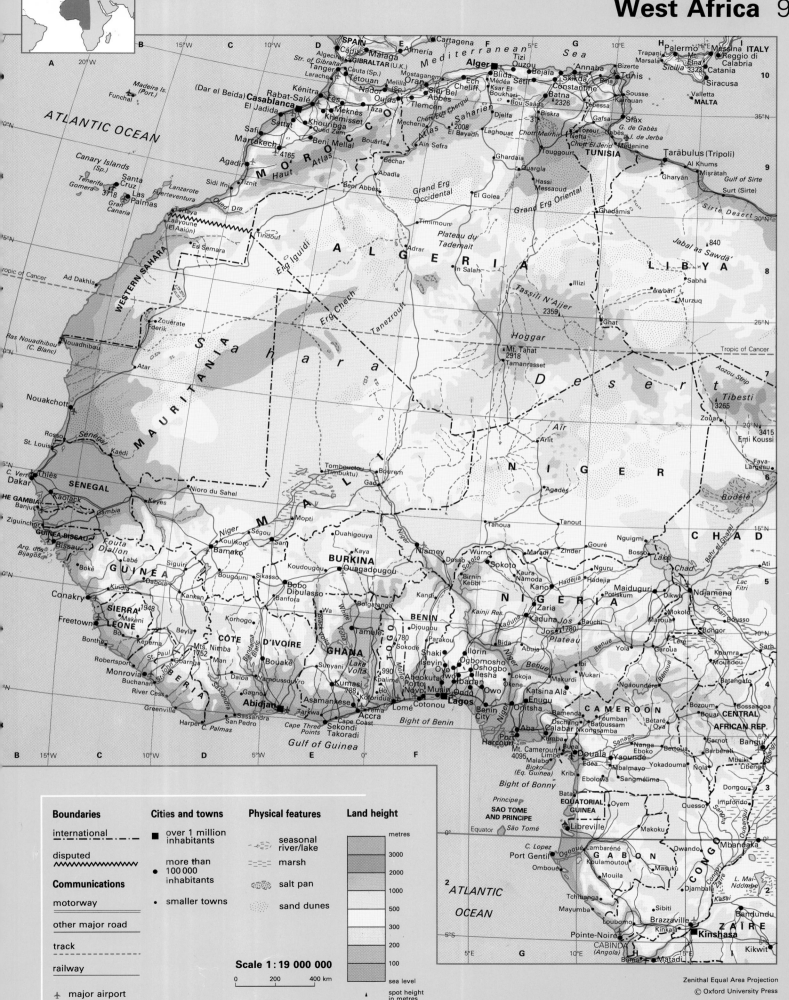

Boundaries

international ·－·－·－

disputed wwwww

Communications

motorway ━━━━

other major road ━━━━

track ━━━━

railway ━━━━

✈ major airport

Cities and towns

■ over 1 million inhabitants

● more than 100 000 inhabitants

• smaller towns

Physical features

seasonal river/lake

marsh

salt pan

sand dunes

Land height

metres
3000
2000
1000
500
300
200
100
sea level
▲ spot height in metres

Scale 1 : 19 000 000

0   200   400 km

Zenithal Equal Area Projection

© Oxford University Press

Zenithal Equal Area Projection

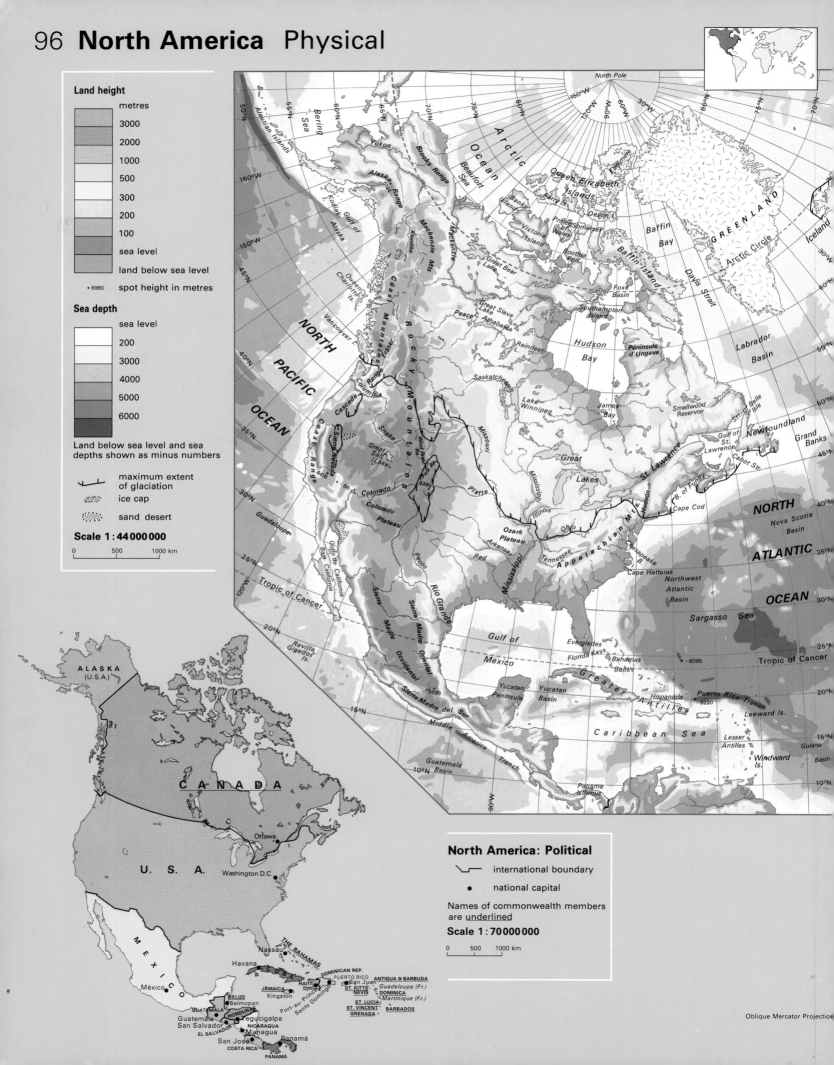

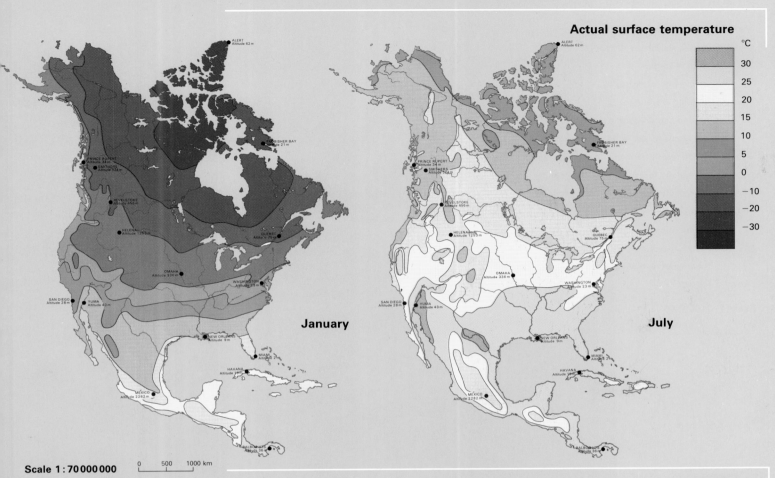

Actual surface temperature

°C
30
25
20
15
10
5
0
−10
−20
−30

January

July

Scale 1 : 70 000 000

0   500   1000 km

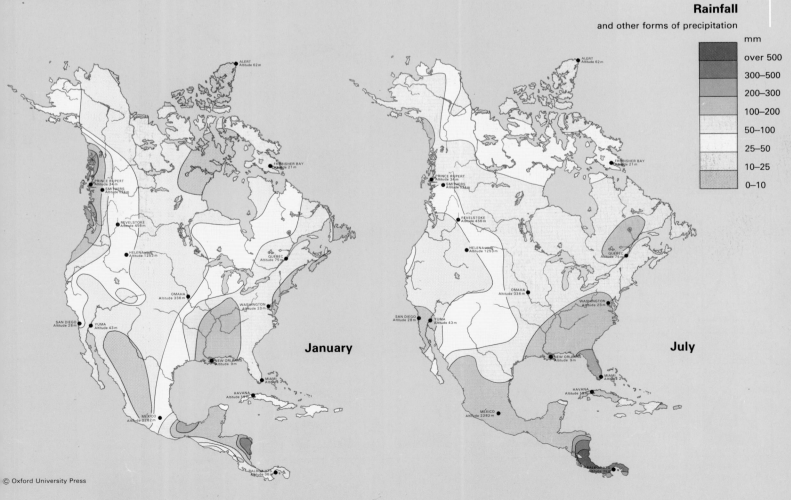

Rainfall

and other forms of precipitation

mm
over 500
300–500
200–300
100–200
50–100
25–50
10–25
0–10

January

July

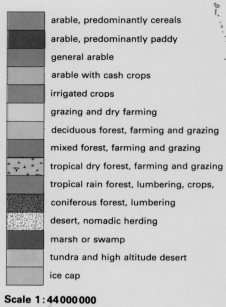

arable, predominantly cereals
arable, predominantly paddy
general arable
arable with cash crops
irrigated crops
grazing and dry farming
deciduous forest, farming and grazing
mixed forest, farming and grazing
tropical dry forest, farming and grazing
tropical rain forest, lumbering, crops,
coniferous forest, lumbering
desert, nomadic herding
marsh or swamp
tundra and high altitude desert
ice cap

Scale 1 : 44 000 000

0   500   1000 km

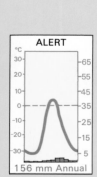

ALERT
°C
30-   -65
20-   -55
10-   -45
0-   -35
-10-   -25
-20-   -15
-30-   -5
156 mm Annual

FROBISHER BAY
°C
30-   -65
20-   -55
10-   -45
0-   -35
-30-   -25
                       -15
                       -5
415 mm Annual

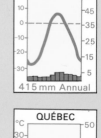

SMITHERS
°C   -50
30-
20-   -35
10-   -25
0-   -15
                       -5
512 mm Annual

PRINCE RUPERT
°C   -50
30-
20-   -35
10-   -25
0-   -15
                       -5
2415 mm Annual

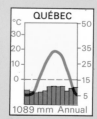
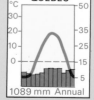

REVELSTOKE
°C   -50
30-
20-   -35
10-   -25
0-   -15
                       -5
1096 mm Annual

QUÉBEC
°C   -50
30-
20-   -35
10-   -25
0-   -15
                       -5
1089 mm Annual

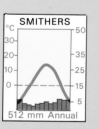
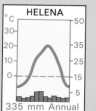

HELENA
°C   -50
30-
20-   -35
10-   -25
0-   -15
                       -5
335 mm Annual

WASHINGTON
°C   -50
30-
20-   -35
10-   -25
0-   -15
                       -5
1036 mm Annual

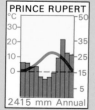
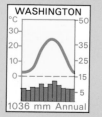

SAN DIEGO
°C   -50
30-
20-   -35
10-   -25
0-   -15
                       -5
264 mm Annual

OMAHA
°C   -50
30-
20-   -35
10-   -25
0-   -15
                       -5
736 mm Annual

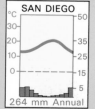
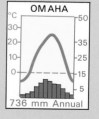

YUMA
°C   -50
30-
20-   -35
10-   -25
0-   -15
                       -5
86 mm Annual

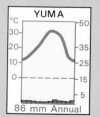

Rainfall figures on graphs in tens of
millimetres except for annual totals

Oblique Mercator Projection

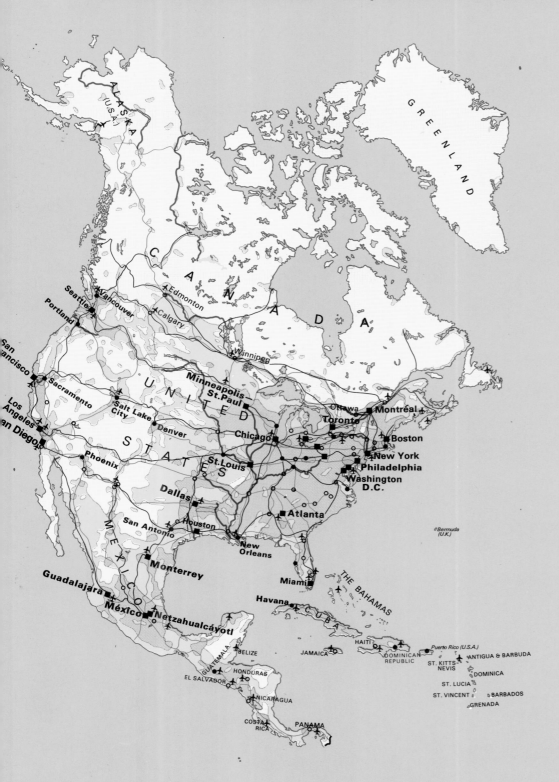

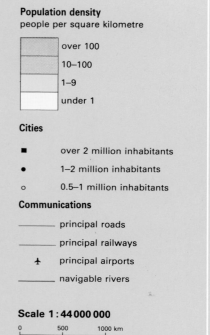

Population density
people per square kilometre

over 100
10–100
1–9
under 1

Cities

■ over 2 million inhabitants
● 1–2 million inhabitants
○ 0.5–1 million inhabitants

Communications

—— principal roads
—— principal railways
✈ principal airports
—— navigable rivers

Scale 1 : 44 000 000

0   500   1000 km

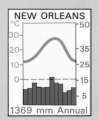

NEW ORLEANS
°C
30
20
10
0
50
35
25
15
5
1369 mm Annual

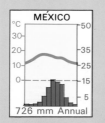

MÉXICO
°C
30
20
10
0
50
35
25
15
5
726 mm Annual

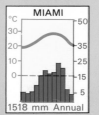

MIAMI
°C
30
20
10
0
50
35
25
15
5
1518 mm Annual

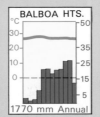

BALBOA HTS.
°C
30
20
10
0
50
35
25
15
5
1770 mm Annual

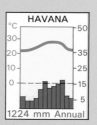

HAVANA
°C
30
20
10
0
50
35
25
15
5
1224 mm Annual

Oxford University Press

Boundaries

international

internal

national park

Physical features

marsh

ice cap

sand dunes

Communications

motorway

other major road

railway

canal

✈ major airport

Land height

metres
3000
2000
1000
500
300
200
100
sea level

▲ spot height in metres

Cities and towns

■ over 1 million inhabitants

● more than 100 000 inhabitants

• smaller towns

Scale 1:19 000 000

0   200   400 km

Zenithal Equidistant Projection

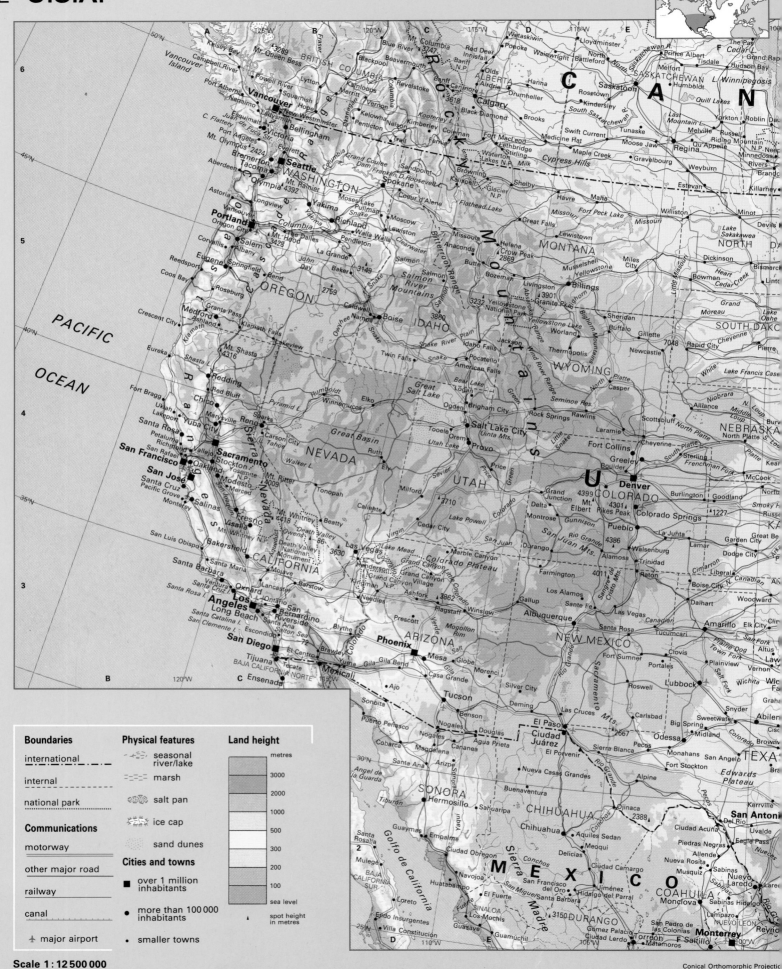

Boundaries

international — ⋅ —
internal ⋯⋯
national park ⋅⋅⋅⋅⋅

Communications

motorway
other major road
railway
canal
✈ major airport

Physical features

🌿 seasonal river/lake
marsh
salt pan
ice cap
sand dunes

Cities and towns

■ over 1 million inhabitants
● more than 100 000 inhabitants
• smaller towns

Land height

metres
3000
2000
1000
500
300
200
100
sea level

▲ spot height in metres

Scale 1 : 12 500 000

0   125   250 km

Conical Orthomorphic Projection

Boundaries

international

internal

national park

Communications

motorway

other major road

railway

canal

✈ major airport

Cities and towns

◊ built-up areas

■ over 1 million
inhabitants

● more than 100 000
inhabitants

• smaller towns

Physical features

seasonal
river/lake

marsh

Land height

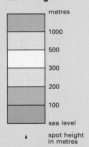

metres

1000

500

300

200

100

sea level

▲ spot height
in metres

Scale 1: 6 250 000

0   25   50 km

Conical Orthomorphic Projection

© Oxford University Press

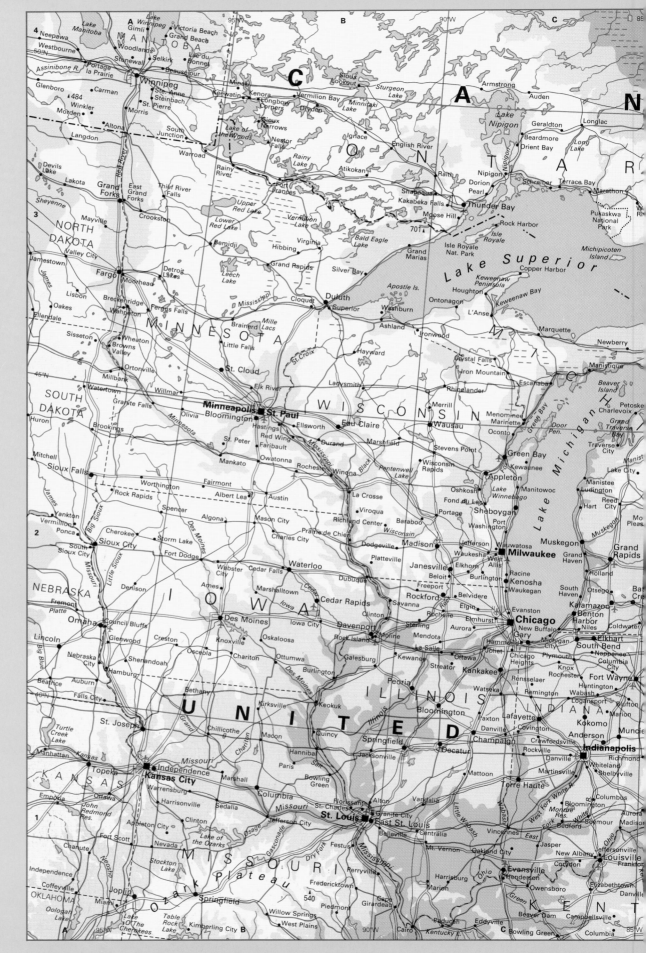

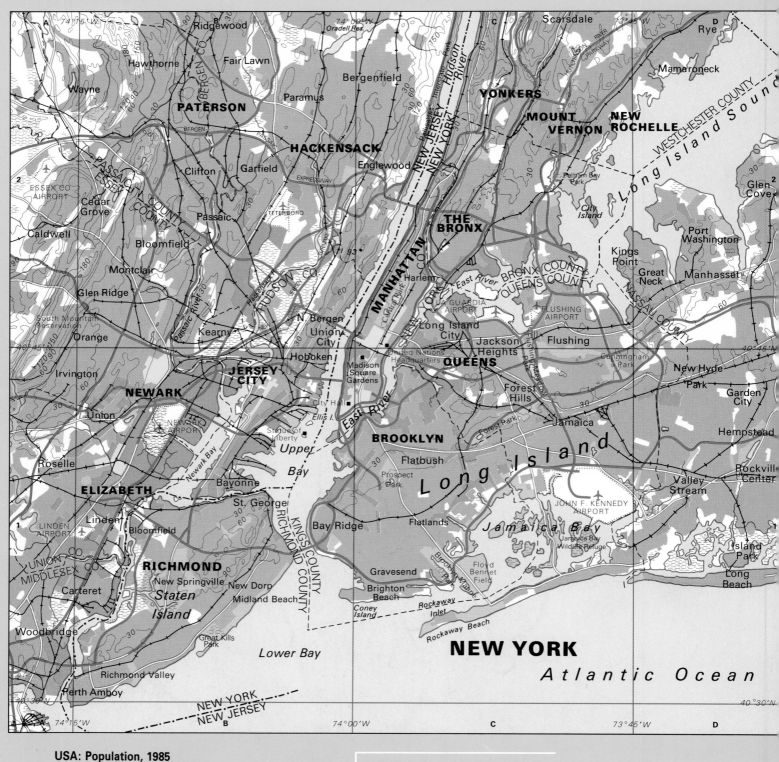

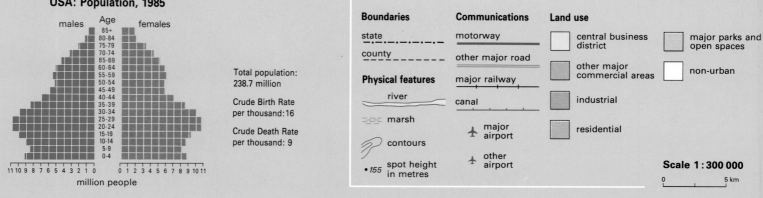

USA: Population, 1985

males | Age | females
85+
80-84
75-79
70-74
65-69
60-64
55-59
50-54
45-49
40-44
35-39
30-34
25-29
20-24
15-19
10-14
5-9
0-4

11 10 9 8 7 6 5 4 3 2 1 0   0 1 2 3 4 5 6 7 8 9 10 11

million people

Total population: 238.7 million

Crude Birth Rate per thousand: 16

Crude Death Rate per thousand: 9

Boundaries

state

county

Physical features

river

marsh

contours

•155 spot height in metres

Communications

motorway

other major road

major railway

canal

✈ major airport

✈ other airport

Land use

central business district

other major commercial areas

industrial

residential

major parks and open spaces

non-urban

Scale 1 : 300 000

0   5 km

SAN GABRIEL MOUNTAINS

ANGELES NATIONAL FOREST

Van Norman Lake
San Fernando
SAN FERNANDO AIRPORT
Sunland
Tujunga
La Crescenta
La Canada
Altadena
MOUNT LUKENS 1853
Big Tujunga Reservoir
Cogswell Reservoir
San Gabriel Reservoir
Mount Wilson Observatory 1740
SAN FERNANDO VALLEY
Van Nuys
North Hollywood
HOLLYWOOD BURBANK AIRPORT
BURBANK
Brand Park
Devils Gate Reservoir
Rose Bowl
PASADENA
Eaton Wash Reservoir
Big Santa Anita Reservoir
Sawpit Canyon Reservoir
Morris Reservoir
Arcadia
Azusa
Sepulveda Dam Recreational Area
Los Angeles River
GLENDALE
Griffith Park
Hollywood Reservoir
Hollywood Bowl
Santa Fe Flood Control Basin
Glendora
STA. MONICA MOUNTAINS
Stone Canyon Reservoir
Beverly Hills
Hollywood
Franklin Canyon Reservoir
Silver Lake Reservoir
Elysian Park
ALHAMBRA
San Gabriel
Temple City
El Monte Airport
Baldwin Park
Covina
LOS ANGELES
Civic Center
Rosemead
El Monte
SAN BERNADINO FREEWAY
West Covina
West Los Angeles
SANTA MONICA FREEWAY
East Los Angeles
Monterey Park
La Puente
SANTA MONICA
Culver City
SANTA MONICA AIRPORT
Montebello
Whittier Narrows Dam Reservoir Area
Rio Hondo
Pico-Rivera
POMONA FREEWAY
Marina del Rey
Whittier
San Gabriel River
INGLEWOOD
HARBOR FREEWAY
SOUTH GATE
DOWNEY
LOS ANGELES COUNTY
ORANGE COUNTY
La Habra
LOS ANGELES AIRPORT
Hawthorne
NORWALK
Manhattan Beach
COMPTON
Los Angeles River
LONG BEACH FREEWAY
Bellflower
SANTA ANA FREEWAY
Fullerton Reservoir
Lawndale
COMPTON AIRPORT
Gardena
Buena Park
Brea Reservoir
FULLERTON
FULLERTON AIRPORT
RIVERSIDE FREEWAY
TORRANCE
LAKEWOOD
Knott's Berry Farm
ANAHEIM
Redondo Beach
Carson
Coyote Creek
LONG BEACH AIRPORT
TORRANCE AIRPORT
Disneyland
GARDEN GROVE
Orange
PALOS VERDES HILLS
San Pedro
LONG BEACH
Santa Ana River
Westminster
SANTA ANA
Marineland of the Pacific
San Pedro Channel
San Pedro Bay
Sunset Beach
SAN DIEGO FREEWAY
Fountain Valley
Huntington Beach

Pacific Ocean

33°45'N

34°15'N

34°00'N

118°15'W

118°00'W

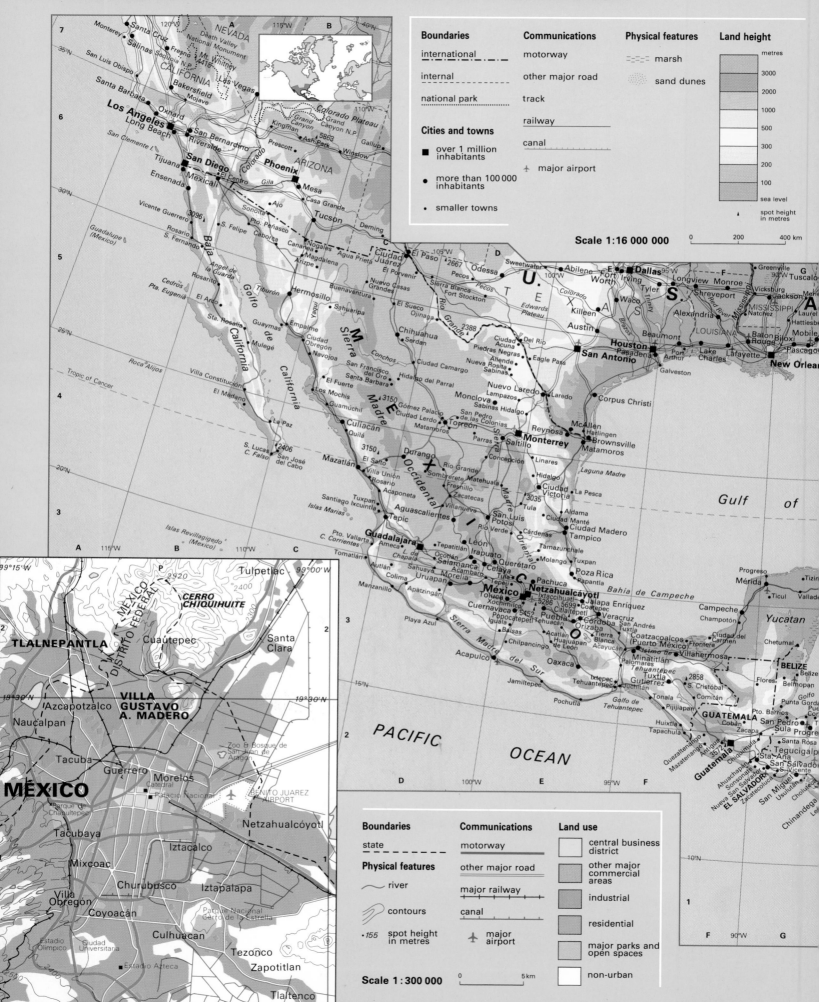

Scale 1:3 000 000

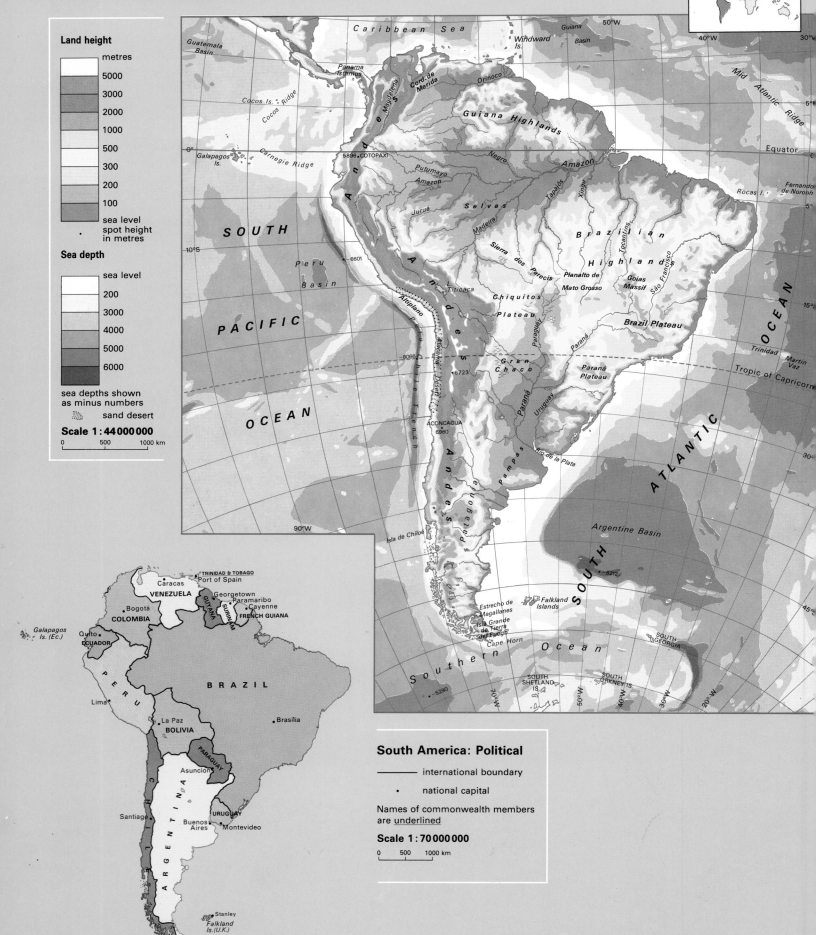

Land height

metres
- 5000
- 3000
- 2000
- 1000
- 500
- 300
- 200
- 100
- sea level
- . spot height in metres

Sea depth

- sea level
- 200
- 3000
- 4000
- 5000
- 6000

sea depths shown as minus numbers

sand desert

Scale 1:44 000 000

0   500   1000 km

Caribbean Sea

Guatemala Basin

Panama Isthmus

Windward Is.

Guiana Basin

50°W

40°W

30°W

Cocos Is.

Cocos Ridge

Carnegie Ridge

Cord. de Merida

Orinoco

Guiana Highlands

Mid Atlantic Ridge

5°N

0°

Galapagos Is.

5896 . COTOPAXI

Putumayo

Amazon

Negro

Amazon

Equator

Rocas I.

Fernando de Noronh

SOUTH

Juruá

Selvas

Tapajós

Xingu

Madeira

Sierra dos Parecis

B r a z i l i a n

5°S

10°S

Peru Basin

— 6601

Tocantins

São Francisco

H i g h l a n d s

Planalto de Mato Grosso

Goias Massif

PACIFIC

Altiplano

Titicaca

Chiquitos Plateau

Paraguay

Brazil Plateau

15°S

— 8066

A n d e s

— 6723

Gran Chaco

Paraná

Paraná Plateau

Trinidad

Martin Vaz

Tropic of Capricorn

OCEAN

Chile Trench

Atacama Desert

ACONCAGUA 6960

Paraná

Uruguay

Rio de la Plata

A T L A N T I C

O C E A N

90°W

Pampas

Patagonia

Isla de Chiloé

Argentine Basin

S O U T H

30°S

— 6212

45°S

Estrecho de Magallanes

Falkland Islands

Isla Grande de Tierra del Fuego

Cape Horn

Southern Ocean

SOUTH GEORGIA

— 5290

SOUTH SHETLAND IS.

SOUTH ORKNEY IS.

70°W

50°W

40°W

30°W

20°W

South America: Political

——— international boundary

• national capital

Names of commonwealth members are underlined

Scale 1:70 000 000

0   500   1000 km

Galapagos Is. (Ec.)

TRINIDAD & TOBAGO
Port of Spain

Caracas
VENEZUELA

Bogotá
COLOMBIA

Quito
ECUADOR

GUYANA
Georgetown
Paramaribo **SURINAM**
Cayenne
FRENCH GUIANA

P E R U

Lima

B R A Z I L

La Paz
BOLIVIA

Brasília

PARAGUAY

Asunción

Santiago

A R G E N T I N A

Buenos Aires

URUGUAY

Montevideo

• Stanley
Falkland
Is.(U.K.)

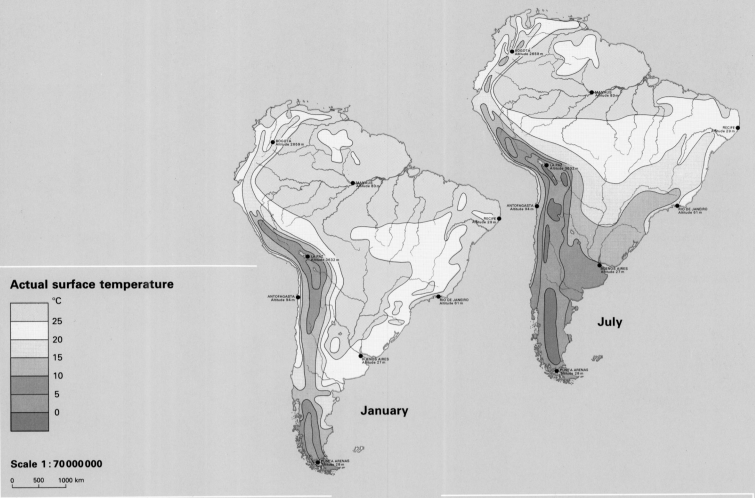

Actual surface temperature

°C

25
20
15
10
5
0

Scale 1 : 70 000 000

0   500   1000 km

January

July

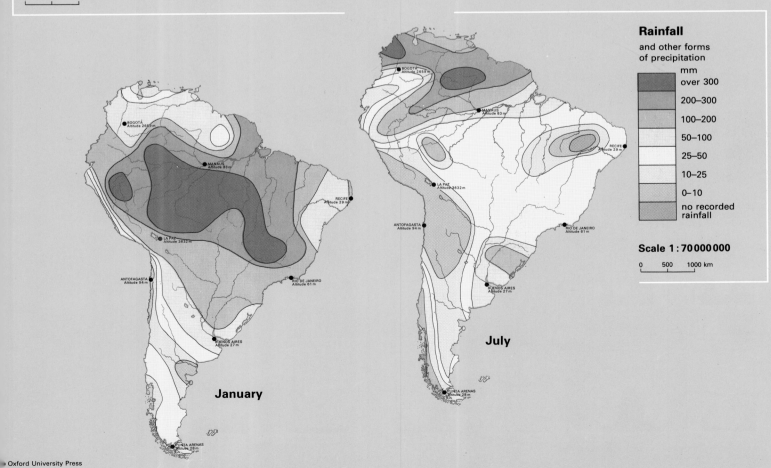

Rainfall

and other forms
of precipitation

mm

over 300
200–300
100–200
50–100
25–50
10–25
0–10
no recorded
rainfall

Scale 1 : 70 000 000

0   500   1000 km

January

July

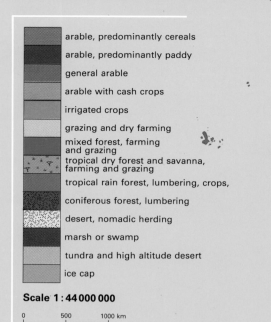

arable, predominantly cereals

arable, predominantly paddy

general arable

arable with cash crops

irrigated crops

grazing and dry farming

mixed forest, farming
and grazing

tropical dry forest and savanna,
farming and grazing

tropical rain forest, lumbering, crops,

coniferous forest, lumbering

desert, nomadic herding

marsh or swamp

tundra and high altitude desert

ice cap

Scale 1 : 44 000 000

0   500   1000 km

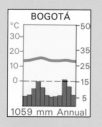

BOGOTÁ

1059 mm Annual

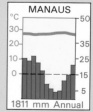

MANAUS

1811 mm Annual

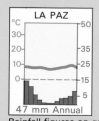

LA PAZ

47 mm Annual

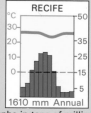

RECIFE

1610 mm Annual

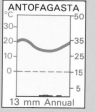

ANTOFAGASTA

13 mm Annual

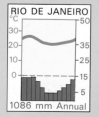

RIO DE JANEIRO

1086 mm Annual

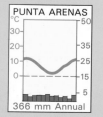

PUNTA ARENAS

366 mm Annual

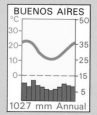

BUENOS AIRES

1027 mm Annual

Rainfall figures on graphs in tens of millimetres
except for annual totals

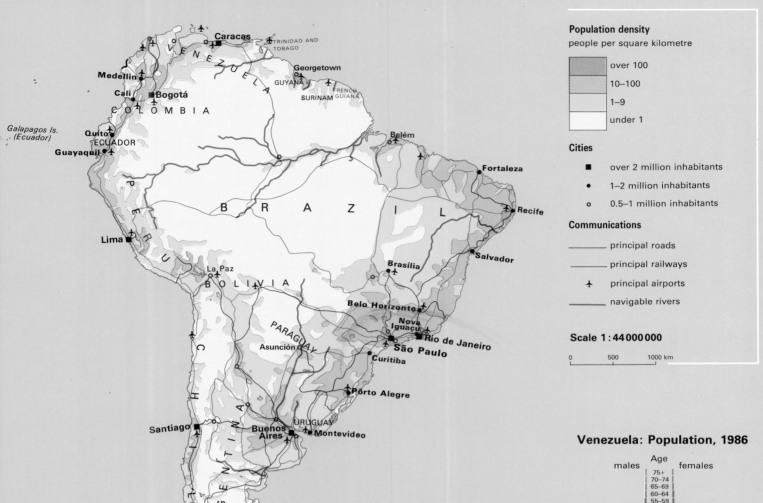

Population density

people per square kilometre

	over 100
	10–100
	1–9
	under 1

Cities

■ over 2 million inhabitants

● 1–2 million inhabitants

○ 0.5–1 million inhabitants

Communications

—— principal roads

—— principal railways

✈ principal airports

—— navigable rivers

Scale 1 : 44 000 000

0   500   1000 km

Venezuela: Population, 1986

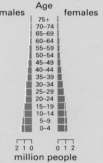

Age

males   females

75+
70–74
65–69
60–64
55–59
50–54
45–49
40–44
35–39
30–34
25–29
20–24
15–19
10–14
5–9
0–4

2 1 0   0 1 2
million people

Total population 17.8 million

Crude Birth Rate per thousand: 32

Crude Death Rate per thousand: 5

Argentina: Population, 1985

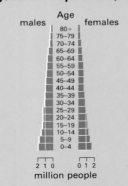

Age

males   females

80+
75–79
70–74
65–69
60–64
55–59
50–54
45–49
40–44
35–39
30–34
25–29
20–24
15–19
10–14
5–9
0–4

2 1 0   0 1 2
million people

Total population 30.6 million

Crude Birth Rate per thousand: 24

Crude Death Rate per thousand: 9

Brazil: Population, 1985

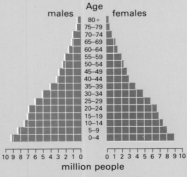

Age

males   females

80+
75–79
70–74
65–69
60–64
55–59
50–54
45–49
40–44
35–39
30–34
25–29
20–24
15–19
10–14
5–9
0–4

10 9 8 7 6 5 4 3 2 1 0   0 1 2 3 4 5 6 7 8 9 10
million people

Total population 135.6 million

Crude Birth Rate per thousand: 30

Crude Death Rate per thousand: 8

Peru: Population, 1985

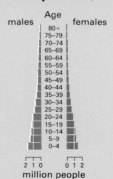

Age

males   females

80+
75–79
70–74
65–69
60–64
55–59
50–54
45–49
40–44
35–39
30–34
25–29
20–24
15–19
10–14
5–9
0–4

2 1 0   0 1 2
million people

Total populations 19.7 million

Crude Birth Rate per thousand: 33

Crude Death Rate per thousand: 10

blique Mercator Projection

© Oxford University Press

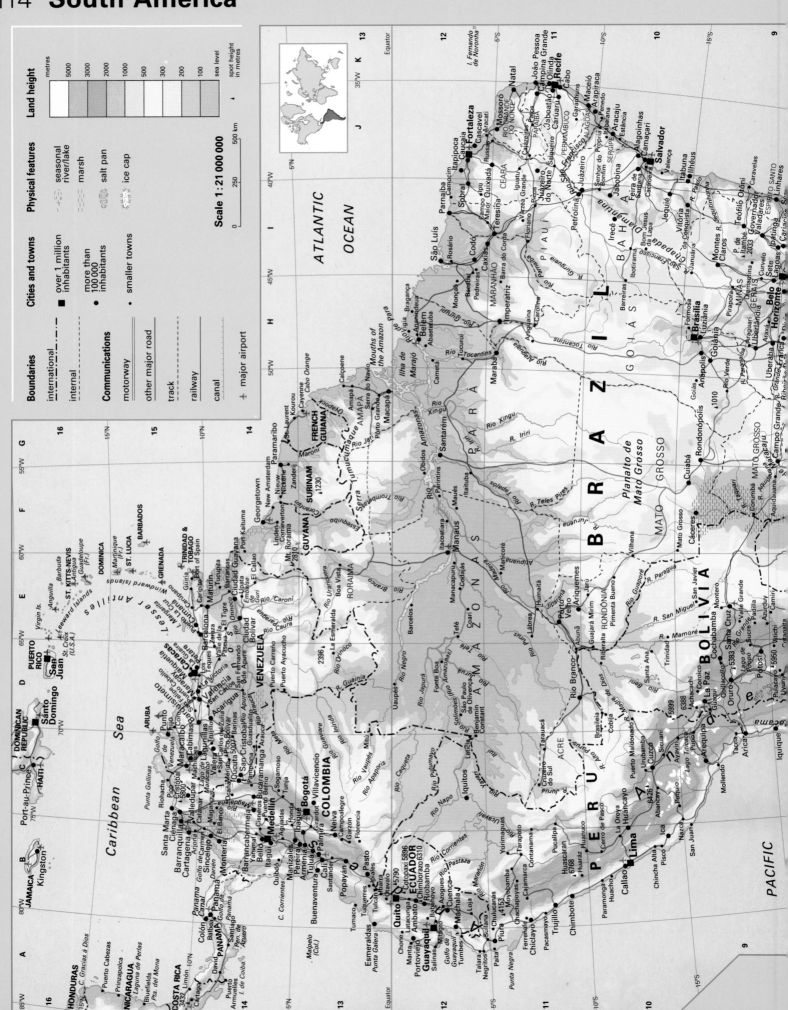

Land height

metres	
5000	
3000	
2000	
1000	
500	
300	
200	
100	
sea level	
	spot height in metres

Physical features

- seasonal river/lake
- marsh
- salt pan
- ice cap

Cities and towns

- ■ over 1 million inhabitants
- ● more than 100 000 inhabitants
- • smaller towns

Boundaries

- international
- internal

Communications

- motorway
- other major road
- track
- railway
- canal
- ✈ major airport

Scale 1:21 000 000

0   250   500 km

ATLANTIC OCEAN

Caribbean Sea

PACIFIC

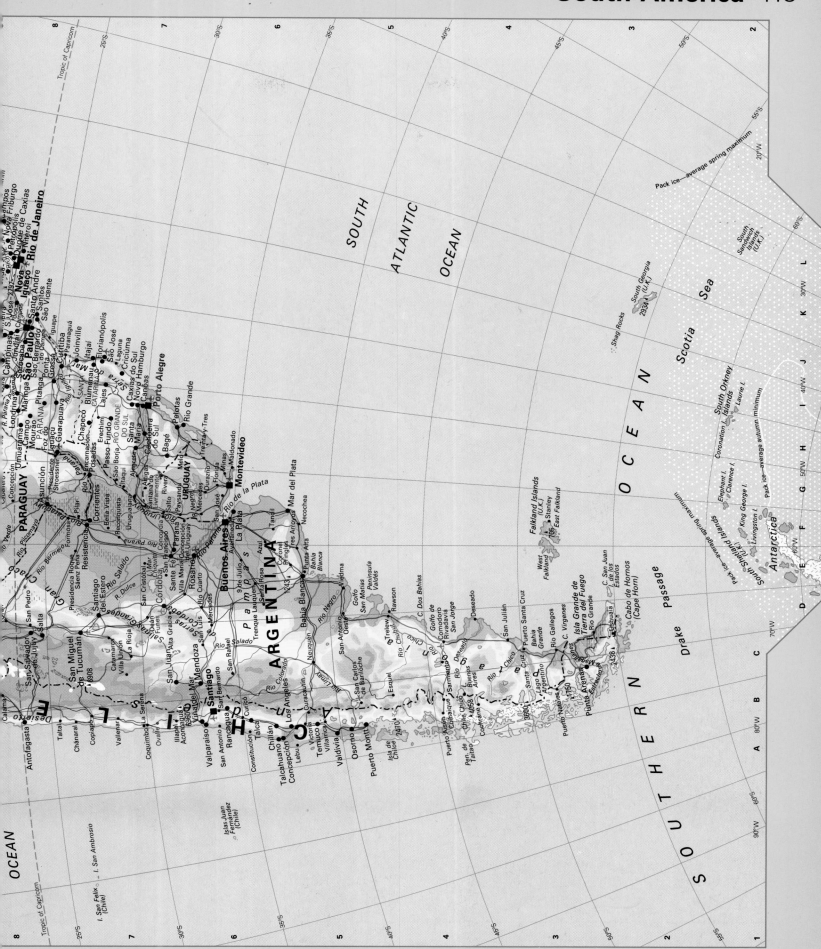

Transverse Mercator Projection

© Oxford University Press

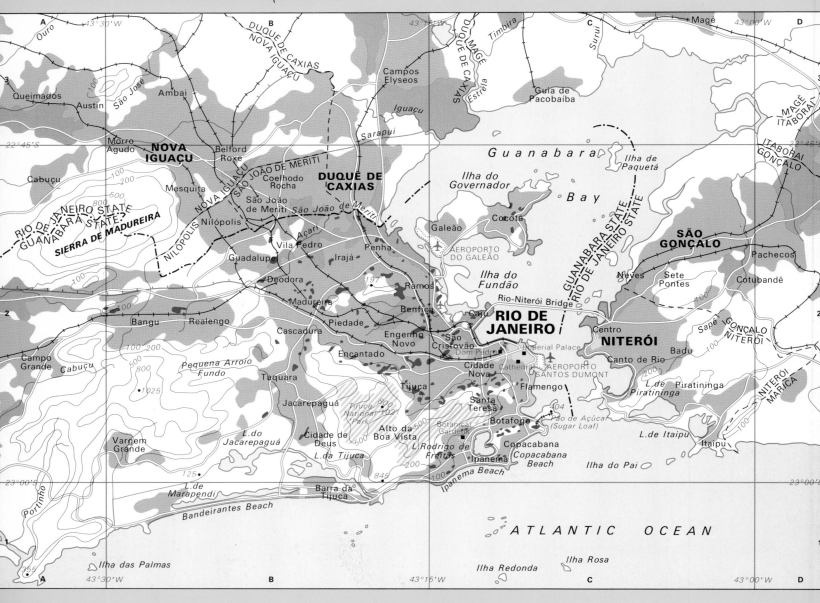

A
Ouro
43°30'W
B
43°15'W
DUQUE DE CAXIAS
NOVA IGUAÇU
43°?5'W
C
Magé
43°00'W
D
Timbira
Surui
MAGÉ ITABORAÍ
Queimados
Austin
São José
Ambai
Campos Elyseos
Iguaçu
Estrêla
MAGÉ
Guia de Pacobaiba
ITABORAÍ GONÇALO
22°45'S
Morro Agudo
NOVA IGUAÇU
Belford Roxe
Sarapui
G u a n a b a r a
Ilha de Paquetá
Cabuçu
Mesquita
Coelhodo Rocha
DUQUE DE CAXIAS
Ilha do Governador
B a y
SÃO GONÇALO
RIO DE JANEIRO STATE
GUANABARA STATE
Nilópolis
São João de Meriti
São João de Meriti
Cocotá
Pachecos
SIERRA DE MADUREIRA
NILÓPOLIS
Nilópolis
Açari
Penha
Galeão
AEROPORTO DO GALEÃO
Cótubandê
Guadalupe
Vila Pedro
Irajá
Ilha do Fundão
Neves
Sete Pontes
Deodora
Ramos
GUANABARA STATE
RIO DE JANEIRO STATE
GONÇALO
2
Madureira
197
Benfica
Rio-Niterói Bridge
Centro NITERÓI
Sapê
NITERÓI
2
Bangu
Realengo
Piedade
Caju
RIO DE JANEIRO
Badu
Campo Grande
Cabuçu
Cascadura
Engenho Novo
São Cristóvão
Imperial Palace
Canto de Rio
Pequena Arroío Fundo
Taquara
Encantado
Cidade Nova
Cathedral
Dom Pedro
AEROPORTO SANTOS DUMONT
L. de Piratininga
Piratininga
Jacarepaguá
Tijuca
Flamengo
NITERÓI MARICÁ
1025
Tijuca National Park
Santa Teresa
104
Pão de Açúcar (Sugar Loaf)
L. de Itaipu
Vargem Grande
L. do Jacarepaguá
Cidade de Deus
Alto da Boa Vista
Botanical Gardens
Botafogo
L. da Tijuca
125
845
L. Rodrigo de Freitas
Copacabana
Copacabana Beach
Itaipu
23°00'S
Ipanema
Ipanema Beach
Ilha do Pai
23°00'S
L. de Marapendi
Barra da Tijuca
Bandeirantes Beach
A T L A N T I C   O C E A N
Portinho
355
Ilha das Palmas
Ilha Rosa
Ilha Redonda
A
43°30'W
B
43°15'W
43°15'W
C
43°00'W
D

Boundaries

state

district

Communications

major road

major railway

cable car

canal

✈ major airport

✈ other airport

Physical features

river

contours

•155 spot height in metres

Land use

central business district

industrial

residential

pueblos jóvenes (Lima)

favelas (Rio de Janeiro)

major parks and open spaces

non-urban

Scale 1:300 000

0   5 km

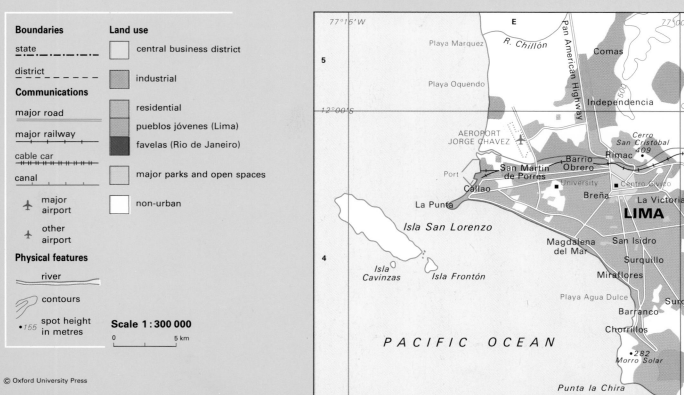

77°15'W
E
Pan American Highway
77°00'W
F
Playa Marquez
R. Chillón
Comas
500
1000
5
1316 Cerro Santa Maria
5
Playa Oquendo
Independencia
12°00'S
12°00'S
AEROPORT JORGE CHAVEZ
Cerro San Cristóbal 409
R. Rímac
Port
San Martin de Porres
Barrio Obrero
Rimac
Callao
University
Centro Cívico
El Agustino
La Punta
Breña
La Victoria
LIMA
La Molir
Isla San Lorenzo
Magdalena del Mar
San Isidro
Monterrico
4
Surquillo
Cerro San Francisco
4
Isla Cavinzas
Isla Frontón
Miraflores
Playa Agua Dulce
Surco
Barranco
Pamplona
Chorrillos
282 Morro Solar
Pan American Highway
P A C I F I C   O C E A N
Villa el Salvador
Punta la Chira
77°15'W
E
77°00'W
F

Boundaries

international ‑‑‑‑‑

disputed ∿∿∿∿∿

Communications

✈ major airport (inset only)

Cities and towns

■ over 1 million inhabitants

● more than 100 000 inhabitants

● smaller towns

national capitals are underlined

Physical features

ice cap

Land height

	metres
	5000
	3000
	2000
	1000
	500
	300
	200
	100
	sea level
	land below sea level

Sea depth

	sea level
	200
	3000
	4000
	5000
	6000

▲ spot height in metres

land below sea level and sea depths shown as minus numbers

Scale 1 : 63 000 000

0   500   1000   1500 km

Falkland Islands (U.K.)

Jason Is.
West Falkland
King George Bay
Queen Charlotte Bay
C. Meredith
George I.
Weddell I.
Pebble I.
Mt Adam 705
San Carlos
Goose Green
Port Darwin
Mt Usborne 681
Bay of Harbours
C. Dolphin
Macbride Head
Berkeley Sound
Stanley
Lively I.
East Falkland
Falkland Sound

Scale 1 : 7 500 000

0   100 km

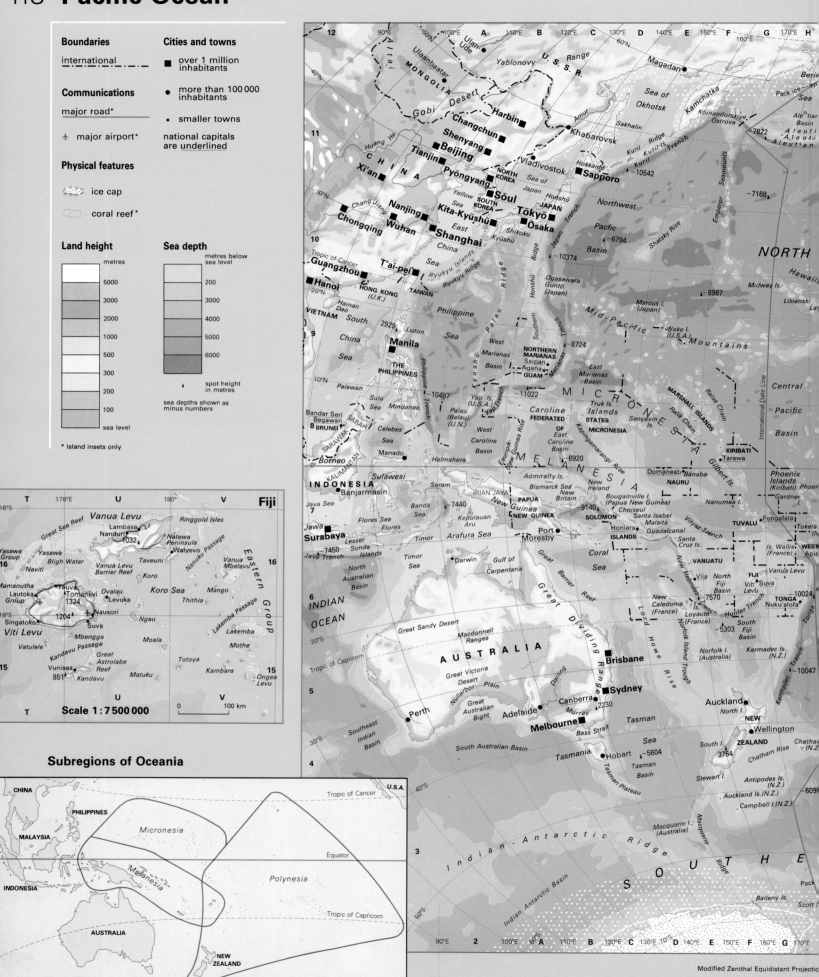

Boundaries

international — — — —

Communications

major road*

✈ major airport*

Physical features

❆ ice cap

⬭ coral reef*

Cities and towns

■ over 1 million inhabitants

● more than 100 000 inhabitants

• smaller towns

national capitals are underlined

Land height

metres
5000
3000
2000
1000
500
300
200
100
sea level

Sea depth

metres below sea level
200
3000
4000
5000
6000

▲ spot height in metres

sea depths shown as minus numbers

* Island insets only

Fiji

Scale 1 : 7 500 000

0   100 km

Subregions of Oceania

Modified Zenithal Equidistant Projection

CANADA

ALASKA (U.S.A.)
Mt. McKinley 6194
Mt. Logan 5951
Anchorage
Gulf of Alaska
Kodiak I.
Nunivak I.
St. Lawrence I.
Bering Strait
Queen Charlotte Is.
Vancouver I.
Vancouver
Seattle
Winnipeg
Saskatchewan
Great Slave Lake
Hudson Bay
Churchill
Canadian Shield
Great Lakes
Minneapolis St. Paul
Chicago
Toronto
Arctic Circle
Rocky Mountains

UNITED STATES
Salt Lake City
Gorda Rise
Mendocino Seascarp
San Francisco
Los Angeles
Mt. Elbert 4399
Colorado
Houston
Rio Grande
New Orleans
Miami
THE BAHAMAS
La Habana
CUBA
Gulf of Mexico

PACIFIC OCEAN
–6474
Murray Seascarp
–6108
Guadalupe (Mexico)
Is. Revillagigedo (Mexico)
Clarion Fracture Zone
–5106
Clipperton I. (France)
Clipperton Fracture Zone
–5298

MEXICO
Guadalajara
México 5452
Acapulco
Middle America Trench
GUATEMALA
Guatemala
BELIZE
HONDURAS
EL SALVADOR
–6662
NICARAGUA
Tegucigalpa
Managua
San José
COSTA RICA
PANAMÁ
Panamá
Guatemala Basin
Yucatan Basin
Cayman Trench
JAMAICA
Kingston
HAITI
DOMINICAN REPUBLIC
–9220 Puerto Rico Trench
PUERTO RICO (U.S.A.)
Leeward Is.
DOMINICA
ST. LUCIA
BARBADOS
GRENADA
TRINIDAD & TOBAGO
Caribbean Sea
Venezuelan Basin
Barranquilla
Maracaibo
Caracas
VENEZUELA
Orinoco
Georgetown
Paramaribo
Cayenne
GUYANA
SURINAM
FRENCH GUIANA
Guyana Basin

NORTH ATLANTIC OCEAN
Tropic of Cancer

Honolulu
Hawaii
East Pacific Basin
Nihoa
Niihau
Hawaiian Ridge
Neckel

Hawaiian Islands (U.S.A.)

Christmas Island Ridge
Palmyra Atoll (U.S.A.)
Tabuaaran I. (Kiribati)
Kiritimati I. (Kiribati)
Line (Kiribati) Islands
Malden I.
–6584
Caroline I.
Marquesas Islands (France)
–6768
–6601
Lima
Islas Galápagos (Ecuador)
Carnegie Ridge
Quito –6310
ECUADOR
Manaus
Amazonas
Equator

PERU
Peru Basin
–5469
Galápagos Rise
Nasca Ridge
Cocos Ridge
I. del Coco (Costa Rica)
Medellín
COLOMBIA
Bogotá
Cali 5750

SAMOA
American Samoa
–6144
Palmerston Atoll (N.Z.)
Cook Is. (N.Z.)
Society Is. (France)
Tahiti
French Polynesia
Tubuai I. (France)
Austral Ridge
Tuamotu Ridge
Tuamotu Archipelago (France)
Gambier Is.
Oano I.
Ducie I.
Pitcairn Islands (U.K.)
Easter I. (Chile)
Sala y Gomez (Chile)
Easter Island Fracture Zone

SOUTH PACIFIC OCEAN
–1088
South West Pacific Basin
Challenger Fracture Zone
Eltanin Fracture Zone
Pacific – Antarctic Ridge

East Pacific Ridge

Peru-Chile Trench
L. Titicaca
La Paz –6388
Santa Cruz
BOLIVIA
Chaco
PARAGUAY
Asunción
–8066
–6755
Gran Chaco
Córdoba –6960
Valparaíso
Santiago
Concepción
Chile Basin
I. San Felix (Chile)
Islas Juan Fernández (Chile)

Brasília
Mato Grosso
BRAZIL
Rio de Janeiro
São Paulo
Tropic of Capricorn
Paraná
Rosario
URUGUAY
Porto Alegre
Buenos Aires
Montevideo

ARGENTINA
Paraná
Patagonia
Isla de Chiloé
Isla Wellington
Pto. Santa Cruz
Isla Grande de Tierra del Fuego
C. de Hornos
Falkland Is. (U.K.)
Argentine Basin
Rio Grande Rise

South East Pacific Basin
Antarctic Circle
spring maximum
Pack ice — autumn minimum

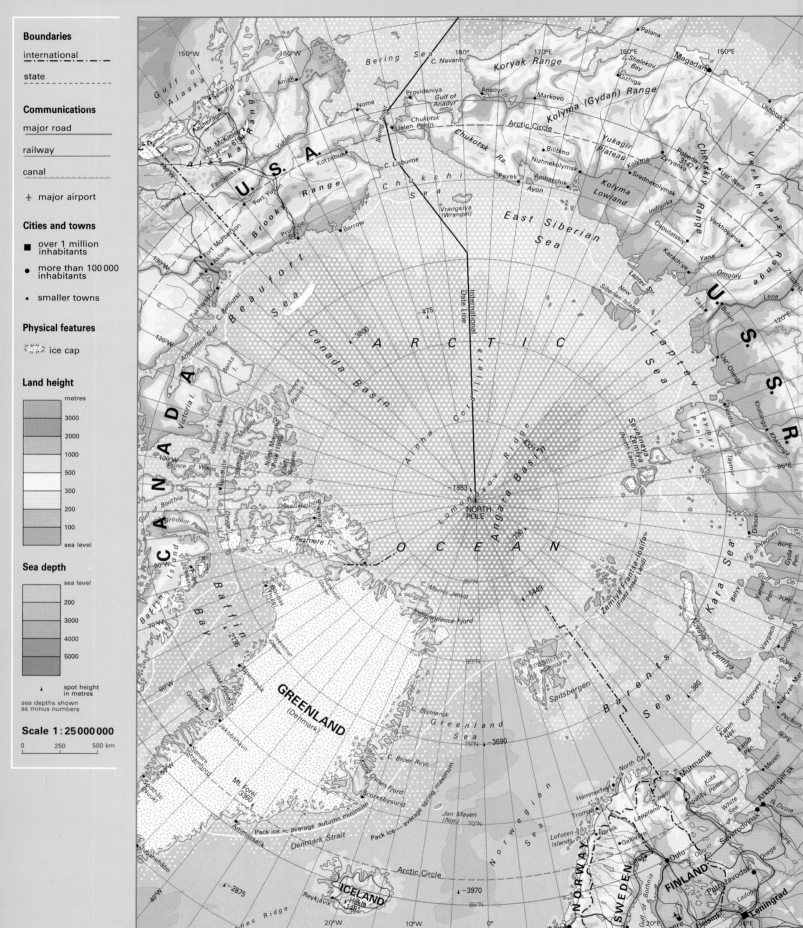

Boundaries

international

state

Communications

major road

railway

canal

✈ major airport

Cities and towns

■ over 1 million inhabitants

● more than 100 000 inhabitants

● smaller towns

Physical features

ice cap

Land height

metres
3000
2000
1000
500
300
200
100
sea level

Sea depth

sea level
200
3000
4000
5000

spot height in metres

sea depths shown as minus numbers

Scale 1:25 000 000

0   250   500 km

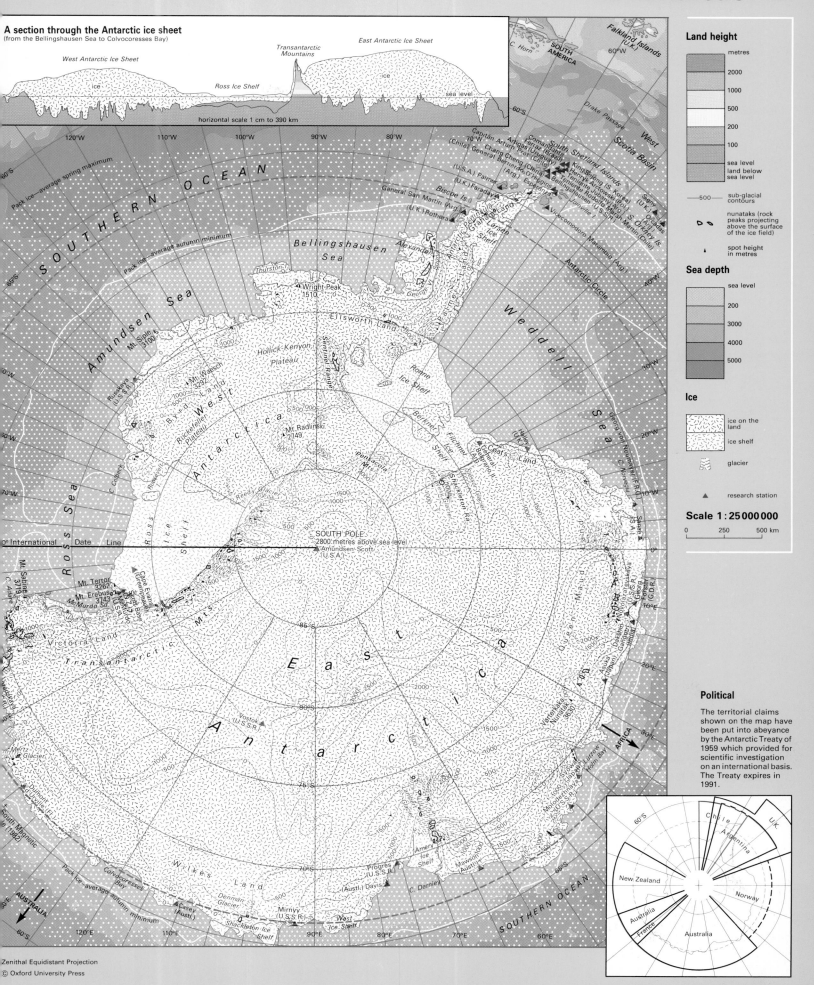

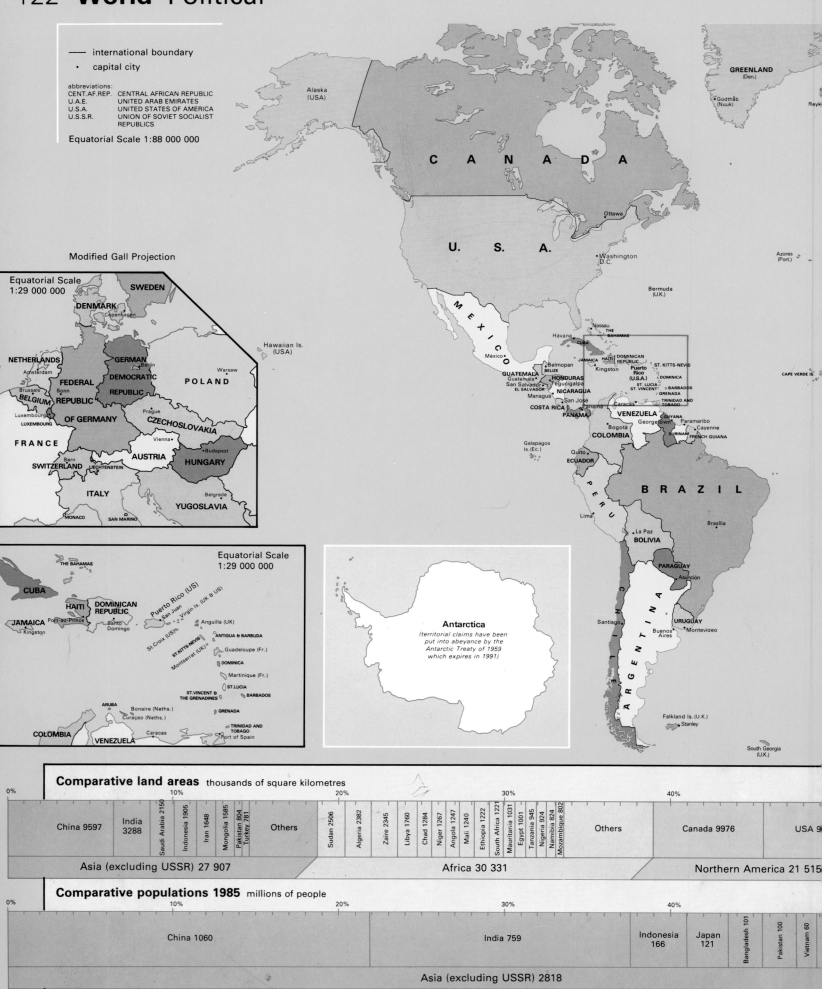

— international boundary
• capital city

abbreviations:
CENT.AF.REP.   CENTRAL AFRICAN REPUBLIC
U.A.E.   UNITED ARAB EMIRATES
U.S.A.   UNITED STATES OF AMERICA
U.S.S.R.   UNION OF SOVIET SOCIALIST
               REPUBLICS

Equatorial Scale 1:88 000 000

Modified Gall Projection

Equatorial Scale
1:29 000 000

SWEDEN
DENMARK
Copenhagen
NETHERLANDS
Amsterdam
GERMAN
DEMOCRATIC
Berlin
REPUBLIC
FEDERAL
Bonn
REPUBLIC
OF GERMANY
POLAND
Warsaw
BELGIUM
Brussels
LUXEMBOURG
Luxembourg
FRANCE
Prague
CZECHOSLOVAKIA
SWITZERLAND
Bern
Vienna
AUSTRIA
HUNGARY
Budapest
LIECHTENSTEIN
ITALY
Belgrade
MONACO
SAN MARINO
YUGOSLAVIA

Equatorial Scale
1:29 000 000

THE BAHAMAS
CUBA
HAITI
DOMINICAN
REPUBLIC
Puerto Rico (US)
San Juan
JAMAICA
Port-au-Prince
Santo
Domingo
Virgin Is. (UK & US)
Anguilla (UK)
Kingston
St.Croix (US)
ST.KITTS-NEVIS
ANTIGUA & BARBUDA
Montserrat (UK)
Guadeloupe (Fr.)
DOMINICA
Martinique (Fr.)
ST.LUCIA
ST.VINCENT &
THE GRENADINES
BARBADOS
ARUBA
Bonaire (Neths.)
GRENADA
Curaçao (Neths.)
TRINIDAD AND
TOBAGO
COLOMBIA
Caracas
Port of Spain
VENEZUELA

Antarctica
(territorial claims have been
put into abeyance by the
Antarctic Treaty of 1959
which expires in 1991)

GREENLAND
(Den.)
Godthåb
(Nuuk)
Reyk

Alaska
(USA)

C A N A D A
Ottawa

U. S. A.
Washington
D.C.

Azores
(Port.)

Bermuda
(U.K.)

Hawaiian Is.
(USA)

MEXICO
México
Havana
CUBA
Nassau
THE BAHAMAS
JAMAICA HAITI
DOMINICAN
REPUBLIC
ST. KITTS-NEVIS
Kingston
Puerto
Rico
(U.S.A.)
DOMINICA
ST. LUCIA
ST.VINCENT
BARBADOS
GRENADA
TRINIDAD AND
TOBAGO
GUATEMALA
Belmopan
BELIZE
Guatemala
San Salvador
EL SALVADOR
HONDURAS
Tegucigalpa
NICARAGUA
Managua
San José
COSTA RICA
PANAMA
Panamá
Caracas
VENEZUELA
GUYANA
Georgetown
SURINAM
Paramaribo
Cayenne
FRENCH GUIANA
Bogotá
COLOMBIA

CAPE VERDE Is.

Galapagos
Is.(Ec.)
Quito
ECUADOR
P E R U
Lima
La Paz
BOLIVIA
B R A Z I L
Brasília
PARAGUAY
Asunción
C H I L E
Santiago
A R G E N T I N A
Buenos
Aires
URUGUAY
Montevideo
Falkland Is. (U.K.)
Stanley
South Georgia
(U.K.)

Comparative land areas thousands of square kilometres

| 0% | | 10% | | | | | 20% | | | | | | | | | | | 30% | | | | | | | 40% | | |

Asia (excluding USSR) 27 907:
China 9597 | India 3288 | Saudi Arabia 2150 | Indonesia 1905 | Iran 1648 | Mongolia 1585 | Pakistan 804 | Turkey 781 | Others

Africa 30 331:
Sudan 2506 | Algeria 2382 | Zaire 2345 | Libya 1760 | Chad 1284 | Niger 1267 | Angola 1247 | Mali 1240 | Ethiopia 1222 | South Africa 1221 | Mauritania 1031 | Egypt 1001 | Tanzania 945 | Nigeria 924 | Namibia 824 | Mozambique 802 | Others

Northern America 21 515:
Canada 9976 | USA 9

Comparative populations 1985 millions of people

| 0% | | 10% | | | | | 20% | | | | | | | | | | | 30% | | | | | | | 40% | | |

Asia (excluding USSR) 2818:
China 1060 | India 759 | Indonesia 166 | Japan 121 | Bangladesh 101 | Pakistan 100 | Vietnam 60

Jan Mayen (Den.)

NORWAY SWEDEN FINLAND

Faeroes (Den.)
Oslo Stockholm Helsinki

U. S. S. R.

Moscow

DENMARK Copenhagen

UNITED KINGDOM
London

NETH. G.D.R.
Amsterdam Berlin
Bonn POLAND Warsaw

BELG. F.R.G.
Brussels Prague
LUX. CZECH.

FRANCE SWITZ. AUST. HUNGARY
Paris Bern Vienna Budapest ROMANIA
ITALY Belgrade Bucharest

MONACO YUGOSLAVIA
ANDORRA Rome BULGARIA
PORTUGAL Sofiya
Lisbon SPAIN ALBANIA
Madrid Tirane GREECE Ankara
Athens TURKEY

MONGOLIA
Ulaanbaatar

CHINA

Beijing (Peking)

NORTH KOREA
Pyongyang
SOUTH KOREA
Seoul JAPAN
Tōkyō

MOROCCO
Rabat-Sale

TUNISIA MALTA
Tunis
Alger
Tripoli

NICOSIA CYPRUS SYRIA
LEBANON Beirut Damascus
ISRAEL Baghdad
Jerusalem Amman IRAQ
JORDAN

Tehrān

AFGHANISTAN
Kābul Islamabad

New Delhi

NEPAL
Kathmandu BHUTAN
Thimpu

T'ai-pei
TAIWAN

Aaiun

ALGERIA LIBYA EGYPT
Cairo

KUWAIT
Al Kuwayt
BAHRAIN
QATAR Doha
Ar Riyād Abu Dhabi
U.A.E. Masqat

PAKISTAN

INDIA

Dhaka BANGLA DESH

Hong Kong (U.K.)

MYANMA (Burma)
Rangoon (Yangon)

Hanoi
Vientiane LAOS
VIETNAM

MAURITANIA
Nouakchott

MALI NIGER CHAD
SUDAN
Khartoum

SAUDI ARABIA
San'a SOUTH YEMEN
YEMEN Aden
DJIBOUTI Djibouti

Socotra (S. Yemen)

SRI LANKA
Colombo

THAILAND
Bangkok
KAMPUCHEA
Phnom Penh

Manila
PHILIPPINES

THE GAMBIA
Bamako
BURKINA
Ouagadougou
Niamey Ndjamena

Addis Ababa
ETHIOPIA

SOMALIA
Mogadishu

MALDIVES

MALAYSIA
Kuala Lumpur
BRUNEI Bandar Seri Begawan

GUINEA
SIERRA LEONE
Monrovia LIBERIA

CÔTE D'IVOIRE
GHANA TOGO BENIN
Yamoussoukro
Accra Lome Porto Novo

NIGERIA
Abuja

CENT. AF. REP.
Bangui

UGANDA
Kampala
KENYA
Nairobi

SEYCHELLES

SINGAPORE

EQUATORIAL GUINEA
Malabo

CAMEROON
Yaounde

RWANDA
Kigali
BURUNDI
Bujumbura

INDONESIA
Jakarta

NAURU

GABON
Libreville
CONGO
Brazzaville

ZAIRE
Kinshāsa
Cabinda (Angola)

TANZANIA
Dodoma

COMOROS

PAPUA NEW GUINEA
Port Moresby

SOLOMON IS.
Honiara

TUVALU

ANGOLA
Luanda

ZAMBIA
Lusaka

MALAWI
Lilongwe

MADAGASCAR
Antananarivo

MAURITIUS
Réunion (Fr.)

VANUATU
Vila

FIJI
Suva

NAMIBIA
Windhoek

BOTSWANA
Gaborone

ZIMBABWE
Harare

MOZAMBIQUE
Maputo
Mbabane SWAZILAND

New Caledonia (Fr.)
Noumea

REPUBLIC OF SOUTH AFRICA
Pretoria
Maseru LESOTHO

AUSTRALIA
Canberra

NEW ZEALAND
Wellington

Kerguelen (Fr.)

	60%						70%		80%				90%		100%

Greenland 2176 | Brazil 8512 | Argentina 2767 | Mexico 1973 | Colombia 1139 | Bolivia 1099 | Venezuela 912 | Chile 757 | Others | Antarctica 14 000 | Australia 7687 | New Zealand 269 | France 547 | Spain 505 | Sweden 450 | Others | USSR 22 400

Central and South America 20 566 | Antarctica 14 000 | Oceania 8 509 | Europe (excluding USSR) 4 876 | USSR 22 400

	60%						70%		80%				90%		100%

South Korea 41 | Burma 37 | Others | Nigeria 95 | Egypt 50 | Ethiopia 44 | South Africa 32 | Zaire 30 | Tanzania 22 | Morocco 22 | Algeria 22 | Sudan 22 | Others | USA 238 | Canada 25 | Brazil 136 | Mexico 79 | Argentina 31 | Colombia 29 | Peru 20 | Venezuela 17 | Others | Australia 16 | FRG 61 | Italy 57 | UK 56 | France 55 | Spain 39 | Poland 37 | Yugoslavia 23 | Romania 23 | Others | USSR 279

Africa 555 | Northern America 264 | Central and South America 405 | Oceania 25 | Europe (excluding USSR) 491 | USSR 279

Land height and sea depth

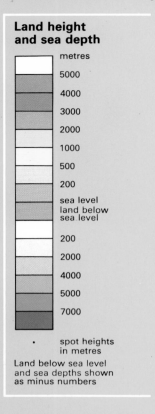

metres
- 5000
- 4000
- 3000
- 2000
- 1000
- 500
- 200

sea level
land below
sea level
- 200
- 2000
- 4000
- 5000
- 7000

• spot heights in metres

Land below sea level and sea depths shown as minus numbers

Equatorial Scale 1:88 000 000

Modified Gall Projection

Plate tectonics

The present positions of the major tectonic plates are shown with the white areas representing the smaller plates.

Plate boundaries

— lines of shallow focus earthquakes

= sea ridges which are actively spreading

➡ direction of sea-floor spreading

— major fracture zones

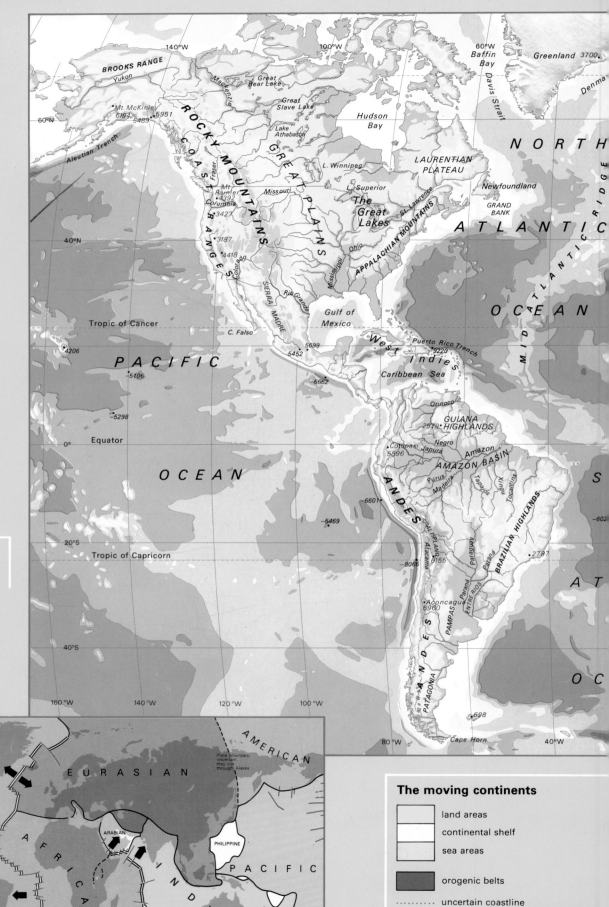

The moving continents

land areas

continental shelf

sea areas

orogenic belts

·········· uncertain coastline

·········· uncertain continental shelf edge

Lines of latitude and longitude indicate position on the globe.

The graticules show how earlier positions of the continents compare with the present

Gall Projection

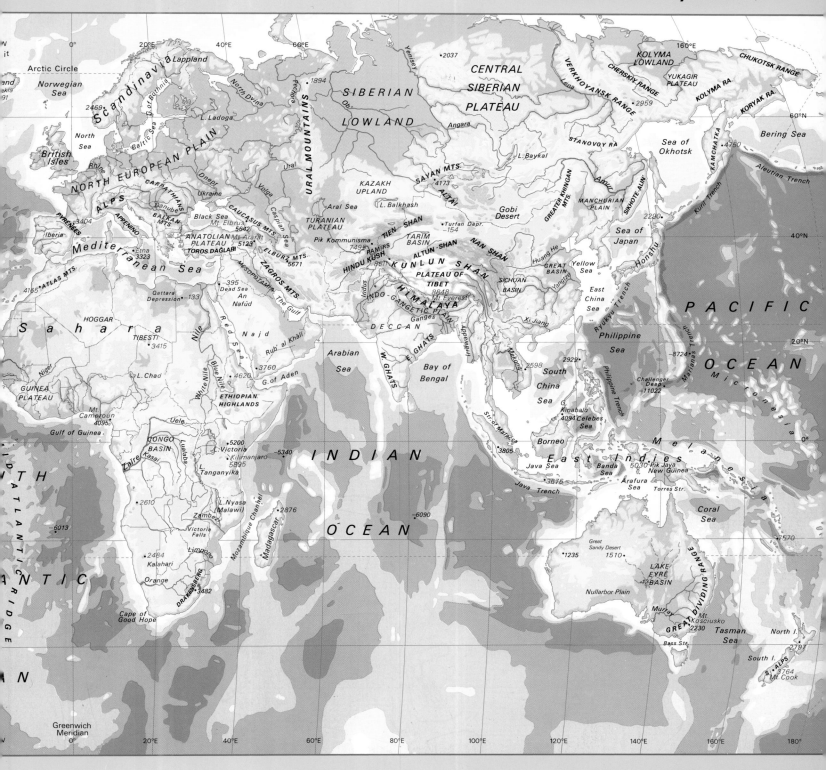

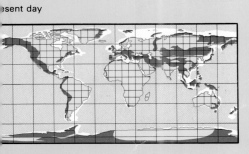

Present day

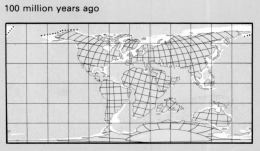

100 million years ago

200 million years ago

Oxford University Press

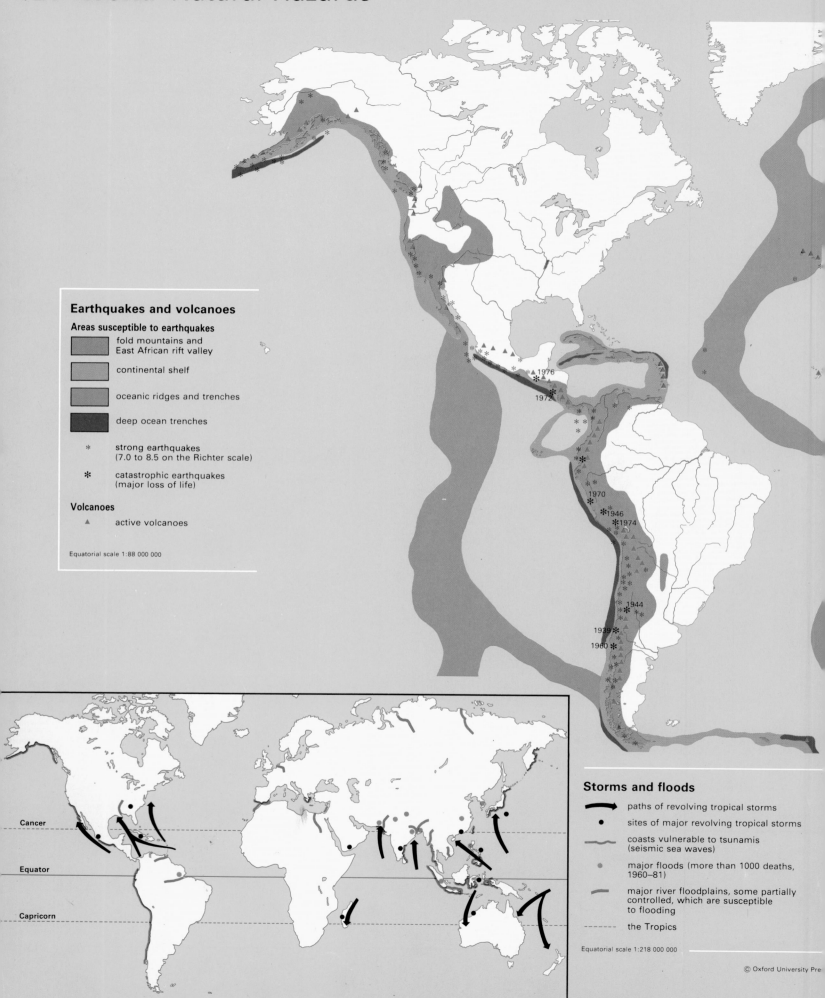

Earthquakes and volcanoes

Areas susceptible to earthquakes

	fold mountains and East African rift valley
	continental shelf
	oceanic ridges and trenches
	deep ocean trenches
*	strong earthquakes (7.0 to 8.5 on the Richter scale)
✳	catastrophic earthquakes (major loss of life)

Volcanoes

▲	active volcanoes

Equatorial scale 1:88 000 000

Storms and floods

➜	paths of revolving tropical storms
•	sites of major revolving tropical storms
∿	coasts vulnerable to tsunamis (seismic sea waves)
●	major floods (more than 1000 deaths, 1960–81)
	major river floodplains, some partially controlled, which are susceptible to flooding
- - -	the Tropics

Equatorial scale 1:218 000 000

Cancer

Equator

Capricorn

1976
1972
1970
1946
1974
1944
1939
1960

© Oxford University Pre

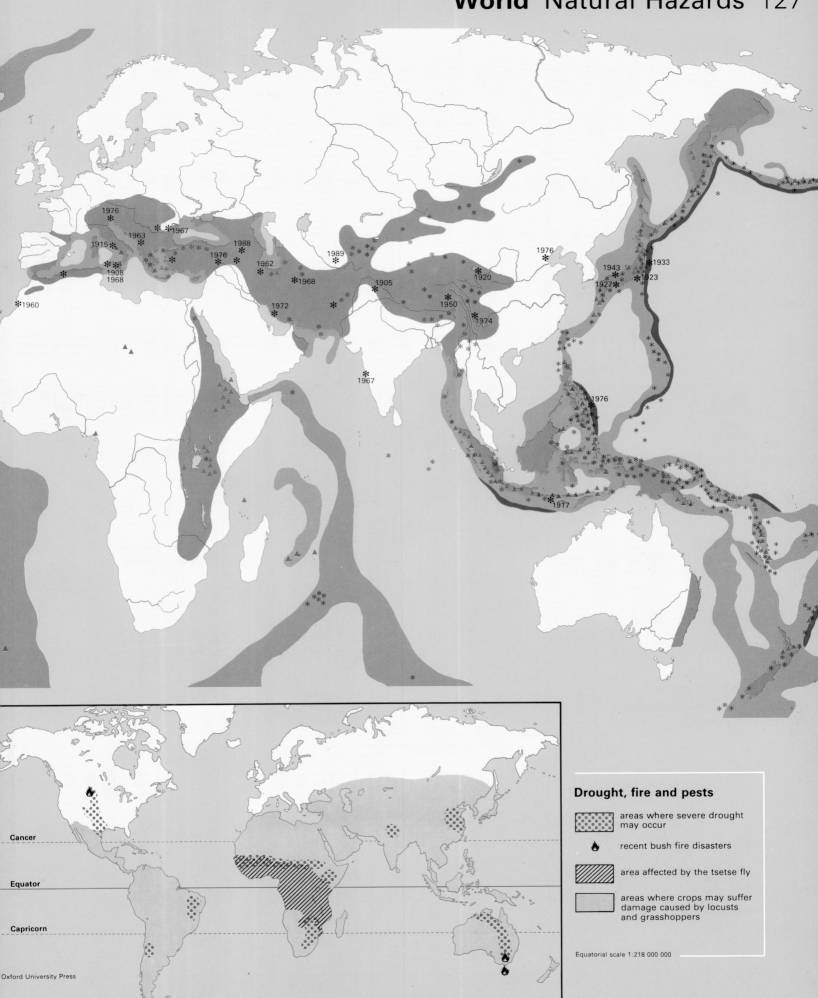

1976
1915
1963
1967
1908
1968
1960
1976
1988
1989
1976
1976
1943
1933
1962
1968
1920
1927
1923
1972
1905
1950
1974
1967
1976
1917

Drought, fire and pests

areas where severe drought may occur

recent bush fire disasters

area affected by the tsetse fly

areas where crops may suffer damage caused by locusts and grasshoppers

Cancer

Equator

Capricorn

Equatorial scale 1:218 000 000

Oxford University Press

Rainfall
and other forms of precipitation

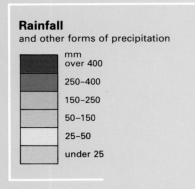

	mm
	over 400
	250–400
	150–250
	50–150
	25–50
	under 25

Temperature, ocean currents

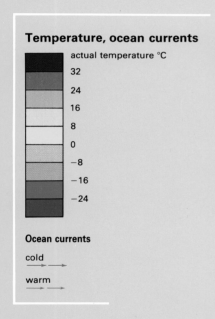

actual temperature °C

	32
	24
	16
	8
	0
	−8
	−16
	−24

Ocean currents

cold

warm

Pressure and winds
Pressure reduced to sea level

1035 millibars
1030
1025
1020
1015
1010
1005
1000
995

H high pressure cell

L low pressure cell

Prevailing winds
Arrows fly with the wind:
the heavier the arrow, the
more regular ('constant')
the direction of the wind

Equatorial Scale 1:218 000 000

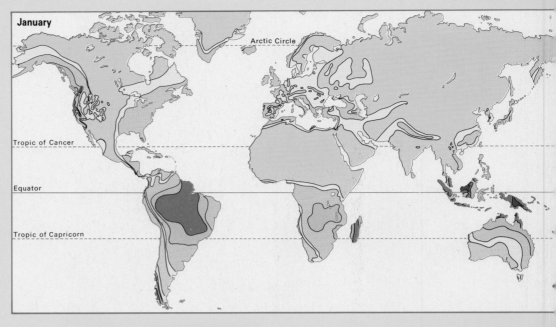

January

January

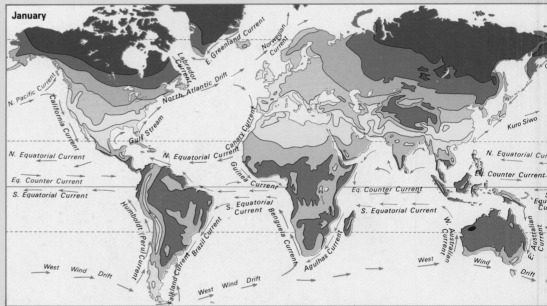

January

Modified Gall Projection

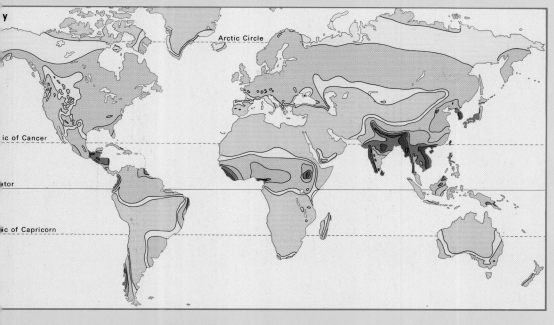

Arctic Circle

ic of Cancer

itor

ic of Capricorn

temperature 27°C and
over at mean sea level

Northern hemisphere
Maximum frequency August - September

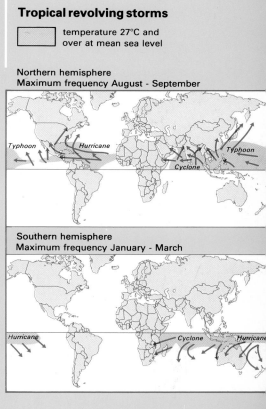

Typhoon   Hurricane   Typhoon
                        Cyclone

Southern hemisphere
Maximum frequency January - March

Hurricane   Cyclone   Hurricane

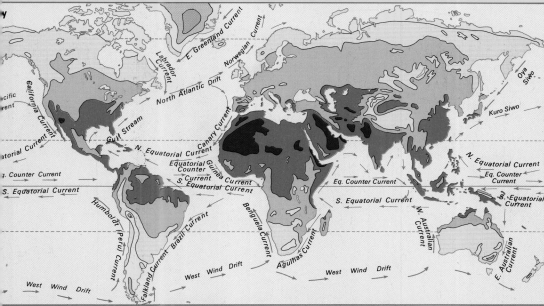

E. Greenland Current
Labrador Current
Norwegian Current
North Atlantic Drift
California Current
Gulf Stream
Canary Current
N. Equatorial Current
Equatorial Guinea Current
Counter Current
S. Equatorial Current
atorial Current
Counter Current
S. Equatorial Current
Humboldt (Peru) Current
Benguela Current
Brazil Current
Falkland Current
Agulhas Current
West Wind Drift
West Wind Drift
Eq. Counter Current
S. Equatorial Current
N. Equatorial Current
Eq. Counter Current
S. Equatorial Current
W. Australian Current
E. Australian Current
Kuro Siwo
Oya Siwo

Air masses

— --- fronts

Arctic
Polar
Temperate
Equatorial

1010
1015
L
L
1015
1020
1015
Westerlies
1015
L
H
1020
L
1000
Westerlies
1015
1025
E. Trades
N.E. Trades
S.W. Monsoon
S.E. Monsoon
N.E. Trades
S.E. Trades
S.E. Trades
S.E. Monsoon
1010
1015
H
1020
H
H
(Roaring Forties)
Westerlies
Westerlies
1015
1010
1005

January

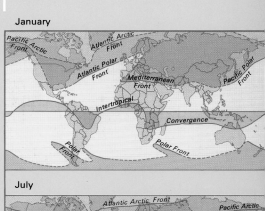

Pacific Arctic Front   Atlantic Arctic Front
Atlantic Polar Front   Mediterranean Front   Pacific Polar Front
Intertropical
Convergence
Polar Front   Polar Front

July

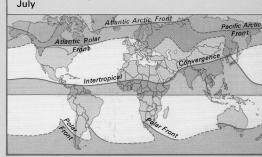

Atlantic Arctic Front
Atlantic Polar Front   Pacific Arctic Front
                        Pacific Polar Front
Intertropical   Convergence
Polar Front   Polar Front

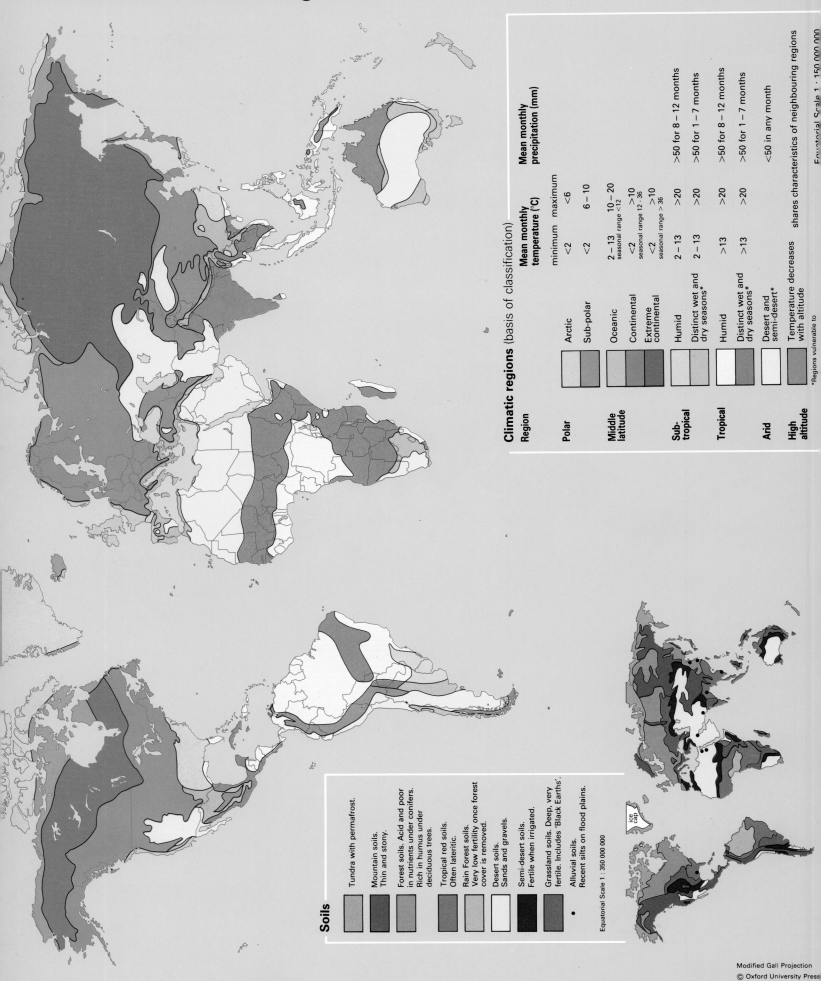

Climatic regions (basis of classification)

Region		Mean monthly temperature (°C)		Mean monthly precipitation (mm)
		minimum	maximum	
Polar	Arctic	<2	<6	
	Sub-polar	<2	6 – 10	
Middle latitude	Oceanic	2 – 13	10 – 20	
	Continental	<2 seasonal range <12	>10	
	Extreme continental	<2 seasonal range > 36	>10 seasonal range 12 - 36	
Sub-tropical	Humid	2 – 13	>20	>50 for 8 – 12 months
	Distinct wet and dry seasons*	2 – 13	>20	>50 for 1 – 7 months
Tropical	Humid	>13	>20	>50 for 8 – 12 months
	Distinct wet and dry seasons*	>13	>20	>50 for 1 – 7 months
Arid	Desert and semi-desert*			<50 in any month
High altitude	Temperature decreases with altitude		shares characteristics of neighbouring regions	

*Regions vulnerable to

Equatorial Scale 1 : 150 000 000

Soils

Tundra with permafrost.

Mountain soils. Thin and stony.

Forest soils. Acid and poor in nutrients under conifers. Rich in humus under deciduous trees.

Tropical red soils. Often lateritic.

Rain Forest soils. Very low fertility once forest cover is removed.

Desert soils. Sands and gravels.

Semi-desert soils. Fertile when irrigated.

Grassland soils. Deep, very fertile. Includes 'Black Earths'.

Alluvial soils. Recent silts on flood plains.

Equatorial Scale 1 : 350 000 000

ice cap

Modified Gall Projection

© Oxford University Press

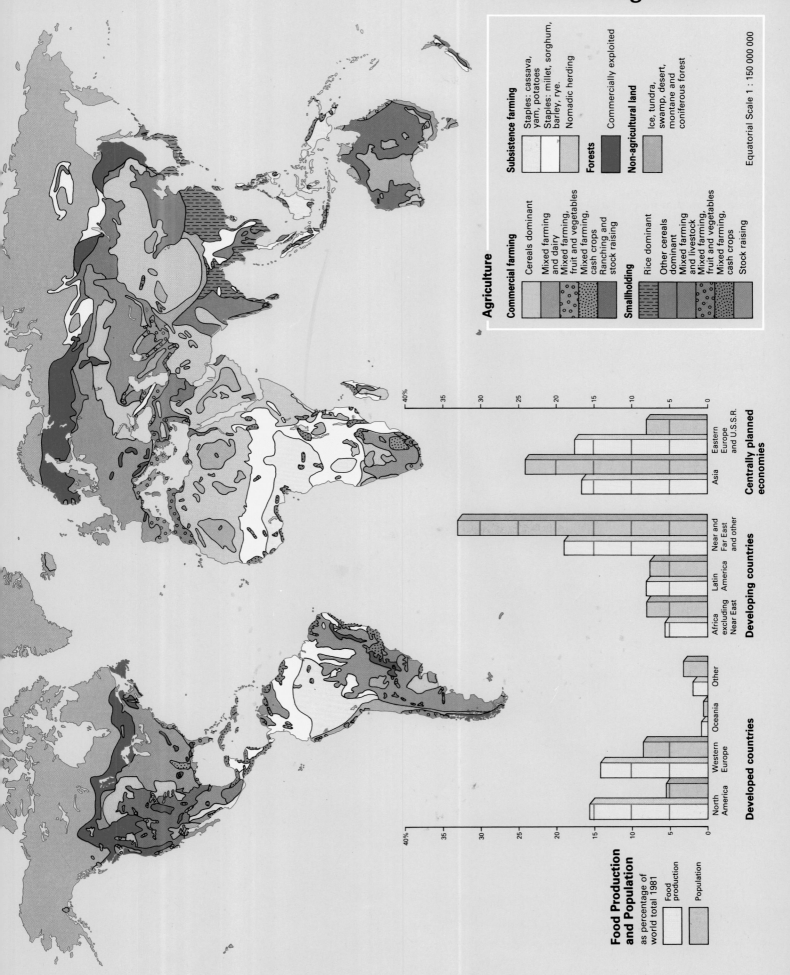

Agriculture

Commercial farming

- Cereals dominant
- Mixed farming and dairy
- Mixed farming, fruit and vegetables
- Mixed farming, cash crops
- Ranching and stock raising

Smallholding

- Rice dominant
- Other cereals dominant
- Mixed farming and livestock
- Mixed farming, fruit and vegetables
- Mixed farming, cash crops
- Stock raising

Subsistence farming

- Staples: cassava, yam, potatoes
- Staples: millet, sorghum, barley, rye.
- Nomadic herding

Forests

- Commercially exploited

Non-agricultural land

- Ice, tundra, swamp, desert, montane and coniferous forest

Equatorial Scale 1 : 150 000 000

Centrally planned economies

Eastern Europe and U.S.S.R. — Asia

Developing countries

Near and Far East and other — Latin America — Africa excluding Near East

Developed countries

North America — Western Europe — Oceania — Other

Food Production and Population

as percentage of world total 1981

- Food production
- Population

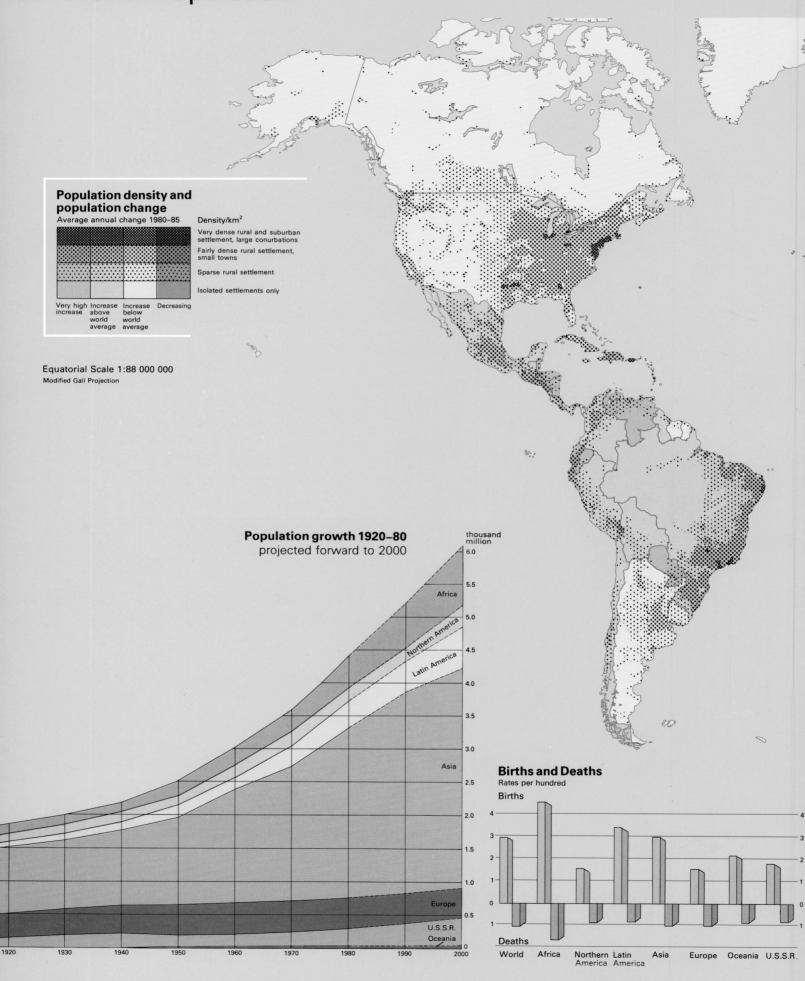

Population density and population change
Average annual change 1980–85

Density/km²

Very dense rural and suburban settlement, large conurbations

Fairly dense rural settlement, small towns

Sparse rural settlement

Isolated settlements only

Very high increase

Increase above world average

Increase below world average

Decreasing

Equatorial Scale 1:88 000 000

Modified Gall Projection

Population growth 1920–80
projected forward to 2000

thousand million

6.0
5.5

Africa

5.0

Northern America

4.5

Latin America

4.0
3.5
3.0

Asia

2.5
2.0
1.5
1.0

Europe

0.5

U.S.S.R.
Oceania

0

1920 1930 1940 1950 1960 1970 1980 1990 2000

Births and Deaths
Rates per hundred

Births

4
3
2
1
0
1

Deaths

World Africa Northern America Latin America Asia Europe Oceania U.S.S.R.

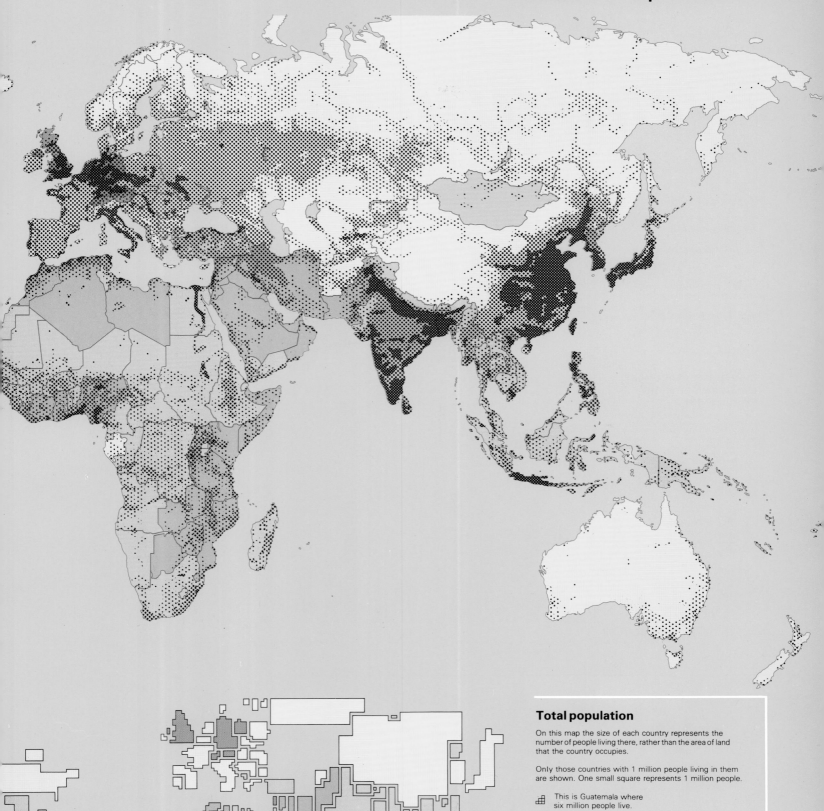

Total population

On this map the size of each country represents the number of people living there, rather than the area of land that the country occupies.

Only those countries with 1 million people living in them are shown. One small square represents 1 million people.

This is Guatemala where six million people live.

Population change

The colours on this map represent the same rates of population increase or decrease shown on the legend to the main map above.

Very high increase - 3 per cent and over

Increase above world average - 1.67 to 3 per cent

Increase below world average - less than 1.67 per cent

Decreasing

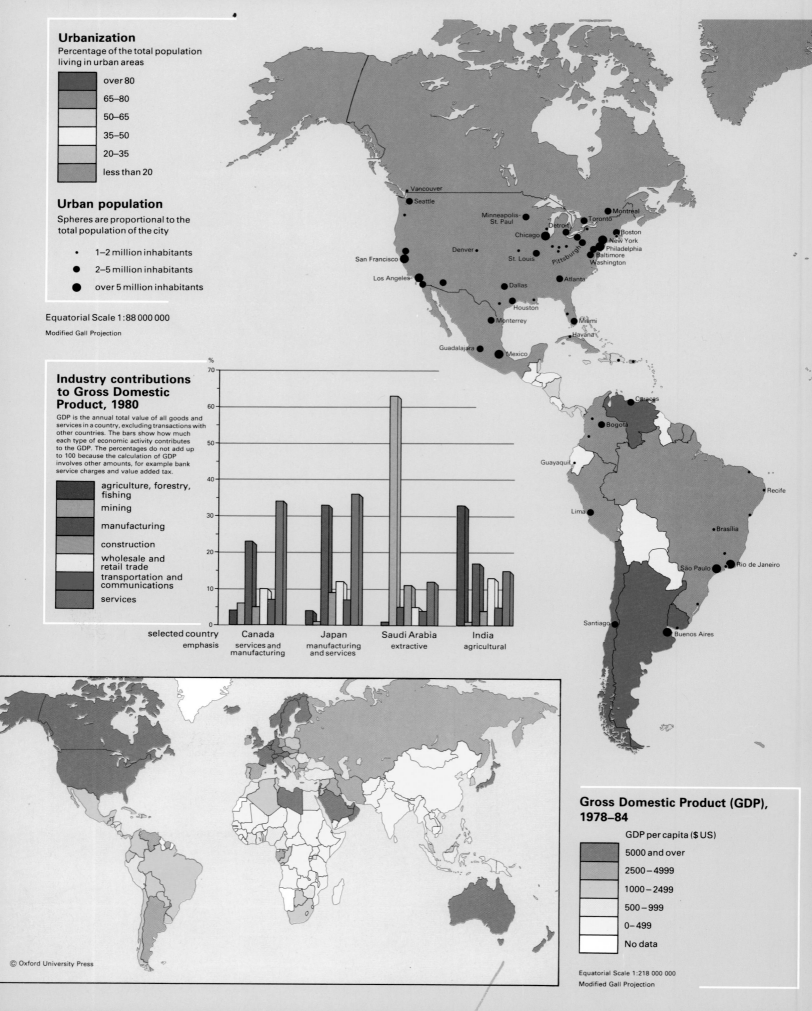

Urbanization

Percentage of the total population living in urban areas

- over 80
- 65–80
- 50–65
- 35–50
- 20–35
- less than 20

Urban population

Spheres are proportional to the total population of the city

- · 1–2 million inhabitants
- ● 2–5 million inhabitants
- ● over 5 million inhabitants

Equatorial Scale 1:88 000 000

Modified Gall Projection

Industry contributions to Gross Domestic Product, 1980

GDP is the annual total value of all goods and services in a country, excluding transactions with other countries. The bars show how much each type of economic activity contributes to the GDP. The percentages do not add up to 100 because the calculation of GDP involves other amounts, for example bank service charges and value added tax.

- agriculture, forestry, fishing
- mining
- manufacturing
- construction
- wholesale and retail trade
- transportation and communications
- services

selected country emphasis

Canada — services and manufacturing

Japan — manufacturing and services

Saudi Arabia — extractive

India — agricultural

© Oxford University Press

Gross Domestic Product (GDP), 1978–84

GDP per capita ($ US)

- 5000 and over
- 2500–4999
- 1000–2499
- 500–999
- 0–499
- No data

Equatorial Scale 1:218 000 000

Modified Gall Projection

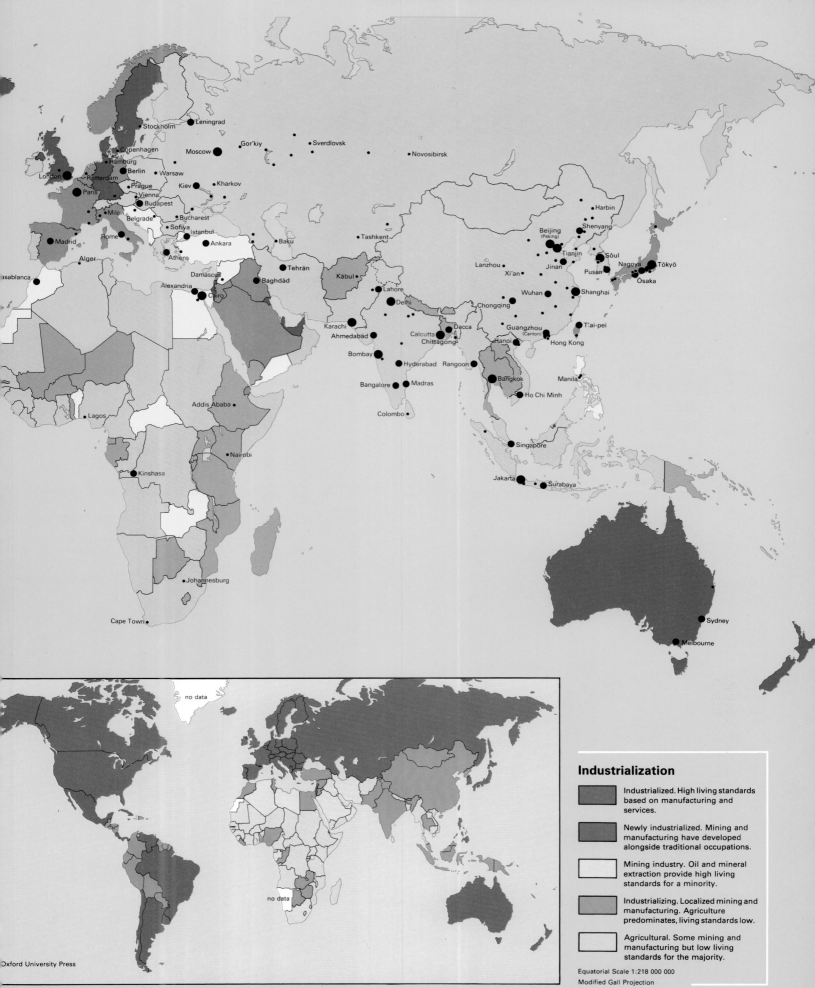

Stockholm • Leningrad
Gor'kiy • Sverdlovsk
Copenhagen • Moscow • Novosibirsk
Hamburg
Berlin • Warsaw
London Rotterdam
Prague • Kiev • Kharkov
Paris Vienna Budapest
Milan Belgrade • Bucharest Harbin
Rome Sofiya Istanbul Shenyang
Madrid Athens Ankara Baku Tashkent Beijing
(Peking)
Alger Damascus Tehrān Lanzhou Tianjin Jinan Sŏul
Casablanca Alexandria Baghdād Kābul Xi'an Pusan Nagoya Tōkyō
Cairo Lahore Wuhan Shanghai Ōsaka
Delhi Chongqing
Karachi Calcutta Dacca Guangzhou T'ai-pei
Ahmedābād Chittagong (Canton)
Bombay Hyderābād Rangoon Hanoi Hong Kong
Addis Ababa Bangalore Madras Bangkok Manila
Lagos Colombo Ho Chi Minh
Nairobi Singapore
Kinshasa Jakarta Surabaya

Johannesburg

Cape Town Sydney
Melbourne

no data

no data

Oxford University Press

Industrialization

	Industrialized. High living standards based on manufacturing and services.
	Newly industrialized. Mining and manufacturing have developed alongside traditional occupations.
	Mining industry. Oil and mineral extraction provide high living standards for a minority.
	Industrializing. Localized mining and manufacturing. Agriculture predominates, living standards low.
	Agricultural. Some mining and manufacturing but low living standards for the majority.

Equatorial Scale 1:218 000 000
Modified Gall Projection

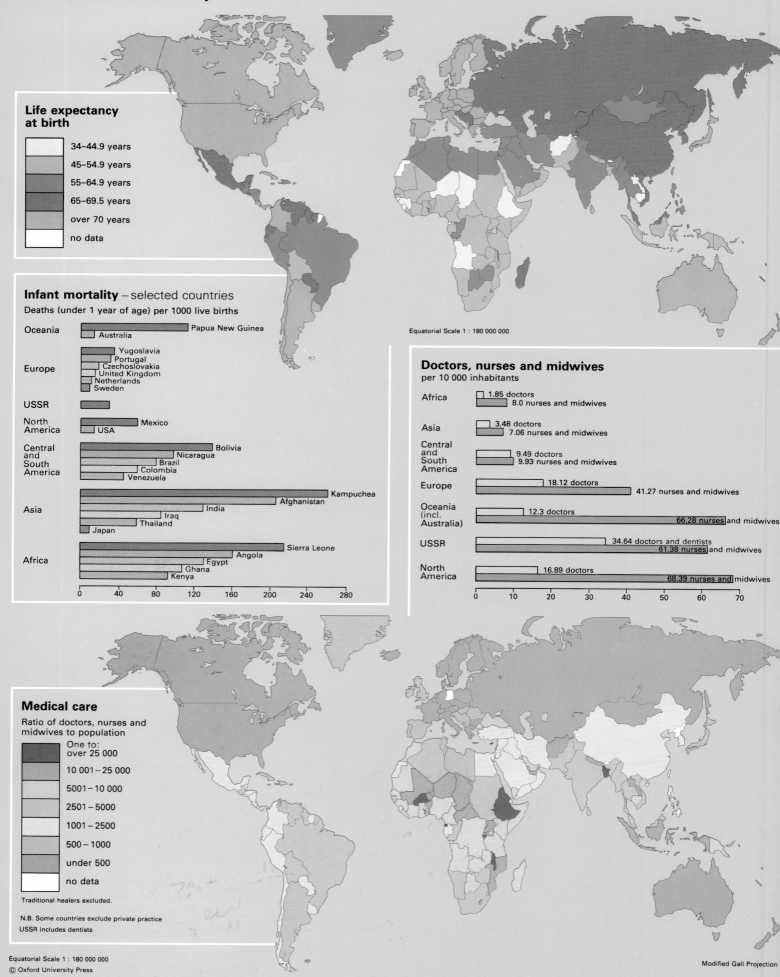

Life expectancy at birth

- 34–44.9 years
- 45–54.9 years
- 55–64.9 years
- 65–69.5 years
- over 70 years
- no data

Infant mortality – selected countries

Deaths (under 1 year of age) per 1000 live births

Oceania
- Papua New Guinea
- Australia

Europe
- Yugoslavia
- Portugal
- Czechoslovakia
- United Kingdom
- Netherlands
- Sweden

USSR

North America
- Mexico
- USA

Central and South America
- Bolivia
- Nicaragua
- Brazil
- Colombia
- Venezuela

Asia
- Kampuchea
- Afghanistan
- India
- Iraq
- Thailand
- Japan

Africa
- Sierra Leone
- Angola
- Egypt
- Ghana
- Kenya

0   40   80   120   160   200   240   280

Equatorial Scale 1 : 180 000 000

Doctors, nurses and midwives

per 10 000 inhabitants

Africa
- 1.85 doctors
- 8.0 nurses and midwives

Asia
- 3.48 doctors
- 7.06 nurses and midwives

Central and South America
- 9.49 doctors
- 9.93 nurses and midwives

Europe
- 18.12 doctors
- 41.27 nurses and midwives

Oceania (incl. Australia)
- 12.3 doctors
- 66.28 nurses and midwives

USSR
- 34.64 doctors and dentists
- 61.38 nurses and midwives

North America
- 16.89 doctors
- 68.39 nurses and midwives

0   10   20   30   40   50   60   70

Medical care

Ratio of doctors, nurses and midwives to population

One to:
- over 25 000
- 10 001 – 25 000
- 5001 – 10 000
- 2501 – 5000
- 1001 – 2500
- 500 – 1000
- under 500
- no data

Traditional healers excluded.

N.B. Some countries exclude private practice
USSR includes dentists

Equatorial Scale 1 : 180 000 000

© Oxford University Press

Modified Gall Projection

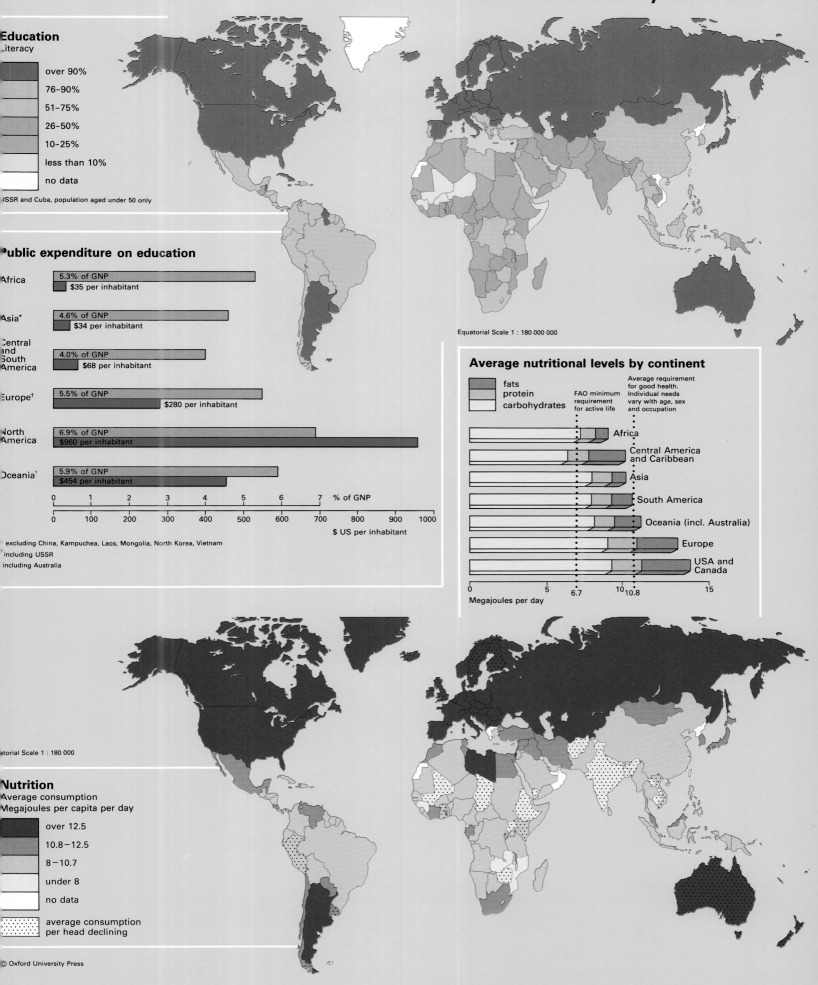

Education
Literacy

- over 90%
- 76–90%
- 51–75%
- 26–50%
- 10–25%
- less than 10%
- no data

USSR and Cuba, population aged under 50 only

Equatorial Scale 1 : 180 000 000

Public expenditure on education

Africa
5.3% of GNP
$35 per inhabitant

Asia*
4.6% of GNP
$34 per inhabitant

Central and South America
4.0% of GNP
$68 per inhabitant

Europe†
5.5% of GNP
$280 per inhabitant

North America
6.9% of GNP
$960 per inhabitant

Oceania¹
5.9% of GNP
$454 per inhabitant

| 0 | 1 | 2 | 3 | 4 | 5 | 6 | 7 | % of GNP |
| 0 | 100 | 200 | 300 | 400 | 500 | 600 | 700 | 800 | 900 | 1000 |

$ US per inhabitant

* excluding China, Kampuchea, Laos, Mongolia, North Korea, Vietnam
† including USSR
¹ including Australia

Average nutritional levels by continent

- fats
- protein
- carbohydrates

FAO minimum requirement for active life

Average requirement for good health. Individual needs vary with age, sex and occupation

- Africa
- Central America and Caribbean
- Asia
- South America
- Oceania (incl. Australia)
- Europe
- USA and Canada

| 0 | 5 | 6.7 | 10.8 | 15 |

Megajoules per day

Equatorial Scale 1 : 180 000

Nutrition
Average consumption
Megajoules per capita per day

- over 12.5
- 10.8–12.5
- 8–10.7
- under 8
- no data
- average consumption per head declining

© Oxford University Press

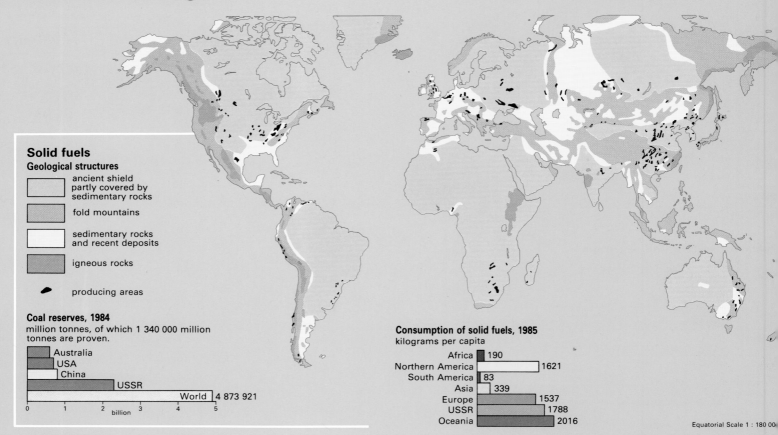

Solid fuels
Geological structures

ancient shield
partly covered by
sedimentary rocks

fold mountains

sedimentary rocks
and recent deposits

igneous rocks

producing areas

Coal reserves, 1984
million tonnes, of which 1 340 000 million tonnes are proven.

- Australia
- USA
- China
- USSR
- World 4 873 921

0   1   2   3   4   5
billion

Consumption of solid fuels, 1985
kilograms per capita

Africa	190
Northern America	1621
South America	83
Asia	339
Europe	1537
USSR	1788
Oceania	2016

Equatorial Scale 1 : 180 00

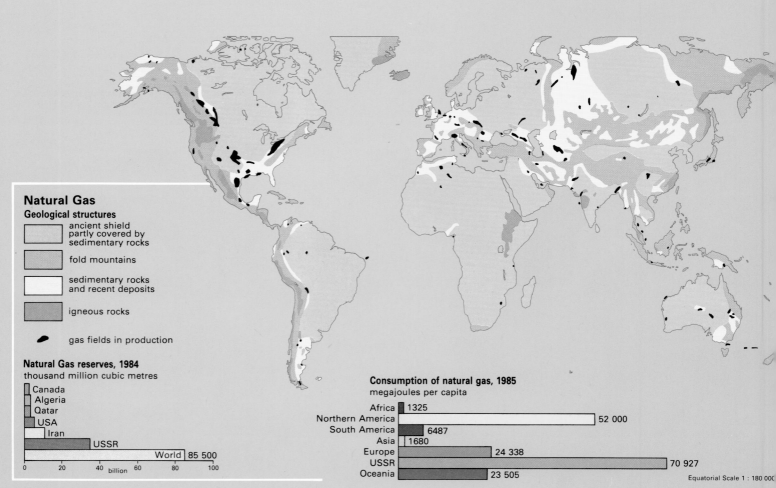

Natural Gas
Geological structures

ancient shield
partly covered by
sedimentary rocks

fold mountains

sedimentary rocks
and recent deposits

igneous rocks

gas fields in production

Natural Gas reserves, 1984
thousand million cubic metres

- Canada
- Algeria
- Qatar
- USA
- Iran
- USSR
- World 85 500

0   20   40   60   80   100
billion

Consumption of natural gas, 1985
megajoules per capita

Africa	1325
Northern America	52 000
South America	6487
Asia	1680
Europe	24 338
USSR	70 927
Oceania	23 505

Equatorial Scale 1 : 180 000

Modified Gall Proje

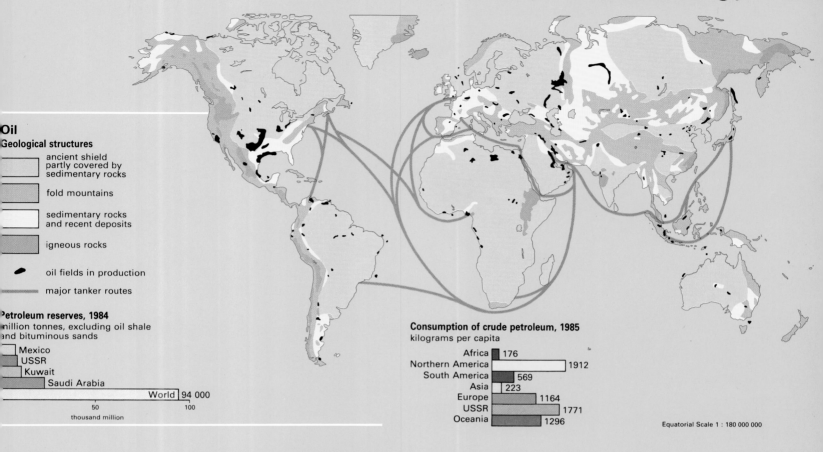

Oil

Geological structures

- ancient shield partly covered by sedimentary rocks
- fold mountains
- sedimentary rocks and recent deposits
- igneous rocks

- ◾ oil fields in production
- major tanker routes

Petroleum reserves, 1984
million tonnes, excluding oil shale and bituminous sands

- Mexico
- USSR
- Kuwait
- Saudi Arabia
- World | 94 000

```
50                    100
thousand million
```

Consumption of crude petroleum, 1985
kilograms per capita

Region	Value
Africa	176
Northern America	1912
South America	569
Asia	223
Europe	1164
USSR	1771
Oceania	1296

Equatorial Scale 1 : 180 000 000

Electricity

Net installed capacity, 1985
megawatts

- less than 100
- 100–1000
- 1000–5000
- 5000–10 000
- 10 000–50 000
- more than 50 000
- no data

- • nuclear power stations

Uranium reserves, 1984
metric tonnes, excluding
332 000 estimated reserves

- Canada
- South Africa
- USA
- Australia
- World | 2 315 000

```
1         2         3
  million
```

Equatorial Scale 1 : 180 000 000

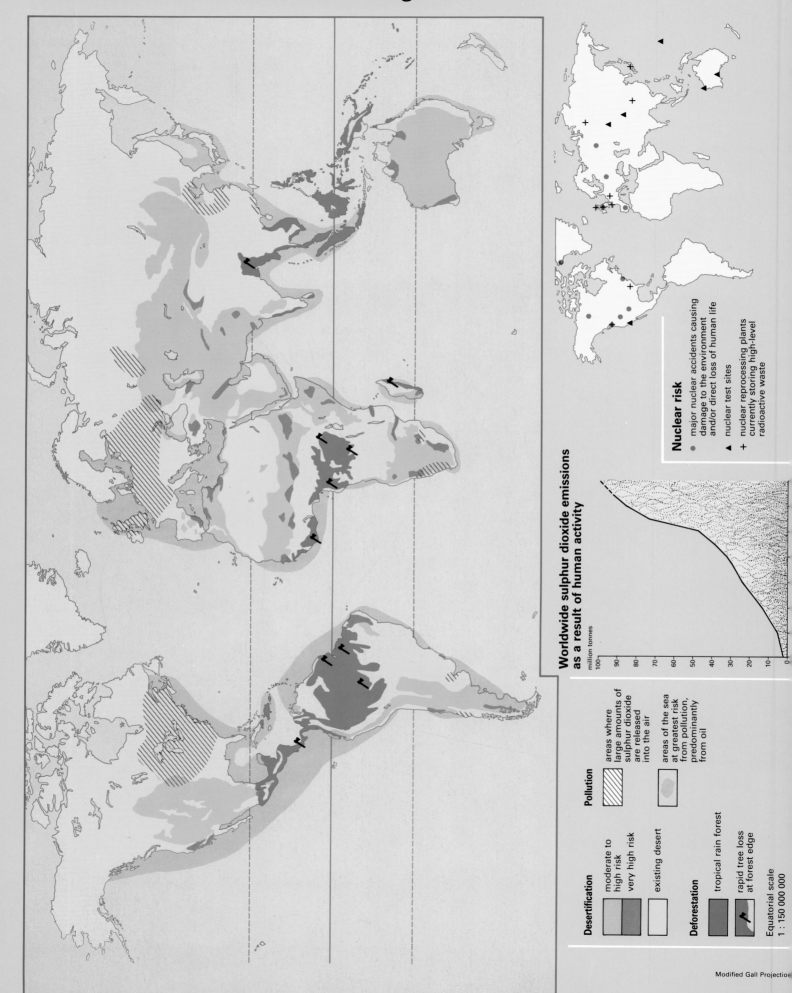

Worldwide sulphur dioxide emissions as a result of human activity

million tonnes

100
90
80
70
60
50
40
30
20
10
0

Nuclear risk

● major nuclear accidents causing damage to the environment and/or direct loss of human life

▲ nuclear test sites

+ nuclear reprocessing plants currently storing high-level radioactive waste

Desertification

moderate to high risk

very high risk

existing desert

Deforestation

tropical rain forest

rapid tree loss at forest edge

Pollution

areas where large amounts of sulphur dioxide are released into the air

areas of the sea at greatest risk from pollution, predominantly from oil

Equatorial scale
1 : 150 000 000

Modified Gall Projection

Major world wildlife conservation projects

A selection of World Wildlife Fund projects active in 1988

- ■ Project mainly concerned with a specific plant or animal species

- ■ Project mainly concerned with the conservation and management of specific locations

Many of the projects mapped involve surveys, the setting up of reserves, the provision of resources and programmes of conservation education.

Equatorial scale 1 : 350 000 000

Recycling of waste, 1980–2

Bars show the percentage of the finished product that is recycled.

Aluminium

Iron and Steel

Paper

100

75

% 50

25

0

International conservation agreements, 1986

World Heritage Convention; Convention on International Trade in Endangered Species of Wild Fauna and Flora (CITES); the Bonn Convention on Conservation of Migratory Species of Wild Animals; the (Ramsar) Convention on Wetlands of International Importance.

States which have signed

World Heritage Sites, at December 1987

- ● natural
- ● cultural
- ● natural and cultural

all 4 agreements

3 agreements

2 agreements

1 agreement

other countries

areas of United Nations Environmental Programme (Regional Seas Programme)

Equatorial scale 1 : 150 000 000

© Oxford University Press

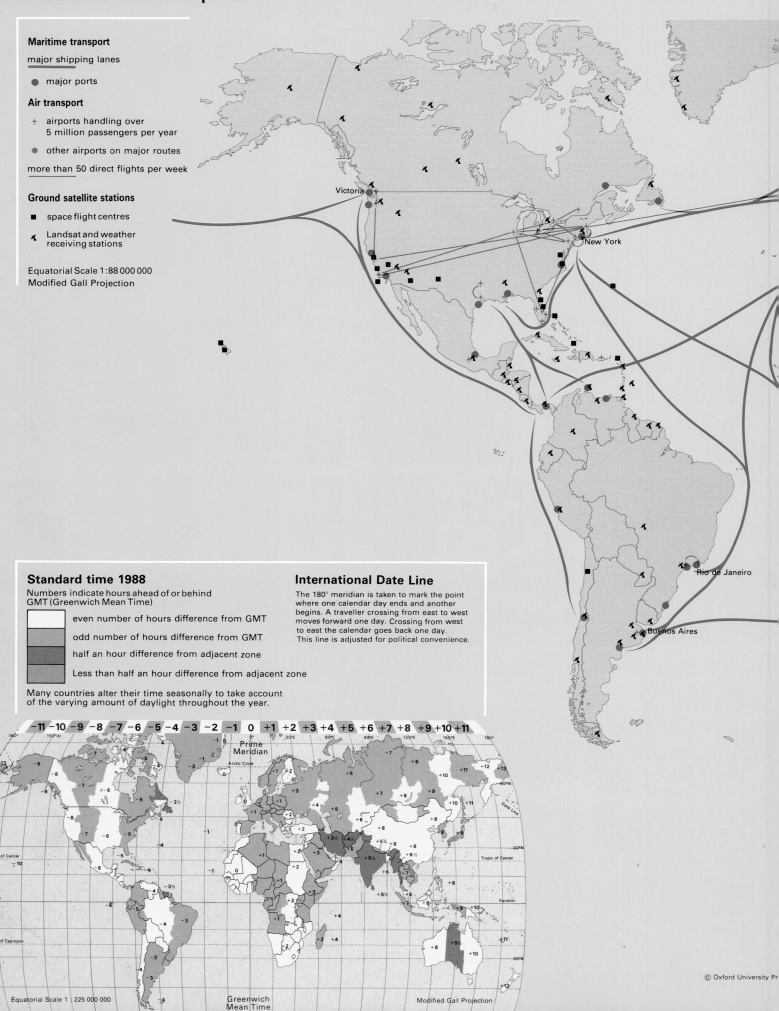

Maritime transport

major shipping lanes

● major ports

Air transport

✈ airports handling over 5 million passengers per year

● other airports on major routes

more than 50 direct flights per week

Ground satellite stations

■ space flight centres

✈ Landsat and weather receiving stations

Equatorial Scale 1:88 000 000
Modified Gall Projection

Victoria

New York

Rio de Janeiro

Buenos Aires

Standard time 1988

Numbers indicate hours ahead of or behind GMT (Greenwich Mean Time)

even number of hours difference from GMT

odd number of hours difference from GMT

half an hour difference from adjacent zone

Less than half an hour difference from adjacent zone

Many countries alter their time seasonally to take account of the varying amount of daylight throughout the year.

International Date Line

The 180° meridian is taken to mark the point where one calendar day ends and another begins. A traveller crossing from east to west moves forward one day. Crossing from west to east the calendar goes back one day. This line is adjusted for political convenience.

Equatorial Scale 1 : 225 000 000

Greenwich Mean Time

Modified Gall Projection

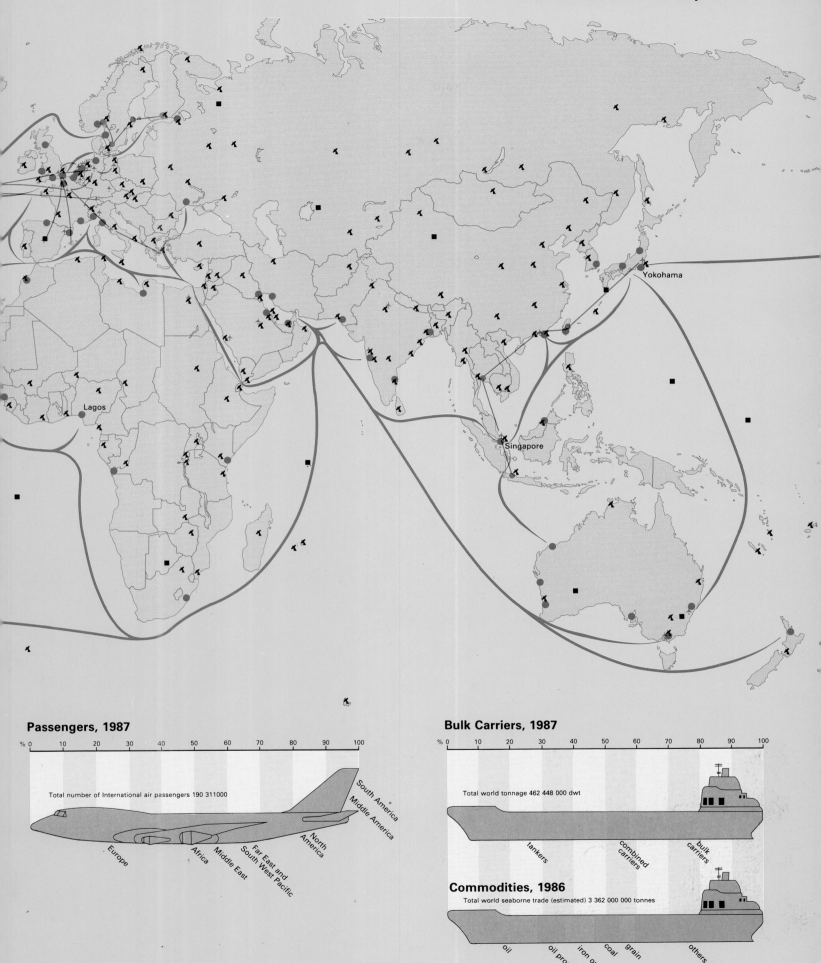

Yokohama

Lagos

Singapore

Passengers, 1987

% 0   10   20   30   40   50   60   70   80   90   100

Total number of International air passengers 190 311000

South America
Middle America
North America
Far East and South West Pacific
Middle East
Africa
Europe

Bulk Carriers, 1987

% 0   10   20   30   40   50   60   70   80   90   100

Total world tonnage 462 448 000 dwt

tankers
combined carriers
bulk carriers

Commodities, 1986

Total world seaborne trade (estimated) 3 362 000 000 tonnes

oil
oil products
iron ore
coal
grain
others

Share of world trade for selected countries, 1977-87

percentage growth

percentage decline

World trade, 1987

On this map the size of each country represents the share that country has of total world trade, rather than the area of land that the country occupies.

Only those countries with more than 0.01% of world trade are shown

a country shown by a square of this size would have 1% of world trade

a country shown by a square of this size would have 0.01% of world trade

Share of world trade, 1977-87

	49 percent and over
	5-49 percent } growth
	0-5 percent growth or decline — little or no change
	5-49 percent } decline
	49 percent and over

© Oxford University Press

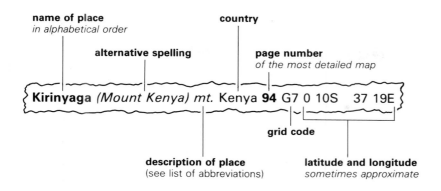

name of place
in alphabetical order

alternative spelling

country

page number
of the most detailed map

Kirinyaga *(Mount Kenya) mt.* Kenya **94** G7 0 10S 37 19E

grid code

description of place
(see list of abbreviations)

latitude and longitude
sometimes approximate

How to use the gazetteer

To find a place on an atlas map use either the grid code or latitude and longitude.

For more information on latitude and longitude look at page 4.

Grid code

Latitude and Longitude

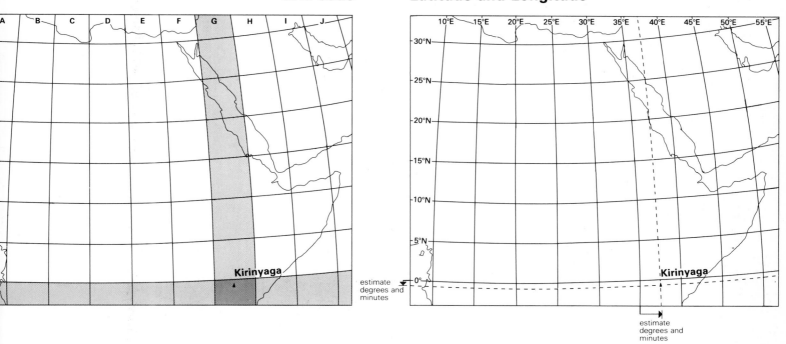

Kirinyaga is in grid square G7

Kirinyaga is at latitude 0 10S longitude 37 19E

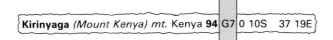

Kirinyaga *(Mount Kenya) mt.* Kenya **94** G7 0 10S 37 19E

Kirinyaga *(Mount Kenya) mt.* Kenya **94** G7 0 10S 37 19E

A

Aa *r.* France **64** B2 50 90N 2 10E
Aachen F.R.G. **63** A2 50 46N 6 06E
Aalsmeer Netherlands **64** D4 52 16N 4 45E
Aalst Belgium **64** D2 50 57N 4 03E
Aalten Belgium **64** C3 51 56N 6 35E
Aaper Wald *hills* F.R.G. **62** B2 51 17N 6 50E
Aare *r.* Switzerland **61** C2 47 00N 7 05E
Aarschot Belgium **64** D2 50 59N 4 50E
Aba Nigeria **93** G4 5 06N 7 21E
Ābādān Iran **79** G5 30 20N 48 15E
Abadla Algeria **93** E9 31 01N 2 45W
Abaetetuba Brazil **114** H12 1 45S 48 54W
Abakan *r.* U.S.S.R. **71** K6 52 00N 90 00E
Abakan U.S.S.R. **71** L6 53 43N 91 25E
Abancay Peru **114** C10 13 37S 72 52W
Abashiri Japan **82** D3 44 02N 144 17E
Abbai *(Blue Nile) r.* Ethiopia **94** G10 11 00N 37 00E
Abbe, Lake Ethiopia **94** H10 11 00N 44 00E
Abbeville France **61** B3 50 06N 1 51E
Abbeyfeale Limerick Irish Republic **48** B2 52 24N 9 18W
Abbeyleix Laois Irish Republic **48** D2 52 55N 7 20W
Abbey Town Cumbria England **44** A1 54 50N 3 17W
Abbots Bromley Staffordshire England **35** C3 52 49N 1 52W
Abbotsbury Dorset England **31** E2 50 40N 2 36W
Abbots Langley Hertfordshire England **34** B3 51 43N 0 25W
Ābd al Kūrī *i.* Socotra **79** H1 11 55N 52 20E
Abéché Chad **94** D10 13 49N 20 49E
Åbenrå Denmark **63** A3 55 03N 9 26E
Abeokuta Nigeria **93** F4 7 10N 3 26E
Aberaeron Dyfed Wales **38** B2 52 15N 4 15W
Aberargie Tayside Scotland **45** D2 56 20N 3 23W
Abercarn Gwent Wales **38** C1 51 39N 3 08W
Aberchirder Grampian Scotland **46** F4 57 33N 2 38W
Aberdare Mid Glamorgan Wales **38** C1 51 43N 3 27W
Aberdare National Park Kenya **94** G7 0 30S 37 00E
Aberdaron Gwynedd Wales **38** B2 52 49N 44 43W
Aberdeen Grampian Scotland **46** F4 57 10N 2 04W
Aberdeen Maryland U.S.A. **105** E1 39 31N 76 10W
Aberdeen South Dakota U.S.A. **103** G6 45 28N 98 30W
Aberdeen Washington U.S.A. **102** B6 46 58N 123 49W
Aberdyfi Gwynedd Wales **38** B2 52 33N 4 02W
Aberfeldy Tayside Scotland **46** E3 56 37N 3 54W
Aberffraw Gwynedd Wales **38** B3 53 12N 4 28W
Aberfoyle Central Scotland **45** B2 56 11N 4 23W
Abergavenny Gwent Wales **38** C1 51 50N 3 00W
Abergele Clwyd Wales **38** C3 53 17N 3 34W
Abernethy Tayside Scotland **45** D2 56 20N 3 19W
Aberporth Dyfed Wales **38** B2 52 07N 4 34W
Abersoch Gwynedd Wales **38** B2 52 50N 4 31W
Abertillery Gwent Wales **38** C1 51 45N 3 09W
Aberystwyth Dyfed Wales **38** B2 52 25N 4 05W
Abhā Saudi Arabia **78** F2 18 14N 42 31E
Abidjan Côte d'Ivoire **93** E4 5 19N 4 01W
Abilene Texas U.S.A. **102** G3 32 27N 99 45W
Abingdon Oxfordshire England **32** A2 51 41N 1 17W
Abington Strathclyde Scotland **46** E2 55 29N 3 42W
Abitibi, Lake Canada **105** D3 49 00N 80 00W
Abitibi River *r.* Ontario Canada **105** D3 50 00N 81 00W
Aboyne Grampian Scotland **46** F4 57 05N 2 50W
Abram Greater Manchester England **42** C2 53 31N 2 36W
Absaroka Range *mts.* U.S.A. **102** D6 45 00N 110 00W
Abu Dhabi *see* Abū Ẓabī
Abu Durba Egypt **78** N9 28 29N 33 20E
Abu Hamed Sudan **78** D2 19 32N 33 20E
Abuja Nigeria **93** G4 9 10N 7 11E
Abu Kamal Syria **78** F5 34 29N 40 56E
Abunã Brazil **114** D11 9 41S 65 20W
Abu Tig Egypt **78** D4 27 06N 31 17E
Abū Ẓabī *(Abu Dhabi)* United Arab Emirates **79** H3 24 28N 54 25E
Acambaro Mexico **108** D4 20 01N 100 42W
Acaponeta Mexico **108** C4 22 30N 105 25W
Acapulco Mexico **108** E3 16 51N 99 56W
Açari *r.* Brazil **116** B2 22 50S 43 22W
Acarigua Venezuela **114** D14 9 35N 69 12W
Acatlán Mexico **108** E3 18 12N 98 02W
Acayucán Mexico **108** E3 17 59N 94 58W
Accra Ghana **93** E4 5 33N 0 15W
Accrington Lancashire England **42** C3 53 46N 2 21W
Achacachi Bolivia **114** D9 16 01S 68 44W
Achill Island Irish Republic **48** A3 53 55N 10 05W
Achinsk U.S.S.R. **71** L7 56 20N 90 33E
Achnasheen Highland Scotland **46** C4 57 35N 5 06W
Ackleton Shropshire England **35** A2 52 34N 2 21W
Acklins Island The Bahamas **109** J4 22 30N 74 30W
Ackworth Moor Top *tn.* West Yorkshire England **43** G2 53 39N 1 20W
Acle Norfolk England **33** D3 52 38N 1 33E
Acock's Green West Midlands England **35** C2 52 26N 1 50W
Aconcagua *mt.* Argentina **115** C6 32 40S 70 02W
Acre *admin.* Brazil **114** C11 8 30S 71 30W
Ada Oklhoma U.S.A. **108** G3 34 47N 96 41W
Adachi Japan **83** C4 35 46N 139 48E
Adaga *r.* Spain **66** B3 40 45N 4 45W
Adamawa Mountains *mts.* Africa **88** 7 00N 13 00E
Adam, Mount Falkland Islands **117** M16 51 36S 60 00W
Adam's Bridge India/Sri Lanka **77** D1 9 10N 79 30E
Adana Turkey **78** E6 37 00N 35 19E
Adapazari Turkey **78** D7 40 45N 30 23E
Adare, Cape Antarctica **121** 71 30S 170 24E
Adda *r.* Italy **61** C2 45 00N 9 00E
Ad Dakhla Western Sahara **93** B7 23 50N 15 58W
Ad Dammām Saudi Arabia **79** H4 26 25N 50 06E
Ad Dawḥah *(Doha)* Qatar **79** H4 25 15N 51 36E
Ad Dilam Saudi Arabia **79** G3 23 59N 47 06E
Addingham West Yorkshire England **43** E3 53 57N 1 53W
Ad Dir'īyah Saudi Arabia **79** G3 24 45N 46 32E
Addis Ababa *see* Ādis Ābeba
Ad Dīwānīyah Iraq **78** F5 32 00N 44 57E
Addlestone Surrey England **34** B2 51 22N 0 31W
Adelaide Australia **86** F3 34 56N 138 36E
Aden South Yemen **79** G1 12 50N 45 03E
Aden, Gulf of **79** G1 12 30N 47 30E
Adirondack Mountains New York U.S.A. **105** F2 44 00N 74 00W
Ādīs Ābeba *(Addis Ababa)* Ethiopia **94** G9 9 03N 38 42E
Adlington Lancashire England **42** C2 53 37N 2 38W
Admiralty Islands Papua New Guinea **86** H9 2 30S 147 00E
Adoni India **77** D3 15 38N 77 16E
Adour *r.* France **61** A1 43 30N 1 30W
Adra Spain **66** B2 36 45N 3 01W
Adrar Algeria **93** E8 27 51N 0 19W
Adrian Michigan U.S.A. **105** D2 41 55N 84 01W
Adriatic Sea Mediterranean Sea **68** B3 43 00N 15 00E
Adur *r.* West Sussex England **33** B1 50 55N 0 20W
Adwa Ethiopia **78** E1 14 12N 38 56E
Adwick le Street South Yorkshire England **43** G2 53 34N 1 11W
Aegean Sea Mediterranean Sea **68** D2 39 00N 24 00E
Ærø *i.* Denmark **63** B2 54 52N 10 20E
AFGHANISTAN **79** J5
Afognak Island *i.* Alaska U.S.A. **100** E4 58 10N 152 50W
Afyon Turkey **78** D6 38 46N 30 32E
Agadès Niger **93** G6 17 00N 7 56E
Agadir Morocco **93** D9 30 30N 9 40W
Agana Guam **118** E9 13 28N 144 45E
Agano *r.* Japan **82** C2 37 50N 139 30E
Agartala India **77** G4 23 49N 91 15E
Agawa Ontario Canada **101** S2 47 22N 84 37W
Agboyi Creek *r.* Nigeria **92** C3 6 37N 3 30E
Agege Nigeria **92** C3 6 41N 3 24E
Agen France **61** B1 44 12N 0 38E
Aghalee Antrim Northern Ireland **49** C1 54 32N 6 16W
Agod G.R.A. Ibadan Nigeria 7 25N 3 58E
Agout *r.* France **61** B1 43 50N 1 50E
Agra India **77** D5 27 09N 78 00E
Agram Yugoslavia *see* Zagreb
Agri *r.* Italy **68** C3 40 00N 16 00E
Agrigento Italy **68** B2 37 19N 13 35E
Agrinion Greece **68** D2 38 38N 21 25E
Agua Prieta Mexico **108** C6 31 20N 109 32W
Aguadas Colombia **114** B14 5 36N 75 30W
Aguadilla Puerto Rico **109** K3 18 27N 67 08W
Aguascalientes Mexico **108** D4 21 51N 102 18W
Agueda *r.* Spain **66** A3 40 50N 6 50W
Aguilas Spain **66** B2 37 25N 1 35W
Agulhas Basin Indian Ocean **117** K2 45 00S 25 00E
Agulhas, Cape Republic of South Africa **95** D1 34 50S 20 00E
Ahaus F.R.G. **64** G4 52 04N 7 01E
Ahklun Mountains Alaska U.S.A. **100** C4 60 00N 161 00W
Ahmadabad India **77** C4 23 03N 72 40E
Ahmadnagar India **77** C3 19 08N 74 48E
Ahmar Mountains Ethiopia **94** H9 9 00N 41 00E
Ahr *r.* F.R.G. **64** F2 50 00N 6 00E
Ahrensburg F.R.G. **63** B2 53 41N 10 14E
Ahuachapán El Salvador **108** G2 13 57N 89 49W
Ahvāz Iran **79** G5 31 17N 48 43E
Ailsa Craig *i.* Scotland **46** C2 55 16N 5 07W
Ain *r.* France **61** C2 46 30N 5 30E
Aïn Sefra Algeria **93** E9 32 45N 0 35W
Ainsdale Merseyside England **42** A2 53 37N 3 03W
Aïn Témouchent Algeria **66** B2 35 18N 1 09W
Aintree Merseyside England **42** B2 53 29N 2 57W
Aïr *mts.* Niger **93** G6 19 10N 8 20E
Airdrie Alberta Canada **100** M3 51 20N 114 00W
Airdrie Strathclyde Scotland **45** C1 55 52N 3 59W
Aire *r.* France **64** D1 49 15N 5 00E
Aire *r.* North Yorkshire/Humberside England **40** D2 53 40N 1 00W
Aire & Calder Navigation *can.* England **43** G3 53 40N 1 00W
Aire-sur-l'Adour France **61** A1 43 42N 0 15W
Aire-sur-la-Lys France **64** B2 51 40N 2 25E
Airton North Yorkshire England **43** D4 54 02N 2 09W
Aishihik Yukon Territory Canada **100** H5 62 00N 137 30W
Aisne *admin.* France **64** C1 49 40N 4 00E
Aisne *r.* France **61** B2 49 30N 3 00E
Aiviekste *r.* U.S.S.R. **67** F2 57 00N 26 40E
Aix-en-Provence France **61** C1 43 31N 5 27E
Aix-les-Bains France **61** C2 45 41N 5 55E
Aiyion Greece **68** D2 38 15N 22 05E
Aizu-Wakamatsu Japan **82** C2 37 30N 139 58E
Ajaccio Corsica **61** C1 41 55N 8 43E
Ajax Ontario Canada **105** E2 43 48N 79 00W
Ajdābiyā Libya **94** D14 30 46N 20 14E
Ajegunle Nigeria **92** C3 6 24N 3 24E
Ajlūn Jordan **78** O11 32 20N 35 45E
Ajmer India **77** C5 26 29N 74 40E
Akabira Japan **82** D3 43 40N 141 55E
Akaroa New Zealand **87** B2 43 50S 172 59E
Akashi Japan **82** B1 34 39N 135 00E
Aketi Zaïre **94** D8 2 42N 23 51E
Akhelóös *r.* Greece **68** D2 39 00N 21 00E
Akhisar Turkey **68** E2 38 54N 27 50E
Akimiski Island *i.* Northwest Territories Canada **101** S3 53 00N 81 00W
Akita Japan **82** D2 39 44N 140 05E
'Akko Israel **78** O11 32 55N 35 04E
Aklavik Northwest Territories Canada **100** I6 68 15N 135 02W
Akobo Sudan **94** F9 7 50N 33 05E
Akola India **77** D4 20 40N 77 05E
Ak'ordat Ethiopia **78** E2 15 26N 37 45E
Akpatok Island *i.* Northwest Territories Canada **101** V5 60 30N 68 00W
Ákra Akrítas *c.* Greece **68** D2 36 43N 21 52E
Ákra Kafirévs *c.* Greece **68** D2 38 10N 24 35E
Ákra Maléa *c.* Greece **68** D2 36 27N 23 12E
Akranes Iceland **67** H6 64 19N 22 05W
Ákra Taínaron *c.* Greece **68** D2 36 23N 22 29E
Akron Ohio U.S.A. **105** D2 41 04N 81 31W
Aksum Ethiopia **78** E1 14 10N 38 45E
Aktyubinsk U.S.S.R. **70** H6 50 16N 57 13E
Akureyri Iceland **67** I7 65 41N 18 04W
Alabama *r.* Alabama U.S.A. **103** I3 31 00N 88 00W
Alabama *state.* U.S.A. **103** I3 32 00N 87 00W
Alagoas *admin.* Brazil **114** J11 9 30S 37 00W
Alagoinhas Brazil **114** J10 12 09S 38 21W
Alagón *r.* Spain **66** A3 40 00N 6 30W
Alajuela Costa Rica **109** H2 10 00N 84 12W
Alakanuk Alaska U.S.A. **100** C5 62 39N 164 48W
Alakol' *l.* U.S.S.R. **71** K5 46 00N 82 00E
Al'Amārah Iraq **79** G5 31 51N 47 10E
Alamosa Colorado U.S.A. **102** E4 37 28N 105 54W
Åland *i.* Finland **67** D3 60 15N 20 00E
Alanya Turkey **78** D6 36 32N 32 02E
Al Artāwīyah Saudi Arabia **79** G4 26 31N 45 21E
Ala Shan *mts.* China F5/F6 40 00N 102 30E
Alaska *state* U.S.A. **100** D5 63 10N 157 30W
Alaska, Gulf of U.S.A. **100** F4 58 00N 147 00W
Alaska Peninsula Alaska U.S.A. **100** D4 56 30N 159 00W
Alaska Range *mts.* Alaska U.S.A. **100** E5 62 30N 152 30W
Alatna Alaska U.S.A. **100** E6 66 33N 152 49W
Al 'Ayn United Arab Emirates **79** I3 24 10N 55 43E
Alay Range *mts.* U.S.S.R. **70** J3 39 00N 70 00E
Alayor Balearic Islands **66** F4 39 56N 4 08E
Albacete Spain **66** B2 39 00N 1 52W
Alba Iulia Romania **69** D2 46 04N 23 33E
ALBANIA **68** C3
Albany Australia **86** B3 34 57S 117 54E
Albany Georgia U.S.A. **103** J3 31 37N 84 10W
Albany New York U.S.A. **105** F2 42 40N 73 49W
Albany Oregon U.S.A. **102** B5 44 38N 123 07W
Albany River Ontario Canada **101** S3 52 00N 84 00W
Al Başrah Iraq **79** G5 30 30N 47 50E
Al Baydā' Libya **94** D14 32 00N 21 30E
Alberche *r.* Spain **66** B3 40 10N 4 45W
Albert France **61** B2 50 00N 2 40E
Alberta *province* Canada **100** L3 54 00N 117 30W
Albert-Kanaal *can.* Belgium **64** D3 51 10N 5 00E
Albert, Lake Uganda/Zaïre **94** F8 2 00N 31 00E
Albert Lea Minnesota U.S.A. **104** B2 43 38N 93 16W
Albertville France **61** C2 45 40N 6 24E
Albi France **61** B1 43 56N 2 08E
Al Bi'r Saudi Arabia **78** P9 28 50N 36 16E
Ålborg Denmark **67** B2 57 05N 9 50E
Albrighton Shropshire England **35** B2 52 38N 2 16W
Albuquerque New Mexico U.S.A. **102** E4 35 05N 106 38W
Al Buraymī Oman **79** I3 24 16N 55 48E
Albury Australia **86** H2 36 03S 146 53E
Alcalá de Henares Spain **66** B3 40 28N 3 22W
Alcamo Italy **68** B2 37 58N 12 58E
Alcañiz Spain **66** B3 41 03N 0 09W
Alcázar de San Juan Spain **66** B2 39 24N 3 12W
Alcester Warwickshire England **35** C1 52 13N 1 52W
Alcira Spain **66** B2 39 10N 0 27W
Alcoy Spain **66** B2 38 42N 0 29W
Alcudia Balearic Islands **66** E4 39 51N 3 06E
Aldabra Islands Indian Ocean **95** I6 9 00S 46 00E
Aldama Mexico **108** E4 22 54N 98 05W
Aldan *r.* U.S.S.R. **71** P7 59 00N 132 30E
Aldan U.S.S.R. **71** O7 58 44N 125 22E
Aldbourne Wiltshire England **31** F3 51 30N 1 37W
Aldbrough Humberside England **40** D2 53 50N 0 06W
Alde *r.* Suffolk England **33** D3 52 10N 1 30E
Aldeburgh Suffolk England **33** D3 52 09N 1 35E
Aldergrove Antrim North Ireland **49** C1 54 38N 6 09W
Alderley Edge Cheshire England **42** D1 53 18N 2 15W
Alderney *i.* Channel Islands British Isles **31** G6 49 43N 2 12W
Aldershot Surrey England **33** B2 51 15N 0 47W
Aldridge West Midlands England **35** C2 52 36N 1 55W
Aldsworth Gloucestershire England **31** F3 51 48N 1 46W
Alegrete Brazil **115** F7 29 45S 55 40W
Aleksandrovsk-Sakhalinskiy U.S.S.R. **71** Q6 50 55N 142 12E
Alençon France **61** B2 48 25N 0 05E
Alenuihaha Channel Hawaiian Islands **119** Y18 20 20N 156 20W
Aleppo *see* Halab
Alès France **61** B1 44 08N 4 05E
Alessàndria Italy **68** A3 44 55N 8 37E
Ålesund Norway **67** B3 62 28N 6 11E
Aleutian Basin Pacific Ocean **118** I13 54 00N 178 00W
Aleutian Islands Alaska U.S.A. **100** A3 54 00N 173 00W
Aleutian Range *mts.* Alaska U.S.A. **100** D4 56 30N 159 00W
Aleutian Ridge Pacific Ocean **118/119** I13 53 55N 178 00W
Aleutian Trench Pacific Ocean **118/119** I13 50 55N 178 00W
Alexander Archipelago *is.* Alaska U.S.A. **100** H4 57 00N 137 30W
Alexander Bay *tn.* Republic of South Africa **95** C2 28 40S 16 30E
Alexander Island Antarctica **121** 71 00S 70 00W
Alexandra New Zealand **87** A1 45 14S 169 26E
Alexandria *(El Iskandarîya)* Egypt **78** C5 31 13N 29 55E
Alexandria Louisiana U.S.A. **103** H3 31 19N 92 29W
Alexandria Romania **69** E1 43 59N 25 19E
Alexandria Strathclyde Scotland **45** A1 55 59N 4 36W
Alexandria Virginia U.S.A. **105** E1 38 49N 77 06W
Alexandria Bay *tn.* New York U.S.A. **105** E2 44 20N 75 55W
Alexandroúpolis Greece **68** E3 40 51N 25 53E
Alfambra *r.* Spain **66** B3 40 40N 1 00W
Alfiós *r.* Greece **68** D2 37 00N 22 00E
Alford Grampian Scotland **46** F4 57 13N 2 42W
Alford Lincolnshire England **36** E3 53 17N 0 11E
Alfred Ontario Canada **105** F3 45 33N 74 52W
Alfreton Derbyshire England **36** C3 53 06N 1 23W
Al Fuḩayḩīl Kuwait **79** G4 29 07N 47 02E
Algarve *geog. reg.* Portugal **51** 37 30N 8 00W
Algeciras Spain **66** A2 36 08N 5 27W
Alger *(Algiers)* Algeria **93** F10 36 50N 3 00E
ALGERIA **93** F8
Alghero Italy **68** A3 40 34N 8 19E
Algiers *see* Alger
Algona Iowa U.S.A. **104** B2 43 04N 94 11W
Al Ḩadīthah Iraq **78** F5 34 06N 42 25E
Alhambra California U.S.A. **107** B3 34 05N 118 10W
Al Hariq Saudi Arabia **79** G3 23 34N 46 35E
Al Hasakah Syria **78** F6 36 32N 40 44E
Al Hillah Iraq **78** F5 32 28N 44 29E
Al Hoceima Morocco **66** B2 35 14N 3 56W
Al Hudaydah Yemen **78** F1 14 50N 42 58E
Al Hufūf Saudi Arabia **79** G4 25 20N 49 34E
Aliákmon *r.* Greece **68** D3 40 00N 22 00E
Alicante Spain **66** B2 38 21N 0 29W
Alice Texas U.S.A. **103** G2 27 45N 98 06W
Alice Springs Australia **86** E5 23 42S 133 52E
Aligarh India **77** D5 27 54N 78 04E
Aling Kangri *mt.* China **81** B4 32 51N 81 03E
Alipur India **76** K2 22 32N 88 19E
Alivérion Greece **68** D2 38 24N 24 02E
Aliwal North Republic of South Africa **95** E1 30 42S 26 43E
Al Jahrah Kuwait **79** G4 29 22N 47 40E
Al Jawf Libya **94** D12 24 12N 23 18E
Al Jawf Saudi Arabia **78** E4 29 49N 39 52E
Al Jubayl Saudi Arabia **79** G4 26 59N 49 40E
Aljustrel Portugal **66** A2 37 52N 8 10W
Al Khums Libya **94** B14 32 39N 14 16E
Alkmaar Netherlands **64** D4 52 38N 4 44E
Al Kufrah Oasis Libya **94** D12 24 10N 23 15E
Al Kūt Iraq **79** G5 32 30N 45 51E
Al Kuwayt Kuwait **79** G4 29 20N 48 00E
Al Lādhiqīyah Syria **78** E6 35 31N 35 47E
Allahabad India **77** E5 25 27N 81 50E
Allegheny Mountains U.S.A. **105** E1 40 00N 79 00W
Allegheny Reservoir U.S.A. **105** E2 42 00N 79 00W
Allen *r.* Northumberland England **44** B1 54 58N 2 20W
Allendale Town Northumberland England **44** B1 54 54N 2 15W
Allende Mexico **108** D5 28 22N 100 50W
Allentown Pennsylvania U.S.A. **105** E2 40 37N 75 30W
Alleppey India **77** D1 9 30N 76 22E
Aller *r.* F.R.G. **63** A2 52 00N 9 00E
Allerton Merseyside England **42** B2 53 23N 2 56W
Allesley West Midlands England **35** D2 52 26N 1 33W
Alliance Nebraska U.S.A. **102** F5 42 08N 102 54W
Allier *r.* France **61** B2 46 40N 3 00E
Alliston Ontario Canada **105** E2 44 09N 79 51W
Al Līth Saudi Arabia **78** F3 20 10N 40 20E
Alloa Central Scotland **45** C2 56 07N 3 49W
Alma Michigan U.S.A. **105** D2 43 23N 84 40W
Alma Québec Canada **105** F3 48 32N 71 41W
Alma-Ata U.S.S.R. **71** J4 43 19N 76 55E
Almada Portugal **66** A2 38 40N 9 09W
Almadén Spain **66** B2 38 47N 4 50W
Al Madīnah Saudi Arabia **78** E3 24 30N 39 35E
Al Manāmah Bahrain **79** H4 26 12N 50 38E
Almansa Spain **66** B2 38 52N 1 06W
Almanzora *r.* Spain **66** B2 37 15N 2 10W
Al Mayādīn Syria **78** F6 35 01N 40 28E
Almelo Netherlands **64** F4 52 21N 6 40E
Almere Netherlands **64** E4 52 22N 5 12E
Almere-Haven Netherlands **65** E3 52 21N 5 11E
Almería Spain **66** B2 36 50N 2 26W
Älmhult Sweden **67** C2 56 32N 14 10E
Al Miqdādīyah Iraq **78** F5 33 58N 44 58E
Almodôvar Portugal **66** A2 37 31N 8 03W
Almond *r.* Tayside Scotland **46** E3 56 25N 3 27W
Almondbury West Yorkshire England **43** E2 53 37N 1 48W
Almonte Ontario Canada **105** E3 45 13N 76 12W
Al Mubarraz Saudi Arabia **79** G4 25 26N 49 37E
Al Mukallā South Yemen **79** G1 14 34N 49 09E
Al Mukhā Yemen **78** F1 13 20N 43 16E
Aln *r.* Northumberland England **44** C2 55 30N 1 45W
Alness Highland Scotland **46** D4 57 41N 4 15W
Alnwick Northumberland England **44** C2 55 25N 1 42W
Alor *i.* Indonesia **80** G2 8 00S 124 30E
Alpena Michigan U.S.A. **105** D3 45 04N 83 27W
Alpes Maritimes *mts.* France/Italy **61** C1 44 15N 6 45E
Alpha Cordillera *ridge* Arctic Ocean **120** 85 00N 120 00W
Alphen aan den Rijn Netherlands **65** C2 52 08N 4 40E
Alpi Carniche *mts.* Europe **68** B4 46 00N 13 00E
Alpi Cozie *mts.* Europe **61** C1 45 00N 7 00E
Alpi Dolomitiche *mts.* Italy **68** B4 46 00N 12 00E
Alpi Graie *mts.* Europe **61** C2 45 00N 7 00E
Alpi Lepontine *mts.* Switzerland **61** C2 46 26N 8 30E
Alpine Texas U.S.A. **102** F3 30 22N 103 40W
Alpi Pennine *mts.* Switzerland/Italy **61** C2 45 55N 7 30E
Alpi Retiche *mts.* Switzerland **61** C2 46 25N 9 45E
Alps *mts.* France/Switzerland/Italy **61** C2 46 00N 7 30E
Al Qunfudhah Saudi Arabia **78** F2 19 09N 41 07E
Alrewas Staffordshire England **35** C3 52 45N 1 43W
Alsager Cheshire England **40** B2 53 06N 2 19W
Alsdorf F.R.G. **64** F2 50 53N 6 10E
Alston Cumbria England **44** B1 54 49N 2 26W
Alta Norway **67** E4 69 57N 23 10E
Altadena California U.S.A. **107** B3 34 12N 118 08W
Altaelv *r.* Norway **67** E4 69 50N 23 30E
Alta Gracia Argentina **115** E6 31 42S 64 25W
Altai *mts.* Mongolia **81** D7 47 00N 92 30E
Altamaha *r.* Georgia U.S.A. **103** J3 32 00N 82 00W
Altamura Italy **68** C3 40 49N 16 34E
Altay China **81** C7 47 48N 88 07E
Altay *mts.* U.S.S.R. **71** K6 51 00N 89 00E
Altenburg G.D.R. **63** B2 50 59N 12 27E
Altenessen F.R.G. **62** C2 51 29N 7 02E
Altmühl *r.* F.R.G. **63** B1 49 00N 10 00E
Altnaharra Highland Scotland **46** D5 58 16N 4 27W
Alto da Boa Vista Brazil **116** B2 22 58S 43 17W
Altofts West Yorkshire England **43** F3 53 42N 1 26W
Alto Molocue Mozambique **95** G4 15 38S 37 42E
Alton Hampshire England **33** B2 51 09N 0 59W
Alton Illinois U.S.A. **104** B1 38 55N 90 10W
Altona Manitoba Canada **104** A3 49 06N 97 35W
Altoona Pennsylvania U.S.A. **105** E2 40 32N 78 23W
Alto Purus, R. Peru **114** C10 10 30S 72 00W
Altrincham Greater Manchester England **42** C2 53 24N 2 21W
Altun Shan *mts.* China **81** C5 37 30N 86 00E
Altus Oklahoma U.S.A. **102** G3 34 39N 99 21W
Alur Setar Malaysia **80** C5 6 06N 100 23E
Alva Central Scotland **45** C2 56 09N 3 49W
Alva Oklahoma U.S.A. **102** G4 36 48N 98 40W
Alvechurch Hereford & Worcester England **35** C2 52 21N 1 57W
Al Wajh Saudi Arabia **78** E4 26 16N 32 28E
Alwar India **77** D5 27 32N 76 35E
Alwen *r.* Clwyd Wales **38** C3 53 00N 3 30W
Alyth Tayside Scotland **46** E3 56 37N 3 13W
Amadeus, Lake Australia **86** E5 24 00S 132 30E
Amadi Sudan **94** F9 5 32N 30 20E
Amadjuak Lake Northwest Territories Canada **101** U6 65 00N 71 00W
Amagasaki Japan **82** C1 34 42N 135 23E
Amakusa-shotō *is.* Japan **82** A1 32 50N 130 05E
Amapá *admin.* Brazil **114** G13 2 00N 52 30W
Amapá Brazil **114** G13 2 00N 50 50W
Amarillo Texas U.S.A. **102** F4 35 14N 101 50W
Amazon *see* Rio Amazonas
Amazonas *admin.* Brazil **114** D12–F12 4 30S 65 00W
Amazon, Mouths of the Brazil **114** H13 1 00N 50 00W
Ambaí Brazil **116** B3 22 43S 43 27W
Ambala India **77** D6 30 19N 76 49E
Ambarchik U.S.S.R. **71** S9 69 39N 162 27E
Ambato Ecuador **114** B12 1 18S 78 39W
Amberg F.R.G. **63** B1 49 26N 11 52E
Amble Northumberland England **44** C2 55 20N 1 34W
Ambleside Cumbria England **44** B1 54 26N 2 58W
Amblève *r.* Belgium **64** F2 50 22N 6 10E
Ambon Indonesia **80** H3 3 41S 128 10E
Ambovombe Madagascar **95** I2 25 10S 46 06E
Amderma U.S.S.R. **71** I9 66 44N 61 35E
Amdo China **81** D4 32 22N 91 07E
Ameca Mexico **108** D4 20 34N 104 03W
Ameland *i.* Netherlands **64** E5 53 28N 5 45E
American Falls *tn.* Idaho U.S.A. **102** D5 42 47N 112 50W
American Samoa Pacific Ocean **119** J6 15 00S 170 00S
Amersfoort Netherlands **64** E4 52 09N 5 23E
Amersham Buckinghamshire England **34** B3 51 40N 0 38W
Amery Ice Shelf Antarctica **121** 70 00S 70 00E
Ames Iowa U.S.A. **104** B2 42 02N 93 33W
Amesbury Wiltshire England **31** F3 51 10N 1 47W
Amfípolis Greece **68** D3 40 48N 23 52E
Amga *r.* U.S.S.R. **71** P8 60 00N 130 00E
Amga U.S.S.R. **71** P8 61 51N 131 59E
Amgun' *r.* U.S.S.R. **71** P6 52 00N 137 00E
Amherst Nova Scotia Canada **101** W2 44 09N 76 45W
Amherst Virginia U.S.A. **105** E1 37 35N 79 04W
Amiens France **61** B2 49 54N 2 18E
Amlia Island Alaska U.S.A. **100** A3 52 05N 173 30W
Amlwch Gwynedd Wales **38** B3 53 25N 4 20W

Amman Jordan 78 O10 31 57N 35 56E
Ammanford Dyfed Wales 38 C1 51 48N 3 59W
Ammassalik Greenland 101 BB6 65 45N 37 45W
Ammersee l. F.R.G. 63 B1 48 00N 11 00E
Amne Machin Shan mts. China 72 35 00N 100 00E
Ampana Indonesia 80 G3 0 54S 121 35E
Amper r. F.R.G. 63 B1 48 00N 11 00E
Ampthill Bedfordshire England 34 B4 52 02N 0 30W
Amravati India 77 D4 20 58N 77 50E
Amritsar India 77 D6 31 35N 74 56E
Amroha India 77 D5 28 54N 78 29E
Amrum i. F.R.G. 63 A2 54 00N 8 00E
Amstelveen Netherlands 65 D3 52 18N 4 52E
Amsterdam Netherlands 65 D3 52 22N 4 54E
Amsterdam New York U.S.A. 105 F2 42 56N 74 12W
Amsterdam Rijnkanaal can. Netherlands 65 E2 51 15N 5 00E
Amstetten Austria 69 B2 48 08N 14 52E
Am Timan Chad 94 D10 10 59N 20 18E
Amudar'ya (Oxus) r. U.S.S.R. 70 I3 38 00N 64 00E
Amund Ringnes Island Northwest Territories Canada 101 P8 78 00W 96 00W
Amundsen Gulf Northwest Territories Canada 100 K7 70 30N 125 00W
Amundsen Sea Southern Ocean 121 72 00S 130 00W
Amundsen-Scott r.s. South Pole Antarctica 121 90 00S
Amungen l. Sweden 67 D3 61 10N 15 35E
Amur (Heilong Jiang) r. U.S.S.R./China 81 K8 52 30N 126 30E
Amursk U.S.S.R 71 P6 50 16N 136 55E
Anabar r. U.S.S.R. 71 N10 71 30N 113 00E
Anaconda Montana U.S.A. 102 D6 46 09N 112 56W
Anadyr' r. U.S.S.R. 71 T9 65 00N 175 00E
Anadyr' U.S.S.R. 71 T8 64 50N 178 00E
Anadyr', Gulf of U.S.S.R. 71 U8 65 00N 178 00W
Anaheim California U.S.A. 107 C2 33 50N 117 56W
Anai Mudi mt. India 77 D2 10 20N 77 15E
Anan Japan 82 B1 33 54N 134 40E
Ananindeua Brazil 114 H12 1 22S 48 20W
Anantapur India 77 D2 14 42N 77 05E
Anápolis Brazil 114 H9 16 19S 48 58W
Anatolian Plateau Turkey 72 39 00N 39 00E
Anatom i. Vanuatu 86 L5 20 10S 169 50E
Anchorage Alaska U.S.A. 100 F5 61 10N 150 00W
Ancona Italy 68 B3 43 37N 13 31E
Ancroft Northumberland England 44 B2 55 42N 2 00W
Anda China 81 K7 46 25N 125 20E
Andalsnes Norway 67 B3 62 33N 7 43E
Andaman Islands India 77 G2 12 00N 94 00E
Andaman Sea Indian Ocean 80 B6 12 30N 97 00E
Andenne Belgium 64 E2 50 29N 5 06E
Anderlecht Belgium 64 D2 50 50N 4 20E
Andermatt Switzerland 61 C2 46 38N 8 36E
Anderson Indiana U.S.A. 104 C2 40 05N 85 41W
Anderson r. Northwest Territories Canada 100 J6 69 42N 129 01W
Anderson South Carolina U.S.A. 103 J3 34 30N 82 39W
Andes mts. South America 114/115 B13–C5
Andhra Pradesh admin. India 77 D3 16 00N 79 00E
Andizhan U.S.S.R. 70 J4 40 40N 72 12E
Andkhvoy Afghanistan 79 K6 36 58N 65 00E
ANDORRA 66 C3
Andorra la Vella Andorra 66 C3 42 30N 1 30E
Andover Hampshire England 32 A2 51 13N 1 28W
Andraitx Balearic Islands 66 E4 39 35N 2 25E
Andreas Isle of Man British Isles 41 F1 54 22N 4 26W
Andrésy France 60 A2 48 59N 2 03E
Andreyevka U.S.S.R. 81 B7 45 50N 80 34E
Andropov (Rybinsk) U.S.S.R. 70 F7 58 03N 38 50E
Ándros i. Greece 68 D2 37 49N 24 54E
Andros i. The Bahamas 109 I4 24 00N 78 00W
Androscoggin River U.S.A. 105 F2 44 00N 70 00W
Androth Island India 77 C2 10 51N 73 41E
Andújar Spain 66 B2 38 02N 4 03W
Andulo Angola 95 C5 11 29S 16 43E
Angara r. U.S.S.R. 71 L7 58 00N 96 00E
Angara Basin Arctic Ocean 120 80 00N
Angarsk U.S.S.R. 71 M6 52 31N 103 55E
Angel de la Guarda i. Mexico 108 B5 29 00N 113 30W
Angeles National Forest California U.S.A. 107 B4 34 15N 118 10W
Ångermanälven r. Sweden 67 D3 64 30N 16 15E
Angers France 61 A2 47 29N 0 32W
Angle Dyfed Wales 38 A1 51 41N 5 06W
Anglesey i. Gwynedd Wales 38 B3 53 18N 4 25W
Angliers Québec Canada 105 E3 47 33N 79 14W
ANGOLA 95 C5
Angola Basin Atlantic Ocean 117 I5 15 00S 3 00E
Angola Plateau Africa 88 14 00S 17 00E
Angoulême France 61 B2 45 40N 0 10E
Anguilla i. Leeward Islands 109 L3 18 14N 63 05W
Anjo Japan 82 C1 34 56N 137 05E
Ankaratra mt. Madagascar 95 I4 19 25S 47 12E
Anklam G.D.R. 63 B2 53 52N 13 42E
Ann Arbor Michigan U.S.A. 105 D2 42 18N 83 43W
Annaba Algeria 93 G10 36 55N 7 47E
An Nabk Saudi Arabia 78 E5 31 21N 37 20E
An Nabk Syria 78 E5 34 02N 36 43E
An Nafud d. Saudi Arabia 78 F4 28 20N 40 30E
An Najaf Iraq 78 F5 31 59N 44 19E
Annam Range hills Asia 72 15 00N 107 00E
Annan Dumfries & Galloway Scotland 46 E1 54 59N 3 16W
Annan r. Dumfries & Galloway Scotland 46 E2 55 15N 3 40W
Annandale v. Dumfries & Galloway Scotland 46 E2 55 15N 3 25W
Annapolis Maryland U.S.A. 105 E1 38 59N 76 30W
Annapurna mt. Nepal 77 E5 28 34N 83 50E
An Nāsirīyah Iraq 79 G5 31 04N 46 17E
Annbank Strathclyde Scotland 46 D2 55 28N 4 30W
Ann, Cape U.S.A. 105 F2 42 39N 70 37W
Annecy France 61 C2 45 54N 6 07E
Annfield Plain Durham England 44 C1 54 52N 1 45W
Anniston Alabama U.S.A. 103 I3 33 38N 85 50W
Annotto Bay tn. Jamaica 109 R8 18 16N 76 47W
Anqing China 81 I4 30 46N 119 40E
Ansari Nagar India 76 L4 28 33N 77 12E
Ansbach F.R.G. 63 B1 49 18N 10 36E
Anshan China 81 J6 41 05N 122 58E
Anshun China 81 G3 26 15N 105 51E
Anstey Leicestershire England 36 C2 52 40N 1 10W
Anston South Yorkshire England 43 G2 53 22N 1 13W
Anstruther Fife Scotland 46 F3 56 14N 2 42W
Ansty Warwickshire England 35 D2 52 26N 1 24W
Antakya Turkey 78 E6 36 12N 36 10E
Antalya Turkey 78 D6 36 53N 30 42E
Antananarivo (Tananarive) Madagascar 95 I4 18 52S 47 30E
Antarctica 121
Antarctic Peninsula Antarctica 121 68 00S 65 00W
Antequera Spain 66 B2 37 01N 4 34W
Antibes France 61 C1 43 35N 7 07E
Antigua Guatemala 108 F2 14 33N 90 42W
Antigua i. Antigua & Barbuda 109 L3 17 09N 61 49W
ANTIGUA & BARBUDA 109 L3
Antipodes Islands Southern Ocean 118 H3 49 42S 178 50E
Antofagasta Chile 115 C8 23 40S 70 23W
Antrim North Ireland 49 C2 54 43N 6 13W
Antrim Mountains Northern Ireland 48 E4/5 55 00N 6 10W
Antseranana Madagascar 95 I5 12 19S 49 17E
Antwerpen admin. Belgium 64 D3 51 20N 4 45E
Antwerpen (Anvers) Belgium 64 D3 51 13N 4 25E
Anuradhapura Sri Lanka 77 E1 8 20N 80 25E
Anvers see Antwerpen
Anxi China 81 E6 40 32N 95 57E
Anyang China 81 H5 36 04N 114 20E
Anzhero-Sudzhensk U.S.S.R. 71 K7 56 10N 86 01E
Aomori Japan 82 D3 40 50N 140 43E
Aosta Italy 68 A4 45 43N 7 19E
Aozou Strip Chad 94 C12 23 00N 17 00E
Apapa Nigeria 92 C3 6 22N 3 25E
Aparri The Philippines 80 G7 18 22N 121 40E
Apatity U.S.S.R. 70 F9 67 32N 33 21E
Apatzingán Mexico 108 D3 19 05N 102 20W
Apeldoorn Netherlands 64 E4 52 13N 5 57E
Apennines see Appennini
Apia Western Samoa 118 I6 13 48S 171 45W
Apolda G.D.R. 63 B2 51 02N 11 31E
Apostle Islands Wisconsin U.S.A. 104 B3 47 00N 90 00W
Appalachian Mountains U.S.A. 103 J4 37 00N 82 00W
Appennini (Apennines) mts. Italy 68 B3
Appennino Abruzzese mts. Italy 68 B3 42 00N 14 00E
Appennino Ligure mts. Italy 68 A3 44 00N 9 00E
Appennino Lucano mts. Italy 68 C3 40 00N 15 00E
Appennino Tosco-Emiliano mts. Italy 68 B3 44 00N 12 00E
Appingedam Netherlands 64 F5 53 18N 6 52E
Appleby-in-Westmoreland Cumbria England 44 B1 53 36N 2 29W
Appledore Devon England 31 C3 51 03N 4 12W
Appleton City Missouri U.S.A. 104 B1 38 10N 94 03W
Appleton Wisconsin U.S.A. 104 C2 44 17N 88 24W
Appomattox Virginia U.S.A. 105 E1 37 21N 78 51W
'Aqaba Jordan 78 O9 29 32N 35 00E
'Aqaba, Gulf of Middle East 78 O9 28 40N 34 40E
Aquidauana Brazil 114 F8 20 27S 55 45W
Ara India 77 E5 25 34N 84 40E
Ara r. Japan 83 C3 35 39N 139 51E
Arabian Sea Indian Ocean 79 J2 17 00N 60 00E
Aracaju Brazil 114 J10 10 54S 37 07W
Aracati Brazil 114 J12 4 32S 37 45W
Arad Romania 69 D2 46 10N 21 19E
Arafura Sea Australia/Indonesia 86 E8/F8 10 00S 135 00E
Aragón r. Spain 66 B3 42 15N 1 40W
Araguaina Brazil 114 H11 7 16S 48 18W
Araguari Brazil 114 H9 18 38S 48 13W
Arāk Iran 79 G5 34 05N 49 42E
Arakan Yoma mts. Myanma 77 G3 18 00N 94 00E
Araks (Aras, Araxes) r. U.S.S.R./Turkey/Iran 78 F6 39 30N 45 00E
Aral Sea U.S.S.R. 70 H5 45 00N 60 00E
Aral'sk U.S.S.R. 70 I5 46 56N 61 43E
Aranda de Duero Spain 66 B3 41 40N 3 41W
Aran Fawddwy mt. Gwynedd Wales 38 C2 52 47N 3 41W
Aran Island Irish Republic 48 C4/5 55 00N 8 30W
Aran Islands Irish Republic 48 B3 53 10N 9 50W
Aranjuez Spain 66 B3 40 02N 3 37W
Arapiraca Brazil 114 J11 9 45S 36 40W
Ar'ar Saudi Arabia 78 F5 30 58N 41 03E
Araraquara Brazil 115 H8 21 46S 48 08W
Ararat, Mount see Bü Ağri Daği
Aras (Araks, Araxes) r. Turkey/U.S.S.R./Iran 79 G6 38 40N 46 30E
Arauca Colombia 114 C14 7 04N 70 41W
Araure Venezuela 109 K1 9 36N 69 15W
Araxá Brazil 114 H9 19 37S 46 50W
Araxes (Araks, Aras) r. Iran/U.S.S.R./Turkey 79 G6 38 40N 46 30E
Arbil Iraq 78 F6 36 12N 44 01E
Arbroath Tayside Scotland 46 F3 56 34N 2 35W
Arc r. France 61 C2 45 15N 6 10E
Arcachon France 61 A1 44 40N 1 11W
Arcadia California U.S.A. 107 B3 34 09N 118 00W
Archipelago Dehalak is. Ethiopia 78 F2 15 45N 40 12E
Arctic Bay tn. Northwest Territories Canada 101 R7 73 05N 85 20W
Arctic Ocean 120
Ardabil Iran 79 G6 38 15N 48 18E
Ardbeg Strathclyde Scotland 46 B2 55 39N 6 05W
Ardee Louth Irish Republic 48 E3 53 52N 6 33W
Ardennes admin. France 64 D1 49 35N 4 35E
Ardennes mts. Belgium 64 E2 50 10N 5 45E
Ardila r. Spain 66 A2 38 15N 6 50W
Ardmore Oklahoma U.S.A. 103 G3 34 11N 97 08W
Ardmore Strathclyde Scotland 45 A1 55 59N 4 41W
Ardnamurchan, Point of c. Highland Scotland 46 B3 56 44N 6 13W
Ardres France 64 A2 50 51N 1 59E
Ardrossan Strathclyde Scotland 46 D2 55 39N 4 49W
Ards Peninsula Northern Ireland 48 F4 54 25N 5 30W
Ardvasar Highland Scotland 46 C4 57 03N 5 55W
Arendal Norway 67 B2 58 27N 8 56E
Arequipa Peru 114 C9 16 25S 71 32W
Arezzo Italy 68 B3 43 28N 11 53E
Arga r. Spain 66 B3 42 30N 1 50W
Argentan France 61 B2 48 45N 0 01W
Argenteuil France 60 A2 48 57N 2 14E
ARGENTINA 115 D5
Argentine Basin Atlantic Ocean 117 D2 42 00S 45 00W
Argeşul r. Romania 69 E1 44 00N 26 00E
Argun (Ergun He) r. U.S.S.R./China 81 I8 52 00N 120 00E
Argyle, Lake Australia 86 D6 17 00S 128 30E
Århus Denmark 67 C2 56 15N 10 10E
Arica Chile 114 C9 18 30S 70 20W
Ariège r. France 61 B1 42 50N 1 40E
Arinagour Strathclyde Scotland 46 B3 56 37N 6 31W
Aripuanā r. Brazil 114 E11 7 00S 60 30W
Ariquemes Brazil 114 E11 9 55S 63 06W
Arisaig Highland Scotland 46 C3 56 51N 5 51W
Arisaig, Sound of Highland Scotland 46 C3 56 50N 5 50W
Arizona state U.S.A. 102 D3 34 00N 112 00W
Arizpe Mexico 108 B6 30 20N 110 11W
Arjeplog Sweden 67 D4 66 04N 18 00E
Arjona Colombia 114 B15 10 14N 75 22W
Arkalyk U.S.S.R. 70 I6 50 17N 66 51E
Arkansas r. U.S.A. 103 H4 35 00N 93 00W
Arkansas state U.S.A. 103 H3 34 00N 93 00W
Arkansas City Kansas U.S.A. 103 G4 37 03N 97 02W
Arkendale North Yorkshire England 43 F4 54 02N 1 24W
Arkhangel'sk U.S.S.R. 70 G8 64 32N 40 40E
Arklow Wicklow Irish Republic 48 E2 52 48N 6 09W
Arkona, Cape G.D.R. 63 B2 54 41N 13 26E
Arlanza r. Spain 66 B3 42 00N 3 30W
Arlanzón r. Spain 66 B3 42 00N 4 00W
Arles France 61 B1 43 41N 4 38E
Arlit Niger 93 G6 18 50N 7 00E
Arlon Belgium 64 E1 49 41N 5 49E
Armadale Highland Scotland 46 C4 57 05N 5 54W
Armadale Lothian Scotland 45 C1 55 54N 3 42W
Armagh Armagh Northern Ireland 48 E4 54 21N 6 39W
Armavir U.S.S.R. 70 G5 44 59N 41 10E
Armenia Colombia 114 B13 4 32N 75 40W
Armenia see Armyanskaya S.S.R.
Armentières France 61 B3 50 41N 2 53E
Armidale Australia 86 I3 30 32S 151 40E
Armstrong Ontario Canada 104 C4 50 20N 89 02W
Armthorpe South Yorkshire England 43 G2 53 32N 1 03W
Armyanskaya S.S.R. rep. U.S.S.R. 70 G4/G3 40 00N 45 00E
Arnhem Netherlands 64 E3 52 00N 5 53E
Arnhem Land geog. reg. Australia 86 E7 13 00S 133 00E
Arno r. Italy 68 B3 43 00N 10 00E
Arnold Nottinghamshire England 36 C2 53 00N 1 09W
Arnprior Central Scotland 45 B2 56 08N 4 15W
Arnprior Ontario Canada 105 E3 45 26N 76 24W
Arnsberg F.R.G. 63 A2 51 23N 8 03E
Arnstadt G.D.R. 63 B2 50 50N 10 57E
Arquipélago dos Bijagós is. Guinea Bissau 93 B5 11 20N 16 40W
Ar Ramādī Iraq 78 F5 33 27N 43 19E
Ar Ramlah Jordan 78 O9 29 28N 35 58E
Arran i. Strathclyde Scotland 46 C2 55 35N 5 15W
Ar Raqqah Syria 78 E6 35 57N 39 03E
Arras France 61 B3 50 17N 2 46E
Ar Riyāḍ Saudi Arabia 79 G3 24 39N 46 46E
Arta Balearic Islands 66 E4 39 42N 3 20E
Arta Greece 68 D2 39 10N 20 59E
Artane Dublin Irish Republic 49 B2 53 23N 6 12W
Arthur Ontario Canada 105 D2 43 50N 80 32W
Arthur's Pass New Zealand 87 B2 42 55S 171 34E
Arthur's Seat sum. Lothian Scotland 45 D1 55 57N 3 11W
Artigas r.s. Antarctica 121 62 11S 58 51W
Artigas Uruguay 115 F6 30 25S 56 28W
Arua Uganda 94 F8 3 02N 30 56E
ARUBA 114 D15 12 30N 70 00W
Arun r. West Sussex England 33 B1 51 00N 0 30W
Arunachal Pradesh admin. India 77 H5 28 00N 95 00E
Arundel West Sussex England 33 B1 50 51N 0 34W
Arusha Tanzania 94 G7 3 23S 36 40E
Aruwimi r. Zaire 94 E8 2 00N 25 00E
Arvika Sweden 67 C2 59 41N 12 38E
Arzew Algeria 66 B2 35 50N 0 19W
Asahi-dake mt. Japan 82 D3 43 42N 142 54E
Asahikawa Japan 82 D3 43 46N 142 23E
Asaka Japan 83 B4 35 47N 139 37E
Asamankese Ghana 93 E4 5 45N 0 45W
Asansol India 77 F4 23 40N 86 59E
Åsarna Sweden 67 C3 62 40N 14 20E
Asbury Park New Jersey U.S.A. 105 F2 40 14N 74 00W
Ascension Island Atlantic Ocean 117 G6 7 57S 14 22W
Aschaffenburg F.R.G. 63 A1 49 58N 9 10E
Aschersleben G.D.R. 63 B2 51 46N 11 28E
Ascoli Piceno Italy 68 B3 42 52N 13 35E
Ascot Berkshire England 34 A2 51 25N 0 41W
Aseb Ethiopia 78 F1 13 01N 42 47E
Asenovgrad Bulgaria 68 D3 42 00N 24 53E
Ash Kent England 33 D2 51 17N 1 16E
Ash Surrey England 34 A1 51 15N 0 44W
Ashbourne Derbyshire England 36 C2 53 01N 1 43W
Ashbourne Meath Irish Republic 49 A2 53 31N 6 24W
Ashburton Devon England 31 D2 50 31N 3 45W
Ashburton New Zealand 87 B2 43 54S 171 46E
Ashburton r. Australia 86 B5 22 30S 116 00E
Ashby Canal Leicestershire England 35 D2 52 37N 1 25W
Ashby-de-la-Zouch Leicestershire England 35 D3 52 46N 1 28W
Ashdod Israel 78 O10 31 48N 34 48E
Åshen l. Sweden 67 C2 56 45N 14 40E
Asheville North Carolina U.S.A. 103 J4 35 35N 82 35W
Ashfield Central Scotland 45 C2 56 12N 3 59W
Ashford Kent England 33 C2 51 09N 0 53E
Ashford Surrey England 34 B2 51 26N 0 27W
Ashford in the Water Derbyshire England 43 E1 53 13N 1 43W
Ashfork Arizona U.S.A. 102 D4 35 13N 112 29W
Ashgill Strathclyde Scotland 45 C1 55 44N 3 55W
Ashikaga Japan 82 C2 36 21N 139 26E
Ashina Japan 83 B1 35 13N 139 36E
Ashington Northumberland England 44 C2 55 11N 1 34W
Ashizuri-misaki c. Japan 82 B1 32 42N 133 00E
Ashkhabad U.S.S.R. 70 H3 37 58N 58 24E
Ashland Kentucky U.S.A. 105 D1 38 28N 82 40W
Ashland Oregon U.S.A. 102 B5 42 14N 122 44W
Ashland Wisconsin U.S.A. 104 B3 46 34N 90 54W
Ashok Nagar India 76 L4 28 38N 77 07E
Ashqelon Israel 78 O10 31 40N 34 35E
Ash Shāriqah United Arab Emirates 79 I4 25 20N 55 20E
Ash Shurayf Saudi Arabia 78 E4 25 50N 39 00E
Ashstead Surrey England 34 C1 51 19N 0 18W
Ashtabula Ohio U.S.A. 105 D2 41 53N 80 47W
Ashton-in-Makerfield Greater Manchester
Ashton-under-Lyne Greater Manchester
Ashwell Hertfordshire England 33 B3 52 03N 0 09W
Asilah Morocco 66 A2 35 32N 6 04W
Asir Mountains Saudi Arabia 78 F2 18 00N 44 00E
Askeaton Limerick Irish Republic 48 C2 52 36N 8 58W
Askern South Yorkshire England 43 G2 53 37N 1 09W
Askham Bryan North Yorkshire England 43 G3 53 55N 1 10W
Askrigg North Yorkshire England 40 B3 54 19N 2 04W
Asmera Ethiopia 78 E2 15 20N 38 58E
Asnières France 60 B2 48 55N 2 17E
Aspatria Cumbria England 44 A1 54 46N 3 20W
Aspiring, Mount New Zealand 87 A2 44 23S 168 46E
Aspley Guise Bedfordshire England 34 B4 52 01N 0 37W
Aspull Greater Manchester England 42 C2 53 33N 2 36W
Assam admin. India 77 G5 26 20N 92 00E
As Samawah Iraq 79 G5 31 18N 45 18E
Asse Belgium 64 D2 50 55N 4 12E
Assen Netherlands 64 F5 53 00N 6 34E
Assis Brazil 115 G8 22 37S 50 25W
Assisi Italy 68 B3 43 04N 12 37E
As Suq Saudi Arabia 78 F3 21 55N 42 02E
As Suwaydā' Syria 78 P11 32 43N 36 33E
Astārā U.S.S.R. 79 G6 38 27N 48 53E
Asti Italy 68 A3 44 54N 8 13E
Astipálaia i. Greece 68 E2 36 00N 26 00E
Astley Cross Hereford & Worcester England 35 B1 52 19N 2 20W
Aston South Yorkshire England 43 G2 53 22N 1 18W
Aston West Midlands England 35 C2 52 30N 1 54W
Aston Clinton Buckinghamshire England 34 A3 51 48N 0 44W
Astoria Oregon U.S.A. 102 B6 46 12N 123 50W
Astrakhan' U.S.S.R. 70 G5 46 22N 48 04E
Astwood Bank Hereford & Worcester England 35 C1 52 15N 1 55W
Asuka r.s. Antarctica 121 71 32S 24 08E
Asunción Paraguay 115 F7 25 15S 57 40W
Aswa r. Uganda 94 F8 3 30N 32 30E
Aswân Egypt 78 D3 24 05N 32 56E
Aswan Dam Egypt 78 D3 23 40N 31 50E
Asyût Egypt 78 D4 27 14N 31 07E
Atacama Desert see Desierto de, Atacama
Atar Mauritania 93 C7 20 32N 13 08W
Atbara r. Sudan 78 D2 17 28N 34 30E
Atbara Sudan 78 D2 17 42N 34 00E
Atbasar U.S.S.R. 70 I6 51 49N 68 18E
Atchison Kansas U.S.A. 103 G4 39 33N 95 09W
Ath Belgium 64 C2 50 38N 3 47E
Athabasca Alberta Canada 100 M3 54 44N 113 15W
Athabasca, Lake Alberta/Saskatchewan Canada 100 N4 59 10N 109 30W
Athabasca River Alberta Canada 100 M4 57 30N 111 00W
Athboy Meath Irish Republic 48 E3 53 37N 6 55W
Athenry Galway Irish Republic 48 C3 53 18N 8 45W
Athens Georgia U.S.A. 103 J3 33 57N 83 24W
Athens Greece see Athínai
Athens Ohio U.S.A. 105 D1 39 20N 82 06W
Athens Pennsylvania U.S.A. 105 E2 41 57N 76 31W
Atherstone Warwickshire England 35 D2 52 35N 1 31W
Atherton Greater Manchester England 42 C2 53 31N 2 31W
Athínai (Athens) Greece 68 D2 38 00N 23 44E
Athlone Westmeath Irish Republic 48 D3 53 25N 7 56W
Áthos mt. Greece 68 D3 40 10N 24 19E
Athy Kildare Irish Republic 48 E2 52 59N 6 59W
Ati Chad 94 C10 13 11N 18 20E
Atikokan Ontario Canada 104 B3 48 45N 91 38W
Atikonak Lake Newfoundland Canada 101 W3 52 40N 64 35W
Atka Island Alaska U.S.A. 100 A3 52 05N 174 40W
Atlanta Georgia U.S.A. 103 J3 33 45N 84 23W
Atlantic City New Jersey U.S.A. 105 F1 39 23N 74 27W
Atlantic-Indian Ridge Atlantic Ocean 117 I1 53 00S 3 00E
Atlantic Ocean 117
Atlas Saharien mts. Algeria 93 F9 33 30N 1 00E
Atlin British Columbia Canada 100 I4 59 31N 133 41W
Atlin Lake British Columbia Canada 100 I4 59 31N 133 41W
Atrek r. Iran/U.S.S.R. 79 H6 37 00N 54 50E
At Tā'if Saudi Arabia 78 F3 21 15N 40 21E
Attawapiskat Ontario Canada 101 S3 53 00N 82 30W
Attawapiskat River Ontario Canada 101 R3 53 00N 86 00W
Attersee l. Austria 63 B1 47 00N 13 00E
Attleborough Norfolk England 33 D3 52 31N 1 01E
Auas Mountains Namibia 95 C3 23 00S 17 00E
Aubagne France 61 C1 43 17N 5 35E
Aube r. France 61 B2 48 40N 3 55E
Aubenas France 61 B1 44 37N 4 24E
Aubervilliers France 60 B2 48 55N 2 22E
Auburn Maine U.S.A. 105 F2 44 04N 70 26W
Auburn Nebraska U.S.A. 104 A2 40 22N 95 41W
Auburn New York U.S.A. 105 E2 42 57N 76 34W
Auch France 61 B1 43 40N 0 36E
Auchengray Strathclyde Scotland 45 C1 55 46N 3 37W
Auchterarder Tayside Scotland 45 C2 56 18N 3 43W
Auchtermuchty Fife Scotland 45 D2 56 17N 3 15W
Auckland New Zealand 87 B3 36 55S 174 47E
Auckland Islands Southern Ocean 118 G2 50 35S 116 00E
Aude r. France 61 B1 43 00N 2 00E
Auden Ontario Canada 104 C4 50 14N 87 54W
Audenshaw Greater Manchester England 42 D2 53 29N 2 06W
Audley Staffordshire England 36 B3 53 03N 2 20W
Aue G.D.R. 63 B2 50 35N 12 42E
Aughton Lancashire England 42 B2 53 33N 2 55W
Aughton South Yorkshire England 43 G2 53 22N 1 19W
Augsburg F.R.G. 63 B1 48 21N 10 54E
Augusta Australia 86 B3 34 19S 115 09E
Augusta Georgia U.S.A. 103 J3 33 29N 82 00W
Augusta Maine U.S.A. 105 G2 44 17N 69 50W
Auldhouse Strathclyde Scotland 45 B1 55 43N 4 12W
Aulnay-sous-Bois France 60 C2 48 57N 2 31E
Aulne r. France 61 A2 48 10N 4 00W
Aurangābād India 77 D3 19 52N 75 22E
Aurich F.R.G. 63 A2 53 28N 7 29E
Aurillac France 61 B1 44 56N 2 26E
Aurora Illinois U.S.A. 104 C2 41 45N 88 20W
Aurora Indiana U.S.A. 104 D1 39 03N 84 55W
Aurora Ontario Canada 105 E2 43 00N 79 28W
Au Sable r. Michigan U.S.A. 105 D2 45 00N 84 00W
Austerfield South Yorkshire England 43 G2 53 27N 1 00W
Austin Brazil 116 A3 22 43S 43 31W
Austin Minnesota U.S.A. 104 B2 43 40N 92 58W
Austin Texas U.S.A. 103 G3 30 18N 97 47W
AUSTRALIA 86
Australian Capital Territory (A.C.T.) admin. Australia 86 H2 35 00S 144 00E
Austral Ridge Pacific Ocean 119 K5 24 00S 155 30W
AUSTRIA 69 B2
Autlān Mexico 108 D3 19 48N 104 20W
Autun France 61 B2 46 58N 4 18E
Auxerre France 61 B2 47 48N 3 35E
Auyuittuq National Park Northwest Territories
Avallon France 61 B2 47 30N 3 54E
Avebury Wiltshire England 31 F3 51 27N 1 51W
Aveiro Portugal 66 A3 40 38N 8 40W
Aveley Essex England 34 D2 51 30N 0 15E
Avellaneda Argentina 115 F6 34 40S 58 20W
Avesnes-sur-Helpe France 64 C2 50 08N 3 57E
Avesta Sweden 67 D3 60 09N 16 10E
Aveyron r. France 61 B1 44 30N 2 05E
Avezzano Italy 68 B3 42 02N 13 26E
Aviemore Highland Scotland 46 E4 57 12N 3 50W

Boldon Tyne and Wear England **44** C1 54 57N 1 27W
Bolesławiec Poland **69** C3 51 16N 34E
Bolgatanga Ghana **93** E5 10 44N 0 53W
Bolgrad U.S.S.R. **69** E2 45 42N 28 35E
Bolivar, Pico *mt.* Venezuela **114** C14 8 33N 71 03W
BOLIVIA 114 E9
Bollin *r.* Cheshire England **42** D1 53 18N 2 10W
Bollington Cheshire England **42** D1 53 18N 2 06W
Bollnäs Sweden **67** D3 61 20N 16 25E
Bolmen *l.* Sweden **67** C2 56 55N 13 45E
Bologna Italy **68** B3 44 30N 11 20E
Bolsover Derbyshire England **43** G1 53 15N 1 17W
Bolton Greater Manchester England **42** C2 53 35N 2 26W
Bolus Head *c.* Irish Republic **48** A1 51 45N 10 10W
Bolzano Italy **68** B4 46 30N 11 22E
Bom Jesus da Lapa Brazil **114** I10 13 16S 43 23W
Boma Zaïre **95** B6 5 50S 13 03E
Bombay India **77** C3 18 56N 72 51E
Bomu *r.* Central Africa **94** D8 4 50N 24 00E
Bonaire *i.* Lesser Antilles **109** K2 12 15N 68 27W
Bonaparte Archipelago Australia **86** D7 19 00S 126 00E
Bonar Bridge *tn.* Highland Scotland **46** D4 57 53N 4 21W
Bondo Zaïre **94** D8 1 22S 23 54E
Bo'ness Central Scotland **45** C2 56 01N 3 37W
Bongor Chad **94** C10 10 18N 15 20E
Bonhill Strathclyde Scotland **45** A1 55 59N 4 34W
Bonifacio Corsica **61** C1 41 23N 9 10E
Bonn F.R.G. **63** A2 50 44N 7 06E
Bonny, Bight of *b.* W. Africa **93** G3 2 10N 7 30E
Bonnybridge Central Scotland **45** C1 55 59N 3 54W
Bonnyrigg Lothian Scotland **45** D1 55 52N 3 08W
Bonthe Sierra Leone **93** C4 7 32N 12 30W
Boorama Somalia **94** H9 9 56N 43 13E
Boosaaso Somalia **94** I10 11 18N 49 10E
Boothia, Gulf of Northwest Territories Canada **101** R6 69 00N 88 00W
Boothia Peninsula Northwest Territories Canada **101** Q7 70 30N 94 30W
Bootle Cumbria England **44** A1 54 17N 3 23W
Bootle Merseyside England **42** A2 53 28N 3 00W
Borås Sweden **67** C2 57 44N 12 55E
Bordeaux France **61** A1 44 50N 0 34W
Borden Peninsula Northwest Territories Canada **101** S7 73 00N 82 30W
Border Forest Park Northumberland England **44** B2 55 17N 2 30W
Borders *reg.* Scotland **46** F2 55 30N 3 00W
Bordon Camp Hampshire England **33** B2 51 07N 0 53W
Borehamwood Hertfordshire England **34** C2 51 40N 0 16W
Borgholm Sweden **67** D2 56 51N 16 40E
Borislav U.S.S.R. **69** D2 49 18N 23 28E
Borisov U.S.S.R. **69** E3 54 09N 28 30E
Borken F.R.G. **64** F3 51 50N 6 52E
Borkum F.R.G. **63** A2 53 35N 6 40E
Borkum *i.* F.R.G. **63** A2 53 00N 6 00E
Borlänge Sweden **67** D3 60 29N 15 25E
Bormida di Spigno *r.* Italy **61** C1 44 17N 8 14E
Borneo *i.* Asia **80** E4 0 00 114 00E
Bornholm *i.* Denmark **67** C2 55 02N 15 00E
Boroughbridge North Yorkshire England **40** C3 54 05N 1 24W
Borough Green Kent England **34** D1 51 17N 0 19E
Borrowash Derbyshire England **35** D3 52 55N 1 24W
Bor Sudan **94** F9 6 18N 31 34E
Borth Dyfed Wales **38** B2 52 29N 4 03W
Borūjerd Iran **79** G5 33 55N 48 48E
Borzya U.S.S.R. **71** N6 50 24N 116 35E
Boscastle Cornwall England **30** C2 50 41N 4 42W
Boskoop Netherlands **65** C2 52 04N 4 39E
Bosna *r.* Yugoslavia **68** C3 45 00N 18 00E
Bosphorus *sd.* Europe/Asia **51** 41 00N 29 00E
Bossangoa Central African Republic **94** C9 6 27N 17 21E
Bosso Niger **93** H5 13 43N 13 19E
Boston Lincolnshire England **36** D2 52 59N 0 01W
Boston Massachusetts U.S.A. **105** F2 42 20N 71 05W
Boston Mountains Arkansas U.S.A. **103** H4 36 00N 94 00W
Boston Spa West Yorkshire England **43** F3 53 54N 1 21W
Botafogo Brazil **116** C2 22 57S 43 11W
Bothnia, Gulf of Sweden/Finland **67** D3 61 00N 19 10E
Botlek Netherlands **65** B1 51 53N 4 17E
Botley Buckinghamshire England **34** B3 51 43N 0 35W
Botoşani Romania **69** E2 47 44N 26 41E
Botrange *sum.* Belgium **64** F2 50 30N 6 05E
BOTSWANA 95 D3
Bottesford Leicestershire England **36** D2 52 56N 0 48W
Bottrop F.R.G. **62** B3 51 31N 6 55E
Bouaké Côte d'Ivoire **93** D4 7 42N 5 00W
Bouar Central African Republic **94** C9 5 58N 15 35E
Bouârfa Morocco **93** E9 32 30N 1 59W
Boucherville Québec Canada **105** F3 45 00N 73 00W
Boufarik Algeria **66** C2 36 36N 2 54E
Bougainville Island Papua New Guinea **86** J8 6 50S 155 00E
Bougouni Mali **93** D5 11 25N 7 28W
Bougzoul Algeria **66** C2 35 42N 2 51E
Bouillon Belgium **64** E1 49 47N 5 04E
Boulder Colorado U.S.A. **102** E5 40 02N 105 16W
Bouligny France **64** E1 49 16N 5 40E
Boulogne-Billancourt France **60** B2 48 50N 2 15E
Boulogne-sur-Mer France **61** B3 50 43N 1 37E
Bourem Mali **93** E6 16 59N 0 20W
Bourg-en-Bresse France **61** C2 46 12N 5 13E
Bourges France **61** B2 47 05N 2 23E
Bourke Australia **86** H3 30 09S 145 59E
Bourne Lincolnshire England **36** D2 52 46N 0 23W
Bourne End Buckinghamshire England **34** A2 51 34N 0 42W
Bournemouth Dorset England **31** F2 50 43N 1 54W
Bournville West Midlands England **35** C2 52 25N 1 56W
Bourton-on-the-Water Gloucestershire England **31** F3 51 53N 1 46W
Bou Saâda Algeria **93** F10 35 10N 4 09E
Bousso Chad **94** C10 10 32N 16 45E
Bouvet Island Southern Ocean **117** I1 54 26S 3 24E
Bovey *r.* Devon England **31** D2 50 40N 3 50W
Bovey Tracey Devon England **31** D2 50 36N 3 40W
Bovingdon Hertfordshire England **34** B3 51 44N 0 32W
Bowen Australia **86** H6 20 00S 148 10E
Bowes Durham England **44** B1 54 30N 2 01W
Bowland, Forest of *hills* Lancashire England **42** C3 54 00N 2 35W
Bowling Green Kentucky U.S.A. **104** C1 37 00N 86 29W
Bowling Green Missouri U.S.A. **104** B1 39 21N 91 11W
Bowling Green Ohio U.S.A. **105** D2 41 22N 83 40W
Bowman North Dakota U.S.A. **102** F6 46 11N 103 26W
Bowmore Strathclyde Scotland **46** B2 55 45N 6 17W
Bowness-on-Windermere Cumbria England **44** B1 54 22N 2 55W
Boxmeer Netherlands **64** E3 51 39N 5 57E
Boxtel Netherlands **64** E3 51 36N 5 20E
Boyle Roscommon Irish Republic **48** C3 53 58N 8 18W
Boyne *r.* Irish Republic **48** E3 53 40N 6 35W
Boyoma Falls Zaïre **94** E8 0 18N 25 30E
Bozeman Montana U.S.A. **102** D6 45 40N 111 00W
Bozoum Central African Republic **94** C9 6 16N 16 22E
Braase-mermeer *l.* Netherlands **65** C2 52 13N 4 38E
Brabant *admin.* Belgium **64** D2 50 45N 4 30E
Brabourne Lees Kent England **33** D2 51 08N 1 00E
Brač *i.* Yugoslavia **68** C3 43 00N 16 00E
Brackley Northamptonshire England **36** C2 52 02N 1 09W
Bracknell Berkshire England **34** A2 51 26N 0 46W
Braco Tayside Scotland **45** C2 56 16N 3 54W
Bradenton Florida U.S.A. **103** J2 27 29N 82 33W
Bradford Pennsylvania U.S.A. **105** E2 41 57N 78 39W
Bradford West Yorkshire England **43** E3 53 48N 1 45W
Bradford-on-Avon Wiltshire England **31** E3 51 22N 2 15W
Bradshaw Greater Manchester **42** C2 53 36N 2 24W
Bradwell Derbyshire England **43** E1 53 20N 1 45W
Bradwell-on-Sea Essex England **33** C2 51 44N 0 54E
Bradworthy Devon England **31** C2 50 54N 4 24W
Brady Texas U.S.A. **102** G3 31 08N 99 22W
Braehead Strathclyde Scotland **45** C1 55 44N 3 40W
Braemar Grampian Scotland **46** E4 57 01N 3 23W
Braga Portugal **66** A3 41 32N 8 26W
Bragança Brazil **114** H12 1 02S 46 46W
Bragança Portugal **66** A3 41 47N 6 46W
Brahmapur India **77** E3 19 21N 84 51E
Brahmaputra *r.* India **77** G5 26 40N 93 00E
Braidwood Strathclyde Scotland **45** C1 55 42N 3 50W
Brăila Romania **69** E2 45 17N 27 58E
Brailsford Derbyshire England **35** D3 52 59N 1 36W
Braine l'Alleud Belgium **64** D2 50 41N 4 22E
Brainerd Minnesota U.S.A. **104** B3 46 20N 94 10W
Braintree Essex England **33** C2 51 53N 0 32E
Braithwell South Yorkshire England **43** G2 53 27N 1 12W
Bramcote Warwickshire England **35** D2 52 56N 1 15W
Bramhall Greater Manchester England **42** D2 53 23N 2 10W
Bramham West Yorkshire England **43** F3 53 53N 1 21W
Bramhope West Yorkshire England **43** F3 53 53N 1 37W
Bramley South Yorkshire England **43** G2 53 26N 1 15W
Bramley Surrey England **34** B1 51 11N 0 35W
Brampton Cumbria England **44** B1 54 57N 2 43W
Brampton Ontario Canada **105** E2 43 42N 79 46W
Brampton South Yorkshire England **43** F2 53 30N 1 22W
Brandenburg G.D.R. **63** B2 52 25N 12 34E
Branderburgh Grampian Scotland **46** E4 57 43N 3 18W
Brandon Durham England **44** C1 54 46N 1 38W
Brandon Manitoba Canada **101** P2 49 50W 99 57W
Brandon Suffolk England **33** C3 52 27N 0 37E
Brandon Vermont U.S.A. **105** F2 43 47N 73 05W
Brandon Mountain Irish Republic **48** A2 52 10N 10 10W
Brandon Point *c.* Irish Republic **48** A2 52 15N 10 05W
Brantford Ontario Canada **105** D2 43 09N 80 17W
Brasileia Brazil **114** D10 10 59S 68 45W
Brasilia Brazil **114** H9 15 45S 47 57W
Braşov Romania **69** E2 45 39N 25 35E
Brasschaat Belgium **64** D3 51 17N 4 30E
Bratislava Czechoslovakia **69** C2 48 10N 17 10E
Bratsk U.S.S.R. **71** M7 56 20N 101 50E
Bratsk Reservoir U.S.S.R. **71** M7 56 00N 102 00E
Brattleboro Vermont U.S.A. **105** F2 42 51N 75 36W
Braughing Hertfordshire England **34** D3 51 55N 0 01E
Braunau Austria **63** B1 48 16N 13 03E
Braunschweig F.R.G. **63** B2 52 15N 10 30E
Braunton Devon England **31** C3 51 07N 4 10W
Brawley California U.S.A. **102** C3 32 59N 115 30W
Bray Berkshire England **34** A2 51 30N 0 42W
Bray Wicklow Irish Republic **49** B1 53 12N 6 06W
Bray Head *c.* Irish Republic **49** B1 53 12N 6 05W
Bray Head *c.* Irish Republic **48** A1 51 50N 10 15W
Brayton North Yorkshire England **43** G3 53 46N 1 06W
BRAZIL 114 G10
Brazil Basin Atlantic Ocean **117** F5 10 00S 26 00W
Brazilian Highlands Brazil **110** 10 00S 50 00W
Brazil Plateau Brazil **110** 20 00S 45 00W
Brazos *r.* Texas U.S.A. **103** G3 32 00N 97 00W
Brazzaville Congo **92** A2 4 14S 15 14E
Brdy *mts.* Czechoslovakia **63** B1 49 00N 14 00E
Brea Reservoir California U.S.A. **107** C2 33 54N 117 56W
Breaston Derbyshire England **36** C2 52 56N 1 12W
Brechin Tayside Scotland **46** F3 56 44N 2 40W
Breckenridge Minnesota U.S.A. **104** A3 46 14N 96 35W
Breckland *geog. reg.* Norfolk England **33** C3 52 30N 0 50E
Brecon Powys Wales **38** C1 51 57N 3 24W
Brecon Beacons National Park Powys Wales **38** C2 51 53N 3 30W
Breda Netherlands **64** D3 51 35N 4 46E
Bredbury Greater Manchester England **42** D2 53 25N 2 07W
Bregenz Austria **63** A1 47 31N 9 46E
Breidha Fjördur *b.* Iceland **67** H7 65 15N 23 00W
Brekstad Norway **67** B3 63 50N 9 50E
Bremen *admin.* F.R.G. **63** A2 53 00N 9 00E
Bremen F.R.G. **63** A2 53 05N 8 48E
Bremerhaven F.R.G. **63** A2 53 33N 8 35E
Bremerton Washington U.S.A. **102** B6 47 34N 122 40W
Breña Peru **116** E4 12 04S 77 04W
Brenham Texas U.S.A. **103** G3 30 09N 96 24W
Brenig Reservoir Clwyd Wales **38** C3 53 28N 3 32W
Brenner Pass Austria / Italy **69** B2 47 02N 11 32E
Brent Greater Manchester England **34** C2 51 34N 0 17W
Brentford Greater London England **34** C2 51 29N 0 19W
Brent Pelham Hertfordshire England **34** D3 51 57N 0 05E
Brentwood Essex England **34** D2 51 38N 0 18E
Brescia Italy **68** B4 45 33N 10 13E
Bressay *i.* Shetland Islands Scotland **47** B2 60 08N 1 05W
Brest France **61** A2 48 23N 4 30W
Brest U.S.S.R. **70** E6 52 08N 23 40E
Bretherton Lancashire England **42** B3 53 41N 2 48W
Brewerton New York U.S.A. **105** E2 43 15N 76 09W
Brewood Staffordshire England **35** B3 52 41N 2 10W
Brezhnev *see* Naberezhnyye Chelny
Bria Central African Republic **94** D9 6 32N 22 00E
Briançon France **61** C1 44 53N 6 39E
Bricket Wood Hertfordshire England **34** B3 51 43N 0 22W
Bride Isle of Man England **41** F1 54 23N 4 24W
Bridgend Lothian Scotland **45** C1 55 58N 3 32W
Bridgend Mid Glamorgan Wales **38** C1 51 31N 3 35W
Bridgend Strathclyde Scotland **45** B1 55 55N 4 05W
Bridge of Allan *tn.* Central Scotland **45** C2 56 09N 3 58W
Bridge of Weir *tn.* Strathclyde Scotland **45** A1 55 52N 4 35W
Bridgeport Connecticut U.S.A. **105** F2 41 12N 73 12W
Bridgeton New Jersey U.S.A. **105** E1 39 26N 75 14W
Bridgetown Barbados **109** M2 13 06N 59 37W
Bridgnorth Shropshire England **35** A2 52 33N 2 25W
Bridgwater Somerset England **31** D3 51 08N 3 00W
Bridgwater Bay Somerset England **31** D3 51 15N 3 20W
Bridlington Humberside England **40** D3 54 05N 0 12W
Bridlington Bay Humberside England **40** D3 54 03N 0 10W
Bridport Dorset England **31** E2 50 44N 2 46W
Brie-Comte-Robert France **60** C1 48 41N 2 37E
Brielle Netherlands **65** A1 51 54N 4 09E
Brielse Meer *l.* Netherlands **65** A1 51 56N 4 09E
Brienz Switzerland **61** C2 46 46N 8 02E
Brierfield Lancashire England **42** D2 53 50N 2 14W
Brierley Hill *tn.* West Midlands England **35** B2 52 29N 2 07W
Briey France **61** C2 49 15N 5 57E
Brig Switzerland **61** C2 46 19N 8 00E
Brigg Humberside England **40** D2 53 34N 0 30W
Brigham City Utah U.S.A. **102** D5 41 30N 112 02W
Brighouse West Yorkshire England **43** E3 53 42N 1 47W
Brightlingsea Essex England **33** D2 51 49N 1 02E
Brighton East Sussex England **33** B1 50 50N 0 10W
Brighton Beach *tn.* New York U.S.A. **106** C1 40 34N 73 58W
Brignoles France **61** C1 43 25N 6 03E
Brimington Derbyshire England **43** F1 53 16N 1 23W
Brindisi Italy **68** C3 40 37N 17 57E
Brinsworth South Yorkshire England **43** F2 53 23N 1 22W
Brisbane Australia **86** I4 27 30S 153 00E
Bristol Avon England **31** E3 51 27N 2 35W
Bristol Bay Alaska U.S.A. **100** D4 57 30N 159 00W
Bristol Channel England/Wales **31** D3 51 20N 3 50W
British Columbia *province* Canada **100** J4 56 50N 125 30W
British Mountains U.S.A./Canada **100** G6 65 40N 142 30W
Briton Ferry *tn.* West Glamorgan Wales **38** C1 51 38N 3 49W
Britt Ontario Canada **105** D3 45 46N 80 35W
Brittany Peninsula France **51** 48 00N 4 00W
Brittas Dublin Irish Republic **49** A1 53 14N 6 27W
Brive-la-Gaillarde France **61** B2 45 09N 1 32E
Brixham Devon England **31** D2 50 23N 3 30W
Brixton Greater London England **34** C2 51 28N 0 06W
Brno Czechoslovakia **69** C2 49 13N 16 40E
Broad Bay Western Isles Scotland **46** B5 58 15N 6 10W
Broadford Highland Scotland **46** C4 57 14N 5 54W
Broadheath Hereford & Worcester England **35** B1 52 12N 2 19W
Broad Law *sum.* Borders Scotland **46** E2 55 30N 3 22W
Broad Meadow Water *r.* Irish Republic **49** B2 53 30N 6 15W
Broadstairs Kent England **33** D2 51 22N 1 27E
Broadstone Dorset England **31** E2 50 45N 2 00W
Broadway Hereford and Worcester England **36** C2 52 02N 1 50W
Brock *r.* Lancashire England **42** B3 53 53N 2 44W
Brockenhurst Hampshire England **32** A1 50 49N 1 34W
Brockham Surrey England **34** C1 51 14N 0 18W
Brockton Massachusetts U.S.A. **105** F2 42 06N 71 01W
Brockville Ontario Canada **105** E2 44 35N 75 44W
Brocton Staffordshire England **35** B3 52 48N 2 03W
Brodeur Peninsula Northwest Territories Canada **101** R7 72 00N 87 30W
Brodick Strathclyde Scotland **46** C2 55 35N 5 09W
Brody U.S.S.R. **69** E3 50 05N 25 08E
Broer Ruys, Cape Greenland **120** 73 30N 20 20W
Broken Hill *tn.* Australia **86** G3 31 57S 141 30E
Bromley Greater London England **34** D2 51 31N 0 01W
Bromsgrove Hereford and Worcester England **35** B1 50 20N 2 03W
Bromyard Hereford and Worcester England **36** B2 52 11N 2 30W
Brønnøysund Norway **67** C4 65 38N 12 15E
Bronx New York U.S.A. **105** F2 40 50N 73 52W
Brookfield Strathclyde Scotland **45** A1 55 51N 4 32W
Brookhouse Lancashire England **42** B4 54 06N 2 42W
Brookings South Dakota U.S.A. **104** A2 44 19N 96 47W
Brooklyn New York U.S.A. **106** C1 40 41N 73 57W
Brookmans Park Hertfordshire England **34** C3 51 43N 0 11W
Brooks Alberta Canada **100** M3 50 35N 111 54W
Brooks Range *mts.* Alaska U.S.A. **100** E6 67 55N 155 00W
Brookville Pennsylvania U.S.A. **105** E2 41 10N 79 06W
Broome Australia **86** C6 17 58S 122 15E
Brora Highland Scotland **46** E5 58 01N 3 51W
Broseley Shropshire England **35** A2 52 37N 2 29W
Brotton Cleveland England **44** D1 54 34N 0 56W
Brough Cumbria England **44** B1 54 32N 2 19W
Brough Humberside England **40** D2 53 44N 0 35W
Broughshane Antrim Northern Ireland **48** E4 54 54N 6 12W
Broughton Buckinghamshire England **34** A4 52 04N 0 42W
Broughton Clwyd Wales **38** C3 53 10N 3 00W
Broughton Lancashire England **42** B3 53 49N 2 44W
Broughton in Furness Cumbria England **44** A1 54 17N 3 13W
Broughty Ferry *tn.* Tayside Scotland **46** F3 56 28N 2 53W
Brown Clee Hill Shropshire England **36** B2 52 27N 2 35W
Brownhills West Midlands England **35** C2 52 39N 1 55W
Browning Montana U.S.A. **102** D6 48 33N 113 00W
Brown's Town Jamaica **109** Q8 18 28N 77 22W
Browns Valley *tn.* Minnesota U.S.A. **104** A3 45 35N 96 50W
Brownsville Texas U.S.A. **103** G2 25 54N 97 30W
Brown Willy *sum.* Cornwall England **30** C2 50 35N 4 36W
Brownwood Texas U.S.A. **102** G3 31 42N 98 59W
Broxburn Lothian Scotland **45** D1 55 57N 3 29W
Bruay-en-Artois France **61** B3 50 29N 2 33E
Bruce Mines *tn.* Ontario Canada **105** D3 46 19N 83 48W
Bruce Peninsula Ontario Canada **105** D3 45 00N 81 20W
Bruchsal F.R.G. **63** A1 49 07N 8 35E
Brue *r.* Somerset England **31** E3 51 10N 2 50W
Bruges *see* Brugge
Brugg Switzerland **66** C2 47 29N 8 13E
Brugge *(Bruges)* Belgium **64** C3 51 13N 3 14E
Brühl F.R.G. **64** F2 50 50N 6 55E
BRUNEI 80 E4
Brunoy France **60** C1 48 40N 2 31E
Brunssum Netherlands **64** E2 50 57N 5 59E
Brunswick Georgia U.S.A. **103** J3 31 09N 81 30W
Brunswick Maine U.S.A. **105** G2 43 55N 69 59W
Brunton Fife Scotland **45** D2 56 23N 3 08W
Brussel *see* Bruxelles
Brussels *see* Bruxelles
Bruton Somerset England **31** E3 51 07N 2 27W
Bruxelles *(Brussel, Brussels)* Belgium **64** D2 50 50N 4 21E
Bryan Texas U.S.A. **103** G3 30 41N 96 24W
Bryansk U.S.S.R. **70** F6 53 15N 34 09E
Bryher *i.* Isles of Scilly England **30** A1 49 57N 6 21W
Brymbo Clwyd Wales **38** C3 53 05N 3 03W
Brynamman Dyfed Wales **38** C1 51 49N 3 52W
Brynmawr Gwent Wales **38** C1 51 49N 3 11W
Brzeg Poland **69** C3 50 52N 17 27E
Bū Ağri Daği *(Mt. Ararat)* Turkey **78** F6 39 44N 44 15E
Bucaramanga Colombia **114** C14 7 08N 73 10W
Buchanan Liberia **93** C4 5 57N 10 02W
Buchan Ness *c.* Grampian Scotland **46** G4 57 28N 1 47W
Bucharest *see* Bucureşti
Buchlyvie Central Scotland **45** B2 56 07N 4 18W
Bucholz F.R.G. **62** 51 25N 6 45E
Buckfastleigh Devon England **31** D2 50 29N 3 46W
Buckhaven Fife Scotland **45** D2 56 11N 3 03W
Buckie Grampian Scotland **46** F4 57 40N 2 58W
Buckingham Buckinghamshire England **33** B2 52 00N 1 00W
Buckingham Québec Canada **105** E3 45 35N 75 25W
Buckinghamshire *co.* England **33** B3 51 50N 0 50W
Buckley Clwyd Wales **38** C3 53 10N 3 05W
Bucknall Staffordshire England **35** B4 53 02N 2 09W
Bucksport Maine U.S.A. **105** G2 44 35N 68 47W
Bucureşti *(Bucharest)* Romania **69** E1 44 25N 26 07E
Budapest Hungary **69** C2 47 30N 19 03E
Bude Cornwall England **30** C2 50 50N 4 33W
Bude Bay Cornwall England **30** C2 50 50N 4 40W
Büderich F.R.G. **62** A1 51 15N 6 20E
Budjala Zaïre **94** C8 2 38N 19 48E
Budleigh Salterton Devon England **31** D2 50 38N 3 20W
Buea Cameroon **93** G3 4 09N 9 13E
Buena Park *tn.* California U.S.A. **107** B2 33 52N 118 02W
Buenaventura Mexico **108** C5 29 50N 107 30W
Buenos Aires Argentina **115** F6 34 40S 58 30W
Buenos Aires, Lake Argentina/Chile **115** C3 47 00S 72 00W
Buer F.R.G. **62** C3 51 35N 7 05E
Buffalo New York U.S.A. **105** E2 42 52N 78 55W
Buffalo Lake Northwest Territories Canada **100** L5 60 40N 115 30W
Buffalo Narrows *tn.* Saskatchewan Canada **100** N4 55 52N 108 28W
Buffalo River *tn.* Northwest Territories Canada **100** M5 61 20N 114 30W
Buffalo Wyoming U.S.A. **102** E5 44 21N 106 40W
Buff Bay *tn.* Jamaica **109** R8 18 18N 76 40W
Bug *r.* Europe **69** D3 51 00N 24 00E
Builth Wells Powys Wales **38** C2 52 09N 3 24W
Bujumbura Burundi **95** E7 3 22S 29 19E
Bukachacha U.S.S.R. **71** N6 53 00N 116 58E
Bukama Zaïre **95** E6 9 13S 25 52E
Bukavu Zaïre **94** E7 2 30S 28 50E
Bukhara U.S.S.R. **70** I3 39 47N 64 26E
Bukittinggi Indonesia **80** C3 0 18S 100 20E
Bukoba Tanzania **94** F7 1 19S 31 49E
Bula Indonesia **80** I3 3 07S 130 27E
Bulandshahr India **77** D5 28 30N 77 49E
Bulawayo Zimbabwe **95** E3 20 10S 28 43E
Bulford Wiltshire England **33** F3 51 12N 1 46W
BULGARIA Europe **68** D3
Bulkington Warwickshire England **35** D2 52 28N 1 25W
Bull Shoals Lake U.S.A. **103** H4 36 00N 93 00W
Buller *r.* New Zealand **87** B2 41 50S 172 20E
Bulun U.S.S.R. **71** O10 70 45N 127 20E
Bumba Zaïre **94** D8 2 10N 22 30E
Bumbu *r.* Zaïre **92** A1 4 22S 15 18E
Bunbury Australia **86** B3 33 20S 115 34E
Bunclody Wexford Irish Republic **48** E2 52 38N 6 40W
Buncrana Donegal Irish Republic **48** D5 55 08N 7 27W
Bundaberg Australia **86** I5 24 50S 152 21E
Bundoran Donegal Irish Republic **48** C4 54 28N 8 17W
Bungay Suffolk England **33** D3 52 28N 1 26E
Bungo-suido *sd.* Japan **82** B1 33 00N 132 30E
Bunia Zaïre **94** F8 1 33N 30 13E
Bura Kenya **94** H7 1 06S 39 58E
Buraydah Saudi Arabia **78** F4 26 20N 43 59E
Burbage Leicestershire England **35** D2 52 31N 1 20W
Burbank California U.S.A. **107** A3 34 10N 118 25W
Burdur Turkey **78** D6 37 44N 30 17E
Bure *r.* Norfolk England **33** D3 52 47N 1 20E
Bureya *r.* U.S.S.R. **71** P6 52 00N 133 00E
Burford Oxfordshire England **32** A2 51 49N 1 38W
Burg G.D.R. **63** B2 52 17N 11 51E
Burgas Bulgaria **68** E3 42 30N 27 29E
Burgess Hill West Sussex England **33** B1 50 58N 0 08W
Burghead *tn.* Grampian Scotland **46** E4 57 42N 3 30W
Burgh le Marsh Lincolnshire England **36** E3 53 10N 0 15E
Burgos Spain **66** B3 42 21N 3 41W
Burham Beeches Buckinghamshire England **34** B2 51 33N 0 36W
Burhanpur India **77** D4 21 18N 76 08E
Burhou *i.* Channel Islands British Isles **31** G6 49 43N 2 15W
Buri Khali India **76** J2 22 30N 88 10E
BURKINA 93 E5
Burks Falls *tn.* Ontario U.S.A. **105** E3 45 37N 79 25W
Burley in Wharfedale West Yorkshire England **43** E3 53 55N 1 45W
Burlington Colorado U.S.A. **102** F4 39 17N 102 17W
Burlington Iowa U.S.A. **104** B2 40 50N 91 07W
Burlington Ontario Canada **105** E2 43 19N 79 48W
Burlington Vermont U.S.A. **105** F2 44 28N 73 14W
Burlington West Virginia U.S.A. **105** E1 39 20N 78 56W
Burlington Wisconsin U.S.A. **104** C2 42 41N 88 17W
BURMA *see* MYANMA
Burnfoot Tayside Scotland **45** C2 56 13N 3 37W
Burnham Market Norfolk England **33** C3 52 57N 0 44E
Burnham on Crouch Essex England **33** C2 51 38N 0 49E
Burnham-on-Sea Somerset England **31** D3 51 15N 3 00W
Burnie Australia **86** H1 41 03S 145 55E
Burnley Lancashire England **42** D3 53 48N 2 14W
Burnsall North Yorkshire England **43** E4 54 03N 1 57W
Burntisland *tn.* Fife Scotland **45** D2 56 03N 3 15W
Burntwood Staffordshire England **35** C3 52 40N 1 56W
Burry Port Dyfed Wales **38** D1 51 42N 4 15W
Bursa Turkey **78** C7 40 12N 29 04E
Bur Safâga Egypt **78** D4 26 43N 33 55E
Burscough Bridge *tn.* Lancashire England **42** B2 53 37N 2 51W
Burslem Staffordshire England **35** B4 53 02N 2 12W
Burston Staffordshire England **35** B3 52 52N 2 05W
Burton Cheshire England **42** A1 53 16N 3 02W
Burton Agnes Humberside England **40** D3 54 03N 0 19W
Burton Latimer Northamptonshire England **36** D2 52 22N 0 40W
Burton upon Trent Staffordshire England **35** D3 52 48N 1 36W

Buru *i.* Indonesia 80 H3 3 20S 126 30E
BURUNDI 95 E/F7
Burwell Cambridgeshire England 33 C3 52 16N 0 19E
Burwell Nebraska U.S.A. 102 G5 41 48N 99 09W
Bury Greater Manchester England 42 D2 53 36N 2 17W
Bury St. Edmunds Suffolk England 33 C3 52 15N 0 43E
Busby Strathclyde Scotland 45 B1 55 47N 4 16W
Büshehr Iran 79 H4 28 57N 50 52E
Bushey Hertfordshire England 34 B2 51 39N 0 22W
Bushmills Northern Ireland 48 E5 55 12N 6 32W
Busira *r.* Zaïre 94 C7 1 00S 20 00E
Bussum Netherlands 65 E3 52 16N 5 09E
Busto Arsizio Italy 68 A4 45 37N 8 51E
Buta Zaïre 94 D8 2 49N 24 50E
Butare Rwanda 94 F7 2 35S 29 44E
Bute *i.* Strathclyde Scotland 46 C2 55 50N 5 05W
Bute, Sound of Strathclyde Scotland 46 C2 55 45N 5 10W
Butler Pennsylvania U.S.A. 105 E2 40 51N 79 55W
Buton *i.* Indonesia 80 G3 5 00S 122 40E
Butovo U.S.S.R. 70 M1 55 30N 37 32E
Butte Montana U.S.A. 102 D6 46 00N 112 31W
Buttermere *l.* Cumbria England 44 A1 54 32N 3 16W
Buttershaw West Yorkshire England 43 E3 53 45N 1 49W
Buttevant Cork Irish Republic 48 C2 52 14N 8 40W
Butt of Lewis *c.* Western Isles Scotland 46 B5 58 30N 6 20W
Butuan The Philippines 80 H5 8 56N 125 31E
Buulobarde Somalia 94 I8 3 50N 45 33E
Buxtehude F.R.G. 63 A2 53 29N 9 42E
Buxton Derbyshire England 43 E1 53 15N 1 55W
Bydgoszoz Poland 69 C3 53 16N 18 00E
Byfield Northamptonshire England 36 C2 52 11N 1 14W
Byfleet Surrey England 34 B1 51 21N 0 29W
Bygland Norway 67 B2 58 50N 7 49E
Bylot Island Northwest Territories Canada 101 T7 73 30N 79 00W
Byrd Land *geog. reg.* Antarctica 121 77 00S 130 00W
Byrranga Mountains U.S.S.R. 71 L10 75 00N 100 00E
Bytom Poland 69 C3 50 21N 18 51E

C

Cabanatuan The Philippines 80 G7 15 30N 120 58E
Cabano Québec Canada 105 G3 47 40N 68 56W
Cabimas Venezuela 114 C15 10 26N 71 27W
Cabinda *admin.* Angola 95 B6 5 30S 12 20E
Cabo Brazil 114 J11 8 16S 35 00W
Cabo Blanco *c.* Costa Rica 109 G1 9 36N 85 06W
Cabo Caballeria *c.* Balearic Islands 66 F5 40 05N 4 05E
Cabo Catoche *c.* Mexico 109 G4 21 38N 87 08W
Cabo Corrientes *c.* Colombia 114 B14 5 29N 77 36W
Cabo Corrientes *c.* Mexico 108 C4 20 25N 105 42W
Cabo d'Artrutx Balearic Islands (Spain) 66 E4 39 55N 3 49E
Cabo de Barberia *c.* Balearic Islands 66 D4 38 40N 1 20E
Cabo de Cala Figuera *c.* Balearic Islands 66 E4 39 27N 2 31E
Cabo de Creus *c.* Spain 66 C3 42 19N 3 19E
Cabo de Finisterre *c.* Spain 66 A3 42 52N 9 16W
Cabo de Formentor *c.* Balearic Islands 66 E4 39 58N 3 13E
Cabo de Gata *c.* Spain 66 B2 36 44N 2 10W
Cabo de Hornos *(Cape Horn)* Chile 115 D1 56 00S 67 15W
Cabo de la Nao *c.* Spain 66 C2 38 44N 0 14E
Cabo Delgado *c.* Mozambique 95 H5 10 45S 40 45E
Cabo de Palos *c.* Spain 66 B2 37 38N 0 40W
Cabo de Peñas *c.* Spain 66 A3 43 39N 5 50W
Cabo de Salinas *c.* Balearic Islands 66 E4 39 16N 3 04E
Cabo de São Vicente *c.* Portugal 66 A2 37 01N 8 59W
Cabo de Tortosa *c.* Spain 66 C3 40 44N 0 54E
Cabo Dos Bahías *c.* Argentina 115 D4 45 00S 65 30W
Cabo Espichel *c.* Portugal 66 A2 38 24N 9 13W
Cabo Falso *c.* Mexico 108 B4 22 50N 110 00W
Cabo Freu Balearic Islands 66 E4 39 45N 3 27E
Cabo Gracias á Dios *c.* Nicaragua 109 H3 15 00N 83 10W
Cabo Guardafui *c.* Somalia 94 J10 11 49N 51 15E
Cabonga Réservoir Québec Canada 105 E3 47 00N 76 00W
Cabo Orange *c.* Brazil 114 G13 4 25N 51 32W
Cabo Ortegal *c.* Spain 66 A3 43 46N 7 54W
Cabora Bassa Dam Mozambique 95 F4 16 00S 33 00E
Caborca Mexico 108 B6 30 42N 112 10W
Cabo San Juan *c.* Argentina 115 E2 54 45S 63 46W
Cabo Santa Elena *c.* Costa Rica 109 G2 10 54N 85 56W
Cabot Strait Nova Scotia/Newfoundland Canada 101 W2 47 10N 59 30W
Cabo Virgenes *c.* Argentina 115 D2 52 20S 68 00W
Cabra Dublin Irish Republic 49 B2 53 22N 6 17W
Cabrera *i.* Balearic Islands 66 E4 39 00N 2 59E
Cabuçu Brazil 116 A2 22 46S 43 33W
Cabuçu *r.* Brazil 116 A2 22 55S 43 31W
Cabriel *r.* Spain 66 B2 39 20N 1 15W
Čačak Yugoslavia 68 D3 43 54N 20 22E
Cáceres Brazil 114 F9 16 05S 57 40W
Cáceres Spain 66 A2 39 29N 6 23W
Cachoeira Brazil 114 J10 12 35S 38 59W
Cachoeira do Sul Brazil 115 G6 30 03S 52 52W
Cachoeiro de Itapemirim Brazil 115 I8 20 51S 41 07W
Caddington Bedfordshire England 34 B3 51 52N 0 27W
Cader Idris *mt.* Gwynedd Wales 38 C2 52 42N 3 54W
Cadiz Spain 66 A2 36 32N 6 18W
Cadiz The Philippines 80 G6 10 57N 123 18E
Cádiz, Gulf of Spain 66 A2 36 30N 7 15W
Caen France 61 A2 49 11N 0 22W
Caerleon Gwent Wales 38 D1 51 37N 2 57W
Caernarfon Gwynedd Wales 38 B3 53 08N 4 16W
Caernarfon Bay Gwynedd Wales 38 B3 53 05N 4 30W
Caerphilly Mid Glamorgan Wales 38 C1 51 35N 3 14W
Caersws Powys Wales 38 C2 52 31N 3 26W
Cagayan de Oro The Philippines 80 G5 8 29N 124 40E
Cágliari Italy 68 A2 39 13N 9 08E
Caguas Puerto Rico 109 K3 18 41N 66 04W
Caha Mountains Irish Republic 48 B1 51 40N 9 40W
Cahir Tipperary Irish Republic 48 D2 52 21N 7 56W
Cahirciveen Kerry Irish Republic 48 A1 51 57N 10 13W
Cahore Point *c.* Wexford Irish Republic 48 E2 52 34N 6 11W
Cahors France 61 B1 44 28N 0 26E
Caicos Passage *sd.* West Indies 109 J4 22 20N 72 30W
Cairngorm *mt.* Grampian Scotland 46 E4 57 07N 3 40W
Cairngorms *mts.* Highland/Grampian Scotland 46 E4 57 10N 3 30W
Cairnryan Dumfries & Galloway Scotland 46 C1 54 58N 5 02W
Cairns Australia 86 H6 16 51S 145 43N
Cairo *(El Qâ'hira)* Egypt 78 D5 30 03N 31 15E
Cairo Illinois U.S.A. 104 C1 37 01N 89 09W
Caister-on-Sea Norfolk England 33 D3 52 39N 1 44E
Caistor Lincolnshire England 36 D3 53 30N 0 20W
Cajamarca Peru 114 B11 7 09S 78 32W
Cajàzeiras Brazil 114 J11 6 52S 38 31W
Caju Brazil 116 C2 22 53S 43 13W
Cakovec Yugoslavia 68 C4 46 24N 16 26E
Calabar Nigeria 93 G3 4 56N 8 22E
Calahorra Spain 66 B3 49 19N 1 58W
Calais France 61 B3 50 57N 1 52E
Calama Chile 115 D8 22 30S 68 55W
Calamar Colombia 114 C15 10 16N 74 55W
Calamian Group *is.* The Philippines 80 F6 12 00N 120 00E
Calapan The Philippines 80 G6 13 23N 121 10E
Calatayud Spain 66 B3 41 21N 1 39W
Calçoene Brazil 114 G13 2 30N 50 55W
Calcutta India 76 K2 22 30N 88 20E
Caldas da Rainha Portugal 66 A3 39 24N 9 08W
Calder *r.* Lancashire England 42 B3 53 55N 2 43W
Calder *r.* Lancashire England 42 C3 53 48N 2 22W
Calder *r.* West Yorkshire England 43 F3 53 42N 1 29W
Caldercruix Strathclyde Scotland 45 C1 55 53N 3 55W
Caldermill Strathclyde Scotland 45 B1 55 39N 4 08W
Caldew *r.* Cumbria England 44 A1 54 45N 3 00W
Caldey Island Dyfed Wales 38 B1 51 38N 4 42W
Caldicot Gwent Wales 38 D1 51 36N 2 45W
Caldwell Idaho U.S.A. 102 C5 43 39N 116 40W
Caldwell New Jersey U.S.A. 106 A2 40 49N 74 16W
Calf of Man *i.* Isle of Man British Isles 41 F1 54 03N 4 49W
Calgary Alberta Canada 100 M3 51 05N 114 05W
Cali Colombia 114 B13 3 24N 76 30W
Calicut India 77 D2 11 15N 75 45E
Caliente Nevada U.S.A. 102 D4 37 36N 114 31W
California Central Scotland 45 C1 55 58N 3 45W
California *state* U.S.A. 102 C4 35 00N 119 00W
Callan Kilkenny Irish Republic 48 D2 52 33N 7 23W
Callander Central Scotland 45 B2 56 15N 4 13W
Callao Peru 116 E4 12 04S 77 08W
Callington Cornwall England 31 C2 50 30N 4 18W
Calne Wiltshire England 31 F3 51 27N 2 00W
Calow Derbyshire England 43 F1 53 13N 1 24W
Caltanissetta Italy 68 B2 37 29N 14 04E
Calver Derbyshire England 43 F1 53 16N 1 38W
Calverton Nottinghamshire England 36 C3 53 03N 1 05W
Calvi Corsica 61 C1 42 34N 8 44E
Calvia Balearic Islands 66 E4 39 33N 2 29E
Calvinia Republic of South Africa 95 C1 31 25S 19 47E
Cam *r.* Cambridgeshire England 33 C3 52 20N 0 15E
Camaçari Brazil 114 J10 12 44S 38 16W
Camacupa Angola 95 C5 12 03S 17 50E
Camagüey Cuba 109 I4 21 25N 77 55W
Camberley Surrey England 34 A2 51 21N 0 45W
Camblesforth North Yorkshire England 43 G3 53 43N 1 02W
CAMBODIA *(KAMPUCHEA)* 80 C6
Camborne Cornwall England 30 B2 50 12N 5 19W
Cambrai France 61 B3 50 10N 3 14E
Cambrian Mountains Wales 38 C2 52 15N 3 45W
Cambridge Cambridgeshire England 33 C3 52 12N 0 07E
Cambridge Jamaica 109 Q8 18 18N 77 54W
Cambridge Maryland U.S.A. 103 K4 38 34N 76 04W
Cambridge New Zealand 87 C3 37 53S 175 29E
Cambridge Ohio U.S.A. 105 D2 40 02N 81 36W
Cambridge Ontario Canada 105 D2 43 22N 80 20W
Cambridge Bay *tn.* Northwest Territories Canada 101 N6 69 09N 105 00W
Cambridgeshire *co.* England 33 B3 52 30N 0 00
Cambusbarron Central Scotland 45 C2 56 07N 3 59W
Camden Greater London England 34 C2 51 33N 0 10W
Camden New Jersey U.S.A. 105 E1 39 57N 75 06W
Cameia National Park Angola 95 D5 12 00S 22 00E
Camel *r.* Cornwall England 30 C2 5 30N 4 40W
Camelford Cornwall England 30 C2 50 37N 4 41W
Camelon Central Scotland 45 C2 56 00N 3 50W
CAMEROON 93 H4
Cametá Brazil 114 H12 2 12S 49 30W
Camiri Bolivia 114 E8 20 08S 63 33W
Camocim Brazil 114 I12 2 55S 40 50W
Camorta *i.* Nicobar Islands 77 G1 7 30N 93 30E
Campbell Island Southern Ocean 118 G2 52 30S 169 10E
Campbell River *tn.* British Columbia Canada 100 J2 50 00N 125 18W
Campbellsville Kentucky U.S.A. 104 C1 37 20N 85 21W
Campbellton New Brunswick Canada 101 V2 48 00N 66 30W
Campbeltown Strathclyde Scotland 46 C2 55 26N 5 36W
Campeche Mexico 108 F3 19 50N 90 30W
Campina Grande Brazil 114 J11 7 15S 35 50W
Campinas Brazil 115 H8 22 54S 47 06W
Campine *see* Kempen land
Campoalegre Colombia 114 B13 2 49N 75 19W
Campobasso Italy 68 B3 41 33N 14 39E
Campo Grande Brazil 114 G8 20 24S 54 35W
Campo Grande Brazil 116 A2 22 55S 43 33W
Campo Maior Brazil 114 I12 4 50S 42 12W
Campo Mourão Brazil 115 G8 24 01S 52 24W
Campos Brazil 115 I8 21 46S 41 21W
Campos del Puerto Balearic Islands 66 E4 39 26N 3 01E
Campos Elyseos Brazil 116 B3 22 42S 43 16W
Campsie Fells *hills* Central Scotland 45 B2 56 00N 4 15W
Cam Ranh Vietnam 80 C6 11 54N 109 14E
CANADA 101/102
Canada Basin Arctic Ocean 120 80 00N 140 00W
Canadian *r.* U.S.A. 102 F4 35 00N 104 00W
Canadian Shield *mts.* Canada 119 Q13 50 00N 90 00W
Canakkale Turkey 78 C7 40 09N 26 25E
Canal de l'Ourcq France 60 C2 48 55N 2 32E
Canal des Ardennes France 64 D1 49 50N 4 30E
Canal du Midi France 61 B1 43 20N 2 00E
Cananea Mexico 108 B6 30 59N 110 20W
Canary Basin Atlantic Ocean 117 F9 26 20N 30 00W
Canary Islands Spain 93 B8 28 30N 15 10W
Canaveral, Cape Florida U.S.A. 103 J2 28 28N 80 28W
Canberra Australia 86 H2 35 18S 149 08E
Cangamba Angola 95 C5 13 40S 19 47E
Cangzhou China 81 I5 38 19N 116 54E
Caniapiscau *r.* Québec Canada 101 V4 57 30N 68 40W
Canisp *mt.* Highland Scotland 46 C5 58 07N 5 03W
Canmore Alberta Canada 100 L3 51 07N 115 18W
Canna *i.* Highland Scotland 46 B4 57 05N 6 35W
Cannanore India 77 D2 11 53N 75 23E
Cannes France 61 C1 43 33N 7 00E
Cannich Highland Scotland 46 D4 57 21N 4 46W
Cannington Somerset England 31 D3 51 09N 3 04E
Cannock Staffordshire England 35 B3 52 42N 2 01W
Canõas Brazil 115 G7 28 55S 51 10W
Canso Nova Scotia Canada 101 W2 45 20N 61 00W
Cantabrian Mountains *see* Cordillera Cantabrica
Canterbury Kent England 33 D2 51 17N 1 05E
Canterbury Bight *b.* New Zealand 87 B2 44 00S 172 30E
Canterbury Plains New Zealand 87 B2 43 30S 172 00E
Can Tho Vietnam 80 D6 10 03N 105 46E
Canto de Rio Brazil 116 C2 22 55S 43 06W
Canton Ohio U.S.A. 105 D2 40 48N 81 23W
Canton *see* Guangzhou
Canvey Island *i.* Essex England 33 C2 51 32N 0 33E
Canvey Island *tn.* Essex England 33 C2 51 32N 0 35E
Cap Blanc *see* Ras Nouâdhibou
Cap Bon *c.* Tunisia 68 B2 37 08N 11 00E
Cap Corse *c.* Corsica 61 C1 43 00N 9 21E
Cap d'Ambre *c.* Madagascar 95 I5 12 00S 49 15E
Cap de la Hague *c.* France 61 A2 49 44N 1 56W
Cap de la Madeleine *tn.* Québec Canada 105 F3 46 22N 72 31W
Cap des Trois Fourches *c.* Morocco 66 B2 35 26N 2 57W
Cape Basin Atlantic Ocean 117 I3 36 00S 6 00E
Cape Breton Island Nova Scotia Canada 101 X2 46 45N 60 00W
Cape Charles *tn.* Virginia U.S.A. 105 E1 37 17N 76 01W
Cape Coast *tn.* Ghana 93 E4 5 10N 1 13W
Cape Cod Bay U.S.A. 105 F2 41 00N 70 00W
Cape Dorset *tn.* Northwest Territories Canada 101 T5 64 10N 76 40W
Cape Dyer *tn.* Northwest Territories Canada 101 W6 66 30N 61 20W
Cape Evans *r.s.* Antarctica 121 77 38S 166 24E
Cape Girardeau *tn.* Missouri U.S.A. 104 C1 37 19N 89 31W
Capel Surrey England 34 C1 51 10N 0 20W
Capelle aan den IJssel Netherlands 65 C1 51 56N 4 36E
Cape May *tn.* New Jersey U.S.A. 105 F1 38 56N 74 54W
Cape Province *admin.* Republic of South Africa 95 D1 31 00S 22 00E
Cape Rise Indian Ocean 117 J3 42 00S 11 00E
Cape Town Republic of South Africa 95 C1 33 56S 18 28E
Cape Verde Basin Atlantic Ocean 117 E8 11 00N 35 00W
Cape Verde Islands Atlantic Ocean 117 F8 16 00N 24 00W
Cape York Peninsula Australia 86 G7 12 30S 142 30E
Cap Ferret France 61 A1 44 42N 1 16W
Cap Gris Nez *c.* France 64 A2 50 52N 1 35E
Cap-Haïtien Haiti 109 J3 19 47N 72 17W
Capitán Arturo Prat *r.s.* Antarctica 121 62 30S 59 41W
Capo Carbonara *c.* Italy 68 A2 39 07N 9 33E
Capo Passero *c.* Italy 68 C2 36 42N 15 09E
Capo Santa Maria di Leuca *c.* Italy 68 C2 39 47N 18 22E
Capo San Vito *c.* Italy 68 B2 38 12N 12 43E
Cappoquin Waterford Irish Republic 48 D2 52 08N 7 50W
Capri *i.* Italy 68 B3 40 33N 14 15E
Capricorn Channel Australia 86 I5 23 00S 152 30E
Caprivi Strip Namibia 95 D4 17 30S 27 50E
Cap Ste. Marie *c.* Madagascar 95 I2 25 34S 45 10E
Cap Vert *c.* Senegal 93 B5 14 43N 17 33W
Caracal Romania 69 D1 44 07N 24 18E
Caracas Venezuela 114 D15 10 35N 66 56W
Caratinga Brazil 114 I9 19 50S 42 06W
Caravelas Brazil 114 J9 17 45S 39 15W
Carbondale Pennsylvania U.S.A. 105 E2 41 35N 75 31W
Carcassonne France 61 B1 43 13N 2 21E
Carcroft South Yorkshire England 43 G2 53 35N 1 12W
Carcross Yukon Territory Canada 100 I5 60 11N 134 41W
Cardamon Hills India 77 D1 9 50N 77 00E
Cárdenas Mexico 108 E4 22 00N 99 41W
Cardenden Fife Scotland 45 D2 56 08N 3 15W
Cardiff South Glamorgan Wales 38 C1 51 30N 3 13W
Cardigan Dyfed Wales 38 B2 52 06N 4 40W
Cardigan Bay Wales 38 B2 52 30N 4 30W
Cardross Strathclyde Scotland 45 A1 55 58N 4 38W
Carei Romania 69 D2 47 40N 22 28E
Cariacica Brazil 114 I8 20 15S 40 23W
Caribbean Sea Central America 109 I3 15 00N 75 00W
Caribou Mountains Alberta Canada 100 L4 59 00N 115 30W
Caripito Venezuela 114 E15 10 07N 63 07W
Carleton Place Ontario Canada 105 E3 45 08N 76 09W
Carlingford Lough *b.* Ireland 48 E4 54 05N 6 10W
Carlisle Cumbria England 44 B1 54 54N 2 55W
Carlow Carlow Irish Republic 48 D2 52 50N 6 55W
Carlow *co.* Irish Republic 48 D2 52 40N 6 55W
Carloway Western Isles Scotland 46 B5 58 17N 6 48W
Carlsbad New Mexico U.S.A. 102 F3 32 25N 104 14W
Carlton North Yorkshire England 43 G3 53 43N 1 02W
Carlton in Lindrick Nottinghamshire England 43 G2 53 22N 1 06W
Carlton-on-Trent Nottinghamshire England 36 D3 53 10N 0 48W
Carluke Strathclyde Scotland 45 C1 55 45N 3 51W
Carmacks Yukon Territory Canada 100 H5 62 04N 136 21W
Carman Manitoba Canada 104 A3 49 32N 97 59W
Carmarthen Dyfed Wales 38 B1 51 51N 4 20W
Carmarthen Bay Dyfed Wales 38 B1 51 40N 4 30W
Carmel Church Virginia U.S.A. 105 E1 37 54N 77 25W
Carmel Head Gwynedd Wales 38 B3 53 24N 4 34W
Carmen Colombia 114 B14 9 46N 75 06W
Carmunnock Strathclyde Scotland 45 B1 55 47N 4 15W
Carnarvon Australia 86 A5 24 51S 113 45E
Carndonagh Donegal Irish Republic 48 D5 55 15N 7 15W
Carnedd Llewelyn *mt.* Gwynedd Wales 38 C3 53 10N 3 58W
Carnegie, Lake Australia 86 C4 27 00S 124 00E
Carnegie Ridge Pacific Ocean 119 R7 1 30S 95 00W
Carn Eige *mt.* Highland Scotland 46 C4 57 22N 5 07W
Carnforth Lancashire England 40 B3 54 08N 2 46W
Carnlough Northern Ireland 48 F4 54 59N 5 59W
Car Nicobar *i.* Nicobar Islands 77 G1 9 00N 93 00E
Carnot Central African Republic 94 C8 4 59N 15 56E
Carnoustie Tayside Scotland 46 F3 56 30N 2 44W
Carnsore Point *c.* Wexford Irish Republic 48 E2 52 10N 6 22W
Carnwath Strathclyde Scotland 45 C1 55 43N 3 38W
Carolina Brazil 114 H11 7 20S 47 25W
Caroline Island Pacific Ocean 119 L7 10 00S 150 00W
Caroline Islands Pacific Ocean 118 E8 8 00N 148 00E
Carpathians *mts.* Europe 69 D2 49 00N 22 00E
Carpaţii Meridionali *mts.* Romania 69 D2 45 00N 24 00E
Carpentaria, Gulf of Australia 86 F7 13 30S 138 00E
Carpentras France 61 C1 44 03N 5 03E
Carrauntoohill *mt.* Irish Republic 48 B1 52 00N 9 45W
Carrbridge Highland Scotland 46 E4 57 17N 3 49W
Carrickfergus Antrim Northern Ireland 49 D2 54 43N 5 49W
Carrickmacross Monaghan Irish Republic 48 E3 53 58N 6 43W
Carrick-on-Shannon Leitrim Irish Republic 48 C3 53 57N 8 05W
Carrick-on-Suir Tipperary Irish Republic 48 D2 52 21N 7 25W
Carrigaline Cork Irish Republic 48 C1 51 48N 8 24W
Carrigtohill Cork Irish Republic 48 C1 51 55N 8 16W
Carrington Lothian Scotland 45 D1 55 50N 3 05W
Carrion *r.* Spain 66 B3 42 30N 4 45W
Carron *r.* Central Scotland 45 C2 56 05N 3 55W
Carron Valley Reservoir Central Scotland 45 B2 56 02N 4 05W
Carryduff Down Northern Ireland 49 D1 54 31N 5 53W
Carson California U.S.A. 107 A2 33 49N 118 16W
Carson City Nevada U.S.A. 102 C4 39 10N 119 46W
Carstairs Strathclyde Scotland 45 C1 55 42N 3 42W
Cartagena Colombia 114 B15 10 24N 75 33W
Cartagena Spain 66 B2 37 36N 0 59W
Cartago Costa Rica 109 H1 9 50N 83 52W
Carteret New Jersey U.S.A. 106 B1 40 34N 74 13W
Carterton Oxfordshire England 32 A2 51 45N 1 35W
Cartwright Newfoundland Canada 101 X3 53 40N 57 00W
Caruarú Brazil 114 J11 8 15S 35 55W
Carúpano Venezuela 114 E15 10 39N 63 14W
Casablanca *(Dar el Beida)* Morocco 93 D9 33 39N 7 35W
Casa Grande Arizona U.S.A. 102 D3 32 52N 111 46W
Cascade Range *mts.* North America 102 B6 48 00N 121 00W
Cascadura Brazil 116 B2 22 53S 43 21W
Cascais Portugal 66 A2 38 41N 9 25W
Cascavel Brazil 114 J12 4 10S 38 15W
Caserta Italy 68 B3 41 04N 14 20E
Casey *r.s.* Antarctica 121 66 17S 77 58E
Cashel Tipperary Irish Republic 48 D2 52 31N 7 53W
Casper Wyoming U.S.A. 102 E5 42 50N 106 20W
Caspian Sea Iran/U.S.S.R. 70 G4 41 00N 50 00E
Cassiar Mountains British Columbia Canada 100 I4 59 15N 129 49W
Cassino Italy 68 B3 41 29N 13 50E
Castellane France 61 C1 43 50N 6 30E
Castellón de la Plana Spain 66 B2 39 59N 0 03W
Castelnaudary France 61 B1 43 18N 1 57E
Castelo Branco Portugal 66 A2 39 50N 7 30W
Castlebar Mayo Irish Republic 48 B3 53 52N 9 17W
Castlebay Western Isles Scotland 46 A3 56 57N 7 28W
Castleblayney Monaghan Irish Republic 48 E4 54 07N 6 44W
Castle Bromwich West Midlands England 35 C2 52 30N 1 45W
Castle Cary Somerset England 31 E3 51 06N 2 31W
Castlecomer Kilkenny Irish Republic 48 D2 52 48N 7 12W
Castleconnell Limerick Irish Republic 48 C2 52 43N 8 30W
Castlederg Northern Ireland 48 D4 54 42N 7 36W
Castle Donington Leicestershire England 35 D3 52 51N 1 19W
Castle Douglas Dumfries & Galloway Scotland 46 E1 54 57N 3 56W
Castleford West Yorkshire England 43 F3 43 44N 1 21W
Castleisland Kerry Irish Republic 48 B2 52 14N 9 27W
Castlerea Roscommon Irish Republic 48 C3 53 46N 8 29W
Castleton Derbyshire England 43 E2 53 21N 1 46W
Castletown Highland Scotland 46 E5 58 35N 3 23W
Castletown Isle of Man British Isles 41 F1 54 04N 4 38W
Castletownbere Cork Irish Republic 48 B1 51 39N 9 55W
Castres France 61 B1 43 36N 2 14E
Castricum Netherlands 64 D4 52 33N 4 40E
Castries St. Lucia 109 L2 14 01N 60 59W
Castrop-Rauxel F.R.G. 62 D3 51 33N 7 18E
Castrovillari Italy 68 C2 39 48N 16 12E
Catamarca Argentina 115 D7 28 28S 65 46W
Catánia Italy 68 C2 37 31N 15 06E
Catanzaro Italy 68 C2 38 54N 16 36E
Cataract, 1st (R. Nile) Egypt 78 D3 24 00N 32 45E
Cataract, 2nd (R. Nile) Sudan 78 D3 21 40N 31 12E
Cataract, 3rd (R. Nile) Sudan 78 D2 19 45N 30 25E
Cataract, 4th (R. Nile) Sudan 78 D2 18 40N 32 10E
Cataract, 5th (R. Nile) Sudan 78 D2 18 25N 33 52E
Caterham Surrey England 34 C1 51 17N 0 04W
Catford Greater London England 34 D2 51 26N 0 00
Cat Island The Bahamas 109 I4 24 30N 75 30W
Catrine Strathclyde Scotland 46 D2 55 30N 4 20W
Catshill Hereford and Worcester England 35 B2 52 22N 2 03W
Catskill Mountains New York U.S.A. 105 F2 42 00N 74 00W
Catterick Garrison North Yorkshire England 40 C3 54 23N 1 40W
Caucaia Brazil 114 J12 3 44S 38 45W
Caucasus Mountains U.S.S.R. 70 G4 43 00N 43 00E
Cauldhame Central Scotland 45 B2 56 07N 4 12W
Cavan Cavan Irish Republic 48 D3 53 58N 7 21W
Cavan *co.* Irish Republic 48 D4 54 02N 7 10W
Cawood North Yorkshire England 43 G3 53 50N 1 07W
Caxias Brazil 114 I12 4 53S 43 20W
Caxias do Sul Brazil 115 G7 29 14S 51 10W
Cayenne French Guiana 114 G13 4 55N 52 18W
Cayman Trench Caribbean Sea 119 R9 15 00N 80 00W
Cayuga Lake New York U.S.A. 105 E2 43 00N 77 00W
Cea *r.* Spain 66 A3 42 40N 5 10W
Ceanannus Mór *(Kells)* Meath Irish Republic 48 E3 53 44N 6 53W
Ceara *admin.* Brazil 114 I11/J11 5 30S 40 00W
Cebu *i.* The Philippines 72 10 30N 123 30E
Cebu The Philippines 80 G6 10 17N 123 56E
Cedar *r.* U.S.A. 104 B2 42 00N 92 00W
Cedar City Utah U.S.A. 102 D4 37 40N 113 04W
Cedar Creek *r.* North Dakota U.S.A. 102 F6 46 00N 102 00W
Cedar Falls *tn.* Iowa U.S.A. 104 B2 42 34N 92 26W
Cedar Grove New Jersey U.S.A. 106 B2 40 51N 74 14W
Cedar Lake Manitoba Canada 101 O3 53 40N 100 30W
Cedar Rapids *tn.* Iowa U.S.A. 104 B2 41 59N 91 39W
Cedros *i.* Mexico 108 A5 28 00N 115 00W
Ceduna Australia 86 E3 32 07S 133 42E
Ceerigaabo Somalia 94 I10 10 40N 47 20E
Cefn-mawr Clwyd Wales 38 C2 52 59N 3 02W
Cegléd Hungary 69 C2 47 10N 19 47E
Ceiriog *r.* Clwyd Wales 38 C2 52 52N 3 10W
Celaya Mexico 108 D4 20 32N 100 48W
Celbridge Kildare Irish Republic 49 A2 53 20N 6 32W
Celebes *see* Sulawesi
Celebes Sea Indonesia 80 G4 3 00N 122 30E
Celje Yugoslavia 68 C4 46 15N 15 16E
Cellarhead Staffordshire England 35 B4 53 02N 2 04W
Celle F.R.G. 63 B2 52 37N 10 05E
Cemaes Gwynedd Wales 38 B3 53 24N 4 27W
Central *reg.* Scotland 46 D3 56 10N 4 20W
CENTRAL AFRICAN REPUBLIC 94 C9
Central Cordilleras *hills* Spain 51
Centralia Illinois U.S.A. 104 C1 38 32N 89 08W
Central Pacific Basin Pacific Ocean 118 I9 10 00N 177 00W
Central Plain Ireland 51 53 30N 8 00W
Central Siberian Plateau U.S.S.R. 71 M/N9–M/N8 65 00N

94 25W
Cobán Guatemala **108** F3 15 28N 90 20W
Cobar Australia **86** H3 31 32S 145 51E
Cobbinshaw Reservoir Lothian Scotland **45** C1 55 48N 3 34W
Cobh Cork Irish Republic **48** C1 51 51N 8 17W
Cobham Surrey England **34** B1 51 20N 0 24W
Cobija Bolivia **114** D10 11 01S 68 45W
Cobourg Ontario Canada **105** E2 43 58N 78 11W
Coburg F.R.G. **63** B2 50 15N 10 58E
Cochabamba Bolivia **114** D9 17 26S 66 10W
Cochin India **77** D1 9 56N 76 15E
Cochrane Chile **115** C3 47 16S 72 33W
Cochrane Ontario Canada **105** D3 49 04N 81 02W
Cockburn Island *i.* Ontario Canada **105** D3 46 00N 83 00W
Cockerham Lancashire England **42** B3 53 59N 2 50W
Cockermouth Cumbria England **44** A1 54 40N 3 21W
Cocksburnspath Borders Scotland **46** F2 55 58N 2 27W
Cocos Basin Indian Ocean **72** 5 00S 96 00E
Cocos Island *see* Isla del Coco
Cocos Ridge Pacific Ocean **119** R8 4 00N 90 00W
Cocota Brazil **116** C2 22 48S 43 11W
Codajás Brazil **114** E12 3 55S 62 00W
Cod, Cape *p.* Massachusetts U.S.A. **105** G2 42 00N 70 00W
Codó Brazil **114** I12 4 28S 43 51W
Codrington Antigua & Barbuda **109** L3 17 43N 61 49W
Codsall Staffordshire England **35** B2 52 37N 2 12W
Coelhodo Rocha Brazil **116** B2 22 46S 43 21W
Coesfeld F.R.G. **63** A2 51 57N 7 10E
Coeur d'Alene Idaho U.S.A. **102** C6 47 40N 116 46W
Coevorden Netherlands **64** F4 52 39N 6 45E
Coffeyville Kansas U.S.A. **104** A1 37 02N 95 37W
Coggeshall Essex England **33** C2 51 52N 0 41E
Coghinhas *r.* Italy **61** C1 40 00N 9 00E
Cognac France **61** A2 45 42N 0 19W
Cogswell Reservoir California U.S.A. **107** C3 34 14N 117 59W
Coihaique Chile **115** C3 45 35S 72 08W
Coimbatore India **77** D2 11 00N 76 57E
Coimbra Portugal **66** A3 40 12N 8 25W
Colbeck, Cape Antarctica **121** 77 00S 158 00W
Colchester Essex England **33** C2 51 54N 0 54E
Cold Lake *tn.* Alberta Canada **100** M3 54 28N 110 15W
Coldrain Tayside Scotland **45** D2 56 12N 3 28W
Coldstream Borders Scotland **46** F2 55 39N 2 15W
Coldwater Michigan U.S.A. **104** C2 41 57N 85 01W
Colebrook New Hampshire U.S.A. **105** F2 44 53N 71 30W
Coleford Gloucestershire England **31** E3 51 48N 2 37W
Coleman Alberta Canada **100** M2 49 38N 114 28W
Coleraine Northern Ireland **48** E5 55 08N 6 40W
Coleshill Warwickshire England **35** C2 52 30N 1 42W
Colima Mexico **108** D3 19 14N 103 41W
Colinton Lothian Scotland **45** D1 55 54N 3 15W
Colintraive Strathclyde Scotland **46** C2 55 56N 5 09W
Coll *i.* Strathclyde Scotland **46** B3 56 40N 6 35W
College Alaska U.S.A. **100** F5 64 54N 147 55W
Collie Australia **86** B3 33 20S 116 06E
Collines de la Puisaye *hills* France **61** B2 47 35N 3 18E
Collines de l'Armagnac *hills* France **61** B1 43 30N 0 30E
Collines de Normandie *hills* France **61** A2 48 58N 0 55W
Collines du Perche *hills* France **61** B2 48 30N 0 50E
Collines du Sancerrois *hills* France **61** B2 47 15N 2 30E
Collingham West Yorkshire England **43** F3 53 55N 1 25W
Collingwood New Zealand **87** B2 40 41S 172 41E
Collingwood Ontario Canada **105** D2 44 30N 80 14W
Collooney Sligo Irish Republic **48** C4 54 11N 8 29W
Colmar France **61** C2 48 05N 7 21E
Colne Lancashire England **42** D3 53 52N 2 09W
Colne *r.* Essex England **33** C2 51 53N 0 45E
Colney Heath Hertfordshire England **34** C3 51 44N 0 14W
Cologne *see* Köln
Colombes France **60** B2 48 55N 2 15E
COLOMBIA **114** C13
Colombo Sri Lanka **77** D1 6 55N 79 52E
Colón Panama **109** I1 9 21N 79 54W
Colonsay *i.* Strathclyde Scotland **46** B3 56 05N 6 15W
Colorado *r.* North America **102** D3 33 00N 114 00W
Colorado *r.* Texas U.S.A. **103** G2 29 00N 96 00W
Colorado *state* U.S.A. **102** E4 39 00N 106 00W
Colorado Plateau Arizona U.S.A. **102** D4 36 00N 111 00W
Colorado Springs *tn.* Colorado U.S.A. **102** F4 38 50N 104 50W
Colsterworth Lincolnshire England **36** D2 52 48N 0 37W
Coltishall Norfolk England **33** D3 52 44N 1 22E
Columbia Kentucky U.S.A. **104** C1 37 05N 85 19W
Columbia Missouri U.S.A. **104** B1 38 58N 92 20W
Columbia *r.* North America **102** B6 46 00N 120 00W
Columbia South Carolina U.S.A. **103** J3 34 00N 81 00W
Columbia City Indiana U.S.A. **104** C2 41 09N 85 20W
Columbia, Mount British Columbia/Alberta Canada **100** L3 52 09N 117 25W
Columbus Georgia U.S.A. **103** J3 32 28N 84 59W
Columbus Indiana U.S.A. **104** C1 39 12N 85 57W
Columbus Mississippi U.S.A. **103** I3 33 30N 88 27W
Columbus Nebraska U.S.A. **103** G5 41 27N 97 21W
Columbus Ohio U.S.A. **105** D2 39 59N 83 03W
Colville *r.* Alaska U.S.A. **100** D6 69 00N 158 00W
Colvocorresses Bay Antarctica **121** 66 00S 120 00E
Colwyn Bay *tn.* Clwyd Wales **38** C3 53 18N 3 43W
Comandante Ferraz *r.s.* Antarctica **121** 62 05S 58 23W
Comas Peru **116** E5 11 57S 77 03W
Combe Martin Devon England **31** C3 51 13N 4 02W
Comber Down Northern Ireland **49** D1 54 33N 5 45W
Comilla Bangladesh **77** G4 23 28N 91 10E
Comitán Mexico **108** F3 16 18N 92 09W
Como Italy **68** A4 45 48N 9 05E
Comodoro Rivadavia Argentina **115** D3 45 50S 67 30W
Comorin, Cape India **77** D1 8 04N 77 35E
Comoro Archipelago *is.* Indian Ocean **88** 12 00S 44 00E
COMOROS **95** H5
Compiègne France **61** B2 49 25N 2 50E
Compton California U.S.A. **107** B2 33 55N 118 14W
Conakry Guinea **93** C4 9 30N 13 43W
Concepción Chile **115** C5 36 50S 73 03W
Concepción Mexico **108** D4 24 38N 101 25W
Concepción Paraguay **115** F8 23 22S 57 26W
Concepción del Uruguay Argentina **115** F6 32 30S 58 15W
Conchos *r.* Mexico **108** C5 27 30N 107 00W
Concord New Hampshire U.S.A. **105** F2 43 13N 71 34W
Concordia Argentina **115** F6 31 25S 58 00W
Concordia Kansas U.S.A. **103** G4 39 35N 97 39W
Condom France **61** B1 43 58N 0 23E
Condorrat Strathclyde Scotland **45** B1 55 57N 4 02W
Conduit *r.* Israel **78** O11 32 25N 35 00E
Conecuh *r.* Alabama U.S.A. **103** I3 31 00N 87 00W
Conejera *i.* Balearic Islands **66** E4 39 11N 2 58E
Coney Island New York U.S.A. **106** C1 40 34N 74 00W
Conflans-Ste. Honorine France **60** A3 49 01N 2 09E
Congleton Cheshire England **40** B2 53 10N 2 13W
CONGO **94** C7
Congo *(Zaire) r.* Congo **94** C7 2 00S 17 00E
Congresbury Avon England **31** E3 51 23N 2 48W
Coningsby Lincolnshire England **36** D3 53 07N 0 10W
Conisbrough South Yorkshire England **43** G2 53 29N 1 13W
Coniston Cumbria England **44** A1 54 22N 3 05W
Coniston Ontario Canada **105** D3 46 29N 80 51W
Coniston Water *l.* Cumbria England **44** A1 54 20N 3 05W
Connah's Quay *tn.* Clwyd Wales **38** C3 53 13N 3 03W
Connecticut *r.* U.S.A. **103** L5 43 00N 72 00W
Connecticut *state* U.S.A. **105** F2 41 00N 73 00W
Connemara National Park Mayo Irish Republic **48** B3 53 30N 9 55W
Conon Bridge *tn.* Highland Scotland **46** D4 57 33N 4 26W
Consett Durham England **44** C1 54 51N 1 49W
Constanța Romania **69** E1 44 12N 28 40E
Constantine Algeria **93** G10 36 22N 6 40E
Constitución Chile **115** C5 31 05S 57 51W
Contanama Peru **114** B11 7 19S 75 04W
Contrary Head Isle of Man British Isles **41** F1 54 13N 4 45W
Conwy Gwynedd Wales **38** C3 53 17N 3 50W
Conwy *r.* Gwynedd Wales **38** C3 53 00N 3 47W
Cookham Berkshire England **34** A2 51 34N 0 43W
Cook Inlet Alaska U.S.A. **100** E5 60 00N 152 30W
Cook Islands Pacific Ocean **119** K6 19 30S 159 50W
Cookley Hereford & Worcester England **35** B2 52 25N 2 14W
Cook, Mount New Zealand **87** B2 43 37S 170 08E
Cookstown Northern Ireland **48** E4 54 39N 6 45W
Cook Strait New Zealand **87** B2 41 00S 174 30E
Cooktown Australia **86** H6 15 29S 145 15E
Coolgardie Australia **86** C3 31 01S 121 12E
Cooper Creek *r.* Australia **86** F4 28 00S 138 00E
Coosa *r.* U.S.A. **103** I3 33 00N 86 00W
Coos Bay *tn.* Oregon U.S.A. **102** B5 43 23N 124 12W
Cootehill Cavan Irish Republic **48** D4 54 04N 7 05W
Copacabana Brazil **116** C2 22 58S 43 11W
Copacabana Beach Brazil **116** C2 22 59S 43 11W
Copenhagen *see* København
Copiapó Chile **115** C7 27 20S 70 23W
Copper *r.* Alaska U.S.A. **100** F5 60 30N 144 50W
Copper Cliff *tn.* Ontario Canada **105** D3 46 28N 81 05W
Copper Harbor *tn.* Michigan U.S.A. **104** C3 47 28N 87 54W
Coppermine Northwest Territories Canada **100** L6 67 49N 115 12W
Coppermine *r.* Northwest Territories Canada **100** M6 67 00N 114 50W
Coppull Lancashire England **42** B2 53 37N 2 40W
Copthorne West Sussex England **34** C1 51 09N 0 08W
Coquet *r.* Northumberland England **44** C2 55 20N 1 50W
Coquimbo Chile **115** C7 29 57S 71 25W
Coral Ontario Canada **105** D4 50 13N 81 41W
Coral Harbour *tn.* Northwest Territories Canada **101** S5 64 10N 83 15W
Coral Sea Pacific Ocean **86** I7 15 00S 154 00E
Corantijn *r.* Surinam **114** F13 4 30N 57 30W
Corbeil-Essonnes France **60** C1 48 36N 2 29E
Corbridge Northumberland England **44** B1 54 58N 2 01W
Corby Northamptonshire England **36** D2 52 49N 0 32W
Cordillera Cantabrica *(Cantabrian Mountains)* Spain **66** A3 43 00N 5 30W
Cordillera de Mérida *mts.* Venezuela **109** J1 8 00N 72 00W
Córdoba Argentina **115** E6 31 25S 64 11W
Córdoba Mexico **108** E3 18 55N 96 55W
Cordoba Spain **66** B2 37 53N 4 46W
Cordova Alaska U.S.A. **100** F5 60 29N 145 52W
Corfe Castle Dorset England **31** E2 50 38N 2 04W
Corfu *see* Kérkira
Corinth Mississippi U.S.A. **103** I3 34 58N 88 30W
Cork *co.* Irish Republic **48** C1 51 58N 8 40W
Cork Cork Irish Republic **48** C1 51 54N 8 28W
Cork Harbour Irish Republic **48** C1 51 50N 8 10W
Corley Warwickshire England **35** D2 52 28N 1 32W
Çorlu Turkey **68** E3 41 11N 27 48E
Cormeilles-en-Parisis France **60** A2 48 58N 2 11E
Corner Brook *tn.* Newfoundland Canada **101** X2 48 58N 57 58W
Corning New York U.S.A. **105** E2 42 10N 77 04W
Cornwall *co.* England **31** C2 50 25N 4 50W
Cornwall Ontario Canada **105** F3 45 02N 74 45W
Cornwallis Island Northwest Territories Canada **101** O7 74 40N 97 30W
Coro Venezuela **114** D15 11 20N 70 00W
Coroico Bolivia **114** D9 16 09S 67 45W
Coromandel Coast India **77** D2 12 30N 81 30E
Coronation Gulf Northwest Territories Canada **100** M6 68 15N 112 30W
Coronation Island South Orkney Islands **115** H0 61 00S 45 00W
Coronel Pringles Argentina **115** E5 37 56S 61 25W
Corpus Christi Texas U.S.A. **103** G2 27 47N 97 26W
Corran Highland Scotland **46** C3 56 43N 5 14W
Corrientes Argentina **115** F7 27 30S 58 48W
Corrieverton Guyana **114** F14 5 53N 57 10W
Corse *(Corsica) i.* France **61** C1 42 00N 9 00E
Corsham Wiltshire England **31** E3 51 26N 2 11W
Corsica *see* Corse
Corstorphine Lothian Scotland **45** D1 55 57N 3 18W
Corte Corsica **61** C1 42 18N 9 08E
Cortland New York U.S.A. **105** E2 42 36N 76 10W
Çoruh *r.* Turkey **78** F7 40 45N 40 45E
Corumbá Brazil **114** F9 19 00S 57 35W
Corunna *see* La Coruña
Corvallis Oregon U.S.A. **102** B5 44 34N 123 16W
Corwen Clwyd Wales **38** C2 52 59N 3 22W
Corydon Indiana U.S.A. **104** C1 38 12N 86 09W
Coseley West Midlands England **35** B2 52 33N 2 06W
Cosenza Italy **68** C2 39 17N 16 16E
Cossipore India **76** K2 22 37N 88 23E
Costa Blanca *geog. reg.* Spain **66** B2 38 15N 0 20W
Costa Brava *geog. reg.* Spain **66** C3 41 40N 3 50E
Costa del Sol *geog. reg.* Spain **66** B2 36 40N 4 40W
COSTA RICA **109** H1/2
Cotagaita Bolivia **114** D8 20 47S 65 40W
Côteau Québec Canada **105** F3 45 16N 74 16W
CÔTE D'IVOIRE **93** E4
Côte d'Or *hills* France **61** B2 47 00N 4 30E
Cotentin *p.* France **51** 49 30N 1 30W
Côtes du Nivernais *plat.* France **61** B2 47 15N 3 20E
Cotonou Benin **93** F4 6 24N 2 31E
Cotopaxi *mt.* Ecuador **114** B12 0 40S 78 28W
Cotswold Hills Gloucestershire England **31** E3 51 40N 2 10W
Cottbus *admin.* G.D.R. **63** B2 52 00N 14 00E
Cottbus G.D.R. **63** B2 51 43N 14 21E
Cottenham Cambridgeshire England **33** C3 52 18N 0 09E
Cotubandê Brazil **116** C2 22 51S 43 00W
Couesnon *r.* France **61** A2 48 30N 1 40W
Coulommiers France **61** B2 48 49N 3 05E
Coulsdon Greater London England **34** C1 51 19N 0 07W
Council Bluffs *tn.* Iowa U.S.A. **104** A2 41 14N 95 54W
Countesthorpe Leicestershire England **36** C2 52 33N 1 09W
Coupar Angus Tayside Scotland **46** E3 56 33N 3 17W
Courtrai *see* Kortrijk
Couvin Belgium **64** D2 50 03N 4 30E
Cove Bay *tn.* Grampian Scotland **46** F4 57 05N 2 05W
Coven Staffordshire England **35** B2 52 39N 2 08W
Coventry West Midlands England **35** D2 52 25N 1 30W
Coverack Cornwall England **30** B2 50 01N 5 05W
Covilhã Portugal **66** A3 40 17N 7 30W
Covina California U.S.A. **107** C3 34 04N 117 53W
Covington Indiana U.S.A. **104** C2 40 10N 87 23W
Covington Kentucky U.S.A. **105** D1 39 04N 84 30W
Cowbridge South Glamorgan Wales **38** C1 51 28N 3 27W
Cowdenbeath Fife Scotland **45** D2 56 07N 3 21W
Cowes Isle of Wight England **32** A1 50 45N 1 18W
Cowie Central Scotland **45** C2 56 05N 3 52W
Cox's Bazar Bangladesh **77** G4 21 25N 91 59E
Coyoacán Mexico **108** P1 19 20N 99 10W
Coyote Creek *r.* California U.S.A. **107** B2 33 50N 118 05W
Craigavon Armagh Northern Ireland **48** E4 54 28N 6 25W
Craigellachie Grampian Scotland **46** E4 57 29N 3 12W
Craiglockhart Lothian Scotland **45** D1 55 55N 3 15W
Craignure Strathclyde Scotland **46** C3 56 28N 5 42W
Crail Fife Scotland **46** F3 56 16N 2 38W
Crailsheim F.R.G. **63** B1 49 09N 10 06E
Craiova Romania **69** D1 44 18N 23 47E
Cramlington Northumberland England **44** C2 55 05N 1 35W
Cramond Lothian Scotland **45** D1 55 58N 3 16W
Cranage Cheshire England **42** C1 53 13N 2 22W
Cranberry Staffordshire England **35** B3 52 55N 2 16W
Cranbourne Berkshire England **34** B2 51 25N 0 40W
Cranbrook Kent England **33** C2 51 06N 0 33E
Cranfield Bedfordshire England **34** B4 52 05N 0 35W
Cranleigh Surrey England **34** B1 51 09N 0 30W
Crathie Grampian Scotland **46** E4 57 02N 3 12W
Craven Arms Shropshire England **36** B2 52 26N 2 50W
Crawford Strathclyde Scotland **46** E2 55 28N 3 40W
Crawfordsville Indiana U.S.A. **104** C2 40 03N 86 54W
Crawley West Sussex England **34** C1 51 07N 0 12W
Crays Hill *tn.* Essex England **34** E2 51 35N 0 27E
Credenhill Hereford and Worcester England **36** B2 52 05N 2 48W
Crediton Devon England **31** D2 50 47N 3 39W
Cree *r.* Saskatchewan Canada **100** N4 58 00N 106 30W
Cree Lake Saskatchewan Canada **100** N4 57 30N 106 30W
Creil France **61** B2 49 16N 2 29E
Cremona Italy **68** B4 45 08N 10 01E
Cres *i.* Yugoslavia **68** B3 45 00N 14 00E
Crescent City California U.S.A. **102** B5 41 46N 124 13W
Creston Iowa U.S.A. **104** B2 41 04N 94 20W
Crestview Florida U.S.A. **103** I3 30 44N 86 34W
Creswell Derbyshire England **43** G1 53 16N 1 12W
Crete *see* Kriti
Crêteil France **60** B2 48 47N 2 28E
Crete, Sea of Mediterranean Sea **68** D2 36 00N 25 00E
Creuse *r.* France **61** B2 46 45N 0 45E
Crewe Cheshire England **40** B2 53 05N 2 27W
Crewkerne Somerset England **31** E2 50 53N 2 48W
Crianlarich Central Scotland **46** D4 56 23N 4 37W
Criccieth Gwynedd Wales **38** B2 52 55N 4 14W
Criciúma Brazil **115** H7 28 45S 49 25W
Crickhowell Powys Wales **38** C1 51 53N 3 09W
Cricklade Wiltshire England **31** F3 51 39N 1 51W
Crieff Tayside Scotland **45** C2 56 23N 3 52W
Crigglestone West Yorkshire England **43** F2 53 38N 1 32W
Crimea *see* Krim
Crinan Strathclyde Scotland **46** C3 56 06N 5 35W
Crockham Hill *tn.* Kent England **34** D1 51 14N 0 04E
Croftamie Central Scotland **45** B2 56 03N 4 26W
Crofton West Yorkshire England **43** F2 53 39N 1 26W
Cromarty Highland Scotland **46** D4 57 40N 4 02W
Cromarty Firth *est.* Highland Scotland **46** D4 57 40N 4 20W
Cromer Norfolk England **33** D3 52 56N 1 18E
Cromwell New Zealand **87** A1 45 03S 169 14E
Crook Durham England **44** C1 54 43N 1 44W
Crooked Island The Bahamas **109** J4 22 45N 74 10W
Crookston Minnesota U.S.A. **104** A3 47 47N 96 36W
Crosby Merseyside England **42** A2 53 30N 3 02W
Cross Fell *sum.* Cumbria England **44** B1 54 43N 2 29W
Crossford Fife Scotland **45** D2 56 04N 3 30W
Crossford Strathclyde Scotland **45** C1 55 42N 3 54W
Crossgates Fife Scotland **45** D2 56 05N 3 24W
Cross Hands Dyfed Wales **38** B1 51 48N 4 05W
Crosshaven Cork Irish Republic **48** C1 51 48N 8 17W
Crosshill Fife Scotland **45** D2 56 09N 3 18W
Crossmaglen Northern Ireland **48** E4 54 05N 6 37W
Crossmolina Mayo Irish Republic **48** B4 54 06N 9 20W
Croston Lancashire England **42** B2 53 40N 2 47W
Crotone Italy **68** C2 39 05N 17 08E
Crouch *r.* Essex England **33** C2 51 38N 0 42E
Crowborough East Sussex England **33** C2 51 03N 0 09E
Crowland Lincolnshire England **36** D2 52 41N 0 11W
Crowle Hereford & Worcester England **35** B1 52 12N 2 07W
Crowle Humberside England **40** D2 53 37N 0 49W
Crow Peak *mt.* Montana U.S.A. **102** D6 46 19N 111 56W
Crowthorne Berkshire England **34** B2 51 23N 0 49W
Croyde Devon England **31** C3 51 08N 4 15W
Croydon Australia **86** G6 18 10S 142 15E
Croydon Greater London England **34** C2 51 23N 0 06W
Crumlin Dublin Irish Republic **49** B1 53 19N 6 18W
Crumlin Northern Ireland **49** C1 54 37N 6 14W
Crumlin *r.* Northern Ireland **49** C1 54 37N 6 03W
Crummock Water *l.* Cumbria England **44** A1 54 34N 3 18W
Cruzeiro do Sul Brazil **114** C11 7 40S 72 39W
Crymmych Dyfed Wales **38** B1 51 59N 4 40W
Crystal Falls *tn.* Michigan U.S.A. **104** C3 46 06N 88 11W
Crystal Palace Greater London England **34** C2 51 24N 0 04W
Cuando *r.* Southern Africa **95** D4 16 00S 21 30E
Cuango *r.* Angola **95** C6 9 00S 18 30E
Cuanza *r.* Angola **95** C6 9 40S 15 00E
Cuautepec Mexico **108** P2 19 32N 99 08W
CUBA **109** I4
Cubango *r.* Angola **95** C4 17 00S 18 00E
Cuckfield West Sussex England **33** B2 51 00N 0 09W
Cuckney Nottinghamshire England **43** G1 53 15N 1 08W
Cúcuta Colombia **114** C14 7 55N 73 31W
Cuddalore India **77** D2 11 43N 79 46E
Cuddapah India **77** D2 14 30N 78 50E
Cudworth South Yorkshire England **43** F2 53 35N 1 25W
Cuenca Ecuador **114** B12 2 54S 79 00W
Cuenca Spain **66** B3 40 04N 2 07W
Cuernavaca Mexico **108** E3 18 57N 99 15W
Cuffley Hertfordshire England **34** C3 51 47N 0 07W
Cuiabá Brazil **114** F9 15 32S 56 05W
Cuillin Hills Skye Scotland **46** B4 57 15N 6 15W
Cuito *r.* Angola **95** C4 17 30S 19 30E
Culcheth Cheshire England **42** C2 53 27N 2 31W
Culemborg Netherlands **64** E3 51 58N 5 14E
Culhuacan Mexico **108** P1 19 19N 99 06W
Culiacán Mexico **108** C4 24 50N 107 23W
Cullen Grampian Scotland **46** F4 57 41N 2 49W
Cullompton Devon England **31** D2 50 52N 3 24W
Cullybackey Antrim Northern Ireland **48** E4 54 53N 6 21W
Culver City California U.S.A. **107** A3 34 01N 118 24W
Culverstone Green Kent England **34** E2 51 20N 0 21E
Cumaná Venezuela **114** E15 10 29N 64 12W
Cumberland *r.* U.S.A. **103** I4 37 00N 86 00W
Cumberland *tn.* Maryland U.S.A. **105** E1 39 40N 78 47W
Cumberland Peninsula Northwest Territories Canada **101** W6 67 00N 65 00N
Cumberland Plateau U.S.A. **103** I4 36 00N 85 00W
Cumberland Sound Northwest Territories Canada **101** V6 65 30N 66 00W
Cumbernauld Strathclyde Scotland **45** C1 55 57N 4 00W
Cumbria *co.* England **44** B1 54 30N 2 45W
Cumbrian Mountains Cumbria England **44** A1/B1 54 30N 3 00W
Cumnock Strathclyde Scotland **46** D2 55 27N 4 16W
Cunene *r.* Angola/Namibia **95** B4 17 00S 13 30E
Cuneo Italy **68** A3 44 24N 7 33E
Cunnamula Australia **86** H4 28 04S 145 40E
Cupar Fife Scotland **45** D2 56 19N 3 01W
Curaçao *i.* Lesser Antilles **109** K2 12 20N 68 20W
Curacautín Chile **115** C5 38 28S 71 52W
Cure *r.* France **61** B2 47 40N 3 40E
Curicó Chile **115** C5 35 00S 71 15W
Curitiba Brazil **115** H7 25 25S 49 25W
Currie Lothian Scotland **45** D1 55 51N 3 20W
Curvelo Brazil **114** I9 18 45S 44 27W
Cutnall Green Hereford & Worcester England **35** B1 52 18N 2 11W
Cuttack India **77** F4 20 26N 85 56E
Cuxhaven F.R.G. **63** A2 53 52N 8 42E
Cuyahoga Falls *tn.* Ohio U.S.A. **105** D2 41 08N 81 27W
Cuzco Peru **114** C10 13 32S 71 57W
Cwmbran Gwent Wales **38** C1 51 39N 3 00W
Cyclades *see* Kikládhes
Cypress Hills Alberta/Saskatchewan Canada **100** N2 48 40N 108 00W
CYPRUS **78** D5
CZECHOSLOVAKIA **69** C2
Częstochowa Poland **69** C3 50 49N 19 07E

D

Dabola Guinea **93** C5 10 48N 11 02W
Dachau F.R.G. **63** B1 48 15N 11 26E
Dadra & Nagar Haveli *admin.* India **77** C4 20 00N 73 00E
Dagenham Greater London England **34** D2 51 33N 0 08E
Dagnall Buckinghamshire England **34** B3 51 50N 0 34W
Da Hinggan Ling *(Greater Khingan Range) mts.* China **81** J7/J8 50 00N 122 00E
Dāhod India **77** C4 22 48N 74 18E
Dahongliutan Kashmir **77** D7 35 55N 79 10E
Dahuk Iraq **78** F6 36 58N 43 01E
Daio-zaki *c.* Japan **82** C1 34 16N 136 55E
Dairût Egypt **78** D4 27 34N 30 48E
Daito Japan **82** B2 35 25N 132 55E
Dakar Senegal **93** B5 14 38N 17 27W
Dakhla Oasis Egypt **94** E13 26 00N 28 00E
Dakshin Gangotri *r.s.* Antarctica **121** 70 05S 12 00E
Da Lat Vietnam **80** D6 11 56N 108 25E
Dalbandin Pakistan **76** A5 28 56N 64 30E
Dalbeattie Dumfries & Galloway Scotland **46** E1 54 56N 3 49W
Dalby Australia **86** I4 27 11S 151 12E
Dalgarven Strathclyde Scotland **45** A1 55 41N 4 42W
Dalgety Bay *tn.* Fife Scotland **45** D2 56 03N 3 18W
Dalhart Texas U.S.A. **102** F4 36 05N 102 32W
Dalian China **81** J5 38 53N 121 37S
Dalkeith Lothian Scotland **45** C1 55 51N 3 04W
Dalkey Dublin Irish Republic **49** B1 53 17N 6 06W
Dallas Texas U.S.A. **103** G3 32 47N 96 48W
Dalmally Strathclyde Scotland **46** D3 56 24N 4 58W
Dalmary Central Scotland **45** B2 56 08N 4 23W
Dalmellington Strathclyde Scotland **46** D2 55 19N 4 24W
Dalmeny Lothian Scotland **45** D1 55 58N 3 22W
Daloa Côte d'Ivoire **93** D4 6 56N 6 28W
Dalry Strathclyde Scotland **45** A1 55 43N 4 44W
Dalton Georgia U.S.A. **103** J3 34 46N 84 59W
Dalton Lancashire England **42** B2 53 34N 2 48W
Dalton-in-Furness Cumbria England **44** A1 54 09N 3 11W
Dalwhinnie Highland Scotland **46** D3 56 56N 4 14W
Daly *r.* Australia **86** E7 14 00S 132 00E
Daly Waters *tn.* Australia **86** E6 16 13S 133 20E
Daman India **77** C4 20 25N 72 58E
Damanhûr Egypt **78** D5 31 03N 30 28E
Damascus *see* Dimashq
Damāvand Iran **79** H6 35 47N 52 04E
Damāvand *mt.* Iran **79** H6 35 56N 52 08E
Damba Angola **95** C6 6 44S 15 20E
Damoh India **77** D4 23 50N 79 30E
Dampier Australia **86** B5 20 45S 116 48E
Danakil *geog. reg.* Africa **88** 14 00N 40 00E
Da Nang Vietnam **80** D7 16 04N 108 14E
Danau Toba *l.* Indonesia **80** B4 2 40N 98 50E
Danbury Connecticut U.S.A. **105** F2 41 24N 73 26W
Danbury Essex England **33** C2 51 44N 0 33E
Danderhall Lothian Scotland **45** D1 55 55N 3 06W
Dandong China **81** J6 40 08N 124 24E
Dangori India **77** H5 27 40N 95 35E
Danli Honduras **109** G2 14 02N 86 30W
Dannevirke New Zealand **87** C2 40 12S 176 08E
Danube *see* Donau, Duna, Dunarea, Dunav
Danville Illinois U.S.A. **104** C2 40 09N 87 37W
Danville Indiana U.S.A. **104** C1 39 44N 86 31W
Danville Kentucky U.S.A. **104** D1 37 40N 84 49W
Danville Pennsylvania U.S.A. **105** E2 40 58N 76 37W
Danville Virginia U.S.A. **103** K4 36 34N 79 25W
Dar'ā Syria **78** P11 32 37N 36 06E

Darbhanga India **77** F5 26 10N 85 54E
Dardanelles *sd.* Turkey **78** C6 40 08N 26 10E
Dar el Beida *see* Casablanca
Dar es Salaam Tanzania **95** G6 6 51S 39 18E
Darfield South Yorkshire England **43** F2 53 34N 1 22W
Dargaville New Zealand **87** B3 35 57S 173 53E
Darjiling India **77** F5 27 02N 88 20E
Darlaston West Midlands England **35** B2 52 34N 2 02W
Darling *r.* Australia **86** G3 31 30S 144 00E
Darling Downs *mts.* Australia **86** H4 28 00S 148 30E
Darlington Durham England **44** C1 54 31N 1 34W
Darmstadt F.R.G. **63** A1 49 52N 8 39E
Darnah Libya **94** D14 32 46N 22 39E
Darnley, Cape Antarctica **121** 67 16S 69 53E
Daroca Spain **66** B3 41 07N 1 25W
Dart *r.* Devon England **31** D2 50 28N 3 50W
Dartford Kent England **34** D2 51 27N 0 13E
Dartmoor National Park Devon England **31** D2 50 35N 3 50W
Dartmouth Devon England **31** D2 50 21N 3 35W
Dartmouth Nova Scotia Canada **101** W1 44 40N 63 35W
Darton South Yorkshire England **43** F2 53 36N 1 32W
Daru Papua New Guinea **86** G8 9 05S 143 10E
Darvel Strathclyde Scotland **46** D2 55 37N 4 18W
Darwen Lancashire England **42** C3 53 42N 2 28W
Darwin Australia **86** E7 12 23S 130 44E
Daryācheh-ye Orūmīyeh *(L. Urmia) l.* Iran **79** G6 37 20N 45 55E
Dasht-e Lut *geog. reg.* Iran **79** I5 32 00N 57 00E
Dasht-e-Kavir *geog. reg.* Iran **79** H5 34 30N 54 30E
Dasht-i-Margo *d.* Afghanistan **79** J5 30 30N 62 30E
Datchet Berkshire England **34** B2 51 30N 0 35W
Datong China **81** H6 40 02N 113 33E
Datong He *r.* China **81** F5 37 30N 102 00E
Datong Shan *mts.* China **81** E5 38 00N 99 00E
Datteln-Hamm-Kanal *can.* F.R.G. **62** E3 51 40N 7 35E
Datu Piang The Philippines **80** G5 7 02N 124 30E
Daugavpils U.S.S.R. **70** E7 55 52N 26 31E
Daun F.R.G. **64** F2 50 11N 6 50E
Dauphin Manitoba Canada **101** P3 51 09N 100 05W
Davangere India **77** D2 14 30N 75 52E
Davao The Philippines **80** H5 7 05N 125 38E
Davenham Cheshire England **42** C1 53 14N 2 31W
Davenport Iowa U.S.A. **104** B2 41 32N 90 36W
Daventry Northamptonshire England **36** C2 52 16N 1 09W
David Panama **109** H1 8 26N 82 26W
Davis *r.s.* Antarctica **121** 68 17S 77 58E
Davis Inlet *tn.* Newfoundland Canada **101** W4 55 51N 60 52W
Davis Strait Canada/Greenland **101** X6 69 00N 60 00W
Davos Switzerland **61** C2 46 47N 9 50E
Dawley Shropshire England **35** A2 52 40N 2 28W
Dawlish Devon England **31** D2 50 35N 3 28W
Dawna Range *mts.* Thailand **80** B7 17 30N 98 00E
Dawson Yukon Territory Canada **100** H5 64 04N 139 24W
Dawson Creek *tn.* British Columbia Canada **100** K4 55 44N 120 15W
Dax France **61** A1 43 43N 1 03W
Dayr az Zawr Syria **78** F6 35 20N 40 02E
Dayton Ohio U.S.A. **105** D1 39 45N 84 10W
Daytona Beach *tn.* Florida U.S.A. **103** J2 29 11N 81 01W
De Aar Republic of South Africa **95** D1 30 40S 24 01E
Dead Sea Israel/Jordan **78** O10 31 35N 35 30E
Deal Kent England **33** D2 51 14N 1 24E
Dean Funes Argentina **115** E6 30 25S 64 22W
Dean National Forest Park Gloucestershire England **31** E3 51 46N 2 25W
Deanston Central Scotland **45** B2 56 12N 4 05W
Dearne *r.* South Yorkshire England **43** G2 53 37N 1 02W
Dearne South Yorkshire England **43** G2 53 32N 1 20W
Dease *r.* British Columbia Canada **100** J4 58 30N 129 00W
Dease Lake *tn.* British Columbia Canada **100** J4 58 05N 130 04W
Death Valley California U.S.A. **102** C4 36 00N 117 00W
Death Valley National Monument California/Nevada U.S.A. **108** A7 37 30N 117 30W
Deben *r.* Suffolk England **33** D3 52 02N 1 25E
Debenham Suffolk England **33** D3 52 13N 1 11E
De Bilt Netherlands **65** E2 52 06N 5 10E
Debrecen Hungary **69** D2 47 30N 21 37E
Debre Mark'os Ethiopia **94** G10 10 19N 37 41E
Debre Tabor Ethiopia **94** G10 11 50N 38 06E
De Burg Netherlands **64** D5 53 04N 4 46E
Decatur Alabama U.S.A. **103** I3 34 36N 87 00W
Decatur Illinois U.S.A. **104** C1 39 51N 88 57W
Deccan *plat.* India **77** D3 18 00N 78 00E
Déception Québec Canada **101** U5 62 10N 74 45W
Děčín Czechoslovakia **63** B2 50 48N 14 15E
Deddington Oxfordshire England **32** A2 51 59N 1 19W
Dee *r.* Dumfries & Galloway Scotland **46** D1 54 55N 4 00W
Dee *r.* Grampian Scotland **46** F4 57 05N 2 10W
Dee *r.* Wales/England **38** C3 53 16N 3 10W
Deep Cut Surrey England **34** A1 51 18N 0 44W
Deep River *tn.* Ontario Canada **105** E3 46 04N 77 29W
Deeps, The *b.* Shetland Islands Scotland **47** B2 60 10N 1 25W
Deer Lake *tn.* Newfoundland Canada **101** X2 49 11N 57 27W
Degeh Bur Ethiopia **94** H9 8 11N 43 31E
Dehra Dun India **77** D6 30 19N 78 03E
Deinze Belgium **64** C2 50 59N 3 32E
Dej Romania **69** D2 47 08N 23 55E
Dekese Zaïre **95** D7 3 28S 21 24E
Delamere Cheshire England **42** C1 53 13N 2 40W
Delamere Forest *hills* Cheshire England **42** B1 53 14N 2 38W
Delaware Ohio U.S.A. **105** D2 40 18N 83 06W
Delaware *state* U.S.A. **105** E1 39 00N 75 00W
Delaware Bay U.S.A. **105** E1 39 00N 75 00W
Delft Netherlands **65** B2 52 00N 4 22E
Delfzijl Netherlands **64** F5 53 19N 6 56E
Delhi India **76** L4 28 40N 77 14E
Delhi Cantonment India **76** L4 28 35N 77 08E
De Lier Netherlands **65** A1 51 59N 4 13E
Delitzsch G.D.R. **63** B2 51 32N 12 20E
Dellen *l.* Sweden **67** D3 61 50N 16 45E
Dellys Algeria **66** C2 36 57N 3 55E
Delmenhorst F.R.G. **63** A2 53 03N 8 37E
De Long Mountains Alaska U.S.A. **100** C6 68 30N 162 00W
Delph Greater Manchester England **42** D2 53 34N 2 02W
Del Rio Texas U.S.A. **102** F2 29 23N 100 56W
Delta Colorado U.S.A. **102** E4 38 42N 108 04W
Dembī Dolo Ethiopia **94** G9 8 34N 34 50E
Demer *r.* Belgium **64** D3 51 02N 4 52E
Deming New Mexico U.S.A. **102** E3 32 17N 107 46W
Denain France **61** B3 50 19N 3 24E
Denbigh Clwyd Wales **38** C3 53 11N 3 25W
Denby Dale West Yorkshire England **43** F2 53 35N 1 38W
Dender *r.* Belgium **64** C2 50 50N 3 55E
Dendermonde Belgium **64** D3 51 02N 4 06E
Den Haag *(The Hague) see* 's-Gravenhage
Den Helder Netherlands **64** D5 52 58N 4 46E
Denison Iowa U.S.A. **104** A2 42 01N 95 20W
Denison Texas U.S.A. **103** G3 33 47N 96 34W
Denizli Turkey **78** C6 37 46N 29 05E
Denman Glacier Antarctica **121** 67 00S 100 00E
DENMARK **67** B2/C2
Denmark Strait Greenland/Iceland **101** DD6 67 00N 26 00W
Denny Central Scotland **45** C2 56 02N 3 55W
Denpasar Indonesia **80** F2 8 40S 115 14E
Denton Greater Manchester England **42** D2 53 27N 2 07W
Denton Texas U.S.A. **103** G3 33 14N 97 18W
D'Entrecasteaux Islands Papua New Guinea **86** I8 9 30S 150 30E
Denver Colorado U.S.A. **102** E4 39 45N 105 00W
Deodora Brazil **116** B2 22 51S 43 22W
De Panne Belgium **64** B3 51 06N 2 35E
Dépression du Mourdi *dep.* Chad **94** D11 17 00N 22 00E
Deputatskiy U.S.S.R. **71** P9 69 15N 139 59E
Dera Ghazi Khan Pakistan **77** C6 30 05N 70 44E
Dera Ismail Khan Pakistan **77** C6 31 51N 70 56E
Derby Australia **86** C6 17 19S 123 38E
Derby Derbyshire England **35** D3 52 55N 1 30W
Derbyshire *co.* England **36** C3 53 15N 1 35W
Derrynasaggart Mountains Irish Republic **48** B1 51 55N 9 10W
Dersingham Norfolk England **33** C3 52 51N 0 30E
Derwent *r.* Cumbria England **44** A1 54 40N 3 20W
Derwent *r.* Derbyshire England **36** C3 53 00N 1 30W
Derwent *r.* Durham/Northumberland England **44** B1 54 50N 2 05W
Derwent *r.* North Yorkshire England **40** D3 54 10N 0 40W
Derwent Reservoir Derbyshire England **43** E2 53 25N 1 45W
Derwent Water *l.* Cumbria England **44** A1 54 35N 3 09W
Desborough Northamptonshire England **36** D2 52 27N 0 49W
Desē Ethiopia **94** G10 11 05N 39 40E
Deseado Argentina **115** D3 47 44S 65 56W
Desford Leicestershire England **35** E2 52 39N 1 17W
Desierto de, Atacama *(Atacama Desert) d.* Chile **114/115** C8 22 30S 70 00W
Des Moines Iowa U.S.A. **104** B2 41 35N 93 35W
Des Moines *r.* U.S.A. **104** B2 40 00N 92 00W
Desna *r.* U.S.S.R. **70** F6 52 00N 32 30E
Dessau G.D.R. **63** B2 51 51N 12 15E
Desvres France **64** A2 50 40N 1 50E
Detmold F.R.G. **63** A2 51 55N 8 52E
Detroit Michigan U.S.A. **105** D2 42 23N 83 05W
Detroit Lakes *tn.* Minnesota U.S.A. **104** A3 46 49N 95 49W
Detroit River North America **105** D2 42 00N 83 00W
Deurne Netherlands **64** E3 51 28N 5 47E
Deva Romania **69** D2 45 53N 22 55E
Deventer Netherlands **64** F4 52 15N 6 10E
Deveron *r.* Grampian Scotland **46** E4 57 25N 3 03W
Devil's Bridge Dyfed Wales **38** C2 52 23N 3 51W
Devils Gate Reservoir California U.S.A. **107** B3 34 11N 118 10W
Devils Lake *tn.* North Dakota U.S.A. **104** A3 48 08N 98 50W
Devizes Wiltshire England **31** E3 51 22N 1 59W
Devon *co.* England **31** C2 50 45N 3 50W
Devon Island Northwest Territories Canada **101** R8 75 10N 85 00W
Devonport Australia **86** H1 41 09S 146 16E
Dewsbury West Yorkshire England **43** F3 53 42N 1 37W
Dezfūl Iran **79** G5 32 23N 48 28E
Dezhou China **81** I5 37 29N 116 11E
Dhaka Bangladesh **77** G4 23 42N 90 22E
Dhamār Yemen **78** F1 14 33N 44 30E
Dhanbad India **77** F4 23 47N 86 32E
Dharoor *r.* Somalia **94** I10 10 00N 54 00E
Dhārwād India **77** D3 15 30N 75 04E
Dhodhekánisos *(Dodecanese) is.* Greece **68** E2 37 00N 27 00E
Dhoraji India **76** C4 21 42N 70 32E
Dhule India **77** C4 20 52N 74 50E
Diamantina Brazil **114** I9 18 17S 43 37W
Diamantina *r.* Australia **86** G5 24 00S 142 00E
Dibrugarh India **77** G5 27 29N 94 56E
Dickinson North Dakota U.S.A. **102** F6 46 54N 102 48W
Didcot Oxfordshire England **32** A2 51 37N 1 15W
Diekirch Luxembourg **64** F1 49 52N 6 10E
Diemel *r.* F.R.G. **63** A2 52 00N 9 00E
Diemen Netherlands **65** D3 52 21N 4 57E
Diepholz F.R.G. **63** A2 52 37N 8 22E
Dieppe France **61** B2 49 55N 1 05E
Diest Belgium **64** E2 50 58N 5 03E
Digby Nova Scotia Canada **101** V1 44 37N 65 47W
Digne France **61** C1 44 05N 6 14E
Dijon France **61** C2 47 20N 5 02E
Diksmuide Belgium **64** B3 51 02N 2 52E
Dikson U.S.S.R. **71** K10 73 32N 80 39E
Dikwa Nigeria **93** H5 12 01N 13 55E
Dili *see* Oekusi
Dillingham Alaska U.S.A. **100** D4 59 03N 158 30W
Dimashq *(Damascus)* Syria **78** P11 33 30N 36 19E
Dimitrovgrad Bulgaria **68** E3 42 03N 25 34E
Dinajpur Bangladesh **77** F5 25 38N 88 44E
Dinan France **61** A2 48 27N 2 02W
Dinant Belgium **64** D2 50 16N 4 55E
Dinara Planina *(Dinaric Alps) mts.* Yugoslavia **68** C3 44 00N 17 00E
Dinard France **61** A2 48 38N 2 03W
Dinaric Alps *see* Dinara Planina
Dinas-Mawddwy Gwynedd Wales **38** C2 52 43N 3 41W
Dinas Powis South Glamorgan Wales **38** C1 51 25N 3 14W
Dindigul India **77** D2 10 23N 78 00E
Dingle Kerry Irish Republic **48** A2 52 08N 10 15W
Dingle Bay Irish Republic **48** A2 52 05N 10 15W
Dingwall Highland Scotland **46** D4 57 35N 4 29W
Dinkel *r.* Europe **64** G4 52 00N 7 00E
Dinnington South Yorkshire England **43** G2 53 22N 1 12W
Dinslaken F.R.G. **62** A3 51 34N 6 43E
Dintel Mark *r.* Netherlands **64** D3 51 35N 4 25E
Dipolog The Philippines **80** G5 8 34N 123 23E
Dir Pakistan **77** C7 35 12N 71 54E
Dirē Dawa Ethiopia **94** H9 9 35N 41 50E
Disappointment, Lake Australia **86** C5 23 00S 123 00E
Disko Greenland **101** Y6 70 00N 54 00W
Disko Bugt *b.* Greenland **101** Y6 69 00N 54 00W
Diss Norfolk England **33** D3 52 23N 1 06W
Ditan China **82** G1 39 58N 116 24E
Ditton Kent England **34** E1 51 18N 0 27E
Diu India **76** C4 20 41N 71 03E
Divinópolis Brazil **114** I8 20 08S 44 55W
Divis *sum.* Northern Ireland **49** C1 54 37N 6 02W
Divriği Turkey **78** E6 39 23N 38 06E
Dixon Entrance *sd.* U.S.A./Canada **100** I3 54 00N 132 30W
Diyarbakir Turkey **78** F6 37 55N 40 14E
Djambala Congo **94** B7 2 32S 14 43E
Djelfa Algeria **93** F9 34 43N 3 14E
DJIBOUTI **78** F1
Djibouti Djibouti **78** F1 11 35N 43 11E
Djoué *r.* Congo **92** A2 4 17S 15 12E
Djougou Benin **93** F4 9 40N 1 47E
Dnepr *r.* U.S.S.R. **70** F5 47 30N 33 00E
Dnepropetrovsk U.S.S.R. **70** F5 48 29N 35 00E
Dnestr *r.* U.S.S.R. **70** E5 48 00N 27 30E
Doagh Northern Ireland **49** C2 54 44N 6 03W
Dobreta-Turnu-Severin Romania **69** D1 44 36N 22 39E
Dobrogea *geog. reg.* Romania **69** E1 44 00N 29 00E
Docking Norfolk England **33** C3 52 55N 0 38E
Dodder *r.* Dublin Irish Republic **49** A1 53 15N 6 20W
Dodecanese *see* Dhodhekánisos
Dodford Hereford & Worcester England **35** B2 52 21N 2 05W
Dodge City Kansas U.S.A. **102** F4 37 45N 100 02W
Dodgeville Wisconsin U.S.A. **104** B2 42 57N 90 08W
Dodman Point Cornwall England **30** C2 50 13N 4 48W
Dodoma Tanzania **95** G6 6 10S 35 40E
Dodworth South Yorkshire England **43** F2 53 33N 1 32W
Doetinchem Netherlands **64** F3 51 58N 6 17E
Dogai Coring *l.* China **77** F6 34 30N 89 00E
Dōgo *i.* Japan **82** B2 36 20N 133 15E
Doha *see* Ad Dawḩah
Dokkum Netherlands **64** F5 53 20N 6 00E
Dolbeau Québec Canada **105** F3 48 52N 72 15W
Dôle France **61** C2 47 05N 5 30E
Dolgellau Gwynedd Wales **38** C2 52 44N 3 53W
Dolina U.S.S.R. **69** D2 49 00N 23 59E
Dollar Central Scotland **45** C2 56 09N 3 41W
Dollard *b.* Netherlands/F.R.G. **64** G5 53 20N 7 15E
Dolo Ethiopia **94** H8 4 11N 42 03E
Dolphin, Cape Falkland Islands **117** M16 51 15S 58 55W
Dolphinton Strathclyde Scotland **45** D1 55 43N 3 26W
Domaneab Nauru **118** G7 0 35S 166 40E
Domažlice Czechoslovakia **63** B1 49 27N 12 56E
Dombas Norway **67** B3 62 05N 9 07E
DOMINICA **109** L3
DOMINICAN REPUBLIC **109** K3
Domont France **60** B3 49 02N 2 21E
Don *r.* Grampian Scotland **46** F4 57 15N 2 55W
Don *r.* South Yorkshire England **43** G2 53 37N 1 02W
Don *r.* U.S.S.R. **70** G6 50 00N 41 00E
Donabate Dublin Irish Republic **49** B2 53 30N 6 09W
Donaghadee Down Northern Ireland **48** F4 54 39N 5 33W
Donau *(Danube) r.* F.R.G./Austria **69** C2 48 00N 16 00E
Donauwörth F.R.G. **63** B1 48 44N 10 48E
Don Benito Spain **66** A2 38 57N 5 52W
Doncaster South Yorkshire England **43** G2 53 32N 1 07W
Donegal *co.* Irish Republic **48** C4/D4 54 55N 8 00W
Donegal Donegal Irish Republic **48** C4 54 39N 8 07W
Donegal Bay Irish Republic **48** C4 54 30N 8 30W
Donegal Mountains Irish Republic **48** C4/5 55 00N 8 05W
Donetsk U.S.S.R. **70** F5 48 00N 37 50E
Dongba China **82** H1 39 58N 116 35E
Dongchuan China **81** F3 26 07N 103 05E
Dongen Netherlands **64** D3 51 38N 4 56E
Dongola Sudan **78** D2 19 10N 30 27E
Dongou Congo **94** C8 2 02N 18 02E
Donington Lincolnshire England **36** D2 52 55N 0 12W
Donisthorpe Leicestershire England **35** D3 52 43N 1 31W
Dønna *i.* Norway **67** C4 66 05N 12 30E
Donnacona Québec Canada **105** F3 46 41N 71 45W
Donnington Shropshire England **35** A3 52 43N 2 25W
Donting Hu *l.* China **81** H3 29 00N 112 30E
Doon *r.* Scotland **46** D2 55 25N 4 30W
Door Peninsula Wisconsin U.S.A. **104** C3 45 00N 87 00W
Dora Bàltea *r.* Italy **61** C2 45 00N 7 00E
Dora Riparia *r.* Italy **61** C2 45 00N 7 00E
Dorchester Dorset England **31** E2 50 43N 2 26W
Dorchester Oxfordshire England **32** A2 51 39N 1 10W
Dordogne *r.* France **61** B1 44 55N 0 30E
Dordon Warwickshire England **35** D2 52 36N 1 37W
Dordrecht Netherlands **64** D3 51 48N 4 40E
Dore *r.* France **61** B2 45 40N 3 30E
Dore South Yorkshire England **43** F1 53 20N 1 33W
Dori *r.* Afghanistan **79** K5 31 20N 65 00E
Dorion Ontario Canada **104** C3 48 49N 88 33W
Dorking Surrey England **34** B1 51 14N 0 20W
Dormagen F.R.G. **64** F3 51 06N 6 50E
Dormansland Surrey England **34** D1 51 10N 0 01E
Dornbirn Austria **63** A1 47 25N 9 46E
Dornie Highland Scotland **46** C4 57 17N 5 31W
Dornoch Highland Scotland **46** D4 57 52N 4 02W
Dornoch Firth *est.* Highland Scotland **46** E4 57 55N 3 55W
Dorridge West Midlands England **35** C2 52 22N 1 45W
Dorset *co.* England **31** E2 50 50N 2 20W
Dorsten F.R.G. **64** F3 51 38N 6 58E
Dortmund F.R.G. **64** A3 51 32N 7 27E
Dortmund-Ems-Kanal *can.* F.R.G. **62** D3 51 40N 7 20E
Dosso Niger **93** F5 13 03N 3 10E
Dothan Alabama U.S.A. **103** I3 31 12N 85 25W
Douai France **61** B3 50 22N 3 05E
Douarnenez France **61** A2 48 05N 4 20W
Doubs *r.* France **61** C2 47 20N 6 25E
Douglas Alaska U.S.A. **100** I4 58 15N 134 24W
Douglas Arizona U.S.A. **102** E3 31 21N 109 34W
Douglas Isle of Man British Isles **41** F1 54 09N 4 29W
Douglas *r.* Lancashire England **42** B2 53 38N 2 48W
Doullens France **61** B3 50 09N 2 21E
Doune Central Scotland **45** B2 56 11N 4 04W
Dounreay Highland Scotland **46** E5 58 34N 3 44W
Dourados Brazil **115** G8 22 09S 54 52W
Douro *r.* Portugal **66** A3 41 00N 8 30W
Dovaia Cameroon **93** G3 4 04N 9 43E
Dove *r.* Derbyshire/Staffordshire England **36** C2 52 50N 1 35W
Dovedale *v.* Derbyshire England **36** C3 53 10N 1 45W
Dover Delaware U.S.A. **105** E1 39 10N 75 32W
Dover Kent England **33** D2 51 08N 1 19E
Dover New Hampshire U.S.A. **105** F2 43 12N 70 55W
Dover Foxcroft Maine U.S.A. **105** G3 45 12N 69 16W
Doveridge Derbyshire England **35** C3 52 54N 1 50W
Dover, Strait of *(Pas de Calais)* English Channel **33** D2 51 00N 1 20E
Dovrefjell *mts.* Norway **67** B3 62 15N 9 10E
Downey California U.S.A. **107** B2 33 56N 118 25W
Downham Market Norfolk England **33** C3 52 36N 0 23E
Downpatrick Down Northern Ireland **48** F4 54 20N 5 43W
Downpatrick Head *c.* Irish Republic **48** B4 54 20N 9 15W
Downton Wiltshire England **31** F2 51 00N 1 44W
Dōzen *is.* Japan **82** B2 36 05N 133 00E
Drachten Netherlands **64** F5 53 07N 6 06E
Dragan *l.* Sweden **67** D3 64 05N 15 20E
Draguignan France **61** C1 43 32N 6 28E
Drakensberg *mts.* Republic of South Africa **95** E1 30 00S 28 00E
Drake Passage *sd.* Southern Ocean **115** C1–E1 58 00S 66 00W
Dráma Greece **68** D3 41 10N 24 11E
Drammen Norway **67** C2 59 45N 10 15E
Drancy France **60** B2 48 55N 2 28E
Drau *r.* Austria **69** B2 46 00N 14 00E
Drava *r.* Europe **68** C4 45 00N 18 00E
Draveil France **60** B1 48 41N 2 25E
Draycote Water *l.* Warwickshire England **35** E1 52 18N 1 20W
Dreghorn Strathclyde Scotland **46** D2 55 37N 4 37W
Drenthe *admin.* Netherlands **64** F4 52 55N 6 45E
Dresden *admin.* G.D.R. **63** B2 51 00N 14 00E
Dresden G.D.R. **63** B2 51 03N 13 45E
Dreswick Point Isle of Man British Isles **41** F1 54 03N 4 37W
Dreux France **61** B2 48 44N 1 23E
Drighlington West Yorkshire England **43** E3 53 45N 1 40W
Drin *r.* Albania **68** D3 42 00N 20 00E
Drina *r.* Yugoslavia **68** C3 43 00N 19 00E
Drogheda Meath Irish Republic **48** E3 53 43N 6 21W
Drogobyč U.S.S.R. **69** D2 49 22N 23 33E
Droichead Nua *(Newbridge)* Kildare Irish Republic
Droitwich Hereford and Worcester England **35** B1 52 16N 2 09W
Drôme *r.* France **61** C1 44 50N 5 00E
Dromore Down Northern Ireland **48** E4 54 25N 6 09W
Dronfield Derbyshire England **43** F1 53 19N 1 27W
Drongan Strathclyde Scotland **46** D2 55 29N 4 30W
Dronten Netherlands **64** E4 53 21N 5 41E
Droylesden Greater Manchester England **42** D2 53 29N 2 09W
Drum Tayside Scotland **45** C2 56 12N 3 33W
Drumbeg Northern Ireland **49** D1 54 32N 5 59W
Drumheller Alberta Canada **100** M3 51 28N 112 40W
Drummond Island Michigan U.S.A. **105** D3 46 00N 84 00W
Drummondville Québec Canada **105** F3 45 52N 72 30W
Drummore Dumfries & Galloway Scotland **46** D1 54 42N 4 54W
Drumnadrochit Highland Scotland **46** D4 57 20N 4 30W
Dryden Ontario Canada **104** B3 49 48N 92 48W
Dry Fork *r.* Missouri U.S.A. **104** B1 38 00N 91 00W
Drymen Central Scotland **45** B2 56 04N 4 27W
Dschang Cameroon **93** H4 5 28N 10 02E
Dubawnt Lake Northwest Territories Canada **101** O5 68 15N 102 00W
Dubayy United Arab Emirates **79** I4 25 14N 55 17E
Dubbo Australia **86** H3 32 16S 148 41E
Dublin *(Baile Átha Cliath)* Dublin Irish Republic **49** B2 53 20N 6 15W
Dublin *co.* Irish Republic **48** E3 53 25N 6 10W
Dublin Georgia U.S.A. **103** J3 32 31N 82 54W
Dublin Bay Dublin Irish Republic **49** B1 53 20N 6 05W
Dubno U.S.S.R. **69** E3 50 28N 25 40E
Dubrovnik Yugoslavia **68** C3 42 40N 18 07E
Dubuque Iowa U.S.A. **104** B2 42 31N 90 41W
Ducie Island Pitcairn Islands **119** N5 24 40S 124 48W
Duddon Cheshire England **42** B1 53 11N 2 44W
Duddon *r.* Cumbria England **44** A1 54 10N 3 10W
Dudelange Luxembourg **64** F1 49 28N 6 05E
Dudinka U.S.S.R. **71** K9 69 27N 86 13E
Dudley Tyne and Wear England **44** C2 55 10N 1 20W
Dudley West Midlands England **35** B2 52 30N 2 05W
Duero *(Douro) r.* Spain/Portugal **66** A3 41 25N 6 30W
Duffield Derbyshire England **35** D4 52 59N 1 29W
Dufftown Grampian Scotland **46** E4 57 26N 3 08W
Dugi Otok *i.* Yugoslavia **68** C3 44 00N 15 00E
Duisburg F.R.G. **62** B2 51 26N 6 45E
Duiveland *i.* Netherlands **64** C3 51 37N 4 00E
Dukinfield Greater Manchester England **42** D2 53 29N 2 06W
Duleek Meath Irish Republic **48** E3 53 39N 6 25W
Dülmen F.R.G. **64** G3 51 49N 7 17E
Duluth Minnesota U.S.A. **104** B3 46 45N 92 10W
Dulverton Somerset England **31** D3 51 03N 3 33W
Dumbarton Strathclyde Scotland **45** A1 55 57N 4 35W
Dum Dum India **76** K2 22 37N 88 24E
Dumfries Dumfries & Galloway Scotland **46** E2 55 04N 3 37W
Dumfries and Galloway *reg.* Scotland **46** D2 55 10N 4 00W
Dumont d'Urville *r.s.* Antarctica **121** 66 40S 140 01E
Dümpten F.R.G. **62** B2 51 28N 6 50E
Dumyāt Egypt **78** D5 31 26N 31 48E
Duna *(Danube) r.* Hungary **69** C2 46 00N 19 00E
Dunadry Northern Ireland **49** C2 54 41N 6 08W
Dunarea *(Danube) r.* Romania **69** E1 44 00N 28 00E
Dunaújváros Hungary **69** C2 47 00N 18 55E
Dunav *(Danube) r.* Yugoslavia/Bulgaria **68** C4 45 00N 20 00E
Dunbar Lothian Scotland **46** F3 56 00N 2 31W
Dunbeath Highland Scotland **46** E5 58 15N 3 25W
Dunblane Central Scotland **45** C2 56 12N 3 59W
Dunboyne Meath Irish Republic **49** A2 53 25N 6 29W
Duncan Oklahoma U.S.A. **103** G3 34 30N 97 57W
Duncan Passage *sd.* Andaman Islands **77** G2 11 00N 93 00E
Duncansby Head *c.* Highland Scotland **46** E5 58 39N 3 02W
Dunchurch Warwickshire England **35** E2 52 20N 1 16W
Dundalk Louth Irish Republic **48** E4 54 01N 6 25W
Dundalk Bay Irish Republic **48** E3 53 55N 6 15W
Dundas Ontario Canada **105** E2 43 16N 79 57W
Dundas *(Thule)* Greenland **101** V8 76 30N 68 58W
Dundee Tayside Scotland **46** E3 56 28N 3 00W
Dundonald Down Northern Ireland **49** D1 54 36N 5 48W
Dundrum Dublin Irish Republic **49** B1 53 17N 6 15W
Dunedin New Zealand **87** B1 45 52S 170 30E
Dunfermline Fife Scotland **45** D2 56 04N 3 29W
Dungannon Northern Ireland **48** E4 54 31N 6 46W
Dungarvan Waterford Irish Republic **48** D2 52 05N 7 37W

Dungeness *c.* Kent England **33** C1 50 55N 0 58E
Dungiven Northern Ireland **48** E4 54 55N 6 55W
Dungloe Donegal Irish Republic **48** C4 54 57N 8 22W
Dunham-on-the-Hill Cheshire England **42** B1 53 15N 2 48W
Dunholme Lincolnshire England **36** D3 53 18N 0 29W
Dunipace Central Scotland **45** C2 56 02N 3 55W
Dunkeld Tayside Scotland **46** E3 56 34N 3 35W
Dunkerque *(Dunkirk)* France **61** B3 51 02N 2 23E
Dunkery Beacon *sum.* Somerset England **31** D3 51 11N 3 35W
Dunkirk New York U.S.A. **105** E2 42 29N 79 21W
Dunkirk *see* Dunkerque
Dún Laoghaire Dublin Irish Republic **49** B1 53 17N 6 08W
Dunleer Louth Irish Republic **48** E3 53 50N 6 24W
Dunley Hereford & Worcester England **35** B1 52 18N 2 19W
Dunlop Strathclyde Scotland **45** A1 55 43N 4 32W
Dunmanus Bay Irish Republic **48** B1 51 30N 9 50W
Dunmanway Cork Irish Republic **48** B1 51 43N 9 06W
Dunmurry Antrim Northern Ireland **49** C1 54 33N 6 00W
Dunnet Head *c.* Highland Scotland **46** E5 58 40N 3 25W
Dunnington North Yorkshire England **43** H3 53 57N 0 59W
Dunnington Warwickshire England **35** C1 52 11N 1 55W
Dunoon Strathclyde Scotland **46** D2 55 57N 4 56W
Duns Borders Scotland **46** F2 55 47N 2 20W
Dunscroft South Yorkshire England **43** G2 53 34N 1 05W
Dunshaughlin Meath Irish Republic **49** A2 53 31N 6 33W
Dunstable Bedfordshire England **34** B3 51 53N 0 32W
Dunster Somerset England **31** D3 51 12N 3 27W
Dunston Staffordshire England **35** B3 52 46N 2 06W
Duntochar Strathclyde Scotland **45** B1 55 55N 4 25W
Dunvegan Highland Scotland **46** B4 57 26N 6 35W
Duque de Caxias Brazil **116** B2 22 46S 43 18W
Durance *r.* France **61** C1 43 50N 5 15E
Durand Wisconsin U.S.A. **104** B2 44 37N 91 56W
Durango Colorado U.S.A. **102** E4 37 16N 107 53W
Durango Mexico **108** D4 24 01N 104 40W
Durant Oklahoma U.S.A. **103** G3 33 59N 96 24W
Durazno Uruguay **115** F6 33 22S 56 31W
Durban Republic of South Africa **95** F2 29 53S 31 00E
Düren F.R.G. **63** A2 50 48N 6 30E
Durgapur India **77** J1 22 47N 87 44E
Durgāpur India **76** J1 22 27N 88 08E
Durg-Bhilai India **77** E4 21 12N 81 20E
Durham *co.* England **44** B1/C1 54 40N 2 00W
Durham Durham England **44** C1 54 47N 1 34W
Durham North Carolina U.S.A. **103** K4 36 00N 78 54W
Durlston Head *c.* Dorset England **31** E2 50 35N 1 57W
Durness Highland Scotland **46** D5 58 33N 4 45W
Durrës Albania **68** C3 41 18N 19 28E
Durrington Wiltshire England **31** F3 51 12N 1 48W
Dursey Head *c.* Irish Republic **48** A1 51 20N 10 10W
Dursey Island Irish Republic **48** A1 51 36N 10 12W
Dursley Gloucestershire England **31** E3 51 42N 2 21W
Dushanbe U.S.S.R. **70** I3 38 38N 68 51E
Düssel *r.* F.R.G. **62** C1 51 14N 7 01E
Düsseldorf F.R.G. **62** B1 51 13N 6 47E
Dutch Harbor *tn.* Alaska U.S.A. **100** B3 53 55N 166 36W
Duyun China **81** G3 26 16N 107 29E
Dvina, North *see* Severnaya Dvina
Dyce Grampian Scotland **46** F4 57 12N 2 11W
Dyfed *co.* Wales **38** B1 52 00N 4 25W
Dyfi *r.* Powys Wales **38** C2 52 38N 3 50W
Dyfrdwy *r.* Clwyd Wales **38** D2/3 53 00N 2 50W
Dykehead Central Scotland **45** B2 56 09N 4 15W
Dyle *r.* Belgium **64** D2 50 38N 4 35E
Dymchurch Kent England **33** C2 51 02N 1 00E
Dzhambul U.S.S.R. **70** J4 42 50N 71 25E
Dzhetygara U.S.S.R. **70** I6 52 14N 61 10E
Dzhezkazgan U.S.S.R. **70** I5 47 44N 67 42E
Dzhugdzhur Range *mts.* U.S.S.R. **71** P7 57 00N 137 00E
Dzungarian Basin *see* Junggar Pendi

E

Eagle Alaska U.S.A. **100** G5 64 46N 141 20W
Eagle Lake Maine U.S.A. **105** G3 46 00N 69 00W
Eagle Pass *tn.* Texas U.S.A. **102** F2 28 44N 100 31W
Eaglescliff Cleveland England **44** C1 54 31N 1 22W
Eaglesham Strathclyde Scotland **45** B1 55 44N 4 15W
Ealing Greater London England **34** C2 51 31N 0 18W
Earby Lancashire England **42** D3 53 56N 2 08W
Earls Colne Essex England **33** C2 51 56N 0 42E
Earl Shilton Leicestershire England **35** E2 52 35N 1 18W
Earlswood Warwickshire England **35** C2 52 22N 1 50W
Earn *r.* Tayside Scotland **45** C2 56 45N 3 40W
Easington Durham England **44** C1 54 47N 1 21W
Easington Humberside England **40** E2 53 40N 0 07E
Easingwold North Yorkshire England **40** C3 54 07N 1 11W
East Antarctica *geog. reg.* Antarctica **121**
Eastbourne East Sussex England **33** C1 50 46N 0 17E
East Calder Lothian Scotland **45** D1 55 54N 3 27W
East Cape New Zealand **87** C3 37 42S 178 35E
East Caroline Basin Pacific Ocean **118** E8 4 00N 148 00E
East China Sea China/Japan **81** K4 32 00N 126 00E
East Dean East Sussex England **33** C1 50 45N 0 13E
East Dereham Norfolk England **33** C3 52 41N 0 56E
Easter Island Pacific Ocean **119** P5 27 05S 109 20W
Easter Island Fracture Zone Pacific Ocean **119** Q5 24 00S 100 00W
Eastern Ghats *geog. reg.* India **77** D2–E3 15 00N 80 00E
Eastern Group *is.* Fiji **118** V16 17 40S 178 30W
Eastern Sayan *mts.* U.S.S.R. **71** L6 53 00N 97 30E
East Falkland *i.* Falkland Islands **117** M15 52 00S 58 50W
Eastfield North Yorkshire England **40** D3 54 15N 0 25W
East Fork White River Indiana U.S.A. **104** C1 39 00N 87 00W
East Frisian Islands *see* Ostfriesische Inseln
East Grand Forks Minnesota U.S.A. **104** A3 47 56N 96 59W
East Grinstead West Sussex England **34** C1 51 08N 0 01W
Eastham Merseyside England **42** B1 53 19N 2 58W
East Ilsley Berkshire England **32** A2 51 32N 1 17W
Eastington Gloucestershire England **31** E3 51 45N 2 20W
East Keswick West Yorkshire England **43** F3 53 53N 1 27W
East Kilbride Strathclyde Scotland **45** B1 55 46N 4 10W
East Leake Nottinghamshire England **36** C2 52 50N 1 11W
Eastleigh Hampshire England **32** A1 50 58N 1 22W
East Linton Lothian Scotland **46** F2 55 59N 2 39W
East Liverpool Ohio U.S.A. **105** D2 40 38N 80 36W
East London Republic of South Africa **95** E1 33 00S 27 54E
East Los Angeles California U.S.A. **107** B3 34 02N 118 12W
Eastmain Québec Canada **101** T3 52 10N 78 30W
East Marianas Basin Pacific Ocean **118** F9 13 00N 153 00E
East Markham Nottinghamshire England **43** H1 53 15N 0 54W
Easton Dorset England **31** E2 50 32N 2 26W
Easton Maryland U.S.A. **105** E1 38 46N 76 05W
Easton Pennsylvania U.S.A. **105** E2 40 41N 75 13W
East Pacific Basin Pacific Ocean **119** K9 16 00N 153 00E
East Pacific Ridge Pacific Ocean **119** O5 20 00S 113 00W
East Pacific Rise Pacific Ocean **119** P9 13 00N 103 00W
East Retford Nottinghamshire England **43** H1 53 19N 0 56W
East Rift Valley East Africa **94** G9 6 00N 37 00E
East St. Louis Illinois U.S.A. **104** B1 38 34N 90 04W
East Siberian Sea Arctic Ocean **120** 72 00N 165 00E
East Stour *r.* Kent England **33** C2 51 08N 0 55E
East Sussex *co.* England **33** C1 50 55N 0 10E
East Wemyss Fife Scotland **45** D2 56 10N 3 05W
Eastwood Nottinghamshire England **35** E4 53 01N 1 18W
Eaton Bray Befordshire England **34** B3 51 53N 0 36W
Eaton Socon Bedfordshire England **33** B3 52 13N 0 18W
Eaton Wash Reservoir California U.S.A. **107** B3 34 10N 118 05W
Eau Claire *tn.* Wisconsin U.S.A. **104** B2 44 50N 91 30W
Eauripik–New Guinea Rise Pacific Ocean **118** E8 2 00N 142 00E
Ebbw Vale Gwent Wales **38** C1 51 47N 3 12W
Ebensburg Pennsylvania U.S.A. **105** E2 40 28N 78 44W
Eberswalde-Finow G.D.R. **63** B2 52 50N 13 53E
Ebinur Hu *l.* China **81** B6/7 45 00N 83 00E
Ebolowa Cameroon **93** H3 2 56N 11 11E
Ebro *r.* Spain **66** C3 41 00N 0 30E
Ebute Metta Nigeria **92** C3 6 27N 3 28E
Ecclefechan Dumfries & Galloway Scotland **46** E2 55 03N 3 17W
Eccles Greater Manchester England **42** C2 53 29N 2 21W
Ecclesfield South Yorkshire England **43** F2 53 27N 1 27W
Eccleshall Staffordshire England **35** B3 52 52N 2 15W
Ech Cheliff Algeria **93** F10 36 05N 1 15E
Echo Bay *tn.* Northwest Territories Canada **100** L6 65 50N 117 30W
Echternach Luxembourg **64** F1 49 49N 6 25E
Ecija Spain **66** A2 37 33N 5 04W
Eckernförde F.R.G. **63** A2 54 28N 9 50E
Eckington Derbyshire England **43** F1 53 91N 1 21W
Écouen France **60** B3 49 01N 2 22E
ECUADOR **114** B12
Edale Derbyshire England **43** E2 53 22N 1 49W
Edam Netherlands **64** E4 52 30N 5 02E
Eday *i.* Orkney Islands Scotland **47** E2 59 11N 2 47W
Ed Damer Sudan **78** D2 17 37N 33 59E
Ed Debba Sudan **94** F11 18 02N 30 56E
Eddleston Borders Scotland **45** D1 55 43N 3 13W
Eddrachillis Bay Highland Scotland **46** C5 58 25N 5 15W
Eddystone Rocks English Channel **31** C2 50 10N 4 16W
Eddyville Kentucky U.S.A. **104** C1 37 03N 88 02W
Ede Netherlands **64** E4 52 03N 5 40E
Edéa Cameroon **93** H3 3 47N 10 13E
Eden Antrim Northern Ireland **49** D2 54 44N 5 47W
Eden North Carolina U.S.A. **103** K4 37 00N 80 00W
Eden *r.* Cumbria England **44** B1 54 50N 2 45W
Eden *r.* Surrey England **33** B2 51 10N 0 05W
Edenbridge Kent England **34** D1 51 12N 0 04E
Edenderry Offaly Irish Republic **48** D3 53 21N 7 35W
Edenthorpe South Yorkshire England **43** G2 53 33N 1 03W
Eder *r.* F.R.G. **63** A2 51 00N 9 00E
Edgbaston West Midlands England **35** C2 52 26N 1 55W
Edgewood Maryland U.S.A. **105** E1 39 25N 76 18W
Edgmond Shropshire England **35** A3 52 45N 2 25W
Edgware Greater London England **34** C2 51 36N 0 16W
Edgworth Lancashire England **42** C2 53 39N 2 24W
Édhessa Greece **68** D3 40 48N 22 03E
Edinboro Pennsylvania U.S.A. **105** D2 41 53N 80 08W
Edinburgh Lothian Scotland **45** D1 55 57N 3 13W
Edirne Turkey **68** E3 41 40N 26 34E
Edlesborough Buckinghamshire England **34** B3 51 53N 0 35W
Edmonton Alberta Canada **100** M3 53 34N 113 25W
Edmonton Greater London England **34** C2 51 37N 0 04W
Edmundston New Brunswick Canada **105** G3 47 22N 68 20W
Edo *r.* Japan **83** C3 35 38N 139 53E
Edogawa Japan **83** C3 35 41N 139 51E
Edremit Turkey **68** E2 39 34N 27 01E
Edward, Lake Zaïre/Uganda **94** E7 0 30S 29 00E
Edwards Plateau Texas U.S.A. **102** F3 31 00N 100 00W
Eeklo Belgium **64** C3 51 11N 3 34E
Eems *(Ems) est.* Netherlands/F.R.G. **64** F5 53 25N 6 55E
Éfaté *i.* Vanuatu **86** L5 17 30S 168 00E
Eger Hungary **69** C2 47 53N 20 28E
Egham Surrey England **34** B2 51 26N 0 34W
Eglinton Northern Ireland **48** D5 55 01N 7 11W
Egmont, Cape New Zealand **87** B3 39 15S 173 46E
Egmont, Mount New Zealand **87** B3 39 18S 174 05E
Egremont Cumbria England **44** A1 54 29N 3 33W
Egridir Gölü Turkey **78** D6 37 52N 30 51E
EGYPT **78** D4
Eifel *p.* F.R.G. **63** A2 50 00N 7 00E
Eigg *i.* Highland Scotland **46** B3 56 55N 6 10W
Eight Degree Channel Indian Ocean **77** C1 8 00N 73 30E
Eighty Mile Beach Australia **86** C6 19 00S 121 00E
Einbeck F.R.G. **63** A2 51 49N 9 53E
Eindhoven Netherlands **64** E3 51 26N 5 30E
Eisenach G.D.R. **63** B2 50 59N 10 19E
Eisenhüttenstadt G.D.R. **63** B2 52 10N 14 42E
Ekibastuz U.S.S.R. **71** J6 51 50N 75 10E
El Aaiún *see* Laayoune
El Agustino Peru **116** F4 12 03S 76 58W
El Arco Mexico **108** B5 28 00N 113 25W
El 'Arîsh Egypt **78** N10 31 08N 33 48E
Elat Israel **78** O9 29 33N 34 57E
Elâzig Turkey **78** E6 38 41N 39 14E
El Banco Colombia **114** C14 9 04N 73 59W
Elbasan Albania **68** D3 41 07N 20 05E
El Bayadh Algeria **93** F9 33 40N 1 00E
El Bayadh Algeria **66** C2 36 35N 1 18E
Elbe *(Labe) r.* Europe **63** A2 53 00N 9 00E
Elberfeld F.R.G. **62** C2 51 17N 7 09E
Elbert, Mount Colorado U.S.A. **102** E4 39 05N 106 27W
Elbeuf France **61** B2 49 17N 1 01E
Elblag Poland **69** C3 54 10N 19 25E
Elburg Netherlands **64** E4 52 27N 5 50E
Elburz Mountains Iran **79** H6 36 15N 51 00E
El Callao Venezuela **114** E14 7 18N 61 48W
El Centro California U.S.A. **102** C3 32 47N 115 33W
Elche Spain **66** B2 38 16N 0 41W
Elda Spain **66** B2 38 29N 0 47W
Elderslie Strathclyde Scotland **45** B1 55 50N 4 29W
El Dorado Arkansas U.S.A. **103** H3 33 12N 92 40W
El Dorado Kansas U.S.A. **103** G4 37 51N 96 52W
Eldoret Kenya **94** G8 0 31N 35 17E
Eleiyele Nigeria **92** E4 7 25N 3 53E
Elekuro Nigeria **92** E4 7 21N 3 57E
Elephant Island South Shetland Islands **115** G0 62 00S 55 00W
Eleuthera *i.* The Bahamas **109** I5 25 05N 76 30W
El Faiyûm Egypt **78** D4 29 19N 30 50E
El Fasher Sudan **94** E10 13 37N 25 22E
El Ferrol del Caudillo Spain **66** A3 43 29N 8 14W
El Fuerte Mexico **108** C5 26 28N 108 35W
Elgin Grampian Scotland **46** E4 57 39N 3 20W
Elgin Illinois U.S.A. **104** C2 42 03N 88 19W
El Gîza Egypt **78** D5 30 01N 31 12E
Elgol Highland Scotland **46** B4 57 09N 6 06W
El Golea Algeria **93** F9 30 35N 2 51E
Elgon, Mount Uganda/Kenya **94** F8 1 07N 34 35E
El Iskandarîya *see* Alexandria
Elista U.S.S.R. **70** G5 46 18N 44 14E
Elizabeth Australia **86** F3 34 45S 138 39E
Elizabeth City North Carolina U.S.A. **103** K4 36 18N 76 16W
Elizabeth New Jersey U.S.A. **106** B1 40 39N 74 13W
Elizabethtown Kentucky U.S.A. **104** C1 37 41N 85 51W
El Jadida Morocco **93** D9 33 19N 8 35W
El Jafr Jordan **78** P10 30 16N 36 11E
Elk City Oklahoma U.S.A. **102** G4 35 25N 99 26W
El Khârga Egypt **78** D4 25 27N 30 32E
Elkhart Indiana U.S.A. **104** C2 41 52N 85 56W
Elkhorn *r.* Nebraska U.S.A. **103** G5 42 00N 98 00W
Elkhorn Wisconsin U.S.A. **104** C2 42 40N 88 34W
Elkins West Virginia U.S.A. **105** E1 38 56N 79 53W
Elko Nevada U.S.A. **102** C5 40 50N 115 46W
Elk River *r.* West Virginia U.S.A. **105** D1 38 00N 81 00W
Elk River *tn.* Minnesota U.S.A. **104** B3 45 19N 93 31W
Elland West Yorkshire England **43** E3 53 41N 1 50W
Ellef Ringnes Island Northwest Territories Canada **101** O8 78 30N 102 00W
Ellendale North Dakota U.S.A. **104** A3 46 00N 98 31W
Ellesmere Island Northwest Territories Canada **101** S8 77 30N 82 30W
Ellesmere Port Cheshire England **42** B1 53 17N 2 54W
Ellesmere Shropshire England **36** B2 52 54N 2 54W
Ellis Island New Jersey U.S.A. **106** B1 40 42N 74 02W
Ellon Grampian Scotland **46** F4 57 22N 2 05W
Ellsworth Land *geog. reg.* Antarctica **121** 75 00S 80 00W
Ellsworth Maine U.S.A. **105** G2 44 34N 68 24W
Ellsworth Wisconsin U.S.A. **104** B2 44 44N 92 29W
El Mahalla El Kubra Egypt **78** D5 30 59N 31 10E
El Médano Mexico **108** B4 24 35N 111 29W
Elmhurst Illinois U.S.A. **104** C2 41 54N 87 56W
el Milk *r.* Sudan **94** E11 17 00N 29 00E
El Minya Egypt **78** D4 28 06N 30 45E
Elmira New York U.S.A. **105** E2 42 06N 76 50W
El Monte California U.S.A. **107** B3 34 04N 118 01W
Elmshorn F.R.G. **63** A2 53 46N 9 40E
El Muglad Sudan **94** E10 11 01N 27 50E
El Obeid Sudan **94** F10 13 11N 30 10E
El Paso Texas U.S.A. **102** E3 31 45N 106 30W
El Porvenir Mexico **108** C6 31 15N 105 48W
El Puerto de Sta. Maria Spain **66** A2 36 36N 6 14W
El Qâ'hira *see* Cairo
El Qunaytirah Syria **78** O11 33 08N 35 49E
El Reno Oklahoma U.S.A. **103** G4 35 32N 97 57W
El Salto Mexico **108** C4 23 47N 105 22W
EL SALVADOR **108** G2
Elsenham Essex England **34** D3 51 55N 0 14E
Elstead Surrey England **34** A1 51 11N 0 43W
Elstree Hertfordshire England **33** B2 51 39N 0 18W
El Sueco Mexico **108** C5 29 54N 106 22W
Eltanin Fracture Zone Pacific Ocean **119** M2 52 00S 135 00W
Eltham Greater London England **34** D2 51 27N 0 03E
El Tigre Venezuela **114** E14 8 44N 64 18W
Elton Cheshire England **42** B1 53 16N 2 49W
El Tûr Egypt **78** N9 28 14N 33 37E
Eluru India **77** E3 16 45N 81 10E
Elvas Portugal **66** A2 38 53N 7 10W
Ely Cambridgeshire England **33** C3 52 24N 0 16E
Ely Nevada U.S.A. **102** D4 39 15N 114 53W
Elyria Ohio U.S.A. **105** D2 41 22N 82 06W
Emāmrūd Iran **79** H6 36 15N 54 59E
Emba *r.* U.S.S.R. **70** H5 47 30N 56 00E
Emba U.S.S.R. **70** H5 48 47N 58 05E
Embalse de Guri *l.* Venezuela **114** E14 7 30N 62 30W
Embleton Northumberland England **44** C2 55 30N 1 37W
Embrun France **61** C1 44 33N 6 30E
Emden F.R.G. **63** A2 53 23N 7 13E
Emerald Australia **86** H5 23 30S 148 08E
Emi Koussi *mt.* Chad **94** C11 19 52N 18 31E
Emmeloord Netherlands **64** E4 52 43N 5 46E
Emmen Netherlands **64** F4 52 47N 6 55E
Emmerich F.R.G. **63** A2 51 49N 6 16E
Empalme Mexico **108** B5 28 00N 110 49W
Emperor Seamounts Pacific Ocean **118** G12 42 00N 169 00E
Emporia Kansas U.S.A. **104** A1 38 24N 96 10W
Ems *r.* F.R.G. **63** A2 53 00N 7 00E
Emscher *r.* F.R.G. **62** D3 51 35N 7 25E
Emsworth Hampshire England **33** B1 50 51N 0 56W
Enard Bay Highland Scotland **46** C5 58 10N 5 25W
Encantado Brazil **116** B2 22 54S 43 18W
Encarnación Paraguay **115** F7 27 20S 55 50W
Endeh Indonesia **80** G2 8 51S 121 40E
Endicott Mountains Alaska U.S.A. **100** E6 67 35N 154 00W
Endon Staffordshire England **35** B4 53 05N 2 07W
Enfield Greater London England **34** C2 51 39N 0 05W
Engel's U.S.S.R. **70** G6 51 30N 46 07E
Engenno Novo Brazil **116** B2 22 54S 43 16W
Enggano *i.* Indonesia **80** C2 5 10S 102 40E
Enghien France **60** B2 48 58N 2 19E
England United Kingdom **29** 53 00N 2 00W
Englehart Ontario Canada **105** E3 47 50N 79 52W
Englewood New Jersey U.S.A. **106** C2 40 53N 73 58W
English Channel *(La Manche)* U.K./France **61** A2 50 00N 2 30W
English River *tn.* Ontario Canada **104** B3 49 14N 90 58W
Enid Oklahoma U.S.A. **103** G4 36 24N 97 54W
Enkhuizen Netherlands **64** E4 52 42N 5 17E
Enna Italy **68** B2 37 34N 14 16E
En Nahud Sudan **94** E10 12 41N 28 28E
Ennerdale Water *l.* Cumbria England **44** A1 54 31N 3 22W
Ennis Clare Irish Republic **48** C2 52 50N 8 59W
Enniscorthy Wexford Irish Republic **48** E2 52 30N 6 34W
Enniskerry Wicklow Irish Republic **49** B1 53 12N 6 10W
Enniskillen Northern Ireland **48** D4 54 21N 7 38W
Ennistymon Clare Irish Republic **48** B2 52 57N 9 15W
Enns *r.* Austria **69** B2 48 00N 14 00E
Enontekiö Finland **67** E4 68 25N 23 40E
Enschede Netherlands **64** F4 52 13N 6 55E
Ensenada Mexico **108** A6 31 53N 116 38W
Entebbe Uganda **94** F8 0 04N 32 27E
Enugu Nigeria **93** G4 6 20N 7 29E
Enville Staffordshire England **35** B2 52 29N 2 15W
Epe Netherlands **64** E4 52 21N 5 59E
Épernay France **61** B2 49 02N 3 58E
Épinal France **61** C2 48 10N 6 28E
Epping Essex England **34** D3 51 42N 0 08E
Epping Forest Essex England **34** D2 51 40N 0 04E
Epsom Surrey England **34** C1 51 20N 0 16W
Epworth Humberside England **40** D2 53 31N 0 50W
EQUATORIAL GUINEA **93** H3
Erbes Kopf *mt.* F.R.G. **64** G1 49 42N 7 07E
Erding F.R.G. **63** B1 48 17N 11 55E
Erdington West Midlands England **35** C2 52 31N 1 50W
Erebus, Mount Antarctica **121** 77 40S 167 20E
Erechim Brazil **115** G7 27 35S 52 15W
Erenhot China **81** H6 43 50N 112 00E
Erft *r.* F.R.G. **64** F2 50 00N 6 00E
Erfurt *admin.* G.D.R. **63** B2 51 00N 11 00E
Erfurt G.D.R. **63** B2 50 58N 11 02E
Erg Chech *geog. reg.* Algeria **93** E7 24 30N 3 00W
Ergene *r.* Turkey **68** E3 41 00N 27 00E
Erg Iguidi *geog. reg.* Algeria **93** D8 26 00N 6 00W
Ergun He *see* Argun
Erie Pennsylvania U.S.A. **105** D2 42 07N 80 05W
Erie, Lake North America **105** D2 42 00N 82 00W
Erimo-misaki *c.* Japan **82** D3 41 55N 143 13E
Eriskay *i.* Western Isles Scotland **46** A4 57 05N 7 10W
Erith Greater London England **34** D2 51 29N 0 11E
Eritrea *see* Ertra
Erkelenz F.R.G. **64** F3 51 05N 6 18E
Erkrath F.R.G. **62** B1 51 13N 6 54E
Erlangen F.R.G. **63** B1 49 36N 11 02E
Ermelo Netherlands **64** E4 52 18N 5 38E
Erode India **77** D2 11 21N 77 43E
Errigal Mountain Irish Republic **48** C5 55 02N 8 07W
Erris Head *c.* Irish Republic **48** A4 54 20N 10 00W
Errol New Hampshire U.S.A. **105** F2 44 47N 71 10W
Errol Tayside Scotland **45** D2 56 23N 3 15W
Erromango *i.* Vanuatu **86** L6 19 00S 169 00E
Er Roseires Sudan **94** F10 11 52N 34 23E
Erskine Strathclyde Scotland **45** B1 55 54N 4 28W
Ertra *(Eritrea) admin.* Ethiopia **78** F1 14 40N 40 15E
Erzgebirge *(Krušnéhory) mts.* Europe **63** B2 50 00N 13 00E
Erzincan Turkey **78** E6 39 44N 39 30E
Erzurum Turkey **78** F6 39 57N 41 17E
Esashi Japan **82** D3 41 54N 140 09E
Esbjerg Denmark **67** B2 55 20N 8 20E
Escanaba Michigan U.S.A. **104** C3 45 47N 87 04W
Escaut *r.* France **64** C2 50 30N 3 28E
Esch-sur-Alzette Luxembourg **64** E1 49 30N 5 59E
Eschwege F.R.G. **63** B2 51 11N 10 03E
Eschweiler F.R.G. **63** A2 50 49N 6 16E
Escondido California U.S.A. **102** C3 33 07N 117 05W
Eşfahān Iran **79** H5 32 41N 51 41E
Esher Surrey England **34** B2 51 22N 0 22W
Esk *r.* Cumbria England **44** A1 54 25N 3 15W
Esk *r.* North Yorkshire England **40** D3 54 30N 0 50W
Esk *r.* Scotland/England **46** E2 55 15N 3 05W
Eskilstuna Sweden **67** D2 59 22N 16 31E
Eskimo Lakes Northwest Territories Canada **100** I6 68 30N 132 30W
Eskimo Point *tn.* Northwest Territories Canada **101** Q5 61 10N 94 15W
Eskişehir Turkey **78** D6 39 46N 30 30E
Esmeraldas Ecuador **114** B13 0 56N 79 40W
Espanola Ontario Canada **105** D3 46 15N 81 46W
Esperance Australia **86** C3 33 49S 121 52E
Esperanza *r.s.* Antarctica **121** 63 24S 56 59W
Espirito Santo *admin.* Brazil **114** J9 18 40S 40 00W
Espiritu Santo *i.* Vanuatu **86** L6 15 10S 167 00E
Espoo Finland **67** E3 60 10N 24 40E
Esquel Argentina **115** C4 42 55S 71 20W
Esquimalt British Columbia Canada **100** K2 48 25N 123 29W
Es Semara Western Sahara **93** C8 26 25N 11 30W
Essen Belgium **64** D3 51 28N 4 28E
Essen F.R.G. **62** C2 51 27N 6 57E
Essequibo *r.* Guyana **114** F13 2 30N 58 00W
Essex *co.* England **33** C2 51 46N 0 30E
Esslingen F.R.G. **63** A1 48 45N 9 19E
Estevan Saskatchewan Canada **101** O2 49 09N 103 00W
Estância Brazil **114** J10 11 15S 37 28W
Eston Cleveland England **44** C1 54 34N 1 07W
Estonia *see* Estonskaya S.S.R.
Estonskaya S.S.R. *rep.* U.S.S.R. **67** F2 59 00N 25 00E
Estrecho de Magallanes *sd.* Chile **115** C2 53 00S 71 00W
Estrêla *r.* Brazil **116** C3 22 42S 43 14W
Étampes France **61** B2 48 26N 2 10E
Étaples France **61** B3 50 31N 1 39E
Etawah India **77** D5 26 46N 79 01E
ETHIOPIA **94** G9
Ethiopian Highlands Africa **88** 8 00N 37 00E
Etna *mt.* Italy **68** C2 37 45N 15 00E
Eton Berkshire England **34** B2 51 31N 0 37W
Etosha National Park Namibia **95** C4 18 30S 16 00E
Etosha Pan *salt l.* Namibia **95** C4 18 30S 16 30E
Ettelbruck Luxembourg **64** F1 49 51N 6 06E
Etten-Leur Netherlands **64** D3 51 34N 4 37E
Ettrick Borders Scotland **46** E2 55 25N 3 05W
Euboea *see* Evvoia
Eucla Australia **86** D3 31 40S 128 51E
Euclid Ohio U.S.A. **105** D2 41 34N 81 33W
Eugene Oregon U.S.A. **102** B5 44 03N 123 04W
Eupen Belgium **64** F2 50 38N 6 02E
Euphrates *r.* Iraq **79** F5 34 40N 42 00E
Eure *r.* France **61** B2 48 45N 1 30E
Eureka California U.S.A. **102** B5 40 49N 124 10W
Europoort Netherlands **65** A1 51 55N 4 10E
Euskirchen F.R.G. **63** A2 50 40N 6 47E
Eutsuk Lake British Columbia Canada **100** J3 54 10N 126 50W
Euxton Lancashire England **42** B3 53 41N 2 41W
Evans Strait Northwest Territories Canada **101** S5 63 15N 82 30W
Evanston Illinois U.S.A. **104** C2 42 02N 87 41W
Evansville Indiana U.S.A. **104** C1 38 00N 87 33W
Evanton Highland Scotland **46** D4 57 40N 4 20W
Evenlode *r.* Oxfordshire England **32** A2 51 50N 1 30W
Evercreech Somerset England **31** E3 51 09N 2 30W

Galley Head *c.* Irish Republic **48** C1 51 35N 8 55W
Gallipoli Italy **68** C3 40 03N 17 59E
Gallipoli Turkey *see* Gelibolu
Gallipolis Ohio U.S.A. **105** D1 38 49N 82 14W
Gallup New Mexico U.S.A. **102** E4 32 32N 108 46W
Galston Strathclyde Scotland **46** D2 55 36N 4 24W
Galtymore *sum.* Irish Republic **48** C2 52 22N 8 10W
Galty Mountains Irish Republic **48** C2 52 20N 8 10W
Galveston Texas U.S.A. **103** H2 29 17N 94 48W
Galway *co.* Irish Republic **48** C3 53 25N 8 45W
Galway Galway Irish Republic **48** B3 53 16N 9 03W
Galway Bay Irish Republic **48** B3 53 15N 9 15W
Gambell Alaska U.S.A. **100** A5 63 46N 171 45W
Gambia *r.* Senegal **93** C5 13 45N 13 15W
GAMBIA, THE 93 B5
Gambier Islands Pitcairn Islands **119** N5 23 10S 135 00W
Gananoque Ontario Canada **105** E2 44 21N 76 11W
Gand *see* Gent
Gandak *r.* India **77** E5 26 30N 84 30E
Gander Newfoundland Canada **101** Y2 49 00N 54 15W
Ganga *(Ganges) r.* India **77** E4 25 30N 82 00E
Ganga, Mouths of the India **77** F4 21 30N 89 00E
Ganganagar India **77** C5 29 54N 73 56E
Gangdisê Shan *mts.* China **81** B4 31 00N 82 30E
Ganges *see* Ganga
Gangtok India **77** F5 27 20N 88 39E
Ganzhou China **81** H3 25 52N 114 51E
Gao Mali **93** E6 16 19N 0 09W
Gap France **61** C1 44 33N 6 05E
Garanhuns Brazil **114** J11 8 53S 36 28W
Garbsen F.R.G. **63** A2 52 25N 9 36E
Gard *r.* France **61** B1 44 05N 4 20E
Gardena California U.S.A. **107** A2 33 53N 118 19W
Garden City Kansas U.S.A. **102** F4 37 57N 100 54W
Garden City New York U.S.A. **106** D1 40 43N 73 39W
Garden Grove California U.S.A. **107** C2 33 48N 117 52W
Garden Reach India **76** K2 22 32N 88 16E
Gardēz Afghanistan **79** K5 33 37N 69 07E
Gardner Island Pacific Ocean **118** I7 4 40S 174 32W
Garelochhead Strathclyde Scotland **46** D3 56 05N 4 50W
Garfield New Jersey U.S.A. **106** B2 40 52N 74 05W
Garforth West Yorkshire England **43** F3 53 48N 1 22W
Gargrave North Yorkshire England **43** D3 53 59N 2 06W
Gargunnock Central Scotland **45** B2 56 08N 4 05W
Garissa Kenya **94** G7 0 27S 39 39E
Gariya India **76** K1 22 27N 88 23E
Garland Texas U.S.A. **103** G3 32 55N 96 37W
Garmisch-Partenkirchen F.R.G. **63** B1 47 30N 11 05E
Garonne *r.* France **61** A1 44 45N 0 15E
Garoua Cameroon **93** H4 9 17N 13 22E
Garron Point *c.* Northern Ireland **48** E/F5 55 05N 6 00W
Garry Lake Northwest Territories Canada **101** O6 66 20N 100 00W
Garstang Lancashire England **42** B3 53 55N 2 47W
Gartempe *r.* France **61** B2 46 10N 1 10E
Garth Powys Wales **38** C2 52 08N 3 32W
Garthorpe Humberside England **40** D2 53 40N 0 42W
Gartocharn Strathclyde Scotland **45** A2 56 02N 4 32W
Garulia India **76** K3 22 49N 88 23E
Garve Highland Scotland **46** D4 57 37N 4 42W
Gary Indiana U.S.A. **104** C2 41 34N 87 20W
Garyarsa China **77** E6 31 46N 80 21E
Garzón Colombia **114** B13 2 14N 75 37W
Gasconade *r.* Missouri U.S.A. **104** B1 38 00N 92 00W
Gascoyne *r.* Australia **86** A5 25 00S 114 00E
Gasherbrum *mt.* Kashmir **77** D7 35 46N 76 38E
Gaspé Québec Canada **101** W2 48 50N 64 30W
Gastonia North Carolina U.S.A. **103** J4 35 14N 81 12W
Gatchina U.S.S.R. **67** G2 59 32N 30 05E
Gatehouse of Fleet Dumfries & Galloway Scotland **46** D1 54 53N 4 11W
Gateshead Tyne and Wear England **44** C1 54 58N 1 35W
Gateside Strathclyde Scotland **45** A1 55 44N 4 36W
Gatineau Québec Canada **105** E3 45 29N 75 40W
Gatmore Central Scotland **45** B2 56 08N 4 23W
Gauhati India **77** G5 26 10N 91 45E
Gávdhos *i.* Greece **68** D1 34 00N 24 00E
Gave d'Oloron *r.* France **61** A1 43 15N 0 40W
Gave du Pau *r.* France **61** A1 43 20N 0 30W
Gävle Sweden **67** D3 60 41N 17 10E
Gaya India **77** F4 24 48N 85 00E
Gaydon Warwickshire England **35** D1 52 45N 0 34E
Gaylord Michigan U.S.A. **105** D3 45 02N 84 41W
Gaza Israel **78** O10 31 30N 34 28E
Gaza Strip *territory* Israel **78** O10 31 28N 34 05E
Gaziantep Turkey **78** E6 37 04N 37 21E
Gbarnga Liberia **93** D4 7 02N 9 26W
Gdańsk Poland **69** C3 54 22N 18 41E
Gdańsk, Gulf of Baltic Sea **69** C3 54 00N 19 00E
Gdynia Poland **69** C3 54 31N 18 30E
Gebel el Tîh *p.* Egypt **78** N9 29 30N 33 45E
Gebel Katherina *hill* Egypt **78** O9 28 30N 33 57E
Gebel Mûsa *(Mount Sinai) mt.* Egypt **78** N9 28 32N 33 59E
Gedaref Sudan **78** E1 14 01N 35 24E
Gediz *r.* Turkey **78** C6 38 40N 27 30E
Geel Belgium **64** D3 51 10N 5 00E
Geelong Australia **86** G2 38 10S 144 26E
Gejiu China **81** F2 23 25N 103 05E
Gela Italy **68** B2 37 04N 14 15E
Gelderland *admin.* Netherlands **64** F4 52 05N 6 10E
Geldern F.R.G. **64** F3 51 31N 6 19E
Geldrop Netherlands **64** E3 51 25N 5 34E
Geleen Netherlands **64** E2 50 58N 5 45E
Gelibolu *(Gallipoli)* Turkey **68** E3 40 25N 26 41E
Gelligaer Mid Glamorgan Wales **38** C1 51 39N 3 15W
Gelsenkirchen F.R.G. **62** C3 51 30N 7 05E
Gembloux Belgium **64** D2 50 34N 4 42E
Gemsbok National Park Botswana **95** D2 26 00S 21 00E
Genalē *r.* Ethiopia **94** H9 6 00N 40 00E
Gendringen Netherlands **64** F3 51 53N 6 24E
Geneina Sudan **94** D10 13 27N 22 30E
General Belgrano II *r.s.* Antarctica **121** 77 52S 34 37W
General Bernardo O'Higgins *r.s.* Antarctica **121** 63 19S 57 54W
General San Martin *r.s.* Antarctica **121** 68 08S 67 04W
Geneva New York U.S.A. **105** E2 42 53N 76 59W
Geneva *see* Genève
Geneva, Lake *see* Lac Léman
Genève *(Geneva)* Switzerland **61** C2 46 13N 6 09E
Genil *r.* Spain **66** B2 37 20N 4 45W
Genk Belgium **64** B2 50 58N 5 30E
Gennevilliers France **60** B2 48 56N 2 17E
Genoa *see* Genova
Genova *(Genoa)* Italy **68** A3 44 24N 8 56E
Gent *(Gand)* Belgium **64** C3 51 02N 3 42E
George *r.* Québec Canada **101** V4 58 00N 65 30W
George Island Falkland Islands **117** M15 52 20S 59 45W
Georgetown Delaware U.S.A. **105** E1 38 43N 75 05W
Georgetown Guyana **114** F14 6 46N 58 10W
George Town Malaysia **80** C5 5 30N 100 28E
Georgetown South Carolina U.S.A. **103** K3 33 23N 79 18W
George VI Sound Antarctica **121** 72 00S 67 00W
Georg Forster *r.s.* Antarctica **121** 70 46S 11 50E
Georgia *see* Gruzinskaya *(Georgian)* S.S.R.
Georgia *state* U.S.A. **103** J3 33 00N 83 00W
Georgian Bay Ontario Canada **105** D3 45 00N 81 00W
Georgian S.S.R. *see* Gruzinskaya S.S.R.
Georgina *r.* Australia **86** F5 22 00S 137 00E
Georg von Neumayer *r.s.* Antarctica **121** 70 37S 08 22W
Gera *admin.* G.D.R. **63** B2 50 00N 11 00E
Gera G.D.R. **63** B2 50 51N 12 11E
Gera *r.* G.D.R. **63** B2 50 00N 10 00E
Geraardsbergen Belgium **64** C2 50 47N 3 53E
Geraldton Australia **86** A4 28 49S 114 36E
Geraldton Ontario Canada **104** C3 49 44N 86 59W
GERMAN DEMOCRATIC REPUBLIC *(G.D.R.)* **63** B2
Gerona Spain **66** C3 41 59N 2 49E
Gerrards Cross Buckinghamshire England **34** B2 51 35N 0 34W
Getafe Spain **66** B3 40 18N 3 44W
Gettysburg Pennsylvania U.S.A. **105** E1 39 50N 77 16W
Ghaghara *r.* India **77** E4 26 20N 83 30E
GHANA 93 E4
Ghanzi Botswana **95** D3 21 42S 21 39E
Ghardaïa Algeria **93** F9 32 20N 3 40E
Gharyān Libya **94** B14 32 10N 13 01E
Ghāt Libya **94** B12 24 58N 10 11E
Ghaziabad India **77** D5 28 39N 77 26E
Ghazni Afghanistan **79** K5 33 33N 68 26E
Gheorghe Gheorghiu-Dej Romania **69** E2 46 17N 26 45E
Ghisonaccia Corsica **61** C1 42 01N 9 24E
Giant's Causeway Northern Ireland **48** E5 55 10N 6 30W
Gibraltar *territory* U.K. **66** A2 36 09N 5 21W
Gibraltar, Strait of Spain/Morocco **66** A2 35 58N 5 30W
Gibson Desert Australia **86** C5 25 00S 123 00E
Gīdolē Ethiopia **94** G9 5 38N 37 28E
Gien France **61** B2 47 41N 2 37E
Giessen F.R.G. **63** A2 50 35N 8 42E
Giffnock Strathclyde Scotland **45** B1 55 49N 4 16W
Gifu Japan **82** C2 35 27N 136 46E
Gigha Isles Strathclyde Scotland **46** C2 55 40N 5 45W
Gigüela *r.* Spain **66** B2 39 40N 3 15W
Gijón Spain **66** A3 43 32N 5 40W
Gila *r.* U.S.A. **102** D3 33 00N 114 00W
Gila Bend Arizona U.S.A. **102** D3 32 56N 112 42W
Gilbert *r.* Australia **86** G6 17 00S 142 30E
Gilbert Islands Pacific Ocean **118** H7 0 00 173 00E
Gildersome West Yorkshire England **43** F3 53 45N 1 37W
Gilfach Goch Mid Glamorgan Wales **38** C1 51 38N 3 30W
Gilgit Kashmir **77** C7 35 54N 74 20E
Gillam Manitoba Canada **101** Q4 56 25N 94 45W
Gillette Wyoming U.S.A. **102** E5 44 18N 105 30W
Gillingham Dorset England **31** E3 51 02N 2 17W
Gillingham Kent England **33** C2 51 24N 0 33E
Gilmerton Tayside Scotland **45** C2 56 23N 3 50W
Gilsland Northumberland England **44** B1 55 00N 2 35W
Gimli Manitoba Canada **104** A4 50 39N 97 00W
Gīnīr Ethiopia **94** H9 7 06N 40 40E
Gippsland *geog. reg.* Australia **86** H2 37 30S 147 00E
Girardot Colombia **114** C13 4 19N 74 47W
Girga Egypt **78** D4 26 17N 31 58E
Gironde *r.* France **61** A2 45 30N 0 45W
Girvan Strathclyde Scotland **46** D2 55 15N 4 51W
Gisborne New Zealand **87** C3 38 41S 178 02E
Gisburn Lancashire England **42** D3 53 57N 2 15W
Giurgiu Romania **69** E1 43 53N 25 58E
Givet France **64** D2 50 08N 4 49E
Gizhiga U.S.S.R. **71** S8 62 00N 160 34E
Gjirokastër Albania **68** D3 40 05N 20 10E
Gjoa Haven *tn.* Northwest Territories Canada **101** P6 68 39N 96 09W
Glace Bay *tn.* Nova Scotia Canada **101** X2 46 11N 59 58W
Gladbeck F.R.G. **62** B3 51 34N 6 59E
Gladstone Australia **86** I5 23 52S 151 16E
Glåma *r.* Norway **67** C3 60 15N 12 00E
Glanaman Dyfed Wales **38** C1 51 47N 3 55W
Glanton Northumberland England **44** C2 55 26N 1 54W
Glarner Alpen *mts.* Switzerland **61** C2 46 50N 9 00E
Glasgow Strathclyde Scotland **45** B1 55 53N 4 15W
Glas Maol *mt.* Tayside Scotland **46** E3 56 52N 3 22W
Glassford Strathclyde Scotland **45** B1 55 42N 4 02W
Glasson Lancashire England **42** B3 54 00N 2 51W
Glastonbury Somerset England **31** E3 51 09N 2 43W
Glauchau G.D.R. **63** B2 50 48N 12 32E
Glenavy Antrim Northern Ireland **49** C1 54 36N 6 13W
Glenavy *r.* Northern Ireland **49** C1 54 36N 6 03W
Glenboig Strathclyde Scotland **45** B1 55 52N 4 04W
Glenboro Manitoba Canada **104** A3 49 35N 99 20W
Glencarse Tayside Scotland **45** D2 56 23N 3 19W
Glencoe Highland Scotland **46** C3 56 40N 5 04W
Glencree *r.* Wicklow Irish Republic **49** B1 53 09N 6 15W
Glendale California U.S.A. **107** B3 34 09N 118 20W
Glendora California U.S.A. **107** C3 34 07N 117 53W
Glen Finglas Reservoir Central Scotland **45** B2 56 15N 4 25W
Glenfoot Tayside Scotland **45** D2 56 20N 3 20W
Glengarnock Strathclyde Scotland **45** A1 55 44N 4 40W
Glengormley Antrim Northern Ireland **49** D2 54 41N 5 58W
Glen Grove *tn.* New York U.S.A. **106** D2 40 52N 73 38W
Glenluce Dumfries & Galloway Scotland **46** D1 54 53N 4 49W
Glen Mor *v.* Highland Scotland **46** D4 57 10N 4 50W
Glenridding Cumbria England **44** B1 54 33N 2 58W
Glen Ridge New Jersey U.S.A. **106** B2 40 47N 74 13W
Glenrothes Fife Scotland **45** D2 56 12N 3 10W
Glens Falls *tn.* New York U.S.A. **105** F2 43 17N 73 41W
Glenties Donegal Irish Republic **48** C4 54 47N 8 17W
Glenveagh National Park Donegal Irish Republic **48** D5 55 00N 8 00W
Glenwood Iowa U.S.A. **104** A2 41 04N 95 46W
Gliwice Poland **69** C3 50 20N 18 40E
Globe Arizona U.S.A. **102** D3 33 23N 110 48W
Głogów Poland **69** C3 51 40N 16 06E
Glossop Derbyshire England **42** E2 53 27N 1 57W
Gloucester Gloucestershire England **31** E3 51 53N 2 14W
Gloucester Ontario Canada **105** E3 45 16N 75 39W
Gloucestershire *co.* England **31** E3 51 50N 2 20W
Gloversville New York U.S.A. **105** F2 43 03N 74 21W
Glovertown Newfoundland Canada **101** Y2 48 40N 54 03W
Glusburn North Yorkshire England **43** D3 53 55N 2 01W
Glyder Fawr *mt.* Gwynedd Wales **38** B3 53 05N 4 02W
Glyncorrwg West Glamorgan Wales **38** C1 51 41N 3 38W
Glyn Neath West Glamorgan Wales **38** C1 51 46N 3 38W
Gmunden Austria **63** B1 47 56N 13 48E
Gniezno Poland **69** C3 52 32N 17 32E
Gnosall Staffordshire England **35** B3 52 47N 2 15W
Goa, Damān & Diu *admin.* India **77** C3 15 00N 74 00E
Goalpara India **77** G5 26 10N 90 38E
Goat Fell *mt.* Arran Scotland **46** C2 55 39N 5 11W
Gobabis Namibia **95** C3 22 30S 18 58E
Gobi Desert Mongolia **81** E6–G6 48 30N 100 00E
Goch F.R.G. **63** A2 51 40N 6 10E
Godalming Surrey England **34** B1 51 11N 0 37W
Godāvari *r.* India **77** D3/E3 19 00N 80 00E
Goderich Ontario Canada **105** D2 43 43N 81 43W
Godhavn *tn.* Greenland **101** Y6 69 18N 53 40W
Godhra India **77** C4 22 49N 73 40E
Godmanchester Cambridgeshire England **33** B3 52 19N 0 11W
Gods Lake Manitoba Canada **101** Q3 54 40N 94 20W
Godstone Surrey England **34** C1 51 15N 0 04W
Godthåb *(Nuuk)* Greenland **101** Y5 64 10N 51 40W
Godwin Austen *see* K2
Goes Netherlands **64** C3 51 30N 3 54E
Goiânia Brazil **114** H9 16 43S 49 18W
Goiás *admin.* Brazil **114** H10 12 30S 48 00W
Goiás Brazil **114** G9 15 57S 50 07W
Goias Massif *hills* South America **110** 15 00S 53 00E
Gökçeada *i.* Turkey **68** E3 40 00N 25 00E
Golan heights *territory* Israel **78** O11 33 00N 35 50E
Golborne Greater Manchester England **42** C2 53 29N 2 36W
Golcar West Yorkshire England **43** E2 53 39N 1 51W
Gold Coast *tn.* Australia **86** I4 27 59S 153 22E
Golden Bay New Zealand **87** B2 40 40S 173 00E
Golden Vale *v.* Irish Republic **48** C2 52 30N 8 05W
Golders Green Greater London England **34** C2 51 35N 0 13W
Goldsboro North Carolina U.S.A. **103** K4 35 23N 78 00W
Goldsworthy Australia **86** B5 20 20S 119 31E
Goldthorpe South Yorkshire England **43** G2 53 32N 1 19W
Golfe de St-Malo *g.* France **61** A2 48 55N 2 30W
Golfe du Lion *g.* France **61** B1 43 10N 4 00E
Golfo de California *g.* Mexico **108** B5 27 00N 111 00W
Golfo de Guayaquil *g.* Ecuador **114** A12 3 00S 81 30W
Golfo de Honduras *g.* Caribbean Sea **108/9** G3 17 00N 87 30W
Golfo de Panamá *g.* Panama **109** I1 8 00N 79 00W
Golfo de San Jorge *g.* Argentina **115** D3 47 00S 66 00W
Golfo de Tehuantepec *g.* Mexico **108** E3/F3 15 30N 95 00W
Golfo de Venezuela *g.* Venezuela **114** C15 12 00N 71 30W
Golfo di Cágliari Italy **68** A2 39 00N 9 00E
Golfo di Catania Italy **68** C2 37 30N 15 20E
Golfo di Gaeta *g.* Italy **68** B3 41 00N 13 00E
Golfo di Genova *g.* Italy **68** A3 44 00N 9 00E
Golfo di Squillace *g.* Italy **68** C2 33 30N 17 00E
Golfo di Táranto *g.* Italy **68** C3 40 00N 17 00E
Golfo di Venèzia Adriatic Sea **68** B4 45 00N 13 00E
Golfo San Matías *g.* Argentina **115** E4 42 00S 64 00W
Golmud China **81** D5 36 22N 94 55E
Golo *r.* Corsica **61** C1 42 30N 9 10E
Golspie Highland Scotland **46** E4 57 58N 3 58W
Gombe Zaire **92** A2 4 19S 15 17E
Gomel' U.S.S.R. **70** F6 52 25N 31 00E
Gomera *i.* Canary Islands **93** B8 28 08N 17 14W
Gomersal West Yorkshire England **43** E3 53 43N 1 41W
Gómez Palacio Mexico **108** D5 25 39N 103 30W
Gomshall Surrey England **34** B1 51 13N 0 27W
Gonder Ethiopia **94** G10 12 39N 37 29E
Gondia India **77** E4 21 23N 80 14E
Gonesse France **60** B2 48 59N 2 27E
Good Hope, Cape of Republic of South Africa **95** C1 34 30S 19 00E
Goodland Kansas U.S.A. **102** F4 39 20N 101 43W
Gooimeer *l.* Netherlands **65** E3 52 18N 5 08E
Goole Humberside England **43** H3 53 42N 0 52W
Goondiwindi Australia **86** I4 28 30S 150 17E
Goose Bay *tn.* Newfoundland Canada **101** W3 53 15N 60 20W
Goose Green Falkland Islands **117** M16 51 52S 59 00W
Goostrey Cheshire England **42** D1 53 14N 2 19W
Göppingen F.R.G. **63** A1 48 43N 9 39E
Gora Kamen' *mt.* U.S.S.R. **71** L9 69 06N 94 59E
Gorakhpur India **77** E5 26 45N 83 23E
Gora Narodnaya *mt.* U.S.S.R. **71** I9 65 02N 60 01E
Gora Pobeda *mt.* U.S.S.R. **71** Q9 65 10N 146 00E
Gorda Rise Pacific Ocean **119** M12 43 00N 130 00W
Gordon Landing *tn.* Yukon Territory Canada **100** H5 63 38N 135 27W
Gorē Ethiopia **94** G9 8 10N 35 29E
Gore New Zealand **87** A1 46 06S 168 58E
Gore Bay *tn.* Ontario Canada **105** D3 45 54N 82 28W
Gorebridge Lothian Scotland **45** D1 55 51N 3 02W
Gorey Wexford Irish Republic **48** E2 52 40N 6 18W
Gorgān Iran **79** H6 36 50N 54 29E
Gorinchem Netherlands **64** D3 51 50N 4 59E
Goring Oxfordshire England **32** A2 51 32N 1 09W
Gorizia Italy **68** B4 45 57N 13 37E
Gorki U.S.S.R. **69** F3 54 17N 30 59E
Gor'kiy U.S.S.R. **70** G7 56 20N 44 00E
Görlitz G.D.R. **63** B2 51 09N 15 00E
Gormanston Meath Irish Republic **48** E3 53 38N 6 14W
Gorno-Altaysk U.S.S.R. **81** C8 51 59N 85 56E
Goroka Papua New Guinea **86** H8 6 02S 145 22E
Gorontalo Indonesia **80** G4 0 33N 123 05E
Gorseinon West Glamorgan Wales **38** B1 51 41N 4 02W
Gort Galway Irish Republic **48** C3 53 04N 8 50W
Gorumna Island Irish Republic **48** B3 53 15N 9 55W
Goryn' *r.* U.S.S.R. **69** E3 51 00N 26 00E
Gorzów Wielkopolski Poland **69** C3 52 42N 15 12E
Gosforth Tyne and Wear England **44** C2 55 01N 1 37W
Goslar F.R.G. **63** B2 51 55N 10 25E
Gosport Hampshire England **32** A1 50 48N 1 08W
Gostivar Yugoslavia **68** D3 41 47N 20 55E
Göta älv *r.* Sweden **67** C2 58 00N 12 00E
Göteborg Sweden **67** C2 57 45N 12 00E
Gotha G.D.R. **63** B2 50 57N 10 43E
Gotland *i.* Sweden **67** D2 57 30N 18 40E
Göttingen F.R.G. **63** A2 51 32N 9 57E
Gottwaldov Czechoslovakia **69** C2 49 14N 17 40E
Gouda Netherlands **65** C2 52 00N 4 42E
Gough Island Atlantic Ocean **117** H2 40 20S 10 00W
Gouin, Réservoir Québec Canada **105** F3 48 00N 75 00W
Goulburn Australia **86** H3 34 47S 149 43E
Gouré Niger **93** H5 13 59N 10 15E
Gourock Strathclyde Scotland **46** D2 55 58N 4 49W
Goussainville France **60** B3 49 02N 2 28E
Govan Strathclyde Scotland **45** B1 55 51N 4 22W
Governador Valadares Brazil **114** I9 18 51S 41 57W
Govind Ballash Pant Sagar *l.* India 24 00N 83 00E
Gower *p.* West Glamorgan Wales **38** B1 51 35N 4 10W
Gozo *i.* Malta **68** B2 35 00N 14 00E
Grabroc Hill *tn.* Strathclyde Scotland **45** B1 55 44N 4 26W
Gracefield Québec Canada **105** E3 46 05N 76 05W
Grafham Water *l.* Cambridgeshire England **33** B3 52 18N 0 20W
Grafton Australia **86** I4 29 40S 152 56E
Grafton West Virginia U.S.A. **105** D1 39 21N 80 03W
Graham Texas U.S.A. **102** G3 33 07N 98 36W
Graham Island British Columbia Canada **100** I3 53 50N 133 00W
Graham Land *geog. reg.* Antarctica **121** 67 00S 64 00W
Grahamstown Republic of South Africa **95** E1 33 18S 26 32E
Graiguenamanagh Carlow Irish Republic **48** D2 52 32N 6 56W
Grain Kent England **33** C2 51 28N 0 43E
Grampian *reg.* Scotland **46** E4/F4 57 30N 3 00W
Grampian Mountains Scotland **46** D3–E3
Granada Nicaragua **109** G2 11 58N 85 59W
Granada Spain **66** B2 37 10N 3 35W
Granard Longford Irish Republic **48** D3 53 47N 7 30W
Granby Québec Canada **105** F3 45 23N 72 44W
Gran Canaria *i.* Canary Islands **93** B8 28 00N 15 35W
Gran Chaco *geog. reg.* Argentina **115** E8 25 00S 62 30W
Grand *r.* U.S.A. **104** B1 40 00N 94 00W
Grand Rapids *tn.* Manitoba Canada **101** P3 53 12N 99 19W
Grand Bahama *i.* The Bahamas **109** I5 27 00N 78 00W
Grand Banks Atlantic Ocean **96** 47 00N 47 00W
Grand Beach *tn.* Manitoba Canada **104** A4 50 34N 96 38W
Grand Canal Irish Republic **49** A1 53 18N 6 33W
Grand Canyon U.S.A. **102** D4 36 04N 112 07W
Grand Canyon National Park Arizona/Utah
Grand Canyon Village Arizona U.S.A. **102** D4 36 02N 112 09W
Grand Cayman *i.* Caribbean Sea **109** H3 19 20N 81 15W
Grand Coulee Dam Washington U.S.A. **102** C6 47 59N 118 58W
Grande Cache Alberta Canada **100** L3 53 50N 118 30W
Grand Erg Occidental *geog. reg.* Algeria **93** F9 30 35N 0 30E
Grand Erg Oriental *geog. reg.* Algeria **93** G9 30 15N 6 45E
Grande Rivière de la Baleine *r.* Québec Canada **101** T4 55 15N 77 00W
Grande Terre *i.* Lesser Antilles **109** L3 17 00N 61 40W
Grand Falls *tn.* New Brunswick Canada **101** V2 47 02N 67 46W
Grand Forks North Dakota U.S.A. **104** A3 47 57N 97 05W
Grand Haven Michigan U.S.A. **104** C2 43 04N 86 13W
Grand Island *tn.* Nebraska U.S.A. **103** G5 40 56N 98 21W
Grand Junction Colorado U.S.A. **102** E4 39 04N 108 33W
Grand Lake Newfoundland Canada **101** X2 49 00N 57 20W
Grand Marais Minnesota U.S.A. **104** B3 47 45N 90 20W
Grand Prairie *tn.* Alberta Canada **100** L4 55 10N 118 52W
Grand *r.* South Dakota U.S.A. **102** F6 46 00N 102 00W
Grand Rapids *tn.* Michigan U.S.A. **104** C2 42 57N 86 40W
Grand Rapids *tn.* Minnesota U.S.A. **104** B3 47 13N 93 31W
Grand Traverse Bay *b.* Michigan U.S.A. **104** C3 45 00N 85 00W
Grand Union Canal England **34** B3 51 45N 0 35W
Grand Union Canal West Midlands England **35** C/D1 52 18N 1 40W
Grane Norway **67** C4 65 35N 13 25E
Grange Hill *tn.* Jamaica **109** P8 18 19N 78 11W
Grangemouth Central Scotland **45** C2 56 01N 3 44W
Grange-over-Sands Cumbria England **44** B1 54 33N 3 09W
Granite City Illinois U.S.A. **104** B1 38 43N 90 04W
Granite Falls *tn.* Minnesota U.S.A. **104** A2 44 49N 95 31W
Granite Peak Montana U.S.A. **102** E6 45 10N 109 50W
Grantham Lincolnshire England **36** D2 52 55N 0 39W
Grantown-on-Spey Highland Scotland **46** E4 57 20N 3 58W
Grants Pass Oregon U.S.A. **102** B5 42 26N 123 20W
Granville France **61** A2 48 50N 1 35W
Granville Lake Manitoba Canada **101** O4 56 00N 101 00W
Grasmere Cumbria England **44** A1 54 28N 3 02W
Grasse France **61** C1 43 40N 6 56E
Grassington North Yorkshire England **43** D1 54 04N 1 59W
Grassmoor Derbyshire England **43** F1 53 11N 1 44W
Gravelbourg Saskatchewan Canada **100** N2 49 53N 106 33W
Gravelines France **64** B2 50 59N 2 08E
Gravenhurst Ontario Canada **105** E2 44 55N 79 22W
Gravesend Kent England **34** E2 51 27N 0 24E
Gravesend New York U.S.A. **106** C1 40 36N 73 58W
Gray France **61** C2 47 27N 5 35E
Grayling Michigan U.S.A. 105 D2 44 40N 84 43W
Grays Essex England **34** D2 51 29N 0 20E
Graz Austria **69** C2 47 05N 15 22E
Greasby Merseyside England **42** A2 53 23N 3 10W
Great Abaco *i.* The Bahamas **109** I5 26 40N 77 00W
Great Altcar Lancashire England **42** A2 53 32N 3 01W
Great Astrolabe Reef Fiji **118** U15 18 45S 178 50E
Great Bardfield Essex England **34** E3 51 57N 0 26E
Great Barrier Island New Zealand **87** C3 35 10S 175 30E
Great Barrier Reef Australia **86** G7–H6 15 00S 146 00E
Great Basin Nevada U.S.A. **102** C4 40 00N 117 00W
Great Bear Lake Northwest Territories Canada **100** K6 66 00N 120 00W
Great Bend Kansas U.S.A. **102** G4 38 22N 98 47W
Great Bernera *i.* Western Isles Scotland **46** B5 58 13N 6 49W
Great Blasket Island Irish Republic **48** A2 52 05N 10 30W
Great Brickhill Bedfordshire England **34** A3 51 57N 0 41W
Great Bridgeford Staffordshire England **35** B3 52 51N 2 10W
Great Broughton North Yorkshire England **40** C3 54 27N 1 10W
Great Chesterford Essex England **33** C3 52 04N 0 11E
Great Coates Humberside England **40** D2 53 35N 0 08W
Great Dividing Range *mts.* Australia **86** G7–H2
Great Driffield Humberside England **40** D3 54 01N 0 26W
Great Dunmow Essex England **34** E3 51 53N 0 22E
Great Eccleston Lancashire England **42** B3 53 51N 2 53W
Greater Antilles *is.* West Indies **109** H4–K3
Greater Khingan Range *mts. see* Da Hinggan Ling
Greater London *admin.* England **34** C2 51 30N 0 10W
Greater Manchester *admin.* England **42** D2 53 30N 2 15W
Great Exuma *i.* The Bahamas **109** I4 23 30N 76 00W
Great Falls *tn.* Montana U.S.A. **102** D6 47 30N 111 16W

Kalat Pakistan **76** B5 29 01N 66 38E
Kalémié Zaïre **95** E6 5 57S 29 10E
Kalevala U.S.S.R. **67** G4 65 15N 31 08E
Kalgoorlie Australia **86** C3 30 49S 121 29E
Kaliavesi *l.* Finland **67** F3 63 00N 27 20E
Kalimantan *admin.* Indonesia **80** E3 2 00S 112 00E
Kálimnos *i.* Greece **68** E2 37 00N 26 00E
Kalinin U.S.S.R. **70** F7 56 49N 35 57E
Kaliningrad U.S.S.R. **70** E6 54 40N 20 30E
Kalispell Montana U.S.A. **102** D6 48 12N 114 19W
Kalisz Poland **69** C3 51 46N 18 02E
Kalix älv *r.* Sweden **67** E4 66 40N 22 30E
Kalkajl India **76** M4 28 32N 77 16E
Kallsjön *l.* Sweden **67** C3 63 30N 13 05E
Kalmar Sweden **67** D2 56 39N 16 20E
Kalmthout Belgium **64** D3 51 23N 4 29E
Kalomo Zambia **95** E4 17 02S 26 29E
Kalpeni Island India **77** C2 10 05N 73 15E
Kaluga U.S.S.R. **70** F6 54 31N 36 16E
Kalutara Sri Lanka **77** D1 6 35N 79 59E
Kama *r.* U.S.S.R. **70** H7 57 00N 54 00E
Kamaishi Japan **82** D2 39 18N 141 52E
Kamakura Japan **83** B2 35 19N 139 33E
Kamarān *i.* Yemen **78** F2 15 21N 42 40E
Kamarhati India **76** K2 22 40N 88 22E
Kambara *i.* Fiji **118** V15 18 57S 178 58W
Kamchatka *p.* U.S.S.R. **71** R7 57 30N 160 00E
Kamchatka Bay U.S.S.R **71** S7 55 00N 164 00E
Kamchiya *r.* Bulgaria **68** E3 43 00N 27 00E
Kamenets Podol'skiy U.S.S.R. **69** E2 48 40N 26 36E
Kamensk-Ural'skiy U.S.S.R. **70** I7 56 29N 61 49E
Kames Strathclyde Scotland **46** C2 55 54N 5 15W
Kamet *mt.* India **77** D6 30 55N 79 36E
Kamina Zaïre **95** E6 8 46S 25 00E
Kamloops British Columbia Canada **100** K3 50 39N 120 24W
Kampala Uganda **94** F8 0 19N 32 35E
Kampen Netherlands **64** E4 52 33N 5 55E
Kamp-Lintfort F.R.G. **64** F3 51 30N 6 33E
KAMPUCHEA *see* CAMBODIA
Kamyshin U.S.S.R. **70** G6 50 05N 45 24E
Kanagawa Japan **83** B2 35 29N 139 38E
Kananga Zaïre **95** D6 5 53S 22 26E
Kanawha *r.* West Virginia U.S.A. **105** D1 38 00N 82 00W
Kanazawa Japan **82** C2 36 35N 136 38E
Kanazawa Japan **83** B2 35 20W 139 37E
Kanbe Myanma **80** B7 16 15N 95 40E
Kanchipuram India **77** D2 12 50N 79 44E
Kānchrāpāra India **76** K3 22 56N 88 26E
Kandahār Afghanistan **79** K5 31 35N 65 45E
Kandalaksha U.S.S.R. **70** F9 67 09N 32 31E
Kandavu *i.* Fiji **118** U15 19 10S 178 30E
Kandavu Passage *sd.* Fiji **118** U15 18 50S 178 00E
Kandi Benin **93** F4 11 05N 2 59E
Kandla India **76** B4 23 03N 70 11E
Kandy Sri Lanka **77** E1 7 17N 80 40E
Kane Pennsylvania U.S.A. **105** E2 41 40N 78 48W
Kaneohe Hawaiian Islands **119** Y18 21 25N 157 48W
Kangan Iran **79** H4 27 51N 52 07E
Kangar Malaysia **80** C5 6 28N 100 10E
Kangaroo Island Australia **86** F2 35 50S 137 50E
Kangnŭng South Korea **81** K5 37 48N 127 52E
Kanin Peninsula U.S.S.R **70** G9 68 00N 45 00E
Kankakee Illinois U.S.A. **104** C2 41 08N 87 52W
Kankan Guinea **93** D5 10 22N 9 11W
Kanker India **77** E4 20 17N 81 30E
Kannapolis North Carolina U.S.A. **103** J4 35 30N 80 36W
Kano Nigeria **93** G5 12 00N 8 31E
Kanoya Japan **82** B1 31 22N 130 50E
Kanpur India **77** E5 26 27N 80 14E
Kansas *r.* Kansas U.S.A. **104** A1 39 00N 95 00W
Kansas *state* U.S.A. **102–103** G4 38 00N 98 00W
Kansas City Kansas U.S.A. **104** B1 39 05N 94 37W
Kansas City Missouri U.S.A. **104** B1 39 02N 94 33W
Kansk U.S.S.R. **71** L7 56 11N 95 48E
Kanturk Cork Irish Republic **48** C2 52 10N 8 55W
Kanye Botswana **95** D3 24 59S 25 19E
Kao-hsiung Taiwan **81** J2 22 36N 120 17E
Kaolack Senegal **93** B5 14 09N 16 08W
Kapaa Hawaiian Islands **119** X19 22 04N 159 20W
Kap Farvel *(Cape Farewell) c.* Greenland **101** AA4 60 00N 44 00W
Kapfenberg Austria **69** C2 47 27N 15 18E
Kapingamarangi Rise Pacific Ocean **118** F8 3 00N 154 00E
Kaposvár Hungary **69** C2 46 21N 17 49E
Kapsukas U.S.S.R. **69** D3 54 31N 23 20E
Kapuskasing Ontario Canada **105** D3 49 25N 82 26W
Kara Bogaz Gol *b.* U.S.S.R. **70** H4 42 00N 53 00E
Kara Kum *geog. reg.* U.S.S.R. **70** H4–I3 40 00N 60 00E
Kara Sea U.S.S.R **71** I11/J10 75 00N 70 00E
Karabük Turkey **78** D7 41 12N 32 36E
Karachi Pakistan **76** B4 24 51N 67 02E
Karaganda U.S.S.R. **71** J5 49 53N 73 07E
Karaginskiy *i.* U.S.S.R. **71** S7 58 00N 164 00E
Karaikkudi India **77** D2 10 04N 78 46E
Karaj Iran **79** H6 35 48N 50 58E
Karak Jordan **78** O10 31 11N 35 42E
Karakoram *mts.* Asia **72** 36 00N 76 00E
Karakoram Pass Kashmir/China **77** D7 35 33N 77 51E
Karama Jordan **78** O10 31 58N 35 34E
Karasburg Namibia **95** C2 28 00S 18 43E
Karasjok Norway **67** F4 69 27N 25 30E
Karbalā' Iraq **78** F5 32 37N 44 03E
Karcag Hungary **69** D2 47 19N 20 53E
Kariba Dam Zambia / Zimbabwe **95** E4 16 31S 28 50E
Kariba, Lake Zambia / Zimbabwe **95** E4 17 00S 28 00E
Karibib Namibia **95** C3 21 59S 15 51E
Karisimbi, Mount Rwanda / Zaïre **94** E7 1 32S 29 27E
Karlino Poland **69** C3 54 02N 15 52E
Karl-Marx-Stadt *admin.* G.D.R. **63** B2 50 00N 13 00E
Karl-Marx-Stadt G.D.R. **63** B2 50 50N 12 55E
Karlovac Yugoslavia **68** C4 45 30N 15 34E
Karlovy Vary Czechoslovakia **69** B3 50 13N 12 52E
Karlskoga Sweden **67** C2 59 19N 14 33E
Karlskrona Sweden **67** D2 56 10N 15 35E
Karlsruhe F.R.G. **63** A1 49 00N 8 24E
Karlstad Sweden **67** C2 59 24N 13 32E
Karnafuli Reservoir Bangladesh **77** 22 30N 92 20E
Karnal India **77** D5 29 41N 76 58E
Karnataka *admin.* India **77** D2 14 40N 75 30E
Karol Bagh India **76** L4 28 39N 77 11E
Kárpathos *i.* Greece **68** E2 35 30N 27 12E
Karpenision Greece **68** D2 38 55N 21 47E
Kars Turkey **78** F7 40 35N 43 05E
Karsakpay U.S.S.R. **70** I5 47 47N 66 43E
Karshi U.S.S.R. **79** K6 38 53N 65 45E
Karwar India **77** C2 14 50N 74 09E
Kasai *r.* Angola / Zaïre **95** C7 4 00S 19 00E
Kasama Zambia **95** F5 10 10S 31 11E
Kasaragod India **77** C2 12 30N 74 59E
Kasa-Vubu Zaïre **92** A1 4 21S 15 19E
Kasempa Zambia **95** E5 13 28S 25 48E
Kasese Uganda **94** F8 0 10N 30 06E
Kāshān Iran **79** H5 33 59N 51 35E
Kashi China **81** A5 39 29N 76 02E
Kashiwazaki Japan **82** C2 37 22N 138 33E
Kaskö Finland **67** E3 62 23N 21 10E
Kásos *i.* Greece **68** E2 35 00N 28 00E
Kassala Sudan **78** E2 15 24N 36 30E
Kassel F.R.G. **63** A2 51 18N 9 30E
Kasserine Tunisia **68** A2 35 13N 8 43E
Kastoria Greece **68** D3 40 33N 21 15E
Kaśur Pakistan **77** C6 31 07N 74 30E
Kataba Zambia **95** E4 16 02S 25 03E
Katase Japan **83** A2 35 18N 139 30E
Katchall *i.* Nicobar Is. (India) **77** G1 7 30N 93 30E
Katerini Greece **68** D3 40 15N 22 30E
Katha Myanma **81** E2 24 11N 96 20E
Katherine Australia **86** E7 14 29S 132 20E
Kathiawar *p.* India **76/77** C4 21 10N 71 00E
Kathmandu Nepal **77** F5 27 42N 85 19E
Katihar India **77** F5 25 33N 87 34E
Katowice Poland **69** C3 50 15N 18 59E
Katrineholm Sweden **67** D2 58 59N 16 15E
Katsina Ala Nigeria **93** G4 7 10N 9 30E
Kattakurgan U.S.S.R **79** K6 39 54N 66 13E
Kattegat *sd.* Denmark/Sweden **67** C2 57 00N 11 00E
Katwijk aan Zee Netherlands **65** B2 52 12N 4 24E
Kauai *i.* Hawaiian Islands **119** X18 22 00N 159 30W
Kauai Channel Hawaiian Islands **119** X18 21 45N 158 50W
Kaufbeuren F.R.G. **63** B1 47 53N 10 37E
Kaula *i.* Hawaiian Islands **119** W18 21 35N 160 40W
Kaulakahi Channel Hawaiian Islands **119** X18 21 58N 159 50W
Kaunas U.S.S.R **70** E6 54 52N 23 55E
Kaura Namoda Nigeria **93** G5 12 39N 6 38E
Kavajë Albania **68** C3 41 11N 19 33E
Kavála Greece **68** D3 40 56N 24 25E
Kavaratti Island India **77** C2 10 32N 72 43E
Kawagoe Japan **82** C2 35 55N 139 30E
Kawaguchi Japan **83** B4 35 47N 139 44E
Kawaihae Hawaiian Islands **119** Z18 20 02N 155 50W
Kawasaki Japan **83** C3 35 30N 139 45E
Kawawa Japan **83** B3 35 31N 139 33E
Kawerau New Zealand **87** C3 38 03S 176 43E
Kaya Burkina **93** E5 13 04N 1 09W
Kayes Mali **93** C5 14 26N 11 28W
Kayseri Turkey **78** E6 38 42N 35 28E
Kazach'ye U.S.S.R. **71** P10 70 46N 136 15E
Kazakhskaya S.S.R. *rep.* U.S.S.R. **70** H5–I5 49 00N 60 00E
Kazakh Upland U.S.S.R. **71** J5 47 00N 75 00E
Kazan' U.S.S.R. **70** G7 55 45N 49 10E
Kazanlŭk Bulgaria **68** E3 42 37N 25 23E
Kazatin U.S.S.R. **69** E2 49 41N 28 49E
Kāzerūn Iran **79** H4 29 35N 51 40E
Kazym *r.* U.S.S.R. **71** I8 63 00N 67 30E
Kéa *i.* Greece **68** D2 37 00N 24 00E
Keady Northern Ireland **48** E4 54 15N 6 42W
Kearney Nebraska U.S.A. **102** G5 40 42N 99 04W
Kearny New Jersey U.S.A. **106** B2 40 45N 74 07W
Kearsley Greater Manchester England **42** C2 53 33N 2 22W
Kecskemét Hungary **69** C2 46 56N 19 43E
Kediri Indonesia **80** E2 7 45S 112 01E
Keele *r.* Northwest Territories Canada **100** J5 64 15N 126 00W
Keene New Hampshire U.S.A. **105** F2 42 55N 72 17W
Keetmanshoop Namibia **95** C2 26 36S 18 08E
Keewatin Ontario Canada **104** B3 49 47N 94 30W
Kefallinia *i.* Greece **68** D2 38 00N 20 00E
Keflavik Iceland **67** H6 64 01N 22 35W
Kegworth Leicestershire England **35** E3 52 50N 1 16W
Kehl F.R.G. **63** A1 48 35N 7 50E
Keighley West Yorkshire England **43** E3 53 52N 1 54W
Keitele *l.* Finland **67** F3 63 10N 26 24E
Keith Grampian Scotland **46** F4 57 32N 2 57W
K'elafo Ethiopia **94** H9 5 37N 44 10E
Kelkit *r.* Turkey **78** E7 40 20N 37 40E
Kells *see* Ceanannus Mór
Kelowna British Columbia Canada **100** L2 49 50N 119 29W
Kelsall Cheshire England **42** B1 53 13N 2 43W
Kelsey Bay *tn.* British Columbia Canada **100** J3 50 22N 125 29W
Kelso Borders Scotland **46** F2 55 36N 2 25W
Kelty Fife Scotland **45** D2 56 08N 3 24W
Kelvedon Essex England **33** C2 51 51N 0 42E
Kemberton Shropshire England **35** A2 52 36N 2 24W
Kemerovo U.S.S.R. **71** K7 55 25N 86 05E
Kemi Finland **67** E4 65 46N 24 34E
Kemijärvi *l.* Finland **67** F4 66 42N 27 30E
Kemijöki *r.* Finland **67** F4 67 15N 27 45E
Kempenland *(Campine) admin.* Belgium **64** E3 51 08N 15 22E
Kempston Bedfordshire England **33** B3 52 07N 0 30W
Kempten F.R.G. **63** B1 47 44N 10 19E
Kemptville Ontario Canada **105** E3 45 01N 75 39W
Kemsing Kent England **34** D1 51 18N 0 14E
Kenai Alaska U.S.A. **100** E5 60 35N 151 19W
Kendal Cumbria England **44** B1 54 20N 2 45W
Kendalakshskiy Zaliv *(White Sea)* U.S.S.R. **67** G4 66 55N 32 40E
Kendari Indonesia **80** G3 3 57S 122 36E
Kenema Sierra Leone **93** C4 7 57N 11 11W
Kengtung Myanma **80** B8 21 16N 99 39E
Kenilworth Warwickshire England **35** D2 52 21N 1 34W
Keningau Malaysia **80** F5 5 21N 116 11E
Kénitra Morocco **93** D9 34 20N 6 34W
Kenmare Kerry Irish Republic **48** B1 51 53N 9 35W
Kenmare River *b.* Irish Republic **48** B1 51 40N 9 00W
Kennebunk Maine U.S.A. **105** F2 43 24N 70 33W
Kennet Fife Scotland **45** C2 56 06N 3 43W
Kennet *r.* Berkshire England **32** A2 51 25N 1 25W
Kennington Kent England **33** C2 51 09N 0 55E
Kennoway Fife Scotland **45** D2 56 12N 3 03W
Kenora Ontario Canada **104** B3 49 47N 94 26W
Kenosha Wisconsin U.S.A. **104** C2 42 34N 87 50W
Kensington & Chelsea Inner London England **34** C2 51 29N 0 10W
Kent *co.* England **33** C2 51 10N 0 45E
Kentford Suffolk England **33** C3 52 16N 0 30E
Kenton Greater London England **34** C2 51 33N 0 16W
Kenton Ohio U.S.A. **105** D2 40 38N 83 38W
Kent Peninsula Northwest Territories Canada **101** N6 68 30N 106 00W
Kentucky *r.* Kentucky U.S.A. **104** D1 38 00N 85 00W
Kentucky *state* U.S.A. **103** I4 37 00N 85 00W
Kentucky Lake Kentucky U.S.A. **104** C1 37 00N 88 00W
KENYA **94** G8
Kenya, Mount *see* Kirinyaga
Keokuk Iowa U.S.A. **104** B2 40 23N 91 25W
Kepulauan Anambas *is.* Indonesia **80** D4 3 00N 106 40E
Kepulauan Aru *is.* Indonesia **80** I2 7 00S 134 00E
Kepulauan Kai *is.* Indonesia **80** I2 5 30S 133 00E
Kepulauan Lingga *is.* Indonesia **80** C3 0 30S 104 00E
Kepulauan Mentawai *is.* Indonesia **80** B3 2 00S 99 00E
Kepulauan Obi *is.* Indonesia **80** H3 1 40S 127 30E
Kepulauan Riau *is.* Indonesia **80** C4 1 00N 104 20E
Kepulauan Sangir *is.* Indonesia **80** H4 2 30N 125 20E
Kepulauan Sula *is.* Indonesia **80** G3/H3 2 00S 125 00E
Kepulauan Talaud *is.* Indonesia **80** H4 4 00N 126 50E
Kepulauan Tanimbar *is.* Indonesia **80** I2 7 30S 132 00E
Kerala *admin.* India **77** D2 10 10N 76 30E
Kerch' U.S.S.R **70** F5 45 22N 36 27E
Kerema Papua New Guinea **86** H8 7 59S 145 46E
Keren Ethiopia **78** E2 15 46N 38 30E
Keresley West Midlands England **35** D2 52 27N 1 32W
Kerguelen *is.* Indian Ocean **123** 49 30S 69 30E
Kerikeri New Zealand **87** B3 35 12S 173 59E
Kerki U.S.S.R. **79** K6 37 53N 65 10E
Kérkira *(Corfu) i.* Greece **68** C2 39 00N 19 00E
Kérkira Greece **68** C2 39 38N 19 55E
Kerkrade Netherlands **64** F2 50 52N 6 04E
Kermadec Islands Pacific Ocean **118** I5 30 00S 178 30W
Kermadec Trench Pacific Ocean **118** I4 33 00S 177 00W
Kermān Iran **79** I5 30 18N 57 05E
Kermānshāh Iran **79** G5 34 19N 47 04E
Kerme Körfezi *b.* Turkey **68** E2 37 00N 27 00E
Kerpen F.R.G. **64** F2 50 52N 6 42E
Kerrera *i.* Strathclyde Scotland **46** C3 56 25N 5 34W
Kerrville Texas U.S.A. **102** G3 30 03N 99 09W
Kerry *co.* Irish Republic **48** B2 52 10N 9 30W
Kerry Head *c.* Irish Republic **48** B2 52 25N 9 55W
Kert *r.* Morocco **66** B2 35 00N 3 30W
Kerulen *r.* Mongolia **81** H7 47 30N 112 30E
Kesagami Lake Ontario Canada **105** D4 50 00N 80 00W
Keşan Turkey **68** E3 40 52N 26 37E
Kessingland Suffolk England **33** D3 52 25N 1 42E
Keswick Cumbria England **44** A1 54 37N 3 08W
Ket' *r.* U.S.S.R. **71** K7 58 30N 86 30E
Ketapang Indonesia **80** E3 1 50S 109 59E
Ketchikan Alaska U.S.A. **100** I4 55 25N 131 40W
Kethel Netherlands **65** B1 51 56N 4 21E
Kętrzyn Poland **69** D3 54 05N 21 24E
Kettering Northamptonshire England **36** D2 52 24N 0 44W
Kettering Ohio U.S.A. **105** D1 39 42N 84 11W
Kettwig F.R.G. **62** B2 51 22N 6 55E
Kewanee Illinois U.S.A. **104** C2 41 14N 89 56W
Kewaunee Wisconsin U.S.A. **104** C2 44 27N 87 31W
Keweenaw Bay Wisconsin U.S.A. **104** C3 47 00N 88 00W
Keweenaw Peninsula Michigan U.S.A. **104** C3 47 00N 88 00W
Kexbrough South Yorkshire England **43** F2 53 34N 1 32W
Keynsham Avon England **31** E3 51 26N 2 30W
Keyworth Nottinghamshire England **36** C2 52 52N 1 05W
Khabarovsk U.S.S.R. **71** P5 48 32N 135 08E
Khairpur Pakistan **79** K4 27 30N 68 50E
Khalkidhikí *p.* Greece **68** D3 40 30N 23 00E
Khalkis Greece **68** D2 38 28N 23 36E
Khambhat India **77** C4 22 19N 72 39E
Khambhat, Gulf of India **77** C4 20 30N 72 00E
Khamman India **77** E3 17 16N 80 13E
Khānābad Afghanistan **79** K6 36 42N 69 08E
Khānaqīn Iraq **79** G5 34 22N 45 22E
Khandwa India **77** D4 21 49N 76 23E
Khaniá Greece **68** D2 35 31N 24 01E
Khanty-Mansiysk U.S.S.R. **71** I8 61 01N 69 00E
Khān Yūnis Israel **78** O10 31 21N 34 18E
Kharagpur India **77** F4 22 23N 87 22E
Kharan Pakistan **76** B5 28 32N 65 26E
Khardah India **76** K2 22 43N 88 23E
Khārg Island Iran **79** H4 29 14N 50 20E
Khar'kov U.S.S.R. **70** F6 50 00N 36 15E
Khartoum Sudan **78** D2 15 33N 32 35E
Khāsh Iran **79** J4 28 14N 61 15E
Khash *r.* Afghanistan **79** J5 31 30N 62 30E
Khashm el Girba Sudan **78** E1 14 59N 35 59E
Khaskovo Bulgaria **68** E3 41 57N 25 32E
Khatanga *r.* U.S.S.R. **71** M10 72 30N 102 30E
Khatanga U.S.S.R. **71** M10 71 59N 102 31E
Khemisset Morocco **93** D9 33 50N 6 03N
Kheta *r.* U.S.S.R. **71** L10 71 30N 95 00E
Khilok *r.* U.S.S.R. **71** M6 51 00N 107 30E
Khimki U.S.S.R. **70** L2 55 56N 37 26E
Khimki-Khovrino U.S.S.R. **70** L2 55 56N 37 30E
Khimki Reservoir U.S.S.R. **70** L2 55 54N 37 28E
Khios Greece **68** E2 38 23N 26 07E
Khios *i.* Greece **68** E2 38 00N 26 00E
Khiva U.S.S.R **70** I4 41 25N 60 49E
Khmel'nitskiy U.S.S.R. **69** E2 49 25N 26 59E
Kholayarvi U.S.S.R. **67** F4 67 07N 28 50E
Kholmsk U.S.S.R. **71** Q5 47 02N 142 03E
Khon Kaen Thailand **80** C7 16 25N 102 50E
Khorochevo U.S.S.R. **70** L2 55 47N 37 30E
Khorog U.S.S.R. **70** J3 37 22N 71 32E
Khorramābād Iran **79** G5 33 29N 48 21E
Khorramshahr Iran **79** G5 30 25N 48 09E
Khotin U.S.S.R. **69** E2 48 30N 26 31E
Khouang Vietnam **80** C7 19 02N 104 56E
Khouribga Morocco **93** D9 32 54N 6 57W
Khrishnapur Canal India **76** K2 22 34W 88 27E
Khulna Bangladesh **77** F4 22 49N 89 34E
Khyber Pass Afghanistan/Pakistan **79** L5 34 00N 71 00E
Kiantajärvi *l.* Finland **67** F4 65 02N 29 00E
Kibombo Zaïre **95** E7 3 58S 25 54E
Kidderminster Hereford and Worcester England **35** B2 52 23N 2 14W
Kidlington Oxfordshire England **32** A2 51 50N 1 17W
Kidsgrove Staffordshire England **35** B4 53 05N 2 14W
Kidwelly Dyfed Wales **38** B1 51 45N 4 18W
Kiel F.R.G. **63** B2 54 20N 10 08E
Kiel Bay Europe **63** B2 54 00N 10 00E
Kielce Poland **69** D3 50 51N 20 39E
Kielder Water *l.* Northumberland England **44** B2 55 10N 2 30W
Kieta Papua New Guinea **86** J8 6 15S 155 37E
Kiev *see* Kiyev
Kigali Rwanda **94** F7 1 56S 30 04E
Kigoma Tanzania **95** E7 4 52S 29 36E
Kii-suidō *sd.* Japan **82** B1 34 00N 134 45E
Kikinda Yugoslavia **68** D4 45 50N 20 30E
Kikládhes *(Cyclades) is.* Greece **68** D2 37 00N 25 00E
Kikori Papua New Guinea **86** G8 7 25S 144 13E
Kikwit Zaïre **95** C6 5 02S 18 51E
Kilanea Hawaiian Islands **119** X19 22 05N 159 35W
Kilbarchan Strathclyde Scotland **45** A1 55 50N 4 33W
Kilbirnie Strathclyde Scotland **45** A1 55 46N 4 41W
Kilbride Meath Irish Republic **49** A2 53 27N 6 24W
Kilburn Derbyshire England **35** D4 52 59N 1 26W
Kilcock Kildare Irish Republic **48** E3 53 24N 6 40W
Kilcoole Wicklow Irish Republic **49** B1 53 07N 6 04W
Kilcormac Offaly Irish Republic **48** D3 53 10N 7 43W
Kilcullen Kildare Irish Republic **48** E3 53 08N 6 45W
Kildare *co.* Irish Republic **48** E3 53 10N 6 55W
Kildare Kildare Irish Republic **48** E3 53 10N 6 55W
Kilgetty Dyfed Wales **38** B1 51 45N 4 44W
Kilimanjaro *mt.* Tanzania **94** G7 3 04S 37 22E
Kilkee Clare Irish Republic **48** B2 52 41N 9 38W
Kilkeel Northern Ireland **48** E4 54 04N 6 00W
Kilkenny *co.* Irish Republic **48** D2 52 30N 7 10W
Kilkenny Kilkenny Irish Republic **48** D2 52 39N 7 15W
Kilkhampton Cornwall England **30** C2 50 53N 4 29W
Kilkis Greece **68** D3 40 59N 22 52E
Kill Kildare Irish Republic **49** A1 53 15N 6 35W
Killaloe Clare Irish Republic **48** C2 52 48N 8 27W
Killamarsh Derbyshire England **43** G1 53 20N 1 20W
Killarney Kerry Irish Republic **48** B2 52 03N 9 30W
Killarney Manitoba Canada **101** P2 49 12N 99 40W
Killarney National Park Kerry Irish Republic **48** B1 52 10N 9 35W
Killearn Central Scotland **45** B2 56 03N 4 22W
Killeen Texas U.S.A. **103** G3 31 08N 97 44W
Killin Central Scotland **46** D3 56 28N 4 19W
Killiney Dublin Irish Republic **49** B1 53 15N 6 07W
Killinghall North Yorkshire England **43** F3 54 01N 1 34W
Killorglin Kerry Irish Republic **48** B2 52 06N 9 47W
Killpatrick Hills Strathclyde Scotland **45** B1 55 55N 4 25W
Killybegs Donegal Irish Republic **48** C4 54 38N 8 27W
Killyleagh Down Northern Ireland **48** F4 54 24N 5 39W
Kilmacanogue Wicklow Irish Republic **49** B1 53 10N 6 08W
Kilmacolm Strathclyde Scotland **45** A1 55 54N 4 38W
Kilmallock Limerick Irish Republic **48** C2 52 23N 8 34W
Kilmaluag Highland Scotland **46** B4 57 41N 6 17W
Kilmarnock Strathclyde Scotland **46** D2 55 36N 4 30W
Kilrea Northern Ireland **48** E4 54 57N 6 34W
Kilroot Northern Ireland **49** D2 54 43N 5 46W
Kilrush Clare Irish Republic **48** B2 52 39N 9 30W
Kilsallaghan Dublin Irish Republic **49** B2 53 28N 6 19W
Kilsyth Strathclyde Scotland **45** B1 55 59N 4 04W
Kiltan Island India **77** C2 11 30N 73 00E
Kilteel Kildare Irish Republic **49** A1 53 14N 6 31W
Kiltimagh Mayo Irish Republic **48** C3 53 51N 9 00W
Kilwa Masoko Tanzania **95** G6 8 55S 39 31S
Kilwinning Strathclyde Scotland **45** A1 55 40N 4 42W
Kilyos Turkey **68** E3 41 14N 29 02E
Kimbanseke Zaïre **92** B1 4 24S 15 24E
Kimberley British Columbia Canada **100** L2 49 40N 115 58W
Kimberley Nottinghamshire England **35** E3 53 00N 1 17W
Kimberley Republic of South Africa **95** D2 28 45S 24 46E
Kimberley Plateau Australia **86** D6 17 30S 126 00E
Kimberling City Missouri U.S.A. **104** B1 36 40N 93 25W
Kimbolton Cambridgeshire England **33** B3 52 18N 0 24W
Kinabalu *see* Gunung Kinabalu
Kinbasket Lake British Columbia Canada **100** L3 51 57N 118 02W
Kinbrace Highland Scotland **46** E5 58 15N 3 56W
Kinbuck Central Scotland **45** C2 56 13N 3 57W
Kincardine Fife Scotland **45** C2 56 03N 3 43W
Kincardine Ontario Canada **105** D2 44 11N 81 38W
Kinderdijk Netherlands **65** C1 51 53N 4 39E
Kindersley Saskatchewan Canada **100** N3 51 27N 109 08W
Kindia Guinea **93** C5 10 03N 12 49W
Kindu Zaïre **95** E7 3 00S 25 56E
Kineton Warwickshire England **36** C2 52 10N 1 30W
King George Bay Falkland Islands **117** L16 51 50S 61 00W
King George Island South Shetland Islands **115** F0 62 00S 58 00W
Kinghorn Fife Scotland **45** D2 56 04N 3 11W
King Island Australia **86** G2 40 00S 144 00E
Kingissepp U.S.S.R. **67** E2 59 22N 28 40E
Kingman Arizona U.S.A. **102** D4 35 12N 114 02W
Kingsbridge Devon England **31** D2 50 17N 3 46W
Kingsbury Warwickshire England **35** C2 52 35N 1 40W
Kingsclere Hampshire England **32** A2 51 20N 1 14W
Kingscourt Cavan Irish Republic **48** E3 53 53N 6 48W
King Sejong *r.s.* Antarctica **121** 62 13S 58 45W
Kingskerswell Devon England **31** D2 50 30N 3 37W
Kings Langley Hertfordshire England **34** B3 51 43N 0 28W
King's Lynn Norfolk England **33** C3 52 45N 0 24E
King Sound Australia **86** C6 16 00S 123 00E
Kings Point *tn.* New York U.S.A. **106** C2 40 49N 73 45W
Kingsport Tennessee U.S.A. **103** J4 36 33N 82 34W
Kingsteignton Devon England **31** D2 50 33N 3 35W
Kingston Jamaica **109** R7 17 58N 76 48W
Kingston New York U.S.A. **105** F2 41 55N 74 00W
Kingston Ontario Canada **105** E2 44 14N 76 30W
Kingston upon Hull Humberside England **40** D2 53 45N 0 20W
Kingston upon Thames Greater London England **34** C2 51 25N 0 18W
Kingstown St. Vincent & The Grenadines **109** L2 13 12N 61 14W
Kingsville Ontario Canada **105** D2 42 02N 82 44W
Kingsville Texas U.S.A. **103** G2 27 32N 97 53W
King's Walden Hertfordshire England **34** C3 51 54N 0 19W
Kingswinford West Midlands England **35** B2 52 29N 2 10W
Kingswood Avon England **31** E3 51 28N 2 30W
Kingswood Surrey England **34** C1 51 17N 0 12W
Kington Hereford and Worcester England **36** A2 52 12N 3 01W
Kingussie Highland Scotland **46** D4 57 05N 4 03W
King William Island Northwest Territories Canada **101** P6 69 00N 97 30W
Kinkala Congo **95** B7 4 18S 14 49E
Kinkell Bridge *tn.* Tayside Scotland **45** C2 56 20N 3 12W
Kinlochard Central Scotland **45** B2 56 12N 4 29W
Kinlochewe Highland Scotland **46** C4 57 36N 5 20W
Kinlochleven Highland Scotland **46** D3 56 42N 4 58W
Kinloch Rannoch Tayside Scotland **46** D3 56 42N 4 11W
Kinloss Grampian Scotland **46** E4 57 38N 3 33W
Kinnairds Head *c.* Grampian Scotland **46** F4 57 40N 2 00W
Kinross Tayside Scotland **45** D2 56 13N 3 27W
Kinsale Cork Irish Republic **48** C1 51 42N 8 32W
Kinsaley Dublin Irish Republic **49** B2 53 25N 6 10W

Kinshasa Zaïre 92 A2 4 18S 15 18E
Kintambo Zaïre 92 A1 4 21S 15 16E
Kintillo Tayside Scotland 45 D2 56 20N 3 24W
Kintore Grampian Scotland 46 F4 57 13N 2 21W
Kintyre p. Strathclyde Scotland 46 C2 55 30N 5 35W
Kinver Staffordshire England 35 B2 52 27N 2 14W
Kinzig r. F.R.G. 63 A2 50 00N 9 00E
Kiparissiakós Kólpos g. Greece 68 D2 37 00N 21 00E
Kipili Tanzania 95 F6 7 30S 30 39E
Kippax West Yorkshire England 43 F3 53 46N 1 22W
Kippen Central Scotland 45 B2 56 08N 4 11W
Kippure mt. Irish Republic 49 B1 53 10N 6 20W
Kirby Muxloe Leicestershire England 35 E2 52 38N 1 14W
Kirchhörde F.R.G. 62 D2 51 27N 7 27E
Kirensk U.S.S.R. 71 M7 57 45N 108 02E
Kirgizskaya S.S.R. rep. U.S.S.R. 70/71 J4 42 00N 75 00E
KIRIBATI Pacific Ocean 118 H8
Kirikiri Nigeria 92 C3 6 22N 3 22E
Kirikkale Turkey 78 D6 39 51N 33 32E
Kirinyaga (Mount Kenya) mt. Kenya 94 G7 0 10S 37 19E
Kiritimati Island Kiribati 119 K8 2 10N 157 00W
Kirkağaç Turkey 68 E2 39 06N 27 40E
Kirkburton West Yorkshire England 43 E2 53 37N 1 42W
Kirkby Merseyside England 42 B2 53 29N 2 54W
Kirkby in Ashfield Nottinghamshire England 36 C3 53 13N 1 15W
Kirkby Lonsdale Cumbria England 44 B1 54 13N 2 36W
Kirkbymoorside North Yorkshire England 40 C3 54 16N 0 55W
Kirkby Overblow North Yorkshire England 43 F3 53 57N 1 30W
Kirkby Stephen Cumbria England 44 B1 54 28N 2 20W
Kirkcaldy Fife Scotland 45 D2 56 07N 3 10W
Kirkconnel Dumfries & Galloway Scotland 46 D2 55 23N 4 00W
Kirkcudbright Dumfries & Galloway Scotland 46 D1 54 50N 4 03W
Kirkfieldbank Strathclyde Scotland 45 C1 55 41N 3 50W
Kirkham Lancashire England 42 B3 53 47N 2 53W
Kirkintilloch Strathclyde Scotland 45 B1 55 57N 4 10W
Kirkland Lake tn. Ontario Canada 105 D3 48 10N 80 02W
Kirklareli Turkey 68 E3 41 45N 27 12E
Kirkliston Lothian Scotland 45 D1 55 58N 3 25W
Kirk Michael Isle of Man British Isles 41 F1 54 17N 4 35W
Kirkmuirhill Strathclyde Scotland 45 C1 55 39N 3 55W
Kirknewton Lothian Scotland 45 D1 55 53N 3 25W
Kirkolm Dumfries & Galloway Scotland 46 C1 54 58N 5 04W
Kirk Sandall South Yorkshire England 43 G2 53 34N 1 04W
Kirksville Missouri U.S.A. 104 B2 40 12N 92 35W
Kirkūk Iraq 78 F6 35 28N 44 26E
Kirkwall Orkney Islands Scotland 47 E1 58 59N 2 58W
Kirov U.S.S.R. 70 G7 58 00N 49 38E
Kirovabad U.S.S.R. 70 G4 40 39N 46 20E
Kirovakan U.S.S.R. 78 F7 40 49N 44 30E
Kirovograd U.S.S.R. 70 E5 48 31N 32 15E
Kirriemuir Tayside Scotland 46 E3 56 41N 3 01W
Kirti Nagar India 76 L4 28 39N 77 09E
Kirton Lincolnshire England 36 D2 52 56N 0 04W
Kiruna Sweden 67 E4 67 53N 20 15E
Kiryū Japan 82 C2 36 26N 139 18E
Kisangani Zaïre 94 E8 0 33N 25 14E
Kisarazu Japan 83 C2 35 22N 139 55E
Kisenso Zaïre 92 B1 4 24S 15 21E
Kishinev U.S.S.R. 70 E5 47 00N 28 50E
Kishiwada Japan 82 C1 34 28N 135 22E
Kiskunfélegyháza Hungary 69 C2 46 42N 19 52E
Kiskunhalas Hungary 69 C2 46 26N 19 29E
Kismaayo Somalia 94 H7 0 25S 42 31E
Kisumu Kenya 94 F7 0 08S 34 47E
Kita Japan 83 B4 35 46N 139 43E
Kita-Kyūshū Japan 82 B1 33 52N 130 49E
Kitami Japan 82 D3 43 51N 143 54E
Kitchener Ontario Canada 105 D2 43 27N 80 30W
Kíthira i. Greece 68 D2 36 00N 23 00E
Kíthnos i. Greece 68 D2 37 00N 24 00E
Kitimat British Columbia Canada 100 J3 54 05N 128 38W
Kittanning Pennsylvania U.S.A. 105 E2 40 49N 79 31W
Kittery Maine U.S.A. 105 F2 43 05N 70 45W
Kitwe Zambia 95 E5 0 08S 30 30E
Kitzbühel Austria 63 B1 47 27N 12 23E
Kitzbühler Alpen mts. Austria 63 B1 47 00N 12 00E
Kitzingen F.R.G. 63 B1 49 45N 10 11E
Kivu, Lake Zaïre/Rwanda 94 E7 2 00S 29 00E
Kiyev (Kiev) U.S.S.R. 70 F6 50 25N 30 30E
Kiyevskoye Vodokhranilishche res. U.S.S.R. 69 F3 51 00N 30 00E
Kiyose Japan 83 B4 35 46N 139 32E
Kizil Irmak r. Turkey 78 D7 40 30N 34 00E
Kizyl Arvat U.S.S.R. 79 I6 39 00N 56 23E
Kladno Czechoslovakia 69 B3 50 10N 14 07E
Klagenfurt Austria 69 B2 46 38N 14 20E
Klaipėda U.S.S.R. 70 E7 55 43N 21 07E
Klamath r. U.S.A. 102 B5 42 00N 123 00W
Klamath Falls tn. Oregon U.S.A. 102 B5 42 14N 121 47W
Klarälven r. Sweden 67 C3 60 45N 13 00E
Klatovy Czechoslovakia 69 B2 49 24N 13 17E
Kleine Emscher can. F.R.G. 62 A3 51 35N 6 45E
Klerksdorp Republic of South Africa 95 E2 26 52S 26 39E
Kleve F.R.G. 63 A2 51 47N 6 11E
Kłodzko Poland 69 C3 50 28N 16 40E
Kløfta Norway 67 C3 60 04N 11 06E
Klondike r. Yukon Canada 96 62 00N 135 00W
Kluane National Park Yukon Territory Canada 100 H5 60 30N 139 00W
Klyuchevskaya Sopka mt. U.S.S.R. 71 S7 56 03N 160 38E
Knaphill Surrey England 34 B1 51 19N 0 37W
Knaresborough North Yorkshire England 43 F4 54 00N 1 27W
Knebworth Hertfordshire England 34 C3 51 52N 0 10W
Knighton Powys Wales 38 C2 52 21N 3 03W
Knockadoon Head c. Irish Republic 48 D1 51 50N 7 50W
Knockholt Pound Kent England 34 D1 51 19N 0 07E
Knokke-Heist Belgium 64 C3 51 21N 3 19E
Knossós hist. site Greece 78 C6 35 18N 25 10E
Knott End-on-Sea Lancashire England 42 B3 53 56N 2 59W
Knottingley West Yorkshire England 43 G3 53 43N 1 14W
Knowle West Midlands England 35 C2 52 23N 1 43W
Knowsley Merseyside England 42 B2 53 26N 2 52W
Knox Indiana U.S.A. 104 C2 41 17N 86 37W
Knoxville Iowa U.S.A. 104 B2 41 26N 93 05W
Knoxville Tennessee U.S.A. 103 J4 36 00N 83 57W
Knutsford Cheshire England 42 C1 53 18N 2 23W
Kōbe Japan 82 C1 34 40N 135 12E
København (Copenhagen) Denmark 67 C2 55 43N 12 34E
Koblenz F.R.G. 63 A2 50 21N 7 36E
Kobrin U.S.S.R. 69 D3 52 16N 24 22E
Kobuk r. Alaska U.S.A. 100 D6 67 00N 157 30W
Koca r. Turkey 68 E2 39 00N 27 00E
Koch Bihār India 77 F5 26 18N 89 32E
Kōchi Japan 82 B1 33 33N 133 32E
Kodiak Alaska U.S.A. 100 E4 57 49N 152 30W
Kodiak Island Alaska U.S.A. 100 E4 57 20N 153 40W
Kodiara Japan 83 A3 35 44N 139 28E
Kodok Sudan 94 F9 9 51N 32 07E
Koforidua Ghana 93 E4 6 01N 0 12W
Kofu Japan 82 C2 35 42N 138 34E
Koganei Japan 83 B3 35 42N 139 30E
Kohat Pakistan 77 C6 33 37N 71 30E
Kohima India 77 G5 25 40N 94 08E
Koh-i-Mazar mt. Afghanistan 79 K5 32 30N 66 23E
Kohoku Japan 83 B3 35 30N 139 39E
Kohtla-Järve U.S.S.R. 67 F2 59 28N 27 20E
Koito r. Japan 83 C2 35 20N 139 52E
Kokand U.S.S.R. 70 J4 40 33N 70 55E
Kokchetav U.S.S.R. 71 I6 53 18N 69 25E
Kokkola Finland 67 E3 62 45N 30 06E
Kokomo Indiana U.S.A. 104 C2 40 30N 86 09W
Koksoak r. Québec Canada 101 V4 58 00N 69 00W
Kola Peninsula U.S.S.R. 70 F9 67 30N 37 30E
Kolar Gold Fields tn. India 77 D2 12 54N 78 16E
Kolding Denmark 67 B2 55 29N 9 30E
Kolguyev i. U.S.S.R. 70 G9 69 00N 49 30E
Kolhapur India 77 C3 16 40N 74 20E
Kolín Czechoslovakia 69 C3 50 02N 15 11E
Köln (Cologne) F.R.G. 63 A2 50 56N 6 57E
Kolobrzeg Poland 69 C3 54 10N 15 35E
Kolomyya U.S.S.R. 69 E2 48 31N 25 00E
Kolpashevo U.S.S.R. 71 K7 58 21N 82 59E
Kolvereid Norway 67 C3 64 53N 11 35E
Kolwezi Zaïre 95 E5 10 45S 25 25E
Kolyma r. U.S.S.R. 71 R9 66 30N 152 00E
Kolyma Lowland U.S.S.R. 71 R9 69 00N 155 00E
Kolyma (Gydan) Range mts. U.S.S.R. 71 R8 63 00N 160 00E
Komae Japan 83 B3 35 38N 139 36E
Komandorskiye Ostrova is. U.S.S.R. 118 G13 55 00N 166 30E
Komárno Czechoslovakia 69 C2 47 46N 18 05E
Komatsu Japan 82 C2 36 25N 136 27E
Komotiní Greece 68 E3 41 06N 25 25E
Kompong Cham Cambodia 80 D6 11 59N 105 26E
Kompong Chhnang Cambodia 80 C6 12 16N 104 39E
Kompong Som Cambodia 80 C6 11 03N 103 41E
Komrat U.S.S.R. 69 E2 46 18N 28 40E
Komsomol'sk-na-Amure U.S.S.R. 71 P6 50 32N 136 59E
Kondūz Afghanistan 79 K6 36 45N 68 51E
Kong Christian X Island geog. reg. Greenland 101 DD8 75 00N 27 30W
Kongolo Zaïre 95 E6 5 20S 27 00E
Kong Oscars Fjord Greenland 101 EE7 72 30N 23 00W
Königswinter F.R.G. 64 G2 50 41N 7 11E
Konin Poland 69 C3 52 12N 18 12E
Konnagar India 76 K2 22 42N 88 20E
Konosha U.S.S.R. 70 G8 60 58N 40 08E
Konya Turkey 78 D6 37 51N 32 30E
Kootenay Lake British Columbia Canada 100 L3 50 00N 117 15W
Koper Yugoslavia 68 B4 45 31N 13 44E
Kopychintsy U.S.S.R. 69 E2 49 10N 25 58E
Korbach F.R.G. 63 A2 51 16N 8 53E
Korçë Albania 68 D3 40 38N 20 44E
Korčula i. Yugoslavia 68 C3 43 00N 17 00E
Korea Bay China/North Korea 81 J5 39 00N 124 00E
Korea Strait South Korea/Japan 81 K4/L4 33 00N 129 00E
Korhogo Côte d'Ivoire 93 D4 9 22N 5 31W
Korinthiakós Kólpos g. Greece 68 D2 38 00N 22 00E
Kórinthos Greece 68 D2 37 56N 22 55E
Kōriyama Japan 82 D2 37 23N 140 22E
Korla China 81 C6 41 48N 86 10E
Koro i. Fiji 118 U16 17 20S 179 25E
Koro Sea Fiji 118 U16 17 35S 180 00
Korosten U.S.S.R. 69 E3 51 00N 28 30E
Korsakov U.S.S.R. 71 Q5 46 36N 142 50E
Kortrijk (Courtrai) Belgium 64 C2 50 50N 3 17E
Koryak Range mts. U.S.S.R. 71 T8 62 00N 170 00E
Kos i. Greece 68 E2 36 00N 27 00E
Kosciusko, Mount Australia 86 H2 36 28S 148 17E
Košice Czechoslovakia 69 D2 48 44N 21 15E
Kosti Sudan 78 D1 13 11N 32 28E
Kostroma U.S.S.R. 70 G7 57 46N 40 59E
Kostrzyn Poland 69 B3 52 35N 14 40E
Koszalin Poland 69 C3 54 10N 16 10E
Kota India 77 D5 25 11N 75 58E
Kota Baharu Malaysia 80 C5 6 07N 102 15E
Kota Kinabalu Malaysia 80 F5 5 59N 116 04E
Köthen G.D.R. 63 B2 51 46N 11 59E
Kotka Finland 67 F3 60 26N 26 55E
Kotlas U.S.S.R. 70 G8 61 15N 46 35E
Kōtō Japan 83 C3 35 40N 139 49E
Kotri Pakistan 76 B5 25 22N 68 18E
Kotto r. Central African Republic 94 D9 7 00N 22 30E
Kotuy r. U.S.S.R. 71 M9 67 30N 102 00E
Kotzebue Alaska U.S.A. 100 C6 66 51N 162 40W
Kotzebue Sound Alaska U.S.A. 100 C6 66 40N 162 20W
Koudougou Burkina 93 E5 12 15N 2 23W
Koulamoutou Gabon 93 H2 1 12S 12 29E
Koulikoro Mali 93 D5 12 55N 7 31W
Koumra Chad 94 C9 8 56N 17 32E
Kounradskiy U.S.S.R. 81 A7 46 58N 74 59E
Kourou French Guiana 114 G14 5 08N 52 37W
Kouvola Finland 67 F3 60 54N 26 45E
Kovel' U.S.S.R. 69 D3 51 12N 24 48E
Koyukuk r. Alaska U.S.A. 100 E6 66 00N 154 00W
Kozáni Greece 68 D3 40 18N 21 48E
Kpalimé Togo 93 F4 6 55N 0 44E
Kragujevac Yugoslavia 68 D3 44 01N 20 55E
Kra, Isthmus of Asia 72 10 00N 104 00E
Kraków Poland 69 C3 50 03N 19 55E
Kraljevo Yugoslavia 68 D3 43 44N 20 41E
Kranj Yugoslavia 68 B4 46 15N 14 20E
Krasnodar U.S.S.R. 70 F5 45 02N 39 00E
Krasnovodsk U.S.S.R. 70 H4 40 01N 53 00E
Krasnoyarsk U.S.S.R. 71 L7 56 05N 92 46E
Krasny Stroitel U.S.S.R. 70 M1 55 31N 37 08E
Krefeld F.R.G. 63 A2 51 20N 6 32E
Kremenets U.S.S.R. 69 E3 50 05N 25 48E
Krems Austria 69 C2 48 25N 15 36E
Kribi Cameroon 93 G3 2 56N 9 56E
Krim (Crimea) p. U.S.S.R. 70 F5 46 00N 34 00E
Krimpen Netherlands 65 C1 51 54N 4 35E
Krishna r. India 77 D3 16 00N 79 00E
Kristiansand Norway 67 B2 58 08N 8 01E
Kristianstad Sweden 67 C2 56 02N 14 10E
Kristiansund Norway 67 B3 63 06N 7 58E
Kriti (Crete) i. Greece 68 D1 35 00N 25 00E
Krivoy Rog U.S.S.R. 70 F5 47 55N 33 24E
Krk i. Yugoslavia 68 B4 45 00N 14 00E
Kronshtadt U.S.S.R. 67 F3 60 00N 29 40E
Krosno Poland 69 D2 49 40N 21 46E
Kruger National Park Republic of South Africa 95 F3 24 00S 32 00E
Krugersdorp Republic of South Africa 95 E2 26 06S 27 46E
Kruševac Yugoslavia 68 D3 43 34N 21 20E
Krušnéhory see Erzgebirge
Ksar El Boukhari Algeria 93 F10 35 55N 2 47E
Ksar-el-Kebir Morocco 66 A2 35 04N 5 56W
Kuala Lumpur Malaysia 80 C4 3 08N 101 42E
Kuala Terengganu Malaysia 80 C5 5 20N 103 07E
Kuantan Malaysia 80 C4 3 50N 103 19E
Kubiri Japan 83 B1 35 13N 139 42E
Kuching Malaysia 80 E4 1 32N 110 20E
Kudat Malaysia 80 F5 6 54N 116 47E
Kufstein Austria 63 B1 47 36N 12 11E
Kuhmo Finland 67 F3 64 04N 29 30E
Kuito Angola 95 C5 12 25S 16 56E
Kujū-san mt. Japan 82 B1 33 07N 131 14E
Kukës Albania 68 D3 42 05N 20 24E
Kuldiga U.S.S.R. 67 E2 56 58N 21 58E
Kulmbach F.R.G. 63 B2 50 06N 11 28E
Kuma r. U.S.S.R. 70 G4 45 00N 45 00E
Kumagaya Japan 82 C2 36 09N 139 22E
Kumamoto Japan 82 B1 32 50N 130 42E
Kumanovo Yugoslavia 68 D3 42 07N 21 40E
Kumasi Ghana 93 E4 6 45N 1 35W
Kumba Cameroon 93 G3 4 39N 9 26E
Kumbakonam India 77 D2 10 59N 79 24E
Kumukahi, Cape Hawaiian Islands 119 Z17 19 30N 154 50W
Kumul see Hami
Kunar r. Asia 79 L5 35 30N 71 20E
Kunashir i. U.S.S.R. 82 E3 44 30N 146 20E
Kungrad U.S.S.R. 70 H4 43 06N 58 54E
Kunlun Shan mts. China 81 B5/C5 36 30N 85 00E
Kunming China 81 F3 25 04N 102 41E
Kunming Hu l. China 82 G2 40 00N 116 15E
Kunsan South Korea 81 K5 35 57N 126 42E
Kuntsevo U.S.S.R. 70 L1 55 43N 37 25E
Kununurra Australia 86 D6 15 42S 128 50E
Kuopio Finland 67 F3 62 54N 27 40E
Kupa r. Yugoslavia 68 C4 45 00N 15 00E
Kupang Indonesia 80 G1 10 13S 123 38E
Kupferdreh F.R.G. 62 C2 51 24N 7 06E
Kura r. U.S.S.R. 70 G4 41 00N 47 30E
Kurashiki Japan 82 B1 34 36N 133 43E
Kure Japan 82 B1 34 14N 132 32E
Kureyka r. U.S.S.R. 71 L9 67 30N 91 00E
Kurgan U.S.S.R. 70 I7 55 30N 65 20E
Kuria Muria Islands Oman 79 I2 17 30N 56 00E
Kurihama Japan 83 B1 35 12N 139 41E
Kurikka Finland 67 E3 62 36N 22 25E
Kuril Islands U.S.S.R. 71 R5/R6 50 00N 155 00E
Kuril Ridge Pacific Ocean 118 F12 47 50N 152 00E
Kuril Trench Pacific Ocean 118 F12 45 40N 154 00E
Kurnool India 77 D3 15 51N 78 01E
Kursk U.S.S.R. 70 F6 51 45N 36 14E
Kurskiy Zaliv g. U.S.S.R. 69 D4 55 00N 21 00E
Kurume Japan 82 B1 33 20N 130 29E
Kushiro Japan 82 D3 42 58N 144 24E
Kushka Afghanistan 79 J6 35 14N 62 15E
Kuskokwim r. Alaska U.S.A. 100 C5 61 30N 160 45W
Kuskokwim Bay Alaska U.S.A. 100 C4 58 50N 164 00W
Kuskokwim Mountains Alaska U.S.A. 100 D5 62 00N 158 00W
Kustanay U.S.S.R. 70 I6 53 15N 63 40E
Kütahya Turkey 78 C6 39 25N 29 56E
Kutno Poland 69 C3 52 13N 19 20E
Kuujjuaq Québec Canada 101 V4 58 25N 68 55W
Kuujjuarapik Québec Canada 101 T4 55 15N 77 30W
Kuusamo Finland 67 F4 65 57N 29 15E
Kuvango Angola 95 C5 14 27S 16 20E
KUWAIT 79 G4
Kuybyshev U.S.S.R. 70 H6 53 10N 50 10E
Kuytun China 81 B6 44 30N 85 00E
Kuzey Anadolu Dağlari mts. Turkey 78 E7 41 15N 36 20E
Kuz'minki U.S.S.R. 70 N1 55 41N 37 45E
Kwangju South Korea 81 K5 35 07N 126 52E
Kwango r. Zaïre 95 C6 6 00S 17 00E
Kwe Kwe Zimbabwe 95 E4 18 55S 29 49E
Kwethluk Alaska U.S.A. 100 C5 60 46N 161 34W
Kwigillingok Alaska U.S.A. 100 C4 59 50N 163 10W
Kwilu r. Zaïre 95 C6 6 00S 19 00E
Kyaukpyu Myanma 77 G3 19 27N 93 33E
Kyleakin Highland Scotland 46 C4 57 16N 5 44W
Kyle of Lochalsh Highland Scotland 46 C4 57 17N 5 43W
Kyle of Tongue b. Highland Scotland 46 D5 58 40N 4 25W
Kylestrome Highland Scotland 46 C5 58 16N 5 02W
Kyoga, Lake Uganda 94 F8 2 00N 34 00E
Kyoga-misaki c. Japan 82 C2 35 48N 135 12E
Kyōto Japan 82 C2 35 02N 135 45E
Kyronjöki r. Finland 67 E3 63 00N 21 30E
Kyūshū i. Japan 82 B1 32 20N 131 00E
Kyūshū Palau Ridge Pacific Ocean 118 D9 15 00N 135 00E
Kyustendil Bulgaria 68 D3 42 16N 22 40E
Kyzyl U.S.S.R. 71 L6 51 45N 94 28E
Kyzyl Kum d. U.S.S.R. 70 I4 43 00N 65 00E
Kzyl-Orda U.S.S.R. 70 I4 44 52N 65 28E

L

Laascaanood Somalia 94 I9 8 35N 46 55E
La Asunción Venezuela 109 L2 11 06N 63 53W
Laâyoune (El Aaiún) Western Sahara 93 C8 27 10N 13 11W
la Baule-Escoublac France 61 A2 47 18N 2 22W
Labé Guinea 93 C5 11 17N 12 11W
Labe see Elbe
Labrador geog. reg. Newfoundland Canada 101 W3 54 00N 63 00W
Labrador Basin Atlantic Ocean 117 C12 58 00N 50 00W
Labrador City Newfoundland Canada 100 V3 52 54N 66 50W
Labrador Sea Canada/Greenland 101 X4 59 00N 56 00W
Lábrea Brazil 114 E11 7 20S 64 46W
Labytnangi U.S.S.R. 71 I9 66 43N 66 28E
Lac Alaotra l. Madagascar 95 I4 17 30S 54 00E
Lac à l'Eau Claire l. Québec Canada 101 U4 56 20N 74 30W
Lac Bienville l. Québec Canada 101 U4 55 30N 78 00W
La Canada California U.S.A. 107 B3 34 12N 118 12W
Lac Caniapiscau l. Québec Canada 101 V3 54 20N 69 00W
La Ceiba Honduras 109 G3 15 45N 86 45W
la Chaux-de-Fonds Switzerland 61 C2 47 07N 6 51E
la Ciotat France 61 C1 43 10N 5 36E
La Coruña (Corunna) Spain 66 A3 43 22N 8 24W
La Cresenta California U.S.A. 107 B3 34 13N 118 14W
La Crosse Wisconsin U.S.A. 104 B2 43 48N 91 04W
Lac de la Forêt d'Orient l. France 61 B2 48 15N 4 20E
Lac de Neuchâtel l. Switzerland 61 C2 46 45N 6 40E
Lac du Bonnet tn. Manitoba Canada 104 A4 50 16N 96 03W
Lac du Der-Chantecoq l. France 61 B2 48 35N 4 45E
Lac Fitri l. Chad 94 C10 13 00N 17 30E
Lac Joseph l. Québec Canada 101 V3 52 30N 65 15W
Lache Cheshire England 42 B1 53 12N 2 54W
Lachlan r. Australia 86 H3 33 30S 145 30E
Lachute Québec Canada 105 F3 45 39N 74 21W
Lackawanna New York U.S.A. 105 E2 42 49N 78 49W
Lac la Martre tn. Northwest Territories Canada 100 L5 63 00N 117 30W
Lac la Ronge l. Saskatchewan Canada 101 N3 54 30N 107 25W
Lac Léman (Lake Geneva) l. Switzerland 61 C2 46 20N 6 20E
Lac Mai-Ndombe l. Zaïre 94 C7 2 00S 18 20E
Lac Manouané l. Québec Canada 105 F4 51 00N 71 00W
Lac Mattagami l. Québec Canada 105 E3 50 00N 78 00W
Lac Minto l. Québec Canada 101 T4 57 35N 75 00W
Lac Mistassini l. Québec Canada 101 U3 51 00N 73 20W
Lac Moero see Mweru, Lake
Lacolle Québec Canada 105 F3 45 04 73 22W
Lac Payne l. Québec Canada 101 U4 59 25N 74 00W
Lac St.-Jean l. Québec Canada 105 F3 48 00N 72 00W
Lac St. Joseph l. Ontario Canada 101 Q3 51 30N 91 40W
Lac Seul l. Ontario Canada 101 Q3 50 20N 92 00W
Lacul Razelm l. Romania 69 E1 45 00N 29 00E
Ladakh Range mts. Kashmir 77 D6 34 30N 78 30E
Ladbroke Warwickshire England 35 D1 52 14N 1 23W
la Défense France 60 A2 48 53N 2 14E
Ladoga, Lake see Ladozhskoye Ozero
Ladozhskoye Ozero (Lake Ladoga) l. U.S.S.R. 70 F8 61 00N 30 00E
Ladybank Fife Scotland 45 D2 56 17N 3 08W
Ladybower Reservoir Derbyshire England 43 E2 53 23N 1 42W
Ladysmith British Columbia Canada 100 K2 48 57N 123 50W
Ladysmith Republic of South Africa 95 E2 28 34S 29 47E
Ladysmith Wisconsin U.S.A. 104 B3 45 27N 91 07W
Lae Papua New Guinea 86 H8 6 45S 147 00E
Laedalsøyri Norway 67 B3 61 05N 7 15E
La Esmeralda Venezuela 114 D13 3 11N 65 33W
Lafayette Indiana U.S.A. 104 C2 40 25N 86 54W
Lafayette Louisiana U.S.A. 103 G3 30 12N 92 18W
La Fé Cuba 109 H4 22 02N 84 15W
la Flèche France 61 A2 47 42N 0 04W
Lagan r. Northern Ireland 49 D1 54 34N 5 58W
Lågen r. Norway 67 B3 61 40N 9 45E
Laghouat Algeria 93 F9 33 49N 2 55E
Lago Argentino l. Argentina 115 C2 50 10S 72 30W
Lago da Tijuca l. Brazil 116 B2 22 59S 43 22W
Lago de Chapala l. Mexico 108 D4 20 05N 103 00W
Lago de Itaipu l. Brazil 116 C2 22 58S 43 03W
Lago de Maracaibo l. Venezuela 114 C14 9 50N 71 30W
Lago de Marapendi l. Brazil 116 B1 23 01S 43 24W
Lago de Nicaragua l. Nicaragua 109 G2 11 50N 86 00W
Lago de Piratininga l. Brazil 116 C2 22 57S 43 05W
Lago de Poopó l. Bolivia 114 D9 18 30S 67 20W
Lago di Bolsena l. Italy 68 B3 42 00N 12 00E
Lago di Como l. Italy 68 A4 46 00N 9 00E
Lago di Garda l. Italy 68 B4 45 00N 10 00E
Lago d'Iseo l. Italy 61 C2 45 00N 10 00E
Lago do Jacarepaguá l. Brazil 116 B2 22 58S 43 23W
Lago Maggiore l. Italy 68 A4 46 00N 8 00E
Lago Rodrigo de Freitas l. Brazil 116 C2 22 58S 43 13W
Lagos Nigeria 92 C3 6 27N 3 28E
Lagos Portugal 66 A2 37 05N 8 40W
Lagos Island tn. Nigeria 92 C3 6 24N 3 28E
Lagos Lagoon Nigeria 92 D3 6 30N 3 33E
Lago Titicaca l. Peru/Bolivia 114 D9 16 00S 69 30W
La Grande Oregon U.S.A. 102 C6 45 21N 118 05W
La Grande 2, Réservoir Québec Canada 101 T3 54 00N 77 00W
La Grande 3, Réservoir Québec Canada 101 U3 54 10N 72 30W
La Grande Rivière r. Québec Canada 100 U3 59 00N 74 00W
La Grange Georgia U.S.A. 103 I3 33 02N 85 02W
La Guaira Venezuela 114 D15 10 38N 66 55W
Laguna Brazil 115 H7 28 29S 48 45W
Laguna Caratasca l. Honduras 109 H3 15 05N 84 00W
Laguna de Perlas l. Nicaragua 109 H2 12 30N 83 30W
Laguna Madre l. Mexico 108 E4 24 30N 97 30W
Laguna Mar Chiquita l. Argentina 115 E6 30 30S 62 30W
Lagunillas Venezuela 114 C15 10 07N 71 16W
La Habana (Havana) Cuba 109 H4 23 07N 82 25W
La Habra California U.S.A. 107 C2 33 56N 117 59W
Lahaina Hawaiian Islands 119 Y18 20 23N 156 40W
Lahn r. F.R.G. 63 A2 50 00N 8 00E
Lahore Pakistan 77 C6 31 34N 74 22E
Lahr F.R.G. 63 A1 48 21N 7 52E
Lahti Finland 67 F3 61 00N 25 40E
Lairg Highland Scotland 46 D5 58 01N 4 25W
Lajes Brazil 115 G7 27 48S 50 20W
Lajpat Nagar India 76 M4 28 34N 77 15E
La Junta Colorado U.S.A. 102 F4 37 59N 103 34W
Lake Charles tn. Louisiana U.S.A. 103 H3 30 13N 93 13W
Lake City Michigan U.S.A. 104 C2 44 22N 85 12W
Lake District National Park Cumbria England 44 A1 54 30N 3 15W
Lake Harbour tn. Northwest Territory Canada 101 V5 62 50N 69 50W
Lakeland Florida U.S.A. 103 J2 28 02N 81 59W
Lakemba i. Fiji 118 V15 18 10S 178 49W
Lakemba Passage sd. Fiji 118 V15 18 10S 179 00W
Lakenheath Suffolk England 33 C3 52 25N 0 31E
Lakeport California U.S.A. 102 B4 39 04N 122 56W
Lake River tn. Ontario Canada 101 S3 54 30N 82 30W
Lakeview Oregon U.S.A. 102 B5 42 13N 120 21W
Lakewood California U.S.A. 107 B2 33 49N 118 08W
Lakewood Ohio U.S.A. 105 D2 41 29N 81 50W
Lakota North Dakota U.S.A. 104 A3 48 02N 98 20W
Laksefjord fj. Norway 67 F5 70 40N 26 30E
Lakselv Norway 67 E5 70 03N 24 55E
Lakshadweep admin. India 77 C1 9 30N 73 00E
La Línea de la Concepción Spain 66 A2 36 10N 5 21W
Lalitpur India 77 D4 24 42N 78 24E
la Louvière Belgium 64 D2 50 29N 4 12E
La Maddalena Sardinia 61 C1 41 13N 9 25E
La Mancha admin. Spain 66 B2 39 10N 2 45W

La Manche *see* English Channel
Lamar Colorado U.S.A. **102** F4 38 04N 102 37W
Lambaréné Gabon **93** H2 0 41S 10 13E
Lambasa Fiji **118** U16 16 25S 179 24E
Lambay Island Irish Republic **49** B2 53 29N 6 01W
Lambeg Northern Ireland **49** C1 54 30N 6 02W
Lambert Glacier Antarctica **121** 73 00S 70 00E
Lambeth Greater London England **34** C2 51 30N 0 07W
Lambourn Berkshire England **32** A2 51 31N 1 31W
Lamego Portugal **66** A3 41 05N 7 49W
Lamia Greece **68** D2 38 55N 22 26E
Lamlash Strathclyde Scotland **46** C2 55 32N 5 08W
Lammermuir Hills Lothian/Borders Scotland **46** F2 55 50N 2 45W
La Molina Peru **116** F4 12 05S 76 57W
Lampazos Mexico **108** D5 27 00N 100 30W
Lampedusa *i.* Italy **68** B2 35 00N 12 00E
Lampeter Dyfed Wales **38** B2 52 07N 4 05W
Lamu Kenya **94** H7 2 17S 40 54E
Lanai *i.* Hawaiian Islands **119** Y18 20 50N 156 55W
Lanai City Hawaiian Islands **119** Y18 20 50N 156 56W
Lanark Strathclyde Scotland **45** C1 55 41N 3 48W
Lancang Jiang *r.* China **81** E4–F2 30 00N 98 00E
Lancashire *co.* England **40** B2 53 50N 2 30W
Lancaster California U.S.A. **102** C3 34 42N 118 09W
Lancaster Lancashire England **42** B4 54 03N 2 48W
Lancaster New Hampshire U.S.A. **105** F2 44 29N 71 34W
Lancaster Ohio U.S.A. **105** D1 39 43N 82 37W
Lancaster Pennsylvania U.S.A. **105** E2 40 01N 76 19W
Lancaster Canal Lancashire England **42** B3 53 55N 2 50W
Lancaster Sound Northwest Territories Canada **101** R7 74 00N 87 30W
Lancing West Sussex England **33** B1 50 50N 0 19W
Landau F.R.G. **63** A1 49 12N 8 07E
Landerneau France **61** A2 48 27N 4 16W
Landes *geog. reg.* France **61** A1 44 15N 1 00E
Landgraaf Netherlands **64** F2 50 55N 6 02E
Landianchang China **82** G1 39 58N 116 17E
Land's End *c.* Cornwall England **30** B2 50 03N 5 44W
Landshut F.R.G. **63** B1 48 31N 12 10E
Landskrona Sweden **67** C2 55 53N 12 50E
Lanesborough Roscommon Irish Republic **48** C3 53 40N 8 00W
Langdon North Dakota U.S.A. **104** A3 48 46N 98 21W
Langeland *i.* Denmark **63** B2 55 00N 10 00E
Langeoog *i.* F.R.G. **63** A2 53 00N 7 00E
Langford Bedfordshire England **34** C4 52 04N 0 15W
Langholm Dumfries & Galloway Scotland **46** E2 55 09N 3 00W
Langjökull *ice cap* Iceland **67** H6 64 45N 20 00W
Langold Nottinghamshire England **43** G2 53 24N 1 08W
Langon France **61** A1 44 33N 0 14W
Langøy *i.* Norway **67** C4 68 45N 15 00E
Langport Somerset England **31** E3 51 02N 2 50W
Langres France **61** C2 47 53N 5 20E
Langwith Nottinghamshire England **43** G1 53 13N 1 12W
Lannion France **61** A2 48 44N 3 27W
L'Annonciation Québec Canada **105** F3 46 24N 74 52W
Lansdowne House *tn.* Ontario Canada **101** R3 52 05N 88 00W
L'Anse Michigan U.S.A. **104** C3 46 45N 88 27W
Lansing Michigan U.S.A. **105** D2 42 44N 85 34W
Lanzarote *i.* Canary Islands **93** B8 29 00N 13 38W
Lanzhou China **81** F5 36 01N 103 45E
Laoag The Philippines **80** G7 18 14N 120 36E
Lao Cai Vietnam **81** F2 22 30N 103 57E
Laois *co.* Irish Republic **48** D2 52 59N 7 25W
Laon France **61** B2 49 34N 3 37E
La Oroya Peru **114** B10 11 36S 75 54W
LAOS 80 C7
La Paz Bolivia **114** D9 16 30S 68 10W
La Paz Mexico **108** B4 24 10N 110 17W
La Pesca Mexico **108** E4 23 46N 97 47W
Lapford Devon England **31** D2 50 52N 3 47W
La Plata Argentina **115** F5 34 52S 57 55W
Lappajärvi *l.* Finland **67** E3 63 13N 23 40E
Lappland *geog. reg.* Sweden/Finland **67** E4 67 30N 20 05E
Laprairie Québec Canada **105** F3 45 24N 73 30W
Laptev Sea Arctic Ocean **71** O11 76 00N 125 00E
Laptev Strait U.S.S.R. **71** Q10 73 00N 141 00E
Lapua Finland **67** E3 62 57N 23 00E
La Puebla Balearic Islands **66** E4 39 46N 3 01E
La Puente California U.S.A. **107** C3 34 01N 117 58W
La Punta Peru **116** E4 12 04S 77 09W
L'Aquila Italy **68** B3 42 22N 13 24E
Lār Iran **79** H4 27 42N 54 19E
Larache Morocco **93** D10 35 12N 6 10W
Laramie Wyoming U.S.A. **102** E5 41 20N 105 38W
Larbert Central Scotland **45** C2 56 02N 3 51W
Laredo Texas U.S.A. **102** G2 27 32N 99 22W
Largs Strathclyde Scotland **46** D2 55 48N 4 52W
La Rioja Argentina **115** D7 29 26S 66 50W
Lárisa Greece **68** D2 39 38N 22 25E
Lark *r.* Suffolk/Cambridgeshire England **33** C3 52 25N 0 25E
Larkana Pakistan **76** B5 27 32N 68 18E
Larkhall Strathclyde Scotland **45** C1 55 45N 3 59W
Larnaca Cyprus **78** D5 34 54N 33 29E
Larne Antrim Northern Ireland **48** F4 54 51N 5 49W
La Roche-en-Ardenne Belgium **64** E2 50 11N 5 35E
la Rochelle France **61** A2 46 10N 1 10W
la Roche-sur-Yon France **61** A2 46 40N 1 25W
La Romana Dominican Republic **109** K3 18 27N 68 57W
Larsen Ice Shelf Antarctica **121** 67 00S 62 00W
La Salle Illinois U.S.A. **104** C2 41 20N 89 06W
La Serena Chile **115** C7 29 54S 71 18W
Las Cruces New Mexico U.S.A. **102** E3 32 18N 106 47W
Lashio Myanma **81** E2 22 58N 97 48E
Las Marismas *geog. reg.* Spain **66** A2 36 55N 6 00W
Las Palmas Canary Islands **93** B8 28 08N 15 27W
La Spezia Italy **68** A3 44 07N 9 48E
Lassodie Fife Scotland **45** D2 56 07N 3 24W
L'Assomption Québec Canada **105** F3 45 48N 73 27W
Last Mount Lake Saskatchewan Canada **100** N3 51 40N 106 55W
Las Vegas Nevada U.S.A. **102** C4 36 10N 115 10W
Las Vegas New Mexico U.S.A. **102** E4 35 36N 105 15W
Latacunga Ecuador **114** B12 0 58S 78 36W
Latheron Highland Scotland **46** E5 58 17N 3 22W
Latina Italy **68** B3 41 28N 12 53E
La Tuque Québec Canada **105** F3 47 26N 72 47W
Latur India **77** D3 18 24N 76 34E
Latvia *see* Latviyskaya S.S.R.
Latviyskaya S.S.R. *rep.* U.S.S.R. **67** E2 57 10N 24 20E
Lauder Borders Scotland **46** F2 55 43N 2 45W
Lauf F.R.G. **63** B1 49 30N 11 16E
Laugharne Dyfed Wales **38** B1 51 47N 4 28W
Launceston Australia **86** H1 41 25S 147 07E
Launceston Cornwall England **30** C2 50 38N 4 21W
Laurel Mississippi U.S.A. **103** I1 31 41N 89 09W
Laurencekirk Grampian Scotland **46** F3 56 50N 2 29W
Laurie Island South Orkney Islands **115** I0 60 51S 44 30W
Lausanne Switzerland **61** C2 46 32N 6 39E
Laut *i.* Indonesia **80** F3 4 00S 116 40E
Lautoka Fiji **118** T16 17 36S 177 28E
Lauzon Québec Canada **105** F3 46 49N 71 10W
Laval France **61** A2 48 04N 0 45W
La Vega Dominican Republic **109** J3 19 15N 70 33W
Lavenham Suffolk England **33** C3 52 06N 0 47E
Laverton Australia **86** C4 28 49S 122 25E
La Victoria Peru **116** E4 12 04S 77 01W
La Victoria Venezuela **114** D15 10 16N 67 21W
Law Strathclyde Scotland **45** C1 55 44N 3 51W
Lawndale California U.S.A. **107** A2 33 52N 118 21W
Lawrence Kansas U.S.A. **103** G4 38 58N 95 15W
Lawrence Massachusetts U.S.A. **105** F2 42 41N 71 12W
Lawton Oklahoma U.S.A. **102** G3 34 36N 98 25W
Laxey Isle of Man British Isles **41** F1 54 14N 4 24W
Laxford Bridge Highland Scotland **46** C5 58 22N 5 01W
Lay *r.* France **61** A2 46 32N 1 15W
Laylā Saudi Arabia **79** G3 22 16N 46 45E
Laysan *i.* Hawaiian Islands **118** I10 25 46N 171 44W
Lazonby Cumbria England **44** B1 54 46W 2 41W
Leadburn Lothian Scotland **45** D1 55 47N 3 14W
Leamington Ontario Canada **105** D2 42 03N 82 35W
Leatherhead Surrey England **34** B1 51 18N 0 20W
LEBANON 78 D5
Lebanon Missouri U.S.A. **103** H4 37 40N 92 40W
Lebanon New Hampshire U.S.A. **105** F2 43 39N 72 17W
Lebanon Pennsylvania U.S.A. **105** E2 40 21N 76 25W
le Blanc France **61** B2 46 38N 1 04E
le Blanc-Mesnil France **60** B2 48 56N 2 28E
Lebu Chile **115** C5 37 38S 73 43W
Lecce Italy **68** C3 40 21N 18 11E
Lech *r.* Europe **63** B1 48 00N 11 00E
Lechlade Gloucestershire England **31** F3 51 43N 1 41W
Lechtaler Alpen *mts.* Austria **63** B1 47 00N 10 00E
le Creusot France **61** B2 46 48N 4 27E
Ledbury Hereford and Worcester England **36** B2 52 02N 2 25W
Ledmore Highland Scotland **46** D5 58 03N 4 58W
Ledsham Cheshire England **42** B1 53 17N 2 59W
Leduc Alberta Canada **100** M3 53 17N 113 30W
Lee *r.* Irish Republic **48** C1 51 50N 8 50W
Leech Lake Minnesota U.S.A. **104** B3 47 00N 94 00W
Leeds West Yorkshire England **43** F3 53 50N 1 35W
Leeds & Liverpool Canal England **42** D3 53 50N 2 15W
Leek Staffordshire England **36** B3 53 06N 2 01W
Lee-on-the-Solent Hampshire England **32** A1 50 48N 1 12W
Leer F.R.G. **63** A2 53 14N 7 27E
Leerdam Netherlands **65** E1 51 53N 5 05E
Leeuwarden Netherlands **64** E5 53 12N 5 48EW
Leeuwin, Cape Australia **86** B3 34 24S 115 09E
Leeward Islands Lesser Antilles **109** L3 17 30N 64 00W
Leganés Spain **66** B3 40 20N 3 46W
Legnica Poland **69** C3 51 12N 16 10E
Legoniel Northern Ireland **49** D1 54 37N 5 59W
Leh Kashmir **77** D6 34 09N 77 35E
le Havre France **61** B2 49 30N 0 06E
Leicester Leicestershire England **36** C2 52 38N 1 05W
Leicestershire *co.* England **36** C2/D2 52 40N 1 00W
Leiden Netherlands **65** C2 52 10N 4 30E
Leiderdorp Netherlands **65** C2 52 08N 4 33E
Leidschendam Netherlands **65** B2 52 05N 4 24E
Leie *r.* Belgium **64** C2 50 50N 3 20E
Leigh Greater Manchester England **42** C2 53 30N 2 33W
Leigh Kent England **34** D1 51 12N 0 13E
Leighton Buzzard Bedfordshire England **34** B3 51 55N 0 41W
Leine *r.* F.R.G./G.D.R. **63** A2 52 00N 10 00E
Leipzig *admin.* G.D.R. **63** B2 51 00N 12 00E
Leipzig G.D.R. **63** B2 51 20N 12 25E
Leiria Portugal **66** A2 39 45N 8 49W
Leiston Suffolk England **33** D3 52 13N 1 34E
Leith Lothian Scotland **45** D1 55 59N 3 10W
Leith Hill Surrey England **34** B1 51 11N 0 23W
Leitrim *co.* Irish Republic **48** C4/D4 54 05N 8 00W
Leixlip Kildare Irish Republic **49** A2 53 22N 6 30W
Leizhou Bandao *p.* China **81** H2 21 00N 110 00E
Lek *r.* Netherlands **65** D1 51 48N 4 47E
Lekkous *r.* Morocco **66** A1/2 35 00N 5 40W
Lelystad Netherlands **64** E4 52 32N 5 29E
le Mans France **61** B2 48 00N 0 12E
Lemgo F.R.G. **63** A2 52 02N 8 54E
Lemmer Netherlands **64** E4 52 50N 5 43E
Lena *r.* U.S.S.R. **71** O9 70 00N 125 00E
Lendrick Central Scotland **45** B2 56 14N 4 20W
Leninakan U.S.S.R. **70** G4 40 47N 43 49E
Leningrad U.S.S.R. **70** F7 59 55N 30 25E
Leningradskaya *r.s.* Antarctica **121** 69 30S 159 23E
Lenino U.S.S.R. **70** M1 55 35N 37 10E
Leninogorsk U.S.S.R. **71** K6 50 23N 83 32E
Leninsk-Kuznetskiy U.S.S.R. **71** K6 54 44N 86 13E
Lenkoran' U.S.S.R. **79** G6 38 45N 48 50E
Lennoxtown Strathclyde Scotland **45** B1 55 59N 4 12W
Lennoxville Québec Canada **105** F3 45 22N 71 51W
Lens France **61** B3 50 26N 2 50E
Lensk U.S.S.R. **71** N8 60 48N 114 55E
Leoben Austria **69** C2 47 23N 15 06E
Leominster Hereford and Worcester England **36** B2 52 14N 2 45W
León Mexico **108** D4 21 10N 101 42W
León Nicaragua **108** G2 12 24N 86 52W
Leon *r.* Texas U.S.A. **103** G3 32 00N 98 00W
León Spain **66** A3 42 35N 5 34W
Leonora Australia **86** C4 28 54S 121 20E
Lepel' U.S.S.R. **69** E3 54 48N 28 40E
le Puy France **61** B2 45 03N 3 53E
le Raincy France **60** C2 48 54N 2 32E
Léré Chad **94** B9 9 41N 14 17E
Lérida *(Lleida)* Spain **66** C3 41 37N 0 38E
Lerwick Shetland Islands Scotland **47** B2 60 09N 1 09W
Les Cayes Haiti **109** J3 18 15N 73 46W
Les Coudreaux France **60** C2 48 54N 2 36E
Les Ecréhou *is.* Channel Islands British Isles **31** H5 49 17N 1 56W
Les Îles Belcher *is.* Northwest Territories Canada **101** T4 56 00N 79 30W
Leskovac Yugoslavia **68** D3 43 00N 21 57E
Leslie Fife Scotland **45** D2 56 13N 3 13W
Lesmahagow Strathclyde Scotland **46** E2 55 38N 3 54W
LESOTHO 95 E2
les Sables-d'Olonne France **61** A2 46 30N 1 47W
Lesse *r.* Belgium **64** E2 50 10N 5 10E
Lesser Antilles *is.* West Indies **109** K2–L3
Lesser Slave Lake Alberta Canada **100** L4 55 25N 115 30W
Lesser Sunda Islands Indonesia **72** 8 00S 120 00E
Lessines Belgium **64** C2 50 43N 3 50E
les Ulis France **60** A1 48 41N 2 11E
Lésvos *i.* Greece **68** E2 39 00N 26 00E
Leszno Poland **69** C3 51 51N 16 35E
Letchworth Hertfordshire England **34** C3 51 58N 0 14W
Letham Fife Scotland **45** D2 56 16N 3 08W
Lethbridge Alberta Canada **100** M2 49 43N 112 48W
Leticia Colombia **114** C12 4 09S 69 57W
le Touquet-Paris-Plage France **61** B3 50 13N 1 36E
le Tréport France **61** B3 50 04N 1 22E
Letterkenny Donegal Irish Republic **48** D4 54 57N 7 44W
Leuchars Fife Scotland **46** F3 56 23N 2 53W
Leuven *(Louvain)* Belgium **64** D2 50 53N 4 42E
Levádhia Greece **68** D2 38 26N 22 53E
Leven Humberside England **40** D2 53 54N 0 19W
Leven *r.* Fife Scotland **45** D2 56 11N 3 20W
Lévêque, Cape Australia **86** C6 16 25S 122 55E
Leverburgh Western Isles Scotland **46** B4 57 45N 7 00W
Leverkusen F.R.G. **63** A2 51 02N 6 59E
Levice Czechoslovakia **69** C2 48 14N 18 35E
Levin New Zealand **87** C2 40 37S 175 18E
Lévis Québec Canada **105** F3 46 47N 71 12W
Levkás *i.* Greece **68** D2 38 00N 20 00E
Levuka Fiji **118** U16 17 42N 178 50E
Lewes Delaware U.S.A. **105** E1 38 47N 75 09W
Lewes East Sussex England **33** C1 50 52N 0 01E
Lewis *i.* Western Isles Scotland **46** B5 58 15N 6 30W
Lewisburg Pennsylvania U.S.A. **105** E2 40 58N 76 55W
Lewisham Greater London England **34** C3 51 27N 0 00
Lewis Pass New Zealand **87** B2 42 22S 172 27E
Lewiston Idaho U.S.A. **102** C6 46 25N 117 00W
Lewiston Maine U.S.A. **105** F2 44 06N 70 14W
Lewiston New York U.S.A. **105** E2 43 11N 79 03W
Lewistown Montana U.S.A. **102** E6 47 04N 109 26W
Lewistown Pennsylvania U.S.A. **105** E2 40 37N 77 36W
Lexington Kentucky U.S.A. **105** D1 38 02N 84 30W
Lexington Virginia U.S.A. **105** E1 37 47N 79 27W
Lexington Park Maryland U.S.A. **105** E1 38 15N 76 28W
Leyburn North Yorkshire England **40** C3 54 19N 1 49W
Leyland Lancashire England **42** B3 53 42N 2 42W
Leysdown on Sea Kent England **33** C2 51 24N 0 55E
Leyte *i.* The Philippines **80** G6 11 00N 124 50E
Leyton Greater London England **34** C2 51 34N 0 01W
Lezhë Albania **68** C3 41 47N 19 39E
Lhasa China **81** D3 29 41N 91 10E
Lhazê China **81** C3 29 08N 87 43E
Liane *r.* France **64** A2 50 40N 1 35E
Lianyungang China **81** I4 34 37N 119 10E
Liao *r.* China **72** 44 00N 121 00E
Liaoyang China **81** J6 41 16N 123 12E
Liaoyuan China **81** K6 42 53N 125 10E
Liard *r.* British Columbia/Northwest Territories Canada **100** K5 61 55N 122 30W
Libenge Zaïre **94** C8 3 39N 18 39E
Liberal Kansas U.S.A. **102** F4 37 03N 100 56W
Liberec Czechoslovakia **69** C3 50 48N 15 05E
LIBERIA 93 D4
Liberton Lothian Scotland **45** D1 55 55N 3 09W
Liberty New York U.S.A. **105** F2 41 47N 74 46W
Libourne France **61** A1 44 55N 0 14W
Libreville Gabon **93** G3 0 30N 9 25E
LIBYA 94 C13
Libyan Desert North Africa **94** D13 25 00N 25 00E
Libyan Plateau 94 E14 31 00N 26 00E
Lichfield Staffordshire England **35** C3 52 42N 1 48W
Lichinga Mozambique **95** G5 13 19S 35 13E
Lickey Hereford & Worcester England **35** B2 52 22N 2 01W
Lickey End Hereford & Worcester England **35** B2 52 21N 2 01W
Licking *r.* Kentucky U.S.A. **105** D1 38 00N 84 00W
Lida U.S.S.R. **69** E3 53 50N 25 19E
Liddel Water *r.* Scotland / **46** F2 55 15N 2 50W
Lidlington Bedfordshire England **34** B4 52 03N 0 34W
LIECHTENSTEIN 61 C2
Liège *admin.* Belgium **64** E2 50 30N 5 45E
Liège Belgium **64** E2 50 38N 5 35E
Lienz Austria **69** B2 46 51N 12 50E
Liepāja U.S.S.R. **67** E2 56 30N 21 00E
Lier Belgium **64** D3 51 08N 4 35E
Liestal Switzerland **61** C2 47 29N 7 43E
Liffey *r.* Irish Republic **49** A2 5 25N 6 25W
Lifford Donegal Irish Republic **48** D4 54 50N 7 29W
Lifou *i.* Is. Loyauté Pacific Ocean **86** L5 21 00S 167 00E
Lightwater Surrey England **34** A2 51 21N 0 41W
Ligurian Sea Mediterranean Sea **68** A3 44 00N 9 00E
Lihue Hawaiian Islands **119** X18 21 59N 159 23W
Likasi Zaïre **95** E5 10 58S 26 47E
Liku Indonesia **80** D4 1 47N 109 19E
Lille France **61** B3 50 39N 3 05E
Lillehammer Norway **67** C3 61 06N 10 27E
Lilleshall Shropshire England **35** A3 52 44N 2 21W
Lilley Hertfordshire England **34** B3 51 56N 0 23W
Lilongwe Malawi **95** F5 13 58S 33 49E
Liluah India **76** K2 22 37N 88 20E
Lim *r.* Yugoslavia **68** C3 43 00N 19 00E
Lima Ohio U.S.A. **105** D2 40 43N 84 06W
Lima Peru **116** E4 12 06S 77 03W
Lima *r.* Portugal **66** A3 41 50N 8 40W
Limassol Cyprus **78** D5 34 40N 33 03E
Limavady Northern Ireland **48** E5 55 03N 6 57W
Limay *r.* Argentina **115** D5 39 30S 69 30W
Limbe Cameroon **93** G3 3 58N 9 10E
Limburg *admin.* Belgium **64** E2 50 55N 5 20E
Limburg *admin.* Netherlands **64** E3 51 32N 5 45E
Limburg F.R.G. **63** A2 50 23N 8 04E
Limeira Brazil **115** H8 22 34S 47 25W
Limerick *co.* Irish Republic **48** C2 52 30N 8 40W
Limerick Limerick Irish Republic **48** C2 52 40N 8 38W
Limfjorden *fj.* Denmark **67** B2 57 00N 8 50E
Límnos *i.* Greece **68** E2 39 00N 25 00E
Limoges France **61** B2 45 50N 1 15E
Limón Costa Rica **109** H2 10 00N 83 01W
Limoux France **61** B1 43 03N 2 13E
Limpopo *r.* Southern Africa **95** F3 22 30S 32 00E
Limpsfield Surrey England **34** D1 51 16N 0 01E
Linares Mexico **108** E3 24 54N 99 38W
Linares Spain **66** B2 38 05N 3 38W
Lincoln Lincolnshire England **36** D3 53 14N 0 33W
Lincoln Maine U.S.A. **105** G3 45 23N 68 30W
Lincoln Nebraska U.S.A. **104** A2 40 49N 96 41W
Lincolnshire *co.* England **36** D3 53 10N 0 20W
Lincoln Wolds *hills* Lincolnshire England **36** D3 53 25N 0 05W
Linden Guyana **114** F14 5 59N 58 19W
Linden New Jersey U.S.A. **106** B1 40 37N 74 13W
Lindis Pass New Zealand **87** A2 44 33S 169 43E
Lindsay Ontario Canada **105** E2 44 21N 78 44W
Line Islands Kiribati **119** K7 0 00 160 00W
Lingen F.R.G. **63** A2 52 32N 7 19E
Lingfield Surrey England **34** C1 51 11N 0 01W
Lingwala Zaire **92** A2 4 19S 15 18E
Linhares Brazil **114** J9 19 22S 40 04W
Linköping Sweden **67** D2 58 25N 15 35E
Linlithgow Lothian Scotland **45** C1 55 59N 3 37W
Linsell Sweden **67** C3 62 10N 13 50E
Linslade Bedfordshire England **34** A3 51 55N 0 42W
Linstead Jamaica **109** Q8 18 08N 77 02W
Linthwaite West Yorkshire England **43** E2 53 38N 1 52W
Linton Cambridgeshire England **33** C3 52 06N 0 17E
Linton North Dakota U.S.A. **102** F6 46 17N 100 14W
Linwood Strathclyde Scotland **45** A1 55 51N 4 30W
Linxia China **81** F5 35 31N 103 08E
Linz Austria **69** B2 48 19N 14 18E
Lipetsk U.S.S.R. **70** F6 52 37N 39 36E
Liphook Hampshire England **33** B2 51 05N 0 49W
Lippe *r.* F.R.G. **64** G3 51 00N 7 00E
Lippstadt F.R.G. **63** A2 51 41N 8 20E
Lisboa *(Lisbon)* Portugal **66** A2 38 44N 9 08W
Lisbon North Dakota U.S.A. **104** A3 46 28N 97 30W
Lisbon *see* Lisboa
Lisburn Northern Ireland **49** C1 54 31N 6 03W
Lisburne, Cape Alaska U.S.A. **100** B6 68 54N 166 18W
Liscannor Bay Irish Republic **48** B2 52 55N 9 30W
Lisianski *i.* Hawaiian Islands **118** I10 26 04N 173 58W
Lisieux France **61** B2 49 09N 0 14E
Liskeard Cornwall England **30** C2 50 28N 4 28W
Lismore Australia **86** I4 28 48S 153 17E
Lismore *i.* Strathclyde Scotland **46** C3 56 30N 5 30W
Lismore Waterford Irish Republic **48** D2 52 08N 7 55W
Lisnaskea Northern Ireland **48** D4 54 15N 7 27W
Liss Hampshire England **33** B2 51 03N 0 55W
Lisse Netherlands **65** C3 52 16N 4 34E
Listowel Kerry Irish Republic **48** B2 52 27N 9 29W
Litani *r.* Lebanon **78** O11 33 35N 35 40E
Litherland Merseyside England **42** A2 53 28N 2 59W
Lithgow Australia **86** I3 33 30S 150 09E
Lithuania *see* Litovskaya S.S.R.
Litovskaya S.S.R. *rep.* U.S.S.R. **70** E7 56 00N 23 30E
Little Aden South Yemen **79** F1 12 47N 44 55E
Little Andaman *i.* Andaman Islands **77** G2 10 30N 92 40E
Littleborough Greater Manchester England **42** D2 53 39N 2 05W
Little Chalfont Buckinghamshire England **34** B2 51 39N 0 34W
Little Colorado *r.* Arizona U.S.A. **102** D4 36 00N 111 00W
Little Current *tn.* Ontario U.S.A. **105** D3 45 57N 81 56W
Little Dart *r.* Devon England **31** D2 50 52N 3 50W
Little Falls *tn.* Minnesota U.S.A. **104** B3 45 58N 94 20W
Littlehampton West Sussex England **33** B1 50 48N 0 33W
Little Lever Greater Manchester England **42** C2 53 34N 2 23W
Little Minch *sd.* Scotland **46** B4 57 45N 6 30W
Little Missouri *r.* U.S.A. **102** F6 46 00N 104 00W
Little Nicobar *i.* Nicobar Islands **77** G1 7 00N 94 00E
Little Ouse *r.* Norfolk/Suffolk England **33** C3 52 30N 0 30E
Littleport Cambridgeshire England **33** C3 52 28N 0 19E
Little Rock Arkansas U.S.A. **103** H3 34 42N 92 17W
Little Salmon Yukon Territory Canada **100** I5 62 30N 134 30W
Little Sioux *r.* U.S.A. **104** A2 42 00N 96 00W
Little Snake *r.* U.S.A. **102** E5 41 00N 108 00W
Littleton New Hampshire U.S.A. **105** F2 44 18N 71 46W
Little Wabash *r.* Illinois U.S.A. **104** C1 39 00N 88 00W
Little Waltham Essex England **34** E3 51 48N 0 28E
Liuzhou China **81** G2 24 17N 109 15E
Lively Island Falkland Islands **117** M15 52 00S 158 40W
Liverpool Merseyside England **42** B2 53 25N 2 55W
Liverpool Bay Merseyside England **42** A2 53 28N 3 15W
Liversedge West Yorkshire England **43** E3 53 43N 1 41W
Livingston Lothian Scotland **45** C1 55 53N 3 32W
Livingston Montana U.S.A. **102** D6 45 40N 110 33W
Livingstone *see* Maramba
Livingstonia Malawi **95** F5 10 35S 34 10E
Livingston Island South Shetland Islands **115** E0 62 38S 60 30W
Livojöki *r.* Finland **67** F4 65 25N 26 45E
Livorno Italy **68** B3 43 33N 10 18E
Liwale Tanzania **95** G6 9 47S 38 00E
Lizard Cornwall England **30** B1 49 57N 5 13W
Lizard Point Cornwall England **30** B1 49 56N 5 13W
Ljubljana Yugoslavia **68** B4 46 04N 14 30E
Ljungan *r.* Sweden **67** D3 62 35N 16 00E
Ljus Sweden **67** D3 61 57N 16 05E
Ljusnan *r.* Sweden **67** D3 62 05N 15 10E
Llanberis Gwynedd Wales **38** B3 53 07N 4 06W
Llanbister Powys Wales **38** C2 52 21N 3 19W
Llandeilo Dyfed Wales **38** C1 51 53N 3 59W
Llandovery Dyfed Wales **38** C2 51 59N 3 48W
Llandrindod Wells Powys Wales **38** C2 52 15N 3 23W
Llandudno Gwynedd Wales **38** C3 53 19N 3 49W
Llandyssul Dyfed Wales **38** B2 52 02N 4 19W
Llanelli Dyfed Wales **38** B1 51 42N 4 10W
Llanerchymedd Gwynedd Wales **38** B3 53 20N 4 22W
Llanfair Caereinion Powys Wales **38** C2 52 39N 3 20W
Llanfairfechan Gwynedd Wales **38** B3 53 15N 3 58W
Llanfyllin Powys Wales **38** C2 52 46N 3 17W
Llangadfan Powys Wales **38** C2 52 41N 3 28W
Llangadog Dyfed Wales **38** C2 51 57N 3 53W
Llangefni Gwynedd Wales **38** B3 53 16N 4 18W
Llangollen Clwyd Wales **38** C2 52 58N 3 10W
Llangurig Powys Wales **38** C2 52 25N 3 36W
Llangynog Powys Wales **38** C2 52 50N 3 25W
Llanharan Mid Glamorgan Wales **38** C1 51 32N 3 28W
Llanidloes Powys Wales **39** C2 52 27N 3 32W
Llanos *geog. reg.* Venezuela **114** D14 7 30N 67 30W
Llanrhystud Dyfed Wales **38** B2 52 18N 4 09W
Llantrisant Mid Glamorgan Wales **38** C1 51 33N 3 23W
Llantwit Major South Glamorgan Wales **38** C1 51 25N 3 390W
Llanuwchllyn Gwynedd Wales **38** C2 52 52N 3 41W
Llanwrst Gwynedd Wales **38** C3 53 08N 3 48W
Llanwrtyd Wells Powys Wales **38** C2 52 07N 3 38W
Llanybydder Dyfed Wales **38** B2 52 04N 4 09W
Lleida *see* Lérida
Lleyn Peninsula Gwynedd Wales **38** B2 52 53N 4 30W
Llobregat *r.* Spain **66** C3 42 00N 1 50E
Lloydminster Saskatchewan Canada **100** N3 53 18N 110 00W
Lluchmayor Balearic Islands **66** E4 39 29N 2 53E
Llyn Alaw *l.* Gwynedd Wales **38** B3 53 21N 4 26W
Llyn Celyn *l.* Gwynedd Wales **38** B3 53 04N 4 10W

Muirkirk Strathclyde Scotland 46 D2 55 31N 4 04W
Muir of Ord Highland Scotland 46 D4 57 31N 4 27W
Muirton Tayside Scotland 45 C2 56 17N 3 44W
Mukachevo U.S.S.R. 69 D2 48 26N 22 45E
Mulde *r.* G.D.R. 63 B2 51 00N 12 00E
Mulegé Mexico 108 B5 26 54N 112 00W
Mulgrave Nova Scotia Canada 101 W2 45 36N 61 25W
Mulhacén *mt.* Spain 66 B2 37 04N 3 19W
Mülheim an der Ruhr F.R.G. 62 B2 51 25N 6 50E
Mulhouse France 61 C2 47 45N 7 21E
Mull *i.* Strathclyde Scotland 46 B3/C3 56 25N 6 00W
Mullaghareirk Mountains Irish Republic 48 B2 52 15N 9 20W
Mullet, The *c.* Irish Republic 48 A4 54 15N 10 05W
Mull Head *c.* Orkney Islands Scotland 47 E2 59 20N 2 58W
Mullingar Westmeath Irish Republic 48 D3 53 32N 7 20W
Mullion Cornwall England 30 B2 50 01N 5 14W
Mull of Galloway *c.* Dumfries & Galloway Scotland 46 D1 54 38N 4 50W
Mull of Kintyre *c.* Strathclyde Scotland 46 C2 55 17N 5 55W
Mull of Oa *c.* Strathclyde Scotland 46 B2 55 35N 6 20W
Multan Pakistan 77 C6 30 10N 71 36E
Muna *i.* Indonesia 80 G3 5 00S 122 30E
München *(Munich)* F.R.G. 63 B1 48 08N 11 35E
Muncie Indiana U.S.A. 104 C2 40 11N 85 22W
Münden F.R.G. 63 A2 51 25N 9 39E
Mundesley Norfolk England 33 D3 52 53N 1 26E
Mundo *r.* Spain 66 B2 38 30N 2 00W
Mungbere Zaïre 94 E8 2 40N 28 25E
Munger India 77 F5 25 24N 86 29E
Munich *see* München
Municipal Colony Delhi India 76 L4 28 42N 77 12E
Münster F.R.G. 63 A2 51 58N 7 37E
Muojärvi *l.* Finland 67 F4 65 52N 29 30E
Muonio älv *r.* Sweden/Finland 67 E4 68 20N 22 00E
Muqdisho *(Mogadishu)* Somalia 94 I8 2 02N 45 21E
Mur *r.* Europe 69 B2 47 00N 14 00E
Murat *r.* Turkey 78 F6 38 50N 40 20E
Murchison *r.* Australia 86 B4 26 00S 117 00E
Murcia Spain 66 B2 37 59N 1 08W
Mureş *r.* Romania 69 D2 46 00N 22 00E
Murfreesboro Tennessee U.S.A. 103 I4 35 50N 86 25W
Murgab *r.* Afghanistan/U.S.S.R. 79 J6 37 00N 62 30E
Müritz *l.* G.D.R. 63 B2 53 00N 12 00E
Murmansk U.S.S.R. 70 F9 68 59N 33 08E
Murom U.S.S.R. 70 G7 55 34N 42 04E
Muroran Japan 82 D3 42 21N 140 59E
Muroto-misaki *c.* Japan 82 B1 33 13N 134 11E
Murray *r.* Australia 86 G2/G3 34 00S 142 00E
Murray Bridge *tn.* Australia 86 F2 35 10S 139 17E
Murray Seascarp Pacific Ocean 119 M11 32 00N 138 00W
Murrumbidgee *r.* Australia 86 H3 34 30S 146 30E
Murton Durham England 44 C1 54 49N 1 23W
Murwara India 77 E4 23 49N 80 28E
Murzuq Libya 94 B13 25 55N 13 55E
Muş Turkey 78 F6 38 45N 41 30E
Musashino Japan 83 B3 35 43N 139 35E
Musgrave Ranges *mts.* Australia 86 E4 26 00S 132 00E
Mushin Nigeria 92 C3 6 33N 3 25E
Musin Nigeria 93 F4 6 30N 3 15E
Muskegon Michigan U.S.A. 104 C2 43 13N 86 15W
Muskegon *r.* Michigan U.S.A. 104 C2 43 00N 86 00W
Muskogee Oklahoma U.S.A. 103 G4 35 45N 95 21W
Musselburgh Lothian Scotland 45 D1 55 57N 3 04W
Musselshell *r.* Montana U.S.A. 102 E6 47 00N 108 00W
Mustafa Kemalpaşa Turkey 68 E2 40 03N 28 52E
Mutarara Mozambique 95 G4 17 30S 35 06E
Mutare Zimbabwe 95 F4 18 58N 32 40E
Muthill Tayside Scotland 45 C2 56 20N 3 51W
Mutsu Japan 82 D3 41 18N 141 15E
Mutsu-wan *b.* Japan 82 D3 41 05N 140 40E
Muyun Kum *d.* U.S.S.R. 70 I4–J4 44 00N 70 00E
Muzaffarnagar India 77 D5 29 28N 77 42E
Muzaffarpur India 77 F5 26 07N 85 23E
Mwanza Tanzania 94 F7 2 31S 32 56E
Mwaya Tanzania 95 F6 9 33S 33 56E
Mweru, Lake *(Lac Moero)* Zaïre/Zambia 95 E6 8 30S 28 30E
Myanaung Myanma 77 H3 18 17N 95 19E
MYANMA *(BURMA)* 80 B7/B1 E2
Myaungmya Myanma 77 G3 16 33N 94 55E
Mybster Highland Scotland 46 E5 58 27N 3 25W
Myingyan Myanma 81 E2 21 25N 95 20E
Myitkyina Myanma 81 E3 25 24N 97 25E
Mymensingh Bangladesh 77 G4 24 45N 90 23E
Mynydd Du *hills* Dyfed Wales 38 C2 51 50N 3 55W
Mynydd Eppynt *hills* Powys Wales 38 C2 52 02N 3 35W
Mynydd Preseli *hills* Dyfed Wales 38 B1 51 58N 4 45W
Mýrdalsjökull *ice cap* Iceland 67 I6 63 40N 19 00W
Mys Chelyuskin *c.* U.S.S.R. 71 M11 77 44N 103 55E
Mys Kanin Nos *c.* U.S.S.R. 70 G9 68 38N 43 20E
Mys Navarin *c.* U.S.S.R. 71 T8 62 17N 179 13E
Mys Olyutorskiy *c.* U.S.S.R. 71 T7 59 58N 170 25E
Mysore India 77 D2 12 18N 76 37E
Mys Tolstoy *c.* U.S.S.R. 71 R7 59 00N 155 00E
My Tho Vietnam 80 D6 10 21N 106 21E
Mytholmroyd West Yorkshire England 43 E3 53 43N 1 59W
Mže *r.* Czechoslovakia 63 B1 49 00N 13 00E
Mzuzu Malawi 95 F5 11 31S 34 00E

N

Naaldwijk Netherlands 65 A2 52 00N 4 10E
Naarden Netherlands 65 E3 52 18N 5 09E
Naas Kildare Irish Republic 48 E3 53 13N 6 39W
Naberezhnyye Chelny U.S.S.R. 70 H7 55 42N 52 19E
Nabeul Tunisia 68 B2 36 30N 10 44E
Nablus Jordan 78 O11 32 13N 35 16E
Nabq Egypt 78 O9 28 04N 34 26E
Nacogdoches Texas U.S.A. 103 H3 31 36N 94 40W
Nadiad India 77 C4 22 42N 72 55E
Nador Morocco 93 E10 35 10N 3 00W
Nadym U.S.S.R. 71 J9 65 25N 72 40E
Naestved Denmark 67 C2 55 14N 11 47E
Naga The Philippines 80 G6 13 36N 123 12E
Naga Hills India 77 G5/H5 26 00N 95 00E
Nagai Japan 83 B1 35 11N 139 37E
Nagaland *admin.* India 77 G5 26 00N 94 30E
Nagano Japan 82 C2 36 39N 138 10E
Nagaoka Japan 82 C2 37 27N 138 50E
Nagasaki Japan 82 A1 32 45N 129 52E
Nagato Japan 82 B1 34 22N 131 11E
Nagatsuda Japan 83 B3 35 31N 139 30E
Nagercoil India 77 D1 8 11N 77 30E
Nagles Mountains Irish Republic 48 C2 52 10N 8 25W
Nagornyy U.S.S.R. 71 O7 55 57N 124 54E
Nagoya Japan 82 C2 35 08N 136 53E
Nagpur India 77 D4 21 10N 79 12E
Nagqu China 77 G6 31 30N 91 57E
Nagykanizsa Hungary 69 C2 46 27N 17 00E
Nahanni Butte *tn.* Northwest Territories Canada 100 K5 61 30N 123 20W
Nahanni National Park Northwest Territories Canada 100 K5 61 30N 123 20W
Nahariya Israel 78 O11 33 01N 35 05E
Nahe *r.* F.R.G. 63 A1 49 00N 7 00E
Naihāti India 76 K3 22 53N 88 27E
Nailsea Avon England 31 E3 51 26N 2 46W
Nailsworth Gloucestershire England 31 E3 51 42N 2 14W
Nain Newfoundland Canada 101 W4 56 30N 61 45W
Nairn Highland Scotland 46 E4 57 35N 3 53W
Nairobi Kenya 94 G7 1 17S 36 50E
Najd *geog. reg.* Saudi Arabia 78 F4 25 40N 42 30E
Najrān Saudi Arabia 78 F2 17 37N 44 40E
Naka Japan 83 B2 35 25N 139 38E
Nakahara Japan 83 B3 35 34N 139 39E
Nakamura Japan 82 B1 33 02N 132 58E
Nakano Japan 83 B3 35 42N 139 40E
Nakatsu Japan 82 B1 33 37N 131 11E
Nakhichevan' U.S.S.R. 78 F6 39 12N 45 24E
Nakhodka U.S.S.R. 71 P4 42 53N 132 54E
Nakhon Ratchasima Thailand 80 C6 15 00N 102 06E
Nakhon Si Thammarat Thailand 80 B5 8 24N 99 58E
Nakina Ontario Canada 101 R3 50 11N 86 43W
Nakskov Denmark 63 B2 54 50N 11 10E
Nakuru Kenya 94 G7 0 16S 36 05E
Nal *r.* Pakistan 76 B5 26 10N 65 30E
Nal'chik U.S.S.R. 70 G4 43 31N 43 38E
Namangan U.S.S.R. 70 J4 40 59N 71 41E
Nam Co *l.* China 77 G6 30 50N 90 30E
Namdalen *geog. reg.* Norway 67 C3 64 40N 12 00E
Namib Desert Namibia 95 B3 22 00S 14 00E
Namibe Angola 95 B4 15 10S 12 09E
NAMIBIA 95 C3
Nampa Idaho U.S.A. 102 C5 43 35N 116 34W
Nampula Mozambique 95 G4 15 09S 39 14E
Namsos Norway 67 C3 64 28N 11 30E
Namtu Myanma 81 E2 23 04N 97 26E
Namur *admin.* Belgium 64 D2 50 10N 4 45E
Namur Belgium 64 D2 50 28N 4 52E
Nanaimo British Columbia Canada 100 K2 49 08N 123 58W
Nanao Japan 82 C2 37 03N 136 58E
Nanchang China 81 I3 28 33N 115 58E
Nanchong China 81 G4 30 54N 106 06E
Nancy France 61 C2 48 42N 6 12E
Nanda Devi *mt.* India 77 E6 30 21N 79 58E
Nānded India 77 D3 19 11N 77 21E
Nanduri Fiji 118 U16 16 26S 179 08E
Nanga Eboko Cameroon 93 H3 4 38N 12 21E
Nangi India 76 J1 22 30N 88 13E
Nanhai *l.* China 82 G1 39 55N 116 22E
Nanjing China 81 I4 32 03N 118 47E
Nan Ling *mts.* China 81 H2/H3 25 00N 112 00E
Nanning China 81 G2 22 50N 108 19E
Nanortalik Greenland 101 Z5 60 10N 45 05W
Nanpan Jiang *r.* China 81 G2 25 00N 106 00E
Nanping China 81 I3 26 40N 118 07E
Nansei-shoto *see* Ryukyu Islands
Nan Shan *mts.* China 72 38 00N 103 00E
Nanterre France 60 A2 48 53N 2 12E
Nantes France 61 A2 47 14N 1 35W
Nantong China 81 J4 32 06N 121 04E
Nantucket Island Massachusetts U.S.A. 105 G2 41 00N 70 00W
Nantucket Sound Massachusetts U.S.A. 105 F2 41 00N 70 00W
Nantwich Cheshire England 40 B2 53 04N 2 32W
Nant-y-moch Reservoir Dyfed Wales 38 C2 52 30N 3 50W
Nanuku Passage *sd.* Fiji 118 V16 16 40S 179 25W
Nanumea Island Pacific Ocean 118 H7 5 30S 175 40E
Nanyang China 81 H4 33 06N 112 31E
Nanyuan China 82 G1 39 48N 116 23E
Nanyuki Kenya 94 G8 0 01N 37 05E
Napanee Ontario Canada 105 E2 44 15N 74 57W
Napier New Zealand 87 C3 39 29S 176 58E
Naples Florida U.S.A. 103 J2 26 09N 81 48W
Naples *see* Napoli
Napoli *(Naples)* Italy 68 B3 40 50N 14 15E
Napoopoo Hawaiian Islands 119 Z17 19 29N 155 55W
Nappanee Indiana U.S.A. 104 C2 41 27N 86 01W
Napton on the Hill Warwickshire England 35 E1 52 15N 1 24W
Nar *r.* Norfolk England 33 C3 52 40N 0 40E
Nara Japan 82 C1 34 41N 135 49E
Narayanganj Bangladesh 77 G4 23 36N 90 28E
Narberth Dyfed Wales 38 B1 51 48N 4 45W
Narbonne France 61 B1 43 11N 3 00E
Narborough Leicestershire England 36 C2 52 35N 1 11W
Nares Deep Atlantic Ocean 117 C9 26 00N 61 10W
Nares Strait Canada/Greenland 101 U8 78 30N 72 30W
Narew *r.* U.S.S.R./Poland 69 D3 53 00N 21 00E
Narmada *r.* India 77 C4/D4 22 00N 75 00E
Narrogin Australia 86 B3 32 57S 117 07E
Narsaq Greenland 101 Z5 61 00N 46 00W
Narsarsuaq Greenland 101 Z5 61 10N 45 20W
Narva U.S.S.R. 67 F2 59 22N 28 17E
Narvik Norway 67 D4 68 26N 17 25E
Nar'yan Mar U.S.S.R. 70 H9 67 37N 53 02E
Nasca Ridge Pacific Ocean 119 R5 20 00S 81 00W
Naseby Northamptonshire England 36 D2 52 23N 0 59W
Nashua New Hampshire U.S.A. 105 F2 42 44N 71 28W
Nashville Tennessee U.S.A. 103 I4 36 10N 86 50W
Näsijärvi *l.* Finland 67 E3 61 45N 24 00E
Nasik India 77 C3 20 00N 73 52E
Näsjo Sweden 67 C2 57 40N 14 40E
Nassau The Bahamas 109 I5 25 05N 77 20W
Nasser, Lake Egypt 78 D3 22 35N 31 40E
Natal Brazil 114 J11 5 46S 35 15W
Natal *province* Republic of South Africa 95 F2 29 00S 31 00E
Natashquan Québec Canada 101 W3 50 10N 61 50W
Natchez Mississippi U.S.A. 103 H3 31 32N 91 24W
Natewa Peninsula Fiji 118 V16 16 40S 180 00
Natron, Lake Tanzania 94 G7 2 00S 36 00E
Natuna Besar *i.* Indonesia 80 D4 4 00N 108 00E
Naturaliste, Cape Australia 86 B3 33 32S 115 01E
Naucalpan Mexico 108 P1 19 28N 99 14W
Naumburg G.D.R. 63 B2 51 09N 11 48E
NAURU 118 G7
Nausori Fiji 118 U15 18 01S 178 31E
Navadwīp India 77 F4 23 24N 88 23E
Navan Meath Irish Republic 48 E3 53 39N 6 41W
Navenby Lincolnshire England 36 D3 53 06N 0 32W
Naver *r.* Highland Scotland 46 D5 58 25N 4 10W
Navia *r.* Spain 66 A3 43 10N 7 05W
Naviti *i.* Fiji 118 T16 17 08S 177 15E
Navoi U.S.S.R. 70 I4 40 04N 65 20E
Navojoa Mexico 108 C5 27 04N 109 28W
Návplion Greece 68 D2 37 34N 22 48E
Navsari India 77 C4 20 58N 73 01E
Náxos *i.* Greece 68 E2 37 00N 25 00E
Nayoro Japan 82 D3 44 21N 142 30E
Nazareth Israel 78 O11 32 41N 35 16E
Nazca Peru 114 C9 14 53S 74 54W
Naze, The *c.* Essex England 33 D2 51 50N 1 20E
Nazilli Turkey 68 E2 37 55N 28 20E
Nazwá Oman 79 I3 22 56N 57 33E
Ndélé Central African Republic 94 D9 8 25N 20 38E
Ndjamena Chad 94 C10 12 10N 14 59E
Ndola Zambia 95 E5 13 00S 28 39E
Neápolis Greece 68 D2 36 31N 23 03E
Neath *r.* West Glamorgan Wales 38 C1 51 40N 3 45W
Neath West Glamorgan Wales 38 C1 51 40N 3 48W
Nebit-Dag U.S.S.R. 70 H3 39 31N 54 24E
Nebraska *state* U.S.A. 102 F5 42 00N 102 00W
Nebraska City Nebraska U.S.A. 104 A2 40 41N 95 50W
Neckar *r.* F.R.G. 63 A1 48 00N 9 00E
Neckei *i.* Hawaiian Islands 119 J10 23 35N 164 42W
Necochea Argentina 115 F5 38 31S 58 46W
Nederrijn *r.* Netherlands 64 E3 51 58N 5 35E
Needham Market Suffolk England 33 D3 52 09N 1 03E
Needles California U.S.A. 102 D3 34 51N 114 36W
Needles, The *rocks* Isle of Wight England 32 A1 50 39N 1 35W
Needwood Forest *hills* Staffordshire England 35 C3 52 25N 1 45W
Neepawa Manitoba Canada 104 A4 50 14N 99 29W
Nefta Tunisia 93 G9 33 53N 7 50E
Nefyn Gwynedd Wales 38 B2 52 56N 4 32W
Negelē Ethiopia 94 G9 5 20N 39 35E
Negev *d.* Israel 78 O10 30 50N 30 45E
Negombo Sri Lanka 77 D1 7 13N 79 51E
Negritos Peru 114 A2 4 42S 81 18W
Negros *i.* The Philippines 80 G5 10 00N 123 00E
Nei Mongol Zizhiqu *(Inner Mongolia Autonomous Region) admin.* China 81 G6–I6 42 30N 112 30E
Neijiang China 81 G3 29 32N 105 03E
Neilston Strathclyde Scotland 45 B1 55 47N 4 27W
Neiva Colombia 114 B13 2 58N 75 15W
Nek'emtē Ethiopia 94 G9 9 04N 36 30E
Nellore India 77 D2 14 29N 80 00E
Nelson Forks British Columbia Canada 100 K4 59 30N 124 00W
Nelson Lancashire England 42 D3 53 51N 2 13W
Nelson Manitoba Canada 100 L2 49 29N 117 17W
Nelson New Zealand 87 B2 41 18S 173 17E
Nelson River Manitoba Canada 101 Q4 57 00N 94 00W
Neman *r.* U.S.S.R. 69 D4 55 00N 22 00E
Nemuro Japan 82 E3 43 22N 145 36E
Nemuro-Kaikyō *sd.* Japan 82 E3 44 00N 146 00E
Nen Jiang *r.* China 81 K8 50 00N 125 00E
Nenagh Tipperary Irish Republic 48 C2 52 52N 8 12W
Nenana Alaska U.S.A. 100 F5 64 35N 149 20W
Nene *r.* Cambridgeshire England 33 C3 52 25N 0 05E
Nenjiang China 81 K7 49 10N 125 15E
Neosho *r.* U.S.A. 104 A1 37 00N 95 00W
NEPAL 77 E5
Nepean Ontario Canada 105 E3 45 16N 75 48W
Nephin Beg Range *mts.* Irish Republic 48 B3/4 54 00N 9 50W
Nerchinsk U.S.S.R. 71 N6 52 02N 116 38E
Neretva *r.* Yugoslavia 68 C3 43 00N 18 00E
Nerva Spain 66 A2 37 41N 6 33W
Neryungri U.S.S.R. 71 O7 56 39N 124 38E
Nes Netherlands 64 E5 53 27N 5 46E
Neskaupstadur Iceland 67 J7 65 10N 13 43W
Ness Cheshire England 42 A1 53 18N 3 03W
Neste *r.* France 61 B1 43 00N 0 15E
Nestor Falls *tn.* Ontario Canada 104 B3 49 06N 93 55W
Netanya Israel 78 O11 32 20N 34 51E
Nete *r.* Belgium 64 D3 51 06N 4 28E
Nether Stowey Somerset England 31 D3 51 09N 3 10W
NETHERLANDS 64 E4
Netherton Central Scotland 45 B1 55 59N 4 19W
Nettetal F.R.G. 64 F3 51 20N 6 14E
Nettilling Lake Northwest Territories Canada 101 U6 66 30N 71 10W
Netzahualcóyotl Mexico 108 P1 19 24N 99 02W
Neubrandenburg *admin.* G.D.R. 63 B2 53 00N 13 00E
Neubrandenburg G.D.R. 63 B2 53 33N 13 16E
Neuburg F.R.G. 63 B1 48 44N 11 12E
Neufchâteau Belgium 64 E1 49 51N 5 26E
Neufchâteau France 61 C2 48 21N 5 42E
Neuchâtel Switzerland 61 C2 46 55N 6 56E
Neufchâtel-en-Bray France 61 B2 49 44N 1 26E
Neufchâtel-sur-Aisne France 64 D1 49 27N 4 02E
Neuilly France 60 B2 48 53N 2 17E
Neuilly Plaisance France 60 C2 48 51N 2 31E
Neumarkt F.R.G. 63 B1 49 17N 11 29E
Neumünster F.R.G. 63 A2 54 05N 9 59E
Neunkirchen F.R.G. 63 A1 49 21N 7 12E
Neuquén Argentina 115 D5 38 55S 68 05W
Neuruppin G.D.R. 63 B2 52 56N 12 49E
Neusiedler See *l.* Austria 69 C2 48 00N 16 00E
Neuss F.R.G. 62 A1 51 12N 6 42E
Neustadt F.R.G. 63 A1 49 21N 8 09E
Neustrelitz G.D.R. 63 B2 53 22N 13 05E
Neu-Ulm F.R.G. 63 B1 48 23N 10 01E
Neuwied F.R.G. 63 A2 50 26N 7 28E
Nevada Missouri U.S.A. 104 B1 37 51N 94 22W
Nevada *state* U.S.A. 102 C4 39 00N 118 00W
Nevers France 61 B2 47 00N 3 09E
Neves Brazil 116 C2 22 51S 43 05W
Neviot Egypt 78 O9 28 58N 34 38E
New *r.* U.S.A. 103 J4 37 00N 81 00W
New Addington Greater London England 34 D2 51 21N 0 01E
New Albany Indiana U.S.A. 104 C1 38 17N 85 50W
New Alresford Hampshire England 32 A2 51 06N 1 10W
New Amsterdam Guyana 114 F14 6 18N 57 30W
Newark Bay New Jersey U.S.A. 106 B1 40 40N 74 08W
Newark Delaware U.S.A. 103 K4 39 42N 75 45W
Newark New Jersey U.S.A. 106 B2 40 43N 74 11W
Newark Ohio U.S.A. 105 D2 40 03N 82 25W
Newark-on-Trent Nottinghamshire England 36 D3 53 05N 0 49W
New Ash Green Kent England 34 D2 51 21N 0 18E
New Bedford Massachusetts U.S.A. 105 F2 41 38N 70 55W
New Bern North Carolina U.S.A. 103 K4 35 05N 77 04W
Newberry Michigan U.S.A. 104 C3 46 22N 85 30W
Newbiggin-by-the-Sea Northumberland England 44 C2 55 11N 1 30W
Newbigging Strathclyde Scotland 45 C1 55 42N 3 33W
Newbold Derbyshire England 43 F1 53 15N 1 28W
New Braunfels Texas U.S.A. 103 G2 29 43N 98 09W
Newbridge Gwent Wales 38 C1 51 41N 3 09W
Newbridge *see* Droichead Nua
Newbridge-on-Wye Powys Wales 38 C2 52 13N 3 27W
New Brighton Merseyside England 42 A2 53 27N 3 03W
New Britain Connecticut U.S.A. 105 F2 41 40N 72 47W
New Britain *i.* Papua New Guinea 86 I8 6 10S 150 00E
New Brunswick *province* Canada 101 V2 47 30N 66 00W
New Buffalo Michigan U.S.A. 104 C2 41 48N 86 44W
New Buildings Northern Ireland 48 D4 54 56N 7 21W
Newburg Grampian Scotland 46 G4 57 18N 2 00W
Newburgh Fife Scotland 45 D2 56 21N 3 15W
Newburgh Lancashire England 42 B2 53 35N 2 48W
Newburgh New York U.S.A. 105 F2 41 30N 74 00W
Newburn Tyne and Wear England 44 C1 54 59N 1 43W
Newbury Berkshire England 32 A2 51 25N 1 20W
New Caledonia *i.* Pacific Ocean 86 K5/L5 22 00S 165 00E
Newcastle Australia 86 I3 32 55S 151 46E
Newcastle Down Northern Ireland 48 F4 54 12N 5 54W
Newcastle Dublin Irish Republic 49 A1 53 18N 6 30W
Newcastle Ontario Canada 105 E2 43 55N 78 35W
New Castle Pennsylvania U.S.A. 105 D2 41 00N 80 22W
Newcastle Wyoming U.S.A. 102 E5 43 52N 104 14W
Newcastle Emlyn Dyfed Wales 38 B2 52 02N 4 28W
Newcastle-under-Lyme Staffordshire England 35 B4 53 00N 2 14W
Newcastle-upon-Tyne Tyne and Wear England 44 C1 54 59N 1 35W
Newcastle West Limerick Irish Republic 48 B2 52 27N 9 03W
New Cumnock Strathclyde Scotland 46 D2 55 24N 4 12W
New Deer Grampian Scotland 46 F4 57 30N 2 12W
New Delhi India 76 M4 28 37N 77 14E
New Dorp New York U.S.A. 106 B1 40 34N 74 06W
New Earswick North Yorkshire England 43 G3 53 59N 1 03W
Newend Hereford & Worcester England 35 C1 52 14N 1 55W
Newent Gloucestershire England 31 E3 51 56N 2 24W
New Forest Hampshire England 32 A1 50 50N 1 40W
Newfoundland Basin Atlantic Ocean 117 D11 44 00N 40 00W
Newfoundland *i.* Newfoundland Canada 101 X2 48 15N 57 00W
Newfoundland *province* Canada 101 W3 52 30N 62 30W
New Georgia Islands Solomon Islands 86 J8 8 00S 157 30E
New G.R.A. Ibadan Nigeria 92 E4 7 22N 3 53E
New Guinea *i.* Pacific Ocean 86 G8 6 00S 142 00E
Newham Greater London England 34 D2 51 30N 0 02E
New Hampshire *state* U.S.A. 105 F2 43 00N 72 00W
New Haven Connecticut U.S.A. 105 F2 41 18N 72 55W
Newhaven East Sussex England 33 C1 50 47N 0 03E
New Hebrides Trench Pacific Ocean 118 G6 15 00S 169 00E
New Holland Humberside England 40 D2 53 42N 0 22W
New Hyde Park New York U.S.A. 106 D1 40 44N 73 42W
New Hythe Kent England 34 E1 51 18N 0 27E
New Iberia Louisiana U.S.A. 103 H2 30 00N 91 51W
Newick East Sussex England 33 C1 50 58N 0 01E
New Ireland *i.* Papua New Guinea 86 I9 3 00S 152 00E
New Jersey *state* U.S.A. 105 F1 39 00N 74 00W
New Liskeard Ontario Canada 105 E3 47 31N 79 41W
New London Connecticut U.S.A. 105 F2 41 21N 72 06W
Newlyn Cornwall England 30 B2 50 06N 5 34W
Newmains Strathclyde Scotland 45 C1 55 47N 3 53W
Newman Australia 86 B5 23 20S 119 34E
Newmarket Cork Irish Republic 48 C2 52 13N 9 00W
Newmarket Suffolk England 33 C3 52 15N 0 25E
Newmarket-on-Fergus Clare Irish Republic 48 C2 52 45N 8 53W
New Mexico *state* U.S.A. 102 E3 35 00N 107 00W
New Milford Pennsylvania U.S.A. 105 E2 41 52N 75 44W
New Mill West Yorkshire England 43 E2 53 35N 1 44W
New Mills Derbyshire England 42 D2 53 23N 2 00W
New Milton Hampshire England 32 A1 50 46N 1 40W
Newnham Gloucestershire England 31 E3 51 49N 2 27W
New Orleans Louisiana U.S.A. 103 H2 30 00N 90 03W
New Philadelphia Ohio U.S.A. 105 D2 40 31N 81 28W
New Plymouth New Zealand 87 B3 39 03S 174 04E
Newport Dyfed Wales 38 B2 52 01N 4 50W
Newport Essex England 34 D3 51 58N 0 13E
Newport Gwent Wales 38 D1 51 35N 3 00W
Newport Isle of Wight England 32 A1 50 42N 1 18W
Newport Maine U.S.A. 105 G2 44 50N 69 17W
Newport Rhode Island U.S.A. 105 F2 41 30N 71 19W
Newport Shropshire England 35 A3 52 47N 2 22W
Newport Vermont U.S.A. 105 F2 44 56N 72 18W
Newport News Virginia U.S.A. 105 E1 36 59N 76 26W
Newport on Tay Fife Scotland 46 F3 56 27N 2 56W
Newport Pagnell Buckinghamshire England 33 B3 52 05N 0 44W
New Providence *i.* The Bahamas 109 I5 25 00N 77 30W
Newquay Cornwall England 30 B2 50 25N 5 05W
New Quay Dyfed Wales 38 B2 52 13N 4 22W
New Radnor Powys Wales 38 C2 52 15N 3 10W
New Rochelle New York U.S.A. 106 C2 40 55N 73 46W
New Romney Kent England 33 C1 50 59N 0 57E
New Ross Wexford Irish Republic 48 E2 52 24N 6 56W
New Rossington South Yorkshire England 43 G2 53 29N 1 04W
Newry Northern Ireland 48 E4 54 11N 6 20W
Newton Lothian Scotland 45 D1 55 59N 3 25W
Newton Massachusetts U.S.A. 105 F2 42 20N 71 13W
Newton Abbot Devon England 31 D2 50 32N 3 36W
Newton Aycliffe Durham England 44 C1 54 37N 1 34W
Newtongrange Lothian Scotland 45 D1 55 52N 3 04W
Newton-le-Willows Merseyside England 42 C2 53 28N 2 37W
Newton Longville Buckinghamshire England 34 A3 51 58N 0 46W
Newton Mearns Strathclyde Scotland 45 B1 55 45N 4 18W
Newtonmore Highland Scotland 46 D4 57 04N 4 08W
Newton St. Boswells Borders Scotland 46 F2 55 34N 2 40W
Newton Stewart Dumfries & Galloway Scotland 46 D1 54 57N 4 29W
Newtown Powys Wales 38 C2 52 32N 3 19W
Newtownabbey Northern Ireland 49 D2 54 40N 5 54W
Newtownards Down Northern Ireland 48 F4 54 36N 5 41W
Newtownbreda Northern Ireland 49 D1 54 33N 5 54W
Newtownmountkennedy Wicklow Irish Republic 48 E3

53 06N 6 07W
Newtownstewart Northern Ireland 48 D4 54 43N 7 24W
New Tredegar Mid Glamorgan Wales 38 C1 51 44N 3 15W
New Ulm Minnesota U.S.A. 103 H5 44 19N 94 28W
New Westminster British Columbia Canada 100 K2 49 10N 122 58W
New York New York U.S.A. 106 C1 40 40N 73 50W
New York *state* U.S.A. 105 E2 43 00N 76 00W
NEW ZEALAND 87
Neyland Dyfed Wales 38 B1 51 43N 4 57W
Neyrīz Iran 79 H4 29 14N 54 18E
Neyshābūr Iran 79 I6 36 13N 58 49E
Ngaba Zaïre 92 A1 4 22S 15 19E
Ngami, Lake Botswana 95 D3 21 00S 23 00E
Ngangla Ringco *l.* China 77 E6 31 40N 83 00E
Nganze Co *l.* China 77 F6 31 00N 87 00E
Ngaoundéré Cameroon 93 H4 7 20N 13 35E
Ngau *i.* Fiji 118 U15 18 00S 179 16E
Ngauruhoe *mt.* New Zealand 87 C3 39 10S 175 40E
Nguigmi Niger 93 H5 14 19N 13 06E
Nguru Nigeria 93 H5 12 53N 10 30E
Nha Trang Vietnam 80 C6 12 15N 109 10E
Nhulunbuy Australia 86 F7 12 30S 136 56E
Niagara Falls *tn.* New York 105 E2 43 06N 79 04W
Niagara Falls *tn.* Ontario Canada 105 E2 43 05N 79 06W
Niamey Niger 93 F5 13 32N 2 05E
Niangara Zaïre 94 E8 3 45N 27 54E
Nias *i.* Indonesia 80 B4 1 30N 97 30E
Nibra India 76 K2 22 35N 88 15E
NICARAGUA 109 G2
Nice France 61 C1 43 42N 7 16E
Nicobar Islands India 77 G1 8 30N 94 00E
Nicosia Cyprus 78 D6 35 11N 33 23E
Nidd *r.* North Yorkshire England 40 C3 54 02N 1 30W
Nied *r.* France 64 F1 49 15N 6 30E
Niedere Tauern *mts.* Austria 63 B1 47 00N 14 00E
Niedersachsen *admin.* F.R.G. 63 A2 52 00N 9 00E
Nienburg F.R.G. 63 A2 52 38N 9 13E
Niers *r.* F.R.G. 64 F3 51 00N 6 00E
Nieuwegein Netherlands 65 E2 52 00N 5 05E
Nieuwe Maas *r.* Netherlands 65 B1 51 54N 4 23E
Nieuwendam Netherlands 65 D3 52 23N 4 57E
Nieuwerkerk aan den IJssel Netherlands 65 C1 51 58N 4 37E
Nieuwe Waterweg Scheur *can.* Netherlands 65 A1 51 55N 4 10E
Nieuwkoopsche Plassen *l.* Netherlands 65 D2 52 08N 4 46E
Nieuw Nickerie Surinam 114 F14 5 52N 57 00W
Nieuwpoort Belgium 64 B3 51 08N 2 45E
Nieuw-Vennep Netherlands 65 C3 52 15N 4 39E
NIGER 93 G6
Niger *r.* Nigeria 93 G4 5 30N 6 15E
Niger Delta Nigeria 88 5 00N 7 00E
NIGERIA 93 G5
Niigata Japan 82 C2 37 58N 139 02E
Niihama Japan 82 B1 33 57N 133 15E
Niihau *i.* Hawaiian Islands 119 W18 21 50N 160 11W
Nii-jima *i.* Japan 82 C1 34 20N 139 15E
Niiza Japan 83 B4 35 48N 139 35E
Nijkerk Netherlands 64 E4 52 12N 5 30E
Nijmegen Netherlands 64 E3 51 50N 5 52E
Nikko Japan 82 C2 36 45N 139 37E
Nikolayev U.S.S.R. 70 F5 46 57N 32 00E
Nikolayevsk-na-Amure U.S.S.R. 71 Q6 53 10N 140 44E
Nikšić Yugoslavia 68 C3 42 48N 18 56E
Nile *r.* Egypt 78 D4 28 30N 30 40E
Nile Delta Egypt 88 31 00N 31 00E
Niles Michigan U.S.A. 104 C2 41 51N 86 15W
Nilgiri Hills India 77 D2 11 00N 76 30E
Nilópolis Brazil 116 B2 22 48S 43 25W
Nîmes France 61 B1 43 50N 4 21E
Nimule Sudan 94 F8 3 35N 32 03E
Ninety Mile Beach New Zealand 87 B4 34 50S 173 00E
Nineveh *hist. site* Iraq 78 F6 36 24N 43 08E
Ningbo China 81 J3 29 54N 121 33E
Ninove Belgium 64 D2 50 50N 4 02E
Niobrara *r.* U.S.A. 102 F5 42 00N 102 00W
Nioro du Sahel Mali 93 D6 15 12N 9 35W
Niort France 61 A2 46 19N 0 27W
Nipigon Ontario Canada 104 C3 49 02N 88 26W
Nipigon *r.* Ontario Canada 104 C3 49 00N 88 00W
Nipigon, Lake Ontario Canada 104 C3 50 00N 88 00W
Niš Yugoslavia 68 D3 43 20N 21 54E
Nishi Japan 83 B2 35 26N 139 37E
Niterói Brazil 116 C2 22 54S 43 06W
Nith *r.* Dumfries & Galloway Scotland 46 E2 55 15N 3 50W
Nithsdale *v.* Dumfries & Galloway Scotland 46 E2 55 15N 3 50W
Nitra Czechoslovakia 69 C2 48 19N 18 04E
Niue *i.* Pacific Ocean 119 J6 19 02S 169 55W
Nive *r.* France 61 A1 43 15N 1 15W
Nivelles Belgium 64 D2 50 36N 4 20E
Nizamabad India 77 D3 18 40N 78 05E
Nizhneangarsk U.S.S.R. 71 M7 55 48N 109 35E
Nizhnekamsk U.S.S.R. 70 H7 55 38N 51 49E
Nizhnekolymsk U.S.S.R. 71 S9 68 34N 160 58E
Nizhnevartovsk U.S.S.R. 71 J8 60 57N 76 40E
Nizhniy Tagil U.S.S.R. 70 I7 58 00N 59 58E
Nizhnyaya *(Lower)* Tunguska *r.* U.S.S.R. 71 L8/M8 64 00N 94 00E
Nízké Tatry *mts.* Czechoslovakia 69 C2 49 00N 19 00E
Nkongsamba Cameroon 93 G3 4 59N 9 53E
Noatak Alaska U.S.A. 100 C6 67 33N 163 10W
Noatak *r.* Alaska U.S.A. 100 C6 67 33N 163 10W
Nobeoka Japan 82 B1 32 36N 131 40E
Nobi Japan 83 B1 35 11N 139 41E
Nogales Arizona U.S.A. 102 D3 31 20N 110 56W
Nogales Mexico 108 B6 31 20N 111 00W
Nogent France 60 C2 48 50N 2 30E
Noguera Ribagorzana *r.* Spain 66 C3 42 25N 0 45E
Noirmont Point *c.* Jersey Channel Islands 31 G5 49 11N 2 07W
Noisy-le-Sec France 60 B2 48 53N 2 27E
Nojima-zaki *c.* Japan 82 C1 34 54N 139 54E
Nola Central African Republic 94 C8 3 28N 16 08E
Nome Alaska U.S.A. 100 B5 64 30N 165 30W
Noord Beveland *i.* Netherlands 64 C3 51 35N 3 45E
Noord-Brabant *admin.* Netherlands 64 D3 51 29N 5 00E
Noord-Holland *admin.* Netherlands 64 D4 52 30N 4 45E
Noordoost Polder Netherlands 64 E4 52 47N 5 45E
Noordwijk Netherlands 64 D4 52 15N 4 25E
Noordwijk aan Zee Netherlands 65 B2 52 14N 4 27E
Noordwijkerhout Netherlands 65 B3 52 15N 4 30E
Noordzeekanaal *can.* Netherlands 65 C3 52 25N 4 45E
Noorvik Alaska U.S.A. 100 C6 66 50N 161 14W
Noranda Québec Canada 105 E3 48 16N 79 03W
Nord *admin.* France 64 D2 50 13N 4 03E
Norden F.R.G. 63 A2 53 36N 7 13E
Nordenham F.R.G. 63 A2 53 30N 8 29E
Norderney *i.* F.R.G. 63 A2 53 00N 7 00E
Norderstedt F.R.G. 63 A2 53 41N 9 58E
Nordfjord *fj.* Norway 67 B3 62 00N 5 15E
Nordfold Norway 67 D4 67 48N 15 20E
Nordfriesische Inseln *(North Frisian Islands) is.* F.R.G. 63 A2 54 00N 8 00E
Nordhausen G.D.R. 63 B2 51 31N 10 48E
Nordhorn F.R.G. 63 A2 52 27N 7 05E
Nordkapp *(North Cape) c.* Norway 67 E5 71 11N 25 40E
Nordrhein-Westfalen *admin.* F.R.G. 63 A2 52 00N 7 00E
Nordstrand *i.* F.R.G. 63 A2 54 00N 8 00E
Nordvik U.S.S.R. 71 N10 74 01N 111 30E
Nore *r.* Irish Republic 48 D2 52 25N 7 02W
Norfolk *co.* England 33 C3 52 45N 1 00E
Norfolk Nebraska U.S.A. 103 G5 42 01N 97 25W
Norfolk Virginia U.S.A. 105 E1 36 54N 76 18W
Norfolk Island Pacific Ocean 118 G5 29 05S 167 59E
Norfolk Island Trough Pacific Ocean 118 G5 27 30S 166 00E
Norfolk Lake Arkansas U.S.A. 103 H4 36 00N 92 00W
Norham Northumberland England 44 B2 55 43N 2 10W
Noril'sk U.S.S.R. 71 K9 69 21N 88 02E
Norman Wells *tn.* Northwest Territories Canada 100 J6 65 19N 126 46W
Normanton Australia 86 G6 17 40S 141 05E
Normanton West Yorkshire England 43 F3 53 42N 1 25W
Norris Lake Tennessee U.S.A. 103 J4 36 00N 84 00W
Norristown Pennsylvania U.S.A. 105 E1 40 07N 75 20W
Norrköping Sweden 67 D2 58 35N 16 10E
Norseman Australia 86 C3 32 15S 121 47E
North Adams Massachusetts U.S.A. 105 F2 42 42N 73 07W
Northallerton North Yorkshire England 40 C3 54 20N 1 26W
Northam Australia 86 B3 31 40S 116 40E
Northam Devon England 31 C3 51 02N 4 14W
North American Basin Atlantic Ocean 117 C10 34 00N 55 00W
Northampton Australia 86 A4 28 27S 114 37E
Northampton Massachusetts U.S.A. 105 F2 42 19N 72 38W
Northampton Northamptonshire England 36 D2 52 14N 0 54W
Northamptonshire *co.* England 36 D2 52 20N 1 00W
North Andaman *i.* Andaman Islands 77 G2 13 00N 93 00E
North Anna *r.* Virginia U.S.A. 105 E1 38 00N 77 00W
North Australian Basin Indian Ocean 118 B6 14 00S 115 00E
North Baddesley Hampshire England 32 A1 50 58N 1 27W
North Ballaculish Highland Scotland 46 C3 56 42N 5 11W
North Barrackpore India 76 K3 22 46N 88 21E
North Battleford Saskatchewan Canada 100 N3 52 47N 108 19W
North Bay *tn.* Ontario Canada 105 E3 46 20N 79 28W
North Bergen New Jersey U.S.A. 106 B2 40 46N 74 02W
North Berwick Lothian Scotland 46 F3 56 04N 2 44W
North Bull Island Dublin Irish Republic 49 B2 53 23N 6 08W
North Canadian *r.* U.S.A. 102 F4 36 00N 100 00W
North Cape New Zealand 87 B4 34 23S 173 04E
North Cape *see* Nordkapp
North Carolina *state* U.S.A. 103 K4 36 00N 80 00W
North Channel Ontario Canada 105 D3 46 00N 83 00W
North Cray Kent England 34 D2 51 26N 0 09E
North Dakota *state* U.S.A. 102 F6 47 00N 102 00W
North Dorset Downs *hills* Dorset England 31 E2 50 40N 2 30W
North Downs *hills* Surrey England 33 B3 51 13N 0 30W
North Duffield North Yorkshire England 43 H3 53 48N 0 57W
Northeastern Atlantic Basin Atlantic Ocean 117 G11 47 00N 18 00W
Northeim F.R.G. 63 A2 51 43N 9 59E
Northern Ireland United Kingdom 48 E4
NORTHERN MARIANAS 118 E9
Northern Territory *territory* Australia 86 E5/E6 19 00S 132 00E
North Esk *r.* Tayside Scotland 46 F3 56 50N 2 50W
North European Plain Europe 51 54 00N 20 00E
North Fiji Basin Pacific Ocean 118 H6 18 00S 173 00E
Northfleet Kent England 34 E2 51 27N 0 20E
North Foreland *c.* Kent England 33 D2 51 23N 1 27E
North Frisian Islands *see* Nordfriesische Inseln
North Hollywood California U.S.A. 107 A3 34 10N 118 22W
North Holmwood Surrey England 34 B1 51 13N 0 20W
Northiam East Sussex England 33 C1 50 59N 0 36E
North Island New Zealand 87 C3 36 40S 177 00E
North Kessock Highland Scotland 46 D4 57 30N 4 15W
NORTH KOREA 81 K5/6
North Land *see* Severnaya Zemlya
Northleach Gloucestershire England 31 F3 51 51N 1 50W
North Little Rock Arkansas U.S.A. 103 H3 34 46N 92 16W
North Loup *r.* Nebraska U.S.A. 102 F5 42 00N 100 00W
Northop Clwyd Wales 42 A1 53 13N 3 08W
North Platte Nebraska U.S.A. 102 F5 41 09N 100 45W
North Platte *r.* U.S.A. 102 F5 42 00N 103 00W
North Pole Arctic Ocean 120 90 00N
North River *tn.* Manitoba Canada 101 Q4 58 55N 94 30W
North Ronaldsay *i.* Orkney Islands Scotland 47 E2 59 23N 2 26W
North Sea Europe 117 I12 55 00N 5 00E
North Shields Tyne and Wear England 44 C2 55 01N 1 26W
North Somercotes Lincolnshire England 36 E3 53 28N 0 08E
North Sound, The Orkney Islands Scotland 47 E2 59 17N 2 45W
North Tawton Devon England 31 D2 50 48N 3 53W
North Tidworth Wiltshire England 31 F3 51 16N 1 40W
North Tyne *r.* Northumberland England 44 B2 54 05N 2 10W
North Uist *i.* Western Isles Scotland 46 A4 57 40N 7 15W
Northumberland *co.* England 44 B2/C2 55 10N 2 00W
Northumberland National Park Northumberland
North Walsham Norfolk England 33 D3 52 50N 1 24E
North Weald Bassett Essex England 34 D3 51 43N 0 10E
North West Cape Australia 86 A5 21 48S 114 10E
North West Christmas Island Ridge Pacific Ocean 119 J8 9 30N 165 00E
Northwestern Atlantic Basin Atlantic Ocean 117 B10 33 00N 70 00W
Northwest Highlands Scotland 46 C4–D5
Northwest Pacific Basin Pacific Ocean 118 F11 35 00N 150 00E
Northwest Territories *territory* Canada 100–101 M6 65 15N 115 00W
Northwich Cheshire England 42 C1 53 16N 2 32W
North York Moors National Park North Yorkshire England 40 D3 54 22N 0 45W
North Yorkshire *co.* England 40 C3 54 05N 1 20W
Norton Kansas U.S.A. 102 G4 39 51N 99 53W
Norton North Yorkshire England 40 D3 54 08N 0 48W
Norton Shropshire England 35 A2 52 36N 2 24W
Norton Sound Alaska U.S.A. 100 C5 64 00N 162 30W
Norvegia, Cape Antarctica 121 71 28S 12 25W
Norwalk California U.S.A. 107 B2 33 56N 118 04W
Norwalk Connecticut U.S.A. 105 F2 41 07N 73 25W
NORWAY 67 B3
Norway House Manitoba Canada 101 P3 53 59N 97 50W
Norwegian Basin Arctic Ocean 117 H13 67 00N 0 00
Norwegian Sea Arctic Ocean 120 70 00N 5 00E
Norwich Connecticut U.S.A. 105 F2 41 32N 72 05W
Norwich Norfolk England 33 D3 52 38N 1 18E
Nose of Howth *c.* Dublin Irish Republic 49 B2 53 23N 6 03W
Noshiro Japan 82 D3 40 13N 140 00E
Nosop *r.* Southern Africa 95 D2 25 00S 20 30E
Noss Head *c.* Highland Scotland 46 E5 58 28N 3 04W
Nosy Bé *i.* Madagascar 95 I5 13 00S 47 00E
Notéc *r.* Poland 69 C3 53 00N 17 00E
Notre Dame Bay Newfoundland Canada 101 X2 49 40N 55 00W
Notre-Dame du Lac *tn.* Québec Canada 105 G3 47 38N 68 49W
Nottaway River Québec Canada 105 E4 51 00N 78 00W
Nottingham Nottinghamshire England 36 C2 52 58N 1 10W
Nottingham Island Northwest Territories Canada 101 T5 62 15N 77 30W
Nottinghamshire *co.* England 36 C3/D3 53 20N 1 00W
Nouadhibou Mauritania 93 B7 20 54N 17 01W
Nouakchott Mauritania 93 B6 18 09N 15 58W
Noumea New Caledonia 86 L5 22 16S 166 26E
Nouzonville France 64 D1 49 49N 4 45E
Nova Friburgo Brazil 115 I8 22 16S 42 34W
Nova Iguaçu Brazil 116 B2 22 45S 43 27W
Novara Italy 68 A4 45 27N 8 37E
Nova Scotia *province* Canada 101 W1 44 30N 65 00W
Nova Scotia Basin Atlantic Ocean 117 C10 39 00N 55 00W
Novaya Zemlya *is.* U.S.S.R. 71 H10 74 00N 55 00E
Novgorod U.S.S.R. 70 F7 58 30N 31 20E
Novi Pazar Yugoslavia 68 D3 43 09N 20 29E
Novi Sad Yugoslavia 68 C4 45 15N 19 51E
Novograd-Volynskiy U.S.S.R. 69 E3 50 34N 27 32E
Novo Hamburgo Brazil 115 G7 29 37S 51 07W
Novokazalinsk U.S.S.R. 70 I5 45 48N 62 06E
Novokuznetsk U.S.S.R. 71 K6 53 45N 87 12E
Novolazarevskaya *r.s.* Antarctica 121 70 46S 11 50E
Novopolotsk U.S.S.R. 69 E4 55 32N 28 39E
Novorossiysk U.S.S.R. 70 F4 44 44N 37 46E
Novosibirsk U.S.S.R. 71 K7 55 04N 83 05E
Novyy Port U.S.S.R. 71 J9 67 38N 72 33E
Novyy Urengoy U.S.S.R. 71 J9 66 00N 77 20E
Nowai *r.* India 76 K2 22 39N 88 28E
Nowa Sól Poland 69 C3 51 49N 15 41E
Nowgong India 77 G5 25 03N 79 27E
Nowy Dwor Poland 69 D3 52 27N 20 41E
Nowy Sącz Poland 69 D2 49 39N 20 40E
Nubian Desert Sudan 78 D3 21 00N 33 00E
Nueces *r.* Texas U.S.A. 102 G2 28 00N 99 00W
Nueltin Lake Northwest Territories Canada 101 P5 60 30N 99 00W
Nueva Rosita Mexico 108 D5 27 58N 101 11W
Nueva San Salvador El Salvador 108 G2 13 40N 89 18W
9 de Julio *(Nueve de Julio) tn.* Argentina 115 E5 35 28S 60 58W
Nuevitas Cuba 109 I4 21 34N 77 18W
Nuevo Casa Grandes Mexico 108 C6 30 22N 107 53W
Nuevo Laredo Mexico 108 E5 27 30N 99 30W
Nu Jiang *(Salween) r.* China 77 G6 31 30N 94 00E
Nuku'alofa Tonga 118 I5 21 09S 175 14W
Nukus U.S.S.R. 70 H4 42 28N 59 07E
Nullabor Plain Australia 86 D3 32 00S 128 00E
Numazu Japan 82 C2 35 08N 138 50E
Numedal *geog. reg.* Norway 67 B3 60 40N 9 00E
Nuneaton Warwickshire England 35 D2 52 32N 1 28W
Nunivak Island Alaska U.S.A. 100 B5 60 00N 166 00W
Nunspeet Netherlands 64 E4 52 22N 5 47E
Nuremberg *see* Nürnberg
Nürnberg *(Nuremberg)* F.R.G. 63 B1 49 27N 11 05E
Nürtingen F.R.G. 63 A1 48 37N 9 20E
Nuseybin Turkey 78 F6 37 05N 41 11E
Nushki Pakistan 76 B5 29 33N 66 01E
Nutak Newfoundland Canada 101 W4 57 30N 61 59W
Nutt's Corner Northern Ireland 49 C1 54 38N 6 09W
Nuussuaq *p.* Greenland 101 Y7 70 50N 53 00W
Nyainqêntanglha Shan *mts.* China 81 C3–E4 30 00N 90 00E
Nyala Sudan 94 D10 12 01N 24 50E
Nyasa, Lake *(Lake Malawi)* Southern Africa 95 F5 12 00S 35 00E
Nyíregyháza Hungary 69 D2 47 57N 21 43E
Nykøbing Denmark 67 C1 54 47N 11 53E
Nyköping Sweden 67 D2 58 45N 17 03E
Nyngan Australia 86 H3 31 34S 147 14E
Nyons France 61 C1 44 22N 5 08E
Nysa *(Neisse) r.* Poland 69 B3 52 00N 14 00E
Nysa Poland 69 C3 50 30N 17 20E
Nyū dō-zaki *c.* Japan 82 C2 40 00N 139 42E

O

Oadby Leicestershire England 36 C2 52 36N 1 04W
Oahe, Lake U.S.A. 102 F6 45 00N 100 00W
Oahu *i.* Hawaiian Islands 119 X18 21 30N 158 10W
Oakenclough Lancashire England 42 B3 53 55N 2 42W
Oakengates Shropshire England 35 A3 52 42N 2 28W
Oakes North Dakota U.S.A. 104 A3 46 08N 98 07W
Oakham Leicestershire England 36 D2 42 21N 72 03W
Oak Hill *tn.* West Virginia U.S.A. 105 D1 37 58N 81 11W
Oakland California U.S.A. 102 B4 37 50N 122 15W
Oakland City Indiana U.S.A. 104 C1 38 21N 87 19W
Oakley Fife Scotland 45 C2 56 05N 3 35W
Oakley Hampshire England 32 A2 51 15N 1 12W
Oak Ridge *tn.* Tennessee U.S.A. 103 J4 36 02N 84 12W
Oakville Ontario Canada 105 E2 43 27N 79 41W
Oamaru New Zealand 87 B1 45 07S 170 58E
Oano Island Pitcairn Islands 119 N5 23 32S 125 00W
Oaxaca Mexico 108 E3 17 05N 96 41N
Ob' *r.* U.S.S.R. 71 I9 65 30N 66 00E
Ob', Gulf of U.S.S.R. 71 J9 68 00N 74 00E
Oba Ontario Canada 101 S2 48 38N 84 17W
Oban Strathclyde Scotland 46 C3 56 25N 5 29W
Ober Österreich *admin.* Austria 63 B1 48 00N 14 00E
Oberhausen F.R.G. 62 B2 51 27N 6 50E
Oberpfälzer Wald *forest* F.R.G. 63 B1 49 00N 12 00E
Oberursel F.R.G. 63 A2 50 12N 8 35E
Obidos Brazil 114 F12 1 52S 55 30W
Obihiro Japan 82 D3 42 56N 143 10E
Obitsu *r.* Japan 83 C2 35 25N 139 53E
Ocala Florida U.S.A. 103 J2 29 11N 82 09W
Ocaña Colombia 114 C14 8 16N 73 21W
Ocean City Maryland U.S.A. 105 E1 38 21N 75 06W
Ochakovo U.S.S.R. 70 L1 55 39N 37 30E
Ochil Hills Scotland 45 C2/D2 56 15N 3 30W
Ocho Rios Jamaica 109 Q8 18 24N 77 06W
Ockley Surrey England 34 B1 51 09N 0 22W
Oconto Wisconsin U.S.A. 104 C2 44 55N 87 52W
Ocotlán Mexico 108 D4 20 21N 102 42W
Ōda Japan 82 B2 35 10N 132 29E
Ōdate Japan 82 D3 40 18N 140 32E
Odawara Japan 82 C2 35 15N 139 08E
Odda Norway 67 B3 60 03N 6 34E
Ödemiş Turkey 68 E2 38 11N 27 58E
Odense Denmark 67 C2 55 24N 10 25E
Odenwald *mts.* F.R.G. 63 A1 49 00N 9 00E
Oder *see* Odra
Odessa Delaware U.S.A. 105 E1 39 27N 75 40W
Odessa Texas U.S.A. 102 F3 31 50N 102 23W
Odessa U.S.S.R. 70 F5 46 30N 30 46E
Odiel *r.* Spain 66 A2 37 32N 7 00W
Odra *(Oder) r.* Europe 69 C3 51 00N 17 00E
Oegstgeest Netherlands 65 B2 52 10N 4 29E
Oekusi *(Dili)* Indonesia 80 H2 8 35S 125 35E
Ofanto *r.* Italy 68 C3 41 00N 15 00E
Offaly *co.* Irish Republic 48 D3 53 15N 7 35W
Offenbach am Main F.R.G. 63 A1 50 06N 8 46E
Offenburg F.R.G. 63 A1 48 29N 7 57E
Ofuna Japan 83 B2 35 21N 139 32E
Ofunato Japan 82 D2 39 04N 141 43E
Ogaden *geog. reg.* Africa 94 I9 7 00N 51 00E
Ogaki Japan 82 C2 35 22N 136 36E
Ogasawara Guntō *i.* Pacific Ocean 118 E10 27 30N 143 00E
Ogawa Japan 83 A3 35 43N 135 29E
Ogbomosho Nigeria 93 F4 8 05N 4 11E
Ogden Utah U.S.A. 102 D5 41 14N 111 59W
Ogdensburg New York U.S.A. 105 E2 44 42N 75 31W
Ogilvie Mountains Yukon Territory Canada 100 H6 65 05N 139 00W
Ogoki *r.* Ontario Canada 101 R3 51 00N 87 00W
Ogooué *r.* Gabon 93 G2 0 50S 9 50E
Ogun *r.* Nigeria 92 C3 6 42N 3 29E
Ogunpa *r.* Nigeria 92 E4 7 19N 3 55E
Ōhata Japan 82 D3 41 22N 141 11E
Ohio *r.* U.S.A. 104 C1 38 00N 88 00W
Ohio *state* U.S.A. 105 D2 40 00N 83 00W
Ohori Japan 83 C2 35 20N 139 52E
Ohře *r.* Czechoslovakia 63 B2 50 00N 14 00E
Ohre *r.* G.D.R. 63 B2 52 00N 11 00E
Ohridsko ezero *l.* Yugoslavia / Albania 68 D3 41 00N 20 00E
Oil City Pennsylvania U.S.A. 105 E2 41 26N 79 44W
Oise *r.* France 61 B2 49 10N 2 10E
Ōita Japan 82 B1 33 15N 131 36E
Ojinaga Mexico 108 D5 29 35N 104 26W
Okanagan *r.* North America 102 C6 49 00N 119 00W
Okara Pakistan 77 C6 30 49N 73 31E
Okavango *r.* Southern Africa 95 C4 17 50S 20 00E
Okavango Basin Botswana 95 D4 19 00S 23 00E
Okaya Japan 82 C2 36 03N 138 00E
Okayama Japan 82 B1 34 40N 133 54E
Okazaki Japan 82 C1 34 58N 137 10E
Oke Ado Nigeria 92 E4 7 21N 3 55E
Okeechobee, Lake Florida U.S.A. 103 J2 27 00N 81 00W
Oke Foko Nigeria 92 E4 7 22N 3 55E
Okehampton Devon England 31 C2 50 44N 4 00W
Okene Nigeria 93 G4 7 31N 6 14E
Oke Ofa Nigeria 92 E4 7 23N 3 58E
Okha U.S.S.R. 71 Q6 53 35N 143 01E
Okhla India 76 M4 28 33N 77 16E
Okhotsk U.S.S.R. 71 Q7 59 20N 143 15E
Okhotsk, Sea of U.S.S.R. 71 Q7 55 00N 148 00E
Oki *is.* Japan 82 B2 36 05N 133 00E
Okinawa *i.* Japan 81 K3 26 30N 128 00E
Oklahoma *state* U.S.A. 103 G4 36 00N 98 00W
Oklahoma City Oklahoma U.S.A. 103 G4 35 28N 97 33W
Oktyabr'skiy U.S.S.R. 71 R6 52 43N 156 14E
Okushiri-tō *i.* Japan 82 C2 42 15N 139 30E
Öland *i.* Sweden 67 D2 56 45N 51 50E
Olbia Italy 68 A3 40 56N 9 30E
Oldbury West Midlands England 35 C2 52 30N 2 00W
Oldcotes Nottinghamshire England 43 G2 53 24N 1 07W
Old Crow Yukon Territory Canada 100 H6 67 34N 139 43W
Oldenburg F.R.G. 63 A2 53 08N 8 13E
Oldenzaal Netherlands 64 F4 52 19N 6 55E
Old Fletton Cambridgeshire England 33 B3 52 34N 0 14W
Oldham Greater Manchester England 42 D2 53 33N 2 07W
Old Harbour Jamaica 109 Q7 17 56N 77 07W
Old Harbour Bay *tn.* Jamaica 109 Q7 17 54N 77 06W
Old Head of Kinsale *c.* Irish Republic 48 C1 51 40N 8 30W
Oldmeldrum Grampian Scotland 46 F4 57 20N 2 20W
Olds Alberta Canada 100 M3 51 50N 114 06W
Old Town Maine U.S.A. 105 G2 44 55N 68 41W
Old Windsor Berkshire England 34 B2 51 28N 0 35E
Olean New York U.S.A. 105 E2 42 05N 78 26W
Olekma *r.* U.S.S.R. 71 O7 59 00N 121 00E
Olekminsk U.S.S.R. 71 O8 60 25N 120 25E
Olenëk *r.* U.S.S.R. 71 O10 72 00N 122 00E
Olenëk U.S.S.R. 71 N9 68 28N 112 18E
Olhão Portugal 66 A2 37 01N 7 50W
Ólimbos *(Olympus) mt.* Greece 68 D3 40 05N 22 21E
Olinda Brazil 114 J11 8 00S 34 51W
Olivia Minnesota U.S.A. 104 B2 44 47N 94 58W
Ollerton Nottinghamshire England 43 G1 53 12N 1 00W
Olney Buckinghamshire England 33 B3 52 09N 0 43W
Olomouc Czechoslovakia 69 C2 49 38N 17 15E
Olongapo The Philippines 80 G6 14 49N 120 17E
Olsztyn Poland 69 D3 53 48N 20 29E
Olt *r.* Romania 69 D1 44 00N 24 00E
Olten Switzerland 61 C2 47 22N 7 55E
Olympia Washington U.S.A. 102 B6 47 03N 122 53W
Olympus *see* Ólimbos
Olympus, Mount Washington U.S.A. 102 B6 47 49N 123 42W
Om' *r.* U.S.S.R. 71 J7 55 00N 79 00E

Omagh Northern Ireland **48** D4 54 36N 7 18W
Omaha Nebraska U.S.A. **104** A2 41 15N 96 00W
OMAN 79 I2
Oman, Gulf of Iran/Oman **79** I3 24 30N 58 30E
Ombersley Hereford & Worcester England **35** B1 52 17N 2 13W
Omboué Gabon **93** G2 1 38S 9 20E
Omdurman Sudan **78** D2 15 37N 32 29E
Omi *r.* Nigeria **92** F4 7 19N 4 01E
Omo *r.* Ethiopia **94** G9 7 00N 37 00E
Omolon *r.* U.S.S.R. **71** R9 65 00N 160 00E
Omoloy *r.* U.S.S.R. **71** P9 69 00N 132 00E
Omsk U.S.S.R. **71** J7 55 00N 73 22E
Omuta Japan **82** B1 33 02N 130 26E
Ona *r.* Nigeria **92** E4 7 28N 3 58E
Ondo Nigeria **93** F4 7 05N 4 55E
Onega, Lake *see* Ozero Onezhskoye
Oneonta New York U.S.A. **105** E2 42 28N 75 04W
Ongea Levu *i.* Fiji **118** V15 19 11S 178 28W
Onitsha Nigeria **93** G4 6 10N 6 47E
Onomichi Japan **82** B1 34 25N 133 11E
Onslow Australia **86** B5 21 41S 115 12E
Onslow Village Surrey England **34** B1 51 14N 0 36W
Ontario California U.S.A. **102** C3 34 04N 117 38W
Ontario *province* Canada **101** Q3 51 00N 91 00W
Ontario, Lake North America **105** E2 43 00N 78 00W
Ontonagon Michigan U.S.A. **104** C3 46 52N 89 18W
Onuki Japan **83** C2 35 16N 139 51E
Oologah Lake Oklahoma U.S.A. **104** A1 36 00N 95 00W
Oostelijk Flevoland *geog. reg.* Netherlands **64** E4 52 30N 5 40E
Oostende Belgium **64** B3 51 13N 2 55E
Oosterhout Netherlands **64** D3 51 39N 4 52E
Oosterschelde *sd.* Netherlands **64** C3 51 30N 3 58E
Oost-Vlaanderen *admin.* Belgium **64** C3 51 10N 3 45E
Oostvoorne Netherlands **65** A1 51 55N 4 06E
Opala Zaïre **94** D7 0 40S 24 20E
Opava Czechoslovakia **69** C2 49 58N 17 55E
Opochka U.S.S.R. **67** F2 56 41N 28 42E
Opole Poland **69** C3 50 40N 17 56E
Oporto *see* Porto
Opotiki New Zealand **87** C3 38 00S 117 18E
Optic Lake *tn.* Manitoba Canada **101** O3 54 47N 101 15W
Oradea Romania **69** D2 47 03N 21 55E
Oradell Reservoir New Jersey U.S.A. **106** B2 40 58N 74 00W
Oran Algeria **93** E10 35 45N 0 38W
Orán Argentina **115** E8 23 07S 64 16W
Orange Australia **86** H3 33 19S 149 10E
Orange California U.S.A. **107** C2 33 43N 117 54W
Orange France **61** B1 44 08N 4 48E
Orange New Jersey U.S.A. **106** B2 40 45N 74 14W
Orange *r.* Southern Africa **95** C2 28 30S 17 30E
Orange Texas U.S.A. **103** H3 30 05N 93 43W
Orangeburg South Carolina U.S.A. **103** J3 33 28N 80 53W
Orange Free State *admin.* Republic of South Africa **95** E2 27 30S 27 30E
Oranienburg G.D.R. **63** B2 52 46N 13 15E
Oranmore Galway Irish Republic **48** C3 53 16N 8 54W
Oraviţa Romania **69** D2 45 02N 21 43E
Orbigo *r.* Spain **66** A3 42 15N 5 45W
Orcadas *r.s.* Antarctica **121** 60 40S 44 44W
Orchies France **64** C2 50 28N 3 15E
Orcia *r.* Italy **68** B3 42 00N 11 00E
Ordzhonikidze U.S.S.R. **70** G4 43 02N 44 43E
Örebro Sweden **67** D2 59 17N 15 13E
Oregon *state* U.S.A. **102** B5 44 00N 120 00W
Oregon City Oregon U.S.A. **102** B6 45 21N 122 36W
Orël U.S.S.R. **70** F6 52 58N 36 04E
Orem Utah U.S.A. **102** D5 40 20N 111 45W
Orenburg U.S.S.R. **70** H6 51 50N 55 00E
Orense Spain **66** A3 42 20N 7 52W
Orford Suffolk England **33** D3 52 06N 1 31E
Orford Ness *c.* Suffolk England **33** D3 52 05N 1 34E
Orge *r.* France **60** B1 48 39N 0 21 9E
Orient Bay *tn.* Ontario Canada **104** C3 49 23N 88 08W
Orihuela Spain **66** B2 38 05N 0 56W
Orillia Ontario Canada **105** E2 44 36N 79 26W
Orissa *admin.* India **77** E4 20 20N 83 00E
Oristano Italy **68** A2 39 54N 8 36E
Orizaba Mexico **108** E3 18 51N 97 08W
Orkney Islands *islands area* Scotland **47** E1 59 00N 3 00W
Orlando Florida U.S.A. **103** J2 28 33N 81 21W
Orléans France **61** B2 47 54N 1 54E
Orly France **60** B1 48 44N 2 24E
Ormskirk Lancashire England **42** B2 53 35N 2 54W
Orne *r.* France **61** A2 48 50N 0 16W
Örnsköldsvik Sweden **67** D3 63 19N 18 45E
Oronsay *i.* Strathclyde Scotland **46** B3 56 00N 6 15W
Orpington Greater London England **34** D2 51 23N 0 05E
Orrell Greater Manchester England **42** B2 53 33N 2 45N
Orsay France **60** A1 48 42N 2 11E
Orsha U.S.S.R. **69** F3 54 30N 30 23E
Orsk U.S.S.R. **70** H6 51 13N 58 35E
Orthez France **61** A1 43 29N 0 46W
Ortigueira Spain **66** A3 43 43N 8 13W
Ortonville Minnesota U.S.A. **104** A3 45 18N 96 28W
Ortze *r.* F.R.G. **63** B2 53 00N 10 00E
Orūmīyeh Iran **78** F6 37 40N 45 00E
Oruro Bolivia **114** D9 17 59S 67 08W
Orwell *r.* Suffolk England **33** D2 52 00N 1 15E
Osage *r.* U.S.A. **104** B1 38 00N 93 00W
Ōsaka Japan **82** C1 34 40N 135 30E
Osceola Iowa U.S.A. **104** B2 41 02N 93 46W
Osgodby North Yorkshire England **43** G3 53 46N 1 01W
Oshawa Ontario Canada **105** E2 43 53N 78 51W
Ō-shima *i.* Japan **82** C1 34 45N 139 25E
Oshkosh Wisconsin U.S.A. **104** C2 44 01N 88 32W
Oshogbo Nigeria **93** F4 7 50N 4 35E
Osijek Yugoslavia **68** C4 45 33N 18 41E
Oskaloosa Iowa U.S.A. **104** B2 41 16N 92 40W
Oslo Norway **67** C2 59 56N 10 45E
Oslofjord *fj.* Norway **67** C2 59 20N 10 37E
Osmaniye Turkey **78** E6 37 04N 36 15E
Osnabrück F.R.G. **63** A2 52 17N 8 03E
Osorno Chile **115** C4 40 35S 73 14W
Oss Netherlands **64** E3 51 46N 5 31E
Ossa, Mount Australia **86** H1 41 52S 146 04E
Ossett West Yorkshire England **43** F3 53 41N 1 35W
Ostankino U.S.S.R. **70** M2 55 50N 37 37E
Österdalälven *r.* Sweden **67** C3 61 40N 13 30E
Østerdalen *geog. reg.* Norway **67** C3 62 00N 10 30E
Osterode F.R.G. **63** B2 51 44N 10 15E
Östervall Sweden **67** D3 62 20N 15 20E
Östersund Sweden **67** C3 63 10N 14 40E
Ostfriesische Inseln *(East Frisian Islands) is.* F.R.G. **63** A2 53 00N 7 00E
Ostrava Czechoslovakia **69** C2 49 50N 18 15E
Ostróda Poland **69** D3 53 42N 19 59E
Ostrołęka Poland **69** D3 53 05N 21 32E
Ostrov U.S.S.R. **67** F2 57 25N 28 20E
Ostrowiec Swietokrzyski Poland **69** D3 50 58N 21 22E
Ostrów Mazowiecki Poland **69** D3 52 50N 21 51E
Ostrów Wielkopolski Poland **69** C3 51 39N 17 50E
Oswaldtwistle Lancashire England **42** C3 53 44N 2 24W
Oswego New York U.S.A. **105** E2 43 27N 76 31W
Oswestry Shropshire England **36** A2 52 52N 3 03W
Ōta Japan **83** B3 35 34N 139 42E
Otaki New Zealand **87** C2 40 45S 175 09E
Otaru Japan **82** D3 43 14N 140 59E
Otava *r.* Czechoslovakia **63** B1 49 00N 13 00E
Otavalo Ecuador **114** B13 0 13N 78 15W
Otford Kent England **34** D1 51 19N 0 12E
O'The Cherokees, Lake Oklahoma U.S.A. **104** B1 37 00N 95 00W
Otley West Yorkshire England **43** E3 53 54N 1 41W
Otra *r.* Norway **67** B2 56 17N 7 30E
Otranto Italy **68** C3 40 08N 18 30E
Otranto, Strait of Adriatic Sea **68** C3 40 00N 19 00E
Otsego Michigan U.S.A. **104** C2 42 26N 85 42W
Otsu Japan **82** C2 35 00N 135 50E
Ottawa Illinois U.S.A. **104** C2 41 21N 88 51W
Ottawa Kansas U.S.A. **104** A1 38 35N 95 16W
Ottawa Ontario Canada **105** E3 45 25N 75 43W
Ottawa *(Rivière des Outaouais) r.* Ontario/Québec Canada **105** E3 46 00N 77 00W
Ottawa Islands Northwest Territories Canada **101** S4 59 10N 80 25W
Otter *r.* Devon England **31** D2 50 50N 3 10W
Otterburn Northumberland England **44** B2 55 14N 2 10W
Otter Rapids *tn.* Ontario Canada **105** D4 50 12N 81 40W
Ottery *r.* Cornwall England **30** C2 50 40N 4 30W
Ottery St. Mary Devon England **31** D2 50 45N 3 17W
Ottumwa Iowa U.S.A. **104** B2 41 02N 92 26W
Ouachita *r.* U.S.A. **103** H3 34 00N 93 00W
Ouachita Mountains U.S.A. **103** G3 34 00N 95 00W
Ouadda Central African Republic **94** D9 8 09N 22 20E
Ouagadougou Burkina **93** E5 12 20N 1 40W
Ouahigouya Burkina **93** E5 13 31N 2 20W
Ouargla Algeria **93** G9 32 00N 5 16E
Ouassel *r.* Algeria **66** C2 35 30N 2 00E
Oubangui *r.* Africa **94** C8 0 00 17 30E
Oudenaarde Belgium **64** C2 50 50N 3 37E
Oude Rijn *r.* Netherlands **65** D2 52 06N 4 46E
Oudtshoorn Republic of South Africa **95** D1 33 35S 22 12E
Oued Dra *r.* Morocco **93** C8 28 10N 11 00W
Oued Zem Morocco **93** D9 32 55N 6 33W
Ouensé Congo **92** A2 4 16S 15 17E
Ouerrha *r.* Morocco **66** A1 34 00N 6 00W
Ouesso Congo **94** C8 1 38N 16 03E
Ouezzane Morocco **66** A1 34 52N 5 35W
Ouham *r.* Central African Republic **94** C9 7 00N 17 30E
Oujda Morocco **93** E9 34 41N 1 45W
Oulton Staffordshire England **35** B3 52 54N 2 09W
Oulu Finland **67** F3 65 02N 25 27E
Oulujärvi *l.* Finland **67** F3 64 20N 27 00E
Oulujoki *r.* Finland **67** F3 64 50N 26 00E
Ounasjoki *r.* Finland **67** F4 67 00N 25 00E
Oundle Northamptonshire England **36** D2 52 29N 0 29W
Our *r.* Luxembourg / F.R.G. **64** F1 50 00N 6 00E
Ouro *r.* Brazil **116** A3 22 40S 43 32W
Ourthe *r.* Belgium **64** E2 50 20N 5 50E
Ou-sanmyaku *mts.* Japan **82** D2 39 20N 141 00E
Ouse *r.* East Sussex England **33** C1 50 55N 0 00
Ouse *r.* North Yorkshire England **40** C2 53 40N 1 00W
Ouseburn North Yorkshire England **43** G4 54 04N 1 20W
Oust *r.* France **61** A2 47 50N 2 30W
Out Skerries *is.* Shetland Islands Scotland **47** C2 60 25N 0 46W
Outbridge South Yorkshire England **43** F2 53 26N 1 34W
Outer Hebrides *is.* Western Isles Scotland **46** A4–B5
Outreau France **64** A2 50 42N 1 36E
Outwell Norfolk England **33** C3 52 37N 0 14E
Outwood Surrey England **34** C1 51 13N 0 06W
Outwood West Yorkshire England **43** F3 53 42N 1 30W
Ovalau *i.* Fiji **118** U16 17 40S 178 47E
Ovalle Chile **115** C6 30 33S 71 16W
Overflakkee *i.* Netherlands **64** D3 51 45N 4 10E
Overijssel *admin.* Netherlands **64** F4 52 23N 6 28E
Overseal Derbyshire England **35** D3 52 44N 1 34W
Overton Clwyd Wales **38** D2 52 58N 2 56W
Overton Hampshire England **32** A2 51 15N 1 15W
Overton Lancashire England **42** B4 54 01N 2 53W
Övertorneå Sweden **67** E4 66 22N 23 40E
Overtown Strathclyde Scotland **45** C1 55 45N 3 55W
Oviedo Spain **66** A3 43 21N 5 50W
Owando Congo **94** C7 0 27S 15 44E
Owatonna Minnesota U.S.A. **104** B2 44 06N 93 10W
Owen Falls Dam Uganda **94** F8 0 29N 33 11E
Owen, Mount New Zealand **87** B2 41 33S 172 33E
Owensboro Kentucky U.S.A. **104** C1 37 45N 87 05W
Owens Lake California U.S.A. **102** C4 36 25N 117 56W
Owen Sound Ontario Canada **105** D2 44 34N 80 56W
Owen Sound *tn.* Ontario Canada **101** S1 44 34N 80 56W
Owen Stanley Range *mts.* Papua New Guinea **86** H8 8 00S 147 30E
Owo Nigeria **93** G4 7 10N 5 39E
Owosso Michigan U.S.A. **105** D2 43 00N 84 11W
Owyhee *r.* U.S.A. **102** C5 43 00N 117 00W
Oxenhope West Yorkshire England **43** E3 53 49N 1 57W
Oxford Oxfordshire England **32** A2 51 46N 1 15W
Oxford Canal England **35** E2 52 24N 1 18W
Oxfordshire *co.* England **32** A2 51 45N 1 20W
Oxnard California U.S.A. **102** C3 34 11N 119 10W
Oxshott Surrey England **34** B2 51 20N 0 21W
Oxted Surrey England **34** C1 51 15N 0 01W
Oxus *see* Amudar'ya
Oyama Japan **82** C2 36 18N 139 48E
Oyapock *r.* Brazil **114** G13 3 00N 52 30W
Oyem Gabon **93** H3 1 34N 11 31E
Oykel *r.* Highland Scotland **46** D4 57 58N 4 40W
Oyo Nigeria **93** F4 7 50N 3 55E
Ozark Plateau Missouri U.S.A. **104** B1 37 00N 93 00W
Ozarks, Lake of the Missouri U.S.A. **104** B1 38 00N 93 00W
Ozero Balkhash *(Lake Balkhash) l.* U.S.S.R. **71** J5 46 00N 75 00E
Ozero Baykal *(Lake Baykal) l.* U.S.S.R. **71** M6 54 00N 109 00E
Ozero Chany *l.* U.S.S.R. **71** J6 55 00N 77 30E
Ozero Chudskoye *(Lake Peipus) l.* U.S.S.R. **67** F2 58 40N 27 30E
Ozero Imandra *l.* U.S.S.R. **67** G4 67 45N 33 00E
Ozero Issyk-Kul' *l.* U.S.S.R. **71** J4 42 30N 77 30E
Ozero Khanka *l.* U.S.S.R./China **71** P5 45 00N 132 30E
Ozero Leksozero *l.* U.S.S.R. **67** G3 64 00N 31 20E
Ozero Nyuk *l.* U.S.S.R. **67** G3 64 30N 31 50E
Ozero Onezhskoye *(Lake Onega) l.* U.S.S.R. **70** F8 62 00N 40 00E
Ozero Pskovskoye *l.* U.S.S.R. **67** F2 58 00N 28 00E
Ozero Pyazero *l.* U.S.S.R. **67** G4 66 00N 31 15E
Ozero Sevan *l.* U.S.S.R. **78** F7 40 35N 44 00E
Ozero Sredneye Kuyto *l.* U.S.S.R. **67** G3 65 00N 31 15E
Ozero Tengiz *l.* U.S.S.R. **70** I6 51 00N 69 00E
Ozero Topozero *l.* U.S.S.R. **67** G4 65 45N 32 10E
Ozero Zaysan *l.* U.S.S.R. **71** K5 48 00N 84 00E
Ozieri Italy **61** C1 40 35N 9 01E

P

Pabjanice Poland **69** C3 51 40N 19 20E
Pabna Bangladesh **77** F4 24 00N 89 15E
Pacasmayo Peru **114** B11 7 27S 79 33W
Pachecos Brazil **116** D2 22 50S 43 00W
Pachuca Mexico **108** E4 20 10N 98 44W
Pacific–Antarctic Ridge Pacific Ocean **119** M2 55 00S 135 00W
Pacific Grove California U.S.A. **102** B4 36 36N 121 56W
Pacific Ocean 118–119
Padang Indonesia **80** C3 1 00S 100 21E
Paddington Greater London England **34** C3 51 31N 0 12W
Paddock Wood *tn.* Kent England **34** E1 51 11N 0 23E
Paderborn F.R.G. **63** A2 51 43N 8 44E
Padiham Lancashire England **42** D3 53 49N 2 19W
Padilla Bolivia **114** E9 19 18S 64 20W
Padova Italy **68** B4 45 24N 11 53E
Padstow Cornwall England **30** C2 50 33N 4 56W
Paducah Kentucky U.S.A. **104** C1 37 03N 88 36W
Paeroa New Zealand **87** C3 37 21S 175 41E
Pag *i.* Yugoslavia **68** B3 44 00N 15 00E
Pagadian The Philippines **80** G5 7 50N 123 30E
Pahala Hawaiian Islands **119** Z17 19 12N 155 28W
Paharganj India **76** L4 28 38N 77 12E
Paignton Devon England **31** D2 50 26N 3 34W
Päijänne *l.* Finland **67** F3 61 30N 25 25E
Pailton Warwickshire England **35** E2 52 26N 1 17W
Painesville Ohio U.S.A. **105** D2 41 43N 81 15W
Paisley Strathclyde Scotland **45** B1 55 50N 4 26W
Paita Peru **114** A11 5 11S 81 09W
PAKISTAN 76/77 A5–C5
Pakokku Myanma **81** E2 21 20N 95 05E
Pakse Laos **80** D6 14 09N 105 50E
Palaiseau France **60** A1 48 43N 2 15E
Palana U.S.S.R. **71** R7 59 05N 159 59E
Palangkaraya Indonesia **80** E3 2 06S 113 55E
Palau *(Belau) i.* Pacific Ocean **118** D8 7 30N 134 30E
Palawan *i.* The Philippines **80** F5/F6 9 00N 114 00E
Palayankottai India **77** D1 8 42N 77 46E
Palembang Indonesia **80** C3 2 59S 104 45E
Palencia Spain **66** B3 41 01N 4 32W
Palermo Italy **68** B2 38 08N 13 23E
Palestine Texas U.S.A. **103** G3 31 45N 95 39W
Palghat India **77** D2 10 46N 76 42E
Palk Strait India **77** D2 10 00N 80 00E
Palliser, Cape New Zealand **87** C2 41 37S 175 16E
Palma de Mallorca Balearic Islands **66** E4 39 35N 2 39E
Palmar Sur Costa Rica **109** H1 8 57N 83 28W
Palmas, Cape Liberia **93** D3 4 25N 7 50W
Palmer Alaska U.S.A. **100** F5 61 35N 149 10W
Palmer *r.s.* Antarctica **121** 64 46S 83 55W
Palmer Land *geog. reg.* Antarctica **121** 72 00S 62 00W
Palmerston Dublin Irish Republic **49** A2 53 22N 6 22W
Palmerston Atoll *is.* Pacific Ocean **119** J6 18 04S 163 10W
Palmerston North New Zealand **87** C2 40 20S 175 39E
Palmira Colombia **114** B13 3 33N 76 17W
Palmyra Atoll *is.* Pacific Ocean **119** K8 5 52N 162 05W
Palomares Mexico **108** E3 17 10N 95 04W
Palopo Indonesia **80** G3 3 01S 120 12E
Palos Verdes Hills California U.S.A. **107** A2 33 46N 118 23W
Palu Indonesia **80** F3 0 54S 119 52E
Pamiers France **61** B1 43 07N 1 36E
Pamirs *mts.* U.S.S.R. **70** J3 38 00N 74 00E
Pamlico Sound North Carolina U.S.A. **103** K4 35 00N 76 00W
Pampas *geog. reg.* Argentina **115** E5 36 00S 63 00W
Pamplona Colombia **114** C14 7 24N 72 38W
Pamplona Peru **116** F4 12 09S 76 58W
Pamplona Spain **66** B3 42 49N 1 39W
PANAMA 109 H1
Panama Canal Panama **109** I1 9 00N 80 00W
Panama City Florida U.S.A. **103** I3 30 10N 85 41W
Panama Isthmus Central America **96** 9 00N 80 00W
Panamá Panama **109** I1 8 57N 79 30W
Panay *i.* The Philippines **80** G6 11 20N 122 30E
Pančevo Yugoslavia **68** D3 44 52N 20 40E
Panchla India **76** J2 22 32N 88 08E
Panchur India **76** K2 22 31N 88 15E
Panevėžys U.S.S.R. **69** D4 55 44N 24 24E
Pangbourne Berkshire England **32** A2 51 29N 1 05W
Pangkalpinang Indonesia **80** D3 2 05S 106 09E
Pangnirtung Northwest Territories Canada **101** V6 66 05N 65 45W
Pānihāti India **76** K2 22 41N 88 23E
Panipat India **77** D5 29 24N 76 58E
Pantar *i.* Indonesia **80** G2 8 00S 124 00E
Pantelleria *i.* Italy **68** B2 36 00N 12 00E
Pantin France **60** B2 48 54N 2 25E
Pao de Açúcar *(Sugar Loaf) mt.* Brazil **116** C2 22 57S 43 09W
Papa Hawaiian Islands **119** Z17 19 12N 155 53W
Pápa Hungary **69** C2 47 20N 17 29E
Papantla Mexico **108** E4 20 30N 97 21W
Papa Stour *i.* Shetland Islands Scotland **47** B2 60 20N 1 42W
Papa Westray *i.* Orkney Islands Scotland **47** E2 59 22N 2 54W
Papenburg F.R.G. **63** A2 53 05N 7 25E
Papendrecht Netherlands **64** D3 51 50N 4 42E
Papua, Gulf of Papua New Guinea **86** H8 8 30S 145 00E
PAPUA NEW GUINEA 86 H8
Pará *admin.* Brazil **114** G12 4 30S 52 30W
Paraburdoo Australia **86** B5 23 15S 117 45E
Paracel Islands South China Sea **80** E7 16 40N 112 00E
PARAGUAY 115 F8
Paraíba *admin.* Brazil **114** J11 7 20S 37 10W
Parakou Benin **93** F4 9 23N 2 40E
Paramaribo Surinam **114** F14 5 52N 55 14W
Paramonga Peru **114** B10 10 42S 77 50W
Paramus New Jersey U.S.A. **106** B2 40 55N 74 03W
Parana *admin.* Brazil **115** G8 24 30S 53 00W
Paraná Argentina **115** E6 31 45S 60 30W
Paranaguá Brazil **115** H7 25 32S 48 36W
Paraná Plateau Brazil **110** 25 00S 50 00W
Parbhani India **77** D3 19 16N 76 51E
Parchim G.D.R. **63** B2 53 26N 11 51E
Pardubice Czechoslovakia **69** C2 50 03N 15 45E
Parepare Indonesia **80** F3 4 00S 119 40E
Parintins Brazil **114** F12 2 38S 56 45W
Paris France **60** B2 48 52N 2 20E
Paris Missouri U.S.A. **104** B1 39 27N 91 59W
Paris Texas U.S.A. **103** G3 33 41N 95 33W
Paris Basin France **51** 48 00N 2 30E
Parish New York U.S.A. **105** E2 43 24N 76 07W
Parkano Finland **67** E3 62 03N 23 00E
Parkersburg West Virginia U.S.A. **105** D1 39 17N 81 33W
Parma Italy **68** B3 44 48N 10 19E
Parma Ohio U.S.A. **105** D2 41 24N 81 44W
Parnaíba Brazil **114** I12 2 58S 41 46W
Parnassós *mt.* Greece **68** D2 38 30N 22 37E
Pärnu U.S.S.R. **67** E2 58 28N 24 30E
Paroo *r.* Australia **86** G4 27 00S 144 00E
Páros *i.* Greece **68** E2 37 00N 25 00E
Parras Mexico **108** D5 25 30N 102 11W
Parrett *r.* Somerset England **31** E3 51 05N 3 00W
Parry, Cape Northwest Territories Canada **100** K7 70 08N 124 34W
Parry Islands Northwest Territories Canada **101** N8 75 15N 109 00W
Parry Sound *tn.* Ontario Canada **105** D3 45 21N 80 03W
Parthenay France **61** A2 46 39N 0 14W
Partick Strathclyde Scotland **45** B1 55 52N 4 18W
Partington Greater Manchester England **42** C2 53 26N 2 26W
Pasadena California U.S.A. **107** B3 34 10N 118 09W
Pasadena Texas U.S.A. **103** G2 29 42N 95 14W
Pascagoula Mississippi U.S.A. **103** I3 30 21N 88 32W
Pas-de-Calais *admin.* France **64** A2 50 45N 2 00E
Pas de Calais *sd. see* Strait of Dover
Passage de la Déroute *sd.* Channel Islands / France **31** G6–H5 49 30N 2 00W
Passage West *tn.* Cork Irish Republic **48** C1 51 52N 8 20W
Passaic New Jersey U.S.A. **106** B2 40 50N 74 08W
Passaic River New Jersey U.S.A. **106** B2 40 46N 74 09W
Passau F.R.G. **63** B1 48 35N 13 28E
Passo Fundo Brazil **115** G7 28 16S 52 20W
Pasto Colombia **114** B13 1 12N 77 17W
Patagonia *geog. reg.* Argentina **115** C2–D4 48 00S 70 00W
Patan India **77** C4 23 51N 72 11E
Patan Nepal **77** F5 27 40N 85 20E
Patchogue New York U.S.A. **105** F2 40 46N 73 01W
Patea New Zealand **87** C3 39 45S 174 29E
Pate Island Kenya **94** H7 2 05S 41 05E
Pateley Bridge *tn.* North Yorkshire England **43** E4 54 05N 1 45W
Paterson New Jersey U.S.A. **106** B2 40 55N 74 08W
Pathankot India **77** D6 32 16N 75 43E
Path of Condie Tayside Scotland **45** D2 56 17N 3 28W
Patiala India **77** D6 30 21N 76 27E
Pātipukur India **76** K2 22 36N 88 24E
Patna India **77** F5 25 37N 85 12E
Patna Strathclyde Scotland **46** D2 55 20N 4 30W
Patos Brazil **114** J11 6 55S 37 15W
Pátrai Greece **68** D2 38 14N 21 44E
Pattingham Staffordshire England **35** B2 52 36N 2 16W
Pau France **61** A1 43 18N 0 22W
Paungde Myanma **77** H3 18 30N 95 30E
Pavia Italy **68** A4 45 12N 9 09E
Pavlodar U.S.S.R. **71** J6 52 21N 76 59E
Pawtucket Massachusetts U.S.A. **105** F2 41 53N 71 23W
Paxton Illinois U.S.A. **104** C2 40 28N 88 07W
Paysandú Uruguay **115** F6 32 21S 58 05W
Pazardzhik Bulgaria **68** D3 42 10N 24 20E
Peacehaven East Sussex England **33** C1 50 47N 0 01E
Peace River British Columbia/Alberta Canada **100** L4 57 30N 117 00W
Peace River *tn.* Alberta Canada **100** L4 56 15N 117 18W
Peak District National Park Derbyshire England **36** C3 53 12N 1 50W
Peake Deep Atlantic Ocean **117** F11 43 00N 20 05W
Peak, The *mt.* Derbyshire England **43** E2 53 24N 1 51W
Pearl Ontario Canada **104** C3 48 41N 88 39W
Pearl *r.* Mississippi U.S.A. **103** H3 32 00N 90 00W
Pearl Harbor Hawaiian Islands **119** X18 21 22N 158 00W
Pebble Island Falkland Islands **117** M16 51 20S 59 40W
Peć Yugoslavia **68** D3 42 40N 20 19E
Pechenga U.S.S.R. **67** G4 69 28N 31 04E
Pechora *r.* U.S.S.R. **70** H9 66 00N 52 00E
Pechora U.S.S.R. **70** H9 65 14N 57 18E
Pecos *r.* U.S.A. **102** F3 30 00N 102 00W
Pecos Texas U.S.A. **102** F3 31 25N 103 30W
Pécs Hungary **69** C2 46 04N 18 15E
Pedreiras Brazil **114** I12 4 32S 44 40W
Pedro Juan Caballero Paraguay **115** F8 22 30S 55 44W
Peebles Borders Scotland **46** E2 55 39N 3 12W
Peekskill New York U.S.A. **105** F2 41 18N 73 56W
Peel Isle of Man England **41** F1 54 14N 4 42W
Peel *r.* Yukon Territory Canada **100** H6 66 00N 135 00W
Peel Fell *sum.* Scotland/England **46** F2 55 17N 2 35W
Peel Sound Northwest Territory Canada **101** P7 73 50N 95 55W
Peene *r.* G.D.R. **63** B2 53 00N 14 00E
Pegasus Bay New Zealand **87** B2 43 00S 173 00E
Pegu Myanma **80** B7 17 18N 96 31E
Pegunungan Barisan *mts.* Indonesia **80** C3 2 30S 102 00E
Pegunungan Moake *mts.* Indonesia **86** F9 4 00S 137 30E
Pegunungan Muller *mts.* Indonesia **80** E4 1 00N 113 40E
Pegunungan Schwaner *mts.* Indonesia **80** E3 1 00S 112 00E
Pegunungan Van Rees *mts.* Indonesia **86** F9 2 30S 138 00E
Pegu Yoma *mts.* Myanma **77** H3 19 00N 96 00E
Peipus, Lake *see* Ozero Chudskoye
Pekalongan Indonesia **80** D2 6 54S 109 37E
Pekanbaru Indonesia **80** C4 0 33N 101 30E
Peking *see* Beijing
Pelee Point Ontario Canada **105** D2 41 45N 82 39W
Pelican Point Namibia **95** B3 22 54S 14 25E
Pelješac *i.* Yugoslavia **68** C3 43 00N 17 00E
Pellworm *i.* F.R.G. **63** A2 54 00N 8 00E
Pelly Lake Northwest Territories Canada **101** O6 65 10N 102 30W
Peloponnese *see* Pelopónnisos
Pelopónnisos *(Peloponnese) geog. reg.* Greece **68** D2 37 00N 22 00E
Pelotas Brazil **115** G6 31 45S 52 20W
Pelsall West Midlands England **35** C2 52 38N 1 58W
Pematangsiantar Indonesia **80** B4 2 59N 99 01E
Pemba Mozambique **95** H5 13 00S 40 30E
Pemba Island Tanzania **95** G6 5 30S 39 50E

Pemba National Park Zaïre 95 E6 9 00S 26 30E
Pembridge Hereford and Worcester England 36 B2 52 14N 2 53W
Pembroke Dyfed Wales 38 B1 51 41N 4 55W
Pembroke Ontario Canada 105 E3 45 49N 77 08W
Pembroke Dock Dyfed Wales 38 B1 51 42N 4 56W
Pembrokeshire Coast National Park Dyfed Wales 38 A1 51 50N 5 25W
Pembury Kent England 33 C2 51 08N 0 19E
Peñarroya-Pueblonuevo Spain 66 A2 38 19N 5 16W
Penarth South Glamorgan Wales 38 C1 51 27N 3 11W
Pencoed Mid Glamorgan Wales 38 C1 51 31N 3 30W
Pendlebury Greater Manchester England 42 D2 53 32N 2 21W
Pendleton Oregon U.S.A. 102 C6 45 40N 118 46W
Penedo Brazil 114 J10 10 16S 36 33W
Penha Brazil 116 B2 22 49S 43 17W
Penicuik Lothian Scotland 45 D1 55 50N 3 14W
Peninsula de Taitao p. Chile 115 C3 46 30N 75 00W
Péninsule d'Ungava p. Québec Canada 101 U5 60 00N 74 00W
Penistone South Yorkshire England 43 F2 53 32N 1 37W
Penketh Cheshire England 40 B2 53 23N 2 40W
Penkridge Staffordshire England 35 B3 52 44N 2 07W
Penmaenmawr Gwynedd Wales 38 C3 53 16N 3 54W
Penner r. India 77 D2 14 30N 77 30E
Pennines hills North West England 40 B3
Pennsylvania state U.S.A. 105 E2 41 00N 78 00W
Penonomé Panama 109 H1 8 30N 80 20W
Penrhyndeudraeth Gwynedd Wales 38 B2 52 56N 4 04W
Penrith Cumbria England 44 B1 54 40N 2 44W
Penryn Cornwall England 30 B2 50 09N 5 06W
Pensacola Florida U.S.A. 103 I3 30 26N 87 12W
Pensacola Mountains Antarctica 121 84 00S 60 00W
Pensby Merseyside England 42 A2 53 21N 3 06W
Penshurst Kent England 34 D1 51 11N 0 11E
Penshiva Cornwall England 30 C2 50 30N 4 25W
Pentenwell Lake Wisconsin U.S.A. 104 C2 44 00N 90 00W
Penticton British Columbia Canada 100 L2 49 29N 119 38W
Pentland Firth sd. Scotland 47 C1 58 45N 3 10W
Pentland Hills Scotland 45 D1 55 45N 3 30W
Pen-y-ghent sum. North Yorkshire England 40 B3 54 10N 2 14W
Penygroes Gwynedd Wales 38 B3 53 04N 4 17W
Penza U.S.S.R. 70 G6 53 11N 45 00E
Penzance Cornwall England 30 B2 50 07N 5 33W
PEOPLE'S DEMOCRATIC REPUBLIC OF YEMEN (P.D.R.Y.) see SOUTH YEMEN
Peoria Illinois U.S.A. 104 C2 40 43N 89 38W
Pequena Arroio Fundo r. Brazil 116 B2 22 54S 43 24W
Pereira Colombia 114 B13 4 47N 75 46W
Perhojöki r. Finland 67 E3 63 30N 24 00E
Peribonca River Québec Canada 105 F3 49 00N 71 00W
Périgueux France 61 B2 45 12N 0 44E
Perm' U.S.S.R. 70 H7 58 01N 56 10E
Pernambuco admin. Brazil 114 J11 8 00S 37 30W
Pernik Bulgaria 68 D3 42 36N 23 03E
Pernis Netherlands 65 B1 51 53N 4 23E
Péronne France 61 B2 49 56N 2 57E
Perovo U.S.S.R. 70 N1 55 44N 37 46E
Perpignan France 61 B1 42 42N 2 54E
Perranporth Cornwall England 30 B2 50 20N 5 09W
Perros-Guirec France 61 A2 48 49N 3 27W
Perryville Missouri U.S.A. 104 C1 37 43N 87 52W
Pershore Hereford and Worcester England 36 B2 52 07N 2 05W
Perth Australia 86 B3 31 58S 115 49E
Perth Ontario Canada 105 E2 44 54N 76 15W
Perth Tayside Scotland 45 D2 56 24N 3 28W
Perth Amboy New Jersey U.S.A. 106 40 31N 74 17W
PERU 114 B10
Peru Basin Pacific Ocean 119 Q6 18 00S 95 00W
Peru-Chile Trench Pacific Ocean 119 S6 13 00S 87 00W
Perugia Italy 68 B3 43 07N 12 23E
Peruwelz Belgium 64 C2 50 30N 3 35E
Pesaro Italy 68 B3 43 54N 12 54E
Pescara Italy 68 B3 42 27N 14 13E
Peshawar Pakistan 77 C6 34 01N 71 40E
Pessac France 61 A1 44 49N 0 37W
Petah Tiqwa Israel 78 O11 32 05N 34 53E
Petaluma California U.S.A. 102 B4 38 13N 122 39W
Pétange Luxembourg 64 E1 49 33N 5 53E
Petare Venezuela 114 D15 10 31N 66 50W
Petauke Zambia 95 F5 14 15S 31 20E
Peterborough Australia 86 F3 33 00S 138 51E
Peterborough Cambridgeshire England 33 B3 52 35N 0 15W
Peterborough Ontario Canada 105 E2 44 19N 78 20W
Peterculter Grampian Scotland 46 F4 57 05N 2 16W
Peterhead Grampian Scotland 46 G4 57 30N 1 46W
Peterlee Durham England 44 C1 54 46N 1 19W
Petersburg Alaska U.S.A. 100 I4 56 49N 132 58W
Petersburg Virginia U.S.A. 105 E1 37 14N 77 24W
Petersfield Hampshire England 33 B2 51 00N 0 56W
Petitot r. British Columbia Canada 100 K4 59 40N 122 30W
Petoskey Michigan U.S.A. 104 D3 45 22N 84 59W
Petra hist. site. Jordan 78 O10 30 19N 35 26E
Petrolina Brazil 114 I11 9 22S 40 30W
Petropavlovsk U.S.S.R. 71 I6 54 53N 69 13E
Petropavlovsk-Kamchatskiy U.S.S.R. 71 R6 53 03N 158 43E
Petrópolis Brazil 115 I8 22 30S 43 06W
Petroşeni Romania 69 D2 45 25N 23 22E
Petrozavodsk U.S.S.R. 70 F8 61 46N 34 19E
Petworth West Sussex England 33 B1 50 59N 0 38W
Pevek U.S.S.R. 71 T9 69 41N 170 19E
Pevensey East Sussex England 33 C1 50 49N 0 20E
Pewsey Wiltshire England 31 F3 51 21N 1 46W
Pewsey, Vale of Wiltshire England 31 F3 51 20N 1 50W
Pfälzer Wald mts. F.R.G. 63 A1 49 00N 8 00E
Pforzheim F.R.G. 63 A1 48 53N 8 41E
Phenix City Alabama U.S.A. 103 I3 32 28N 85 01W
Philadelphia Pennsylvania U.S.A. 105 E1 40 00N 75 10W
Philippeville Belgium 64 D2 50 12N 4 33E
Philippine Sea Pacific Ocean 118 C10 21 00N 130 00E
PHILIPPINES, THE 80 G7–H5
Philippine Trench Pacific Ocean 118 C9 12 00N 127 00E
Philip Smith Mountains Alaska U.S.A. 100 F6 68 20N 148 00W
Phillipsburg New Jersey U.S.A. 105 E2 40 41N 75 12W
Phnom Penh Cambodia 80 C6 11 35N 104 55E
Phoenix Arizona U.S.A. 102 D3 33 30N 112 03W
Phoenix Island Pacific Ocean 118 I7 3 30S 174 30W
Phoenix Islands Kiribati 118 I7 4 40S 177 30W
Phuket Thailand 80 B5 7 52N 98 22E
Piacenza Italy 68 A3 45 03N 9 41E
Piatra Neamt Romania 69 E2 46 53N 26 23E
Piauí admin. Brazil 114 I11 7 30S 43 00W
Pickering North Yorkshire England 40 D3 54 14N 0 46W
Pickering Ontario Canada 105 E2 43 48N 79 11W
Pickering, Vale of North Yorkshire England 40 D3 54 10N 0 45W
Pickle Lake Ontario Canada 101 Q3 52 30N 90 00W
Pico Cristóbal mt. Colombia 114 C15 10 53N 73 48W
Pico de Itambé mt. Brazil 114 I9 18 23S 43 21W
Pico-Rivera California U.S.A. 107 B2 33 59N 118 06W
Picos Brazil 114 I11 7 05S 41 24W
Picton New Zealand 87 B2 41 17S 174 02E
Picton Ontario Canada 105 E2 44 01N 77 09W
Pidurutalagala mt. Sri Lanka 77 E1 7 01N 80 45E
Piedade Brazil 116 B2 22 53S 43 19W
Piedmont Missouri U.S.A. 104 B1 37 09N 90 42W
Piedras Negras Mexico 108 D5 28 40N 100 32W
Pielinen l. Finland 67 F3 63 20N 29 40E
Pierre South Dakota U.S.A. 102 F5 44 23N 100 20W
Pietermaritzburg Republic of South Africa 95 F2 29 36S 30 24E
Pietersburg Republic of South Africa 95 E3 23 54S 29 23E
Pijijiapan Mexico 108 F3 15 42N 93 12W
Pijnacker Netherlands 65 B2 52 00N 4 27E
Pikangikum Lake Ontario Canada 101 Q3 52 15N 94 00W
Pikes Peak Colorado U.S.A. 102 E4 38 50N 105 03W
Pik Kommunizma mt. U.S.S.R. 70 J3 38 59N 72 01E
Pik Pobedy mt. U.S.S.R. 71 J4 42 25N 80 15E
Piła Poland 69 C3 53 09N 16 44E
Pilar Paraguay 115 F7 26 51S 58 20W
Pilgrims Hatch Essex England 34 D2 51 38N 0 17E
Pilica r. Poland 69 D3 52 00N 21 00E
Pimenta Bueno Brazil 114 E10 11 40S 61 14W
Pinang i. Malaysia 80 C5 5 30N 100 20E
Pinar del Rio Cuba 109 H4 22 24N 83 42W
Pindhos mts. Greece 68 D2 40 00N 21 00E
Pine Bluff Arkansas U.S.A. 103 H3 34 13N 92 00W
Pingdingshan China 81 H4 33 50N 113 20E
P'ing-tung Taiwan 81 J2 22 40N 120 30E
Pingxiang China 81 H3 27 35N 113 46E
Piniós r. Greece 68 D2 39 00N 22 00E
Pink Mountain tn. British Columbia Canada 100 K4 57 10N 122 36W
Pinneberg F.R.G. 63 A2 53 40N 9 49E
Pinsk U.S.S.R. 70 E6 52 08N 26 01E
Piombino Italy 68 B3 42 56N 10 32E
Piotrków Trybunalski Poland 69 C3 51 27N 19 40E
Piraiévs Greece 68 D2 37 57N 23 42E
Pirapora Brazil 114 I9 17 20S 44 54W
Piratininga Brazil 116 C2 22 56S 43 04W
Pirbright Surrey England 34 B1 51 18N 0 39W
Pírgos Greece 68 D2 37 40N 21 27E
Pírgos Greece 68 E2 35 00N 25 10E
Pirineos (Pyrénées) mts. Spain/France 66 C3 42 50N 0 30E
Pirin Planina mts. Bulgaria 68 D3 41 00N 23 00E
Pirmasens F.R.G. 63 A1 49 12N 7 37E
Pirna G.D.R. 63 B2 50 58N 13 58E
Pisa Italy 68 B3 43 43N 10 24E
Pisco Peru 114 B10 13 46S 76 12W
Písek Czechoslovakia 69 B2 49 18N 14 10E
Pistoia Italy 68 B3 43 56N 10 55E
Pitanga Brazil 115 G8 24 45S 51 43W
Pitcairn Islands Pacific Ocean 119 N5 25 04S 130 06W
Piteå Sweden 67 E4 65 19N 21 30E
Pite älv r. Sweden 67 D4 66 45N 17 20E
Piteşti Romania 69 D1 44 51N 24 51E
Pitlochry Tayside Scotland 46 E3 56 43N 3 45W
Pitti Island India 77 C2 11 00N 73 00E
Pittsburgh Pennsylvania U.S.A. 105 E2 40 26N 80 00W
Pittsfield Massachusetts U.S.A. 105 F2 42 27N 73 15W
Piura Peru 114 A11 5 15S 80 38W
Pjórsá r. Iceland 67 I6 64 15N 19 00W
Placentia Bay Newfoundland Canada 101 X2 46 50N 55 00W
Plains Strathclyde Scotland 45 C1 55 53N 3 55W
Plainview Texas U.S.A. 102 F3 34 12N 101 43W
Planalto de Mato Grosso geog. reg. Brazil 114 F10 13 00S 56 00W
Plasencia Spain 66 A3 40 02N 6 05W
Plateau de Langres hills France 61 B2 47 40N 4 55E
Plateau des 15 ans tn. Congo 92 A2 4 16S 15 16E
Plateau du Barrois hills France 61 C2 48 30N 5 15E
Plateau du Tademaït plat. Algeria 93 F8 28 45N 2 00E
Plateaux du Limousin hills France 61 B2 45 45N 1 15E
Platte r. U.S.A. 102 F5 41 00N 100 00W
Platteville Wisconsin U.S.A. 104 B2 42 44N 90 29E
Plattsburgh New York U.S.A. 105 F2 44 42N 73 29W
Plauen G.D.R. 63 B2 50 29N 12 08E
Plauer See l. G.D.R. 63 B2 53 00N 12 00E
Playa Agua Dulce beach Peru 116 E4 12 08S 77 02W
Playa Azul Mexico 108 D3 18 00N 102 24W
Playa Conchán beach Peru 116 E4 12 13S 77 01W
Playa Marquez beach Peru 116 E5 11 57S 77 08W
Playa Oquendo beach Peru 116 E5 11 59S 77 08W
Plenty, Bay of New Zealand 87 C3 37 30S 117 00E
Plessisville Québec Canada 105 F3 46 14N 71 46W
Pleven Bulgaria 68 D3 43 25N 24 40E
Płock Poland 69 C3 52 32N 19 40E
Plockton Highland Scotland 46 C4 57 20N 5 40W
Ploieşti Romania 69 E1 44 57N 26 01E
Płoty Poland 69 C3 53 48N 15 14E
Plovdiv Bulgaria 68 D3 42 08N 24 45E
Plunge U.S.S.R. 69 D4 55 52N 21 49E
Plym r. Devon England 31 C2 50 28N 4 05W
Plymouth Devon England 31 C2 50 23N 4 10W
Plymouth Indiana U.S.A. 104 C2 41 20N 86 19W
Plympton Devon England 31 C2 50 23N 4 03W
Plymstock Devon England 31 C2 50 21N 4 07W
Plynlimon mt. Dyfed Wales 38 C3 52 28N 3 47W
Plyussa r. U.S.S.R. 67 F2 58 40N 28 15E
Plzeň Czechoslovakia 69 B2 49 45N 13 25E
Po r. Italy 68 B4 45 00N 11 00E
Pocatello Idaho U.S.A. 102 D5 42 53N 112 26W
Pochutla Mexico 108 E3 15 45N 96 30W
Pocklington Humberside England 40 D2 53 56N 0 46W
Pocomoke City Maryland U.S.A. 105 E1 38 04N 75 35W
Podara India 76 K2 22 34N 88 17E
Podkamennaya (Stony) Tunguska r. U.S.S.R. 71 L8/M8 62 00N 95 00E
Podol'sk U.S.S.R. 70 F7 55 23N 37 32E
P'ohang South Korea 81 K5 36 00N 129 26E
Pohénégamook Québec Canada 105 G3 47 28N 69 17W
Pointe-à-Pitre Lesser Antilles 109 L3 16 14N 61 32W
Pointe au Baril Station tn. Ontario Canada 105 D3 45 36N 80 23W
Point Hope tn. Alaska U.S.A. 100 B6 68 20N 166 50W
Point-Noire tn. Congo 95 B7 4 46S 11 53E
Poissy France 60 A2 48 56N 2 03E
Poitiers France 61 B2 46 35N 0 20E
Pokhara Nepal 77 E5 28 14N 83 58E
POLAND 69 C3
Polbeth Lothian Scotland 45 C1 55 53N 3 32W
Polegate East Sussex England 33 C1 50 50N 0 15E
Polesworth Warwickshire England 35 D2 52 44N 1 36W
Poles'ye geog. reg. U.S.S.R. 70 E6 53 00N 27 30E
Poles'ye Pripyat' (Pripet Marshes) marsh U.S.S.R. 70 E6 52 00N 27 00E
Políyiros Greece 68 D3 40 23N 23 25E
Pollachi India 77 D2 10 38N 77 00E
Pollensa Balearic Islands 66 E4 39 52N 3 01E
Pollokshaws Strathclyde Scotland 45 B1 55 49N 4 19W
Polotsk U.S.S.R. 69 E4 55 30N 28 43E
Polperro Cornwall England 30 C2 50 19N 4 31W
Poltava U.S.S.R. 70 F5 49 35N 34 35E
Poluostrov Rybachiy p. U.S.S.R. 67 G4 69 50N 32 35E
Polynesia geog. reg. Pacific Ocean 119 J4–L9
Pomeranian Bay Baltic Sea 69 B3 54 00N 14 00E
Ponca Nebraska U.S.A. 104 A2 42 35N 96 42W
Ponca City Oklahoma U.S.A. 103 G4 36 41N 97 04W
Ponce Puerto Rico 109 K3 18 01N 66 36W
Pondicherry India 77 D2 11 59N 79 50E
Pondine Dyfed Wales 38 B1 51 34N 4 35W
Pond Inlet tn. Northwest Territories Canada 101 T7 72 40N 77 59W
Ponferrada Spain 66 A3 42 33N 6 35W
Ponoka Alberta Canada 100 M3 52 42N 113 33W
Pont r. Northumberland England 44 C2 55 02N 1 55W
Ponta da Marca c. Angola 95 B4 16 33S 11 43E
Ponta das Salinas c. Angola 95 B5 12 50S 12 54E
Ponta Grossa Brazil 115 G7 25 07S 50 09W
Pont-à-Mousson France 61 C2 48 55N 6 03E
Ponta Porã Brazil 115 F8 22 27S 55 39W
Pontardawe West Glamorgan Wales 38 C1 51 44N 3 52W
Pontardulais West Glamorgan Wales 38 B1 51 43N 4 02W
Pontchartrain, Lake Louisiana U.S.A. 103 H3 30 00N 90 00W
Pontefract West Yorkshire England 43 G3 53 42N 1 18W
Ponteland Northumberland England 44 C2 55 03N 1 44W
Ponte Leccia Corsica 61 C1 42 28N 9 12E
Ponterwyd Dyfed Wales 38 C2 52 25N 3 50W
Pontevedra Spain 66 A3 42 25N 8 39W
Pontiac Michigan U.S.A. 105 D2 42 39N 83 18W
Pontianak Indonesia 80 D3 0 05S 109 16E
Pontivy France 61 A2 48 04N 2 58W
Pontrilas Hereford and Worcester England 36 B1 51 57N 2 53W
Pontycymer Mid Glamorgan Wales 38 C1 51 36N 3 35W
Pontypool Gwent Wales 38 C1 51 43N 3 02W
Pontypridd Mid Glamorgan Wales 38 C1 51 37N 3 22W
Poole Dorset England 31 F2 50 43N 1 59W
Poolewe Highland Scotland 46 C4 57 45N 5 37W
Pooley Bridge tn. Cumbria England 44 B1 54 38N 2 49W
Pool Malebo l. Zaïre 95 C7 5 00S 17 00E
Popayán Colombia 114 B13 2 27N 76 32W
Poperinge Belgium 64 B2 50 52N 2 44E
Poplar Bluff tn. Missouri U.S.A. 103 H4 36 16N 90 25W
Popocatepetl mt. Mexico 108 E3 19 02N 98 38W
Popondetta Papua New Guinea 86 H8 8 45S 148 15E
Porbandar India 76 B4 21 40N 69 40E
Porcupine r. U.S.A./Canada 100 G6 67 15N 144 00W
Pordenone Italy 68 B4 45 58N 12 39E
Pori Finland 67 E3 61 28N 21 45E
Porirua New Zealand 87 B2 41 08S 174 52E
Porlamar Venezuela 109 L2 11 01N 63 54W
Porlock Somerset England 31 D3 51 14N 3 36W
Poronaysk U.S.S.R. 71 Q5 49 13N 143 05E
Porsangen fj. Norway 67 F5 70 40N 25 30E
Porsgrunn Norway 67 B2 59 10N 9 40E
Portadown Armagh Northern Ireland 48 E4 54 26N 6 27W
Portaferry Down Northern Ireland 48 F4 54 23N 5 33W
Portage la Prairie Manitoba Canada 104 A3 49 58N 98 20W
Portage Wisconsin U.S.A. 104 C2 43 33N 89 29W
Port Alberni British Columbia Canada 100 K2 49 11N 124 49W
Portalegre Portugal 66 A2 39 17N 7 25W
Portales New Mexico U.S.A. 102 F3 34 12N 103 20W
Port Alfred Québec Canada 101 U2 48 20N 70 54W
Port Angeles Washington U.S.A. 102 B6 48 06N 123 26W
Port Antonio Jamaica 109 R8 18 10N 76 27W
Portarlington Laois / Offaly Irish Republic 48 D3 53 10N 7 11W
Port Arthur Texas U.S.A. 103 H2 29 55N 93 56W
Port Askaig Strathclyde Scotland 46 B2 55 51N 6 07W
Port Augusta Australia 86 F3 32 30S 137 27E
Port-au-Prince Haiti 109 J3 18 33N 72 20W
Port Austin Michigan U.S.A. 105 D2 44 04N 82 59W
Port Blair Andaman Islands 77 G2 11 40N 92 44E
Port Chalmers New Zealand 87 B1 45 48S 170 38E
Port Colborne Ontario Canada 105 E2 42 53N 79 16W
Port Darwin Falkland Islands 117 M16 51 51S 58 55W
Port-de-Paix Haiti 109 J3 19 56N 72 52W
Port Dinorwic Gwynedd Wales 38 B3 53 11N 4 13W
Port Elgin Ontario Canada 105 D2 44 25N 81 23W
Port Elizabeth Republic of South Africa 95 E1 33 58S 25 36E
Port Ellen Strathclyde Scotland 46 B2 55 39N 6 12W
Port Erin Isle of Man British Isles 41 F1 54 05N 4 45W
Port Gentil Gabon 93 G2 0 40S 8 50E
Port Glasgow Strathclyde Scotland 45 A1 55 56N 4 41W
Port Harcourt Nigeria 93 G3 4 43N 7 05E
Port Hardy British Columbia Canada 100 J3 50 41N 127 30W
Port Hawkesbury Nova Scotia Canada 101 W2 45 36N 61 22W
Porthcawl Mid Glamorgan Wales 38 C1 51 29N 3 43W
Port Hedland Australia 86 B5 20 24S 118 36E
Porthleven Cornwall England 30 B2 50 30N 5 21W
Porthmadog Gwynedd Wales 38 B2 52 55N 4 08W
Port Hope Ontario Canada 105 E2 43 58N 78 18W
Port Huron Michigan U.S.A. 105 D2 42 59N 82 28W
Portile de Fier (Iron Gate) gorge Romania / Yugoslavia 69 D1 44 00N 22 00E
Portimão Portugal 66 A2 37 08N 8 32W
Portinho r. Brazil 116 A1 23 01S 43 33W
Port Isaac Cornwall England 30 C2 50 35N 4 49W
Portishead Avon England 31 E3 51 30N 2 46W
Port Jervis New York U.S.A. 105 F2 41 22N 74 40W
Port Kaituma Guyana 114 F14 7 44N 59 53W
Portland Australia 86 G2 38 21S 141 38E
Portland Bill c. Dorset England 31 E2 50 31N 2 27W
Portland Maine U.S.A. 105 F2 43 41N 70 18W
Portland Oregon U.S.A. 102 B6 45 32N 122 40W
Portland Point c. Jamaica 109 Q7 17 42N 77 11W
Portland, Isle of Dorset England 31 E2 50 33N 2 27W
Portlaoise Laois Irish Republic 48 D3 53 02N 7 17W
Portlaw Waterford Irish Republic 48 D2 52 17N 7 19W
Port Lincoln Australia 86 F3 34 43S 135 49E
Port Macquarie Australia 86 I3 31 28S 152 25E
Portmahomack Highland Scotland 46 E4 57 49N 3 50W
Port Maria Jamaica 109 R8 18 22N 76 54W
Portmarnock Dublin Irish Republic 49 B2 53 26N 6 08W
Port Morant Jamaica 109 R7 17 53N 76 20W
Port Moresby Papua New Guinea 86 H8 9 30S 147 07E
Portnaguran Western Isles Scotland 46 B5 58 17N 6 13W
Portnahaven Strathclyde Scotland 46 B2 55 41N 6 31W
Portnockie Grampian Scotland 46 F4 57 42N 2 54W
Port Nolloth Republic of South Africa 95 C2 29 17S 16 51E
Porto (Oporto) Portugal 66 A3 41 09N 8 37W
Porto Alegre Brazil 115 G6 30 03S 51 10W
Porto Amboim Angola 95 B5 10 47S 13 43E
Portobello Lothian Scotland 45 D1 55 58N 3 07W
Port of Menteith Central Scotland 45 B2 56 11N 4 18W
Port of Ness Western Isles Scotland 46 B5 58 29N 6 13W
Port of Spain Trinidad and Tobago 109 L2 10 38N 61 31W
Pôrto Grande Brazil 114 G13 0 43N 51 23W
Porto Novo Benin 93 F4 6 30N 2 47E
Porto Tórres Italy 61 C1 40 51N 8 24E
Porto-Vecchio Corsica 61 C1 41 35N 9 16E
Pôrto Velho Brazil 114 E11 8 45S 63 54W
Portoviejo Ecuador 114 A12 1 07S 80 28W
Portpatrick Dumfries & Galloway Scotland 46 C1 54 51N 5 07W
Port Perry Ontario Canada 105 E2 44 06N 78 58W
Port Pirie Australia 86 F3 33 11S 138 01E
Portrane Dublin Irish Republic 49 B2 53 29N 6 06W
Portreath Cornwall England 30 B2 50 51N 5 17W
Portree Highland Scotland 46 B4 57 24N 6 12W
Port Royal Jamaica 109 R7 17 55N 76 52W
Portrush Northern Ireland 48 E5 55 12N 6 40W
Port Said Egypt 78 D5 31 17N 32 18E
Port St. Mary Isle of Man British Isles 41 F1 54 04N 4 44W
Portsmouth Hampshire England 32 A1 50 48N 1 05W
Portsmouth New Hampshire U.S.A. 105 F2 43 03N 70 47W
Portsmouth Ohio U.S.A. 105 D1 38 45N 82 59W
Portsmouth Virginia U.S.A. 105 E1 36 50N 76 20W
Portsoy Grampian Scotland 46 F4 57 41N 2 41W
Port Stanley Ontario Canada 105 D2 42 40N 81 14W
Portstewart Northern Ireland 48 E5 55 11N 6 43W
Port Sudan Sudan 78 E2 19 38N 37 07E
Port Talbot West Glamorgan Wales 38 C1 51 36N 3 47W
Porttipahdan tekojärvi l. Finland 67 F4 68 15N 26 00E
PORTUGAL 66 A2
Portumna Galway Irish Republic 48 C3 53 06N 8 13W
Port Washington New York U.S.A. 106 D2 40 50N 73 41W
Port Washington Wisconsin U.S.A. 104 C2 43 23N 87 54W
Port William Dumfries & Galloway Scotland 46 D1 54 46N 4 35W
Porus Jamaica 109 Q8 18 02N 77 25W
Posadas Argentina 115 F7 27 27S 55 50W
Potenza Italy 68 C3 40 38N 15 48E
Potiskum Nigeria 93 H5 11 40N 11 03E
Potomac River U.S.A. 105 E1 38 00N 77 00W
Poto-Poto Congo 92 A2 4 16S 15 17E
Poto-Poto du Djoué Congo 92 A2 4 18S 15 13E
Potosí Bolivia 114 D9 19 34S 65 45W
Potsdam admin. G.D.R. 63 B2 52 00N 12 00E
Potsdam G.D.R. 63 B2 52 24N 13 04E
Potsdam New York U.S.A. 105 F2 44 40N 75 01W
Potten End Hertfordshire England 34 B3 51 46N 0 31W
Potter's Bar Hertfordshire England 34 C3 51 42N 0 11W
Potter's Cross Staffordshire England 35 B2 52 27N 2 12W
Potton Bedfordshire England 33 B3 52 08N 0 14W
Poughkeepsie New York U.S.A. 105 F2 41 43N 73 56W
Poulaphouca Reservoir Wicklow Irish Republic 48 E3 53 10N 6 30W
Poulton-le-Fylde Lancashire England 42 B3 53 51N 3 00W
Pound Bank Hereford & Worcester England 35 A2 52 21N 2 24W
Poverty Bay New Zealand 87 C3 38 40S 178 00E
Povungnituk Québec Canada 101 T4 59 45N 77 20W
Powell, Lake U.S.A. 102 D4 37 00N 110 00W
Powell River tn. British Columbia Canada 100 K2 49 54N 124 34W
Powmill Tayside Scotland 45 C2 56 09N 3 35W
Powys co. Wales 38 C2 52 10N 3 30W
Poyang Hu l. China 81 I3 29 00N 116 30E
Poynton Cheshire England 42 D2 53 21N 2 07W
Poza Rica Mexico 108 E4 20 34N 97 26W
Poznań Poland 69 C3 52 25N 16 53E
Pradesh admin. India 77 E5 26 00N 81 00E
Prague see Praha
Praha (Prague) Czechoslovakia 69 B3 50 06N 14 26E
Prairie de Chien tn. Wisconsin U.S.A. 104 B2 43 02N 91 08W
Prairie Dog Town Fork r. U.S.A. 102 F3 34 00N 101 00W
Prato Italy 68 B3 43 53N 11 06E
Pratt Kansas U.S.A. 102 G4 37 40N 98 45W
Prawle Point c. Devon England 31 D2 50 12N 3 44W
Preesall Lancashire England 42 B3 53 55N 2 57W
Prenzlau G.D.R. 63 B2 53 19N 13 52E
Přerov Czechoslovakia 69 C2 49 28N 17 30E
Prescot Merseyside England 42 B2 53 26N 2 48W
Prescott Arizona U.S.A. 102 D3 34 34N 112 28W
Prescott Ontario U.S.A. 105 E2 44 43N 75 33W
Presidence Zaïre 92 A1 4 20S 15 14E
Presidencia Roque Sáenz Peña Argentina 115 E7 26 45S 60 30W
Presidente Prudente Brazil 115 G8 22 09S 51 24W
Presidente Stroessner Paraguay 115 G7 25 32S 54 34W
Prešov Czechoslovakia 69 D2 49 00N 21 10E
Presque Isle Maine U.S.A. 105 G3 46 42N 68 01W
Prestatyn Clwyd Wales 38 C3 53 20N 3 24W
Prestbury Cheshire England 42 D2 53 16N 2 07W
Presteigne Powys Wales 38 C2 52 17N 3 00W
Preston Lancashire England 42 B3 53 46N 2 42W
Preston Brook tn. Cheshire England 42 B1 53 19N 2 41W
Prestwich Greater Manchester England 42 D2 53 32N 2 17W
Prestwick Strathclyde Scotland 46 D2 55 30N 4 37W
Prestwood Buckinghamshire England 34 A3 51 42N 0 43W
Pretoria Republic of South Africa 95 E2 25 45S 28 12E
Préveza Greece 68 D2 38 59N 20 45E
Příbram Czechoslovakia 69 B2 49 42N 14 01E
Price r. Utah U.S.A. 102 D4 39 00N 110 00W

Q

R

Rhynie Grampian Scotland **46** F4 57 19N 2 50W
Ribble *r.* Lancashire England **42** B3 53 44N 2 56W
Ribblesdale *v.* North Yorkshire England **42** D4 54 00N 2 18W
Ribeirão Prêto Brazil **114** H8 21 09S 47 48W
Riberalta Bolivia **114** D10 10 59S 66 06W
Riccall North Yorkshire England **43** G3 53 51N 1 04W
Richhill Armagh Northern Ireland **48** E4 54 22N 6 33W
Richibucto New Brunswick Canada **101** V2 46 42N 64 54W
Richland Center Wisconsin U.S.A. **104** B2 43 22N 90 24W
Richland Washington U.S.A. **102** C6 46 17N 119 17W
Richmond Australia **86** G5 20 45S 143 05E
Richmond California U.S.A. **102** B4 37 56N 122 20W
Richmond Indiana U.S.A. **104** D1 39 50N 84 51W
Richmond Kentucky U.S.A. **105** D1 37 45N 84 19W
Richmond New York U.S.A. **106** B1 40 36N 74 10W
Richmond New Zealand **87** B2 41 20S 173 10E
Richmond North Yorkshire England **40** C3 54 24N 1 44W
Richmond Virginia U.S.A. **105** E1 37 34N 77 27W
Richmond upon Thames Greater London England **34** C2 51 28N 0 19W
Richmond Valley New York U.S.A. **106** B1 40 31N 74 13W
Rickmansworth Hertfordshire England **34** B2 51 38N 0 29W
Ridderkerk Netherlands **65** C1 51 53N 4 36E
Riddlesden West Yorkshire England **43** E3 53 54N 1 51W
Ridgewood New Jersey U.S.A. **106** B2 40 58N 74 08W
Ried Austria **63** B1 48 13N 13 29E
Riesa G.D.R. **63** B2 51 18N 13 18E
Rieti Italy **68** B3 42 24N 12 51E
Rif Mountains Morocco **66** A2 35 00N 5 00W
Riga U.S.S.R. **67** E2 56 53N 24 08E
Riga, Gulf of U.S.S.R. **67** E2 57 30N 23 30E
Rijeka Yugoslavia **68** B4 45 20N 14 27E
Rijn *(Rhin, Rhein, Rhine) r.* Netherlands **64** F3 51 53N 6 05E
Rijnsburg Netherlands **65** B2 52 11N 4 27E
Rijssen Netherlands **64** F4 52 18N 6 31E
Rijswijk Netherlands **65** B2 52 02N 4 19E
Rimac Peru **116** E4 12 02S 77 02W
Rimini Italy **68** B3 44 03N 12 34E
Rimnicu Vilcea Romania **69** D2 45 06N 24 21E
Rimouski Québec Canada **105** G3 48 27N 68 32W
Ringgold Isles Fiji **118** V16 16 10S 179 50W
Ringkøbing Fjord Denmark **67** B2 56 00N 8 00E
Ringvassøy *i.* Norway **67** D4 69 55N 19 10E
Ringwood Dorset England **32** A1 50 51N 1 47W
Rio Amazonas *r.* Brazil **114** G12 2 00S 53 00W
Río Apaporis *r.* Colombia **114** C13 1 00N 72 30W
Río Apure *r.* Venezuela **114** D14 7 40N 68 00W
Rio Aquidauana *r.* Brazil **114** F9 20 00S 56 00W
Rio Araguaia *r.* Brazil **114** H11 7 20S 49 00W
Río Arauca *r.* Venezuela **114** D14 7 10N 68 30W
Riobamba Ecuador **114** B12 1 44S 78 40W
Río Bermejo Argentina **115** E7 25 00S 61 00W
Rio Branco *r.* Brazil **114** E13 0 00 62 00W
Rio Branco *tn.* Brazil **114** D11 9 59S 67 49W
Río Caqueta *r.* Colombia **114** C12 0 05S 72 30W
Río Caroni *r.* Venezuela **114** E14 7 00N 62 30W
Río Caura *r.* Venezuela **114** E14 6 00N 64 00W
Río Chico *r.* Argentina **115** D4 45 00S 67 30W
Río Chico *r.* Argentina **115** D3 49 00S 70 00W
Río Chillón *r.* Peru **116** E5 11 57S 77 07W
Río Chubut *r.* Argentina **115** D4 43 30S 67 30W
Río Colorado *r.* Argentina **115** D5 37 30S 69 00W
Río Corrientes *r.* Peru **114** B12 2 30S 76 30W
Río Cuarto *tn.* Argentina **115** E6 33 08S 64 20W
Rio de Janeiro *admin.* Brazil **115** I8 22 00S 42 30W
Rio de Janeiro *tn.* Brazil **116** C2 22 53S 43 17W
Río de la Plata *r.* Uruguay / Argentina **115** F5 35 00S 57 00W
Rio de Para *r.* Brazil **114** H12 1 00S 48 00W
Río Deseado *r.* Argentina **115** D3 47 00S 68 00W
Río Dulce *r.* Argentina **115** E7 29 00S 63 00W
Río Gallegos *tn.* Argentina **115** D2 51 35S 68 10W
Río Grande *r.* Bolivia **114** E9 18 00S 65 00W
Rio Grande *r.* Brazil **114** G8 20 00S 50 00W
Rio Grande *r.* Mexico / U.S.A. **108** D5/D6 30 00N 104 00W
Río Grande *tn.* Argentina **115** D2 53 45S 67 46W
Rio Grande *tn.* Brazil **115** G6 32 03S 52 08W
Río Grande *tn.* Mexico **108** D4 23 50N 103 02W
Rio Grande do Norte *admin.* Brazil **114** J11 6 00S 37 00W
Rio Grande do Sul *admin.* Brazil **115** G7 28 00N 52 30W
Rio Grande Rise Atlantic Ocean **117** E3 32 00S 36 00W
Río Guainía *r.* Colombia / Venezuela **114** D13 2 30N 67 30W
Río Guaporé *r.* Brazil / Bolivia **114** E10 13 00S 62 00W
Río Guaviare *r.* Colombia **114** C13 3 00N 70 00W
Rio Gurgueia *r.* Brazil **114** I11 9 00S 44 00W
Rio Gurupi *r.* Brazil **114** H12 4 00S 47 00W
Riohacha Colombia **114** C15 11 34N 72 58W
Rio Hondo *r.* California U.S.A. **107** B3 34 00N 118 07W
Rio Iguaçu *r.* Brazil **115** G7 26 00S 51 00W
Río Inirida *r.* Colombia **114** C13/D13 2 30N 70 00W
Rio Japurá *r.* Brazil **114** D12 2 00S 67 30W
Rio Jari *r.* Brazil **114** G13 2 00N 54 00W
Rio Jequitinhonha *r.* Brazil **114** I9 16 00S 41 00W
Rio Juruá *r.* Brazil **114** D12 4 30S 67 00W
Rio Juruena *r.* Brazil **114** F11 10 00S 57 40W
Rio Madeira *r.* Brazil **114** E11 6 00S 61 30W
Río Madre de Dios *r.* Bolivia **114** D10 12 00S 68 00W
Río Magdalena *r.* Colombia **114** C14 8 00N 73 30W
Río Mamoré *r.* Bolivia **114** E9 15 00S 65 00W
Río Marañón *r.* Peru **114** B12 4 50S 77 30W
Río Meta *r.* Colombia **114** C14 6 00N 71 00W
Río Napo *r.* Peru **114** C12 2 30S 73 30W
Río Negro *r.* Argentina **115** E5 40 00S 65 00W
Rio Negro *r.* Brazil **114** D12 0 05S 67 00W
Río Negro *r.* Uruguay **115** F6 33 00S 57 30W
Río Orinoco *r.* Venezuela **114** E14 8 00N 64 00W
Río Paraguá *r.* Bolivia **114** E10 14 00S 61 30W
Río Paragua *r.* Venezuela **114** E14 6 00N 63 30W
Rio Paraguay *r.* Paraguay / Argentina **115** F7 26 30S 58 00W
Río Paraná *r.* Paraguay / Argentina **115** F7 27 00S 56 00W
Rio Paranaiba *r.* Brazil **114** H9 18 00S 49 00W
Rio Pardo *r.* Brazil **114** J9 15 10S 40 00W
Rio Parnaiba *r.* Brazil **114** I11 7 30S 45 00W
Río Parana Panema *r.* Brazil **115** G8 22 30S 52 00W
Río Pastaza *r.* Peru **114** B12 2 30S 77 00W
Río Pilcomayo *r.* Paraguay / Argentina **115** F8 24 00S 60 00W
Río Rimac *r.* Peru **116** F4 12 01S 76 58W
Río Salado *r.* Argentina **115** E7 28 30S 62 30W
Río Salado *r.* Argentina **115** D5 35 00S 66 30W
Río San Miguel *r.* Bolivia **114** E9 15 00S 63 30W
Rio São Francisco *r.* Brazil **114** J11 8 30S 39 00W
Rio Solimões *r.* Brazil **114** D12 3 30S 69 00W
Rio Tapajós *r.* Brazil **114** F11 6 30S 57 00W
Rio Taquari *r.* Brazil **114** F9 18 00S 57 00W
Rio Tefé *r.* Brazil **114** D12 4 30S 65 30W
Rio Teles Pires *r.* Brazil **114** F11 8 00S 57 00W
Rio Tocantins *r.* Brazil **114** H12 3 00S 49 00W
Rio Trombetas *r.* Brazil **114** F13 1 30N 57 00W
Río Ucayali *r.* Peru **114** C11 6 00S 74 00W
Rio Uraricuera *r.* Brazil **114** E13 3 00N 62 30W
Río Uruguay *r.* Uruguay / Argentina **115** F6 32 00S 57 40W
Río Vaupés *r.* Colombia **114** C13 1 30N 72 00W
Río Verde *r.* Paraguay **115** F8 23 20S 60 00W
Rio Verde *tn.* Brazil **114** G9 17 50S 50 55W
Río Verde *tn.* Mexico **108** D4 21 58N 100 00W
Rio Xingu *r.* Brazil **114** G12 2 30S 52 30W
Río Yavari *r.* Peru/Brazil **114** C12 5 00S 72 30S
Ripley Derbyshire England **35** D4 53 03N 1 24W
Ripley North Yorkshire England **43** F4 54 03N 1 34W
Ripley Surrey England **34** B1 51 18N 0 29W
Ripley West Virginia U.S.A. **105** D1 38 49N 81 44W
Ripon North Yorkshire England **40** C3 54 08N 1 31W
Ripponden West Yorkshire England **43** E3 53 41N 1 57W
Risca Gwent Wales **38** C1 51 37N 3 07W
Rishiri-tō *i.* Japan **82** D4 45 10N 141 20E
Rishrā India **76** K2 22 43N 88 19E
Rishton Lancashire England **42** C3 53 47N 2 24W
Risley Cheshire England **42** C2 53 26N 2 32W
Ritter, Mount California U.S.A. **102** C4 37 40N 119 15W
Rivera Uruguay **115** F6 30 52S 55 30W
River Cess *tn.* Liberia **93** D4 5 28N 9 32W
Riverhead New York U.S.A. **105** F2 40 55N 72 40W
Rivers *tn.* Manitoba Canada **101** O3 50 02N 100 14W
Riverside California U.S.A. **102** C3 33 59N 117 22W
Riverton Manitoba Canada **101** P3 51 00N 97 00W
Riverton New Zealand **87** A1 46 21S 168 02E
Rivière aux Feuilles *r.* Québec Canada **101** U4 57 45N 73 00W
Rivière aux Outardes *r.* Québec Canada **105** G4 50 00N 69 00W
Rivière-du-Loup *tn.* Québec Canada **105** G3 47 49N 69 32W
Roanne France **61** B2 46 02N 4 05E
Roanoke *r.* Virginia U.S.A. **105** D1 37 00N 80 00W
Roanoke Virginia U.S.A. **105** E1 37 15N 79 58W
Robertsport Liberia **93** C4 6 45N 11 22W
Roberval Québec Canada **105** F3 48 31N 72 16W
Robin Hood Bay *tn.* North Yorkshire England **40** D3 54 25N 0 33W
Roblin Manitoba Canada **101** O3 51 15N 101 20W
Robson, Mount British Columbia Canada **100** L3 53 08N 118 18W
Roca Alijos *is.* Mexico **108** A4 24 59N 115 49W
Rocas Island Atlantic Ocean **110** 3 50S 33 50W
Rochdale Greater Manchester England **42** D2 53 38N 2 09W
Rochdale Canal England **42** D3 53 40N 2 05W
Rochefort France **61** A2 45 57N 0 58W
Rochelle Illinois U.S.A. **104** C2 41 55N 89 05W
Rochester Indiana U.S.A. **104** C2 41 03N 86 13W
Rochester Kent England **33** C2 51 24N 0 30E
Rochester Minnesota U.S.A. **104** B2 44 01N 92 27W
Rochester New York U.S.A. **105** E2 43 12N 77 37W
Rochester Northumberland England **44** B2 55 16N 2 16W
Rochford Essex England **33** C2 51 36N 0 43E
Rock *r.* U.S.A. **104** C2 42 00N 89 00W
Rock Rapids *tn.* Iowa U.S.A. **104** A2 43 25N 96 10W
Rock Springs *tn.* Wyoming U.S.A. **102** E5 41 35N 109 13W
Rockall Bank Atlantic Ocean **117** G12 58 00N 15 00W
Rockaway Beach New York U.S.A. **106** C1 40 33N 73 55W
Rockaway Inlet New York U.S.A. **106** C1 40 34N 73 56W
Rockefeller Plateau Antarctica **121** 79 00S 140 00W
Rockford Illinois U.S.A. **104** C2 42 16N 89 06W
Rockhampton Australia **86** I5 23 22S 150 32E
Rock Harbor *tn.* Michigan U.S.A. **104** C3 48 08N 88 30W
Rock Hill South Carolina U.S.A. **103** J3 34 55N 81 01W
Rockingham Forest *hills* Northamptonshire England **36** D2 52 30N 0 30W
Rock Island *tn.* Illinois U.S.A. **104** B2 41 30N 90 34W
Rockland Maine U.S.A. **105** G2 44 06N 69 08W
Rockville Center New York U.S.A. **106** D1 40 40N 73 38W
Rockville Indiana U.S.A. **104** C1 39 45N 87 15W
Rocky Mount *tn.* North Carolina U.S.A. **103** K4 35 56N 77 48W
Rocky Mountains U.S.A./Canada **100** K4–N1
Rocroi France **64** D1 49 56N 4 31E
Rodel Western Isles Scotland **46** B4 57 41N 7 05W
Rodenrijs-Berkel Netherlands **65** B1 51 59N 4 29E
Rodez France **61** B1 44 21N 2 34E
Rodhós Greece **68** E2 36 26N 28 14E
Ródhos *(Rhodes) i.* Greece **68** E2 36 00N 28 00E
Roding *r.* Essex England **33** C2 51 45N 0 15E
Rodopi Planina *mts.* Bulgaria **68** D3 41 00N 25 00E
Roelofarendsveen Netherlands **65** C2 52 11N 4 38E
Roer *r.* Netherlands **64** F3 51 10N 6 03E
Roermond Netherlands **64** F3 51 12N 6 00E
Roes Welcome Sound Northwest Territories Canada **101** R5 63 30N 87 30W
Roeselare Belgium **64** C2 50 57N 3 08E
Rogers City Michigan U.S.A. **105** D3 45 24N 83 50W
Rokugo *r.* Japan **83** C3 35 31N 139 46E
Rolla Missouri U.S.A. **103** H4 37 56N 91 55W
Rolleston Staffordshire England **35** C3 52 51N 1 39W
Roma Australia **86** H4 26 32S 148 46E
Roma *(Rome)* Italy **68** B3 41 53N 12 30E
Roman Romania **69** E2 46 56N 26 56E
ROMANIA **69** D2
Romannobridge Borders Scotland **45** D1 55 44N 3 20W
Romans-sur-Isère France **61** C2 45 03N 5 03E
Rome Georgia U.S.A. **103** I3 34 01N 85 02W
Rome New York U.S.A. **105** E2 43 13N 75 28W
Rome *see* Roma
Romford Greater London England **34** D2 51 35N 0 11E
Romiley Greater Manchester England **42** D2 53 24N 2 09W
Romney Marsh Kent England **33** C2 51 03N 0 58E
Rømø *i.* Denmark **63** A3 55 00N 8 00E
Romorantin-Lanthenay France **61** B2 47 22N 1 44E
Romsey Hampshire England **32** A1 50 59N 1 30W
Romsley Hereford & Worcester England **35** B2 52 25N 2 03W
Ronay *i.* Western Isles Scotland **46** A4 57 30N 7 11W
Ronda Spain **66** A2 36 45N 5 10W
Rondônia *admin.* Brazil **114** E10 11 30S 63 00W
Rondonópolis Brazil **114** G9 16 29S 54 37W
Ronne Ice Shelf Antarctica **121** 77 00S 60 00W
Ronsdorf F.R.G. **62** C1 51 13N 7 13E
Ronse Belgium **64** C2 50 45N 3 36E
Roosendaal Netherlands **64** D3 51 32N 4 28E
Roosevelt Island Antarctica **121** 79 00S 160 00W
Rootpark Strathclyde Scotland **45** C1 55 46N 3 40W
Roraima *admin.* Brazil **114** E13 2 30N 62 30W
Rosario Argentina **115** E6 33 00S 60 40W
Rosário Brazil **114** I12 3 00S 44 15W
Rosario Mexico **108** C4 23 00N 105 51W
Rosario Mexico **108** A6 30 02N 115 46W
Rosarito Mexico **108** B5 28 38N 114 02W
Roscoff France **61** A2 48 43N 3 59W
Roscommon *co.* Irish Republic **48** C3 53 45N 8 10W
Roscommon Roscommon Irish Republic **48** C3 53 38N 8 11W
Roscrea Tipperary Irish Republic **48** D2 52 57N 7 47W
Roseau Dominica **109** L3 15 18N 61 23W
Roseburg Oregon U.S.A. **102** B5 43 13N 123 21W
Rosehearty Grampian Scotland **46** F4 57 42N 2 07W
Roselle New Jersey U.S.A. **106** A1 40 40N 74 16W
Rosemead California U.S.A. **107** B3 34 03N 118 07W
Rosenheim F.R.G. **63** B1 47 51N 12 09E
Rosetown Saskatchewan Canada **100** N3 51 34N 107 59W
Rosewell Lothian Scotland **45** D1 55 51N 3 08W
Roskilde Denmark **67** C2 55 39N 12 07E
Roslin Lothian Scotland **45** D1 55 51N 3 11W
Rosliston Derbyshire England **35** D3 52 45N 1 38W
Ross Ice Shelf Antarctica **121** 80 00S 180 00
Ross River *tn.* Yukon Territory Canada **100** I5 62 02N 132 28W
Rossal Point *c.* Lancashire England **42** A3 53 56N 3 04W
Rossan Point *c.* Irish Republic **48** C4 54 40N 8 50W
Rossano Italy **68** C2 39 35N 16 38E
Rossendale, Forest of *hills* Lancashire England **42** D3 53 45N 2 15W
Rossiyskaya S.F.S.R. *(Russian Soviet Federated Socialist Republic) rep.* U.S.S.R. **71** J8–M8
Rosslare Harbour *tn.* Wexford Irish Republic **48** E2 52 15N 6 22W
Rosso Mauritania **93** B6 16 29N 15 53W
Ross-on-Wye Hereford and Worcester England **36** B1 51 55N 2 35W
Røssvatnet *mt.* Sweden **67** D4 66 00N 15 10E
Rostock *admin.* G.D.R. **63** B2 54 00N 13 00E
Rostock G.D.R. **63** B2 54 06N 12 09E
Rostov-na-Donu U.S.S.R. **70** F5 47 15N 39 45E
Roswell New Mexico U.S.A. **102** F3 33 24N 104 33W
Rosyth Fife Scotland **45** D2 56 03N 3 26W
Rothaar-gebirge *mts.* F.R.G. **63** A2 51 00N 8 00E
Rothbury Northumberland England **44** C2 55 19N 1 55W
Rother *r.* Kent/East Sussex England **33** C2 51 00N 0 40E
Rother *r.* West Sussex England **33** B1 51 00N 0 50W
Rothera *r.s.* Antarctica **121** 67 34S 68 07W
Rotherham South Yorkshire England **43** F2 53 26N 1 20W
Rothes Grampian Scotland **46** E4 57 31N 3 13W
Rothesay Strathclyde Scotland **46** C2 55 51N 5 03W
Rothwell Northamptonshire England **36** D2 52 25N 0 48W
Rothwell West Yorkshire England **43** F3 53 45N 1 29W
Rotorua New Zealand **87** C3 38 07S 176 17E
Rott *r.* F.R.G. **63** B1 48 00N 13 00E
Rottenburg F.R.G. **63** A1 48 42N 12 03E
Rotterdam Netherlands **65** C1 51 54N 4 28E
Rottingdean East Sussex England **33** B1 50 48N 0 04W
Roubaix France **61** B3 50 42N 3 10E
Rouen France **61** B2 49 26N 1 05E
Roundhay West Yorkshire England **43** F3 53 48N 1 30W
Rousay *i.* Orkney Islands Scotland **47** D2 59 10N 3 00W
Rouyn Québec Canada **105** E3 48 15N 79 00W
Rovaniemi Finland **67** F4 66 29N 25 40E
Rovigo Italy **68** B4 45 04N 11 47E
Rovno U.S.S.R. **70** E6 50 39N 26 10E
Rovuma *(Ruvuma) r.* Mozambique **95** G5 11 30S 38 00E
Rowington Warwickshire England **35** C2 52 19N 1 42W
Rowlands Gill Tyne and Wear England **44** C1 54 54N 1 45W
Rowly Surrey England **34** B1 51 10N 0 31W
Roxas The Philippines **80** G6 11 36N 122 45E
Roxburgh New Zealand **87** A1 45 34S 169 21E
Royal Canal Irish Republic **49** A2 53 22N 6 39W
Royal Leamington Spa Warwickshire England **35** D1 52 18N 1 31W
Royal Tunbridge Wells Kent England **33** C2 51 08N 0 16E
Royan France **61** A2 45 38N 1 02W
Roydon Essex England **34** D3 51 46N 0 03E
Royston Cambridgeshire England **33** B2 52 03N 0 01W
Royston South Yorkshire England **43** F2 53 37N 1 27W
Royton Greater Manchester England **42** D2 53 34N 2 08W
Rozel Jersey Channel Islands **31** G5 49 14N 2 03W
Rozenburg Netherlands **65** A1 51 54N 4 15E
Râs Banâs *c.* Egypt **78** E3 23 58N 35 50E
Râs Ghârib Egypt **78** N9 28 22N 33 04E
Râs Kasar *c.* Sudan **78** E2 18 02N 38 33E
Râs Muhammed *c.* Egypt **78** O8 27 44N 34 15E
R.S.F.S.R. *see* Rossiyskaya S.F.S.R.
Ruabon Clwyd Wales **38** C2 52 59N 3 02W
Ruaha National Park Tanzania **95** F6 7 00S 35 00E
Ruapehu *mt.* New Zealand **87** C3 39 18S 176 36E
Rub Al Khālī *d.* Saudi Arabia **79** G2 19 30N 48 00E
Rubha Coigeach *c.* Highland Scotland **46** C5 58 06N 5 26W
Rubha Hunish *c.* Highland Scotland **46** B4 57 40N 6 20W
Rubha Reidh *c.* Highland Scotland **46** C4 57 50N 5 55W
Rubtsovsk U.S.S.R. **71** K6 51 34N 81 11E
Ruby Alaska U.S.A. **100** D5 64 41N 155 35W
Ruddington Nottinghamshire England **36** C2 52 54N 1 09W
Rudnyy U.S.S.R. **70** I6 53 00N 63 05E
Rudolstadt G.D.R. **63** B2 50 44N 11 20E
Rueil-Malmaison France **60** A2 48 52N 2 12E
Rufford Lancashire England **42** B2 53 39N 2 49W
Rufforth North Yorkshire England **43** G3 53 57N 1 07W
Rufiji *r.* Tanzania **95** G6 7 30S 38 40E
Rugby Warwickshire England **35** E2 52 23N 1 15W
Rugeley Staffordshire England **35** C3 52 46N 1 55W
Rügen *i.* G.D.R. **63** B1 54 00N 14 00E
Ruhr *r.* F.R.G. **63** A2 51 00N 7 00E
Ruhrort F.R.G. **62** A2 51 27N 6 44E
Ruislip Greater London England **34** B2 51 35N 0 25W
Rukwa, Lake Tanzania **95** F6 8 00S 33 00E
Rumford Maine U.S.A. **105** F2 44 33N 70 34W
Rumney South Glamorgan Wales **38** C1 51 30N 3 10W
Rumoi Japan **82** D3 43 57N 141 40E
Runanga New Zealand **87** B2 42 24S 171 12E
Runcorn Cheshire England **42** B2 53 20N 2 44W
Rungis France **60** B2 48 45N 2 22E
Rupel *r.* Belgium **64** D3 51 05N 4 20E
Rur *r.* F.R.G. **64** F2 51 00N 6 00E
Ruse Bulgaria **68** E3 43 50N 25 59E
Rush Dublin Irish Republic **48** E3 53 32N 6 06W
Rushall West Midlands England **35** C2 52 37N 1 57W
Rushden Northamptonshire England **36** D2 52 17N 0 36W
Rusk Texas U.S.A. **103** G3 31 49N 95 11W
Russas Brazil **114** J12 4 56S 38 02W
Russell Kansas U.S.A. **102** G4 38 54N 98 51W
Russell Manitoba Canada **101** O3 50 47N 101 17W
Russell New Zealand **87** B3 35 16S 174 10E
Russian Soviet Federated Socialist Republic *see* Rossiyskaya S.F.S.R.
Russkaya *r.s.* Antarctica **121** 74 46S 136 51W
Rustavi U.S.S.R. **78** G7 41 34N 45 03E
Ruston Louisiana U.S.A. **103** H3 32 32N 92 39W
Ruth Nevada U.S.A. **102** D4 39 16N 114 59W
Rutherglen Strathclyde Scotland **45** B1 55 50N 4 12W
Ruthin Clwyd Wales **38** C3 53 07N 3 18W
Rutland Vermont U.S.A. **105** F2 43 37N 72 59W
Rutland Water *l.* Leicestershire **36** D2 52 40N 0 37W
Rutog China **81** A4 33 27N 79 43E
Ruvuma *(Rovuma) r.* Tanzania **95** G5 11 30S 38 00E
Ruwenzori National Park Rwanda **94** E7 0 30S 29 30E
Ruwenzori, Mount *mt.* Uganda/Zaïre **88** 0 23N 29 54E
Ružomberok Czechoslovakia **69** C2 49 04N 19 15E
RWANDA **94** F7
Ryazan' U.S.S.R. **70** F6 54 37N 39 43E
Rybach'ye U.S.S.R. **81** A6 42 28N 76 09E
Rybinsk Reservoir U.S.S.R. **70** F7 59 00N 38 00E
Rybinsk *see* Andropov
Rybnik Poland **69** C3 50 07N 18 30E
Ryde Isle of Wight England **32** A1 50 44N 1 10W
Rye East Sussex England **33** C1 50 57N 0 44E
Rye New York U.S.A. **106** D2 40 58N 73 41W
Rye *r.* North Yorkshire England **40** C3 54 15N 1 10W
Ryhill West Yorkshire England **43** F2 53 38N 1 25W
Ryton-on-Dunsmore Warwickshire England **35** D2 52 22N 1 26W
Ryukyu Islands *(Nansei-shoto)* Japan **81** K3 27 30N 127 30E
Ryukyu Ridge Pacific Ocean **118** C10 25 50N 128 00E
Ryukyu Trench Pacific Ocean **72** 25 00N 128 00E
Rzeszów Poland **69** D3 50 04N 22 00E

S

Saale *r.* F.R.G. **63** B2 50 00N 10 00E
Saale *r.* G.D.R. **63** B2 52 00N 11 00E
Saalfeld G.D.R. **63** B2 50 39N 11 22E
Saar *r.* F.R.G. **64** F1 49 00N 6 00E
Saarbrücken F.R.G. **63** A1 49 15N 6 58E
Saaremaa *i.* U.S.S.R. **67** E2 58 20N 22 00E
Saarland *admin.* F.R.G. **63** A1 49 00N 6 00E
Saarlouis F.R.G. **63** A1 49 19N 6 45E
Šabac Yugoslavia **68** C3 44 45N 19 41E
Sabadell Spain **66** C3 41 33N 2 07E
Sabah *state* Malaysia **80** F5 5 00N 117 30E
Sabaloka Cataract (River Nile) Sudan **78** D2 16 19N 32 40E
Sabanalarga Colombia **109** J2 10 38N 74 55W
Sabhā Libya **94** B13 27 02N 14 26E
Sabi *r.* Zimbabwe / Mozambique **95** F3 20 30S 33 00E
Sabinas Mexico **108** D5 27 50N 101 09W
Sabinas Hidalgo Mexico **108** D5 26 33N 100 10W
Sabine *r.* U.S.A. **103** H3 30 00N 94 00W
Sabine, Mount Antarctica **121** 72 00S 169 00W
Sabkhet el Bardawîl *l.* Egypt **78** N10 31 10N 33 35E
Sable, Cape Florida U.S.A. **103** J2 25 08N 80 07W
Sable Island Nova Scotia Canada **101** X1 43 57N 60 00W
Sabor *r.* Portugal **66** A3 41 22N 6 50W
Sabyā Saudi Arabia **78** F2 17 07N 42 39E
Sabzevār Iran **79** I6 36 15N 57 38E
Saclay France **60** A1 48 43N 2 09E
Sacramento California U.S.A. **102** B4 38 32N 121 30W
Sacramento Mountains U.S.A. **102** E3 33 00N 105 00W
Sacriston Durham England **44** C1 54 50N 1 38W
Sadar Bazar India **76** L4 28 39N 77 12E
Saddleworth Moor England **43** E2 53 30N 1 55W
Sadiya India **77** H5 27 49N 95 38E
Sado *i.* Japan **82** C2 38 20N 138 30E
Sado *r.* Portugal **66** A2 38 15N 8 30W
Saffron Walden Essex England **33** C3 52 01N 0 15E
Safi Morocco **93** D9 32 20N 9 17W
Saga Japan **82** B1 33 16N 130 18E
Sagaing Myanma **77** H4 21 55N 95 56E
Sagami Bay Japan **83** B2 35 15N 139 32E
Sagamihara Japan **82** C2 35 34N 139 22E
Sagar India **77** D4 23 50N 78 44E
Saggart Dublin Irish Republic **49** A1 53 16N 6 26W
Saginaw Michigan U.S.A. **105** D2 43 25N 83 54W
Saginaw Bay Michigan U.S.A. **105** D2 44 00N 84 00W
Sagua la Grande Cuba **109** H4 22 48N 80 06W
Saguenay River Québec Canada **105** F3 48 00N 71 00W
Sagunto Spain **66** B2 39 40N 0 17W
Sahara Desert North Africa **93** E7
Saharanpur India **77** D5 29 58N 77 33E
Sahiwal Pakistan **77** C6 30 41N 73 11E
Sahuaripa Mexico **108** C5 29 00N 109 13W
Sahuayo Mexico **108** D4 20 05N 102 42W
Saïda Algeria **66** C1 34 50N 0 10E
Saïda *(Sidon)* Lebanon **78** O11 33 32N 35 22E
Saidpur Bangladesh **77** F5 25 48N 89 00E
Saikhoa Ghat India **77** H5 27 46N 95 38E
Saimaa *l.* Finland **67** F3 61 15N 27 45E
St. Abb's Head *c.* Borders Scotland **46** F2 55 55N 2 09W
Ste. Agathe des Monts Québec Canada **105** F3 46 03N 74 19W
St. Agnes Cornwall England **30** B2 50 18N 5 13W
St. Agnes *i.* Isles of Scilly England **30** A1 49 54N 6 21W
St. Albans Hertfordshire England **34** B3 51 46N 0 21W
St. Albans *or* **St. Aldhelm's Head** *c.* Dorset
St. Albans Vermont U.S.A. **105** F2 44 49N 73 07W
St.-Amand-les-Eaux France **64** C2 50 27N 3 26E
St. Andrews Bay Fife Scotland **46** F3 56 20N 2 35W
St. Andrews Fife Scotland **46** F3 56 20N 2 48W
Ste. Anne de Beaupré Québec Canada **105** F3 47 02N 70 58W
Sainte Anne des Monts Québec Canada **101** V2 49 07W 66 29W
Ste. Anne Manitoba Canada **104** A3 49 40N 96 40W
St. Ann's Bay *tn.* Jamaica **109** Q8 18 26N 77 12W
St. Ann's Head *c.* Dyfed Wales **38** A1 51 41N 5 10W
St. Anthony Newfoundland Canada **101** X3 51 24N 55 37W
St. Asaph Clwyd Wales **38** C3 53 15N 3 26W
St. Aubin Jersey Channel Islands **31** G5 49 12N 2 10W
St. Augustine Florida U.S.A. **103** J2 29 54N 81 19W
St. Austell Cornwall England **30** C2 50 20N 4 48W
St. Bees Cumbria England **44** A1 54 29N 3 35W

St. Bees Head *c.* Cumbria England **44** A1 54 31N 3 39W
St. Blazey Cornwall England **30** C2 50 22N 4 43W
St. Bride's Bay Dyfed Wales **38** A1 51 50N 5 15W
St-Brieuc France **61** A2 48 31N 2 45W
St. Catharines Ontario Canada **105** E2 43 10N 79 15W
St. Catherine's Point *c.* Isle of Wight England **32** A1 50 34N 1 18W
St.-Chamond France **61** B2 45 29N 4 32E
St. Charles Missouri U.S.A. **104** B1 38 48N 91 29W
St. Clair River North America **105** D2 43 00N 82 00W
St. Clair, Lake North America **105** D2 43 00N 82 00W
St. Clears Dyfed Wales **38** B1 51 50N 4 30W
St-Cloud France **60** A2 48 51N 2 11E
St. Cloud Minnesota U.S.A. **104** B3 45 34N 94 10W
St. Columb Major Cornwall England **30** C2 50 26N 4 56W
St. Croix *i.* West Indies **109** L3 22 45N 65 00W
St. Croix *r.* North America **104** B3 46 00N 93 00W
St. Cyr-l'École France **60** A2 48 47N 2 03E
St. David's Dyfed Wales **38** A1 51 54N 5 16W
St. Davids Tayside Scotland **45** C2 56 22N 3 41W
St. David's Head *c.* Dyfed Wales **38** A1 51 55N 5 19W
St-Denis France **60** B2 48 57N 2 22E
St.-Dié France **61** C2 48 17N 6 57E
St.-Dizier France **61** B2 48 38N 5 58E
St. Elias, Mount U.S.A./Canada **100** G5 60 12N 140 57W
St.-Étienne France **61** B2 45 26N 4 23E
St. Fabien Québec Canada **105** G3 48 19N 68 51W
St.-Félicien Québec Canada **105** F3 48 38N 72 29W
Ste.-Foy Québec Canada **105** F3 46 47N 71 18W
St. Francis *r.* U.S.A. **103** H4 35 00N 90 00W
St. Francis, Cape Republic of South Africa **88** 34 13S 24 51E
St. Gallen Switzerland **61** C2 47 25N 9 23E
St.-Gaudens France **61** B1 43 07N 0 44E
Ste. Geneviève-des-Bois France **60** B1 48 38N 2 19E
Saint George *i.* Alaska/U.S.A. **100** B4 56 34N 169 31W
St. George New York U.S.A. **106** B1 40 48N 74 06W
St. George's Grenada **109** L2 12 04N 61 44W
St. Georges Québec Canada **105** F3 46 08N 70 40W
St. George's Channel British Isles **48** E2 52 00N 6 00W
St.-Germain-en-Laye France **61** B2 48 53N 2 04E
St.-Germain-en-Laye France **60** A2 48 54N 2 04E
St.-Ghislain Belgium **64** C2 50 27N 3 49E
St.-Girons France **61** B1 42 59N 1 08E
St. Govan's Head *c.* Dyfed Wales **38** B1 51 36N 4 55W
St. Helena Bay Republic of South Africa **95** C1 32 00S 17 30E
St. Helena *i.* Atlantic Ocean **117** H5 15 58S 5 43W
St. Helens Merseyside England **42** B2 53 28N 2 44W
St. Helier Jersey Channel Islands **31** G5 49 12N 2 07W
St.-Hubert Belgium **64** E2 50 02N 5 22E
St. Hyacinthe Québec Canada **105** F3 45 38N 72 57W
St. Ignace Michigan U.S.A. **105** D3 45 53N 84 44W
St. Ives Cambridgeshire England **33** B3 52 20N 0 05W
St. Ives Cornwall England **30** B2 50 12N 5 29W
St. Jean de Dieu Québec Canada **105** G3 48 00N 69 05W
St-Jean-de-Luz France **61** A1 43 23N 1 39W
St. Jean Port Joli Québec Canada **105** F3 47 13N 70 16W
St. Jean Québec Canada **105** F3 45 18N 73 16W
St. Jerôme Québec Canada **105** F3 45 47N 74 01W
Saint John New Brunswick Canada **101** V2 45 16N 66 03W
St. John *r.* Liberia **93** D4 6 30N 9 40W
Saint John *r.* North America **103** M6 46 00N 69 00W
St. John's Antigua & Barbuda **109** L3 17 08N 61 50W
St. John's Isle of Man British Isles **41** F1 54 12N 4 40W
St. John's Newfoundland Canada **101** Y2 47 34N 52 41W
St. John's Town of Dalry Dumfries & Galloway Scotland **46** D2 55 07N 4 10W
St. Joseph Island Ontario Canada **105** D3 46 00N 84 00W
St. Joseph Missouri U.S.A. **104** B1 39 45N 94 51W
St. Just Cornwall England **30** B2 50 07N 5 41W
St. Keverne Cornwall England **30** B2 50 03N 5 06W
ST. KITTS-NEVIS **109** L3
St. Laurent French Guiana **114** G14 5 29N 54 03W
St. Laurent *r.* Canada/U.S.A. *see* St. Lawrence
St. Lawrence *(St. Laurent) r.* Canada/U.S.A. **105** G3 48 00N 69 00W
St. Lawrence, Gulf of Canada **101** W2 49 00N 62 30W
St. Lawrence Island Alaska U.S.A. **100** B5 63 15N 169 50W
St. Lawrence Seaway North America **105** E2 44 00N 76 00W
St. Leonard New Brunswick Canada **105** G3 47 10N 67 55W
St. Leonards Dorset England **31** F2 50 50N 1 50W
St-Lô France **61** A2 49 07N 1 05W
St. Louis Missouri U.S.A. **104** B1 38 40N 90 15W
St. Louis Senegal **93** B6 16 01N 16 30W
ST. LUCIA **109** L2
St. Magnus Bay Shetland Islands Scotland **47** B2 60 25N 1 35W
St.-Malo France **61** A2 48 39N 2 00W
St-Mandé France **60** B2 48 50N 2 26E
St. Margaret's at Cliffe Kent England **33** D2 51 10N 1 23E
Ste. Marie Québec Canada **105** F3 46 26N 71 00W
St. Martin Guernsey Channel Islands **31** G5 49 13N 2 03W
St. Martins *i.* Isles of Scilly England **30** A1 49 58N 6 17W
St. Mary Jersey Channel Islands **31** G5 49 14N 2 10W
St. Marys *i.* Isles of Scilly England **30** A1 49 55N 6 18W
St. Marys Ohio U.S.A. **105** D2 40 32N 84 22W
St. Matthew Island Alaska U.S.A. **100** A5 60 30N 172 30W
St. Maur France **60** B2 48 48N 2 30E
St. Mawes Cornwall England **30** B2 50 09N 5 01W
St. Moritz Switzerland **66** C2 46 30N 9 51E
St.-Nazaire France **61** A2 47 17N 2 12W
St. Neots Cambridgeshire England **33** B2 52 14N 0 17W
St.-Niklaas Belgium **64** D3 51 10N 4 09E
St.-Omer France **61** B3 50 45N 2 15E
St. Ouen France **60** A3 49 03N 2 07E
St. Pacôme Québec Canada **105** G3 47 24N 69 58W
St. Pascal Québec Canada **105** G3 47 32N 69 48W
St. Paul Minnesota U.S.A. **104** B3 45 00N 93 10W
Saint Paul Alaska U.S.A. **100** A4 57 09N 170 18W
St. Paul *r.* Liberia **93** C4 7 10N 10 05W
St. Paul Rocks Atlantic Ocean **117** F7 0 23N 29 23W
St. Peter Minnesota U.S.A. **104** B2 44 21N 93 58W
St. Peter Port Guernsey Channel Islands **31** G5 49 27N 2 32W
St. Pierre Manitoba Canada **104** A3 49 28N 96 58W
Saint-Pierre & Miquelon *is.* Atlantic Ocean **101** X2 47 00N 56 20W
St. Pölten Austria **69** C2 48 13N 15 37E
St-Quentin France **61** B2 49 51N 3 17E
St. Remy France **60** A1 48 42N 2 04E
St. Siméon Québec Canada **105** G3 47 50N 69 55W
St. Stephen New Brunswick Canada **101** V2 45 12N 67 18W
St. Thomas *i.* West Indies **109** K3 18 00N 65 30W
St. Thomas Ontario Canada **105** D2 42 46N 81 12W
St-Tropez France **61** C1 43 16N 6 39E
St.-Truiden Belgium **64** E2 50 49N 5 11E
St.-Vieth Belgium **64** F2 50 15N 6 07E
ST. VINCENT AND THE GRENADINES **109** L2
St. Vincent *i.* St. Vincent and The Grenadines **109** L2 13 15N 61 12W
St. Wendel F.R.G. **64** G1 49 28N 7 10E
St.-Yvieix-la-Perche France **61** B2 45 31N 1 12E
Saintes France **61** A2 45 44N 0 38W
Saipan Northern Marianas **118** E9 15 12N 145 43E
Sakai Japan **82** C1 34 35N 135 28E
Sākākah Saudi Arabia **78** F4 29 59N 40 12E
Sakakawea, Lake North Dakota U.S.A. **102** F6 48 00N 103 00W
Sakarya *r.* Turkey **78** D6 40 05N 30 15E
Sakata Japan **82** C2 38 55N 139 51E
Sakhalin *i.* U.S.S.R. **71** Q6 50 00N 143 00E
Sakhalin Bay U.S.S.R. **71** Q6 54 00N 141 00E
Sakurai Japan **83** C2 35 21N 139 55E
Sala y Gomez *i.* Pacific Ocean **119** P5 26 28S 105 28W
Salālah Oman **79** H2 17 00N 54 04E
Salamanca Mexico **108** D4 20 34N 101 12W
Salamanca Spain **66** A3 40 58N 5 40W
Salcombe Devon England **31** D2 50 13N 3 47W
Saldus U.S.S.R. **67** E2 56 38N 22 30E
Sale Greater Manchester England **42** D2 53 26N 2 19W
Salekhard U.S.S.R. **71** I9 66 33N 66 35E
Salem India **77** D2 11 38N 78 08E
Salem Massachusetts U.S.A. **105** F2 42 32N 70 53W
Salem Oregon U.S.A. **102** B5 44 57N 123 01W
Salen Highland Scotland **46** C3 56 43N 5 47W
Salen Strathclyde Scotland **46** C3 56 31N 5 57W
Salerno Italy **68** B3 40 40N 14 46E
Salford Greater Manchester England **42** D2 53 30N 2 16W
Salfords Surrey England **34** C1 51 12N 0 10W
Salgótarján Hungary **69** C2 48 05N 19 47E
Salgueiro Brazil **114** J11 8 04S 39 05W
Salihli Turkey **68** E2 38 29N 28 08E
Salima Malawi **95** F5 13 45S 34 29E
Salina Kansas U.S.A. **103** G4 38 53N 97 36W
Salinas California U.S.A. **102** B4 36 39N 121 40W
Salinas Ecuador **114** A12 2 15S 80 58W
Salinas Grandes *l.* Argentina **115** D6/E7 30 00S 65 00W
Saline Fife Scotland **45** C2 56 07N 3 36W
Salisbury Maryland U.S.A. **105** E1 38 22N 75 37W
Salisbury North Carolina U.S.A. **103** J4 35 20N 80 30W
Salisbury Wiltshire England **31** F3 51 05N 1 48W
Salisbury Island Northwest Territories Canada **101** T5 63 10N 77 20W
Salisbury Plain Wiltshire England **31** F3 51 10N 1 55W
Salmon Idaho U.S.A. **102** D6 45 11N 113 55W
Salmon *r.* Idaho U.S.A. **102** C6 45 00N 116 00W
Salmon River Mountains Idaho U.S.A. **102** C6 45 00N 115 00W
Salo Finland **67** E3 60 23N 23 10E
Salon-de-Provence France **61** C1 43 38N 5 06E
Salonta Romania **69** D2 46 49N 21 40E
Salpausselka *geog. reg.* Finland **67** F3 61 40N 26 00E
Salt Jordan **78** O11 32 03N 35 44E
Salt *r.* Arizona U.S.A. **102** D3 34 00N 110 00W
Salt *r.* Missouri U.S.A. **104** B1 39 00N 91 00W
Salta Argentina **115** D8 24 46S 65 28W
Saltash Cornwall England **31** C2 50 24N 4 12W
Saltburn-by-the-Sea Cleveland England **44** D1 54 35N 0 58W
Saltcoats Strathclyde Scotland **46** D2 55 38N 4 47W
Saltdal Norway **67** D4 67 06N 15 25E
Saltdean East Sussex England **33** B1 50 49N 0 02W
Saltee Islands Wexford Irish Republic **48** E2 52 07N 6 36W
Salten *geog. reg.* Norway **67** D4 67 05N 15 00E
Saltfleet Lincolnshire England **36** E3 53 26N 0 10E
Salt Fork *r.* Texas U.S.A. **102** F3 33 00N 101 00W
Salt Fork *r.* Texas/Oklahoma U.S.A. **102** F4 35 00N 100 00W
Saltillo Mexico **108** D5 25 30N 101 00W
Salt Lake City Utah U.S.A. **102** D5 40 45N 111 55W
Salt Lake *tn.* India **76** K2 22 35N 88 23E
Salto Uruguay **115** F6 31 27S 57 50W
Salton Sea *l.* California U.S.A. **102** C3 33 00N 116 00W
Salvador Brazil **114** J10 12 58S 38 29W
Salween *r.* China *see* Nu Jiang
Salween *r.* Myanma **80** B8 21 00N 98 30E
Salzach *r.* Europe **63** B1 48 00N 13 00E
Salzburg *admin.* Austria **63** B1 47 00N 13 00E
Salzburg Austria **63** B1 47 48N 13 03E
Salzgitter F.R.G. **63** B2 52 13N 10 20E
Salzwedel G.D.R. **63** B2 52 51N 11 10E
Samani Japan **82** D3 42 07N 142 57E
Samar *i.* The Philippines **80** G6 12 30N 125 00E
Samarinda Indonesia **80** F3 0 30S 117 09E
Samarkand U.S.S.R. **70** I3 39 40N 66 57E
Sāmarrā' Iraq **78** F5 34 13N 43 52E
Sambalpur India **77** E4 21 28N 84 04E
Sambor U.S.S.R. **69** D2 49 31N 23 10E
Sambre *r.* France **64** C2 50 15N 4 00E
Samlesbury Lancashire England **42** C3 53 46N 2 38W
Sámos *i.* Greece **68** E2 37 00N 26 00E
Samothráki *i.* Greece **68** E3 40 00N 25 00E
Samsun Turkey **78** E7 41 17N 36 22E
San Mali **93** D5 13 21N 4 57W
San'ā Yemen **78** F2 15 23N 44 14E
Sanae *r.s.* Antarctica **121** 70 18S 02 25E
Sanaga *r.* Cameroon **93** H3 4 30N 12 20E
Sanak Island Alaska U.S.A. **100** C3 54 26N 162 40W
Sanandaj Iran **79** G6 35 18N 47 01E
San Andrés Tuxtla Mexico **108** E3 18 28N 95 15W
San Angelo Texas U.S.A. **102** F3 31 28N 100 28W
San Antonio Abad Balearic Islands **66** D4 38 59N 1 19E
San Antonio Chile **115** C6 33 35S 71 39W
San Antonio Oeste Argentina **115** E4 40 45S 64 58W
San Antonio *r.* Texas U.S.A. **103** G2 29 00N 97 00W
San Antonio Texas U.S.A. **102** G2 29 25N 98 30W
San Bernardino California U.S.A. **102** C3 34 07N 117 18W
San Bernardo Chile **115** C6 33 37S 70 45W
San Carlos Falkland Islands **117** M16 51 00S 58 50W
San Carlos The Philippines **80** G6 10 30N 123 29E
San Carlos The Philippines **80** G7 15 59N 120 22E
San Carlos Venezuela **114** D14 9 39N 68 35W
San Carlos de Bariloche Argentina **115** C4 41 11S 71 23W
San Carlos del Zulia Venezuela **114** C14 9 01N 71 58W
San Clemente Island California U.S.A. **102** C3 33 26N 117 36W
San Clemente Island U.S.A. **102** C3 32 55N 118 30W
San Cristóbal Argentina **115** E6 30 20S 61 14W
San Cristobal *i.* Solomon Islands **86** K7 11 00S 162 00E
San Cristóbal Mexico **108** F3 16 45N 92 40W
San Cristobal Venezuela **114** C14 7 46N 72 15W
Sanda Island Strathclyde Scotland **46** C2 55 18N 5 35W
Sandakan Malaysia **80** F5 5 52N 118 04E
Sanday *i.* Orkney Islands Scotland **47** E2 59 15N 2 30W
Sandbach Cheshire England **40** B2 53 09N 2 22W
Sandford Strathclyde Scotland **45** B1 55 39N 4 02W
Sandhurst Berkshire England **33** B2 51 21N 0 48W
San Diego California U.S.A. **102** C3 32 45N 117 10W
Sandoway Myanma **77** G3 18 28N 94 20E
Sandown Isle of Wight England **32** A1 50 39N 1 09W
Sandpoint *tn.* Idaho U.S.A. **102** C6 48 17N 116 34W
Sandray *i.* Western Isles Scotland **46** A3 56 53N 7 30W
Sandringham Norfolk England **33** C3 52 50N 0 31E
Sandspit British Columbia Canada **100** I3 53 14N 131 50W
Sandusky Ohio U.S.A. **105** D2 41 27N 82 42W
Sandwich Kent England **33** D2 51 17N 1 20E
Sandy Bedfordshire England **33** B3 52 08N 0 18W
Sandy Lake Ontario Canada **101** Q3 52 45N 93 00W
San Felipe Mexico **108** B6 31 03N 114 52W
San Felipe Venezuela **114** D15 10 25N 68 40W
San Feliú de Guixols Spain **66** C3 41 47N 3 02E
San Fernando California U.S.A. **107** A1 34 17N 118 27W
San Fernando de Apure Venezuela **114** D14 7 53N 67 15W
San Fernando Mexico **108** A5 29 59N 115 10W
San Fernando Spain **66** A2 36 28N 6 12W
San Fernando Trinidad and Tobago **109** L2 10 16N 61 28W
Sanford Florida U.S.A. **103** J2 28 49N 81 17W
San Francisco Argentina **115** E6 31 29S 62 06W
San Francisco California U.S.A. **102** B4 37 45N 122 27W
San Francisco del Oro Mexico **108** C5 26 52N 105 50W
San Francisco Dominican Republic **109** J3 19 19N 70 15W
San Francisco Javier Balearic Islands **66** D4 38 43N 1 26E
San Gabriel California U.S.A. **107** B3 34 06N 118 06W
San Gabriel Mountains California U.S.A. **107** B4 34 18N 118 05W
San Gabriel Reservoir California U.S.A. **107** C3 34 12N 117 52W
San Gabriel River California U.S.A. **107** B2 33 58N 118 06W
Sangar U.S.S.R. **71** O8 64 02N 127 30E
Sangerhausen G.D.R. **63** B2 51 29N 11 18E
Sangha *r.* Africa **94** C8 2 00N 17 00E
Sangli India **77** C3 16 55N 74 37E
Sangmélima Cameroon **93** H3 2 57N 11 56E
Sangre de Cristo Mountains New Mexico U.S.A. **102** E4 37 00N 105 00W
San Isidro Peru **116** E4 12 06S 77 02W
San Javier Bolivia **114** E9 16 22S 62 38W
San Joaquin *r.* California U.S.A. **102** B4 37 00N 120 00W
San José Balearic Islands **66** D4 38 55N 1 18E
San Jose California U.S.A. **102** B4 37 20N 121 55W
San José Costa Rica **109** H1 9 59N 84 04W
San José del Cabo Mexico **108** C4 23 01N 109 40W
San José Uruguay **115** F6 34 27S 56 40W
San Juan Argentina **115** D6 31 33S 68 31W
San Juan Bautista Balearic Islands **66** D4 39 05N 1 31E
San Juán Peru **114** B9 15 22S 75 07W
San Juan Puerto Rico **109** K3 18 29N 66 08W
San Juan *r.* U.S.A. **102** D4 37 00N 110 00W
San Julián Argentina **115** D3 49 17S 67 45W
Sānkrāil India **76** J2 22 33N 88 14E
Sankuru *r.* Zaïre **95** D7 4 00S 23 30E
Sanlúcar de Barrameda Spain **66** A2 36 46N 6 21W
San Lucas Mexico **108** C4 22 50N 109 52W
San Luis Argentina **115** D6 33 20S 66 23W
San Luis Obispo California U.S.A. **102** B4 35 16N 120 40W
San Luis Potosí Mexico **108** D4 22 10N 101 00W
San Marcos Texas U.S.A. **103** G2 29 54N 97 57W
SAN MARINO **68** B3 44 00N 12 00E
San Martin de Porres Peru **116** E4 12 03S 77 07W
Sanmenxia China **81** H4 34 46N 111 17E
San Miguel de Tucumán Argentina **115** D7 26 47S 65 15W
San Miguel El Salvador **108** G2 13 28N 88 10W
Sanming China **81** I3 26 16N 117 35E
San Pablo The Philippines **80** G6 14 03N 121 19E
San Pedro Argentina **115** E8 24 12S 64 55W
San Pedro California U.S.A. **107** A2 33 45N 118 19W
San Pedro Bay California U.S.A. **107** B1 33 43N 118 12W
San Pedro Channel California U.S.A. **107** A1 33 43N 118 22W
San Pedro Côte d'Ivoire **93** D3 4 45N 6 37W
San Pedro de las Colonias Mexico **108** D5 25 50N 102 59W
San Pedro Dominican Republic **109** K3 18 30N 69 18W
San Pedro Sula Honduras **108** G3 15 26N 88 01W
Sanquhar Dumfries & Galloway Scotland **46** E2 55 22N 3 56W
San Rafael California U.S.A. **102** B4 37 58N 122 30W
San Rafael Argentina **115** D6 34 35S 68 24W
San Remo Italy **68** A3 43 48N 7 46E
San Salvador El Salvador **108** G2 13 40N 89 10W
San Salvador *i.* The Bahamas **109** J4 24 00N 74 32W
San Salvador de Jujuy Argentina **115** D8 24 10S 65 48W
San Sebastián Spain **66** B3 43 19N 1 59W
San Severo Italy **68** C3 41 41N 15 23E
Sant' Antioco Italy **68** A2 39 04N 8 27E
Santa Ana River California U.S.A. **107** C2 33 46N 117 54W
Santa Ana Bolivia **114** D10 13 46S 65 37W
Santa Ana California U.S.A. **107** C2 33 44N 117 54W
Santa Ana El Salvador **108** G2 14 00N 89 31W
Santa Barbara California U.S.A. **102** C3 33 29N 119 01W
Santa Barbara Mexico **108** C5 26 48N 105 50W
Santa Catalina Island California U.S.A. **102** C3 33 25N 118 25W
Santa Catarina *admin.* Brazil **115** G7 27 00S 51 00W
Santa Clara Cuba **109** I4 22 25N 79 58W
Santa Clara Mexico **108** P2 19 32N 99 03W
Santa Cruz *r.* Argentina **115** D2 50 00S 70 00W
Santa Cruz Bolivia **114** E9 17 50S 63 10W
Santa Cruz California U.S.A. **102** B4 36 58N 122 03W
Santa Cruz Canary Islands **93** B8 28 28N 16 15W
Santa Cruz Jamaica **109** Q8 18 03N 77 43W
Santa Cruz Island California U.S.A. **102** C3 34 00N 119 40W
Santa Cruz Islands Solomon Islands **86** L7 11 00S 167 00E
Santa Eulalia del Rio Balearic Islands **66** D4 38 59N 1 33E
Santa Fé Argentina **115** E6 31 35S 60 50W
Santa Fe New Mexico U.S.A. **102** E4 35 41N 105 57W
Santa Isabel *i.* Solomon Islands **86** J8 7 30S 158 30E
Santa Maria Brazil **115** G7 29 45S 53 40W
Santa Maria California U.S.A. **102** B3 34 56N 120 25W
Santa Marta Colombia **114** C15 11 18N 74 10W
Santa Monica California U.S.A. **107** A3 34 00N 118 25W
Santa Monica Mountains California U.S.A. **107** A3 33 07N 118 27W
Santa Rosa Argentina **115** E5 36 37S 64 17W
Santa Rosa California U.S.A. **102** B4 38 26N 122 43W
Santa Rosa Honduras **108** G2 14 48N 88 43W
Santa Rosa New Mexico U.S.A. **102** F3 34 56N 104 42W
Santa Rosa Island California U.S.A. **102** B3 34 00N 120 05W
Santa Rosalía Mexico **108** B5 27 20N 112 20W
Santa Teresa Brazil **116** C2 22 57S 43 12W
Santa Teresa Gallura Italy **61** C1 41 14N 9 12E
Santana do Livramento Brazil **115** F6 30 52S 55 30W
Santander Colombia **114** B13 3 00N 76 25W
Santander Spain **66** B3 43 28N 3 48W
Santañy Balearic Islands **66** E4 39 22N 3 07E
Santarém Brazil **114** G12 2 26S 54 41W
Santarém Portugal **66** A2 39 14N 8 40W
Santi Nagar India **76** L4 28 40N 77 10E
Santiago Chile **115** C6 33 30S 70 40W
Santiago Dominican Republic **109** J3 19 30N 70 42W
Santiago Panama **109** H1 8 08N 80 59W
Santiago de Compostela Spain **66** A3 42 52N 8 33W
Santiago de Cuba Cuba **109** I4 20 00N 75 49W
Santiago del Estero Argentina **115** E7 27 47S 64 15W
Santiago Ixcuintla Mexico **108** C4 21 50N 105 11W
Santo Andre Brazil **115** H8 23 39S 46 29W
Santo Domingo Dominican Republic **109** K3 18 30N 69 57W
Santos Brazil **115** H8 23 56S 46 22W
Santpoort Netherlands **65** C3 52 25N 4 39E
Santry Dublin Irish Republic **49** B2 53 24N 6 15W
Sanuki Japan **83** C2 35 15N 139 53E
San Vicente El Salvador **108** G2 13 38N 88 42W
São Bernardo do Campo Brazil **115** H8 23 45S 46 34W
São Borja Brazil **115** F7 28 35S 56 01W
São Cristovão Brazil **116** C2 22 54S 43 14W
São Gonçalo Brazil **116** C2 22 49S 43 03W
São João de Meriti Brazil **116** B2 22 47S 43 22W
São João de Meriti *r.* Brazil **116** B2 22 48S 43 20W
São José Brazil **115** H7 27 35S 48 40W
São José do Rio Prêto Brazil **114** H8 20 50S 49 20W
São José dos Campos Brazil **115** H8 23 07S 45 52W
São José *r.* Brazil **116** B3 22 43S 43 29W
São Luís Brazil **114** I12 2 34S 44 16W
São Paulo *admin.* Brazil **114** G8/H8 21 30S 50 00W
São Paulo Brazil **115** H8 23 33S 46 39W
São Paulo de Olivença Brazil **114** D12 3 34S 68 55W
São Tomé *i.* Gulf of Guinea **93** G3 0 25N 6 35E
SÃO TOMÉ AND PRINCIPE **93** G3
São Vicente Brazil **115** H8 23 57S 46 23W
Saône *r.* France **61** B2 46 28N 4 55E
Sapê *r.* Brazil **116** C2 22 53S 43 03W
Sappemeer Netherlands **64** F5 53 10N 6 47E
Sapporo Japan **82** D3 43 05N 141 21E
Saqqez Iran **79** G6 36 14N 46 15E
Sarajevo Yugoslavia **68** C3 43 52N 18 26E
Sarakhs Iran **79** J6 36 32N 61 07E
Saranac Lake *tn.* New York U.S.A. **105** F2 44 19N 74 10W
Saransk U.S.S.R. **70** G6 54 12N 45 10E
Sarapui *r.* Brazil **116** B3 22 44S 43 17W
Sarasota Florida U.S.A. **103** J2 27 20N 82 32W
Sarata U.S.S.R. **69** E2 46 00N 29 40E
Saratov U.S.S.R. **70** G6 51 30N 45 55E
Saravan Iran **79** J4 27 25N 62 17E
Sarawak *state* Malaysia **80** E4 2 30N 112 30E
Sarcelles France **60** B2 48 59N 2 22E
Sardegna *(Sardinia) i.* Italy **68** A3 40 00N 9 00E
Sardindida Plain Kenya **94** G8/9 2 00N 40 00E
Sardinia *see* Sardegna
Sar-e Pol Afghanistan **79** K6 36 13N 65 55E
Sargasso Sea Atlantic Ocean **117** B9 27 00N 66 00W
Sargodha Pakistan **77** C6 32 01N 72 40E
Sarh Chad **94** C9 9 08N 18 22E
Sarīr Calanscio *d.* Libya **94** D13 26 00N 22 00E
Sark *i.* Channel Islands British Isles **31** G5 49 26N 2 22W
Sarmiento Argentina **115** D3 45 38S 69 08W
Sarnia Ontario Canada **105** D2 42 57N 82 24W
Sarny U.S.S.R. **69** E3 51 21N 26 31E
Saronikós Kólpos *g.* Greece **68** D2 38 00N 23 00E
Sarpsborg Norway **67** C2 59 17N 11 06E
Sarrebourg France **61** C2 48 43N 7 03E
Sarreguemines France **61** C2 49 06N 6 55E
Sartène Corsica **61** C1 41 37N 8 58E
Sarthe *r.* France **61** A2 47 45N 0 30W
Sartrou-ville France **60** A2 48 56N 2 11E
Sasebo Japan **82** A1 33 10N 129 42E
Saskatchewan *province* Canada **100** N3 53 50N 109 00W
Saskatchewan *r.* Canada **96** 54 00N 103 00W
Saskatoon Saskatchewan Canada **100** N3 52 10N 106 40W
Sassandra Côte d'Ivoire **93** D3 4 58N 6 08W
Sassandra *r.* Côte d'Ivoire **93** D4 5 50N 6 55W
Sassari Italy **68** A3 40 43N 8 34E
Sassenheim Netherlands **65** C2 52 13N 4 31E
Sassnitz G.D.R. **63** B2 54 32N 13 40E
Satna India **77** E4 24 33N 80 50E
Satpura Range *mts.* India **77** C4/D4 21 40N 75 00E
Sattahip Thailand **80** C6 12 36N 100 56E
Satu Mare Romania **69** D2 47 48N 22 52E
SAUDI ARABIA **78** F3
Sauer *(Sûre) r.* Europe **64** F1 49 45N 6 30E
Sault Ste. Marie Michigan U.S.A. **105** D3 46 29N 84 22W
Sault Ste. Marie Ontario Canada **105** D3 46 32N 84 20W
Saumur France **61** A2 47 16N 0 05W
Saundersfoot Dyfed Wales **38** B1 51 43N 4 43W
Saurimo Angola **95** D6 9 39S 20 24E
Sava *r.* Yugoslavia **68** C3 45 00N 19 00E
Savanna Illinois U.S.A. **104** B2 42 06N 90 07W
Savannah Georgia U.S.A. **103** J3 32 04N 81 07W
Savannah *r.* U.S.A. **103** J3 33 00N 82 00W
Savannakhet Laos **80** C7 16 34N 104 45E
Savanna la Mar Jamaica **109** P8 18 13N 78 08W
Saverne France **63** A1 48 45N 7 22E
Savona Italy **68** A3 44 18N 8 28E
Sawahlunto Indonesia **80** C3 0 41S 100 52E
Sawbridgeworth Hertfordshire England **34** D3 51 50N 0 09E
Sawel *mt.* Northern Ireland **48** D4 54 49N 7 02W
Sawpit Canyon Reservoir California U.S.A. **107** B3 34 10N 117 59W
Sawston Cambridgeshire England **33** C3 52 07N 0 10E
Sawu Sea Indonesia **80** G2 9 30S 122 00E
Saxmundham Suffolk England **33** D3 52 13N 1 29E
Saxthorpe Norfolk England **33** D3 52 50N 1 09E
Sayabec Québec Canada **105** G3 48 35N 67 41W

Skikda Algeria **93** G10 36 53N 6 54E
Skipton North Yorkshire England **43** D3 53 58N 2 01W
Skiros *i.* Greece **68** D2 39 00N 24 00E
Skokholm Island Dyfed Wales **38** A1 51 42N 5 16W
Skomer Island Dyfed Wales **38** A1 51 45N 5 18W
Skopje Yugoslavia **68** D3 42 00N 21 28E
Skövde Sweden **67** C2 58 30N 14 50E
Skovorodino U.S.S.R. **71** O6 54 00N 123 53E
Skowhegan Maine U.S.A. **105** G2 44 46N 69 44W
Skye *i.* Highland Scotland **46** B4 57 20N 6 15W
Slaidburn Lancashire England **42** C3 54 00N 2 26W
Slaithwaite West Yorkshire England **43** E2 53 38N 1 53W
Slamannan Central Scotland **45** C1 55 57N 3 51W
Slaney *r.* Irish Republic **48** E2 52 30N 6 35W
Slatina Romania **69** D1 44 26N 24 22E
Slave Lake *tn.* Alberta Canada **100** M4 55 17N 114 43W
Slave River Alberta/Northwest Territories Canada **100** M4 59 20N 111 10W
Slavonski Brod Yugoslavia **68** C4 45 09N 18 02E
Sleaford Lincolnshire England **36** D2 53 00N 0 24W
Sleat, Sound of Highland Scotland **46** C4 57 00N 5 55W
Sledmere Humberside England **40** D3 54 04N 0 35W
Sleights North Yorkshire England **40** D3 54 26N 0 40W
Slessor Glacier Antarctica **121** 79 00S 22 00W
Sliedrecht Netherlands **64** D3 51 50N 4 46E
Slieve Bloom *hills* Irish Republic **48** D3 53 05N 7 30W
Slieve Callan *sum.* Irish Republic **48** B2 52 50N 9 15W
Slieve Donard *mt.* Northern Ireland **48** F4 54 11N 5 55W
Slieve Gamph *hills* Irish Republic **48** C4 54 10N 8 55W
Slieve Mish Mountains Irish Republic **48** A1 51 12N 10 00W
Slieve Snaght *sum.* Irish Republic **48** D5 55 12N 7 20W
Sligo *co.* Irish Republic **48** C4 54 10N 8 40W
Sligo Sligo Irish Republic **48** C4 54 17N 8 28W
Sligo Bay Irish Republic **48** C4 54 15N 8 55W
Sliven Bulgaria **68** E3 42 40N 26 19E
Slonim U.S.S.R. **69** E3 53 05N 26 21E
Sloten Netherlands **65** D3 52 21N 4 48E
Sloterdijk Netherlands **65** D3 52 23N 4 50E
Slough Berkshire England **33** B2 51 31N 0 36W
Sluch' *r.* U.S.S.R. **69** E3 50 00N 27 00E
Slutsk U.S.S.R. **69** E3 53 02N 27 31E
Slyne Head *c.* Irish Republic **48** A3 53 25N 10 10W
Smallfield Surrey England **34** C1 51 10N 0 07W
Smallwood Reservoir Newfoundland Canada **101** W3 54 00N 63 00W
Smederevo Yugoslavia **68** D3 44 40N 20 56E
Smethwick West Midlands England **35** C2 52 30N 1 58W
Smith Alberta Canada **100** M4 55 10N 114 02W
Smith Mountain Lake Virginia U.S.A. **105** E1 37 00N 79 00W
Smithers British Columbia Canada **100** J3 54 45N 127 10W
Smiths Falls *tn.* Ontario Canada **105** E2 44 54N 76 01W
Smoky Hills Kansas U.S.A. **102** G4 39 00W 100 00W
Smøla *i.* Norway **67** B3 63 25N 8 00E
Smolensk U.S.S.R. **70** F6 54 49N 32 04E
Smolyan Bulgaria **68** D3 41 34N 24 42E
Smyrna Mills Maine U.S.A. **105** G3 46 07N 68 09W
Snaefell *mt.* Isle of Man British Isles **41** F1 54 16N 4 28W
Snake *r.* U.S.A. **102** C6 47 00N 118 00W
Snake River Plain U.S.A. **102** D5 43 00N 114 00W
Sneek Netherlands **64** E5 53 02N 5 40E
Snitterfield Warwickshire England **35** C1 52 14N 1 41W
Snodland Kent England **34** E1 51 20N 0 27E
Snowdon *mt.* Gwynedd Wales **38** B3 53 04N 4 05W
Snowdonia National Park Gwynedd Wales **38** C2 52 55N 3 50W
Snow Lake *tn.* Manitoba Canada **101** P3 54 56N 100 00W
Snowy Mountains Australia **86** H2 36 50S 147 00E
Snyder Texas U.S.A. **102** F3 32 43N 100 54W
Soa-Siu Indonesia **80** H4 0 40N 127 30E
Soay *i.* Highland Scotland **46** B4 57 08N 6 14W
Sobat *r.* Sudan **94** F9 8 00N 33 00E
Sobral Brazil **114** I12 3 45S 40 20W
Sochi U.S.S.R. **70** F4 43 35N 39 46E
Society Islands Pacific Ocean **119** K6 16 30S 153 00W
Socotra *i.* South Yemen **79** H1 12 05N 54 10E
Sodankylä Finland **67** F4 67 26N 26 35E
Söderhamn Sweden **67** D3 61 19N 17 10E
Södertälje Sweden **67** D2 59 11N 17 39E
Sodo Ethiopia **94** G9 6 49N 37 41E
Soest F.R.G. **63** A2 51 34N 8 06E
Soest Netherlands **64** E4 52 10N 5 20E
Sofiya Bulgaria **68** D3 42 40N 23 18E
Sogamosa Colombia **114** C14 5 43N 72 56W
Sognefjorden *fj.* Norway **67** B3 61 05N 5 30E
Sohâg Egypt **78** D4 26 33N 31 42E
Soham Cambridgeshire England **33** C3 52 20N 0 20E
Soignies Belgium **64** D2 50 35N 4 04E
Soissons France **61** B2 49 23N 3 20E
Sokodé Togo **93** F4 8 59N 1 11E
Sokoto Nigeria **93** G5 13 02N 5 15E
Sokoto *r.* Nigeria **93** F5 12 55N 4 30E
Solāpur India **77** D3 17 43N 75 56E
Solent, The *sd.* Isle of Wight England **32** A1 50 45N 1 25W
Soligorsk U.S.S.R. **69** E3 52 50N 27 32E
Solihull West Midlands England **35** C2 52 25N 1 45W
Solikamsk U.S.S.R. **70** H7 59 40N 56 45E
Solingen F.R.G. **62** C1 51 10N 7 05E
Sollefteå Sweden **67** D3 63 09N 17 15E
Sóller Balearic Islands **66** E4 39 46N 2 42E
Solntsevo U.S.S.R. **70** L1 55 36N 37 25E
Sologne *admin.* France **61** B2 47 35N 1 47E
SOLOMON ISLANDS **86** J/K8
Solomon Sea Papua New Guinea **86** I8 7 30S 152 00E
Solothurn Switzerland **61** C2 47 13N 7 32E
Soltau F.R.G. **63** A2 52 59N 9 50E
Solway Firth *est.* Scotland/England **46** E1 54 40N 3 40W
SOMALIA **94** I8/9
Sombor Yugoslavia **68** C4 45 46N 19 09E
Sombrerete Mexico **108** D4 23 38N 103 40W
Somerset *co.* England **31** E3 51 10N 3 00W
Somerset Island Northwest Territories Canada **101** Q7 73 00N 92 30W
Somerton Somerset England **31** E3 51 03N 2 44W
Somme *r.* France **61** B3 50 00N 1 45E
Sommen *l.* Sweden **67** D2 58 05N 15 15E
Somoto Nicaragua **109** G2 13 29N 86 36W
Sompting West Sussex England **33** B1 50 50N 0 21W
Son *r.* India **77** E4 24 00N 81 00E
Sonārpur India **76** K1 22 26N 88 26E
Sønderborg Denmark **67** B1 54 55N 9 48E
Søndre Strømfjord *tn.* Greenland **101** Y6 67 00N 50 59W
Songea Tanzania **95** G5 10 42S 35 39E
Songkhla Thailand **80** C5 7 12N 100 35E
Songhua Jiang *r.* China **81** K7 46 30N 128 00E
Song-koi *r.* Vietnam **80** C8 22 00N 105 00E
Sonneberg G.D.R. **63** B2 50 22N 11 10E
Sonning Common *tn.* Oxfordshire England **33** B2 51 31N 0 59W
Sonoita Mexico **108** B6 31 53N 112 52W
Sonsonate El Salvador **108** G2 13 43N 89 44W
Sopot Poland **69** C3 54 27N 18 31E
Sopron Hungary **69** C2 47 40N 16 35E
Soûr *(Tyre)* Lebanon **78** O11 33 16N 35 12E
Sorel Québec Canada **105** F3 46 03N 73 06W
Soria Spain **66** B3 41 46N 2 28W
Sorocaba Brazil **115** H8 23 30S 47 32W
Soroki U.S.S.R. **69** E2 48 08N 28 12E
Sorong Indonesia **80** I3 0 50S 131 17E
Soroti Uganda **94** F8 1 42N 33 37E
Sørøya *i.* Norway **67** E5 70 35N 22 30E
Sorraia *r.* Portugal **66** A2 38 55N 9 30W
Sorrento Point *c.* Dublin Irish Republic **49** B1 53 17N 6 05W
Sosnowiec Poland **69** C3 50 16N 19 07E
Soudley Shropshire England **35** A3 52 51N 2 24W
Souillac France **61** B1 44 53N 1 29E
Souk Ahras Algeria **68** A2 36 14N 8 00E
Sŏul *(Seoul)* South Korea **81** K5 37 32N 127 00E
Sousse Tunisia **93** H10 35 50N 10 38E
Southall Greater London England **34** B2 51 31N 0 23W
Southam Warwickshire England **35** D1 52 15N 1 23W
Southampton Hampshire England **32** A1 50 55N 1 25W
Southampton Ontario Canada **105** D2 44 29N 81 22W
Southampton Island Northwest Territories Canada **101** R5 64 50N 85 00W
Southampton Water *sd.* Hampshire England **32** A1 50 50N 1 20W
South Andaman *i.* Andaman Islands **77** G2 11 30N 93 00E
South Australia *state* Australia **86** E4/F4
South Australian Basin Indian Ocean **118** C4 38 00S 125 00E
South Bank *tn.* Cleveland England **44** C1 54 35N 1 10W
South Barrule *hill* Isle of Man British Isles **41** F1 54 09N 4 40W
South Bend Indiana U.S.A. **104** C2 41 40N 86 15W
South Benfleet Essex England **33** C2 51 33N 0 34E
Southborough Kent England **33** C2 51 10N 0 15E
South Brent Devon England **31** D2 50 25N 3 50W
South Cape *see* Kalae
South Carolina *state* U.S.A. **103** J3 34 00N 81 00W
South Cave *tn.* Humberside England **40** D2 53 46N 0 35W
South Cerney Gloucestershire England **31** F3 51 41N 1 57W
South China Sea South East Asia **80** E6/E7 15 00N 115 00E
South Dakota *state* U.S.A. **102** F5 45 00N 102 00W
South Darenth Kent England **34** D2 51 24N 0 15E
South Dorset Downs *hills* Dorset England **31** E2 50 40N 2 30W
South Downs *hills* England **33** B1 50 50N 0 30W
South East Cape Australia **86** H1 43 38S 146 48E
Southeast Indian Basin Indian Ocean **118** A4 32 00S 108 00E
South East Pacific Basin Pacific Ocean **119** Q2 53 00S 95 00W
South Elmsall West Yorkshire England **43** G2 53 34N 1 16W
Southend-on-Sea Essex England **33** C2 51 33N 0 43E
Southern Alps *mts.* New Zealand **87** B2 43 30S 170 00E
Southern Honshu Ridge Pacific Ocean **118** E10 25 50N 142 30E
Southern Indian Lake Manitoba Canada **101** P4 57 00N 99 00W
Southern Ocean **118/119**
Southern Uplands Scotland **46** D2–F2
South Esk *r.* Tayside Scotland **46** F3 56 40N 2 55W
South Fiji Basin Pacific Ocean **118** H5 25 00S 176 50E
South Gate California U.S.A. **107** B2 33 56N 118 11W
Southgate Greater London England **34** C2 51 38N 0 07W
South Georgia *i.* South Atlantic Ocean **115** J2 54 00S 36 30W
South Glamorgan *co.* Wales **38** C1 51 29N 3 25W
South Godstone Surrey England **34** C1 51 13N 0 04W
South Haven Michigan U.S.A. **104** C2 42 25N 86 16W
South Hayling Hampshire England **33** B1 50 47N 0 59W
South Island New Zealand **87** A2 43 00S 169 00E
South Junction Manitoba Canada **104** A3 49 03N 95 44W
South Kirkby South Yorkshire England **43** F2 53 34N 1 20W
SOUTH KOREA **81** K5
South Loup *r.* Nebraska U.S.A. **102** G5 42 00N 99 00W
Southminster Essex England **33** C2 51 40N 0 50E
South Molton Devon England **31** D3 51 01N 3 50W
South Nahanni *r.* Northwest Territories Canada **100** J5 61 03N 123 22W
South Negril Point *c.* Jamaica **109** P8 18 16N 78 22W
South Normanton Derbyshire England **36** C3 53 06N 1 20W
South Nutfield Surrey England **34** C1 51 13N 0 09W
South Ockenden Kent England **34** D2 51 32N 0 18E
South Orkney Islands Southern Ocean **115** H1 60 00S 45 00W
South Oxhey Hertfordshire England **34** B2 51 36N 0 23W
South Petherton Somerset England **31** E2 50 58N 2 49W
South Platte *r.* U.S.A. **102** F5 41 00N 103 00W
South Pole Antarctica **121** 90 00S
Southport Merseyside England **42** A2 53 39N 3 01W
South Ronaldsay *i.* Orkney Islands Scotland **47** E1 58 47N 2 56W
South Sandwich Islands South Atlantic Ocean **115** L1 58 00S 36 30W
South Sandwich Trench Southern Ocean **117** F1 55 00S 30 00W
South Shetland Islands Southern Ocean **115** E0 62 00S 60 00W
South Shields Tyne and Wear England **44** C1 55 00N 1 25W
South Sioux City Nebraska U.S.A. **104** A2 42 28N 96 24W
South Suburbs *(Behala)* India **76** K1 22 28N 88 18E
South Tyne *r.* Northumberland England **44** B1 54 52N 2 30W
South Uist *i.* Western Isles Scotland **46** A4 57 20N 7 15W
Southwark Greater London England **34** C3 51 30N 0 06W
Southwest Cape New Zealand **87** A1 47 17S 167 29E
South West Pacific Basin Pacific Ocean **119** K4 35 00S 155 00W
Southwick West Sussex England **33** B1 51 01N 0 14W
Southwold Suffolk England **33** D3 52 20N 1 40E
South Woodham Ferrers Essex England **33** C2 51 38N 0 38E
SOUTH YEMEN *(PEOPLE'S DEMOCRATIC REPUBLIC OF YEMEN)* **79** G2
South Yorkshire *admin.* England **43** F2 53 30N 1 30W
Sovetsk U.S.S.R. **69** D3 55 02N 21 50E
Sovetskaya Gavan' U.S.S.R. **71** Q5 48 57N 140 16E
Sowerby Bridge West Yorkshire England **43** E3 53 43N 1 54W
Sozh *r.* U.S.S.R. **69** F3 53 00N 30 00E
Spa Belgium **64** E2 50 29N 5 52E
SPAIN **66** B2
Spalding Lincolnshire England **36** D2 52 47N 0 10W
Spanish Head *c.* Isle of Man British Isles **41** F1 54 03N 4 46W
Spanish Town Jamaica **109** R7 17 59N 76 58W
Sparks Nevada U.S.A. **102** C4 39 34N 119 46W
Spartanburg South Carolina U.S.A. **103** J3 34 56N 81 57W
Spárti Greece **68** D2 37 05N 22 25E
Spassk-Dal'niy U.S.S.R. **71** P4 44 37N 132 37E
Spean Bridge *tn.* Highland Scotland **46** D3 56 53N 4 54W
Speke Merseyside England **42** B2 53 20N 2 51W
Spellbrook Hertfordshire England **34** D3 51 50N 0 10E
Spence Bay *tn.* Northwest Territories Canada **101** Q6 69 30N 93 20W
Spencer Gulf Australia **86** F3 34 00S 137 00E
Spencer Iowa U.S.A. **104** A2 43 08N 95 08W
Spennymoor *tn.* Durham England **44** C1 54 42N 1 35W
Sperrin Mountains Northern Ireland **48** D4/E4 54 50N 7 00W
Spey *r.* Scotland **46** D4 57 00N 4 30W
Speyer F.R.G. **63** A1 49 18N 8 26E
Spiekeroog *i.* F.R.G. **63** A2 53 47N 7 43E
Spijkenisse Netherlands **64** D3 51 52N 4 19E
Spilsby Lincolnshire England **36** E3 53 11N 0 05E
Spirit River *tn.* Alberta Canada **100** L4 55 46N 118 51W
Spithead *sd.* Hampshire England **32** A1 50 45N 1 10W
Spitsbergen *i.* Arctic Ocean **70** D1 79 00N 15 00E
Spittal an der Drau Austria **69** B2 46 48N 13 30E
Split Yugoslavia **68** C3 43 31N 16 28E
Spokane Washington U.S.A. **102** C6 47 40N 117 25W
Spoleto Italy **68** B3 42 44N 12 44E
Spondon Derbyshire England **35** D3 52 26N 1 25W
Spratly Islands South China Sea **80** E6–F5 10 00N 115 00E
Spree *r.* G.D.R. **63** B2 52 00N 14 00E
Springbok Republic of South Africa **95** C2 29 44S 17 56E
Springburn Strathclyde Scotland **45** B1 55 53N 4 13W
Springdale Newfoundland Canada **101** X2 49 30N 56 06W
Springfield Illinois U.S.A. **104** C1 39 49N 89 39W
Springfield Massachusetts U.S.A. **105** F2 42 07N 72 35W
Springfield Missouri U.S.A. **104** B1 37 11N 93 19W
Springfield Ohio U.S.A. **105** D1 39 55N 83 48W
Springfield Oregon U.S.A. **102** B5 44 03N 123 01W
Springfield Vermont U.S.A. **105** F2 43 18N 72 29W
Springsure Australia **86** H5 24 09S 148 04E
Springville New York U.S.A. **105** E2 42 31N 78 41W
Spurn Head *c.* Humberside England **40** E2 53 36N 0 07E
Squamish British Columbia Canada **100** K2 49 41N 123 11W
Sredinnyy Range *mts.* U.S.S.R. **71** R7 57 00N 158 00E
Srednekolymsk U.S.S.R. **71** R9 67 27N 153 35E
Sretensk U.S.S.R. **71** N6 52 15N 117 52E
Srikakulam India **77** E3 18 19N 84 00E
SRI LANKA **77** E1
Srinagar Kashmir **77** C6 34 08N 74 50E
Stadskanaal *tn.* Netherlands **64** F4 53 00N 6 55E
Staffa *i.* Strathclyde Scotland **46** B3 56 30N 6 15W
Stafford Staffordshire England **35** B3 52 48N 2 07W
Staffordshire *co.* England **36** B2/C2 52 50N 2 00W
Staffs and Worcs Canal England **35** B2 52 25N 2 15W
Staines Surrey England **34** B2 51 26N 0 30W
Stainforth South Yorkshire England **43** G2 54 06N 2 16W
Stake Pool *tn.* Lancashire England **42** B3 53 55N 2 54W
Stalbridge Dorset England **31** E2 50 58N 2 23W
Stalmine Lancashire England **42** B3 53 52N 2 58W
Stalybridge Greater Manchester England **42** D2 53 29N 2 04W
Stamford Lincolnshire England **36** D2 52 39N 0 29W
Stamford Bridge *tn.* Humberside England **40** D2 53 59N 0 55W
Stanbridge Bedfordshire England **34** B3 51 54N 0 35W
Standish Greater Manchester England **42** B2 53 36N 2 41W
Standish Michigan U.S.A. **105** D2 43 59N 83 58W
Standon Hertfordshire England **34** D3 51 53N 0 02E
Stanford le Hope Essex England **34** E2 51 31N 0 26E
Stanhope Durham England **44** B1 54 45N 2 01W
Stanley Durham England **44** C1 54 53N 1 42W
Stanley Falkland Islands **117** M16 51 45S 57 56W
Stanmore Greater London England **34** C2 51 38N 0 19W
Stannington South Yorkshire England **43** F2 53 24N 1 34W
Stanovoy Range *mts.* U.S.S.R. **71** O7 56 00N 122 30E
Stanstead Abbotts Hertfordshire England **34** D3 51 47N 0 01E
Stansted Mountfitchet Essex England **34** D3 51 54N 0 12E
Stapleford Nottinghamshire England **35** E3 52 56N 1 15W
Stapleford Abbotts Essex England **34** D2 51 39N 0 11E
Staplehurst Kent England **33** C2 51 10N 0 33E
Star Fife Scotland **45** D2 56 13N 3 06W
Stara Planina *mts.* Europe **68** D3 43 00N 23 00E
Stara Zagora Bulgaria **68** E3 42 25N 25 37E
Stargard Szczeciński Poland **69** C3 53 21N 15 01E
Starnberger See *l.* F.R.G. **63** B1 47 00N 11 00E
Starogard Gdański Poland **69** C3 53 58N 18 30E
Start Bay Devon England **31** D2 50 16N 3 35W
Start Point *c.* Devon England **31** D2 50 13N 3 38W
Staryy Oskol U.S.S.R. **70** F6 51 20N 37 50E
State College Pennsylvania U.S.A. **105** E2 40 48N 77 52W
Staten Island New York U.S.A. **106** B1 40 35N 74 10W
Staunton Gloucestershire England **31** E3 51 58N 2 19W
Staunton Virginia U.S.A. **105** E1 38 10N 79 05W
Stavanger Norway **67** B2 58 58N 5 45E
Staveley Derbyshire England **43** F1 53 16N 1 20W
Staveley North Yorkshire England **43** F4 54 04N 1 26W
Stavelot Belgium **64** E2 50 25N 5 56E
Staveren Netherlands **64** E4 52 53N 5 21E
Stavropol' U.S.S.R. **70** G5 45 03N 41 59E
Staxton North Yorkshire England **40** D3 54 11N 0 26W
Stebbing Essex England **34** E3 51 54N 0 25E
Stebbins Alaska U.S.A. **100** C5 63 32N 162 20W
Steen River *tn.* Alberta Canada **100** L4 59 40N 117 15W
Steenstrup Glacier Greenland **101** X8 75 00N 56 00W
Steenwijk Netherlands **64** F4 52 47N 6 07E
Steep Holm *i.* Avon England **31** D3 51 21N 3 07W
Steeping *r.* Lincolnshire England **36** E3 53 10N 0 10E
Steiermark *admin.* Austria **63** B1 47 00N 14 00E
Steigerwald *hills* F.R.G. **63** B1 49 00N 10 00E
Stein Netherlands **64** E2 50 58N 5 45E
Steinbach Manitoba Canada **104** A3 49 32N 96 40W
Steinfurt F.R.G. **63** A2 52 09N 7 21E
Stenay France **61** E1 49 29N 5 12E
Stendal G.D.R. **63** B2 52 36N 11 52E
Stenhousemuir Central Scotland **45** C2 56 02N 3 49W
Stepaside Dublin Irish Republic **49** B1 53 15N 6 13W
Stephenville Newfoundland Canada **101** X2 48 33N 58 34W
Stepps Strathclyde Scotland **45** B1 55 52N 4 09W
Sterkrade F.R.G. **62** B3 51 31N 6 52E
Sterling Colorado U.S.A. **102** F5 40 37N 103 13W
Sterling Illinois U.S.A. **104** C2 41 48N 89 43W
Sterlitamak U.S.S.R. **70** H6 53 40N 55 59E
Steubenville Ohio U.S.A. **105** D2 40 22N 80 39W
Stevenage Hertfordshire England **34** C3 51 55N 0 14W
Stevens Point *tn.* Wisconsin U.S.A. **104** C2 44 32N 89 33W
Stewart British Columbia Canada **100** J4 55 56N 130 01W
Stewart Yukon Territory Canada **100** H5 63 15N 139 15W
Stewart Crossing Yukon Territory Canada **100** H5 60 37N 128 37W
Stewart Island New Zealand **87** A1 47 30S 168 00E
Stewarton Strathclyde Scotland **45** A1 55 41N 4 31W
Stewkley Buckinghamshire England **34** A3 51 56N 0 46W
Steyning West Sussex England **33** B1 50 53N 0 20W
Steyr Austria **69** B2 48 04N 14 25E
Stillorgan Dublin Irish Republic **49** B1 53 17N 6 12W
Stilton Cambridgeshire England **33** B3 52 29N 0 17W
Stinchar *r.* Strathclyde Scotland **46** D2 55 10N 4 45W
Štip Yugoslavia **68** D3 41 44N 22 12E
Stirchley Shropshire England **35** A2 52 40N 2 27W
Stirling Alberta Canada **100** M2 49 34N 112 30W
Stirling Central Scotland **45** C2 56 07N 3 57W
Stockbridge Hampshire England **32** A2 51 07N 1 29W
Stockholm Sweden **67** D2 59 20N 18 95E
Stockport Greater Manchester England **42** D2 53 25N 2 10W
Stocksbridge South Yorkshire England **43** F2 53 27N 1 34W
Stocks Reservoir Lancashire England **42** C3 53 59N 2 25W
Stockton California U.S.A. **102** B4 37 59N 121 20W
Stockton Heath Cheshire England **42** C2 53 22N 2 34W
Stockton Lake *res.* Missouri U.S.A. **104** B1 38 00N 94 00W
Stockton-on-Tees Cleveland England **44** C1 54 34N 1 19W
Stoer, Point of *c.* Highland Scotland **46** C5 58 25N 5 25W
Stoke Golding Leicestershire England **35** D2 52 34N 1 24W
Stokenchurch Buckinghamshire England **33** B2 51 40N 0 55W
Stoke Poges Buckinghamshire England **34** B2 51 33N 0 35W
Stoke-on-Trent Staffordshire England **35** B4 53 00N 2 10W
Stokesley North Yorkshire England **40** C3 54 28N 1 11W
Stolberg F.R.G. **63** A2 50 45N 6 15E
Stondon Massey Essex England **34** D3 51 41N 0 17E
Stone Staffordshire England **35** B3 52 54N 2 10W
Stone Canyon Reservoir California U.S.A. **107** A3 34 07N 118 27W
Stonehaven Grampian Scotland **46** F3 56 38N 2 13W
Stonehouse Strathclyde Scotland **45** C1 55 43N 3 59W
Stoneleigh Warwickshire England **35** D2 52 21N 1 31W
Stonewall Manitoba Canada **104** A4 50 08N 97 20W
Stoneyburn Lothian Scotland **45** C1 55 51N 3 37W
Stony Rapids *tn.* Saskatchewan Canada **100** N4 59 14N 103 48W
Stony Stratford Buckinghamshire England **33** B3 52 04N 0 52W
Stony Tunguska *see* Podkamennaya Tunguska
Stora Lulevatten *l.* Sweden **67** D4 67 20N 19 00E
Størdal Norway **67** C3 63 18N 11 48E
Støren Norway **67** C3 63 03N 10 16E
Storm Lake *tn.* Iowa U.S.A. **104** A2 42 39N 95 11W
Stornoway Western Isles Scotland **46** B5 58 12N 6 23W
Storr, The *mt.* Highland Scotland **46** B4 57 30N 6 11W
Storrington West Sussex England **33** B1 50 55N 0 28W
Storsjön *l.* Sweden **67** C3 63 10N 14 10E
Storuman Sweden **67** D4 65 05N 17 10E
Stotfold Bedfordshire England **34** C4 52 01N 0 15W
Stour *r.* Dorset England **31** E2 50 55N 2 15W
Stour *r.* Kent England **33** D2 51 10N 1 10E
Stour *r.* Suffolk/Essex England **33** C2 51 58N 0 55E
Stourbridge West Midlands England **35** B2 52 27N 2 09W
Stourport-on-Severn Hereford and Worcester
Stowmarket Suffolk England **33** D3 52 11N 1 00E
Stow-on-the-Wold Gloucestershire England **31** F3 51 56N 1 44W
Strabane Northern Ireland **48** D4 54 49N 7 27W
Strachur Strathclyde Scotland **46** C3 56 10N 5 04W
Stradbally Laois Irish Republic **48** D2 53 00N 7 08W
Straffan Kildare Irish Republic **49** A1 53 18N 6 37W
Straits of Florida *sd.* Florida U.S.A. **103** J1 25 00N 80 00W
Strakonice Czechoslovakia **63** B1 49 16N 13 54E
Stralsund G.D.R. **63** B2 54 18N 13 06E
Strangford Lough *l.* Northern Ireland **48** F4 54 25N 5 45W
Stranorlar Donegal Irish Republic **48** D4 54 48N 7 46W
Stranraer Dumfries & Galloway Scotland **46** C1 54 55N 5 02W
Strasbourg France **61** C2 48 35N 7 45E
Stratford Ontario Canada **105** D2 43 22N 81 00W
Stratford-upon-Avon Warwickshire England **35** C1 52 12N 1 41W
Strathallan *v.* Tayside Scotland **45** C2 56 30N 3 50W
Strathaven Strathclyde Scotland **45** B1 55 41N 4 05W
Strathclyde *reg.* Scotland **46** C3 56 10N 5 30W
Strathmiglo Fife Scotland **56** D2 56 17N 3 16W
Strathpeffer Highland Scotland **46** D4 57 35N 4 33W
Strathspey *v.* Scotland **46** E4 57 25N 3 30W
Strathy Point *c.* Highland Scotland **46** D5 58 35N 4 02W
Stratton Cornwall England **30** C2 50 50N 4 31W
Straubing F.R.G. **63** B1 48 53N 12 35E
Strausberg G.D.R. **63** B2 52 34N 13 53E
Streatham Greater London England **34** C2 51 26N 0 07W
Streatley Bedfordshire England **34** B3 51 57N 0 27W
Streator Illinois U.S.A. **104** C2 41 07N 88 53W
Stredočeský *admin.* Czechoslovakia **63** B2 50 00N 14 00E
Street Somerset England **31** E3 51 03N 2 45W
Streetly West Midlands England **35** C2 52 34N 1 52W
Strensall North Yorkshire England **43** G4 54 02N 1 03W
Stretford Greater Manchester England **42** D2 53 27N 2 19W

Thame *r.* Buckinghamshire England **33** B2 51 45N 0 55W
Thames New Zealand **87** C3 37 08S 175 35E
Thames *r.* England **32/33** A2–C2
Thane India **77** C3 19 14N 73 02E
Thanh Hoa Vietnam **80** D7 19 49N 105 48E
Thanjavur India **77** D2 10 46N 79 09E
Thar Desert India **77** C5 27 30N 72 00E
Thásos *i.* Greece **68** D3 40 00N 24 00E
Thatcham Berkshire England **32** A2 51 25N 1 15W
Thaxted Essex England **34** E3 51 57N 0 20E
Thayetmyo Myanma **80** B7 19 20N 95 10E
Thebes *hist. site* Egypt **78** D4 25 41N 32 40E
The Bronx New York U.S.A. **106** C2 40 50N 73 55W
The Dalles Oregon U.S.A. **102** B6 45 36N 121 10W
The Den Strathclyde Scotland **45** A1 55 43N 4 40W
The Everglades *swamp* Florida U.S.A. **103** J2 26 00N 81 00W
The Mumbles West Glamorgan Wales **38** B1 51 35N 3 59W
The Pas Manitoba Canada **101** O3 53 49N 101 14W
Thelon *r.* Northwest Territories Canada **101** O5 64 40N 102 30W
Thelwall Cheshire England **42** C2 53 23N 2 31W
Thermaïkós Kólpos *g.* Greece **68** D3 40 00N 22 50E
Thermopolis Wyoming U.S.A. **102** E5 43 39N 108 12W
Thessalon Ontario Canada **105** D3 46 15N 83 34W
Thessaloníki Greece **68** D3 40 38N 22 58E
Thetford Norfolk England **33** C3 52 25N 0 45E
Thetford Mines *tn.* Québec Canada **105** F3 46 06N 71 18W
Theydon Bois Essex England **34** D3 51 40N 0 05E
Thiais France **60** B2 48 45N 2 24E
Thief River Falls *tn.* Minnesota U.S.A. **104** A3 48 12N 96 48W
Thiers France **61** B2 45 51N 3 33E
Thiès Senegal **93** B5 14 49N 16 52W
Thika Kenya **94** G7 1 03S 37 05E
Thimphu Bhutan **77** F5 27 32N 89 43E
Thionville France **61** C2 49 22N 6 11E
Thíra *i.* Greece **68** E2 36 00N 25 00E
Thirsk North Yorkshire England **40** C3 54 14N 1 20W
Thithia *i.* Fiji **118** V16 17 45S 179 20W
Thívai Greece **68** D2 38 19N 23 19E
Tholen *i.* Netherlands **64** D3 51 33N 4 05E
Thomastown Kilkenny Irish Republic **48** D2 52 31N 7 08W
Thomasville Georgia U.S.A. **103** J3 30 50N 83 59W
Thompson Manitoba Canada **101** P4 55 45N 97 54W
Thomson *r.* Australia **86** G5 24 00S 143 30E
Thorganby North Yorkshire England **43** H3 53 28N 0 11W
Thornaby-on-Tees Cleveland England **44** C1 54 34N 1 18W
Thornbury Avon England **31** E3 51 37N 2 32W
Thorne South Yorkshire England **43** H2 53 37N 0 58W
Thorney Cambridgeshire England **33** B3 52 37N 0 07W
Thornhill Dumfries & Galloway Scotland **46** E2 55 15N 3 46W
Thornhill Edge West Yorkshire England **43** F2 53 41N 1 38W
Thornliebank Strathclyde Scotland **45** B1 55 47N 4 19W
Thornton Fife Scotland **45** D2 56 10N 3 09W
Thornton Lancashire England **42** B3 53 53N 3 00W
Thornton West Yorkshire England **43** E3 53 47N 1 52W
Thornwood Common Essex England **34** D3 51 43N 0 07E
Thorpe-le-Soken Kent England **33** D2 51 52N 1 10E
Thouars France **61** A2 46 59N 0 13W
Thrapston Northamptonshire England **36** D2 52 24N 0 32W
Three Kings Islands New Zealand **87** B4 34 00S 172 30E
Three Mile Bay *tn.* New York U.S.A. **105** E2 44 04N 76 12W
Three Points, Cape Ghana **93** E3 4 43N 2 06W
Three Rock Mountain Dublin Irish Republic **49** B1 53 14N 6 14W
Thringstone Leicestershire England **35** D3 52 44N 1 22W
Thrybergh South Yorkshire England **43** G2 53 27N 1 18W
Thuin Belgium **64** D2 50 21N 4 18E
Thule *see* Dundas
Thun Switzerland **61** C2 46 46N 7 38E
Thunder Bay *tn.* Ontario Canada **104** C3 48 27N 89 12W
Thurcroft South Yorkshire England **43** G2 53 24N 1 16W
Thüringer Wald *hills* G.D.R. **63** B2 50 00N 10 00E
Thurles Tipperary Irish Republic **48** D2 52 41N 7 49W
Thursby Cumbria England **44** A1 54 51N 3 03W
Thurso Highland Scotland **46** E5 58 35N 3 32W
Thurso *r.* Highland Scotland **46** E5 58 15N 3 35W
Thurston Island *i.* Antarctica **121** 72 00S 100 00W
Tianjin China **81** I5 39 08N 117 12E
Tianshui China **81** G4 34 25N 105 58E
Tiaret Algeria **66** C2 35 20N 1 20E
Tibberton Shropshire England **35** A3 52 47N 2 28W
Tiber *r.* Italy **68** B3 42 00N 12 00E
Tiberias Israel **78** O11 32 48N 35 32E
Tiberias, Lake *(Sea of Galilee) l.* Israel **78** O11 32 45N 35 30E
Tibesti *mts.* Chad **94** C12 21 00N 17 00E
Tibet Autonomous Region *see* Xizang Zizhiqu
Tibet, Plateau of Asia **72** 33 00N 90 00E
Tiburón *i.* Mexico **108** B5 28 30N 112 30W
Ticehurst East Sussex England **33** C2 51 02N 0 24E
Ticino *r.* Italy / Switzerland **61** C2 45 00N 9 00E
Tickhill South Yorkshire England **43** G2 53 26N 1 06W
Ticul Mexico **108** G4 20 22N 89 31W
Tideswell Derbyshire England **43** E1 53 17N 1 46W
Tiel Netherlands **64** E3 51 53N 5 26E
Tielt Belgium **64** C3 51 00N 3 20E
Tienen Belgium **64** D2 50 48N 4 56E
Tien Shan *(Tyan-Shan') mts.* China **71** J4 41 00N 76 00E
Tierra Blanca Mexico **108** E3 18 28N 96 21W
Tierra del Fuego *see* Isla Grande de Tierra del Fuego
Tietar *r.* Spain **66** A3 40 07N 5 15W
Tiffin Ohio U.S.A. **105** D2 41 07N 83 11W
Tigermore Tayside Scotland **45** C2 56 24N 3 32W
Tighnabruaich Strathclyde Scotland **46** C2 55 56N 5 14W
Tigris *r.* Iraq **79** G5 32 00N 46 00E
Tijuana Mexico **108** A6 32 29N 117 10W
Tijuca Brazil **116** B2 22 56S 43 16W
Tikrit Iraq **78** F5 34 36N 43 42E
Tiksi U.S.S.R. **71** O10 71 40N 128 45E
Tilak Nagar India **76** L4 28 38N 77 07E
Tilburg Netherlands **64** E3 51 34N 5 05E
Tilbury Essex England **34** E2 51 28N 0 23E
Tile Hill West Midlands England **35** D2 52 24N 1 31W
Tillsonburg Ontario Canada **105** D2 42 53N 80 44W
Tillycoultry Central Scotland **45** C2 56 09N 3 45W
Timaru New Zealand **87** B2 44 23S 171 14E
Timbira *r.* Brazil **116** C3 22 40S 43 12W
Timimoun Algeria **93** F8 29 15N 0 14E
Timişoara Romania **69** D2 45 45N 21 15E
Timişul *r.* Romania / Yugoslavia **69** D2 45 00N 21 00E
Timmins Ontario Canada **101** S2 48 30N 81 20W
Timor *i.* Indonesia **80** G2/H2 9 00S 125 00E
Timor Sea Australia / Indonesia **80** H1/H2 10 00S 128 00E
Tindouf Algeria **93** D8 27 42N 8 10W
Tínos *i.* Greece **68** E2 37 00N 25 00E
Tinsley South Yorkshire England **43** F2 53 25N 1 24W
Tintagel Cornwall England **30** B2 50 40N 4 45W
Tintagel Head *c.* Cornwall England **30** B2 50 41N 4 46W
Tipperary *co.* Irish Republic **48** C2/D2 52 30N 8 00W
Tipperary Tipperary Irish Republic **48** C2 52 29N 8 10W
Tipton West Midlands England **35** B2 52 32N 2 05W
Tiptree Essex England **33** C2 51 49N 0 45E
Tiranë Albania **68** C3 41 20N 19 49E
Tiraspol' U.S.S.R. **69** E2 46 50N 29 38E
Tiraz Mountains Namibia **95** C2 25 30S 16 30E
Tiree *i.* Strathclyde Scotland **46** B3 56 30N 6 55W
Tirgovişte Romania **69** E1 44 56N 25 27E
Tirgu Jiu Romania **69** D1 45 03N 23 18E
Tirgu Mureş Romania **69** D2 46 33N 24 34E
Tirol *admin.* Austria **63** B1 47 00N 11 00E
Tirso *r.* Italy **68** A2 40 00N 9 00E
Tiruchchirāppalli India **77** D2 10 50N 78 41E
Tirunelveli India **77** D1 8 45N 77 43E
Tirupati India **77** D2 13 39N 79 25E
Tiruppur India **77** D2 11 05N 77 20E
Tisdale Saskatchewan Canada **100** O3 52 51N 104 01W
Tisza *r.* Hungary / Yugoslavia **69** D2 46 00N 20 00E
Titāgarh India **76** K2 22 44N 88 22E
Titograd Yugoslavia **68** C3 42 28N 19 17E
Titov Veles Yugoslavia **68** D3 41 43N 21 49E
Titova Mitrovica Yugoslavia **68** D3 42 54N 20 52E
Titovo Užice Yugoslavia **68** C3 43 52N 19 50E
Tittensor Staffordshire England **35** B3 52 57N 2 12W
Tiverton Devon England **31** D2 50 55N 3 29W
Tiverton Rhode Island U.S.A. **105** F2 41 38N 71 13W
Tivoli Italy **68** B3 41 58N 12 48E
Tizimín Mexico **108** G4 21 10N 88 09W
Tizi Ouzou Algeria **93** F10 36 44N 4 05E
Tiznit Morocco **93** D8 29 43N 9 44W
Tlalnepantla Mexico **108** P2 19 32N 99 12W
Tlaltenco Mexico **108** P1 19 17N 99 01W
Tlemcen Algeria **93** E9 34 53N 1 21W
Toad River *tn.* British Columbia Canada **100** J4 59 00N 125 10W
Toamasina Madagascar **95** I4 18 10S 49 23E
Tobago *i* Trinidad and Tobago **109** L2 11 15N 60 40W
Tobermory Ontario Canada **105** D3 45 15N 81 39W
Tobermory Strathclyde Scotland **46** B3 56 37N 6 05W
Tobi-shima *i.* Japan **82** C2 39 12N 139 32E
Tobol *r.* U.S.S.R. **71** I7 56 00N 66 00E
Tobol'sk U.S.S.R. **71** I7 58 15N 68 12E
Tocopilla Chile **115** C8 22 05S 70 10W
Toddington Bedfordshire England **34** B3 51 57N 0 32W
Todmorden West Yorkshire England **43** D3 53 43N 2 05W
TOGO **93** F4
Tokelau Islands Pacific Ocean **118** I7 9 00S 168 00W
Tokorozawa Japan **83** A4 35 47N 139 28E
Tokushima Japan **82** B1 34 03N 134 34E
Tokuyama Japan **82** B1 34 04N 131 48E
Tōkyō Japan **83** C3 35 40N 139 45E
Tokyo Bay Japan **83** C2 35 25N 139 45E
Tolbukhin Bulgaria **68** E3 43 34N 27 51E
Toledo Ohio U.S.A. **105** D2 41 40N 83 35W
Toledo Spain **66** B2 39 52N 4 02W
Toliara Madagascar **95** H3 23 20S 43 41E
Tolka *r.* Dublin Irish Republic **49** B2 53 23N 6 19W
Tollygunge India **76** K2 22 30N 88 19E
Tolosa Spain **66** B3 43 09N 2 04W
Toluca Mexico **108** E3 19 20N 99 40W
Tol'yatti U.S.S.R. **70** G6 53 32N 49 24E
Tomakomai Japan **82** D3 42 39N 141 33E
Tomaniivi *mt.* Fiji **118** U16 17 37S 178 01E
Tomar Portugal **66** A2 39 36N 8 25W
Tomaszów Mazowiecka Poland **69** C3 51 33N 20 00E
Tomatin Highland Scotland **46** E4 57 20N 3 59W
Tomatlán Mexico **108** C3 19 54N 105 18W
Tombigbee *r.* U.S.A. **103** I3 32 00N 88 00W
Tombouctou Mali **93** E6 16 49N 2 59W
Tombua Angola **95** B4 15 49S 11 53E
Tomintoul Grampian Scotland **46** E4 57 14N 3 22W
Tom Price, Mount Australia **86** B5 22 49S 117 51E
Tomsk U.S.S.R. **71** K7 56 30N 85 05E
Tonala Mexico **108** F3 16 08N 93 41W
Tonawanda New York U.S.A. **105** E2 43 01N 78 54W
Tonbridge Kent England **34** D1 51 12N 0 16E
Tønder Denmark **63** A2 54 57N 8 53E
TONGA **118** I5
Tonga Trench Pacific Ocean **118** I5 20 00S 173 00W
Tongchuan China **81** G5 35 05N 109 02E
Tongeren Belgium **64** E2 50 47N 5 28E
Tonghai China **81** F2 24 07N 102 45E
Tonghua China **81** K6 41 42N 125 45E
Tongking, Gulf of Vietnam/China **80** D7 19 00N 107 00E
Tongling China **81** I4 30 58N 117 48N
Tongue Highland Scotland **46** D5 58 28N 4 25W
Tonle Sap *l.* Cambodia **80** C6 13 00N 104 00E
Tonopah Nevada U.S.A. **102** C4 38 05N 117 15W
Tønsberg Norway **67** C2 59 16N 10 25E
Tonyrefail Mid Glamorgan Wales **38** C1 51 36N 3 25W
Tooele Utah U.S.A. **102** D5 40 32N 112 18W
Toowoomba Australia **86** I4 27 35S 151 54E
Topeka Kansas U.S.A. **104** A1 39 02N 95 41W
Toppings Greater Manchester England **42** C2 53 38N 2 27W
Topsham Devon England **31** D2 50 42N 3 27W
Tor Bay *b.* Devon England **31** D2 50 27N 3 30W
Torbalı Turkey **68** E2 38 07N 27 08E
Torbay *tn. see* Torquay *or* Paignton
Tordesillas Spain **66** A3 41 30N 5 00W
Torhout Belgium **64** C3 51 04N 3 06E
Torino *(Turin)* Italy **68** A4 45 04N 7 40E
Tormes *r.* Spain **66** A3 41 03N 5 58W
Torne älv *r.* Sweden **67** E4 67 03N 23 02E
Torne-träsk *l.* Sweden **67** D4 68 14N 19 40E
Torngat Mountains *(Monts Torngat)* Newfoundland/Québec Canada **101** W4 59 00N 64 15W
Tornio Finland **67** E4 65 50N 24 10E
Toronto Ontario Canada **105** E2 43 42N 79 25W
Tororo Uganda **94** F8 0 42N 34 12E
Toros Dağlari *mts.* Turkey **78** D6 37 10N 33 10E
Torpichen Lothian Scotland **45** C1 55 56N 3 39W
Torpoint *tn.* Cornwall England **31** C2 50 22N 4 11W
Torquay Devon England **31** D2 50 28N 3 30W
Torrance California U.S.A. **107** A2 33 50N 118 20W
Torrance Strathclyde Scotland **45** B1 55 56N 4 11W
Torre del Greco Italy **68** B3 40 46N 14 22E
Torrelavega Spain **66** B3 43 21N 4 03W
Torrens, Lake Australia **86** F3 31 00S 137 50E
Torreón Mexico **108** D5 25 34N 103 25W
Torres Strait Australia **86** G7/G8 10 00S 142 30E
Torridge *r.* Devon England **31** C2 50 55N 4 05W
Torridon Highland Scotland **46** C4 57 33N 5 31W
Torrington Connecticut U.S.A. **105** F2 41 48N 73 08W
Torrisholme Lancashire England **42** B4 54 05N 2 50W
Tortosa Spain **66** C3 40 49N 0 31E
Toruń Poland **69** C3 53 01N 18 35E
Tory Island Irish Republic **48** C5 55 16N 8 14W
Tory Sound Irish Republic **48** C5 55 15N 8 05W
Tosa-wan *b.* Japan **82** B1 33 20N 133 40E
Toshima Japan **83** B3 35 43N 139 41E
Totland Isle of Wight England **32** A1 50 40N 1 32W
Totnes Devon England **31** D2 50 25N 3 41W
Totoya *i.* Fiji **118** V15 18 56S 179 50W
Totsuka Japan **83** B2 35 23N 139 32E
Tottenham Greater London England **34** C2 51 35N 0 05W
Tottington Greater Manchester England **42** C2 53 37N 2 20W
Totton Hampshire England **32** A1 50 56N 1 29W
Tottori Japan **82** B2 35 32N 134 12E
Touggourt Algeria **93** G9 33 08N 6 04E
Toul France **61** C2 48 41N 5 54E
Toulon France **61** C1 43 07N 5 55E
Toulouse France **61** B1 43 33N 1 24E
Toungoo Myanma **80** B7 18 57N 96 26E
Tourcoing France **61** B3 50 44N 3 10E
Tournai Belgium **64** C2 50 36N 3 24E
Tours France **61** B2 47 23N 0 42E
Towcester Northamptonshire England **36** D2 52 08N 1 00W
Tower Hamlets Greater London England **34** C3 51 30N 0 02W
Tow Law *sum.* Durham England **44** C1 54 45N 1 49W
Townhill Fife Scotland **45** D2 56 05N 3 27W
Townsville Australia **86** H6 19 13S 146 48E
Toyama Japan **82** C2 36 42N 137 14E
Toyohashi Japan **82** C1 34 46N 137 22E
Toyota Japan **82** C2 35 05N 137 09E
Tozeur Tunisia **93** G9 33 55N 8 07E
Trabzona Turkey **78** E7 41 00N 39 43E
Tracy Québec Canada **105** F3 45 59N 73 04W
Trail British Columbia Canada **100** L2 49 04N 117 39W
Tralee Kerry Irish Republic **48** B2 52 16N 9 42W
Tralee Bay Irish Republic **48** B2 52 20N 9 55W
Tramore Waterford Irish Republic **48** D2 52 10N 7 10W
Transantarctic Mountains Antarctica **121** 77 00S 147 00E
Transvaal *province* Republic of South Africa **95** E3 24 30S 28 00E
Trápani Italy **68** B2 38 02N 12 32E
Traunstein F.R.G. **63** B1 47 52N 12 39E
Travers, Mount New Zealand **87** B2 42 01S 172 47E
Traverse City Michigan U.S.A. **104** C2 44 46N 85 38W
Trawden Lancashire England **42** D3 53 51N 2 08W
Trawsfynydd Gwynedd Wales **38** C2 52 54N 3 55W
Tredegar Gwent Wales **38** C1 51 47N 3 16W
Tregaron Dyfed Wales **38** C2 52 13N 3 55W
Tregony Cornwall England **30** C2 50 16N 4 55W
Treinta-y-Tres Uruguay **115** G6 33 16S 54 17W
Trelew Chile **115** D4 43 13S 65 15W
Tremadog Bay Gwynedd Wales **38** B2 52 54N 4 15W
Trenčín Czechoslovakia **69** C2 48 53N 18 00E
Trenque Lauquen Argentina **115** E5 35 56S 62 43W
Trent *r.* Midlands England **36** C2–D3
Trent & Mersey Canal England **35** C3 52 25N 1 40W
Trento Italy **68** B4 46 04N 11 08E
Trenton New Jersey U.S.A. **105** F2 40 15N 74 43W
Trenton Ontario Canada **105** E2 44 07N 77 34W
Trepassey Newfoundland Canada **101** Y2 46 45N 53 20W
Tres Arroyos Argentina **115** E5 38 26S 60 17W
Tresco *i.* Isles of Scilly England **30** A1 49 57N 6 20W
Três Lagoas Brazil **114** G8 20 46S 51 43W
Treviso Italy **68** B4 45 40N 12 15E
Trevose Head *c.* Cornwall England **30** B2 50 33N 5 01W
Trichur India **77** D2 10 32N 76 14E
Trier F.R.G. **63** A1 49 45N 6 39E
Trieste Italy **68** B4 45 39N 13 47E
Tríkkala Greece **68** D2 39 33N 21 46E
Trim Meath Irish Republic **48** E3 53 34N 6 47W
Trincomalee Sri Lanka **77** E1 8 34N 81 13E
Trindade *i.* Atlantic Ocean **117** F4 20 30S 29 20W
Tring Hertfordshire England **34** B3 51 48N 0 40W
TRINIDAD AND TOBAGO **109** L2
Trinidad Bolivia **114** E10 14 46S 64 50W
Trinidad Colorado U.S.A. **102** F4 37 11N 104 31W
Trinidad Cuba **109** H4 21 48N 80 00W
Trinidad *i.* Trinidad and Tobago **109** L2 11 00N 61 30W
Trinity *r.* U.S.A. **103** G3 32 00N 96 00W
Trinity Islands Alaska U.S.A. **100** E4 56 45N 154 15W
Tripoli Lebanon *see* Trâblous
Tripoli Libya *see* Tarābulus
Trípolis Greece **68** D2 37 31N 22 22E
Tripura Mizoram *admin.* India **77** G4 23 40N 92 30E
Tristan da Cunha *i.* Atlantic Ocean **117** G3 37 15S 12 30W
Trivandrum India **77** D1 8 30N 76 57E
Trnava Czechoslovakia **69** C2 48 23N 17 35E
Troisdorf F.R.G. **63** A2 50 49N 7 09E
Trois-Pistoles Québec Canada **105** G3 48 08N 69 10W
Trois Rivières *tn.* Québec Canada **105** F3 46 21N 72 34W
Trollhättan Sweden **67** C2 58 17N 12 20E
Trollheimen *mts.* Norway **67** B3 63 00N 9 00E
Tromsø Norway **67** D4 69 42N 19 00E
Trondheim Norway **67** C3 63 36N 10 23E
Trondheimsfjorden *fj.* Norway **67** C3 63 40N 10 30E
Troon Strathclyde Scotland **46** D2 55 32N 4 40W
Trotternish *p.* Skye Scotland **46** B4 57 00N 6 00W
Trout Lake Northwest Territories Canada **100** K5 61 00N 121 30W
Trouville France **61** B2 49 22N 0 05E
Trowbridge Wiltshire England **31** E3 51 20N 2 13W
Troy Alabama U.S.A. **103** I3 31 49N 86 00W
Troy *hist. site* Turkey **78** C6 39 55N 26 17E
Troy New York U.S.A. **105** F2 42 43N 73 43W
Troyes France **61** B2 48 18N 4 05E
Trujillo Peru **114** B11 8 06S 79 00W
Trujillo Spain **66** A2 39 28N 5 53W
Trujillo Venezuela **114** C14 9 20N 70 38W
Truk Islands Caroline Islands **118** F8 7 30N 152 30E
Truro Cornwall England **30** B2 50 16N 5 03W
Truro Nova Scotia Canada **101** W2 45 24N 63 18W
Truyère *r.* France **61** B1 44 55N 2 47E
Tsangpo *see* Yarlung Zangbo Jiang
Tsavo National Park Kenya **94** G7 3 30S 38 00E
Tselinograd U.S.S.R. **71** J6 51 10N 71 28E
Tsenke *r.* Zaïre **92** B1 4 24S 15 26E
Tshane Botswana **95** D3 24 05S 21 54E
Tshuapa *r.* Zaïre **94** D7 1 00S 23 00E
Tsiéme *r.* Congo **92** A2 4 15S 15 17E
Tsu Japan **82** C1 34 41N 136 30E
Tsuchiura Japan **82** D2 36 05N 140 11E
Tsugaru-kaikyō *sd.* Japan **82** D3 41 30N 140 30E
Tsumeb Namibia **95** C4 19 13S 17 42E
Tsunashima Japan **83** B3 35 31N 139 38E
Tsuruga Japan **82** C2 35 40N 136 05E
Tsuruoko Japan **82** C2 38 42N 139 50E
Tsushima *i.* Japan **82** A1 34 30N 129 20E
Tsuyama Japan **82** B2 35 04N 134 01E
Tua *r.* Portugal **66** A3 41 20N 7 30W
Tuam Galway Irish Republic **48** C3 53 31N 8 50W
Tuamotu Archipelago *is.* Pacific Ocean **119** M6 15 00S 145 00W
Tuamotu Ridge Pacific Ocean **119** L6 19 00S 144 00W
Tubbercurry Sligo Irish Republic **48** C4 54 03N 8 43W
Tübingen F.R.G. **63** A1 48 32N 9 04E
Tubize Belgium **64** D2 50 42N 4 12E
Tubruq Libya **94** D14 32 05N 23 59E
Tubuai Islands Pacific Ocean **119** L5 23 23S 149 27W
Tuchitua Yukon Territory Canada **100** J5 61 20N 129 00W
Tucson Arizona U.S.A. **102** D3 32 15N 110 57W
Tucumcari New Mexico U.S.A. **102** F4 35 11N 103 44W
Tucupita Venezuela **114** E14 9 02N 62 04W
Tucuruí Brazil **114** H12 3 42S 49 44W
Tudela Spain **66** B3 42 04N 1 37W
Tudweiliog Gwynedd Wales **38** B2 52 55N 4 39W
Tugaske Saskatchewan Canada **100** N3 50 54N 106 15W
Tujunga California U.S.A. **107** A3 34 14N 118 16W
Tuktoyaktuk Northwest Territories Canada **100** I6 69 24N 133 01W
Tukums U.S.S.R. **67** E2 56 58N 23 10E
Tula Mexico **108** E4 23 00N 99 41W
Tula Mexico **108** E4 20 01N 99 21W
Tula U.S.S.R. **70** F6 54 11N 37 38E
Tulcan Ecuador **114** B3 0 50N 77 48W
Tulcea Romania **69** E2 45 10N 28 50E
Tulkarm Jordan **78** O11 32 19N 35 02E
Tullamore Offaly Irish Republic **48** D3 53 16N 7 30W
Tulle France **61** B2 45 16N 1 46E
Tullibody Central Scotland **45** C2 56 06N 3 47W
Tullow Carlow Irish Republic **48** D2 52 48N 6 44W
Tuloma *r.* U.S.S.R. **67** G4 69 00N 32 00E
Tulpetlac Mexico **108** P2 19 21N 99 02W
Tulsa Oklahoma U.S.A. **103** G4 36 07N 95 58W
Tuluá Colombia **114** B13 4 05N 76 12W
Tulun U.S.S.R. **71** M6 54 32N 100 35E
Tumaco Colombia **114** B13 1 51N 78 46W
Tumbes Peru **114** A12 3 37S 80 27W
Tumkur India **77** D2 13 20N 77 06E
Tummel *r.* Tayside Scotland **46** D3/E3 56 38N 4 00W
Tunduru Tanzania **95** G5 11 08S 27 21E
Tundzha *r.* Bulgaria **68** E3 42 00N 26 00E
Tungabhadra *r.* India **77** D3 16 00N 77 00E
Tungsten Northwest Territories Canada **100** J5 62 25N 128 40W
Tunis Tunisia **93** H10 36 50N 10 13E
TUNISIA **93** G9
Tunja Colombia **114** C14 5 33N 73 23W
Tunnsjøen *l.* Norway **67** C3 64 45N 13 25E
Tunstall Staffordshire England **35** B4 53 05N 2 13W
Tupelo Mississippi U.S.A. **103** I3 34 15N 88 43W
Tupiza Bolivia **114** D8 21 27S 65 45W
Tupper Lake *tn.* New York U.S.A. **105** F2 44 14N 74 29W
Tupton Derbyshire England **43** F1 53 11N 1 26W
Túquerres Colombia **114** B13 1 06N 77 37W
Tura U.S.S.R. **71** M8 64 20N 100 17E
Turda Romania **69** D2 46 35N 23 50E
Turfan *see* Turpan
Turfan Depression China **81** C6 42 40N 89 30E
Turgay *r.* U.S.S.R. **70** I5 50 00N 64 00E
Turgutlu Turkey **68** E2 38 30N 27 43E
Turia *r.* Spain **66** B2 39 45N 0 55W
Turin *see* Torino
Turkana, Lake Ethiopia / Kenya **94** G8 4 00N 36 00E
TURKEY **78** D6
Turkmenskaya S.S.R. *rep.* U.S.S.R. **70** H3/I3 40 00N 60 00E
Turks and Caicos Islands West Indies **109** J4 21 30N 72 00W
Turks Island Passage *sd.* West Indies **109** J4 21 30N 71 30W
Turku Finland **67** E3 60 27N 22 15E
Turnhout Belgium **64** D3 51 19N 4 57E
Turnu Măgurele Romania **69** D1 43 44N 24 53E
Turpan *(Turfan)* China **81** C6 42 55N 89 06E
Turriff Grampian Scotland **46** F4 57 32N 2 28W
Turtle Creek Lake Kansas U.S.A. **104** A1 39 00N 96 00W
Turukhansk U.S.S.R. **71** K9 65 49N 88 00E
Tuscaloosa Alabama U.S.A. **103** I3 33 12N 87 33W
Tushino U.S.S.R. **70** L2 55 52N 37 26E
Tutbury Staffordshire England **35** C3 52 52N 1 40W
Tuticorin India **77** D1 8 48N 78 10E
Tuttlingen F.R.G. **63** A1 47 59N 8 49E
TUVALU **118** H7
Tuxpan Mexico **108** C4 21 58N 105 20W
Tuxpan Mexico **108** E4 20 58N 97 23W
Tuxtla Gutierrez Mexico **108** F3 16 45N 93 09W
Túy Spain **66** A3 42 03N 8 39W
Tuz Gölü *l.* Turkey **78** D6 38 40N 33 35E
Tuzla Yugoslavia **68** C3 44 33N 18 41E
Twechar Strathclyde Scotland **45** B1 55 57N 4 05W
Tweed *r.* Scotland/England **46** F2 55 45N 2 10W
Twickenham Greater London England **34** B2 51 27N 0 20W
Twin Falls *tn.* Idaho U.S.A. **102** D5 42 34N 114 30W
Twin Lakes *tn.* Alberta Canada **100** L4 60 40N 154 00W
Twycross Leicestershire England **35** D2 52 39N 1 30W
Twyford Berkshire England **33** B2 51 29N 0 53W
Twyford Hampshire England **32** A2 51 01N 1 19W
Tyan-Shan' *(Tien Shan) mts.* U.S.S.R. **71** J4 41 00N 76 00E
Tyldesley Greater Manchester England **42** C2 53 32N 2 29W
Tyler Texas U.S.A. **103** G3 32 22N 95 18W
Tylers Green Buckinghamshire England **34** A2 51 37N 0 42W
Tym *r.* U.S.S.R. **71** K7 59 00N 82 30E
Tynda U.S.S.R. **71** O7 55 10N 124 35E
Tyndrum Central Scotland **46** D3 56 27N 4 44W
Tyne *r.* Northern England **44** C1 55 00N 1 50W
Tyne and Wear *admin.* England **44** B3 55 00N 1 10W
Tynemouth Tyne and Wear England **44** C2 55 01N 1 24W
Tynset Norway **67** C3 62 17N 10 47E
Tyre *see* Soûr
Tyrrhenian Sea Europe **68** B3 40 00N 12 00E
Tyumen' U.S.S.R. **70** I7 57 11N 65 29E

Tyung *r.* U.S.S.R. **71** N8 65 00N 119 00E
Tywi *r.* Dyfed Wales **38** C2 51 53N 3 35W
Tywyn Gwynedd Wales **38** B2 52 35N 4 05W

U

Uaupés Brazil **114** D12 0 07S 67 05W
Ubangi *r.* Central African Republic / Zaïre **94** C8 4 00N 18 00E
Ube Japan **82** B1 33 57N 131 16E
Uberaba Brazil **114** H9 19 47S 47 57W
Uberlândia Brazil **114** H9 18 57S 48 17W
Ubon Ratchathani Thailand **80** D7 15 15N 104 50E
Ubort' *r.* U.S.S.R. **69** E3 51 00N 27 00E
Ubundu Zaïre **94** E7 0 24S 25 30E
Uchiura-wan *b.* Japan **82** D3 42 30N 140 40E
Uckfield East Sussex England **33** C1 50 58N 0 05E
Uda *r.* U.S.S.R. **71** P6 54 00N 134 00E
Udaipur India **77** C4 24 36N 73 47E
Uddevalla Sweden **67** C2 58 20N 11 56E
Uddingston Strathclyde Scotland **45** B1 55 50N 4 06W
Uddjaur *l.* Sweden **67** D4 65 55N 17 50E
Uden Netherlands **64** E3 51 40N 5 37E
Udgir India **77** D3 18 26N 77 11E
Udine Italy **68** B4 46 04N 13 14E
Udon Thani Thailand **80** C7 17 25N 102 45E
Ueda Japan **82** C2 36 27N 138 13E
Uele *r.* Zaïre **94** E8 4 00N 27 00E
Uelen U.S.S.R. **71** U9 66 13N 169 48W
Uelzen F.R.G. **63** B2 52 58N 10 34E
Ufa U.S.S.R. **70** H6 54 45N 55 58E
Uffculme Devon England **31** D2 50 54N 3 21W
Ugab *r.* Namibia **95** C3 21 00S 15 00E
UGANDA **94** F8
Uig Highland Scotland **46** B4 57 35N 6 22W
Uinta Mountains Utah U.S.A. **102** D5 40 00N 111 00W
Uitenhage Republic of South Africa **95** E1 33 46S 25 25E
Uithoorn Netherlands **65** D2 52 14N 4 49E
Uithuizen Netherlands **64** F5 53 24N 6 41E
Ujjain India **77** D4 23 11N 75 50E
Ujung Pandang Indonesia **80** F2 5 09S 119 28E
Ukhta U.S.S.R. **70** H8 63 33N 53 44E
Ukiah California U.S.A. **102** B4 39 09N 123 12W
Ukmerge U.S.S.R. **69** D4 55 14N 24 49E
Ukraine *see* Ukrainskaya S.S.R.
Ukrainskaya S.S.R. *rep.* U.S.S.R. **70** E5 50 00N 27 30E
Ulaanbaatar *(Ulan Bator)* Mongolia **81** G7 47 54N 106 52E
Ulaangom Mongolia **81** D7 49 59N 92 00E
Ulan Bator *see* Ulaanbaatar
Ulan-Ude U.S.S.R. **71** M6 51 55N 107 40E
Ulhasnagar India **77** C3 19 15N 73 08E
Uliastay Mongolia **81** E7 47 42N 96 52E
Ullapool Highland Scotland **46** C4 57 54N 5 10W
Ullenhall Warwickshire England **35** C1 52 17N 1 50W
Ullswater *l.* Cumbria England **44** B1 54 35N 2 55W
Ulm F.R.G. **63** A1 48 24N 10 00E
Ulsan South Korea **81** K5 35 32N 129 21E
Uluberiya India **76** J1 22 28N 88 07E
Ulungur Hu *l.* China **81** C7 47 10N 87 10E
Ulva *i.* Strathclyde Scotland **46** B3 56 30N 6 15W
Ulverston Cumbria England **44** A1 54 12N 3 06W
Ul'yanovsk U.S.S.R. **70** G6 54 19N 48 22E
Uman' U.S.S.R. **69** F2 48 45N 30 10E
Ume älv *r.* Sweden **67** D3 64 45N 18 20E
Umeå Sweden **67** E3 63 50N 20 15E
Umiat Alaska U.S.A. **100** E6 69 25N 152 20W
Umm as Samim *geog. reg.* Oman **79** I3 22 10N 56 00E
Umm Ruwaba Sudan **94** F10 12 50N 31 20E
Umnak Island Alaska U.S.A. **100** B3 53 20N 168 20W
Umtata Republic of South Africa **95** E1 31 35S 28 47E
Umuarama Brazil **115** G8 23 43S 52 57W
Una *r.* Yugoslavia **68** C4 45 00N 17 00E
Unalakleet Alaska U.S.A. **100** C5 63 52N 160 50W
Unalaska Islands Alaska U.S.A. **100** B3 53 40N 166 40W
Unapool Highland Scotland **46** C5 58 14N 5 00W
'Unayzah Saudi Arabia **78** F4 26 06N 43 58E
Ungava Bay Québec Canada **101** V4 59 00N 67 30W
Union New Jersey U.S.A. **106** B1 40 42N 74 14W
Union City New Jersey U.S.A. **106** B2 40 45N 74 01W
UNION OF SOVIET SOCIALIST REPUBLICS *(U.S.S.R.)* **70/71**
Uniontown Pennsylvania U.S.A. **105** E1 39 54N 79 44W
UNITED ARAB EMIRATES *(U.A.E.)* **79** H3
UNITED KINGDOM *(U.K.)* **29**
UNITED STATES OF AMERICA *(U.S.A.)* **102/103**
Unna F.R.G. **63** A2 51 32N 7 41E
Unst *i.* Shetland Islands Scotland **47** C2 60 45N 0 55W
Unstone Derbyshire England **43** F1 53 17N 1 26W
Unstrut *r.* G.D.R. **63** B2 51 00N 10 00E
Upata Venezuela **114** E14 8 02N 62 25W
Upavon Wiltshire England **31** F3 51 18N 1 49W
Upernavik Greenland **101** X7 72 40N 56 05W
Uphall Lothian Scotland **45** C1 55 56N 3 31W
Upington Republic of South Africa **95** D2 28 28S 21 14E
Uplawmoor Strathclyde Scotland **45** B1 55 46N 4 29W
Upminster Greater London England **34** D2 51 34N 0 15E
Upolu Point Hawaiian Islands **119** Z18 20 16N 155 52W
Upper Bay U.S.A. **106** B1 40 40N 74 03W
Upper Hutt New Zealand **87** C2 41 06S 175 06E
Upper Liard Yukon Territory Canada **100** J5 60 00N 129 20W
Upper Lough Erne *l.* Ireland **48** D4 54 15N 7 30W
Uppermill Greater Manchester England **42** D2 53 34N 2 02W
Upper Poppleton North Yorkshire England **43** G3 53 58N 1 09W
Upper Red Lake Minnesota U.S.A. **104** B3 48 04N 94 48W
Upper Tean Staffordshire England **36** C2 52 57N 2 00W
Uppingham Leicestershire England **36** D2 52 35N 0 43W
Uppsala Sweden **67** D2 59 55N 17 38E
Upton Cheshire England **42** B1 53 13N 2 52W
Upton Dorset England **31** E2 50 42N 2 02W
Upton Snodsbury Hereford & Worcester England **35** B1 52 11N 2 04W
Upton-upon-Severn Hereford and Worcester
Upton West Yorkshire England **43** G2 53 37N 1 17W
Ur *hist. site* Iraq **79** G5 30 56N 46 08E
Uraga Japan **83** B1 35 14N 139 43E
Uraga Strait Japan **83** C2 35 17N 139 45E
Urakawa Japan **82** D3 42 10N 142 46E
Ural *r.* U.S.S.R. **70** H5 48 00N 52 00E
Ural Mountains U.S.S.R. **70** H6–H8
Ural'sk U.S.S.R. **70** H6 51 19N 51 20E
Uranium City Saskatchewan Canada **100** N4 59 32N 108 43W
Urawa Japan **82** C2 35 52N 139 40E
Urayasu Japan **83** C3 35 39N 139 54E
Ure *r.* North Yorkshire England **40** C3 54 05N 1 20W
Urengoy U.S.S.R. **71** J9 65 59N 78 30E
Urfa Turkey **78** E6 37 08N 38 45E
Urgench U.S.S.R. **70** I4 41 35N 60 41E
Urk Netherlands **64** E4 52 40N 5 35E
Urmia, Lake *see* Daryacheh-ye Orūmīyeh
Urmston Greater Manchester England **42** C2 53 27N 2 21W
Uroševac Yugoslavia **68** D3 42 21N 21 09E
Urubamba Peru **114** C10 13 20S 72 07W
Uruguaiana Brazil **115** F7 29 45S 57 05W
URUGUAY **115** F6
Ürümqi China **81** C6 43 43N 87 38E
Urziceni Romania **69** E1 44 43N 26 39E
U.S.A. *see* UNITED STATES OF AMERICA
Usa *r.* U.S.S.R. **71** H9 66 00N 57 00E
Usborne, Mount Falkland Islands **117** M16 51 35S 58 57W
Usedom *i.* G.D.R. **63** B2 54 00N 13 00E
Ushaw Moor *tn.* Durham England **44** C1 54 47N 1 39W
Ushuaia Argentina **115** D2 54 48S 68 19W
Usinsk U.S.S.R. **70** H9 65 57N 57 27E
Usk *r.* Wales **38** C1 51 50N 3 10W
Usk Gwent Wales **38** D1 51 43N 2 54W
Usküdar Turkey **78** C7 41 02N 29 02E
Usol'ye-Sibirskoye U.S.S.R. **71** M6 52 48N 103 40E
Ussel France **61** B2 45 32N 2 18E
U.S.S.R. *see* UNION OF SOVIET SOCIALIST REPUBLICS
Ussuri *(Wusul Jiang) r.* U.S.S.R. **71** 47 00N 134 00E
Ussuri *see* Wusul Jiang
Ussuriysk U.S.S.R. **71** P4 43 48N 131 59E
Ústí Czechoslovakia **69** B3 50 40N 14 02E
Ustica *i.* Italy **68** B2 38 00N 13 00E
Ust'-Ilimsk U.S.S.R. **71** M7 58 03N 102 39E
Ust'-Kamchatsk U.S.S.R. **71** S7 56 14N 162 28E
Ust'-Kamenogorsk U.S.S.R. **71** K5 49 58N 82 36E
Ust'-Kut U.S.S.R. **71** M7 56 48N 105 42E
Ust'Maya U.S.S.R. **71** P8 60 25N 134 28E
Ust'-Nera U.S.S.R. **71** Q8 64 35N 143 14E
Ust'Olenëk U.S.S.R. **71** N10 72 59N 119 57E
Ust Urt Plateau U.S.S.R. **70** H4 43 30N 55 00E
Usulután El Salvador **108** G2 13 20N 88 25W
Utah *state* U.S.A. **102** D4 39 00N 112 00W
Utah Lake Utah U.S.A. **102** D5 40 10N 111 50W
Utica New York U.S.A. **105** E2 43 06N 75 15W
Utrecht *admin.* Netherlands **64** E4 52 07N 5 10E
Utrecht Netherlands **65** E2 52 05N 5 07E
Utrera Spain **66** A2 37 10N 5 47W
Utsunomiya Japan **82** C2 36 33N 139 52E
Uttar *admin.* India **77** E4 27 00N 80 00E
Uttaradit Thailand **80** C7 17 38N 100 05E
Uttarpāra-Kotrung India **76** K2 22 39N 88 20E
Uttoxeter Staffordshire England **35** C3 52 54N 1 52W
Uvalde Texas U.S.A. **102** G2 29 14N 99 49W
Uvinza Tanzania **95** F6 5 08S 30 23E
Uvs Nuur *l.* Mongolia **81** D8 50 10N 92 30E
Uwajima Japan **82** B1 33 13N 132 32E
Uxbridge Greater London England **34** B2 51 33N 0 30W
Uyuni Bolivia **114** D8 20 28S 66 47W
Už *r.* Europe **69** D2 48 00N 22 00E
Uzbekskaya S.S.R. *rep.* U.S.S.R. **70** H4/I4 44 00N 60 00E
Uzhgorod U.S.S.R. **69** D2 48 39N 22 15E

V

Vaal *r.* Republic of South Africa **95** E2 27 30S 25 30E
Vaasa Finland **67** E3 63 06N 21 36E
Vác Hungary **69** C2 47 46N 19 08E
Vadodara India **77** C4 22 19N 73 14E
Vaduz Liechtenstein **61** C2 47 08N 9 32E
Vaga *r.* U.S.S.R. **70** G8 62 00N 43 00E
Váh *r.* Czechoslovakia **69** C2 48 00N 18 00E
Vakh *r.* U.S.S.R. **71** K8 61 30N 80 00E
Vakhsh *r.* Asia **70** I3 37 00N 68 00E
Valdepeñas Spain **66** B2 38 46N 3 24W
Valdés, Peninsula Argentina **115** E4 42 30S 63 00W
Valdivia Chile **115** C5 39 46S 73 15W
Val-d'Or Québec Canada **105** E3 48 07N 77 47W
Val d'Or *tn.* Québec Canada **101** T2 48 07N 77 47W
Valdosta Georgia U.S.A. **103** J3 30 51N 83 51W
Valdres *geog. reg.* Norway **67** B3 60 55N 8 40E
Valença Brazil **114** J10 13 22S 39 06W
Valence France **61** B1 44 56N 4 54E
Valencia Spain **66** B2 39 29N 0 24W
Valencia Venezuela **114** D15 10 14N 67 59W
Valencia, Gulf of Spain **66** C2 39 30N 0 20E
Valenciennes France **61** B3 50 22N 3 32E
Valentia Island Irish Republic **48** A1 51 52N 10 20W
Valera Venezuela **114** C14 9 21N 70 38W
Valga U.S.S.R. **67** F2 57 44N 26 00E
Valjevo Yugoslavia **68** C3 44 16N 19 56E
Valkenswaard Netherlands **64** E3 51 21N 5 27E
Valladolid Mexico **108** G4 20 40N 88 11W
Valladolid Spain **66** B3 41 39N 4 45W
Valle de la Pascua Venezuela **114** D14 9 15N 66 00W
Valledupar Colombia **114** C15 10 31N 73 16W
Valle Grande Bolivia **114** E9 18 30S 64 06W
Vallée Jonction Québec Canada **105** F3 46 22N 70 58W
Vallejo California U.S.A. **102** B4 38 05N 122 14W
Vallenar Chile **115** C7 28 36S 70 45W
Valletta Malta **68** B2 35 54N 14 32E
Valley Gwynedd Wales **38** B3 53 17N 4 34W
Valley City North Dakota U.S.A. **104** A3 46 57N 97 58W
Valleyfield Fife Scotland **45** C2 56 04N 3 36W
Valleyfield Québec Canada **105** F3 45 15N 74 08W
Valley Stream *tn.* New York U.S.A. **106** D1 40 39N 73 42W
Valmiera U.S.S.R. **67** F2 57 32N 25 29E
Valparaíso Chile **115** C6 33 05S 71 40W
Van Turkey **78** F6 38 28N 43 20E
Van Buren Maine U.S.A. **105** G3 47 10N 67 59W
Vancouver British Columbia Canada **100** K2 49 13N 123 06W
Vancouver Washington U.S.A. **102** B6 45 38N 122 40W
Vancouver Island British Columbia Canada **100** J2 49 30N 126 00W
Vandalia Illinois U.S.A. **104** C1 38 58N 89 05W
Vänern *l.* Sweden **67** C2 59 00N 13 30E
Van Gölü *l.* Turkey **78** F6 38 33N 42 46E
Vanier Ontario Canada **105** E3 45 27N 75 40W
Vanna *i.* Norway **67** D5 70 05N 19 50E
Vännäs Sweden **67** D3 63 56N 19 50E
Vannes France **61** A2 47 40N 2 44W
Van Norman Lake California U.S.A. **107** A4 34 17N 118 28W
Vantaa Finland **67** E3 60 20N 24 50E
Vanua Levu *i.* Fiji **118** U16 16 20S 179 00E
Vanua Levu Barrier Reef Fiji **118** U16 17 10S 179 00E
Vanua Mbalavu *i.* Fiji **118** V16 17 15S 178 55W
VANUATU **86** L6
Vanves France **60** B2 48 49N 2 17E
Van Wert Ohio U.S.A. **105** D2 40 53N 84 36W
Var *r.* France **61** C1 43 55N 6 55E
Varanasi India **77** E5 25 20N 83 00E
Varangerfjorden *fj.* Norway **67** G4 70 00N 30 00E
Varangerhalvøya *p.* Norway **67** F5 70 22N 29 40E
Varaždin Yugoslavia **68** C4 46 18N 16 21E
Vardar *r.* Yugoslavia **68** D3 41 00N 22 00E
Vardø Norway **67** G5 70 22N 31 06E
Varese Italy **61** C2 45 49N 8 49E
Vargem Grande Brazil **116** B2 22 59S 43 29W
Varkhaus Finland **67** F3 62 20N 27 50E
Varna Bulgaria **68** E3 43 12N 27 57E
Värnamo Sweden **67** C2 57 11N 14 03E
Várzea Grande Brazil **114** I11 6 32S 42 05W
Vaslui Romania **69** E2 46 37N 27 46E
Västerås Sweden **67** D2 59 36N 16 32E
Västerdalälven *r.* Sweden **67** C3 61 15N 18 10E
Västervik Sweden **67** D2 57 45N 16 40E
Vasyugan *r.* U.S.S.R. **71** J7 59 00N 77 00E
Vatersay *i.* Western Isles Scotland **46** A3 56 55N 7 32W
Vatnajökull *ice cap* Iceland **67** I6 64 30N 17 00W
Vättern *l.* Sweden **67** C2 58 20N 14 20E
Vatulele *i.* Fiji **118** T15 18 30S 177 38E
Vaucresson France **60** A2 48 51N 2 08E
Vaughan Ontario Canada **105** E2 43 49N 79 36W
Växjö Sweden **67** C2 56 52N 14 50E
Vaygach *i.* U.S.S.R. **71** H10 70 00N 59 00E
Vecht *r.* Netherlands **64** F4 52 20N 7 15E
Vechta F.R.G. **63** A2 52 44N 8 17E
Vechte *r.* F.R.G. **64** G4 52 00N 7 00E
Veendam Netherlands **64** F5 53 07N 6 53E
Veenendaal Netherlands **64** E4 52 02N 5 34E
Vega *i.* Norway **67** C4 65 38N 11 52E
Veghel Netherlands **64** E3 51 37N 5 33E
Vejle Denmark **67** B2 55 43N 9 33E
Velbert F.R.G. **62** C2 51 22N 7 03E
Veldhoven Netherlands **64** E3 51 24N 5 24E
Velebit *mts.* Yugoslavia **68** C3 44 00N 15 00E
Velikaya *r.* U.S.S.R. **67** F2 57 00N 28 45E
Velikiye-Luki U.S.S.R. **70** F7 56 19N 30 31E
Veliko Tŭrnovo Bulgaria **68** E3 43 04N 25 39E
Vellore India **77** D2 12 56N 79 09E
Velsen Netherlands **65** C3 52 28N 4 39E
Veluwe *geog. reg.* Netherlands **64** E4 52 10N 5 47E
Vendôme France **61** B2 47 48N 1 04E
Venézia Italy **68** B4 45 26N 12 20E
VENEZUELA **114** D14
Venezuelan Basin Caribbean Sea **117** B8 15 00N 65 00W
Vénissieux France **61** B2 45 42N 4 46E
Venlo Netherlands **64** F3 51 22N 6 10E
Venraij Netherlands **64** E3 51 32N 5 59E
Venta *r.* U.S.S.R. **67** E2 56 05N 21 50E
Ventnor Isle of Wight England **32** A1 50 36N 1 11W
Ventspils U.S.S.R. **67** E2 57 22N 21 31E
Ventura California U.S.A. **102** C3 34 16N 119 18W
Veracruz Mexico **108** E3 19 11N 96 10W
Veraval India **76** C4 20 53N 70 28E
Vercelli Italy **68** A4 45 19N 8 26E
Verde *r.* Arizona U.S.A. **102** D3 34 00N 112 00W
Verden F.R.G. **63** A2 52 56N 9 14E
Verdon *r.* France **61** C1 43 45N 6 10E
Verdun-sur-Meuse France **61** C2 49 10N 5 24E
Vereeniging Republic of South Africa **95** E2 26 41S 27 56E
Vergennes Vermont U.S.A. **105** F2 44 11N 73 16W
Verin Spain **66** A3 41 55N 7 26W
Verkhoyansk U.S.S.R. **71** P9 67 35N 133 25E
Verkhoyansk Range *mts.* U.S.S.R. **71** O9–P8 65 00N 130 00E
Vermillion South Dakota U.S.A. **104** A2 42 48N 96 55W
Vermilion Bay *tn.* Ontario Canada **104** B3 49 51N 93 21W
Vermilion Lake Minnesota U.S.A. **104** B3 48 00N 93 00W
Vermont *state* U.S.A. **105** F2 44 00N 73 00W
Vernon British Columbia Canada **100** L3 50 17N 119 19W
Vernon Texas U.S.A. **102** G3 34 10N 99 19W
Véroia Greece **68** D3 40 32N 22 11E
Verona Italy **68** B4 45 26N 11 00E
Verrières France **60** B1 48 44N 2 16E
Versailles France **60** A2 48 48N 2 07E
Verviers Belgium **64** E2 50 36N 5 52E
Vervins France **64** C1 49 50N 3 55E
Verwood Dorset England **31** F2 50 53N 1 52W
Vesdre *r.* Belgium **64** F2 50 35N 6 05E
Vesoul France **61** C2 47 38N 6 09E
Vestfjorden *fj.* Norway **67** C4 68 00N 14 50E
Vestmannaeyjar *is.* Iceland H6 63 28N 20 30W
Vesuvio *mt.* Italy **68** B3 40 49N 14 26E
Vesuvius *see* Vesuvio
Vetlanda Sweden **67** D2 57 26N 15 05E
Veurne Belgium **64** B3 51 04N 2 40E
Vevey Switzerland **61** C2 46 28N 6 51E
Vézère *r.* France **61** B2 45 30N 1 40E
Viana do Castelo Portugal **66** A3 41 41N 8 50W
Viar *r.* Spain **66** A2 37 45N 5 50W
Viborg Denmark **67** B2 56 28N 9 25E
Vicecomodoro Marambio *r.s.* Antarctica **121** 64 14S 56 38W
Vicente Guerrero Mexico **108** A6 30 48N 116 00W
Vicenza Italy **68** B4 45 33N 11 32E
Vichy France **61** B2 46 07N 3 25E
Vicksburg Mississippi U.S.A. **103** H3 32 21N 90 51W
Victoria *r.* Australia **86** E6 131 30S 17 00S
Victoria *state* Australia **86** G2/H2
Victoria British Columbia Canada **100** K2 48 26N 123 20W
Victoria Chile **115** C5 38 20S 72 30W
Victoria Texas U.S.A. **103** G2 28 49N 97 01W
Victoria Beach *tn.* Manitoba Canada **104** A4 50 43N 96 32W
Victoria Falls Zambia / Zimbabwe **95** E4 17 55S 25 51E
Victoria Island Northwest Territories Canada **100** M7 70 45N 115 00W
Victoria Island *tn.* Nigeria **92** D3 6 21N 3 31E
Victoria, Lake East Africa **94** F7 2 00S 33 00E
Victoria Land *geog. reg.* Antarctica **121** 75 00S 157 00E
Victoria Strait Northwest Territories Canada **101** O6 69 00N 100 00W
Victoriaville Québec Canada **105** F3 46 04N 71 57W
Victoria West Republic of South Africa **95** D1 31 25S 23 08E
Vidin Bulgaria **68** D3 44 00N 22 50E
Viedma Argentina **115** E4 40 45S 63 00W
Vienna *see* Wien
Vienne France **61** B2 45 32N 4 54E
Vienne *r.* France **61** B2 45 50N 0 08E
Vientiane Laos **80** C7 17 59N 102 38E
Viersen F.R.G. **64** F3 51 16N 6 24E
Vierwaldstätter See *l.* Switzerland **61** C2 46 55N 8 30E
Vierzon France **61** B2 47 14N 2 03E
VIETNAM **80** D7
Viewpark Strathclyde Scotland **45** B1 55 49N 4 04W
Vigia Brazil **114** H12 0 50S 48 07W
Vigo Spain **66** A3 42 15N 8 44W
Vijayawada India **77** E3 16 34N 80 40E
Vijosë *r.* Europe **68** D3 40 00N 20 00E
Vikna *i.* Norway **67** C3 64 55N 10 55E
Vila Vanuatu **86** L6 17 45S 168 18E
Vila Nova de Gaia Portugal **66** A3 41 08N 8 37W
Vila Pedro Brazil **116** B2 22 49S 43 20W
Vila Real Portugal **66** A3 41 17N 7 45W
Vila Velha Brazil **114** I8 20 23S 40 18W
Vilaine *r.* France **61** A2 47 50N 1 50W
Vilhelmina Sweden **67** D3 64 38N 16 40E
Vilhena Brazil **114** J10 12 40S 60 08W
Villach Austria **69** B2 46 37N 13 51E
Villa Constitución Mexico **108** B5 25 05N 111 45W
Villa el Salvador Peru **116** F4 12 12S 76 57W
Villa Gustavo a Madero Mexico **108** P1 19 29N 99 08W
Villahermosa Mexico **108** F3 18 00N 92 53W
Villalba Spain **66** A3 43 17N 7 41W
Villa María Argentina **115** E6 32 25S 63 15W
Villa Montes Bolivia **114** E8 21 15S 63 30W
Villanueva Mexico **108** D4 22 24N 102 53W
Villa Obregón Mexico **108** P1 19 21N 99 11W
Villarrica Chile **115** C5 39 15S 72 15W
Villarrobledo Spain **66** B2 39 16N 2 36W
Villa Unión Argentina **115** D7 29 27S 62 46W
Villa Unión Mexico **108** C4 23 10N 106 12W
Villavicencio Colombia **114** C13 4 09N 73 38W
Villefranche-sur-Saône France **61** B2 46 00N 4 43E
Villejuif France **60** B2 48 47N 2 23E
Villeneuve d'Ascq France **64** C2 50 37N 3 10E
Villeneuve St. Georges France **60** B1 48 43N 2 27E
Villeneuve-sur-Lot France **61** B1 44 25N 0 43E
Villeparisis France **60** C2 48 56N 2 37E
Villeurbanne France **61** B2 45 46N 4 54E
Villingen-Schwenningen F.R.G. **63** A1 48 03N 8 28E
Vilnius U.S.S.R. **70** E6 54 40N 25 19E
Vilnya *r.* U.S.S.R. **69** E3 54 00N 25 00E
Vils *r.* F.R.G. **63** B1 48 00N 12 00E
Vilvoorde Belgium **64** D2 50 56N 4 25E
Vilyuy *r.* U.S.S.R. **71** O8 64 00N 123 00E
Vilyuysk U.S.S.R. **71** O8 63 46N 121 35E
Viña del Mar Chile **115** C6 33 02S 71 35W
Vinaroz Spain **66** C3 40 29N 0 28E
Vincennes France **60** B2 48 51N 2 27E
Vincennes Indiana U.S.A. **104** C1 38 42N 87 30W
Vindelälven *r.* Sweden **67** D4 65 15N 18 15E
Vindhya Range *mts.* India **77** C4 23 00N 75 00E
Vineland New Jersey U.S.A. **105** E1 39 29N 75 02W
Vinh Vietnam **80** D7 18 42N 105 41E
Vinkeveense Plassen *l.* Netherlands **65** D2 52 15N 4 51E
Vinkovci Yugoslavia **68** C4 45 16N 18 49E
Vinnitsa U.S.S.R. **70** E5 49 11N 28 30E
Vipiteno Italy **68** B4 46 54N 11 27E
Virgin *r.* U.S.A. **102** D4 37 00N 114 00W
Virginia *state* U.S.A. **103** K4 38 00N 77 00W
Virginia Beach *tn.* Virginia U.S.A. **103** K4 36 51N 75 59W
Virginia Cavan Irish Republic **48** D3 53 49N 7 04W
Virginia Minnesota U.S.A. **104** B3 47 30N 92 28W
Virginia Water *tn.* Surrey England **34** B2 51 24N 0 34W
Virgin Islands West Indies **109** L3 18 00N 64 30W
Viroqua Wisconsin U.S.A. **104** B2 43 33N 90 54W
Virovitica Yugoslavia **68** C4 45 50N 17 25E
Virton Belgium **64** E1 49 34N 5 32E
Vis *i.* Yugoslavia **68** C3 43 00N 16 00E
Visalia California U.S.A. **102** C4 36 20N 119 18W
Visby Sweden **67** D2 57 32N 18 15E
Viscount Melville Sound Northwest Territories Canada **101** N7 74 10N 105 00W
Viseu Portugal **66** A3 40 40N 7 55W
Vishakhapatnam India **77** E3 17 42N 83 24E
Vistula *see* Wisła
Vitebsk U.S.S.R. **70** F7 55 10N 30 14E
Viterbo Italy **68** B3 42 24N 12 06E
Vitichi Bolivia **114** D8 20 14S 65 22W
Viti Levu *i.* Fiji **118** T15 18 10S 177 55E
Vitim *r.* U.S.S.R. **71** N7 58 00N 113 00E
Vitim U.S.S.R. **71** N7 59 28N 112 35E
Vitória Brazil **114** I8 20 20S 40 18W
Vitoria Spain **66** B3 42 51N 2 40W
Vitória da Conquista Brazil **114** I10 14 53S 40 52W
Vitry-le-François France **61** B2 48 44N 4 36E
Vitry-sur-Seine France **60** B2 48 47N 2 24E
Vityaz Trench Pacific Ocean **118** G7 9 30S 170 00E
Vivi *r.* U.S.S.R. **71** L9 61 00N 96 00E
Vize *i.* U.S.S.R. **71** J11 79 30N 77 00E
Vizianagaram India **77** E3 18 07N 83 30E
Vlaardingen Netherlands **65** B1 51 54N 4 20E
Vladimir U.S.S.R. **70** G7 56 08N 40 25E
Vladimir Volynskiy U.S.S.R. **69** D3 50 51N 24 19E
Vladivostok U.S.S.R. **71** P4 43 09N 131 53E
Vlanen Netherlands **65** E1 51 59N 5 05E
Vlieland *i.* Netherlands **64** D5 53 16N 5 00E
Vlissingen Netherlands **64** C3 51 27N 3 35E
Vlorë Albania **68** C3 40 29N 19 29E
Vltava *r.* Czechoslovakia **69** B2 49 00N 14 00E
Vogelsberg *mts.* F.R.G. **63** A2 50 00N 9 00E
Vohwinkel F.R.G. **62** C1 51 13N 7 05E
Voi Kenya **94** G7 3 23S 38 35E
Volendam Netherlands **64** E4 52 30N 5 04E
Volga *r.* U.S.S.R. **70** G5/G6 50 00N 45 00E
Volgodonsk U.S.S.R. **70** G5 47 35N 42 08E
Volgograd U.S.S.R. **70** G5 48 45N 44 30E
Volksrust Republic of South Africa **95** E2 27 22S 29 54E
Vologda U.S.S.R. **70** F7 59 10N 39 55E
Vólos Greece **68** D2 39 22N 22 57E
Volta Redonda Brazil **115** I8 22 31S 44 05W
Volta, Lake Ghana **93** E4 7 30N 0 30W
Volturno *r.* Italy **68** B3 41 00N 14 00E
Volzhskiy U.S.S.R. **70** G5 48 48N 44 45E
Voorburg Netherlands **65** B2 52 04N 4 22E
Voorne *geog. reg.* Netherlands **65** A1 51 53N 4 08E
Voorschoten Netherlands **65** B2 52 07N 4 27E
Voorst Netherlands **64** F4 52 10N 6 10E
Vopnafjördur Iceland **67** J7 65 46N 14 50W
Vorarlberg *admin.* Austria **63** A1 47 00N 10 00E
Vorderrhein *r.* Switzerland **61** C2 46 45N 9 15E
Vordingborg Denmark **63** B3 55 01N 11 55E
Voriai Sporadhes *is.* Greece **68** D2 39 00N 24 00E
Vorkuta U.S.S.R. **71** I9 67 27N 64 00E
Voronezh U.S.S.R. **70** F6 51 40N 39 13E
Voroshilovgrad U.S.S.R. **70** F5 48 35N 39 20E
Vørterkaka Nunatak *mt.* Antarctica **121** 71 45S 32 00E
Võrtsjärv *l.* U.S.S.R. **67** F2 58 15N 26 10E
Võru U.S.S.R. **67** F2 57 46N 26 52E
Vosges *mts.* France **61** C2 48 10N 6 50E
Voss Norway **67** B3 60 38N 6 25E

Vostochnyy U.S.S.R. 71 P4 42 52N 132 56E
Vostok *r.s.* Antarctica 121 78 27S 106 51E
Vouga *r.* Portugal 66 A3 40 45N 8 15W
Vouziers France 64 D1 49 25N 4 41E
Voxnan Sweden 67 D3 61 22N 15 39E
Vrangelya *(Wrangel) i.* U.S.S.R. 71 T10 71 30N 180 00
Vranje Yugoslavia 68 D3 42 33N 21 54E
Vratsa Bulgaria 68 D3 43 12N 23 32E
Vrbas *r.* Yugoslavia 68 C3 44 00N 17 00E
Vršac Yugoslavia 68 D4 45 07N 21 19E
Vryburg Republic of South Africa 95 D2 26 57S 24 44E
Vught Netherlands 64 E3 51 40N 5 18E
Vukovar Yugoslavia 68 C4 45 19N 19 01E
Vung Tau Vietnam 80 D6 10 21N 107 04E
Vunisea Fiji 118 U15 19 04S 178 09E
Vyatka *r.* U.S.S.R. 70 G7 58 00N 50 00E
Vyborg U.S.S.R. 67 F3 60 45N 28 41E
Vychegda *r.* U.S.S.R. 70 H8 62 00N 52 00E
Vyrnwy *r.* Powys Wales 38 C2 52 41N 3 25W
Vyrnwy, Lake Powys Wales 38 C2 52 47N 3 30W

W
Wa Ghana 93 E5 10 07N 2 28W
Waal *r.* Netherlands 64 E3 51 50N 5 07E
Waalwijk Netherlands 64 E3 51 42N 5 04E
Wabana Newfoundland Canada 101 Y2 47 40N 52 58W
Wabash Indiana U.S.A. 104 C2 40 47N 85 48W
Wabash *r.* U.S.A. 104 C1 39 00N 87 00W
Wabowden Manitoba Canada 101 P3 54 57N 98 38W
Wabush Lake *tn.* Newfoundland Canada 101 V3 52 45N 66 30W
Waco Texas U.S.A. 103 G3 31 33N 97 10W
Waddeneilanden *(West Frisian Islands)* Netherlands 64 E5 53 25N 5 15E
Waddenzee *sea* Netherlands 64 E5 53 15N 5 15E
Waddesdon Buckinghamshire England 33 B2 51 51N 0 56W
Waddington Lancashire England 42 C3 53 54N 2 24W
Waddington Lincolnshire England 36 D3 53 10N 0 32W
Waddington, Mount British Columbia Canada 100 J3 51 22N 125 14W
Wadebridge Cornwall England 30 C2 50 32N 4 50W
Wadhurst East Sussex England 33 C2 51 04N 0 21E
Wādī al Masīlah *r.* South Yemen 79 H2 16 00N 50 00E
Wadi Araba *r.* Israel 78 O10 30 30N 35 10E
Wadi el'Arish *r.* Egypt 78 N10 30 05N 33 50E
Wadi Halfa Sudan 78 D3 21 55N 31 20E
Wadinxveen Netherlands 65 C2 52 02N 4 39E
Wad Medani Sudan 78 D1 14 24N 33 30E
Waesch, Mount Antarctica 121 77 00S 127 30W
Wageningen Netherlands 64 E3 51 58N 5 40E
Wager Bay Northwest Territories Canada 101 R6 66 00N 89 00W
Wagga Wagga Australia 86 H2 35 07S 147 24E
Wagin Australia 86 B3 33 20S 117 15E
Wah Pakistan 77 C6 33 50N 72 44E
Waha Libya 94 C13 28 10N 19 57E
Wahiawa Hawaiian Islands 119 X18 21 35N 158 05W
Wahpeton North Dakota U.S.A. 104 A3 46 16N 96 36W
Waialua Hawaiian Islands 119 X18 21 35N 158 08W
Waigeo *i.* Indonesia 80 I3 0 00 131 00E
Waihi New Zealand 87 C3 37 22S 175 51E
Waikaremoana, Lake New Zealand 87 C3 38 50S 178 40E
Waikato New Zealand 87 C3 38 00S 175 30E
Wailuku Hawaiian Islands 119 Y18 20 54N 156 30W
Waimate New Zealand 87 B2 44 45S 171 03E
Wainfleet All Saints Lincolnshire England 36 E3 53 06N 0 15E
Wainwright Alaska U.S.A. 100 D7 70 39N 160 10W
Wainwright Alberta Canada 100 M3 53 15N 110 20W
Waipawa New Zealand 87 C3 39 48S 176 36E
Wairoa New Zealand 87 C3 39 03S 177 25E
Waitaki *r.* New Zealand 87 B2 44 30S 170 30E
Waitara New Zealand 87 B3 38 59S 174 13E
Wajima Japan 82 C2 37 23N 136 53E
Wajir Kenya 94 G8 1 46N 40 05E
Wakasa-wan *b.* Japan 82 C2 35 40N 135 30E
Wakatipu, Lake New Zealand 87 A1 45 00S 168 50E
Wakayama Japan 82 C1 34 12N 135 10E
Wake Island Pacific Ocean 118 G10 19 18N 166 36E
Wakefield Rhode Island U.S.A. 105 F2 41 26N 71 30W
Wakefield West Yorkshire England 43 F3 53 42N 1 29W
Wakkanai Japan 82 D4 45 26N 141 43E
Wako Japan 83 B4 35 46N 139 37E
Wałbrzych Poland 69 C3 50 48N 16 19E
Walcheren *i.* Netherlands 64 C3 51 30N 3 30E
Waldorf Maryland U.S.A. 105 E1 38 38N 76 56W
Wales South Yorkshire England 43 G2 53 21N 1 17W
Wales United Kingdom 38
Wales Alaska U.S.A. 100 B6 65 38N 168 09W
Walkden Greater Manchester England 42 C2 53 32N 2 24W
Walker Lake Nevada U.S.A. 102 C4 38 40N 118 43W
Walkern Hertfordshire England 34 C3 51 55N 0 07W
Walkerton Ontario Canada 105 D2 44 08N 81 10W
Wallaceburg Ontario Canada 105 D2 42 34N 82 22W
Wallaroo Australia 86 F3 33 57S 137 36E
Wallasey Merseyside England 42 A2 53 26N 3 03W
Walla Walla Washington U.S.A. 102 C6 46 05N 118 18W
Wallingford Oxfordshire England 32 A2 51 37N 1 08W
Wallsend Tyne and Wear England 44 C2 55 00N 1 31W
Walmer Kent England 33 D2 51 13N 1 24E
Walney, Isle of Cumbria England 44 A1 54 05N 3 15W
Walsall West Midlands England 35 C2 52 35N 1 58W
Walsall Wood *tn.* West Midlands England 35 C2 52 37N 1 56W
Walsenburg Colorado U.S.A. 102 F4 37 36N 104 48W
Walston Strathclyde Scotland 45 D1 55 42N 3 30W
Walsum F.R.G. 62 A3 51 32N 6 41E
Waltham Abbey Essex England 34 D3 51 41N 0 00
Waltham Forest *tn.* Greater London England 34 C2 51 35N 0 00
Waltham on the Wolds Leicestershire England 36 D2 52 49N 0 49W
Walton-le-Dale Lancashire England 42 B3 53 45N 2 41W
Walton-on-Thames Surrey England 34 B2 51 24N 0 25W
Walton-on-the-Hill Staffordshire England 35 B3 52 47N 2 04W
Walton on the Hill Surrey England 34 C1 51 17N 0 15W
Walton on the Naze Essex England 33 D2 51 51N 1 16E
Waltrop F.R.G. 62 D3 51 37N 7 25E
Walvis Bay *tn.* Namibia 95 B3 22 59S 14 31E
Walvis Ridge Atlantic Ocean 117 I4 30 00S 3 00E
Walyevo Fiji 118 V16 17 35S 179 58W
Wamba *r.* Zaïre 95 C6 6 30S 17 30E
Wanaka, Lake New Zealand 87 A2 44 30S 169 00E
Wandsworth Greater London England 34 C2 51 27N 0 11W
Wanganui New Zealand 87 C3 39 56S 175 02E
Wanganui *r.* New Zealand 87 C3 39 30S 175 00E
Wangaratta Australia 86 H2 36 22S 146 20E
Wangerooge *i.* F.R.G. 63 A2 53 47N 7 54E
Wanheim F.R.G. 62 B2 51 23N 6 45E
Wanne-Eickel F.R.G. 62 C3 51 31N 7 09E
Wansbeck *r.* Northumberland England 44 C2 55 10N 1 50W
Wanstead Greater London England 34 D2 51 34N 0 02E
Wantage Oxfordshire England 32 A2 51 36N 1 25W
Wanxian China 81 G4 30 54N 108 20E
Warangal India 77 D3 18 00N 79 35E
Warboys Cambridgeshire England 33 B3 52 24N 0 06W
Warburg F.R.G. 63 A2 51 28N 9 10E
Ward Dublin Irish Republic 49 B2 53 26N 6 20W
Ward *r.* Dublin Irish Republic 49 B2 53 28N 6 19W
Ward's Stone *hill* Lancashire England 42 C4 54 03N 2 38W
Ware British Columbia Canada 100 J4 57 26N 124 41W
Ware Hertfordshire England 34 C3 51 49N 0 02W
Waregem Belgium 64 C2 50 53N 3 26E
Wareham Dorset England 31 E2 50 41N 2 07W
Waremme Belgium 64 E2 50 42N 5 15E
Waren G.D.R. 63 B2 53 32N 12 42E
Warendorf F.R.G. 63 A2 51 57N 8 00E
Warlingham Surrey England 34 C1 51 19N 0 04W
Warminster Wiltshire England 31 E3 51 13N 2 12W
Warmsworth South Yorkshire England 43 G2 53 30N 1 10W
Warnow *r.* G.D.R. 63 B2 53 00N 12 00E
Warrego *r.* Australia 86 H4 27 30S 146 00E
Warren Michigan U.S.A. 105 D2 42 30N 83 02W
Warren Ohio U.S.A. 105 D2 41 15N 80 49W
Warren Pennsylvania U.S.A. 105 E2 41 52N 79 09W
Warrenpoint *tn.* Northern Ireland 48 E4 54 06N 6 15W
Warrensburg Missouri U.S.A. 104 B1 38 46N 93 44W
Warrington Cheshire England 42 C2 53 24N 2 37W
Warrnambool Australia 86 G2 38 23S 142 03E
Warroad Minnesota U.S.A. 104 A3 48 54N 95 20W
Warsaw *see* Warszawa
Warsop Nottinghamshire England 43 G1 53 13N 1 10W
Warszawa *(Warsaw)* Poland 69 D3 52 15N 21 00E
Warta *r.* Poland 69 C3 52 00N 17 00E
Warton Lancashire England 42 B3 53 46N 2 54W
Waruha *r.* India 77 D4 20 30N 79 00E
Warwick Australia 86 I4 28 12S 152 00E
Warwick Rhode Island U.S.A. 105 F2 41 42N 71 23W
Warwick Warwickshire England 35 D1 52 17N 1 34W
Warwickshire *co.* England 36 C2 52 15N 1 40W
Wasaga Beach *tn.* Ontario Canada 105 D2 44 31N 80 02W
Wash, The *b.* Lincolnshire England 36 E2 52 55N 0 10E
Washburn *r.* North Yorkshire England 43 E3 53 56N 1 40W
Washburn Wisconsin U.S.A. 104 B3 46 41N 90 53W
Washingborough Lincolnshire England 36 D3 53 14N 0 28W
Washington District of Columbia U.S.A. 105 E1 38 55N 77 00W
Washington Pennsylvania U.S.A. 105 D2 40 11N 80 16W
Washington *state* U.S.A. 102 B6 47 00N 120 00W
Washington Tyne and Wear England 44 C1 54 54N 1 31W
Wasmes Belgium 64 C2 50 25N 3 51E
Wassenaar Netherlands 65 B2 52 07N 4 23E
Wast Water *l.* Cumbria England 44 A1 54 26N 3 18W
Watampone Indonesia 80 G3 4 33S 120 20E
Watchet Somerset England 31 D3 51 12N 3 20W
Waterbeach Cambridgeshire England 33 C3 52 16N 0 11E
Waterbury Connecticut U.S.A. 105 F2 41 33N 73 03W
Waterbury Vermont U.S.A. 105 F2 44 21N 72 46W
Waterfoot Strathclyde Scotland 45 B1 55 46N 4 18W
Waterford *co.* Irish Republic 48 D2 52 10N 7 30W
Waterford Harbour Irish Republic 48 D2 52 10N 7 00W
Waterford Waterford Irish Republic 48 D2 52 15N 7 06W
Wateringbury Kent England 34 E1 51 16N 0 26E
Waterloo Belgium 64 D2 50 43N 4 24E
Waterloo Iowa U.S.A. 104 B2 42 30N 92 20W
Waterlooville Hampshire England 32 A1 50 53N 1 02W
Waterside Strathclyde Scotland 45 B1 55 21N 4 28W
Watertown New York U.S.A. 105 E2 43 57N 75 56W
Watertown South Dakota U.S.A. 104 A2 44 54N 97 08W
Waterville Maine U.S.A. 105 G2 44 34N 69 41W
Watford Hertfordshire England 34 B2 51 39N 0 24W
Wath upon Dearne South Yorkshire England 43 F2 53 31N 1 21W
Watkins Glen *tn.* New York U.S.A. 105 E2 42 23N 76 53W
Watlington Oxfordshire England 33 A2 51 39N 1 01W
Watseka Illinois U.S.A. 104 C2 40 46N 87 45W
Watson Lake *tn.* Yukon Territory Canada 100 J5 60 07N 128 49W
Watten France 64 B2 50 50N 2 13E
Wattenscheid F.R.G. 62 C2 51 27N 7 07E
Watton Norfolk England 33 C3 52 34N 0 50E
Watton at Stone Hertfordshire England 34 C3 51 52N 0 07W
Wattrelos Belgium 64 C2 50 40N 3 14E
Wattston Strathclyde Scotland 45 C1 55 54N 3 56W
Wau Papua New Guinea 86 H8 7 22S 146 40E
Wau Sudan 94 E9 7 40N 28 04E
Waukegan Illinois U.S.A. 104 C2 42 21N 87 52W
Waukesha Wisconsin U.S.A. 104 C2 43 01N 88 14W
Wausau Wisconsin U.S.A. 104 C2 44 58N 89 40W
Wauwatosa Wisconsin U.S.A. 104 C2 43 04N 88 02W
Waveney *r.* Suffolk/Norfolk England 33 D3 52 30N 1 30E
Wavre Belgium 64 D2 50 43N 4 37E
Wawa Ontario Canada 105 D3 48 04N 84 49W
Waycross Georgia U.S.A. 103 J3 31 12N 82 22W
Wayne New Jersey U.S.A. 106 A2 40 55N 74 15W
Waynesboro Virginia U.S.A. 105 E1 38 04N 78 54W
Weald, The *geog. reg.* Kent England 33 C2 51 05N 0 25E
Wear *r.* Durham England 44 C1 54 40N 1 50W
Weardale *v.* Durham England 44 B1 54 55N 2 10W
Weaver *r.* Cheshire England 42 C1 53 17N 2 40W
Weaverham Cheshire England 42 C1 53 16N 2 35W
Webster City Iowa U.S.A. 104 B2 42 30N 93 50W
Weddell Island Falkland Islands 117 L16 51 55S 61 30W
Weddell Sea Southern Ocean 121 71 00S 40 00W
Wedmore Somerset England 31 E3 51 14N 2 49W
Wednesbury West Midlands England 35 B2 52 34N 2 00W
Wednesfield West Midlands England 35 B2 52 36N 2 04W
Weedon Beck Northamptonshire England 36 C2 52 14N 1 05W
Weert Netherlands 64 E3 51 15N 5 42E
Weesp Netherlands 65 E3 52 19N 5 02E
Wei He *r.* China 81 G4 34 00N 106 00E
Weiden F.R.G. 63 B1 49 40N 12 10E
Weifang China 81 I5 36 44N 119 10E
Weimar G.D.R. 63 B2 50 59N 11 20E
Weipa Australia 86 G7 12 35S 141 56E
Weirton West Virginia U.S.A. 103 J5 40 24N 80 37W
Weisse Elster *r.* G.D.R. 63 B2 51 00N 12 00E
Weissenfels G.D.R. 63 B2 51 12N 11 58E
Weisswasser *tn.* G.D.R. 63 B2 51 31N 14 38E
Wejherowo Poland 69 C3 54 36N 18 12E
Welham Green Hertfordshire England 34 C3 51 44N 0 12W
Welland Ontario Canada 105 E2 45 59N 79 14W
Welland *r.* East Midlands England 36 D2 52 50N 0 00
Wellesbourne Warwickshire England 35 D1 52 12N 1 35W
Wellesley Islands Australia 86 F6 16 30S 139 00E
Wellingborough Northamptonshire England 36 D2 52 19N 0 42W
Wellington Kansas U.S.A. 103 G4 37 17N 97 25W
Wellington New Zealand 87 B2 41 17S 174 47E
Wellington Shropshire England 36 B2 52 43N 2 31W
Wellington Somerset England 31 D2 50 59N 3 15W
Wells Somerset England 31 E3 51 13N 2 39W
Wellsboro Pennsylvania U.S.A. 105 E2 41 45N 77 18W
Wellsford New Zealand 87 B3 36 16S 174 32E
Wells-next-the-Sea Norfolk England 33 C3 52 58N 0 51E
Wels Austria 63 B1 48 10N 14 02E
Welshpool Powys Wales 38 C2 52 40N 3 09W
Welton Humberside England 40 D2 54 47N 3 00W
Welwyn Hertfordshire England 34 C3 51 50N 0 13W
Welwyn Garden City Hertfordshire England 34 C3 51 48N 0 13W
Wem Shropshire England 36 B2 52 51N 2 44W
Wembley Greater London England 34 C2 51 33N 0 18W
Wendover Buckinghamshire England 34 A3 51 46N 0 46W
Wenlock Edge *hills* Shropshire England 36 B2 52 30N 2 45W
Wensleydale *v.* North Yorkshire England 40 B3 54 20N 2 20W
Wensum *r.* Norfolk England 33 D3 52 45N 1 10E
Wenyu He *r.* China 82 H2 40 02N 116 32E
Wenzhou China 81 J3 28 02N 120 40E
Wernigerode G.D.R. 63 B2 51 51N 10 48E
Werra *r.* G.D.R. 63 B2 51 00N 10 00E
Werrington Staffordshire England 35 B4 53 02N 2 06W
Wertach *r.* F.R.G. 63 B1 48 00N 10 00E
Wesel F.R.G. 63 A2 51 39N 6 37E
Weser *r.* F.R.G. 63 A2 53 00N 8 00E
West Allis Wisconsin U.S.A. 104 C2 43 01N 88 00W
West Antarctica *geog. reg.* Antarctica 121 80 00S 120 00W
West Bank *territory* Israel 78 O11 32 00N 35 00E
West Bengal *admin.* India 77 F4 22 00N 88 00E
West Berlin *see* Berlin, West
Westbourne Manitoba Canada 104 A4 50 08N 98 33W
West Bradford Lancashire England 42 C3 53 54N 2 24W
West Bridgford Nottinghamshire England 36 C2 52 56N 1 08W
West Bromwich West Midlands England 35 C2 52 31N 1 59W
Westbrook *tn.* Maine U.S.A. 105 F2 43 41N 70 22W
Westbury Wiltshire England 31 E3 51 16N 2 11W
West Calder Lothian Scotland 45 C1 55 51N 3 35W
West Caroline Basin Pacific Ocean 118 D8 3 00N 136 00E
West Chester Pennsylvania U.S.A. 105 E1 39 58N 75 37W
West Clandon Surrey England 34 B1 51 16N 0 30W
Westcot Surrey England 34 B1 51 13N 0 22W
West Covina California U.S.A. 107 C3 34 04N 117 56W
West Derby Merseyside England 42 B2 53 26N 2 55W
West Drayton Greater London England 34 B2 51 30N 0 28W
West Dvina *see* Zap Dvina
Westeinder Plas *l.* Netherlands 65 C2 52 15N 4 44E
Westerham Kent England 34 D1 51 16N 0 05E
Westerland F.R.G. 63 A2 54 54N 8 19E
Western Australia *state* Australia 86 C4/C5 25 00S 117 00E
Western Desert Egypt 88 30 00N 30 00E
Western Ghats *mts.* India 77 C3/C2 15 30N 74 00E
Western Isles *islands area* Scotland 46 A4–B5
WESTERN SAHARA 93 C7
WESTERN SAMOA 118/119 I6
Western Sayan *mts.* U.S.S.R. 71 L6 52 30N 92 30E
Western Yamuna Canal India 76 L4 28 40N 77 08E
Westerschelde *sd.* Netherlands 64 C3 51 20N 3 45E
Westerwald *geog. reg.* F.R.G. 63 A2 50 00N 8 00E
West Falkland *i.* Falkland Islands 117 L16 51 00S 60 40W
West Felton Shropshire England 36 B2 52 49N 2 58W
Westfield Massachusetts U.S.A. 105 F2 42 07N 72 45W
West Fork White River Indiana U.S.A. 104 C1 39 00N 87 00W
West Frisian Islands *see* Waddeneilanden
West Glamorgan *co.* Wales 38 C1 51 45N 3 55W
West Haddon Northamptonshire England 36 C2 52 20N 1 04W
West Ham Greater London England 34 D2 51 32N 0 01E
Westhill Grampian Scotland 46 F4 57 11N 2 16W
Westhoughton Greater Manchester England 42 C2 53 34N 2 32W
West Ice Shelf Antarctica 121 66 00S 85 00E
West Indies *is.* Caribbean Sea 109 K4 22 00N 69 00W
West Kingsdown Kent England 34 D2 51 20N 0 16E
West Kirby Merseyside England 42 A2 53 22N 3 10W
West Linton Borders Scotland 45 D1 55 46N 3 22W
West Los Angeles California U.S.A. 107 A3 34 02N 118 25W
West Malling Kent England 34 E1 51 18N 0 25E
West Marianas Basin Pacific Ocean 118 D9 16 00N 137 30E
Westmeath *co.* Irish Republic 48 D3 53 30N 7 30W
West Memphis Arkansas U.S.A. 103 H4 35 09N 90 11W
West Mersea Essex England 33 C2 51 47N 0 55E
West Midlands *admin.* England 35 B2–D2 52 28N 1 40W
Westminster California U.S.A. 107 C2 33 45N 117 59W
Westminster Inner London England 34 C2 51 30N 0 09W
Weston West Virginia U.S.A. 105 D1 39 03N 80 28W
Weston-super-Mare Avon England 31 E3 51 21N 2 59W
West Palm Beach *tn.* Florida U.S.A. 103 J2 26 42N 80 05W
Westport Connecticut U.S.A. 105 F2 41 09N 73 22W
Westport Mayo Irish Republic 48 B3 53 48N 9 32W
Westport New Zealand 87 B2 41 46S 171 38E
West Plains *tn.* Missouri U.S.A. 104 B1 36 44N 91 51W
Westray *i.* Orkney Islands Scotland 47 D2 59 18N 3 00W
Westray Firth *sd.* Orkney Islands Scotland 47 D2 59 15N 3 00W
West Rift Valley Africa 88 0 00 30 00E
West Scotia Basin Southern Ocean 121 58 00S 52 00W
West Siberian Lowland U.S.S.R. 71 J7/J8 60 00N 75 00E
West Sussex *co.* England 33 B1 51 00N 0 25W
West Terschelling Netherlands 64 E5 53 22N 5 13E
West Thurrock Essex England 34 D2 51 29N 0 17E
West Virginia *state* U.S.A. 105 D1 39 00N 81 00W
West-Vlanderen *admin.* Belgium 64 B3 51 10N 3 00E
Westward Ho! Devon England 31 C3 51 02N 4 15W
West Wittering West Sussex England 33 B1 50 47N 0 54W
West Yorkshire *admin.* England 43 F3 53 50N 1 30W
Wetar *i.* Indonesia 80 H2 7 30S 126 30E
Wetaskiwin Alberta Canada 100 M3 52 57N 113 20W
Wetherby West Yorkshire England 43 F3 53 56N 1 23W
Wetzlar F.R.G. 63 A2 50 33N 8 30E
Wevelgem Belgium 64 C2 50 48N 3 12E
Wewak Papua New Guinea 86 G9 3 35S 143 35E
Wexford *co.* Irish Republic 48 E2 52 25N 6 35W
Wexford Wexford Irish Republic 48 E2 52 20N 6 27W
Wexford Bay Irish Republic 48 E2 52 25N 6 10W
Wey *r.* Surrey England 33 B2 51 18N 0 30W
Weybridge Surrey England 34 B2 51 22N 0 28W
Weyburn Saskatchewan Canada 100 O2 49 39N 103 51W
Weymouth Dorset England 31 E2 50 37N 2 25W
Weymouth Massachusetts U.S.A. 105 F2 42 14N 70 58W
Whakatane New Zealand 87 C3 37 56S 177 00E
Whaley Bridge Derbyshire England 42 E1 53 20N 1 59W
Whalley Lancashire England 42 C3 53 50N 2 24W
Whalsay *i.* Shetland Islands Scotland 47 C2 60 22N 0 59W
Whangarei New Zealand 87 B3 35 43S 174 20E
Wharfe *r.* North Yorkshire England 40 C2 53 50N 1 15W
Wharfedale *v.* North Yorkshire England 40 C3 54 05N 2 00W
Wharton Cheshire England 42 C1 53 12N 2 31W
Wheathampstead Hertfordshire England 34 C3 51 49N 0 17W
Wheatley Oxfordshire England 32 A2 53 22N 0 52W
Wheaton Minnesota U.S.A. 104 A3 45 49N 96 30W
Wheaton Aston Staffordshire England 35 B3 52 43N 2 12W
Wheeler Lake Alabama U.S.A. 103 I3 34 00N 87 00W
Wheeling West Virginia U.S.A. 105 D2 40 05N 80 43W
Wheldrake North Yorkshire England 43 H3 53 54N 0 57W
Whernside *sum.* North Yorkshire England 44 B1 54 14N 2 23W
Whickham Tyne and Wear England 44 C1 54 57N 1 40W
Whiddy Island Cork Irish Republic 48 B1 51 41N 9 30W
Whipsnade Bedfordshire England 34 B3 51 52N 0 33W
Whiston Merseyside England 42 B2 53 25N 2 50W
Whiston South Yorkshire England 43 G2 53 24N 1 20W
Whitburn Lothian Scotland 45 C1 55 52N 3 42W
Whitburn Tyne and Wear England 44 C1 54 57N 1 21W
Whitby North Yorkshire England 40 D3 54 29N 0 37W
Whitby Ontario Canada 105 E2 43 52N 78 56W
Whitchurch Buckinghamshire England 33 B2 51 53N 0 51W
Whitchurch Hampshire England 32 A2 51 14N 1 20W
Whitchurch Shropshire England 36 B2 52 58N 2 41W
White *r.* U.S.A. 102 F5 43 00N 103 00W
White *r.* U.S.A. 103 H4 35 00N 92 00W
White Bay Newfoundland Canada 101 X3 50 30N 55 15W
Whitecourt Alberta Canada 100 L3 54 10N 115 38W
Whitefield Greater Manchester England 42 D2 53 34N 2 18W
Whitehaven Cumbria England 44 A1 54 33N 3 35W
Whitehead Antrim Northern Ireland 48 F4 54 45N 5 43W
Whitehorse Yukon Territory Canada 100 I5 60 41N 135 08W
White Horse, Vale of Berkshire England 32 A2 51 35N 1 30W
Whitehouse Northern Ireland 49 D1 54 39N 5 55W
Whiteland Indiana U.S.A. 104 C1 39 32N 86 05W
White Mountains New Hampshire U.S.A. 105 F2 44 00N 72 00W
White Nile *see* Bahr el Abiad
White Nile *see* Bahr el Jebel
White Nile Dam Sudan 78 D2 14 18N 32 30E
Whiteparish Wiltshire England 32 F3 51 01N 1 39W
White River *tn.* Ontario Canada 104 C3 48 35N 85 16W
Whitesand Bay Cornwall England C2 50 20N 4 25W
White Sea U.S.S.R. 70 F9 66 00N 37 30E
White Volta *r.* Ghana 93 E4 9 30N 1 30W
Whitfield Kent England 33 D2 51 09N 1 17E
Whithorn Dumfries & Galloway Scotland 46 D1 54 44N 4 25W
Whitland Dyfed Wales 38 B1 51 50N 4 37W
Whitley Bay *tn.* Tyne and Wear England 44 C2 55 03N 1 25W
Whitney Ontario Canada 105 E3 45 29N 78 15W
Whitney, Mount California U.S.A. 102 C4 36 35N 118 17W
Whitstable Kent England 33 D2 51 22N 1 02E
Whittier California U.S.A. 107 B2 33 58N 118 02W
Whittington Derbyshire England 43 F1 53 17N 1 25W
Whittington Shropshire England 36 B2 52 52N 3 00W
Whittlesey Cambridgeshire England 33 B3 52 34N 0 08W
Whitton Humberside England 40 D2 53 43N 0 38W
Whitwell Derbyshire England 43 G1 53 18N 1 12W
Whitwell Hertfordshire England 34 C3 51 52N 0 16W
Whitwick Leicestershire England 35 E3 52 44N 1 20W
Whitworth Lancashire England 42 D2 53 40N 2 10W
Whyalla Australia 86 F3 33 04S 137 34E
Wiarton Ontario Canada 105 D2 44 44N 81 10W
Wiay *i.* Western Isles Scotland 46 A4 57 23N 7 13W
Wichita Kansas U.S.A. 103 G4 37 43N 97 20W
Wichita *r.* Texas U.S.A. 102 F3 33 00N 100 00W
Wichita Falls *tn.* Texas U.S.A. 102 G3 33 55N 98 30W
Wick Highland Scotland 46 E5 58 26N 3 06W
Wickersley South Yorkshire England 43 G2 53 26N 1 17W
Wickford Essex England 33 C2 51 38N 0 31E
Wickham Hampshire England 32 A1 50 54N 1 10W
Wickham Market Suffolk England 33 D3 52 09N 1 22E
Wicklow *co.* Irish Republic 48 E2 52 55N 6 25W
Wicklow Wicklow Irish Republic 48 E2 52 59N 6 03W
Wicklow Head *c.* Irish Republic 48 E2 52 58N 6 00W
Wicklow Mountains Irish Republic 48 E3 53 00N 6 20W
Widford Hertfordshire England 34 D3 51 50N 0 04E
Widnes Cheshire England 42 B2 53 22N 2 44W
Wien *(Vienna)* Austria 69 C2 48 13N 16 22E
Wiener Neustadt Austria 69 C2 47 49N 16 15E
Wieprz *r.* Poland 69 D3 51 00N 23 00E
Wierden Netherlands 64 F4 52 21N 6 35E
Wiesbaden F.R.G. 63 A2 50 05N 8 15E
Wigan Greater Manchester England 42 C2 53 33N 2 38W
Wigginton Staffordshire England 35 C2 52 39N 1 42W
Wigston Leicestershire England 36 C2 52 36N 1 05W

Wigton Cumbria England 44 A1 54 49N 3 09W
Wigtown Dumfries & Galloway Scotland 46 D1 54 52N 4 26W
Wigtown Bay Dumfries & Galloway Scotland 46 D1 54 10N 4 20W
Wijchen Netherlands 64 E3 51 48N 5 44E
Wijde Blik *l.* Netherlands 65 E2 52 13N 5 04E
Wil Switzerland 61 C2 47 28N 9 03E
Wilberfoss Humberside England 40 D2
Wilhelmshaven F.R.G. 63 A2 53 32N 8 07E
Wilhelm-Pieck-Stadt-Guben G.D.R. 63 B2 51 59N 14 42E
Wilkes Land *geog. reg.* Antarctica 121 68 00S 105 00E
Wilkes-Barre Pennsylvania U.S.A. 105 E2 41 15N 75 50W
Willaston Cheshire England 42 A1 53 17N 3 02W
Willebroek Belgium 64 D3 51 04N 4 22E
Willemstad Curaçao 109 K2 12 12N 68 56W
Willenhall West Midlands England 35 B2 52 36N 2 02W
Willesden Greater London England 34 C2 51 33N 0 14W
Williamsburg Virginia U.S.A. 105 E1 37 17N 79 43W
Williams Lake *tn.* British Columbia Canada 100 K3 52 08N 122 09W
Williamson West Virginia U.S.A. 105 D1 37 42N 82 16W
Williamsport Pennsylvania U.S.A. 105 E2 41 16N 77 03W
Williamstown Kentucky U.S.A. 105 D1 38 39N 84 32W
Willington Derbyshire England 35 D3 52 51N 1 34W
Willington Durham England 44 C1 54 43N 1 41W
Williston North Dakota U.S.A. 102 F6 48 09N 103 39W
Williston Lake British Columbia Canada 100 K4 49 27N 80 37W
Williton Somerset England 31 D3 51 10N 3 20W
Willmar Minnesota U.S.A. 104 A3 45 06N 95 03W
Willoughby Warwickshire England 35 E1 52 18N 1 16W
Willow Springs Missouri U.S.A. 104 B1 36 59N 91 59W
Wilmington Delaware U.S.A. 105 E1 39 46N 75 31W
Wilmington Kent England 34 D2 51 25N 0 12E
Wilmington North Carolina U.S.A. 103 K3 34 14N 77 55W
Wilmslow Cheshire England 42 D1 53 20N 2 15W
Wilson North Carolina U.S.A. 103 K4 35 43N 77 56W
Wilton Wiltshire England 31 F3 51 05N 1 52W
Wiltshire *co.* England 31 E3/F3 51 30N 2 00W
Wiluna Australia 86 C4 26 37S 120 12E
Wimbledon Greater London England 34 C2 51 25N 0 13W
Wimborne Minster Dorset England 31 F2 50 48N 1 59W
Wimereux France 64 A2 50 46N 1 37E
Wincanton Somerset England 31 E3 51 04N 2 25W
Winchburgh Lothian Scotland 45 D1 55 57N 3 26W
Winchelsea East Sussex England 33 C1 50 55N 0 42E
Winchester Hampshire England 32 A2 51 04N 1 19W
Winchester Virginia U.S.A. 103 K4 39 11N 78 12W
Wind River Range *mts.* Wyoming U.S.A. 102 E5 43 00N 109 00W
Windermere *l.* Cumbria England 44 B1 54 20N 2 57W
Windermere *tn.* Cumbria England 44 B1 54 23N 2 54W
Windhoek Namibia 95 C3 22 34S 17 06E
Windlesham Surrey England 34 A2 51 22N 0 39W
Windsor Berkshire England 34 B2 51 29N 0 38W
Windsor Newfoundland Canada 101 X2 48 58N 55 40W
Windsor Ontario Canada 105 D2 42 18N 83 00W
Windward Islands Lesser Antilles 109 L2 12 30N 62 00W
Windward Passage *sd.* Cuba/Haiti 109 J3/J4 20 00N 73 00W
Windygates Fife Scotland 45 D2 56 12N 3 03W
Wing Buckinghamshire England 34 A3 51 54N 0 44W
Wingate Durham England 44 C1 54 55N 1 23W
Wingerworth Derbyshire England 43 F1 53 13N 1 28W
Wingham Ontario Canada 105 D2 43 54N 81 19W
Winisk Ontario Canada 101 R4 55 20N 85 15W
Winisk Lake Ontario Canada 101 R3 52 30N 87 30W
Winisk River Ontario Canada 101 R4 54 50N 87 00W
Winkleigh Devon England 31 D2 50 51N 3 56W
Winkler Manitoba Canada 104 A3 49 12N 97 55W
Winnebago, Lake Wisconsin U.S.A. 104 C2 44 00N 88 00W
Winnemucca Nevada U.S.A. 102 C5 40 58N 117 45W
Winnipeg Manitoba Canada 104 A3 49 53N 97 10W
Winnipeg, Lake Manitoba Canada 101 P3 52 30N 97 30W
Winnipegosis, Lake Manitoba Canada 101 O3 52 10N 100 00W
Winnipesaukee, Lake New Hampshire U.S.A. 105 F2 43 00N 72 00W
Winona Minnesota U.S.A. 104 B2 44 02N 91 37W
Winschoten Netherlands 64 G5 53 07N 7 02E
Winscombe Avon England 31 E3 51 28N 2 52W
Winsford Cheshire England 42 C1 53 11N 2 31W
Winslow Arizona U.S.A. 102 D4 35 01N 110 43W
Winslow Buckinghamshire England 33 B2 51 57N 0 54W
Winston-Salem North Carolina U.S.A. 103 J4 36 05N 80 18W
Winterbourne Avon England 31 E3 51 30N 2 31W
Winterswijk Netherlands 64 F3 51 58N 6 44E
Winterthur Switzerland 61 C2 47 30N 8 45E
Winterton-on-Sea Norfolk England 33 D3 52 43N 1 42E
Winton Australia 86 G5 22 22S 143 00E
Wirksworth Derbyshire England 36 C3 53 05N 1 34W
Wirral *p.* Merseyside England 42 A2 53 20N 3 03W
Wisła *r.* Poland 69 C3 53 00N 19 00E
Wisbech Cambridgeshire England 33 C3 52 40N 0 10E
Wiscasset Maine U.S.A. 105 G2 44 01N 69 41W
Wisconsin *state* U.S.A. 104 B3 45 00N 90 00W
Wisconsin *r.* Wisconsin U.S.A. 104 B2 43 00N 90 00W
Wisconsin Rapids *tn.* Wisconsin U.S.A. 104 C2 44 24N 89 50W
Wishaw Strathclyde Scotland 45 C1 55 47N 3 56W
Wismar G.D.R. 63 B2 53 54N 11 28E
Wisłok *r.* Poland 69 D3 50 00N 22 00E
Wissembourg France 61 C2 49 02N 7 57E
Wissey *r.* Norfolk England 33 C3 52 38N 0 50E
Wistow North Yorkshire England 43 G3 53 48N 1 06W
Witham Essex England 33 C2 51 48N 0 38E
Witham *r.* Lincolnshire England 36 D3 53 05N 0 10W
Witheridge Devon England 31 D2 50 55N 3 42W
Withernsea Humberside England 42 E2 53 44N 0 02E
Witley Surrey England 34 B1 51 08N 0 39W
Witney Oxfordshire England 32 A2 51 48N 1 29W
Witten F.R.G. 62 D2 51 25N 7 19E
Wittenberg G.D.R. 63 B2 51 53N 12 39E
Wittenberge G.D.R. 63 B2 52 59N 11 45E
Wittlich F.R.G. 63 A1 49 59N 6 54E
Wittstock G.D.R. 63 B2 53 10N 12 30E
Wiveliscombe Somerset England 31 D3 51 03N 3 19W
Wivenhoe Essex England 33 C2 51 52N 0 58E
Woburn Bedfordshire England 34 B3 51 59N 0 38W
Woburn Sands *tn.* Bedfordshire England 34 B4 52 01N 0 39W
Włocławek Poland 69 C3 52 39N 19 01E
Woerden Netherlands 65 D2 52 05N 4 53E
Woking Surrey England 34 B1 51 20N 0 34W
Wokingham Berkshire England 33 B2 51 25N 0 51W
Woldingham Surrey England 34 C1 51 17N 0 02W
Wolf-Bay *tn.* Québec Canada 101 W3 50 14N 60 40W
Wolfen G.D.R. 63 B2 51 41N 12 17E
Wolfenbüttel F.R.G. 63 B2 52 10N 10 33E
Wolfsberg Austria 69 B2 46 50N 14 50E
Wolfsburg F.R.G. 63 B2 52 27N 10 49E
Wolin Poland 63 B2 53 51N 14 38E
Wollaston Lake Saskatchewan Canada 101 O4 58 20N 103 00W
Wollaston Lake *tn.* Saskatchewan Canada 101 O4 58 05N 103 38W
Wollaston Northamptonshire England 36 D2 52 16N 0 41W
Wollongong Australia 86 I3 34 25S 150 52E
Wolsingham Durham England 44 C1 54 44N 1 52W
Wolverhampton West Midlands England 35 B2 52 36N 2 08W
Wolverton Buckinghamshire England 33 B3 52 04N 0 50W
Wolvey Warwickshire England 35 D2 52 29N 1 21W
Wombourne Staffordshire England 35 B2 52 32N 2 11W
Wombwell South Yorkshire England 43 F2 53 32N 1 24W
Wompah Australia 86 G4 29 04S 142 05E
Wonersh Surrey England 34 B1 51 12N 0 33W
Wŏnju South Korea 81 K5 37 24N 127 52E
Wŏnsan North Korea 81 K5 39 07N 127 26E
Woodbridge New Jersey U.S.A. 106 A1 40 33N 74 16W
Woodbridge Suffolk England 33 D3 52 06N 1 19E
Wood Buffalo National Park Alberta Canada 100 M4 60 00N 113 00W
Woodburn Northern Ireland 49 D2 54 43N 5 50W
Woodford Greater London England 34 D2 51 37N 0 02E
Woodford Halse Northamptonshire England 36 C2 52 10N 1 13W
Wood Green Greater London England 34 C2 51 38N 0 06W
Woodhall Spa Lincolnshire England 36 D3 53 09N 0 14W
Woodhouse South Yorkshire England 43 F2 53 22N 1 23W
Woodlands *tn.* Manitoba Canada 104 A4 50 12N 97 40W
Woodlark Island Papua New Guinea 86 I8 9 00S 152 30E
Woods, Lake of the North America 104 B3 49 00N 94 00W
Woodseaves Staffordshire England 35 B3 52 49N 2 19W
Woodstock New Brunswick Canada 101 V2 46 10N 67 36W
Woodstock Ontario Canada 105 D2 43 07N 80 46W
Woodstock Oxfordshire England 32 A2 51 52N 1 21W
Woodstock Vermont U.S.A. 105 F2 43 37N 72 33W
Woodsville New Hampshire U.S.A. 105 F2 44 08N 72 02W
Woodville New Zealand 87 C2 40 20S 175 54E
Woodward Oklahoma U.S.A. 102 G4 36 26N 99 25W
Wool Dorset England 31 E2 50 41N 2 14W
Woolacombe Devon England 31 C3 51 10N 4 13W
Wooler Northumberland England 44 B2 55 33N 2 01W
Woolwich Greater London England 34 D2 51 29N 0 04E
Woore Shropshire England 35 A3 52 59N 2 24W
Wooster Ohio U.S.A. 105 D2 40 46N 81 57W
Wootton Bassett Wiltshire England 31 F3 51 33N 1 54W
Worcester & Birmingham Canal West Midlands England 35 B1 52 15N 2 08W
Worcester Hereford and Worcester England 35 B1 52 11N 2 13W
Worcester Massachusetts U.S.A. 105 F2 42 17N 71 48W
Worcester Republic of South Africa 95 C1 33 39S 19 26E
Workington Cumbria England 44 A1 54 39N 3 33W
Worksop Nottinghamshire England 43 G1 53 18N 1 07W
Worland Wyoming U.S.A. 102 E5 44 01N 107 58W
Wormhoudt France 64 B2 50 53N 2 28E
Worms F.R.G. 63 A1 49 38N 8 23E
Worms Head *c.* West Glamorgan Wales 38 B1 51 34N 4 20W
Worplesdon Surrey England 34 B1 51 17N 0 37W
Worsbrough South Yorkshire England 43 F2 53 33N 1 29W
Worthing West Sussex England 33 B1 50 48N 0 23W
Worthington Minnesota U.S.A. 104 A2 43 37N 95 36W
Wotton-under-Edge Gloucestershire England 31 E3 51 39N 2 21W
Woverley Hereford & Worcester England 35 B2 52 24N 2 16W
Wragby Lincolnshire England 36 D3 53 39N 1 23W
Wrangell Alaska U.S.A. 100 I4 56 28N 132 23W
Wrangell Mountains Alaska U.S.A. 100 G5 62 00N 143 00W
Wrangle Lincolnshire England 36 E3 53 02N 0 07E
Wrath, Cape Highland Scotland 46 C5 58 37N 5 01W
Wrekin, The *mt.* Shropshire England 36 B2 52 41N 2 32W
Wrexham Clwyd Wales 38 D3 53 03N 3 00W
Wright Peak Antarctica 121 73 15S 94 00W
Wrigley Northwest Territories Canada 100 K5 63 16N 123 39W
Wrinehill Staffordshire England 35 A4 53 02N 2 23W
Writtle Essex England 34 E3 51 44N 0 26E
Wrocław Poland 69 C3 51 05N 17 00E
Wrotham Kent England 34 D1 51 19N 0 19E
Wroughton Wiltshire England 31 F3 51 31N 1 48W
Wroxham Norfolk England 33 D3 52 42N 1 24E
Wuhai China 81 G5 39 40N 106 40E
Wuhan China 81 H4 30 35N 114 19E
Wuhu China 81 I4 31 23N 118 25E
Wukari Nigeria 93 G4 7 49N 9 49E
Wülfrath F.R.G. 62 C2 51 17N 7 03E
Wunstorf F.R.G. 63 A2 52 26N 9 26E
Wupper *r.* F.R.G. 62 D1 51 14N 7 17E
Wuppertal F.R.G. 62 C2 51 15N 7 10E
Wurno Nigeria 93 G5 13 18N 5 29E
Würzburg F.R.G. 63 A1 49 48N 9 57E
Wusul Jiang *(Ussuri) r.* China/U.S.S.R. 81 L7 47 00N 134 00E
Wutongqiao China 81 F3 29 21N 103 48E
Wuxi China 81 J4 31 35N 120 19E
Wuyi Shan *mts.* China 81 I3 26 00N 116 30E
Wuzhou China 81 H2 23 30N 111 21E
Wye Kent England 33 C2 51 11N 0 56E
Wye *r.* Hereford and Worcester England 36 B1 51 58N 2 35W
Wymondham Norfolk England 33 D3 52 34N 1 07E
Wyndham Australia 86 D6 15 30S 128 09E
Wyoming *state* U.S.A. 102 E5 43 00N 108 00W
Wyre *r.* Lancashire England 42 B3 53 52N 2 52W

X

Xaafuun Somalia 94 J10 10 27N 51 15E
Xaidulla China 77 D7 36 27N 77 46E
Xánthi Greece 68 D3 41 07N 24 56E
Xiaguan China 81 F3 25 33N 100 09E
Xiamen China 81 I2 24 28N 118 05E
Xi'an China 81 G4 34 16N 108 54E
Xiangfan China 81 H4 32 05N 112 03E
Xiangtan China 81 H3 27 48N 112 55E
Xianyang China 81 G4 34 22N 108 42E
Xieng Laos 80 C7 19 21N 103 23E
Xigaze China 81 C3 29 18N 88 50E
Xi Jiang *r.* China 81 H2 23 30N 111 00E
Xingtai China 81 H5 37 08N 114 29E
Xining China 81 F5 36 35N 101 55E
Xinjiang Uygur Zizhiqu *(Sinkiang Uighur Autonomous Region) admin.* China 81 B6/C6 41 00N 85 00E
Xinjin China 81 J5 39 25N 121 58E
Xiqing Shan *mts.* China 81 F4 34 00N 102 30E
Xizang Zizhiqu *(Tibet Autonomous Region) admin.* China 81 B4/C4 33 30N 85 00E
Xizhuang China 82 G1 39 51N 116 20E
Xochimiko Mexico 108 E3 19 08N 99 09W
Xuanhua China 81 I6 40 36N 115 01E
Xuchang China 81 H4 34 03N 113 48E
Xuwen China 81 H2 20 25N 110 08E
Xuzhou China 81 I4 34 17N 117 18E

Y

Yaba Nigeria 92 C3 6 29N 3 27E
Yablonovy Range *mts.* U.S.S.R. 71 M6/N6 51 30N 110 00E
Yabrūd Syria 78 P11 33 58N 36 39E
Yaizu Japan 82 C1 34 54N 138 20E
Yakima *r.* Washington U.S.A. 102 B6 47 00N 120 00W
Yakima Washington U.S.A. 102 B6 46 37N 120 30W
Yakutat Alaska U.S.A. 100 H4 59 29N 139 49W
Yakutsk U.S.S.R. 71 O8 62 10N 129 50E
Yalding Kent England 34 E1 51 14N 0 26E
Yalu *r.* China / North Korea 81 K6 42 00N 127 00E
Yamagata Japan 82 D2 38 16N 140 19E
Yamaguchi Japan 82 B1 34 10N 131 28E
Yamal Peninsula U.S.S.R. 71 I10/J10 72 00N 70 00E
Yamato Japan 83 A2 35 29N 139 27E
Yambio Sudan 94 E8 4 34N 28 21E
Yambol Bulgaria 68 E3 42 28N 26 30E
Yamburg U.S.S.R. 71 J9 68 19N 77 09E
Yamoussoukro Côte d'Ivoire 93 D4 6 50N 5 20W
Yamuna *r.* India 76 L4 28 43N 17 13E
Yamunanagar India 77 D6 30 07N 77 17E
Yana *r.* U.S.S.R. 71 P9 69 00N 135 00E
Yanbu'al Baḥr Saudi Arabia 78 E3 24 07N 38 04E
Yancheng China 81 J4 33 23N 120 10E
Yangon *see* Rangoon
Yangquan China 81 H5 37 52N 113 29E
Yangtze *see* Jinsha Jiang
Yanji China 81 K6 42 52N 129 32E
Yanjing China 81 E3 29 01N 98 38E
Yankton South Dakota U.S.A. 104 A2 42 53N 97 24W
Yantai China 81 J5 37 30N 121 22E
Yao Japan 82 C1 34 36N 135 37E
Yaoundé Cameroon 93 H3 3 51N 11 31E
Yap Islands Pacific Ocean 118 D8 9 30N 138 09E
Yap Trench Pacific Ocean 118 D8 10 00N 139 00E
Yaqui *r.* Mexico 108 C5 28 00N 109 50W
Yare *r.* Norfolk England 33 D3 52 37N 1 30E
Yaritagua Venezuela 109 K2 10 05N 69 07W
Yarkant He *r.* China 71 J3 36 00N 76 00E
Yarlung Zangbo Jiang *(Tsangpo) r.* China 81 D3 29 00N 92 30E
Yarmouth Isle of Wight England 32 A1 50 42N 1 29W
Yarmouth Nova Scotia Canada 101 V1 43 50N 66 08W
Yarnfield Staffordshire England 35 B3 52 54N 2 12W
Yaroslavl' U.S.S.R. 70 F7 57 34N 39 52E
Yarrow Water *r.* Borders Scotland 46 E2 55 35N 3 10W
Yarumal Colombia 114 B14 6 59N 75 25W
Yasawa *i.* Fiji 118 T16 16 50S 177 30E
Yasawa Group *is.* Fiji 118 T16 17 00S 177 40E
Yate Avon England 31 E3 51 32N 2 25W
Yateley Hampshire England 33 B2 51 20N 0 51W
Yathkyed Lake Northwest Territories Canada 101 P5 62 30N 97 30W
Yatsushiro Japan 81 B1 32 32N 130 35E
Yatton Avon England 31 E3 51 24N 2 49W
Yauza *r.* U.S.S.R. 65 M2 55 46N 37 40E
Yawatahama Japan 82 B1 33 27N 132 24E
Yaxley Cambridgeshire England 33 B3 52 31N 0 16W
Yazd Iran 79 H5 31 54N 54 22E
Yazoo *r.* Mississippi U.S.A. 103 H3 33 00N 90 00W
Ye Myanma 80 B7 15 15N 97 50E
Ye Xian China 81 I5 37 10N 119 55E
Yeadon West Yorkshire England 43 E3 53 52N 1 41W
Yealmpton Devon England 31 C2 50 21N 3 59W
Yell *i.* Shetland Islands Scotland 47 B2 60 35N 1 10W
Yell Sound Shetland Islands Scotland 47 B2 60 30N 1 15W
Yellowknife Northwest Territories Canada 100 M5 62 30N 114 29W
Yellow Sea *(Huang Hai)* China 81 J5 35 30N 122 30E
Yellowstone *r.* U.S.A. 102 E6 46 00N 108 00W
Yellowstone Lake Wyoming U.S.A. 102 D5 44 30N 110 20W
Yelverton Devon England 31 C2 50 30N 4 05W
YEMEN 78 F2
Yenisey *r.* U.S.S.R. 71 K8 64 00N 87 30E
Yenisey, Gulf of U.S.S.R. 71 J10/K10 72 30N 80 00E
Yeniseysk U.S.S.R. 71 L7 58 27N 92 13E
Yeo *r.* Avon England 31 E3 51 20N 2 50W
Yeo *r.* Dorset / Somerset England 31 E2 51 00N 2 35W
Yeovil Somerset England 31 E2 50 57N 2 39W
Yeppoon Australia 86 I5 23 05S 150 42E
Yerevan U.S.S.R. 70 G4 40 10N 44 31E
Yerres *r.* France 60 C1 48 40N 2 36E
Yesil *r.* Turkey 78 E7 41 00N 36 25E
Yes Tor *sum.* Devon England 31 C2 50 42N 4 00W
Yetts O'Muckhart Central Scotland 45 C2 56 12N 3 37W
Yeu Myanma 77 H4 22 49N 95 26E
Yiannitsá Greece 68 D3 40 46N 22 24E
Yibin China 81 F3 28 42N 104 30E
Yichang China 81 H4 30 46N 111 20E
Yinchuan China 81 G5 38 30N 106 19E
Yingkou China 81 J6 40 40N 122 17E
Yining China 81 B6 43 50N 81 28E
Yirga 'Alem Ethiopia 94 G9 6 48N 38 22E
Yiyang China 81 H3 28 39N 112 10E
Yoakum Texas U.S.A. 103 G2 29 18N 97 20W
Yogyakarta Indonesia 80 E2 7 48S 110 24E
Yoichi Japan 82 D3 43 14N 140 47E
Yokadouma Cameroon 93 I3 3 26N 15 06E
Yokkaichi Japan 82 C1 34 58N 136 38E
Yokohama Japan 83 B2 35 27N 139 38E
Yokosuka Japan 83 B2 35 18N 139 38E
Yokote Japan 82 D2 39 20N 140 31E
Yola Nigeria 93 H4 9 14N 12 32E
Yonago Japan 82 B2 35 27N 133 20E
Yonkers New York U.S.A. 106 C2 40 56N 73 52W
Yonne *r.* France 61 B2 48 00N 3 15E
York North Yorkshire England 43 G3 53 58N 1 05W
York Pennsylvania U.S.A. 105 E1 39 57N 76 44W
York, Cape Australia 86 G7 10 42S 142 32E
York Factory Manitoba Canada 101 Q4 57 08N 92 25W
Yorkshire Dales National Park North Yorkshire
Yorkshire Wolds *hills* Humberside England 40 D3 54 00N 0 45W
Yorkton Saskatchewan Canada 101 O3 51 12N 102 29W
York, Vale of North Yorkshire England 40 C3 54 10N 1 20W
Yŏsu South Korea 81 K4 34 50N 127 30E
You Jiang *r.* China 81 G2 23 30N 107 00E
Youghal Cork Irish Republic 48 D1 51 51N 7 50W
Youngstown Ohio U.S.A. 105 D2 41 05N 80 40W
Yoxall Staffordshire England 35 C3 52 46N 1 46W
Yoxford Suffolk England 33 D3 52 16N 1 30E
Yser *see* Ijzer
Ystalfera West Glamorgan Wales 38 C1 51 47N 3 47W
Ystrad Aeron Dyfed Wales 38 B2 52 10N 4 10W
Ystradgynlais West Glamorgan Wales 38 C1 51 47N 3 45W
Ytterhogdal Sweden 67 C3 62 10N 14 55E
Yu Jiang *r.* China 81 G2 23 00N 109 00E
Yuan Jiang *r.* Asia 72 30 00N 107 00E
Yuba City California U.S.A. 102 B4 39 09N 121 36W
Yūbari Japan 82 D3 43 04N 141 59E
Yucatan *p.* Mexico 108 G3 19 00N 89 00W
Yucatan Basin Caribbean Sea 119 R9 20 00N 85 00W
Yuci China 81 H5 37 40N 112 44E
Yuetot France 61 B2 49 37N 0 45E
YUGOSLAVIA 68 C3
Yukagir Plateau U.S.S.R. 71 R9 66 30N 156 00E
Yü-kitka *l.* Finland 67 F4 66 15N 28 30E
Yukon Delta Alaska U.S.A. 100 C5 62 45N 164 00W
Yukon River U.S.A./Canada 100 D5 63 30N 159 40W
Yukon Territory *territory* Canada 100 H5 64 15N 135 00W
Yuma Arizona U.S.A. 102 D3 32 40N 114 39W
Yumen China 81 E5 39 54N 97 43E
Yun *(Grand Canal)* China 82 H1 39 54N 116 33E
Yurimaguas Peru 114 B11 5 54S 76 07W
Yushu China 77 H6 33 06N 96 48E
Yuzhno-Sakhalinsk U.S.S.R. 71 Q5 46 58N 142 45E
Yverdon Switzerland Switzerland 61 C2 46 47N 6 38E

Z

Zaandam Netherlands 65 D3 52 27N 4 51E
Zaanstad Netherlands 65 D3 52 27N 4 49E
Zābol Iran 79 J5 31 00N 61 32E
Zabrze Poland 69 C3 50 18N 18 47E
Zacapa Guatemala 108 G3 15 00N 89 30E
Zacatecas Mexico 108 D4 22 48N 102 33W
Zacatecoluca El Salvador 108 G2 13 29N 88 51W
Zadar Yugoslavia 68 C3 44 07N 15 14E
Zafra Spain 66 A2 38 25N 6 25W
Żagań Poland 69 C3 51 37N 15 20E
Zagazig Egypt 78 D5 30 36N 31 30E
Zagorsk U.S.S.R. 70 F7 56 20N 38 10E
Zagreb *(Agram)* Yugoslavia 68 C4 45 48N 15 58E
Zagros Mountains Iran 79 G5 32 45N 48 50E
Zāhedān Iran 79 J4 29 32N 60 54E
Zahlé Lebanon 78 O11 33 50N 35 55E
ZAÏRE 94 D7
Zaïre *(Congo) r.* Zaïre 94 C7 2 00S 17 00E
Zákinthos *i.* Greece 68 D2 38 00N 20 00E
Zakopane Poland 69 C2 49 17N 19 54E
Zalaegerszeg Hungary 69 C2 46 53N 16 51E
Zalău Romania 69 D2 47 10N 23 04E
Zambezi *r.* Southern Africa 95 D4 16 00S 23 00E
Zambezi Zambia 95 D5 13 33S 23 08E
ZAMBIA 95 E5
Zamboanga The Philippines 80 G5 6 55N 122 05E
Zamora Spain 66 A3 41 30N 5 45W
Zamość Poland 69 D3 50 43N 23 15E
Zanderij Surinam 114 F14 5 26N 55 14W
Zandvoort Netherlands 65 C3 52 22N 4 32E
Zanesville Ohio U.S.A. 105 D1 39 55N 82 02W
Zanjān Iran 79 G6 36 40N 48 30E
Zanthus Australia 86 C3 31 01S 123 32E
Zanzibar *i.* Tanzania 95 G6 6 10S 39 13E
Zanzibar Tanzania 95 G6 6 10S 39 12E
Zaozhuang China 81 I4 34 53N 117 38E
Zapadnaya *(West)* Dvina *r.* U.S.S.R. 67 E2 56 45N 24 30E
Západočeský *admin.* Czechoslovakia 63 B1 49 00N 13 00E
Zaporozh'ye U.S.S.R. 70 F5 47 50N 35 10E
Zapotitlan Mexico 108 P1 19 18N 99 03W
Zaragoza Spain 66 B3 41 39N 0 54W
Zarand Iran 79 I5 30 50N 56 35E
Zaraza Venezuela 114 D14 9 23N 65 20W
Zargun *mt.* Pakistan 76 B6 30 15N 67 11E
Zaria Nigeria 93 G5 11 01N 7 44E
Zarqa Jordan 78 P11 32 04N 36 05E
Zary Poland 63 C2 51 40N 15 10E
Zeebrugge Belgium 64 C3 51 20N 3 13E
Zeeland *admin.* Netherlands 64 C3 51 25N 3 50E
Zeeuwsch-Vlaanderen *geog. reg.* Netherlands 64 C3 51 20N 3 40E
Zefat Israel 78 O11 32 57N 35 27E
Zeist Netherlands 64 E4 52 05N 5 15E
Zeitz G.D.R. 63 B2 51 03N 12 08E
Zell-am-See *tn.* Austria 69 B2 47 19N 12 47E
Zelten Libya 94 C13 28 15N 19 52E
Zelzate Belgium 64 C3 51 12N 3 49E
Zemlya Frantsa-Iosifa *(Franz Josef Land) is.* U.S.S.R. 71 G12–I12 80 00N 50 00E
Zermatt Switzerland 61 C2 46 01N 7 45E
Zevenaar Netherlands 64 F3 51 55N 6 05E
Zeya *r.* U.S.S.R. 71 O6 53 00N 127 30E
Zeya U.S.S.R. 71 O6 53 48N 127 14E
Zêzere *r.* Portugal 66 A2 39 50N 8 05W
Zgierz Poland 69 C3 51 52N 19 25E
Zgorzelec Poland 69 C3 51 10N 15 00E
Zhangjiakou China 81 H6 40 51N 114 59E
Zhangzhou China 81 I2 24 31N 117 40E
Zhanjiang China 81 H2 21 10N 110 20E
Zhdanov U.S.S.R. 70 F5 47 05N 37 34E
Zhengzhou China 81 H4 34 45N 113 38E
Zhenjiang China 81 I4 32 08N 119 30E
Zhigansk U.S.S.R. 71 O9 66 48N 123 27E
Zhitomir U.S.S.R. 70 E6 50 18N 28 40E
Zhlobin U.S.S.R. 69 F3 52 50N 30 00E
Zhmerinka U.S.S.R. 69 E2 49 00N 28 02E
Zhob Pakistan 76 B6 31 30N 69 30E
Zhonghai *l.* China 82 G1 39 56N 116 22E
Zhuzhou China 81 H3 27 53N 113 07E
Zibo China 81 I5 36 51N 118 01E

Zielona Góra Poland **69** C3 51 57N 15 30E
Zierikzee Netherlands **64** C3 51 39N 3 55E
Zigong China **81** F3 29 25N 104 47E
Ziguinchor Senegal **93** B5 12 35N 16 20W
Žilina Czechoslovakia **69** C2 49 14N 18 40E
ZIMBABWE **95** E4
Zinder Niger **93** G5 13 46N 8 58E
Ziqudukou China **81** E4 33 03N 95 51E
Zittau G.D.R. **63** B2 50 55N 14 50E
Zlatoust U.S.S.R. **70** H7 55 10N 59 38E
Znojmo Czechoslovakia **69** C2 48 52N 16 04E
Zoetermeer Netherlands **65** C2 52 03N 4 30E
Zofingen Switzerland **63** A1 47 18N 7 57E
Zolochev U.S.S.R. **69** D2 49 49N 24 53E
Zomba Malawi **95** G4 15 22S 35 22E
Zonguldak Turkey **78** D7 41 26N 31 47E
Zottegem Belgium **64** C2 50 52N 3 49E
Zouar Chad **94** C12 20 30N 16 30E
Zouérate Mauritania **93** C7 22 44N 12 21W
Zrenjanin Yugoslavia **68** D4 45 22N 20 23E
Zug Switzerland **63** B1 47 10N 8 31E
Zugspitze mt. Austria **63** B1 47 25N 11 00E
Zuid Beveland i. Netherlands **64** C3 51 28N 3 48E
Zuidelijk Flevoland geog. reg. Netherlands **64** E4 52 25N 5 18E
Zuid-Holland admin. Netherlands **64** D3 51 50N 4 28E
Zuid-Willemsvaart can.. Netherlands **64** E3 51 35N 5 30E
Zújar r. Spain **66** A2 38 35N 5 30W
Zunyi China **81** G3 27 35N 106 48E
Zürich Switzerland **61** C2 47 23N 8 33E
Zürichsee l. Switzerland **63** A1 47 00N 8 00E
Zushi Japan **83** B2 35 17N 139 35E
Zutphen Netherlands **64** F4 52 08N 6 12E
Zvishavane Zimbabwe **95** F3 20 20S 30 02E
Zwanenburg Netherlands **65** D3 52 22N 4 45E
Zweibrücken F.R.G. **63** A1 49 15N 7 22E
Zwevegem Belgium **64** C2 50 48N 3 20E
Zwickau G.D.R. **63** B2 50 43N 12 30E
Zwickau Mulde r. G.D.R. **63** B2 51 00N 12 00E
Zwijndrecht Netherlands **64** D3 51 49N 4 39E
Zwolle Netherlands **64** F4 52 31N 6 06E
Zyrardów Poland **69** D3 52 02N 20 28E
Zyryanka U.S.S.R. **71** R9 65 42N 150 49E
Zyryanovsk U.S.S.R. **71** K5 49 45N 84 16E

Abbreviations used in the gazetteer

admin.	administrative area
A.C.T.	Australian Capital Territory
b.	bay or harbour
c.	cape, point or headland
can.	canal
co.	county
d.	desert
dep.	depression
est.	estuary
fj.	fjord
F.R.G.	Federal Republic of Germany
g.	gulf
G.D.R.	German Democratic Republic
geog. reg.	geographical region
G.R.A.	Government Residential Area
hist. site.	historical site
i.	island
is.	islands
ist.	isthmus
l.	lake, lakes, lagoon
mt.	mountain
mts.	mountains
p.	peninsula
plat.	plateau
pn.	plain
r.	river
rd.	road
r.s.	research station
reg.	region
rep.	republic
res.	reservoir
salt l.	salt lake
sd.	sound, strait or channel
S.S.R.	Soviet Socialist Republic
sum.	summit
tn.	town
U.A.E.	United Arab Emirates
U.K.	United Kingdom
U.S.A.	United States of America
U.S.S.R.	Union of Soviet Socialist Republics
v.	valley
vol.	volcano

Abbreviations used on the maps

A.C.T.	Australian Capital Territory
Ákr.	Ákra
App.	Appennino
Arch.	Archipelago
Arg.	Argentina
Arq.	Arquípelago
Austl.	Australia
C.	Cape; Cabo; Cap
Col.	Colombia
D.C.	District of Columbia
Den.	Denmark
E.	East
Ec.	Ecuador
Eq.	Equatorial
Fj.	Fjord
Fr.	France
F.R.G.	Federal Republic of Germany
G.	Gunung; Gebel
G.D.R.	German Democratic Republic
I.	Island; Île; Isla; Ilha
Is.	Islands; Îles; Islas; Ilhas
J.	Jezioro
Jez.	Jezero
Kep.	Kepulauan
M.	Muang
Mt.	Mount; Mountain; Mont
Mte.	Monte
Mts.	Mountains; Monts
N.	North
Nat. Pk.	National Park
Neths.	Netherlands
N.P.	National Park
N.Z.	New Zealand
Pa.	Passage
Peg.	Pegunungan
Pen.; Penin.	Peninsula
Pl.	Planina
Port.	Portugal
P.P.	Pulau-pulau
proj.	projected
Pt.	Point
Pta.	Punta
Pte.	Pointe
Pto.	Porto; Puerto
R.	River; Rio
Ra.	Range
Res.	Reservoir
Résr.	Réservoir
R.S.F.S.R.	Russian Soviet Federated Socialist Republic
S.	South; San
S.A.	South Africa
Sa.	Sierra
Sd.	Sound
Sev.	Severnaya
Sp.	Spain
S.S.R.	Soviet Socialist Republic
St.	Saint
Ste.	Sainte
Str.	Strait
Terr.	Territory
U.A.E.	United Arab Emirates
u/c.	under construction
U.K.	United Kingdom
U.N.	United Nations
U.S.A.	United States of America
U.S.S.R.	Union of Soviet Socialist Republics
W.	West

Glossary

Ákra	cape (Greek)		Lago	lake (Italian; Portuguese; Spanish)
Älv	river (Swedish)		Laguna	lagoon (Spanish)
Bahia	bay (Spanish)		Ling	mountain range (Chinese)
Bahr	stream (Arabic)		Llyn	lake (Welsh)
Baie	bay (French)		-misaki	cape (Japanese)
Bugt	bay (Danish)		Mont	mountain (French)
Cabo	cape (Portuguese; Spanish)		Montagne	mountain (French)
Cap	cape (French)		Monts	mountains (French)
Capo	cape (Italian)		Monti	mountains (Italian)
Cerro	hill (Spanish)		More	sea (Russian)
Chaîne	mountain range (French)		Muang	city (Thai)
Chapada	hills (Portuguese)		Mys	cape (Russian)
Chott	salt lake (Arabic)		-nada	gulf; sea (Japanese)
Co	lake (Chinese)		Ostrova	islands (Russian)
Collines	hills (French)		Ozero	lake (Russian)
Cordillera	mountain range (Spanish)		Pegunungan	mountain range (Indonesian)
Costa	coast (Spanish)		Pendi	basin (Chinese)
Côte	coast (French)		Pic	summit (French; Spanish)
-dake	peak (Japanese)		Pico	summit (Spanish)
Danau	lake (Indonesian)		Pik	summit (Russian)
Dao	island (Chinese)		Planalto	plateau (Portuguese)
Dasht	desert (Persian; Urdu)		Planina	mountain range (Bulgarian; Serbo-Croat)
Djebel	mountain (Arabic)		Poluostrov	peninsula (Russian)
Do	island (Korean; Vietnamese)		Puerto	port (Spanish)
Embalse	reservoir (Spanish)		Pulau-pulau	islands (Indonesian)
Erg	dunes (Arabic)		Puncak	mountain (Indonesian)
Estrecho	strait (Spanish)		Punta	cape (Italian; Spanish)
Estreito	strait (Portuguese)		Ras; Râs	cape (Arabic)
Gebel	mountain (Arabic)		Ra's	cape (Persian)
Golfe	gulf, bay (French)		Rio	river (Portuguese)
Golfo	gulf, bay (Italian; Spanish)		Rio	river (Spanish)
Gölü	lake (Turkish)		Rivière	river (French)
Gora	mountain (Russian)		Rubha	cape (Gaelic)
Gunto	islands (Japanese)		Salina	salt pan (Spanish)
Gunung	mountain (Indonesian; Malay)		-san	mountain (Japanese)
Hafen	harbour (German)		-sanchi	mountains (Japanese)
Hai	sea (Chinese)		-sanmyaku	mountain range (Japanese)
Ho	river (Chinese)		Sebkra	salt pan (Arabic)
Hu	lake (Chinese)		See	lake (German)
Île; Isle	island (French)		Selat	strait (Indonesian)
Ilha	island (Portuguese)		Seto	strait (Japanese)
Inseln	islands (German)		Shan	mountains (Chinese)
Isla	island (Spanish)		-shima	island (Japanese)
Istmo	isthmus (Spanish)		-shotō	islands (Japanese)
Jabal; Jebel	mountain (Arabic)		Sierra	mountain range (Spanish)
Jezero	lake (Serbo-Croat)		Song	river (Vietnamese)
Jezioro	lake (Polish)		-suidō	strait (Japanese)
Jiang	river (Chinese)		Tassili	plateau (Berber)
-jima	island (Japanese)		Tau	island (Chinese)
-kaikyō	strait (Japanese)		Teluk	bay (Indonesian)
Kamen'	rock (Russian)		-tō	island (Japanese)
Kap	cape (Danish)		Tonle	lake (Cambodian)
Kepulauan	islands (Indonesian)		-wan	bay (Japanese)
-ko	lake (Japanese)		-zaki	cape (Japanese)
Lac	lake (French)		Zaliv	bay (Russian)

The publishers would like to thank the following individuals for their assistance in the preparation of this atlas:

Dr K. Atkinson, Dr J. Dickenson, Professor Andrew Goudie, Michael Grove, Jerry Harris, Anne Inie, Dr J. Lockwood, William Radice, Dr Fiona Ross, Ian Whitelaw.

The following institutions and societies:

Brewers' Society; Brick Development Association; British Carpet Manufacturers Association; British Coal; British Gas; British Hardmetal Association; British Home Furnishing Bureau; British Independent Steel Producers Association; British Leather Confederation; British Nuclear Fuels; British Paper and Board Industry Federation; British Printing Industries Federation; British Rail; British Rubber Manufacturers Association; British Shipbuilders; British Textile Confederation; British Textile Employers Association; Business Equipment Trade Association; Cement Makers Federation; Central Electricity Generating Board; Central Statistical Office; Central Statistics Office, Dublin; Chartered Institute of Transport; Chemical Industries Association; Civil Aviation Authority; Clothing and Allied Products Industry Training Board; Conservation Monitoring Centre; Countryside Commission; Countryside Commission for Scotland; C.S.E. Aviation; Department of Agriculture for Fisheries for Northern Ireland; Department of Education, Dublin; Department of Energy, Dublin; Department for Enterprise; Department of the Environment; Department of the Environment, Dublin; Department of the Environment for Northern Ireland; Department of Forestry and Agriculture, Ireland; Department of Industry and Commerce, Dublin; Department of Tourism and Transport; Department of Transport; D.W.H. Consultancies; Electricity Supply Board, Dublin; Engineering Industry Training Board; English Tourist Board; Federation of Milk Marketing Boards; Forest and Wildlife Service, Dublin; Forestry Commission; Glass and Glazing Federation; Glass Manufacturers Federation; Greenpeace; Industrial Development Authority, Dublin; Industrial Development Board for Northern Ireland; Industry Department for Scotland; Institute of Petroleum; International Institute for Environment and Development; International Tin Research Institute; International Union for the Conservation of Nature; Irish Sea Fisheries Board; Irish Tourist Board; Irish Wild Bird Conservancy; Jersey State Board of Administration, Customs and Excise; Light Metal Founders Association; Manx Electricity Authority; Meteorological Office; Milk Marketing Board; Ministry of Agriculture, Fisheries and Food; National Federation of Hide and Skin Markets; National Sport Council, Ireland; National Union of the Footwear, Leather and Allied Trades; Northern Ireland Department of Agriculture; North of Scotland Hydro-Electric Board; Nuclear Electricity Information Group; Northern Ireland Electricity; Office of Public Works, Dublin; Oxfordshire County Council; Petroleum Information Bureau; Port Authorities, Isle of Man and Channel Islands; Railway Industry Association of Great Britain; Regional Councils, Scotland; Royal Aircraft Establishment; Royal Automobile Club; Royal Society for the Protection of Birds; Scottish Office; Scott Polar Research Institute; Sea Fish Authority (U.K.); Sea Fish Industry Authority; Shoe and Allied Trades Research Association; Society of British Aerospace Companies Ltd.; Society of Motor Manufacturers and Traders Ltd.; Soil Survey; South of Scotland Electricity Board; Sport for Television; The Aluminium Federation; The Bookseller; U.K. Iron and Steel Statistics Bureau; U.K. Petroleum Industry Association; UNESCO; United Engineering Steels Ltd.; Water Authorities in England and Wales; Wool Industry Bureau of Statistics; World Wide Fund for Nature; Zinc Development Association.

And the many companies, too numerous to list here, who supplied data.

The distribution of locusts and grasshoppers, shown on page 127, is based on A. Steedman (Ed.) The Locust Handbook (2nd edn.) 1988 London: Overseas Development Natural Resources Institute, with permission.

The Moving Continents maps on pages 124–5 are based on Smith, Hurley and Briden Phaneroxoic paleocontinental world maps, Cambridge University Press 1981, with permission.

The weather summary and synoptic chart on page 54 are based on information supplied by the Met. Office.

The seasonal rainfall maps on pages 53, 73, 84, 97 and 111 are based on A. Street-Perott, M. Beran, R. Radcliffe (Eds.) Variations in the Global Water Budget 1983 Dordrecht: D. Reidel Publishing Company. Reprinted by permission of Kluwer Academic Publishers.

Peters projection courtesy of Professor Doctor Arno Peters

The illustrations are by Autographics Illustration (pages 11, 28) and Mike Saunders (page 11).

The publishers would like to thank the following for permission to reproduce photographs:

Daily Telegraph Colour Library on page 4 (top and bottom left) National Remote Sensing Centre on pages 4 (bottom right), 7 and 28 University of Dundee on page 54 (all).